THE FIGURE OF MINERVA
IN MEDIEVAL LITERATURE

The Figure of Minerva
in Medieval Literature

William F. Hodapp

D. S. BREWER

© William F. Hodapp 2019

All Rights Reserved. Except as permitted under current legislation no part of this work may be photocopied, stored in a retrieval system, published, performed in public, adapted, broadcast, transmitted, recorded or reproduced in any form or by any means, without the prior permission of the copyright owner

The right of William F. Hodapp to be identified as the author of this work has been asserted in accordance with sections 77 and 78 of the Copyright, Designs and Patents Act 1988

First published 2019
D. S. Brewer, Cambridge

ISBN 978 1 84384 539 3

D. S. Brewer is an imprint of Boydell & Brewer Ltd
PO Box 9, Woodbridge, Suffolk IP12 3DF, UK
and of Boydell & Brewer Inc.
668 Mt Hope Avenue, Rochester, NY 14620–2731, USA
website: www.boydellandbrewer.com

A CIP catalogue record for this book is available
from the British Library

The publisher has no responsibility for the continued existence or accuracy of URLs for external or third-party internet websites referred to in this book, and does not guarantee that any content on such websites is, or will remain, accurate or appropriate

This publication is printed on acid-free paper

For Laura Jean

Contents

Illustrations	ix
Acknowledgements	x
Abbreviations	xii
Introduction	**1**
1 The Roman Minerva and Elements of Medieval Classicism	**11**
Reception and Transformation of the Antique in the Middle Ages	14
The Roman Minerva	18
Ideas of Wisdom: Antique and Medieval	21
Mythography: Interpreting Myth	32
2 The Sapiential Tradition: Minerva as Redemptress	**44**
The Medieval Sapiential Tradition	44
John Lydgate's *Reson and Sensuallyte*	55
Reson and Sensuallyte: Translatio and Reception	56
Minerva: Iconography and the Judgment of Paris	59
The Poem's Primary Concerns and Minerva's Central Role	69
Gavin Douglas and Wisdom's Path to Honor	75
3 The Martianus Tradition: Minerva as Mistress of the Liberal Arts	**81**
The Liberal Arts and the Martianus Tradition	82
Liberal Arts in Classical and Medieval Cultures: A Brief Survey	82
Martianus Capella in the Middle Ages	91
The Court of Sapience: A Fifteenth-Century Compendium of Learning	101
Dame Sapyence and the Four Daughters of God	103
Minerva: Iconography and the Liberal Arts	106
John Skelton and *The Garland of Laurel*	113
4 The *Patrona* Tradition: Minerva as Protectress and Benefactor	**120**
Minerva *Patrona* in Roman Literature	121
Minerva *Patrona* in Medieval Literature	129
Twelfth-Century Epic: Walter of Châtillon and Joseph of Exeter	131
Guido delle Colonne, John Lydgate, and the Matter of Troy	139
Christine de Pizan's *L'Epìstre d'Othea*	142

	Stephen Hawes and Minerva *patrona principis*	151
	The Example of Vertu	152
	The Pastime of Pleasure	154
5	**The Patristic Tradition: Minerva as Idol**	**162**
	Idols and Idolatry in Jewish and Christian Cultures	163
	Minerva and the Fathers: The Goddess in Patristic Writing	168
	Minerva as Idol in Medieval Literature: The Catalog of Deities	178
	The Assembly of Gods and Minerva as Idol	186
	Minerva-Othea and Idolatry	188
	The Poem's Primary Concerns and Minerva-Othea's Worldly Wisdom	193
	William Dunbar's Minerva-Athena Imagery in *The Golden Targe*	195
6	**The Ovidian Tradition: Minerva as Venus' Ally**	**203**
	Ovid's Venus and Minerva	204
	The Ovidian Tradition	215
	John Lydgate's *Temple of Glas*	227
	Minerva and Venus in James I's *Kingis Quair*	231
	Charles d'Orléans, Venus, Fortune, and Minerva's Bird	239
	Conclusion	**247**
	Bibliography	257
	Index	298

Illustrations

1. Cambridge, Corpus Christi College Ms. 61, fol. iv. By permission of The Parker Library, Corpus Christi College, Cambridge.   13
2. Assisi. Portico of the Temple of Minerva. F. Alinari. Courtesy of Andrew Dickson White Architectural Photographs Collection, #15-5-3090. Division of Rare and Manuscript Collections, Cornell University Library.   15
3. Herrad of Hohenbourg, *Hortus deliciarum*, fol. 32r. By permission of the Warburg Institute (from *The Hortus Deliciarum of Herrad of Hohenbourg (Landsberg)*, ed. Rosalie Green et al. (London, 1979)).   89
4. British Library, Harley Ms. 4431, fol. 95v. © The British Library Board (Harley Ms. 4431).   145
5. British Library, Harley Ms. 4431, fol. 102v. © The British Library Board (Harley Ms. 4431).   147

The author and publisher are grateful to all the institutions and individuals listed for permission to reproduce the materials in which they hold copyright. Every effort has been made to trace the copyright holders; apologies are offered for any omission, and the publisher will be pleased to add any necessary acknowledgement in subsequent editions.

Acknowledgements

Writing is paradoxical: it is at-once an individual and a communal activity – we rely on others even as we labor alone. I have incurred numerous debts from many generous people, beginning with the late Archibald Coolidge, David Chamberlain, and Valerie Lagorio. For having read, listened to, debated, and discussed versions of materials here I wish to thank Bob De Smith, Tim Gustafson, Nickolas Haydock, Travis Johnson, John King, George Killough, Sean Lewis, Jess McCullough, Mark Rankin, Edward Risden, Tom Shippey, Michelle Sweeney, Audrey Thorstad, and Jonathan Wilcox. For help with Hebrew, I wish to thank Marian Diaz and Ethan Schwartz. I particularly thank Nick Haydock. At Nick's encouragement, I began weaving various Minerva threads into chapter ideas. As drafting developed, Nick read carefully and replied insightfully to each chapter. I also wish to thank the anonymous reader for Boydell & Brewer. The results are now better than they were because of the reader's and Nick's efforts.

Many analyses expressed here received initial airing at conferences and lectures. I wish to thank organizers for inviting me to present at the Medieval Consortium, the University of Iowa (Jon Wilcox); the School of Arts and Letters Colloquium, the College of St. Scholastica (Nathan Carroll); the Institute for Medieval Studies, University of Leeds (Audrey Thorstad); the Institute of Medieval and Early Modern Studies, Durham University (John O'Brien); and Hill Museum and Manuscript Library/St. John's University (Matthew Heintzelman). For permission to re-work materials first appearing in print, I am grateful to the editors of *Enarratio: Publications of the Medieval Association of the Midwest* (for material in Chapters 2 and 4) and the editor of *ANQ: A Quarterly Journal of Short Articles, Notes and Reviews* (for material in Chapter 6). In each case, I extensively revised the material, but elements of repetition remain.

I wish to thank the President and Fellows of Wolfson College, Cambridge University, for hosting me as a Visiting Scholar in 2001–2, during which I first worked with many of the manuscripts in this study; the National Endowment for the Humanities and John King and Mark Rankin for inviting me to participate in their Summer Seminar in 2012, during which I conducted bibliographic research on John Skelton and Stephen Hawes; and the US-UK Fulbright Commission for granting me a Durham University-Fulbright Scholar Award in 2015, during which I studied materials related to James I of Scotland and *The Kingis Quair*. I am also grateful to Elizabeth Archibald, Simon James, John McKinnell, Corinne Saunders, and the Department of English Studies at Durham University for support during my Fulbright stay. For assistance with manuscripts, I am grateful to librarians and archivists at Bodleian Library, University of Oxford; the British Library; Cambridge University Library; Hill Museum and Manuscript Library; National Archives of Scotland; National Library of Scotland; Palace Green Library, Durham University; Parker Library, Corpus Christi College, Cambridge; Plantin-Moretus Museum; St. John's College Library, Cambridge; and Trinity College Library, Cambridge. For permissions to reproduce images, I am grateful to the British Library, Cornell University Library, the Parker Library, Corpus Christi College, Cambridge, and the Warburg Institute.

Closer to home, I wish to thank the President and Trustees of the College of St. Scholastica for sabbatical leaves; the College's Faculty Development Committee, School of Arts and Letters, and English Department for research and travel grants; and Bret Amundson, Dean of the School of Arts and Letters, and Ryan Vine, Chair of the English Department, for a grant supporting this publication. In addition, I wish to thank School and Department colleagues for their interest and encouragement, and College librarians Jennifer Lund and Todd White, for whom no text is too remote or query too arcane that it cannot be found or answered. My thanks, too, to the Editorial Board, Caroline Palmer, and the production staff at Boydell & Brewer for their commitment, hard work, and dedication to seeing this project into book form.

Finally, I wish to thank my family, especially my first reader in all things, Laura Jean, to whom I gratefully dedicate this book, and our four children – Patricia, Rachel, Joseph, and Benjamin – who likely know more about Minerva than nearly anyone else their age. Though I acknowledge my debts here with deep gratitude, any mistakes remaining in the book are mine.

Abbreviations

Am.	Ovid's *Amores*
ANRW	*Aufstieg und Niedergang der römischen Welt*
Ars am.	Ovid's *Ars amatoria*
BCCT	Brill's Companions to the Christian Tradition
BD	Geoffrey Chaucer's *Book of the Duchess*
CA	John Gower's *Confessio Amantis*
CCCM	Corpus Christianorum: continuatio mediaevalis
CCSL	Corpus Christianorum Series Latina
CMC	Cambridge Medieval Classics
CP	Boethius' *De consolatione Philosophiae*
CSEL	Corpus Scriptorum Ecclesiasticorum Latinorum
CSML	Cambridge Studies in Medieval Literature
CT	Geoffrey Chaucer's *Canterbury Tales*
Dom.	Suetonius' *De vita Caesarum, Domitian*
DOST	*Dictionary of the Older Scots Tongue*
EEBO	Early English Books Online
EETS ES	Early English Text Society Extra Series
EETS OS	Early English Text Society Original Series
EETS SS	Early English Text Society Supplemental Series
Ep. ex. Pon.	Ovid's *Epistulae ex Ponto*
Her.	Ovid's *Heroides*
HF	Geoffrey Chaucer's *House of Fame*
HMML	Hill Museum and Manuscript Library
Inst. ora.	Quintilian's *Institutio oratoria*
LCL	Loeb Classical Library
MAAP	Medieval Academy of America Publication
MART	Medieval Academy Reprints for Teaching
MED	*Middle English Dictionary*
Met.	Ovid's *Metamorphoses*
MGH	Monumenta Germaniae Historica
MGRLL	Monographs on Greek and Roman Language and Literature
Mit.	Fulgentius' *Mitologiae*
MRAT	Medieval and Renaissance Authors and Texts
MRTS	Medieval and Renaissance Texts and Studies
NIMEV	Boffey and Edwards' *A New Index of Middle English Verse*

OHEL	Oxford History of English Literature
PF	Geoffrey Chaucer's *Parliament of Fowls*
PL	Patrologia Latina
Rem. am.	Ovid's *Remedia amoris*
RR	Guillaume de Lorris and Jean de Meun's *Le Roman de la Rose*
RS	John Lydgate's *Reson and Sensuallyte*
SMC	Studies in Medieval Culture
ST	*Summa Theologiae*
STC	Pollard and Redgrave's *Short-Title Catalogue*
STS	Scottish Text Society
SVM	Second Vatican Mythographer
TB	John Lydgate's *Troy Book*
TC	Geoffrey Chaucer's *Troilus and Criseyde*
TEAS	Twayne's English Authors Series
TKQ	James I of Scotland's *The Kingis Quair*
TVM	Third Vatican Mythographer's *De diis gentium et illorum allegoriis*
USTC	*Universal Short-Title Catalogue*
Ylias	Joseph of Exeter's *Frigii Daretis Yliados libri sex*

Note on Texts and Translations

This study draws on a range of texts from classical and medieval cultures. I quote Middle English and Older Scots texts without translation. In most other instances, I quote the original followed by translation. Unless otherwise noted, translations are mine. Citations of frequently referenced texts appear in the body of this work after the first citation in a note. Citations of Chaucer's texts are to editions in *The Riverside Chaucer,* ed. Benson, and appear in this work without further notation. Unless otherwise noted, citations to biblical texts are to the Latin Vulgate: abbreviations of biblical books follow *The Chicago Manual of Style* and also appear in this work without further notation.

Introduction

Leiden University Library owns a small mid-fifteenth-century anthology of Middle English poetry (Vossius Germ. Gall. Q.9). Written in three hands on a mixture of parchment and paper gatherings, this anthology contains fourteen of John Lydgate's short poems, three excerpts from his *Fall of Princes*, two of Geoffrey Chaucer's short poems, and eight anonymous poems. Because of its contents, the book is generally known among scholars as the "Leyden Lydgate Manuscript" and has offered useful witnesses to several of Lydgate's and the two Chaucer poems. This manuscript also offers the only known witness to four of its eight anonymous poems. In one of these – a two-stanza ballade in rime royal I entitle here "Vpon temse" – the narrator recounts a dream as follows:

> Vpon temse fro London myles iij
> jn my chambir riht as j lay slepyng
> me thought I sawe apperyng vn to me
> the fresh venus mercifully lokyng
> vpon her fyngris many a strange Ring
> of which the stonys gaf so gret clernesse
> that neuer sawe j so fresh a brithnesse
>
> And in her hand me semed that she helde
> depeynted vpon a skyn of velem whiht
> the Resemblance of a floury felde
> and in the meddis a woman stod vp right
> of which the figure so fayre was to my siht
> that neuer in gravyng nor in portrature
> sawe j depict so fayre A creature

Though "Vpon temse" concludes before much happens, leaving us perhaps with a sense of incompleteness, this engagingly brief poem raises a number of interesting questions about medieval poetics and reading practices key to the present study.[1]

---

[1] Manuscript evidence suggests these two stanzas constitute the entire text as the scribe knew it. Found on folio 112r,"Vpon temse" is written in the same hand as the previous 111 folios. Hand 2 begins on folio 112v. For an edition of the poem and description of the manuscript, see van Dorsten, "Leyden 'Lydgate Manuscript'," 318, 321–3. See also *NIMEV* 3844.5.

As with most if not all first-person medieval narratives, the poet of "Vpon temse" creates a world in which a narrator – the poem's "I" – recounts a personal event – the dream – to what Gerald Prince calls a narratee, that is, the narrator's addressee as inscribed in the text.[2] This narratee presumably understands the narrator's discourse completely and is implied throughout but especially in the narrator's twice-used emphatic phrase "that neuer sawe j." In this phrase the personal pronoun "I" implies a "you" to whom the "I" addresses the discourse, the pattern of which is as follows: I (the subject) describe my dream (the object) to you (the implicit indirect object). The dream itself involves two female figures: Venus, who appears to the dreamer-narrator in the first stanza, and a woman depicted in an illumination Venus holds, as presented in the second stanza. Other elements in the poem serve largely to describe the two figures, by which the dreamer-narrator offers readings of them: Venus is "fresh" and "mercifully lokyng," wearing jeweled rings giving off "so gret clernesse," while the woman, in the midst of a "floury felde" painted on "velem whiht," is "so fayre." The dreamer-narrator also offers an evaluative reading of each, repeating their respective key adjectives within a parallel grammatical construct: concerning Venus' rings at the end of stanza one, he states "that neuer sawe j so fresh a brithnesse"; concerning the woman in the painting at the end of stanza two, "that neuer ... / sawe j depict so fayre A creature."

The classical figure Venus, the dream-vision form, and the descriptions of the two figures raise an initial set of interpretive questions. First, what does the poet's use of this particular classical figure imply about the poem's subject matter? In naming the first figure Venus without further explanation, the narrator assumes his narratee understands who she is. Similarly, on another diegetic level, the poet also assumes his audience will understand who she is within the world of the poem. Drawing on an intertextual tradition reaching back to Greco-Roman culture, the poet uses Venus to connote the poem's central subject, love. In fact, without the Roman goddess of love being named, we would be hard pressed to determine love is the poem's subject, as a simple substitution of another Roman deity like Ceres or Juno for "venus" might illustrate. Second, what does the poet's use of the dream-vision form, the poem's dream-world context, suggest about Venus, her painting, and her interactions with the narrator? A "spiritual adventure," as A.C. Spearing describes the genre, the dream-vision provides a vehicle for this poet to explore in part the

---

[2] Prince, "Introduction à l'étude du narrataire," 177–96. On first-person discourse and the audience as inscribed in a text, see J. Allen, "Grammar, Poetic Form, and the Lyric Ego," 199–226; Anscombe, "The First Person," 45–65; Eco, *Role of the Reader*, 3–43; R. Elliott, *Literary Persona*, 3–62; W. Gibson, "Authors, Speakers, Readers, and Mock Readers," 265–9; Ong, "The Writer's Audience," 9–21; Spitzer, "Note on the Poetic and Empirical 'I,'" 414–22; Stevens, "The Performing Self," 193–218; and Rovane, "The Epistemology of First-Person Reference," 147–67. On contemporary narratology, see Abbott, *Cambridge Introduction to Narrative*; Herman and Vervaeck, *Handbook of Narrative Analysis*; J.H. Miller, "Narrative," 66–79; and Prince, *Dictionary of Narratology*. On medieval narrative, see Davenport, *Medieval Narrative*; J. Newman, "Narratology and Literary Theory," 990–8; and Spearing, *Textual Subjectivity*, 1–173, and *Medieval Autographies*.

psychology of human love.³ In approaching the dreamer-narrator with painting in hand, Venus in a sense offered it to him as gift though the gesture is not wholly clear. His response, however, is: the dreamer-narrator was smitten by, as he says, "the figure so fayre … to my siht." Third, what does the poet's use of the narrator's descriptions and judgments imply about the narrator's emotional state? Though we cannot be certain for lack of detail, presumably the narrator has been troubled by a love situation: the goddess' "mercifully lokyng," as the narrator interprets her glance, implies he perhaps needed mercy, and the "fresh … brithnesse" of the stones on her rings suggests her dazzling "fresh" appearance somehow rejuvenated him. His repeated "so fayre" judgment of the solution Venus presumably offered him, the depicted woman, likewise reinforces the impression that the narrator needed rejuvenation. The woman's appearance depicted amid an idyllic landscape – a moment of art existing within art – similarly seems to have refreshed the narrator, as his repeated "so fayre" judgment implies. Finally, the grammatical parallelism in the narrator's readings of Venus and the woman – "that neuer sawe j" phrase – suggests a narrative parallelism between the two figures as they operated within the dream: Venus represents love itself while the woman in the painting, a literal and figurative extension of the goddess, functions presumably as representation of a potential beloved, even if twice removed.

"Vpon temse" illustrates how one medieval poet uses a classical figure within a dream vision to explore an aspect of the human condition. Venus is the poem's central figure: her appearance connotes its subject, and the narrator's reading of her and her gift suggests his attitude and emotional state in relation to that subject. Yet, the poet's use of Venus would be meaningless without an intertextual tradition – the codes and conventional meanings – he assumes readers bring to the poem, and a fair amount of literary and cultural convention underlies this particular poetic image. As readers of medieval literature know, classical figures, allusions, and images such as Venus are ubiquitous in medieval Latin and vernacular poetry. Some years ago, Richard Hamilton Green argued for reconsidering classical figures and allusions in medieval poetry, calling for modern readers "to ask what an instructed medieval reader would have made of the medieval poet's use of the figures and fables of the pagan poets" by examining them within literary and cultural-historical contexts.⁴ In this study, I examine poetic images of the goddess Minerva as she appears in medieval literature, with a particular focus on several English and Scots poems. Unlike with many of her classical counterparts such as Fortune, Saturn, Venus, Cupid, Nature, Genius, Orpheus, and Apollo, scholars in the main have paid little attention to Minerva, with the exception of Margaret J. Ehrhart's discussion of her

---

3   Spearing, *Medieval Dream Poetry*, 6–16. On *visio somniumque* in medieval culture, see also Cherniss, *Boethian Apocalypse*; Davenport, *Medieval Narrative*, 192–209; Depres, *Ghostly Sights*; Kruger, *Dreaming in the Middle Ages*; Le Goff, *Medieval Imagination*, 196–231; Lenz, *Dreams, Medicine, and Literary Practice*; Lynch, *High Medieval Dream Vision* and *Philosophical Visions*; B. Newman, "What Did It Mean to Say 'I Saw'?," 1–43; B. Nolan, *Gothic Visionary Perspective*; Piehler, *Visionary Landscape*; Russell, *English Dream Vision*; and Wehrle, "Dreams and Dream Theory," 329–46.
4   R.H. Green, "Classical Fable and English Poetry," 133.

role in the Judgment of Paris story and Helen Solterer's exploration of the goddess as wisdom figure in the gendered clerical context of master-respondent *disputatio*.[5] Yet, as evidence indicates, Minerva has as rich and varied appearances in medieval literature as any of her classical colleagues. I seek to remedy this lack of attention by exploring major aspects of her imagery as manifest in medieval texts. This study, then, focuses on Minerva imagery within the context of medieval classicism, that is, the interpretation of antiquity, and thereby its transformation, in medieval culture.

Study of medieval classicism has in recent years joined with the emerging field of classical reception studies. Classical reception studies encompass "the inquiry into how and why the texts, images and material cultures of Ancient Greece and Rome have been received, adapted, refigured, used and abused in later times and often other places": an inquiry giving rise to a range of studies from general guides to specific interpretive discussions.[6] Examining and discussing the reception of the classical past in medieval cultures is challenging, though, in light of the modern practice of periodization. The adjective "classical," like its counterpart "medieval," is an early modern invention, developed initially within the context of Renaissance humanistic thinking. While the terms help us to demarcate historically cultures of earlier periods, it is important we remember they are terms we impose. European writers and intellectuals living between 500 and about 1500 CE had no idea they were medieval any more than they thought of Greco-Roman culture as classical. Rather, inheriting from Latin writers the intellectual habit of distinguishing the old (*veteri*) from the new (*novi*), they considered Greco-Roman culture along with Jewish and early Christian cultures under the rubric *antiqui* (the ancients); when writing self-reflectively, they considered themselves *moderni* (the moderns), beginning as early as Cassiodorus (c.485–c.585), or *neoterici* (modern writers).[7] This cultural relationship with the antique past led to what Rita Copeland has tellingly identified as "the principle of medieval saturation in antiquity": many medieval writers integrate the antique with the modern, the old with the new.[8] A task of anyone seeking to understand medieval engagements with aspects of antiquity is both to tease them

---

[5] Ehrhart, *Judgment of the Trojan Prince Paris*; Solterer, *The Master and Minerva*. On Fortuna, see Patch, *Goddess Fortuna*, and Pickering, *Literature and Art*, 168–222; on Saturn, see Klibansky, *Saturn and Melancholy*; on Venus, see Economou, "The Two Venuses," 17–50, Hollander, *Boccaccio's Two Venuses*, Schreiber, "Venus and the Mythographic Tradition," 519–35, Tinkle, *Medieval Venuses and Cupids*, and Twycross, *Medieval Anadyomene*; see Tinkle for Cupid as well; on Natura, see Curtius, *European Literature*, 106–27, Dronke, "Bernard Silvestris, Natura, and Personification," 16–31, Economou, *Goddess Natura*; on Genius, see Chance Nitzsche, *Genius Figure*; on Orpheus, see Friedman, *Orpheus in the Middle Ages*, and Warden, *Orpheus*; on Apollo, see Fumo, *Legacy of Apollo*.

[6] Classical Reception Studies Network, "Classics," para.1. See also Hardwick and Stray, *Companion*, 1–9, and accompanying essays; Kallendorf, *Companion*, 1–4, and accompanying essays; Grafton, Most, and Settis, *Classical Tradition*, vii–x, and entries; Brockliss, Chaudhuri, Lushkov, and Wasdin, *Reception*, 1–16, and accompanying essays; and Copeland, *Oxford History*, 1–20, and accompanying essays.

[7] Cassiodorus, *Variarum libri XII*, 4.51; on *neotericus*, a Latin Grecism, see de Ghellink, "Neotericus, Neoterice," 113–26. See also Curtius, *European Literature*, 251–5, and Copeland, "Introduction," 3–4.

[8] Copeland, "Introduction," 3–13: 7–8.

out from and examine them within their medieval contexts so as to deepen that understanding.

Medieval poets like the author of "Vpon temse" use dream-vision, allegory, and mythography – all initially drawn from antiquity – to explore aspects of the human condition. The narrational landscape of the dream poem, for instance, provides imaginative space to examine questions about love, knowledge, wisdom, death, fortune, fame, and the acts of reading and writing themselves. Not surprisingly, perhaps, allegory – the life-blood of which is a world of ideas – offers a point of conjunction for using classical imagery in dream-visions for, as Jean Seznec pointed out more than half a century ago, medieval writers and artists commonly treat classical figures as representatives of moral or philosophical ideas attributed to them in antiquity.[9] This approach to classical figures, evident as early as the Homeric corpus, was part of the antique inheritance, and medieval writers exploit it in a range of creative and interpretive texts. Thus, for instance, Diana, the virgin huntress, often appears in medieval literature as an allegorical figure for chastity; Mercury, the winged-messenger of Jupiter, for eloquence; and Venus, as we have just seen, for love. Armed with this notion of representation, it would seem we could easily interpret classical figures in medieval poetry. Yet, while correspondence between figures and ideas can exist, becoming almost clichéd metaphors in the high to late Middle Ages, the ideas the figures represent are in themselves often complex. The multivalent nature of Venus, as explained for example by commentators on the ancient poets, illustrates the complex notion of love medieval thinkers inherited from classical culture and reinterpreted in their own. In a passage familiar to scholars of medieval classicism, Bernard Silvestris, a mid-twelfth-century poet and commentator on Virgil's *Aeneid*, describes Aeneas' parentage, saying in part:

> Veneres ergo duas legimus esse, legitimam scilicet et petulantie deam. Legitimam Venerem legimus esse mundanam musicam, id est equalem mundanorum proportionem, quam alii Astream, naturalem iusticiam, vocant. Hec enim est in elementis, in sideribus, in temporibus, in animantibus. Impudicam vero Venerem et petulantie deam dicimus esse carnis concupiscentiam que omnium fornicationum mater est

> (We read there are two Venuses, namely the lawful one and the goddess of wantonness. We read that the lawful Venus is world harmony, that is, the equal proportion of worldly things, which some call Astrea, others natural justice. This harmony is in the elements, the stars, the seasons, and living creatures. But we say the shameless Venus, the goddess of wantonness, is the desire of the flesh, which is the mother of all fornication)[10]

Bernard's distinction echoes Plato's (c.428–347 BCE) between the heavenly and earthly Aphrodite though he did not know Plato's idea directly.[11] While Bernard

---

[9] Seznec, *The Survival of the Pagan Gods*, 4.
[10] *Commentum quod dicitur*, eds. Jones and Jones, 9.
[11] *Symposium*, 180e–182a, in *Lysis; Symposium; Gorgias*, ed. and trans. Lamb.

seems to disparage his shameless Venus, his lawful Venus sounds much like Boethius' (c.480–c.524 CE) "amor" in *De Consolatione Philosophiae*, about which Philosophia declares "O felix hominum genus, / si vestros animos amor / quo caelum regitur regat!" (O happy race of men if the love that rules heaven might also rule your souls).[12]

Similarly, poets who wrote commentaries on their own works in the later Middle Ages followed and often expanded this earlier tradition when interpreting their use of figures such as Venus; thus, in the commentary on Book 7 line 50 of his *Teseida*, where he describes the ascent of Palamon's prayer to Venus' temple, Giovanni Boccaccio (1313–75) writes:

> Marte consistere nello appetito irascibile, così Venere nel concupiscible. La quale Venere è doppia, perciò che l'una si può e dee intendere per ciascuno onesto e licito disiderio, sì come è disiderare d'avere moglie per avere figliuoli, e simili a questo; ed di questa Venere non si paral qui. La seonda Venere è quella per la quale ogni lascivia è disiderata, e che volgarmente è chiamata dea d'amore

> (Mars consists of the irascible appetite, so Venus consists of the concupiscible. This Venus is twofold: thus, one is understood as each honest and licit desire, such as the desire of having a wife in order to have children, and desires similar to this; of this Venus I shall say no more here. The second Venus is that through which all lasciviousness is desired, and she is properly called the goddess of love)[13]

Bernard and Boccaccio emphasize Venus' multivalent nature in order to direct their contemporaries' readings of her as a figure for love. While Bernard implies an association between Venus and the human soul, Boccaccio draws a clear connection, adopting psychological discourse, that is, "appetito irascibile … [e] concupiscible," to place his use of Mars and Venus squarely in the context of medieval psychology: they figuratively represent the sensitive appetites of the soul. Such commentary exhibits a clear concern for, even anxiety over, reading. In addition, however, texts like these can help us ascertain medieval interpretations of a classical figure and "its importance as part of the language of representation," as R.H. Green would have it.[14]

Minerva, like her classical counterpart Venus, is a multivalent figure in medieval literature. As the Roman goddess of strategic warfare, intellectual arts, and practical arts, Minerva is used by medieval poets as a figure for wisdom. However, like Venus, who can represent multiple aspects of love, Minerva can show forth multiple facets of wisdom both divine and human, with the latter ranging from a wisdom seeking intellectual perfection to live in harmony with others or draw closer to divinity, to a wisdom using intellectual cleverness to further self-centered desires.[15] Drawing on a

---

[12] *Philosophiae consolationis*, ed. Weinberger, 2.m8.28–30.
[13] *Teseida*, ed. Battaglia, gloss on 7.50, 197.
[14] R.H. Green, "Classical Fable and English Poetry," 112.
[15] Smith, *Personification of Wisdom*, 1–18, distinguishes between worldly wisdom and divine wisdom. The latter is a characteristic of the Godhead and attribute of the Second Person of the Trinity, and the former is a property of human intellect and includes both

wide range of texts familiar to medieval poets, I have come to distinguish a five-fold paradigm of Minerva imagery: redemptress, mistress of the liberal arts, patroness of princes, idol, and Venus' ally. These distinct facets of the paradigm, or what I call traditions, figure forth equally distinctive aspects of wisdom. Within the first three traditions, Minerva primarily represents divine wisdom itself or human intellectual powers used in pursuit of divine wisdom or ethical living. In these traditions, poets ally Minerva with Sophia-Sapientia of the biblical books of Proverbs, Wisdom, and Ecclesiasticus and other wisdom figures such as Philosophia of Boethius' *De Consolatione Philosophiae*. In the tradition of Minerva as idol, poets depict the goddess within an anti-pagan discourse: here she either represents a demon or human intellectual powers used in pursuit of self-centered desires. Finally, her role as Venus' ally – in light of its Ovidian roots – is perhaps most ambiguous and ultimately comical in a satiric even parodic vein as this tradition draws on, and plays off of, the others.

Though a range of texts appear in this study, these distinct facets of the paradigm are especially evident in several fifteenth- and early sixteenth-century English and Scots allegorical and dream poems. In these poems, classical figures such as Minerva frequently function as what Bernard Silvestris called "interiores animi potentias," or inner powers of the soul (*Commentum quod dicitur*, 47). This book, then, consists of six chapters. In Chapter 1, I overview medieval classicism before explicating the Roman Minerva, ideas of wisdom, and mythography. A synthesis of ideas currently circulating, this discussion provides historical and theoretical contexts for analyzing Minerva imagery in medieval literature. Shifting to the medieval Minerva, I first treat the goddess' role as a wisdom figure in the vein of biblical Sophia-Sapientia in Chapter 2. Minerva's appearance in John Lydgate's *Reson and Sensuallyte* illustrates well this redemptive path of contemplative wisdom. Probing a different yet similar question, Gavin Douglas draws on this same tradition in *Palice of Honoure* to explore various paths to a life of honor. Related to this sapiential tradition, Minerva's strong association with the liberal arts bequeathed most clearly to medieval culture through Martianus Capella's *De nuptiis Philologiae et Mercurii* is the subject of Chapter 3. Within the context of this tradition, I examine *The Court of Sapience* and Minerva's central role in Book II of the poem as well as how the tradition illuminates her role in John Skelton's *Book of Laurel*, in which he probes the relation between wisdom and fame. Chapter 4 then moves us into the realm of politics by exploring the goddess' ancient role as patroness of princes, perhaps most familiar to modern readers from Homer's *Odyssey* but bequeathed to medieval Europe through Latin epic and history. Drawing on her capacity as wise war-leader and diplomat, evident in texts such as John Lydgate's *Troy Book* and Christine de Pizan's *L'Epistre d'Othea*, I particularly explore her roles in Stephen Hawes' *Example of Vertu* and *Pastime of Pleasure*, where she serves as advocate for Christian knighthood. From the viewpoint of medieval Christianity, possibly the most easily recognizable use of Minerva is that of pagan idol. In Chapter 5, I address the Patristic tradition, prevalent throughout

---

positive (knowledge, judgment, counsel, and understanding) and negative (cunning and carnality) aspects. Minerva can represent any of these aspects, including divine wisdom.

the Middle Ages, and analyze her appearances in *The Assembly of Gods*, an anonymous poem that has received very little of the attention it deserves, and William Dunbar's *Golden Targe*. Finally, in Chapter 6, I analyze the contrasting themes of tension and union between Minerva and Venus, and demonstrate that, in certain poems, the goddess of wisdom serves Venus in the latter's work of promoting love. This tradition – rooted in Ovid's poetry and medieval Ovidian poetry – informs particularly her appearances in John Lydgate's *Temple of Glas*, James I's *Kingis Quair*, and the third narrative of Charles d'Orléans' *Fortunes Stabilnes*.

The method I follow here joins close readings of the poems with readings of other primary texts to examine Minerva's roles within the poems. By gaining an understanding for traditions informing specific uses of Minerva as a poetic image, we are better able to appreciate and understand her role in a given poem. Medieval poets and scholars themselves recognize the value of reading texts in relation to other texts. Turning again to Bernard Silvestris, for example, we find him concerned over how to read multivalent poetic figures when he writes:

> Notandum est vero in … misticis voluminibus, ita et in hoc equivocationes et multivocationes esse et integumenta ad diversa respicere … Hic autem diversus integumentorum respectus et multiplex designatio in omnibus misticis observari debet si in una vero veritas stare non poterit
>
> (One must indeed remember in … allegorical works, that there are equivocations and multiple significations and that one considers poetic fictions in diverse ways … Hence, the diverse aspects and multiple interpretations of poetic fictions must be observed in all allegorical matters if in fact the truth will not be able to stand in a single interpretation) (*Commentum quod dicitur*, 9)

When approaching medieval literature, we should bear in mind Bernard's advice to observe "diversus integumentorum respectus et multiplex designatio" as we strive for an informed understanding of it. Such attentive reading can deepen our engagement with the horizon of expectations medieval texts suggest about poets and audiences: an intellectual gesture on our part akin to archaeological excavation as we work to read texts within historical-cultural-literary contexts.[16]

In this study, then, I explore medieval interpretations of Minerva by delineating a five-fold paradigm of imagery medieval writers draw upon when using the goddess to represent wisdom. These images of the goddess, of course, are evident

---

[16] In "Alterity and Modernity," Jauss uses the phrase "horizon of expectations" to describe reconstructed historical-cultural-literary contexts "of the addressees for whom the text was originally composed" (182). See also his "Literary History as a Challenge," 18–23; and Burrow's cautionary "The Alterity of Medieval Literature," 385–90. Framing this study by analogy to archaeology, I draw on Hume's theory of archaeo-historicism, which he posits contra Jauss' historicism, in *Reconstructing Contexts*; see also his "Aims and Limits," 399–422. In *Experience of Beauty*, Carruthers describes her work as "that of a lexical archaeologist" (16); similarly, in *Ennobling Love*, C.S. Jaeger explicates his method as "historical excavation" (1). Both in differing ways illustrate the kind of work I attempt here.

primarily in specific poems. Focus on these poems allows us to explore both intertextual contexts of Minerva and her distinctive role within each poem. Studying conventions informing poetic imagery should lead to deeper understanding of the imagery in specific instances. Such understanding ultimately leads to an even deeper appreciation of how each use of Minerva also, and most importantly, interprets and transforms the traditions from which she derives.

I

The Roman Minerva and Elements of Medieval Classicism

Medieval poets, like those of any other period, did not work in a vacuum, creating verse *ex nihilo*. Rather, as Bonaventure (1221–74) observes about authorship in general, these poets drew on a wide range of available texts for images, ideas, modes, and genres.[1] Reading as much as experience, or rather reading as experience as Mary Carruthers argues, contributed greatly to their writing.[2] At times, this intertextual process is clear, as when Geoffrey Chaucer (c.1340–c.1400) begins *The Book of the Duchess* reading Ovid's tale of Ceyx and Alcione or recounts Virgil's *Aeneid* in Book I of *The House of Fame*; at others, it is not, as when he integrates his translation of Petrarch's Sonnet 132 into *Troilus and Criseyde*. Shot through with allusions, echoes, paraphrases, ideas, and images from other texts, medieval poetry reminds us much of medieval culture itself was largely, to borrow a phrase from Martin Irvine, a textual culture.[3]

---

[1] In the proem to his commentaries on Peter Lombard's *Sentences*, Bonaventure delineates four ways of making a book, all of which involve "aliena" (others' words): the "scriptor," who copies "aliena" exactly; the "compilator," who excerpts and mixes "aliena" from various sources; the "commentator," who adds his own words to explain "aliena"; and the "auctor," who "scribit et sua et aliena, sed sua tamquam principalia, aliena tamquam annexa ad confirmationem" (writes both his own words and those of others, but with his own as the principal words and others' as words added for confirmation). He concludes: "Talis fuit magister, qui sententias quas ponit et Patrum sententiis confirmat. Unde vere debet dici auctor huius libri" (Such was the master who set down his own views and confirmed them with opinions of the Fathers; hence, he truly ought to be called author of these books). *Commentaria in quatuor libros*, proem, q.4.concl., 14–15. See also Minnis, *Medieval Theory of Authorship*, 94–5, 98–9.

[2] Carruthers, *Book of Memory*, 12–13, 156–88.

[3] I borrow the phrase from Irvine's book on *grammatica*, *The Making of Textual Culture*. This point does not deny contributions oral traditions made to medieval textual culture. Niles, *Homo Narrans*, 19–21, challenges Irvine's privileging of *grammatica* and explicates the role of oral poetics in textual production. On the nexus of orality and textuality, see also Amodio, *Writing the Oral Tradition*; Bradbury, *Writing Aloud*; Clanchy, *From Memory to Written Record*; DuBois, *Lyric, Meaning, and Audience*; Stock, *Implications of Literacy*; and the essays in Vitz, Regalado, and Lawrence, eds., *Performing Medieval Narrative*. Lord (e.g., *Epic Singers and Oral Traditions*, 133–85) and Foley (e.g., *Traditional Oral Epic*, 201–39, 329–58) are indispensable here as well.

A dynamic interaction between reading and writing marks this culture, but the intertextual process does not simply end with a text newly composed. As has been long acknowledged, the concept of art for art's sake was foreign to medieval aesthetic sensibility.[4] Medieval poets and artists worked with a sense of audience and a desire to engage them in an interactive experience of perception and interpretation through their art. If we take Chaucer, again, as example, and attend for a moment to the prologues of his early dream poems, we catch glimpses into his poetry workshop and hints of his poetic method. Chaucer reads a text (or several), offers a reading by rewriting it, then expands on it, producing another text to be read by his audience. The audience's act of reading, too, was dynamic: a social practice typically involving the ear as much as the eye.[5] Readers often read aloud either to others in a group, as depicted in the famous "*Troilus* Frontispiece" in which Chaucer himself reads *Troilus and Criseyde* to courtly auditors who simultaneously "read" the poem through their ears (Fig. 1), or to oneself *sotto voce*, but nevertheless aloud.[6] This dynamic of reading, writing, reading, as described by Joyce Coleman, invites the audience to become grammarians and interpret the poem, thereby offering them an opportunity to compose yet another text.[7] When viewing the "*Troilus* Frontispiece" – this visually imagined, yet frozen moment of reading – we can almost hear the

---

[4] Medieval art is rooted in an interactive aesthetic actively seeking to engage audiences. See Carruthers, *Experience of Beauty* and the essays in her edited volume, *Rhetoric Beyond Words*; Camille, *Gothic Idol* and *Image on the Edge*; Eco, *Aesthetics of Thomas Aquinas* and *Art and Beauty*; Mâle, *Gothic Image*; and Robertson, *Preface to Chaucer*, 3–51. Such interactive aesthetics inform art like that produced in insular Gospel books where image, decoration, and text facilitate liturgical and meditative reading, and in choir stall misericords or roof bosses in churches, both of which though mostly out of sight playfully engage viewers within their architectural-liturgical contexts. See Farr, *Book of Kells*, 41–50; and Rose and Hedgecoe, *Stories in Stone*. Medieval writings about art also illustrate this dynamic scholars perceive between image and audience. See texts in Davis-Weyer, *Early Medieval Art*, and Frisch, *Gothic Art*.

[5] Crosby, "Oral Delivery in the Middle Ages," 88, and "Chaucer and the Custom of Oral Delivery," 413–32; Joyce Coleman, "Interactive Parchment," 63–79; and J. Murphy, "Arts of Poetry and Prose," passim. For an extended case study on *TC*, see Quinn, *Olde Clerkis Speche*.

[6] This oral-aural practice stemmed in part from *grammatica*, defined by the ninth-century monk-scholar-bishop Rabanus Maurus as "Prima ergo liberalium artium ... scientia interpretandi poetas atque historicos, et recte scribendi loquendique ratio" (the first of the liberal arts ... the knowledge of interpreting poets and historians, and the system of writing and speaking correctly). *De Clericorum Institutione*, col. 395. *Lectio*, one of four parts of "scientia interpretandi" in classical and medieval *grammatica* (the others being *enarratio*, interpretation, *emendatio*, editing, and *iudicium*, evaluation), laid out "the principles for reading a text aloud from a manuscript." Irvine, *Making of Textual Culture*, 4. On the social practices of reading in a classroom context, see Reynolds, *Medieval Reading*, 7–41. As Saenger, *Space between Words*, explains, silent reading as a common practice developed slowly from the seventh century through the fifteenth, reaching full development only in the early modern era. Even the monastic reading practice of *meditatio* in response to *lectio divina* could involve sub-vocalized murmur as the monk or nun familiarized the text in memory. See Carruthers, *Book of Memory*, 170–4, and with Ziolkowski, *Medieval Craft of Memory*, 21–3.

[7] Joyce Coleman, *Public Reading and the Reading Public*, 97–108.

Figure 1. Cambridge, Corpus Christi College Ms. 61, fol. 1v. By permission of The Parker Library, Corpus Christi College, Cambridge.

poet's voice as the auditors (well, most of them), intent on his words, read the poem carefully through their ears: this oral-aural textual moment serving as pretext to their subsequent interpretive responses.[8]

Like Chaucer, the medieval poets producing the texts examined in this study were readers as well as writers. As they sought to engage their audience through their art, they consciously played with poetic and philosophical codes and conventions gleaned from reading. A foundational source of poetics and ideas for these medieval poets was the specific bits of detritus from the Greco-Roman past that along with Jewish and early Christian culture constituted antiquity in the Middle Ages.[9] In this chapter, I lay out the study's larger contexts by beginning with an overview of medieval classicism, that is, the "reception and transformation," as Ernst Robert Curtius describes it, of antique remains in medieval culture.[10] I then explicate the Roman Minerva before reviewing ideas of wisdom and mythography in relation to the goddess.

Reception and Transformation of the Antique in the Middle Ages

Located on a spur of Mount Subasio in the region of Umbria, Italy, the hillside town of Assisi, perhaps most noted now for its thirteenth-century saints Francis and Clare, has a deep and rich history of socio-economic development and religious worship. Successively an Umbro-Etruscan settlement, a Roman *municipium*, a Frankish village, an Italian *comune*, a holding of the Papal States, and an Italian town, Assisi today is a site of world pilgrimage largely contained within Roman and medieval walls dominated by two late medieval fortresses. As with any settlement, Assisi's buildings and communal spaces reflect, even inscribe, its history. Given sufficient training in the visual grammar of art and architecture, we can read aspects of the city's history in its physical structures, design, and layout as well as in surviving documents. Yet, as any archaeologist or historian would remind us, the detritus of the past – the relics or artifacts that survive – tell only a partial story, revealing vestiges of past cultures and peoples who lived, worked, fought, loved, thought,

---

[8] I do not mean to suggest the *Troilus* frontispiece attempts to capture visually an actual event, a sort of medieval snapshot of a poetry reading complete with identifiable audience members, as some mid-twentieth-century Chaucerians argued (e.g., Galway, "The 'Troilus' Frontispiece," 161–77; Williams, "The 'Troilus and Criseyde' Frontispiece," 173–8). Rather, as Pearsall, "The 'Troilus' Frontispiece," 68–74, Salter, "The 'Troilus' Frontispiece," 15–23, and Joyce Coleman, "Where Chaucer Got His Pulpit," 103–28, respectively demonstrate, the stylized fifteenth-century image depicts an imagined event. For the possible link of the image to Richard II's triumphal re-entry into London in 1392, see Lerer, *Chaucer and His Readers*, 53–5.

[9] I take my use of the term "detritus," here, from Robertson, "Some Observations on Method," 81, who states: "The historian or the student of literature concerns himself with the order and significance of the detritus of the past in the present, not with the past itself, which is unapproachable." See also M. Nolan, "Historicism after Historicism," 63–85, in which she unpacks the image of "jetsam" from Augustine, Ovid, and Gower to illustrate a similar point regarding interpreting artifacts.

[10] Curtius, *European Literature*, 19.

composed poetry, sang songs, raised families, worshipped deities, and died. Still, as I assume throughout this study, examining relics for what they reveal or suggest is an initial step in seeking to understand past cultures and peoples. One such relic in Assisi, located in the Piazza del Comune at the center of the medieval walled town, is the church of Santa Maria sopra Minerva (Fig. 2).

Figure 2. Assisi. Portico of the Temple of Minerva. F. Alinari. A.D. White Architectural Photographs Collection. Courtesy of Cornell University Library.

Surrounded by thirteenth- and fourteenth-century buildings – other architectural relics of Assisi – this church is particularly interesting as it evinces in its physical features historical changes in religious worship and by extension changes in communal-social structures. The most striking feature of the building is its classical façade, which is all that remains visible of a public complex constructed between 28 and 25 BCE at the expense of Cnaeus Titus Caesius and Priscus Caesius, *quadrumviri* of the *municipium*.[11] Six fluted columns topped by Corinthian capitals with carved olive foliage, standing on plinths, support the entablature and the pediment of the roof. The plinths rest on the fourth of nine steps leading to the *pronaos*, or open porch, of the original temple. As a *hexacastylos* (i.e., six-columned) structure, the double-door entrance to the rectangular *cella*, the temple's chamber, would have been in the center of the façade with three columns on either side. Archaeological evidence from below the present-day street level indicates that the temple, part of a larger integrated complex, dominated surrounding structures, including a Roman *schola* on its right, a walled, arcaded and terraced rectangular forum with *tribunale* at its front, and lesser temples dedicated to Hercules, Juno, Mars, and the Dioscuri radiating beyond the front of the forum.[12]

The story of this temple structure from its initial construction in the first century BCE to the present is one of reception and transformation. Initially dedicated to the worship of Minerva, the temple and its forum served the inhabitants of Assisium as a religious, educational, and legal center for approximately 400 years. Following the Christianization of the Empire, the temple functioned in turn as a monastic church, mayoral and magisterial residence, administrative center, civic jail, parish church, and even landmark, appearing in Giotto's (c.1266–1337) frescoes of the life of St. Francis (c.1296–1304), before being re-dedicated in 1539 to Santa Maria sopra Minerva. Currently it is a Franciscan church serving residents and pilgrims. Throughout the building's known history, the people of Assisi used it for multiple public purposes, but primarily as a site of worship and legal proceedings; while the building bridges the town's classical past with its contemporary present, it records traces of intervening years.[13] The building's Roman origins, visibly evident in the façade, also remain evident in its name so that, even today, it is most commonly referred to in Italian as simply "Tempio di Minerva."

This building – particularly its medieval and early modern phases – illustrates how people received relics from antique culture and then at times transformed them for their own purposes. The adaptive use of the antique past is a key marker of medieval classicism. Again, as Curtius notes:

---

[11] Temperini, *Assisi*, 34, 49–50.
[12] Temperini, *Assisi*, 24–31, 57–78; Marcattili, "Templum Castorum et Minervae," 263–94.
[13] The temple's fortunes followed the town's throughout its history. On Assisi, see Temperini, *Assisi*; and Donovan, "Assisi." On the temple's history in particular, see Abate, *La Medievale*, 91–111; Temperini, *Assisi*, 96–106; and Franciscanum.it. And on re-purposing Roman buildings and *spolia* or stones quarried from Roman ruins, see Christie, *From Constantine to Charlemagne*, 93, 94; Greenhalgh, *Marble Past, Monumental Present*, 77–9, 141–52; Hanson, *The Spolia Churches of Rome*, 9–82; and the essays in Hahn, Emmel, and Gotter, eds., *From Temple to Church*.

Antiquity has a twofold life in the Middle Ages: reception and transformation. This transformation can take very various forms. It can mean impoverishment, degeneration, devitalization, misunderstanding; but it can also mean critical collecting (the encyclopedias of Isidore and Raban Maur), schoolboyish copying, skillful imitation of formal patterns, assimilation of cultural values, enthusiastic empathy. All stages and forms of accomplishment are represented.[14]

For Curtius, seeking to explicate continuities from the antique to the modern, the "twofold life" of antiquity he delineates underscores his general assessment that, though "a fallow period of decline which extended from 425–775" occurred in Europe, "the substance of antique culture was never destroyed" in the medieval period.[15] Structures like the Temple of Minerva demonstrate in microcosm the reception and transformation of material remains of antique culture in the medieval and early modern periods.

This reflection on the Temple of Minerva as a case study of sorts also suggests the sweep of medieval classicism, the study of which, as touched on in the Introduction, is joined with the emerging field of classical reception studies. In the Middle Ages, the reception and transformation of the antique touches a wide range of ideas, practices, and technologies, from "grammatica" as explicated by Bede in the eighth century to "memoria" as practiced by Thomas Aquinas in the thirteenth, from Charlemagne's palace chapel at Aachen and Theodulf's oratory at Germigny-des-Prés in the early ninth century to eleventh- and twelfth-century Romanesque churches dotting the European landscape, and from the Old English lyric "The Ruin" with its elegiac rumination on an abandoned Roman city, to the Benedictine cloister modeled in part on the Roman *villa rustica*, or working farm.[16] Often engaged, frequently transformed, relics from the antique past – whether ideas, texts, images, or stones – are foundational to much medieval cultural production, including literary texts.[17] Before examining mythography, an element of medieval classicism key to this inquiry, I will first review the Roman Minerva and ideas of wisdom as foundation for the rest of the study.

---

[14] Curtius, *European Literature*, 19.
[15] Curtius, *European Literature*, 20.
[16] On Bede and "grammatica," see Irvine, *Making of Textual Culture*, 272–98; on Aquinas and "memoria," see Carruthers, *Book of Memory*, 4–8; on Charlemagne, Theodulf, and Romanesque churches, see Beckwith, *Early Medieval Art*, 11–16, 152–76; for "The Ruin," see Krapp and Dobbie, eds., 227–9; on the Benedictine cloister, see J.G. Clark, *Benedictines*, 130–9, and Dimier, *Stones Laid before the Lord*, 235–54.
[17] Curtius views European literature through the lens of the Latin Middle Ages as shaped by the reception and transformation of the antique past. Studies such as those in Godman and Murray, eds., *Latin Poetry*, illustrate how many medieval poets engaged the classical literary past. For surveys, see Wetherbee, "Study of Classical Authors," 99–144; V. Gillespie, "Study of Classical Authors," 145–235; L. Reynolds, introduction to *Texts and Transmission*, xiii–xliii; and L. Reynolds and Wilson, *Scribes and Scholars*, 80–122. For manuscripts and transmission of classical texts, see entries in L. Reynolds, ed., *Texts and Transmission*. For cultural contexts of transmission, see the essays in Wisnovsky, Wallis, Fumo, and Fraenkel, eds., *Vehicles of Transmission*. For classical reception in medieval English literature, see the essays in Copeland, ed., *Oxford History of Classical Reception*.

The Roman Minerva

The adaptive use of the antique past as discussed above illustrates that much of what we know about Greco-Roman culture today stems from vestiges evident in, even filtered through, medieval culture: a culture that considered aspects of the Roman past with suspicion. When viewing the pre-Christian Roman Minerva with a twenty-first-century Western gaze, we might find it difficult at first glance to imagine the system that brought forth a pantheon of deities in response to the vagaries of life and that seemingly welcomed – and subsequently colonized – numerous forms of worship around its hearth at the Temple of Vesta. The incredulous student question – did the average Roman *really* believe in multiple deities? – remains largely unanswerable from our perspective. When we query members of our own culture about religious belief, it is difficult to determine what any person specifically believes short of a direct profession of faith. The distance of time and space makes such a question of the antique past even more challenging to answer, and perhaps ultimately more fruitless. Yet, just as we might when analyzing our own culture today, we can begin to gain a view of belief in the antique world by asking a different question: what did Romans do, that is, how did they behave religiously? Here we tread on surer, if fragmentary, ground, for their relics – bits of texts and temples – give evidence of vibrant religious activity, of life lived under a different gaze: the gaze, or rather gazes, of multiple deities. If we cannot say with certainty that particular pre-Christian Romans believed in multiple deities with the kind of surety creedal assent suggests today, we can say many certainly acted as though they believed, and the pre-Christian Roman Minerva inspired part of that religious behavior.

At the time of Augustus' reign, when Cnaeus Titus Caesius and Priscus Caesius built the Temple of Minerva in Assisium, a religious act they undertook at least in part for the common good, three fundamental features marked Roman religion. First, it encapsulated religious ideas in the various deities who oversaw and divinely inspired particular activities or who guarded particular places.[18] From early on, a strong current of animism, with natural features attended by specific deities, permeated Roman religious practice.[19] Such practice surfaces frequently in stories as well. Tiberinus, the tutelary deity of the Tiber River who figures in Roman foundation myth as the rescuer of Romulus and Remus, also appears in Virgil's (70–19 BCE) prequel foundation story, the *Aeneid*, where he approached a troubled Aeneas in a dream, prophesizing success, instructing him in human and divine alliance building, and promising aid as spiritual river guide to the invading Trojans. Upon waking, Aeneas immediately responded with a ritual prayer supplicating the god before proceeding to carry out Tiberinus' instructions.[20] In addition to places and natural features, particular deities oversaw arenas of human activity. Minerva, in part, was patroness of numerous groups of artisans and artists (fullers, dyers, cobblers, carpenters, shipwrights, weavers, musicians, sculptors, painters, actors, poets), as well as physicians, schoolmasters, schoolchildren, and military strategists.

[18] Dumézel, *Archaic Roman Religion*, 134; Ogilvie, *Romans and Their Gods*, 10.
[19] Shelton, *As the Romans Did*, 262–71.
[20] *Aeneid*, ed. Fairclough, 8.26–101.

In Ostia, for instance, Rome's harbor city some twenty-four miles down river at the mouth of the Tiber, *restioni* – those who made and sold ropes in that busy seaport so dependent on their craft – had a particular devotion to the goddess.[21] Though certainly serious, such devotion from artisans also had a witty side appropriate to Minerva. On the wall of Fullonica de Fabius Ululitremulus (The Fullery of Fabius the Hooting Owl) in Pompeii, a shop where *fulloni*, or fullers – those who cleaned clothes and processed wool – worked, we find this inscription: "Fullones uluamque cano non arma virumq(ue)" (Fullers and the owl I sing not arms and the man).[22] This tongue-in-cheek echo of the opening line of Virgil's *Aeneid* alludes directly to the fullers' patroness Minerva: the owl, as we shall see later in this study, was Minerva's bird signifying wisdom.

Second, Roman religion fostered a syncretic and synthetic approach to religious ideas and practices.[23] Thus, as they did with several deities early in the cultural exchange with Greece, Romans synthesized Menrva, an Italic goddess of intelligence and art, with the Greek goddess Pallas Athena, giving the former – now called Minerva – the latter's attributes, iconography, and mythology.[24] Just as Zeus, then, assisted by Hephaestos' head-splitting blow, gave birth to a fully-armed Athena, so did Jupiter with Vulcan's help bring forth Minerva: an armed virgin goddess born from the head of the father of the gods.[25] Similarly, when Roman legions conquered new territory, they tended to syncretize local with equivalent Roman deities in an effort to appease the former and to synthesize the two religious systems.[26] In Bath, England, for example, the Romans paired the local healing goddess Sulis, who presided over the hot springs, with Minerva as patroness of physicians; Romans and Celts alike worshipped Sulis-Minerva at Bath in her temple complex.[27]

---

[21] Ogilvie, *Romans and Their Gods*, 15.
[22] Ostia-antica, "The Fulleries"; on inscriptions at Pompeii, see Wallace, *Introduction to Wall Inscriptions*.
[23] Palmer, "Juno," 3–56.
[24] On Athena, see Deacy, *Athena*; the collection of essays in Deacy and Villing, eds., *Athena in the Classical World*; and Otto, *Homeric Gods*, 43–60. Minerva's synthesis with Athena happened by the late sixth century BCE: see Graf, "Athena and Minerva," 127–30.
[25] The fable of Pallas Athena/Minerva's birth springing fully armed from Zeus/Jupiter's head is common in ancient and classical literature. An early version in Greek literature comes from Hesiod's *Theogony*, ed. and trans. Most, 887–901, in which Zeus swallows his pregnant wife, Metis, to prevent the fulfillment of a prophecy predicting his overthrow at the hands of a son born of her; later, in 923–34, Pallas Athena springs fully armed from his head. It is also the basis for *Homeric Hymn* 28, where the poet sings of Pallas Athena "to whom wise Zeus himself gave birth out of his august head, in battle armour of shining gold: all the immortals watched in awe, as before Zeus the goat-rider she sprang quickly down from his immortal head with a brandish of her sharp javelin." *Homeric Hymns*, ed. and trans. West, 211. And, in *Fasti*, Ovid speculates that the goddess' shrine, called "Minerva Capta," derives its name from the legend: "an quia de capitis fertur sine matre paterni / vertice cum clipeo prosiluisse suo?" (or did she get the name Capta because it was said that she leapt forth without a mother from the top of her father's head with her shield). *Fasti*, ed. Frazer, rev. Gould, 3.841–2.
[26] Caseau, "Sacred Landscapes," 21–2.
[27] Croon, "Cult of Sul-Minerva," 79–83; Webster, *British Celts*, 42, 55.

Third, based on a notion of piety centered on respect for the ancestral gods of the city-state, Roman religion emphasized public expression of worship whereby individuals, small groups (industries, guilds, families), and residents of towns and cities honored patron deities.[28] For Minerva, public worship culminated in *Quinquatrus*, a five-day annual festival held March 19–23 in which those who claimed the goddess as patroness honored her with processions, games, and sacrifices. Teachers and students in particular celebrated as the former received the *minerval*, their annual stipend, while the latter enjoyed a Roman version of spring break.[29] Writing in *Fasti* near the end of Augustus' reign, Ovid (43 BCE–17 CE) recounts *Quinquatrus* with its various festivities in Minerva's honor, declaring his verse – though curiously not directly addressed to her – an offering of his own: "mille dea est operum: certe dea carminis illa est; / si mereor, studiis adsit amica meis" (she is goddess of a thousand works: she is certainly the goddess of song; if I merit it, may she be friendly to my efforts) (3.833–4). With no central creed, Roman religion was an eclectic, largely tolerant, religious phenomenon tied closely to public life. As R.M. Ogilvie notes, "a Roman was free to think what he [sic] liked about the gods; what mattered was what religious action he performed."[30]

As goddess of wisdom, war, and art, Minerva held a central place in the Roman pantheon. One of three deities making up the Capitoline triad in Rome, the others being her father Jupiter and his sister-wife Juno, Minerva was a particular patroness of the city, the Republic, and eventually the Empire. She oversaw Roman industry through the arts and, in conjunction with Mars' war rage, provided for Rome's military protection and prowess through strategic and diplomatic initiative. Minerva also protected Rome in the guise of the Palladium, her divine statue that once guarded Troy. Housed at the Temple of Vesta, the hearth-center of the Republic and later the Empire, the Palladium was brought to Italy by Aeneas, as one legend had it, following the sack of Troy.[31] According to Ovid, this Trojan relic carried with it Apollo's prophecy: "'aetheriam servate deam, servabitis urbem: / imperium secum transferet illa loci'" (preserve the heavenly goddess and you will preserve the city: she will carry with herself the power of the place) (*Fasti* 6.427–8). Though she had temples on the Aventine, the Quirinal, and Esquiline, and at the base of the Caelian, her worship in Rome began and particularly centered on the Capitoline Hill, the highest of Rome's seven hills, where a temple dedicated to Jupiter Optimus Maximus stood from its founding on September 13, 507 BCE until after the Empire became Christian. This temple structure – the Capitolium – had three *cella*: one for each deity – Jupiter Optimus Maximus in the center, Juno Regina stage right, and Minerva Augusta stage left. Annually, Romans marked this foundation day with ritual festivities. By the late Republic, this ritual included the sacrifice of a white heifer and a banquet at which the senators and magistrates gathered, joined

---

[28] Chuvin, *Chronicle*, 9–10; Ogilvie, *Romans and Their Gods*, 124; Shelton, *As the Romans Did*, 361–71.
[29] Dumézil, *Archaic Roman Religion*, 303.
[30] Ogilvie, *Romans and Their Gods*, 2.
[31] Ogilvie, *Romans and Their Gods*, 90; Ovid, *Fasti* 6.433–4.

by statues of Jupiter, Juno, and Minerva signifying the deities' communion with humans at the table.[32]

The Capitolium and its attendant religious rituals in many ways served as a unifying element in Roman civic-religion as Rome's influence and power spread. Beginning in the third century BCE, Capitolia, copies of the Capitolium, became integral to the public spaces in Roman-controlled towns. In Emporion, a one-time Greek colony on the Mediterranean coast of northern Spain, Romans built the earliest known extant Capitolium outside Rome as part of its forum when the seaport came under Roman influence during the First Punic War (264–41 BCE).[33] Pompeii, too, had an early Capitolium, built in 150 BCE to replace a temple dedicated to Jupiter alone. This spread of Roman architecture received a boost in the Augustan period as the Empire began to take shape. In his *De architectura*, a first-century BCE manual dedicated to Augustus, Vitruvius (c.80–c.15 BCE), after explaining in detail how to lay out a Roman town, writes: "Aedibus vero sacris, quorum deorum maxime in tutela civitas videtur esse, et Iovi et Iunoni et Minervae, in excelissimo loco unde moenium maxima pars conscpiciatur, areae distribuantur" (The building sites should be apportioned with the holy temples of those gods under whose particular protection the state is seen to reside, and of Jupiter, Juno, and Minerva, on the highest site from where the greater part of the city is viewed).[34] Vitruvius' reference here to the Capitoline triad found further expression in stone as Capitolia spread throughout the Empire. In 73 CE, for instance, Vespasian built a Capitolium in Brixia (modern Brescia in northern Italy), and in the reign of Marcus Aurelius, Thugga, a Roman town located southwest of Carthage in modern Tunisia, acquired a Capitolium dating from 166–7 CE.[35] Even Ostia, Rome's harbor town, had its own Capitolium completed during Hadrian's reign in about 120 CE.[36] In each case, Romans built the Capitolium, mimicking the layout of Rome's forum, on the north side of the highest point, thereby dominating the given city's public space.[37] Capitolia such as these expressed the power of Rome, and equally important, captured the protection of its three chief deities by providing holy places for the Capitoline triad to dwell throughout the Empire. Along with Jupiter and Juno, Minerva and her wisdom it seems went wherever Roman soldiers trod.

Ideas of Wisdom: Antique and Medieval

We can best glean the wisdom Minerva represents for Romans, I think, by parsing out what we know about the goddess, beginning with her name. As noted above, *Minerva* comes from an Italic or Etruscan form *Menrva*, the root of which is *mens*, that is, "mind," "thought," "plan," "intelligence," "understanding," "reason," and

---

[32] Ogilvie, *Romans and Their Gods*, 95.
[33] Blagg, "Temple at Bath," 426–7.
[34] Vitruvius, *On Architecture*, ed. Granger, 1.7.1.
[35] Gros, *L'architecture Romane*, 193.
[36] Ostia-antica.org, "Regio I."
[37] Gros, *L'architecture Romane*, 193.

the like. But for Romans she is more than human intelligence alone. The story of her birth, syncretized from Athena, reinforces the overarching divine nature of her mind, thought, plan, intelligence, and so on. Considering her role as patroness of arts, she represents technical skill and theoretical knowledge and understanding: both what and how to do something like weave or teach, and why. As our tongue-in-cheek fuller-poet of Pompeii implies in his graffiti verse, there is more to practicing a craft fully and well than just mechanical know-how. Similarly, when considering her role as Minerva Augusta, patroness of Rome, she represents the arts of both strategic-defensive war and peace-making diplomacy, that is, the use of intelligence in discerning political harmony and in conducting relationships to achieve it. In these instances, the Roman Minerva represents ideas of wisdom that medieval thinkers inherited from the antique world and most would recognize today.

Those who have thought about the concept generally define wisdom as the knowledge of things human and divine and the understanding of what is true and right. As knowledge and understanding, wisdom is practical and speculative, and it encompasses science, the knowledge of tangible things, or what is directly observable, and intelligence, the knowledge of intangible things.[38] Wisdom's practical and speculative aspects imply both mental and physical activity: an ability to perceive, judge, and organize things and to behave accordingly, as the term's etymological roots suggest.[39] It also implies wisdom's fundamental social dimension. In general, one can characterize wisdom in pre-industrial Western societies, including those of antique and medieval Europe, as centered on particular world-views, or models of reality, and subsequent moral codes, or practical advice for living based on a given world-view.[40] When people in the past pursued wisdom in its practical and speculative aspects, they sought to understand their society's world-view and to follow the ethical dictates the world-view espoused.[41] Thus, the rope-makers of Ostia invoked Minerva the goddess of rope-making as they mastered and practiced their

---

[38] Conley, "Wisdom," 967.
[39] Modern English "wisdom" descends from Old English *wisdom*, derived from the roots *wis* ("wise") and *dom* ("judgment"). Its Indo-European roots, *weid* ("to see") and *dhe* ("to set"), have even deeper philological implications for the notions of judgment and order: implications it shares with the Latin infinitives *videre* ("to see") and *facere* ("to do, make"), which similarly derive from these Indo-European roots. *American Heritage Dictionary*, 2100, 2131; *American Heritage Dictionary of Indo-European Roots*, 18, 99. On sight as a metaphor for knowing, see Akbari, *Seeing Through the Veil*, 3–7.
[40] I use "pre-industrial" to indicate traditional societies based on close-knit ties of kinship, religious belief, legal code, etc. Although traditional societies exist today, Western culture is now shaped more by plurality and individualism than by community and tradition.
[41] Bloomfield and Dunn write: "The ancient notion of wisdom then is the natural religion of early humanity. Their myths and tales have as presuppositions, no matter how fantastic the form, the idea of order and rationality. They attempt to answer the most basic question of all – 'why?' 'Why' cannot be asked unless there is present the assumption of order and rationality. In other words to ask 'why' assumes that there is a 'why'. It is this assumption that is basic and fundamental to all rational thinking, and it may be called wisdom." *Role of the Poet*, 108. Answering "why" leads then to a question of "what to do." Bloomfield and Dunn continue: "Practical wisdom rests on a sapiential view of the world, the view that the world makes sense, possesses order, rules and patterns

craft; teachers and students invoked her as goddess of thought as they developed and practiced the liberal arts; and political leaders invoked her as Minerva Augusta, the venerated goddess of political-diplomatic wisdom who discerned why, when, and how to make war and conduct peace.

When Ovid invokes Minerva the goddess of song in hopes she will accept his verse as sufficient offering for *Quinquatrus*, he is alluding to an old notion that poets, too, were wise persons, or at least purveyors of wisdom. This notion stems from the poet's artful use of the chief vehicle for wisdom: language. As the foundational skill necessary for shared knowledge, language is the means by which a society articulates and communicates its world-view through law, the codes of personal and collective conduct for maintaining social and cosmic harmony, and through education.[42] Just as in past societies the wise person was one who saw, understood, and lived according to the societal world-view, so too was the person who could use language effectively and well as leader, legislator, priest, councilor, or educator. Similarly, societies often granted poets the distinction of being wise because part of their function was to see, understand, order, and transmit verbally the society's world-view and moral code in their poetry.[43] Even in their most comic or satirical vein, poets engage this world-view and moral code, sometimes with personally devastating effects as Ovid himself experienced.

The notion that societies considered poets wise is inherent in the words used to label them. Romans called the poet either *vates*, which connotes both prophet and poet, or *poeta* itself, which connotes maker and contriver. Angles and Saxons called the poet *scop*, which derives from the third-person indicative singular form of *scieppan*, that is, to create, form, shape, make, order, arrange, adjudge, assign. Similarly, medieval and early modern Englishmen and Scotsmen called the poet *makar*, which like *poeta* suggests craftsmanship or ordering, and they called composition itself – both process and product – *making*, as Chaucer's famous complaint to "Adam scryveyne" reminds us.[44] This idea of poets as wise craftsmen is ancient, but in the Middle Ages it received new life at the hands of such theorists as Geoffrey of

---

to which individuals if they wish happiness must conform and that everything has its proper place and time" (111).

[42] Bloomfield and Dunn, *Role of the Poet*, 111.

[43] Bloomfield and Dunn, *Role of the Poet*, 1–7, 111–12. Dante illustrates the notion that poetry addresses ethics: "The branch of philosophy which determines the procedure of the work as a whole and in this part [*Paradiso*] is moral philosophy, or ethics, inasmuch as the whole and this part have been conceived for the sake of practical results, not for the sake of speculation." *Letter to Can Grande*, trans. Haller, 16.102. This instance of commentary is emblematic of medieval literary theory influenced by Aristotle, in which people frequently read poetry *sub ponitur ethice*, i.e., as pertaining to ethics. See J. Allen, *Ethical Poetic*, 3–66; *Medieval Grammar*, eds. Copeland and Sluiter, 52–60; and Minnis, *Medieval Theory of Authorship*. But also see Carruthers' cautionary note in *Experience of Beauty*, 8–13.

[44] Mooney, "Chaucer's Scribe," focuses attention on Adam Pinkhurst as addressee of "Chauciers woordes, a Geffrey vn to Adame his owen scryveyne" (Trinity College, Cambridge, R.3.20, 367), Chaucer's one-stanza, likely tongue-in-cheek curse, in which "making" signifies both poetic process and poem:

Vinsauf, who writing in the early thirteenth century characterizes poetic composition as analogous to mathematical design:

> Circinus interior mentis praecircinet omne
> Materiae spatium. Certus praelimitet ordo
> Unde praearripiat cursum stylus, at ubi Gades
> Figat. Opus totum prudens in pectoris arcem
> Contrahe, sitque prius in pectore quam sit in ore
>
> (Let the inner compass of the mind round out the entire extent of the material. Let a certain order predetermine from where the pen sets forth on its course, and where Cadiz is fixed. Draw together prudently the entire work into the storage chest of your breast, and let it be first in the breast before it is in the mouth)[45]

Geoffrey's advice echoes the biblical book of Wisdom 11:21 which asserts that in creation God disposed "omnia mensura et numero et pondere" (all things in measure, number and weight). Geoffrey's assertion that poets need to order their material implies they should similarly and wisely measure, number, and weigh their words as they construct poetry. Such measuring, numbering, and weighing are central to medieval concepts of beauty, for theorists often ground aesthetics in the harmonies produced by order and proportion: in medieval thinking, the beautiful expresses God's wisdom.[46] If God creates the universe and, in so doing, expresses Divine wisdom through the beauty of its order, medieval poets, it would seem, become secondary creators – "sub-creator[s]," to use J.R.R. Tolkien's term[47] – as they construct poetry. While poets often look to the past to preserve and express wisdom in the present, they do so with an eye on the future; when they express world-views and moral codes, poets present a particular understanding of a society's practical and speculative wisdom so that audiences likewise can measure, number, and weigh their lives and act according to that view.[48]

> Adam scryveyne if euer it thee byfalle
> Boece or Troylus for to wryten nuwe,
> Vnder thy long lokkes thuwe most haue the scale
> But affter my *makyng* thowe wryte more truwe,
> So offt adaye I mot thy werk renuwe
> It to correct and eke to rubbe and scrape,
> And al is thorugh thy necglygence and rape. (101–2, emphasis added)

See also William Dunbar's "I that in heill was," *Poems*, 21, in which he eulogizes English and Scottish "makaris"; Sir Philip Sidney's "Defense of Poesie," 411–12, in which he characterizes the poet as a "maker," based on the etymology of the Greek *poiein*, "to make"; and Ebin, *Illuminator*, 49–90.

[45] Geoffrey of Vinsauf, *Poetria Nova*, ed. Faral, 1.55–9. For context, see *Medieval Grammar*, eds. Copeland and Sluiter, 594–6, and J. Murphy, *Rhetoric*, 168–73.

[46] Eco, *Art and Beauty*, 17–42; Robertson, *Preface*, 114–37.

[47] Tolkien, "On Fairy Stories," 37.

[48] Geoffrey's other metaphor for creativity, comparing poetic composition to house building (1.43–7), also emphasizes forethought. As Copeland and Sluiter note in *Medieval Grammar*, 596–7, n.14, this metaphor for poetic composition is traditional. In a different

Art – liberal, mechanical, performing, visual, and poetic – is as Stephen Greenblatt notes "an important agent … in the transmission of culture."[49] In the West, medieval European world-views evident in part through surviving bits of art synthesized ideas from three main socio-linguistic groups: the Celtic, the Germanic, and the Italic. An overarching, and culturally leavening, force was a Christianity rooted in biblical-liturgical Judaism, synthesized with Greco-Roman philosophy, and administered through a Roman system of management and law: all vestiges of the antique past. Fusing Jewish-Christian views of the universe found in the Bible with Greco-Roman views articulated by Ptolemy and Plato, medieval thinkers drew on verbal constructs such as the chain of being, the plane of correspondences, the three estates, and the body politic to understand and explain the universe and humankind's place in it. As both path and end, wisdom in medieval culture centered on "cognitio divinorum" (knowledge of Divine things), as Thomas Aquinas (1225–74) defines "sapientia," and the application of that knowledge.[50] Aquinas further distinguishes "prudentia" from "sapientia." Prudentia is wisdom's ethical dimension that asks and tries to answer, "what shall we do and why?" (*ST* 2a–2ae Q.47–Q.51). Sapientia, on the other hand, is wisdom's theoretical, metaphysical, theological dimension that asks and tries to answer, "what is real, the universe, God?" If prudentia is wisdom on the ground, tending toward the moral and practical, sapientia is wisdom in the stars, tending toward the transcendental and speculative. Citing Augustine, Aquinas clarifies: "dicitur enim sapiens in unoquoque genere qui novit altissimam causam illius generis, per quam potest de omnibus iudicare. Simpliciter autem sapiens dicitur qui novit altissimam causam simpliciter, scilicet Deum (for a wise man in any branch of knowledge is said to be one who knows the highest cause of that kind of knowledge and can judge of all matters by that cause; and a wise man simply is said to be one who knows the cause which is simply highest, namely God) (*ST* 2a–2ae Q.9, A.2).[51]

---

context, Chaucer uses the metaphor to describe Pandarus' technique (*TC* 1.1065–71): a narrational moment that for readers familiar with Geoffrey of Vinsauf illustrates Chaucer's intertextual reading-writing practice.

[49] Greenblatt, "Culture," 228.
[50] Aquinas, *Summa Theologiae*, ed. Caramello, 2a–2ae Q.19, A.7.
[51] Aquinas elaborates on this distinction later when he writes: "secundum philosophum, in principio Metaphys., ad sapientem pertinent considerare causam altissimam, per quam de aliis certissime iudicatur, et secundum quam omnia ordinari oportet. Causa autem altissima dupliciter accipi potest, vel simpliciter, vel in aliquo genere. Ille igitur qui cognoscit causam altissimam in aliquo genere et per eam potest de omnibus quae sunt illius generis iudicare et ordinare, dicitur esse sapiens in illo genere, ut in medicina vel architectura, secundum illud I ad Cor. III, ut sapiens architectus fundamentum posui. Ille autem qui cognoscit causam altissimam simpliciter, quae est Deus, dicitur sapiens simpliciter, inquantum per regulas divinas omnia potest iudicare et ordinare. (According to the Philosopher [i.e., Aristotle], in the beginning of *Metaphysics*, it belongs to wisdom to consider the highest cause, through which a most certain judgment is formed about other causes, and according to which all things should be ordered. Now the highest cause may be understood in two ways, either simply or in some particular genus. Therefore, he who knows the highest cause in any particular genus, and by it is able to judge and order all that belongs to that genus, is said to be wise in that genus, as in medicine or

Such wisdom for Aquinas is both an intellectual virtue, a mental habit to be cultivated (*ST* 1a–2ae Q.57, A.2), and an infused gift of the Holy Spirit (*ST* 2a–2ae Q.45).

Drawing on ideas of wisdom gleaned from the biblical and antique past, medieval Christians like Aquinas sought to understand their "middle place" in the order of creation, that is, between inanimate matter and God, and their "middle place" in the order of time, that is, between time's beginning and its end. Hence, Christians sought – or were so instructed – to live mindful of life's ends: either salvation or damnation, as ubiquitous instances of Last Judgment images in visual and verbal arts indicate.[52] In relation to these two possible ends, medieval Christians viewed life as a spiritual pilgrimage on one of two paths. Jesus himself suggested this view during the Sermon on the Mount: "Intrate per angustam portam: quia lata porta, et spatiosa via est, quae ducit ad perditionem, et multi sunt qui intrant per eam. Quam angusta porta, et arcta via est, quae ducit ad viam: et pauci sunt qui inveniunt eam" (Enter through the narrow gate: because wide is the gate and broad is the way that leads to destruction, and there are many who go through it. How narrow is the gate and strait is the way that leads to life: and there are few who find it) (Mt. 7:13–14). Taking this passage as a starting point, Sir John Clanvowe (1341–91), a contemporary and friend of Chaucer, composed *The Two Ways*, a short prose meditation that provides a view of one late fourteenth-century English knight's understanding of wisdom's role in life.

Clanvowe characterizes the two ways he delineates as two kinds of wisdom. Paraphrasing and quoting Paul's letter to the Romans (8:5–8; 13), he writes:

> And, therfore, [Seynt Poul] teecheth vs that we shulde not walke after the flessh but after the spirit. ffor he seith that the wysdom of the flessh is deeth and that the wisdom of the spirit is lyf and pees. And the wisdom of the flessh is enemy to God … And, therfor, he seith to vs, "Yef we lyuen after the flessh we shulne dyen, that is to seye, we shuln bee dampned; and yef that thorugh the spirit we maken deede the deedys of oure flessh we shuln lyue," that is to seye, we schuln bee sauued.[53]

---

architecture, according to 1 Cor. 3: "As a wise architect, I have laid a foundation" [10]. Yet, he who knows the cause that is simply the highest, which is God, is said to be wise simply as far as he is able to judge and order all things according to divine rules.) *ST* 2a–2ae Q.45 A.2. Paul's simile of the wise architect, which Thomas quotes, parallels Geoffrey of Vinsauf's wise poet-house builder (see n.48).

52 One of the more striking Last Judgment relief sculptures is Gislebertus' twelfth-century west portal tympanum at the Cathedral of Saint-Lazare, Autun, but it is a common theme in stained glass and manuscript painting as well as plastic forms dating from the late antique. Beckwith, *Early Medieval Art*, 215; Davis-Weyer, *Early Medieval Art*, 20–3, 74, 151, 154, 178; Mâle, *Gothic Image*, 355–89; von Simson, *Gothic Cathedral*, 110–14. Thomas of Celano's thirteenth-century sequence, "Dies irae," which became part of the Roman Rite liturgy for the dead, offers an instance of the theme in poetry. Raby, *Christian Latin Poetry*, 443–52. And the episode serves as the culminating pageant in each of the four extant English cycle plays (Chester, N-Town, Towneley, and York). For an exploration of this theme in literature, see B. Nolan, *Gothic Visionary Perspective*.

53 Clanvowe, *Two Ways*, ed. Scattergood, 65.

Though likely he is unaware of the connection, Clanvowe's distinction here between "wisdom of the spirit," or the way of "lyf and pees," and "wysdom of the flessh," or the way of "deeth," is based on an early Jewish-Christian catechetical teaching known as the two ways.[54] In 1 Corinthians 2:4–7, Paul writes:

> Et sermo meus, et praedicatio mea, non in persuasibilibus humanae sapientiae verbis, sed in ostensione spiritus et virtutis: ut fides vestra non sit in sapientia hominum, sed in virtute Dei. Sapientiam autem loquimur inter perfectos, sapientiam vero non hujus seculi, neque principum hujus seculi, qui destruuntur: sed loquimur Dei sapientiam in mysterio, quae abscondita est, quam praedestinavit Deus ante secula in gloriam nostrum

> (And my speech and my preaching was not in persuasive words of human wisdom, but in the showing of the spirit and of virtue, so that your faith might not be in human wisdom but in the virtue of God. Moreover, we speak wisdom among the perfect, but not the wisdom of this world nor of the princes of this world who are ruined: but we speak the wisdom of God in a mystery, which is hidden, and which God ordained before the world for our glory)[55]

In addition to its allusion to the two-ways tradition, the Pauline distinction between "the wisdom of this world" and "the wisdom of God" articulates a then vibrant tension between two forms of education rooted in classical Greek culture. As Paul Olson delineates the struggle, Socratic-Platonic thinking, which insisted that education should lead to understanding the cosmic order and to aligning individual and civic life with it, directly challenged Sophistic thinking, which argued that education should lead to creating social order through language.[56] In his epistles, Paul clearly comes down on the side of Socratic-Platonic thinking (even if unaware of the connection) and in doing so echoes the distinction made in James 3:13–18 when James writes:

> Quis sapiens et disciplinatus inter vos ostendat ex bona conversatione operationem suam in mansuetudine sapientiae. Quod si zelum amarum habetis et contentiones in cordibus vestris nolite gloriari et mendaces esse adversus veritatem. Non ista sapientia desursum descendens sed terrena animalis diabolica. Ubi enim zelus et contentio ibi inconstantia et omne opus pravum quae autem desursum est sapientia primum quidem pudica est deinde pacifica modesta suadibilis plena miseri-

---

[54] *The Didache*, a first-century Christian catechism dating shortly after the Pauline letters, begins "Two Ways there are, one of life and one of death, and there is a great difference between the Two Ways." *The Didache*, trans. Kleist, 15. Rooted in Jewish teaching, this catechetical instruction also appears in *The Epistle of Barnabas*, *Doctrina Aposolorum*, *Apostolic Church Order*, and the *Manual of Discipline*, this last from the Qumran community. Suggs, "Christian Two Ways," 60–7; Niederwimmer, *Didache*, 30–41. On the two ways' possible function as baptismal catechism, its provenance and audience, see Suggs, 72–3, and Rordorf, "Judeo-Christian Ethic," 148–59.

[55] Meyendorff, "Wisdom – Sophia," 391, offers a succinct review of Paul on wisdom.

[56] Olson, *Journey to Wisdom*, 1–40.

cordia et fructibus bonis non iudicans sine simulatione. Fructus autem iustitiae in pace seminatur facientibus pacem

(Let anyone among you who is wise and understanding show his work through good conversation and in the meekness of wisdom. But if you have bitter envy and contention in your hearts do not glory in it nor lie against truth, for that is not wisdom descending from above but worldly, sensual, diabolical. For where there is envy and contention there is inconstancy and every evil work, but wisdom from above is indeed first virtuous, then peaceable, modest, humble, filled with mercy and good fruits, non-judgmental, and without pretence. And the fruit of justice is sown in peace by those making peace)

As he contrasts a worldly, sensual, diabolical wisdom marked by envy and contention with wisdom from above, James provides a litany of qualities that both define and benchmark the latter, marked by virtue, peace, modesty, humility, mercy, meekness, and integrity.

Writings such as these shaped medieval Christian understanding of the nature of wisdom and the distinction between "wysdom of the flessh" and "wisdom of the spirit." Turning again to the *Summa Theologiae*, we note Aquinas paraphrases James 3:15 while examining the spiritual gift of wisdom, stating "dicitur enim Iac. III quaedam sapientia esse terrena, animalis, diabolica" (for it is written in James 3 that a certain wisdom is earthly, sensual, diabolical) (*ST* 2a–2ae Q.45, Obj. 1). Distinguishing kinds of wisdom in relation to their respective ends, he continues:

Quicumque enim avertitur a fine debito, necesse est quod aliquem finem indebitum sibi praestituat, quia omne agens agit propter finem. Unde si praestituat sibi finem in bonis exterioribus terrenis, vocatur sapientia terrena; si autem in bonis corporalibus, vocatur sapientia animalis; si autem in aliqua excellentia, vocatur saptientia diabolica, propter imitationem superbiae Diaboli

(Now whoever is turned away from his due end, it is necessary that he set up some undue end because every agent acts for an end. Wherefore, if he fixes for himself an end in external earthly things, the wisdom is called earthly; if in the goods of the body, the wisdom is called sensual; if in some excellence, the wisdom is called diabolical because it imitates the devil's pride) (*ST* 2a–2ae Q.45, Reply Obj. 1)

These three categories of wisdom – *terrena, animalis, diabolica* – parallel the theme of the three temptations prevalent in medieval culture: the world, the flesh, and the devil.[57] Again for Aquinas, pursuing wisdom of the spirit leads ultimately to the highest cause, God, while pursuing any of these other three leads to a self-centered, finally destructive, end.

Though difficult to pinpoint whether or not Clanvowe read the *Summa*, the ideas on wisdom Aquinas articulates seem fairly common in medieval thinking. As he writes his own summa of sorts, Clanvowe draws on these ideas and others

---

[57] Howard, *Three Temptations*. See also Twycross, *Medieval Anadyomene*, 38–45, for the three temptations theme in Bersuire as related to Venus, the three graces, and the sirens.

to distinguish further virtuous from worldly wisdom. Declaring that the gate to the narrow way is the "dreede of God" and the narrow way itself is keeping God's commandments (59), Clanvowe echoes ideas found in Jewish wisdom literature and appropriated by Christian thinkers. In Ecclesiasticus, for example, Jesus ben Sira describes fear of the Lord as wisdom's beginning, fullness, crown, and root (1:11–25), and wisdom itself as the law and covenant of Moses (24:33). For Clanvowe, and indeed for most medieval Christians, fearing the Lord and keeping his commandments serve as the moral code of virtuous wisdom. On the other hand, worldly wisdom has its own code of behavior that Clanvowe, like Aquinas, suggests through reference to the three temptations. While according to Clanvowe the world tempts people to pursue honor, power, and comforts by counseling conformity, and the flesh tempts them to pursue physical delights by counseling the naturalness of these pursuits, the devil tempts them to rely overmuch on God's mercy (62–3). As a fourteenth-century poet and knight composing a treatise on wisdom and the Christian life, Clanvowe implies the traditional medieval Christian world-view that places humankind on a temporal continuum between time's origin and end, and he explains the moral code based on that world-view by contrasting the wisdom that leads to salvation with the wisdom that leads to damnation.[58]

Clanvowe's *Two Ways* probably did not circulate beyond his group of friends and the courtly environment to which he, as a knight of Richard II's inner circle, belonged.[59] Still, his commentary illustrates well the medieval distinction between virtuous and worldly wisdom, reaching back to early Christian writers fully engaged in the polemical debate between Christian exclusivity and pagan syncretism.[60] While this distinction seems fairly clear, and we find its artistic expression in various texts, two other aspects of wisdom stemming from the antique world were especially at play in medieval culture.[61] In Jewish wisdom literature, writers frequently personify

---

[58] Though the content of *The Two Ways* is traditional, Clanvowe himself associated with a group of knights sympathetic to Wycliffites, and at one point in the treatise refers to simple Christians as those whom "þe world scorneth and hooldeth ... [as] lolleris and loselis, foolis and schameful wrecches ... God holdeth hem moost wise and most worsshipful" (511–14). The Middle English word "loller," meaning loafer or idler, was occasionally applied to Wycliffites, perhaps as an aural pun on Lollard, a label of contempt for those deemed heretical derived from the Middle Dutch *lollaerd* ("mumbler, mutterer"). On Clanvowe and his courtly colleagues, see McFarlane, *Lancastrian Kings*, 139–226.

[59] Two copies of *The Two Ways* are extant: University College Oxford MS 97 (complete) and British Library Ms. Additional 22283 (fragmentary). Both manuscript miscellanies date to within a decade of Clanvowe's death in 1391. Scattergood, introduction to *The Works*, 21–2.

[60] The fourth-century anti-pagan polemicist Lactantius, for instance, contrasts the false wisdom of pagan philosophers, Paul's "wisdom of this world," with the true wisdom of the Incarnation and the Church, Paul's "wisdom of God," in books three and four of *Divinarum Institutiones*. See also the fifth-century poets, Prosper of Aquitaine, *Epigram* 236, ed. Callens and Gastaldo, and Caelius Sedulius, *Carmen Paschale*, ed. Huemer, 1.325–33.

[61] In *Amorosa Visione*, for instance, Boccaccio uses the two-ways metaphor to structure the narrator's dream action in confronting a choice between a narrow gate "a via die vita"

wisdom as a female (Sapientia in the Vulgate), created by God in the beginning, who helped God to order, even create, the universe (Ecclus. 1:1–10, 24:5–11; Prov. 3:19–20, 8:22–31; Wis. 7:25–6) and who now helps God sustain universal harmony through the law (Ecclus. 24:32–4). Biblical Sapientia is a vibrant, playful, creative figure: an expression of the Divine in the universe.[62] When they develop wisdom figures, medieval poets often follow these notions of wisdom's femininity and her ordering and sustaining role. In the twelfth century, to cite just one example, Bernard Silvestris uses these ideas in part to develop Noys in his *Cosmographia*. Echoing biblical Sapientia, Noys says to Natura:

> Porro Nois ego, dei ratio profundius exquisite, quam utique de se, alteram se, Usia prima genuit – non in tempore sed ex eo quo consistit eterno – Noys ego, scientia et arbitraria divine voluntatis ad dispositionem rerum, quemadmodum de consensus eius accipio, sic mee administrationis official circumduco
>
> (Moreover I am Noys, the profound and exquisite reason of God, whom his prime being generated from itself, a second self, not in time, but out of that eternity in which he exists – I, Noys, am the knowledge and judgment of the divine will in disposing things; I thus carry forth the duties of my administration as I receive them from his will)[63]

Noys, as she actively organizes the universe herself and sustains it through Endelichia, the world soul, is arguably the central character in book one. As Barbara Newman states, biblical Sapientia is the "matriarch of medieval goddesses, casting a faint glow of canonicity over them all."[64]

Medieval poets also incorporated the idea whereby Christ as Logos takes on Sapientia's attributes, and wisdom in Trinitarian theology becomes Christ's special attribute.[65] Comparing Proverbs 8:22–36, Ecclesiasticus 24:5–26, and John 1:1–18 reveals this connection. In each passage, Wisdom or Logos follows a four-step

---

(to the way of life) and a broad gate to earthly joy. The narrator chose the broad gate, in spite of his dream guide's advice, and it made all the comic difference as he bumbled his way through a series of experiences leading to frustrated sexual expression with his beloved Fiammetta. His dream guide returned upon his waking and offered to lead him to Fiammetta through the narrow gate. Hollander, *Boccaccio's Two Venuses*, 79–91, takes the mysterious heavenly dream guide as the celestial Venus striving throughout to lead the narrator to rightly ordered love.

[62] B. Newman, *God and the Goddesses*, 190–2.
[63] Bernard Silvestris, *Cosmographia*, ed. Dronke, 1.2.1.5–10.
[64] B. Newman, *God and the Goddesses*, 190.
[65] At the height of the Arian-Catholic conflict over the Trinitarian nature of God, the Arian Emperor Constantius exiled Hilary of Poitiers (c.315–67/8) to Phrygia for his orthodoxy. While there from 356 to 360, Hilary wrote his *De Trinitate*, a twelve-book treatise in which he synthesized earlier thinking linking Christ to biblical Sapientia. Hilary of Poitiers, *De Trinitate*, trans. McKenna, 1.35, 4.21, and 12.36–9. Augustine drew on Hilary extensively in his own treatise on the Trinity, in part attributing Power to the Father, Wisdom to the Son, and Love to the Holy Spirit. Augustine, *De Trinitate*, books 14 and 15.

sequence: it is initially close to God, has a role in creation, dwells among humans, and bestows gifts on humankind.[66] Wisdom-Logos in this pattern mediates between God and the universe.[67] While the idea of Christ as divine wisdom pervades medieval literature, it takes center stage in the fifteenth-century English morality play *Wisdom*, in which Euerlastyng Wysdom, complete with attributes of the Second Person of the Trinity, saves a fallen soul whose three faculties – Mynd, Wnderstondyng, Wyll – have been seduced by Lucifer's worldly wisdom.[68] Developing a *Brautmystic* theme where Anima initially desires and ultimately achieves union with Wysdom, the playwright dramatizes wisdom as both path and end for the individual soul. As Euerlastyng Wysdom calls Mynd in particular to conversion, he states:

> O thou Mynde, remembyr the!
> Turne þi weys, þou gost amyse.
> Se what þi ende ys, þou might not fle:
> Dethe to euery creature certen ys.
> They þat lyue well, þey xall haue blys;
> Thay þat endyn yll, þey go to hell.
> I am Wysdom, sent to tell yow thys:
> Se in what stat þou doyst indwell. (873–80)

Here the metaphor of life as a journey serves as an objective correlative to Mynd's inner state as well as a reminder of the end to which he is tending. This play aptly stages the Pauline distinction between the "wisdom of God" and the "wisdom of this world" in the characters of Wysdom and Lucifer, and Wysdom's reminder that "They þat lyue well, þey xall haue blys; / Thay þat endyn yll, þey go to hell" demonstrates

---

[66] R. Murphy, "Wisdom," 973, writes: "The prologue to the Fourth Gospel presents so many contacts with OT wisdom that one can hardly doubt that the Evangelist was rethinking much of the traditional sapiential heritage in presenting Jesus as the Logos, or Word."

[67] Olson, *Journey to Wisdom*, 19–25.

[68] Lucifer's worldly wisdom is particularly insidious when he initially counsels against devotional practices such as fasting, silence, and tears, which could become excessive, and then advises the soul to leave the contemplative life:

> Wan they haue wastyde by feyntnes,
> Than febyll ther wyttis and fallyn to fondnes,
> Sum into dyspeyer and sum into madness.
>   Wet yt well, God ys not plesyde with thys.
> Lewe, lewe, suche syngler besynes.
> Be in the worlde, vse thyngys nesesse.
> The comyn ys best expres.
>   Who clymyt hye, hys fall gret ys.

Wisdom, ed. Eccles, 437–44. The audience of *Wisdom* is likely monastic, or at least religious, and Lucifer's temptation of Anima – to avoid despairing of perfection by never seeking it – plays on the temptations many medieval writers addressed in treatises on the spiritual life. M. Smith, *Personification*, 123–65.

the contrast between virtuous and worldly wisdom and their conflicting paths to salvation or damnation that Clanvowe articulates in *The Two Ways*.

Like people in other early societies, medieval Christians relied upon speculative and practical wisdom to understand and articulate their world-view and to live according to the moral code founded upon it. They also considered another kind of wisdom that, unless they were particularly wary, could seduce them into overvaluing worldly ends. As Clanvowe suggests, two different spiritual paths characterized by two different kinds of wisdom were open for medieval Christians; of course, as *Wisdom* dramatizes, individuals made their own choices, for which they would be held accountable. The implication, however, is that to choose following the dictates of worldly wisdom is unwise. Developing an *ubi sunt* theme, Paul writes:

> Scriptum est enim: "Perdam sapientiam sapientium, et prudentiam prudentium reprobabo." Ubi sapiens? ubi scriba? ubi conquisitor hujus seculi? Nonne stultam fecit Deus sapientiam hujus mundi? Nam quia in Dei sapientia non cognovit mundus per sapientiam Deum: placuit Deo per stultitiam praedicationis salvos facere credentes
>
> (For it is written: "I shall destroy the wisdom of the wise, and I shall reject the prudence of the prudent." Where is the wise man? Where is the scribe? Where is the seeker of this world? Has not God made the wisdom of this world foolish? For because in the wisdom of God the world, through its wisdom, did not recognize God, it pleased God, through the foolishness of our preaching, to save those who believe) (1 Cor. 1:19–21)

Because of the Incarnation, the wisdom of the worldly wise is now foolishness, Paul says, so follow the "foolishness" I preach and be wise.

Synthesizing Greco-Roman with Jewish-Christian ideas, medieval thinkers distinguished between what has been called virtuous and worldly wisdom. They believed that virtuous wisdom – as intellectual virtue, gift of the Holy Spirit, or moral virtue in the guise of *prudentia* – encompassed the intellectual and moral ideals they should follow in their search to know things human and divine, to understand what is right and true, and to act accordingly. Medieval poets as lovers and purveyors of wisdom engage these ideas in and through their art. Intellectually, part of their search for truth was manifest in their approach to classical mythology and fable, and their reception and transformation of the Roman Minerva – their uses of her as a poetic image – take into account this multi-dimensional view of wisdom.

Mythography: Interpreting Myth

Writing *De natura deorum* in the summer of 45 BCE, just months before being caught up in the politics surrounding Julius Caesar's assassination, Cicero (106–43 BCE) reviews several theories concerning divinity then current in Roman culture through a dialogue between Vellius, an Epicurean, Balbus, a Stoic, and Cotta, an Academic Skeptic. Three theories in particular profoundly influenced subsequent views of Greco-Roman mythology and fable: that the gods were deified mortals; that the gods were personifications of natural and cosmological forces; and that the gods were personifications of moral and intellectual attributes.[69] Tracing these theories through medieval culture and classifying them as the historical, the physical, and the moral traditions, Seznec argues that the Middle Ages appropriated them primarily from Cicero to explain mythological figures in classical literature and to validate their appearance in medieval literature and visual art.[70] Jane Chance goes beyond explanation and validation to demonstrate that Greco-Roman mythology and mythography – the former "a unified system of myth" and the latter "the interpretation of myth" – as received and transformed in the Middle Ages proved an immensely productive cultural force in literature and art.[71] Rather than merely surviving the Middle Ages to be revived in Renaissance glory, classical deities and their stories actually thrived in medieval cultures, albeit transformed and adapted.

When Cicero develops his historical view of the gods in *De natura deorum*, he draws on a tradition propounded in about 300 BCE by the Greek mythographer Euhemerus, who first theorized that the gods were simply noteworthy humans deified by subsequent generations.[72] His historical theory bears his name: euhemerism. Although Cicero himself seems to discount euhemerism as impious towards the traditional Greek and Roman deities, early Christian apologists used the theory to discount the pagan gods as mere mortals who had been inappropriately deified for performing extraordinary tasks. Writing in a time when Christianity was under pressure from the state, Lactantius (c.250–c.325) attacks paganism using euhemerism when he describes how the gods came to exist:

> Quibus ex rebus, cum constet illos homines fuisse, non est obscurum qua ratione dii coeperint nominari. Si enim nulli reges ante Saturnum uel Uranum fuerunt propter hominum raritatem, qui agrestem uitam sine ullo rectore uiuebant: non est dubium quin illis temporibus homines regem ipsum totamque gentem summis laudibus ac nouis honoribus iactare coeperint, ut etiam deos appellarent, siue ob miraculum uirtutis (hoc uere putabant rudes adhuc et simplices), siue (ut fieri solet) in adulationem praesentis potentiae, siue ob beneficia quibus erant ad humanitatem compositi … Itaque homines eorum simulacra finxerunt, ut haberent aliquod ex imaginum contemplatione solatium; progressique longius per amorem meriti, memoriam defunctorum colere coeperunt

---

[69] On allegory and personification, see Auerbach, "Figura," 11–76; Boyarin, "Origen as Theorist," 39–54; Copeland and Struck, Introduction, 1–6; D. Jeffrey, "Reference and Recognition," 1–17; Lamberton, "Language," 73–80; Most, "Helenistic Allegory," 26–38; Obbink, "Early Greek Allegory," 15–25; Paxson, *Poetics of Personification*, 8–34; Struck, "Allegory and Ascent," 57–70; Turner, "Allegory," 71–82; and Whitman, "Retrospective Forward," 3–29, and "Present Perspectives," 33–45.
[70] Seznec, *Survival of the Pagan Gods*, 4. Cicero, *De natura deorum*, ed. Rackham, does not delineate these theories systematically; however, a few highlighted passages demonstrate his general attitude concerning each. On the historical, see Cotta's attack (1.119) and Balbus' defense (2.62); on the physical, see Balbus' presentation (2.49–57) and Cotta's refutation (3.passim); on the moral, see Balbus' presentation (2.63–72) and Vellius' (1.36, 41) and Cotta's (3.61–4) attacks.
[71] Chance, *Medieval Mythography* 1: 2.
[72] Cooke, "Euhemerism," 397.

(Since it is established from these things that these were men, it is not a mystery by what manner they began to be named gods. For if there were no kings before Saturn or Uranus on account of the rarity of men, who were living a wild life without any leader, there is no doubt that in those times men began to raise up the king himself and the entire nation with highest praises and new honors so that they also called them gods either for some miracle of strength [the simple and rustic truly used to think this and still do] or [as is usually done] in adulation of present power, or for benefits to humanity with which they were associated ... Thus men made statues of them so that they might have some solace from contemplating the images)[73]

This passage echoes Wisdom 14 on the origin of idolatry, in which the gods were merely humans deified through popular custom after their death or in their absence.[74] Lactantius also suggests that certain mortals became gods because they were founders of tribes or cities:

Priuatim uero singuli populi gentis aut urbis suae conditores, seu uiri fortitudine insignes erant, seu foeminae castitate mirabiles, summa ueneratione coluerunt; ut Aegyptii Isidem, Mauri Iubam, Macedones Cabirum, Poeni Uranum, Latini Faunum, Sabini Sancum, Romani Quirinum. Eodem utique modo Athenae Mineruam, Samos Iunonem, Paphos Venerem, Lemnos Vulcanum, Naxos Liberum, Apollinem Delphi.

(Privately, distinct peoples honored with highest veneration the founders of their tribe or city, whether they were men distinguished for bravery or women remarkable for chastity; so Egypt honored Isis, the Moors Juba, the Macedonians Cabirus, the Phoenicians Uranus, the Latins Faunus, the Sabines Sancus, the Romans Quirinus. And so in the same way Athens honored Minerva, Samos Juno, Pamphos Venus, Lemnos Vulcan, Naxos Liber, and Delphos Apollo. (*Divinarum Institutiones*, 1.15)

---

[73] Lactantius, *Divinarum Institutiones*, ed. Brandt, 1.15.
[74] Wisdom 14:15–17 reads: "Acerbo enim luctu dolens pater, cito sibi rapti filii fecit imaginem: et illum, qui tunc quasi homo mortuus fuerat, nunc tamquam deum colere coepit, et constituit inter servos suos sacra et sacrificia. Deinde interveniente tempore, convalescente iniqua consuetudine, hic error tamquam lex custoditus est, et tyrannorum imperio colebantur figmenta. Et hos quos in palam homines honorare non poterant propter hoc quod longe essent, e longinquo figura eorum allata, evidentem imaginem regis, quem honorare volebant, fecerunt: ut illum, qui aberat, tamquam praesentem colerent sua sollicitudine" (For a father mourning with bitter sorrow made for himself an image of his son who had been quickly taken away: and he now began to worship as a god that son, who had died as a man, and he constituted holy rites and sacrifices among his servants. Then time having passed, with the wicked custom strengthening, this error was protected as a law, and statues were worshipped by the command of tyrants. And those [kings] who men could not honor in open because they lived far off, the men, having brought their resemblance from afar, made a visible image of the king, whom they wished to honor: so that they by their anxiety might worship him, who was absent, as present).

In late-antique Imperial culture, Lactantius and other Christian apologists deploy euhemerism as a polemical tool to combat a living belief in the gods. Once Christianity becomes well established, however, the need to vilify the gods dissipates, but writers continue to use euhemerism to explain origins. In the seventh century, Isidore of Seville (c.560–636) integrates this passage from Lactantius almost verbatim into his discussion of Greco-Roman deities: a move that enables the theory's widespread dissemination.[75]

The euhemeristic notion of a people's founder becomes rather important in high medieval culture when, much like Celtic bards with genealogy poems, certain writers fulfill a wished for cultural continuity with the Greco-Roman past by developing ethnogenic fables, tracing a people's lineage from a mythological hero, deity, or demigod.[76] Medieval historians, for instance, often incorporate mythological figures into histories and chronicles, melding myth, legend, and history into a narrative that authenticates a people's origins and lends the glory achieved by the mythological figures to their descendants. In particular, the Trojan story appealed to medieval writers primarily because Virgil's *Aeneid*, Ovid's *Heroides*, and three late-antique narratives purporting to be eyewitness accounts of the Trojan war (Dares' *De excidio Troiae historia*, Dictys of Crete's *Ephemeridos belli Troiani libri*, and the anonymous *Excidium Troiae*) were popular in medieval schools. When we recall that the *Aeneid* recounts a foundation myth of Roman Imperial culture, implying that Rome itself is the new Troy, and that the Palladium – Troy's divine statue of Athena – found a new home in Rome at Vesta's hearth, we begin to understand the Trojan story's fruitful influence in Roman and medieval cultures. In twelfth-century England, the attention to Troy gains new momentum when Geoffrey of Monmouth (c.1095–c.1155) composes his *Historia regum Britanniae*, popularizing the idea that Aeneas' great-grandson Brutus, a lineal descendant of Venus, founded the British race and established London, like Rome, as *Troia Nova*.[77] Here, instead of discounting Brutus as a mythological figure or ignoring him altogether, Geoffrey follows the founder model of euhemerized deities expounded by writers such as Lactantius and Isidore and appropriates Brutus for the British; now a historical

---

[75] Isidore of Seville, *Etymologiae*, ed. Lindsay, 8.11. Isidore's encyclopedia was widely popular and deeply influential. Extant today in nearly 1000 known manuscript copies, it had by 800 disseminated throughout Europe. Subsequent extant copies date from every century, including over sixty full and over seventy excerpted fifteenth-century copies. Its *editio princeps* published by G. Zainer at Augsburg in 1472 was the first of eleven editions published by 1500. Barney et al., introduction to *The Etymologies*, 24–8; Cooke, "Euhemerism," 402–7; Henderson, *Medieval World of Isidore of Seville*.

[76] On Celtic bards, see Bloomfield and Dunn, *Role of the Poet*, 33–5, 120–49. On euhemerism and cultural origins, see Seznec *Survival of the Pagan Gods*, 11–22.

[77] Geoffrey of Monmouth, *Historia regum Britanniae*, ed. Wright, 14. Later writers draw on Geoffrey's account. The *Gawain*-poet, for instance, invokes Trojan history to frame *Sir Gawain and the Green Knight*. See Hodapp, "Geoffrey of Monmouth," 18–22; and Federico, *New Troy*, xiii–xxii, 33–45. See also Smalley's discussion of the English public's taste for pseudo-histories: *English Friars*, 9–27.

rather than legendary figure, Brutus dignifies British history as the founder of the race: new Trojans living in a new Troy.[78]

Along with this historical tradition, medieval writers appropriated the classical idea that gods could personify natural phenomena, particularly the planets. In spite of patristic opposition to astrology, early medieval thinkers synthesized biblical cosmology with scientific knowledge from Greco-Roman culture, grounding cosmological theories initially on Plato's *Timaeus*, Macrobius' (fl. c.400–30) *Commentarii in Somnium Scipionis*, and Martianus Capella's (fl. c.400–30) *De nuptiis Philologiae et Mercurii*.[79] In the wake of more interactive contact with Arabic and Byzantine cultures via trade, the Crusades in Asia Minor, and Andalusian Spain's "la convivencia," Greco-Arabic scientific texts began flowing into Europe beginning in the twelfth century, gradually influencing cosmological thinking further.[80] Many medieval people thought that certain stars and the planets – Luna (Diana), Mercury, Venus, Sol (Apollo), Mars, Jupiter, Saturn – could influence human life. Following this astrological science, poets often used the gods to indicate planetary and astral influences on a character's physical and temperamental nature; Chaucer's Wife of Bath offers an example of such characterization. She declares:

> Gat-tothed I was, and that bicam me well;
> I hadde the prente of Seinte Venus seel ...
> For certes, I am al Venerien
> In fellynge, and myn herte is Marcien.
> Venus me yaf my lust, my likerousness,
> And Mars yaf me my sturdy hardynesse.
> Myn ascendent was Taur, and Mars therinne
> Allas, allas, that evere love was synne!
> I folwed ay myn inclinacioun
> By vertu of my constellacioun,
> That made me I koude noght withdrawe
> My chambre of Venus from a goode felawe.
> Yet have I Martes mark upon my face,
> And also in another privee place. (603–4, 609–20)

According to medieval astrological science, the stars under which one was born could influence one's physical and temperamental make-up. The Wife of Bath's horoscope, by her own admission, dictates her physical features ("Gat-tothed") and

---

[78] The myth of London as *Troia Nova* seemed a productive cultural force in late medieval England especially during Ricardian and early Lancastrian rule. See Federico, *New Troy*.
[79] Wedel, *Astrology in the Middle Ages*, 15–24; Lewis, *Discarded Image*, 45–69.
[80] The history of astronomy and astrology in the medieval period is much more complex and varied than this summary suggests. Lewis, *Discarded Image*, 92–121, offers an overview. Charon, *Cosmology*, 19–57, gives more detail, and, though dated, Wedel, *Astrology in the Middle Ages*, 25–100, remains helpful. While Pederson, *Early Physics*, 214–45, presents detailed analyses, Hoskin and Gingerich, "Medieval Latin Astronomy," 68–97, provide a more recent survey. For detailed bibliographic work, Grant's "Astronomy, Cosmology, and Cosmography," 363–8, and Burnett's "Astrology," 369–82, are useful.

moral character ("likerousness ... hardynesse") as well as her personality ("I folwed ay myn inclinacioun"). Chaucer uses Venus and Mars to indicate his character's temperament, and the Wife of Bath herself uses astrological lore to justify herself.[81]

While according to theory the planets and constellations could influence one's physical features and personality from birth, they also could influence one's later life through the fortune they might bring. We find a literary example of this kind of influence in Robert Henryson's (c.1430–c.1500) *Testament of Cresseid*, his poetic response to Chaucer's *Troilus and Criseyde*. After Diomeid deserts Cresseid, she laments her loyalty to Venus and Cupid and has a dream in which Cupid prosecutes her before the planetary deities. In accord with the other gods, Saturn and Cynthia (Diana) sentence her to a loss of beauty and health; Cresseid wakes from the dream a wretched leper and dies shortly thereafter, following a final chance meeting with Troylus in which neither recognizes the other. Henryson, in constructing the trial scene, uses the gods as astrological figures representing the fickleness of fortune or perhaps as objective manifestations of Cresseid's own corrupt inner state: her conscience, in a sense, judging, condemning, and executing punishment. As Nickolas Haydock argues, Cresseid's curse and subsequent punishment at the will of the planetary deities points to a power system that scapegoats its victim to provide "ane mirrour" of warning to other women.[82] Putting aside the question of her moral character and culpability, however, we note that Cresseid herself remains powerless in the world of the narrative to alter the dream's events and swiftly succumbs to the deities' influence. These gods in Chaucer's Wife of Bath Prologue and Henryson's poem illustrate primarily the cosmological tradition of mythography, representing forces that can influence a character's temperament in the one instance and fate in the other.

The historical and physical traditions were prominent in mythographical handbooks and commentaries on ancient authors. Often in these same texts, medieval writers also interpreted the gods as allegorical representatives of philosophical, intellectual, or moral ideas: a set of interpretations rooted in Greco-Roman literary theories that sought underlying meanings in poetic fables.[83] Drawing on the longstanding tradition of allegorical interpretation, Macrobius bequeaths to the Middle Ages a theory of "narratio fabulosa" (fabulous narrative), by which "sacrarum rerum

---

[81] Curry, "Wife of Bath," 166–87.
[82] Haydock, *Situational Poetics*, 155–200; *Testament of Cresseid*, 457, in *Poems and Fables*, ed. Wood.
[83] Though relatively late on the scene, the term *allēgoria* ultimately comes from the Greek word *allegorein*, which when broken down to its roots *allos* ("other") and *agoreuein* ("to speak") literally means "to speak of the other." *The American Heritage Dictionary*, 48; *The American Heritage Dictionary of Indo-European Roots*, 2, 19. At its roots, then, the term allegory implies a referential relationship between a signifying word or image and a signified idea or nexus of ideas. Isidore of Seville offers the standard Medieval Latin definition of allegory as *alieniloquium* (speaking of another thing), stating: "Allegoria est alieniloquium. Aliud enim sonat, et aliud intellegitur (Allegory is speaking of another thing. For it says one thing, and another is understood). *Etymologiae*, 1.37.22. This essential referential element in the antique and medieval concept of allegory underscores the concept's distinct practices of reading and writing.

notio sub pio figmentorum velamine honestis et tecta rebus et vestita nominibus enuntiatur" (the idea of holy things, concealed and clothed with decent events and names, is expressed under a pious covering of fiction).[84] Regarding individual gods, these truths could include a range of positive attributes, negative attributes, or both; for example, while Diana frequently represents chastity as a positive attribute (self-control in sexual matters) and Mars irascibility as a negative attribute (uncontrolled war-rage), Venus – as noted in the Introduction – can represent varieties of love and sexual pleasure from the harmony of the universe and the generative impulse to self-centered desire and base lust.

As Chance reminds us in her three-volume survey, Greco-Roman mythography as received and transformed by medieval writers offers a complex nexus of interpretations and treatments of classical mythology and fable in medieval cultures. Though I emphasize the three approaches here to illustrate briefly their distinct influence on medieval literature, these distinctions are artificial, for medieval commentators and mythographers usually integrate multiple approaches in their interpretations of classical mythology and fable. To illustrate, Pierre Bersuire (c.1290–1362), a fourteenth-century French commentator on Ovid, interprets the gods historically, naturally, and allegorically in *Metamorphosis Ovidiana Moraliter*, justifying his interpretations in the prologue by comparing his moves to scriptural exegesis. As Minnis and Scott translate the passage, Bersuire states:

> If you go through the books of the poets it is quite clear that it is hardly ever, or even never, possible to cite a fable without its containing some truth concerning nature or history ... Therefore, because I see that Scripture uses fables to point out some truth, either of nature or of history, it seemed appropriate for me ... to set my hand to moralizing the fables of the poets, so that in this way I could confirm the mysteries of behaviour and of faith by using the very fictions of men. For a man may, if he can, gather grapes from thorns, suck honey from a rock, take oil from the hardest stone, and build and construct the ark of the covenant from the treasures of the Egyptians.[85]

Echoing Macrobius on the use of fiction and Augustine on scriptural and poetic allegoresis, Bersuire implies his method of explicating the gods, moving from physical to historical to moral meanings.[86] Moreover, Bersuire follows a long tradition of

---

[84] Macrobius, *In somnium Scipionis*, ed. Rinaldi and Rota, 1.2.11.
[85] Minnis and Scott, eds., *Medieval Literary Theory*, 367.
[86] Augustine writes: "Sicut enim Aegyptii non solum idola habebant et onera gravia, quae populus Israel detestaretur et fugeret, sed etiam vasa atque ornamenta de auro et argento, et vestem, quae ille populus exiens de Aegypto, sibi potius tanquam ad usum meliorem clanculo vindicavit ... sic doctrinae omnes Gentium non solum simulata et superstitios figmenta gravesque sarcinas supervacanei laboris habent ... sed etiam liberales disciplinas usui veritatis aptiores, et quaedam morum praecepta utilissima continent (For just as the Egyptians used to have not only idols and heavy burdens, which the people of Israel detested and shunned, but also vases and ornaments of gold and silver, and clothing, which the people leaving Egypt claimed secretly to themselves rather than [the Egyptians] for a better use ... thus all teachings of the pagans not only have simulated and superstitious figments and heavy burdens of superfluous work ... but also contain liberal

scholars who similarly present physical, historical, and/or allegorical readings of classical mythology and fable in their mythographical handbooks and commentaries.

Poets, too, often integrate more than one approach when using classical figures. Returning to the Wife of Bath for a moment, Chaucer suggests a moral dimension as well as an astrological one in his choice of Venus and Mars. The story of Venus and Mars' love affair was familiar in the Middle Ages through Ovid. Briefly, as Ovid narrates the story, the sun exposes the liaison between Venus and Mars to Vulcan, Venus' husband, who then captures them *in flagrante delicto* with a net of fine bronze and reveals their affair to the amusement of the other gods.[87] Chaucer's canon attests to his familiarity with this story and its moral dimension, for his *Complaint of Mars* describes both the astrological conjunction of Venus and Mars in the sign of Taurus and the limits of their affair. The moment Phoebus awakes the lovers in the chamber and Mars springs to action, arming himself and shaking his spear in reply as though he could prevent the sun's rising, is a comical echo of Ovid's dawn song *Amores* 1.13, in which Ovid's persona-lover impotently chides Aurora, the goddess of dawn, not to interrupt his liaison with his beloved: she arrives anyway blushing and on time.[88] Mars ends Chaucer's poem complaining of love's fickleness after Venus' abrupt but unavoidable departure: after all, she cannot help leaving; she moves through her sphere faster than Mars moves through his. As the narrator suggests early in the poem, even their affair seems as much a matter of opportunity as of anything else, saying "Whilom the thridde hevenes lord above, / As wel by hevenysh revolucion / As by desert, hath wonne Venus his love" (29–31). Chaucer's treatment in this poem of the Venus and Mars affair is gently comical in an Ovidian vein: like the *Parliament of Fowls* in its exploration of *fin' amours*, the *Complaint of Mars* feels humorous in an almost parodic way, especially when read aloud. When Chaucer includes Venus and Mars in the Wife of Bath's self-description, he invites an intertextual reading of the Venus–Mars union the Wife invokes: as with these deities, it seems, union with another for the Wife of Bath is an opportunistic venture.[89]

As mentioned in the Introduction, we can understand more fully mythological allusions in reference to both classical poetry and mythographic handbooks and commentaries. Along with the poetry they glossed, these kinds of texts affected poets such as Chaucer who, by the nature of the school curriculum, were exposed to them during courses in grammar and rhetoric. The medieval school curriculum as

---

disciplines more apt for uses of the truth and certain most useful precepts on morals). *De doctrina Christiana*, ed. Migne, 2.40. On Bersuire's influence, see Minnis and Scott, eds., *Medieval Literary Theory*, 317–18, 323–4, 366–72; and Minnis, *Chaucer and Pagan Antiquity*, 12.

[87] Ovid, *Metamorphoses*, ed. Miller, 4.167–89.

[88] Ovid, *Amores*, ed. Showerman, 1.13.47–8. .

[89] Chance's discussion of the Wife of Bath's mythography is instructive; on Venus and Mars, she concludes: "The mythological examples Alisoun uses to describe her own self and her husbands – Venus and Mars, Venus without Bacchus and Ceres, the children of Venus in opposition to the children of Mercury, but figuratively producing a monstrous child, Hermaphroditus, when they do couple – project a powerful image of the Wife's physical and psychological hunger, thirst, emptiness, need." *Mythographic Chaucer*, 214–31: 221.

generally practiced fostered the consumption and imitation of Roman literature.[90] Literate persons would have encountered the classics directly and through mythographic commentary primarily in grammar school, which taught the ability to read, comprehend, write, and speak Latin.[91] The variety of mythographies and commentaries produced in the Middle Ages is extensive as a glance at a chronology of medieval mythographers and their texts reveals.[92] Following Chance's lead, we can categorize the kinds of reference works on classical material available to medieval students and teachers into three general types: commentaries on classical authors, commentaries on certain schoolbooks written in the late-antique period, and handbooks summarizing and commenting on classical fables, particularly those found in Hyginus' *Fabulae*.[93] While it is difficult to demonstrate always a direct influence of one of these texts on a writer's particular use of a figure or fable, there is a general provenance: medieval educators and students used these texts in their studies, and the writers examined here, being literate persons of their times, surely had contact with this kind of material.[94]

[90] Irvine, *Making of Textual Culture*, 118–61, 334–71; C.S. Jaeger, *Envy of Angels*, 128–64; Morse, *Truth and Convention*, 15–84; S. Reynolds, *Medieval Reading*, 7–44; Scaglione, "Classics in Medieval Education," 343–62; Copeland, "The Curricular Classics," 21–33, and "The Trivium and the Classics," 53–76; Woods, "Experiencing the Classics in Medieval Education," 35–52.

[91] Courtenay, *Schools and Scholars*, 15–20; Hunt, *Teaching and Learning Latin*, vols. 1, 2; Irvine, *Making of Textual Culture*, 49–87; Irvine and Thomson, "*Grammatica* and Literary Theory," 15–41; Orme, *English Schools*, 68–70; S. Reynolds, *Medieval Reading*, 61–134; Russell, *Chaucer and the Trivium*, 6–52. Though grammar schools were the primary site for studying Latin language and literature and corresponding mythographies and commentaries, education beyond grammar school was available in different places and at different times to persons mentally capable and financially able to pursue it. Peter Abelard in his *Historia calamitatum*, for example, offers incidentally a description of what was available in Brittany and France in the first quarter of the twelfth century.

[92] Chance, *Medieval Mythography* 1: xxxiii–xxxvii, 2: xxii–xxvi, 3:xxv–xxx. See also Zeeman, "Mythography and Mythographical Collections," 121–50

[93] There were two distinct Virgilian traditions: the eclogue tradition, including *Ecologa Theoduli* and its commentaries, especially Bernard of Utrecht's *Commentum in Theodulum*; and the *Aeneid* tradition, including the commentaries by Fulgentius and Bernard Silvestris. Ovidian commentaries from the twelfth to the fifteenth centuries include such texts as Bersuire on the *Metamorphoses* and Thomas Walsingham (d. 1422), *De archana deorum*. Schoolbooks include Martianus Capella's *De nuptiis Philologiae et Mercurii*, which drew commentaries from Bernard Silvestris, Alexander Neckham, and several others, and Boethius' *De Consolatione Philosophiae*, which inspired influential commentaries from William of Conches in the twelfth century and Nicholas Trivet in the fourteenth, among others. Handbooks include Fulgentius' *Mitologiae*, which inspired other handbooks such as the First, Second, and Third Vatican Mythographers, the Digby Mythographer's *Liber de natura deorum*, John Ridevall's *Fulgentius metafloralis*, and Giovanni Boccaccio's *Genealogie deorum gentilium*, arguably the most extensive handbook of all. See Chance, *Mythographic Art*, 8–12.

[94] Chance argues that "as educated men, [these writers] were all familiar with the school commentaries on the great classical epic poems of Virgil and Ovid ... and with handbooks of medieval mythography, or the rationalizing of classical myth through moralization and allegorization. These texts had been used initially in the medieval schools – from

Medieval writers using Minerva as a wisdom figure also draw upon a long tradition in Latin and Greek literature that ascribes wisdom to her or Pallas Athena. In Homer's *Iliad*, Athena is the goddess of war. Unlike the bloodthirsty Ares, however, who gluts himself on the battlefield, Athena favors strategic warfare, using wisdom as well as strength to fight. For example, during Odysseus and Diomedes' night-raid on the Trojans' allies, she counsels Diomedes to stop slaying Thracians in their sleep, once they have achieved their objective, and to return to the Achaian camp with his booty before he wakes the Trojans and is captured or killed.[95] Her counsel to moderate his attack counters the Mars-like blood-lust that threatens Diomedes' own safety and the success of their mission. Similarly, in the *Odyssey*, she helps Odysseus return safely to Ithaka and defeat Penelope's suitors through strategy as well as prowess. And, at the end of the poem, she helps him restore political order to the state by directly intervening in the brief skirmish outside Laertes' shack and establishing a truce between the suitors' families and Odysseus.[96]

As we saw with the Roman Minerva, Athena is also the patroness of practical arts in Greek literature, especially weaving, and this attribute – along with her wiliness – is evident in the *Odyssey* when she inspires Penelope to delay the suitors by alternately weaving and undoing a burial shroud for Laertes (2.85–128). Athena's strategic and technical wisdom exemplified in Homer surfaces in other Greek literature as well. Two of the thirty-three extant Homeric hymns honor Athena: the first of these praises her strategic military prowess that protects the city and its army; the second catalogues her epithets before recounting her birth fully-armed from Zeus' head.[97] In *Eumenides*, the third play in Aeschylus' *Oresteia* trilogy (c.460 BCE), Athena again asserts herself into a political process when she ends the cycle of retribution begun in *Agamemnon* and developed in *Libation Bearers* by establishing Athens' *areopagus*, the Athenian justice system, including a trial by jury, that offers a more peaceful means of settling disputes than vengeance. The play recounts a foundation myth in which Athena, as the goddess of wisdom, restores familial and civic harmony.[98]

Greek literature was largely unavailable to the Latin West in the Middle Ages, and Homer's texts did not begin arriving until Boccaccio commissioned a Latin translation of the *Iliad* in 1365. Medieval writers, however, inherited Athena's characteristic attributes through Latin literature. Again, the Romans syncretized Greek Pallas Athena with their Minerva so that in a text like *Metamorphoses*, for instance, Ovid refers to Minerva as the goddess of wisdom (4.38), patroness of wise men (8.252), patroness of practical arts (6.23), and goddess of war (2.752, 756), all recognizable attributes of Pallas Athena. Similarly, in a passage in the *Thebaid* that resoundingly echoes the Athena–Diomedes exchange in the *Iliad*, Minerva advises Tydeus not to

---

postclassical times – for students studying grammar and rhetoric; the commentaries and handbooks developed because of the difficulty, in time, in understanding ancient poets … [and their] references to mythology." *Mythographic Art*, 5.
[95] Homer, *Iliad*, ed. Murray, 10.503–14.
[96] Homer, *Odyssey*, ed. Murray, 24.473–548.
[97] *Homeric Hymns*, ed. and trans. West, 11.192–3, and 28.210–11.
[98] Aeschylus, *Oresteia: Agamemnon; Libation Bearers; Eumenides*, ed. Sommerstein. See also Papadopoulou, "Representations of Athena in Greek Tragedy," 304–6.

proceed to Thebes but rather to be satisfied in his victory.[99] Moreover, Roman poets such as Ovid and Statius use Minerva's Latin and Greek names interchangeably: a practice medieval poets and scholars also follow.

Medieval writers tend to use Minerva as a wisdom figure in one of two ways: either as a metonym for wisdom or as "interiorem animi potentiam," to cite Bernard Silvestris' formulation. As a metonym, Minerva functions as a sort of short-hand for positive wisdom. Richard de Bury (1287–1345), in his defense of poetic fables in *Philobiblon*, writes:

> Quamvis nimirum omnes homines natura scire desiderent, non tamen omnes equaliter delectantur addiscere, quinimmo studii labore gustato et sensuum fatigatione percepta plerique nucem abiciunt inconsulte, prius quam testa solute nucleus attingatur … Idcirco prudentia veterum adinvenit remedium, quo lascivum humanum caperetur ingenium quodam modo pio dolo, dum sub voluptatis iconio delicata Minerva delitesceret in occulto
>
> (Although it is true that all men by nature desire to know things, nevertheless not all are equally delighted to learn; on the contrary, when they have experienced the labor of study and find their senses wearied, most unthinkingly throw away the nut before they have broken the shell and reached the kernel … Accordingly the wisdom of the ancients came upon a solution through which the mind of wanton men might be seized by a kind of pious fraud, while under a mask of pleasure the delicate Minerva lurks in secret)[100]

In this passage we see the ubiquitous kernel-and-shell metaphor for reading, which Richard uses to establish with his audience a dichotomy between two kinds of readers: those who throw away the nut and those who do not, that is, Richard and his audience. Playing with this idea, Richard teasingly, I think, invites his reader to crack the shell. His "delicata Minerva" is the wisdom, the *sententia* or philosophical truth, underlying the fable's "voluptatis iconium." By writing "Minerva" in place of "wisdom," Richard rather cleverly uses poetic diction both to defend poetry itself and to draw his audience into allegoresis: the game of interpretation.[101]

---

[99] Statius, *Thebaid*, ed. Shakleton Bailey, 2.682–90.
[100] Richard de Bury, *Philobiblon*, 13.6–9, 15–17.
[101] As Obbink, "Early Greek Allegory," 15, observes: allegoresis, or allegorical interpretation, predates allegorical composition. Allegorical composition, or figurative allegory, however, comes relatively close on the heels of allegoresis. Though Plato mistrusts allegoresis and poetic composition, "The Allegory of the Cave" from *The Republic*, ed. and trans. Emlyn-Jones and Reddy, 7.514a–520a, reminds us that, when it suits him, he engages in figurative allegory – an attempt "to express imagistically what is otherwise abstract or invisible" (Copeland and Struck, introduction to *The Cambridge Companion*, 6). Later Cleanthes (c. 330–230 BCE) composed in his "Hymn to Zeus" what Most, "Hellenistic Allegory," 34, considers the earliest extant allegorical poem. Cleanthes invokes Zeus as a figure for the creative force in the universe, the law that orders all things through the "universal Logos" and leads humans to seek the good. Such figurative expression became part of grammatical and rhetorical instruction in Greco-Roman culture and found definition in texts such as Quintillian's first-century CE *Institutio oratoria*, ed. Butler, 8.6.44–59, where allegory is a tripartite literary figure: a brief trope, a sustained metaphor, or an

As an inner power of the soul, on the other hand, Minerva usually has a more active role as a character and can represent wisdom's various aspects. Bernard Silvestris uses this term particularly to describe the role gods play in poetry, representing "powers of the soul" or, in modern terms, psychological forces. He writes, "Quantam ad interiorem intellectum DEOS vocat interiores animi potentias, ERRANTES quia in primis etatibus erraverunt, AGITATA, commotionibus carnis" (With respect to the inner understanding, [Virgil] calls the inner powers of the soul "gods-wandering" because in the first ages they wandered, having been agitated by the commotions of the flesh) (*Commentum ... Virgilii*, 6.68.47). In medieval poetry Minerva often plays the role of "interiorem animi potentiam." Her role as a euhemerized deity, her place in the natural world, and her function as a metonym for wisdom, however, also inform her appearances in several poems and texts discussed in the following chapters. Like the scholars from whom they drew much of their imagery, medieval classicizing poets integrate the historical and physical traditions as well as the allegorical in their reception and transformative use of Minerva as a figure for wisdom.

---

ironic form of discourse. See also Most, "Hellenistic Allegory," 33–7; and Irvine, *Making of Textual Culture*, 244–50. An early instance of Christian figurative allegory, the anonymous late third-century [Lactantius] *De ave phoenice*, ed. Latin Library, recounts in eighty-five elegiac couplets the life, death, and resurrection of the legendary bird as a figure for Christ.

The Middle English translation of Richard of St. Victor's *Benjamin Minor* attributed to *The Cloud*-author, ed. Hodgson, offers a medieval example of both allegoresis and allegorical composition to delineate medieval psychology and the spiritual life. Paraphrasing the story of Jacob's wives, concubines, and children (Gen. 29:31–30:24, 35:16–21), Richard uses biblical characters as allegorical figures representing the soul's faculties, their relationship to God, and the spiritual virtues infused by God's grace in the soul: Jacob represents God married to the soul; the wives (Leah as will and Rachel as reason) and the concubines (Zelpha as sensuality and Bala as imagination) represent the soul's faculties; and the thirteen children represent spiritual virtues (e.g., Reuben, the first born, is "fear of the Lord," and Benjamin, the last born, is "contemplation"). The allegorical interpretation of these figures also serves as a mnemonic device for remembering the soul's faculties and spiritual virtues. Many mss. include a chart mapping references between biblical characters and ideas: see, for example, Cambridge, University Library, Ms. K.k.6.26, fol. 33r, and Ms. F.f.6.33, fols. 2v–3r.

2

The Sapiential Tradition: Minerva as Redemptress

The medieval sapiential tradition is rooted in Jewish wisdom literature, particularly Job, Ecclesiastes, the Song of Songs, Proverbs, Ecclesiasticus, and the Wisdom of Solomon. When personified in these texts, Hokma/Sophia, or Sapientia in the Vulgate (Ecclus. 1:1–10, 24:5–11; Prov. 3:19–20, 8:22–31; Wis. 7:23–8:1), acts as a living, divine force permeating the universe. As Barbara Newman delineates, the Christian interpretation of biblical Sapientia accrued associations over time, beginning in Patristic writings with her link to Christ as *Verbum Dei*, the creative force in the universe, to developing links with Mary *Theotokos* beginning in the seventh century and Philosophia in the eighth.[1] None of these interpretations and associations superseded the others in the Middle Ages; rather, "as the streams of tradition intermingled, each altered the connotations of the others."[2] These intertextual readings of Sapientia and biblical sapiential literature proved productive for medieval writers and thinkers engaging ideas of wisdom. In this chapter, I explore Minerva's association with Sapientia by examining aspects of the medieval sapiential tradition – especially in relation to love – through reading a number of texts that offer evidence of active reception and creative transformation of biblical Sapientia in the Middle Ages. From this reading, I then turn to her appearances in John Lydgate's *Reson and Sensuallyte* and Gavin Douglas' *Palice of Honoure* where she functions as a redemptress. In this role, Minerva represents the redemptive wisdom one finds through contemplation of the universe and its maker: a wisdom grounded in love.

The Medieval Sapiential Tradition

Two brief Latin texts – both widely known throughout the Middle Ages – set the stage for understanding the medieval sapiential tradition in which Minerva at times takes part. The origin of the first is obscure, but its use and message are clear:

---

[1] B. Newman, *God and the Goddesses*, 194–203. See also Adolf, "Figure of Wisdom," 429–43; Francomano, *Wisdom and Her Lovers*, 19–25.
[2] B. Newman, *God and the Goddesses*, 205.

O Sapientia, quae ex ore Altissimi prodisti
attingens a fine usque ad finem
fortiter suaviter disponensque omnia:
veni ad docendum nos viam prudentiae

(O Wisdom, who comes forth from the mouth of the Most High, reaching from end to end mightily and ordering all things sweetly: come, teach us the way of prudence)[3]

The first of seven so-called "O Antiphons," a set of votive texts in the Roman Rite sung before and after the Gospel canticle, the Magnificat (Lk 1:46–55), in the vespers service of the Divine Office, this brief text helps mark the beginning of the final seven days of Advent in the medieval liturgical calendar.[4] Addressing Sapientia and recounting her origins from the mouth of God (Ecclus. 24:5), an echo of Genesis (1:1–2:3) and read by early Christians as a precursor to the opening words of the Gospel of John (1:1–14), the speakers inscribed in the text name two key attributes – her extensive mighty reach and her sweet ordering of the universe (Wis. 8:1) – before lodging a request "ad docendum nos viam prudentiae": a request articulating a felt need for instruction in right living. Sung each year throughout medieval Europe on December 17, this short poetic text articulates not only a prayer to Christ as Wisdom but also a fundamental understanding of Divine Wisdom as an active agent in the universe.[5] Sapientia's "via prudentiae," it would seem, is a wide-ranging and powerful yet sweet and ordered path leading back to herself: she is both means and end.

---

[3] "O Sapientia," in *Liber Usualis*, ed. Benedictines of Solesmes, 340.

[4] Hiley notes that the O Antiphons "appear to have been composed as a group, for they are all addressed to Christ, and may be linked by an acrostic: reading in reverse order the initial letters of each second word finds the text 'ERO CRAS', which is interpreted as 'Tomorrow I shall be [with you].' The largest bell of the church was rung while they and the Magnificat were sung, and they were assigned in turn to the most prominent members of the ecclesiastical hierarchy: abbot, prior, cellarer, and so on." *Western Plainchant*, 98–9. See also the facsimile in Hiley, 432–3, of British Library Ms. Additional 17302, fol. 8r, which includes music and text for three O Antiphons.

[5] "O Sapientia" echoes biblical wisdom literature. The Proverbs-author, for instance, declares that "Dominus sapientia fundavit terram, stabilivit caelos prudentia. Sapientia illius eruperunt abyssi, et nubes rore concrescunt" (The Lord built the earth with wisdom; He established the heavens with prudence; by His wisdom the depths have erupted and clouds congeal with dew). Prov. 3:19–20. Similarly, the Wisdom-author states: "Omnibus enim mobilibus mobilior est sapientia: attingit autem ubique propter suam munditiam ... Et cum sit una, omnia potest: et in se permanens omnia innovat, et per nationes in animas sanctas se transfert, amicos Dei et prophetas constituit ... Attingit ergo a fine usque ad finem fortiter, et disponit omnia suaviter" (For wisdom is more active than all active things: and now she touches everywhere on account of her purity ... And since she is one, she can do all things: and remaining in herself, she restores all things, and she transfers herself through nations into holy souls; she establishes the friends of God and prophets ... She therefore touches strongly from one end all the way to the other end, and she orders all things sweetly). Wis. 7:24–7, 8:1; see also Wis. 1–2.

46 THE FIGURE OF MINERVA IN MEDIEVAL LITERATURE

The second text, perhaps not as widely known in the Middle Ages as the first, except among certain circles, but clearly as influential, is Boethius' metrum 8 from book two of *Consolatio Philosophiae*. Having just concluded that adverse Fortune is better than favorable Fortune because it clarifies the true good and reveals true friends, Philosophia punctuates for the narrator her mini-treatise on Fortune and the goddess' false goods with this poem:

> concordes uariat uices,
> quod pugnantia semina
> foedus perpetuum tenent,
> quod Phoebus roseum diem
> curru prouehit aureo,
> ut quas duxerit Hesperos
> Phoebe noctibus imperet,
> ut fluctus auidum mare
> certo fine coherceat,
> ne terris liceat uagis
> latos tendere terminos,
> hanc rerum seriem ligat
> terras ac pelagus regens
> et caelo imperitans amor.
> Hic si frena remiserit,
> quicquid nunc amat inuicem
> bellum continuo geret
> et quam nunc socia fide
> pulchris motibus incitant
> certent soluere machinam.
> Hic sancto populos quoque
> iunctos foedere continent,
> hic et coniugii sacrum
> castis nectit amoribus,
> hic fidis etiam sua
> dictat iura sodalibus.
> O felix hominum genus,
> si uestros animos amor
> quo caelum regitur regat!

(With stable confidence the universe varies change through harmony, an everlasting law holds in balance seeds competing with each other, and Phoebus in his golden chariot brings forth a rosy day so that Phoebe might rule nights, which Hesperus leads, contain greedy sea-waves within a fixed boundary, and keep land from wandering to gain wider limits. Ruling earth and sea, and commanding the heavens, Love [*Amor*] binds all these things. If Love's reins slacken, all things that now love mutually would wage continuous war and strive to destroy the universe that they now urge on in mutual trust and beautiful motion. And Love also joins people in a holy bond, ties chaste lovers in bonds of sacred matrimony, and with its law also joins faithful comrades. O happy human race if Love by which the heavens are ruled also rules your hearts.)

Moving from the outer reaches of the heavens to the inner workings of the human heart, from the macrocosm to the microcosm, Philosophia draws out her lesson that Love, Amor, harmonizes all in a mutually beneficial order fostering happiness: even relations among humans if they allow it, as her final sentence – a gesture to a wider audience – implies. Philosophia's Amor sounds much like Sapientia with her wide, powerful reach and sweetly ordered universe: both govern the cosmos and seem to be distinct names of the same, divine force – Sapientia-Amor. While Philosophia instructs her pupil on Amor's harmonizing role in the universe, commenting wryly at the end on human behavior, singers of the antiphon praise Sapientia and invoke her as teacher, requesting aid now in how to live prudently or, in Philosophia's terms, how to live with Love ruling their hearts.

The notion of Sapientia-Amor evident when reading these two texts together underpins the Jewish-Christian formulation of right living in relation to God and others. When asked in the gospels what is the greatest commandment, Jesus quotes Deuteronomy 6:5 that one should love God with one's mind, heart, and soul, and then quoting Leviticus 19:18 he adds a second commandment to love one's neighbor as oneself (Mt. 22:34–40; Mk. 12:29–34; Lk. 10:25–8). Writing in the fourth and fifth centuries CE, Augustine of Hippo (354–430) turns frequently to the theme of love in the guise of *amor*, *caritas*, and *dilectio* as he works out interpretations of Jesus' simple, yet provocative response to this query. Parsing these comments, Hugh Feiss identifies various points in Augustine's thought: love, a striving for something desired, determines a person's goodness or vileness; it dynamically seeks union with the object of desire; it seeks to enjoy rather than merely use the object of desire; it finds expression in the virtues, which are distinct forms of love, and is a gift of the Spirit; it is the root of all virtue, existence, and action; and it has shaped history, which revolves around whether love is God-centered seeking the common good or self-centered seeking domination of other creatures.[6] Augustine's distinction between *caritas* and *cupiditas* encapsulates his thought: "Charitatem voco motum animi ad fruendum Deo propter ipsum, et se atque proximo propter Deum: cupiditatem, autem, motum animi ad fruendum se et proximo et quolibet corpore non propter Deum" (I call charity the motion of the soul toward enjoying God for his own sake, and oneself and one's neighbor for the sake of God; but cupidity is a motion of the soul toward enjoying oneself, one's neighbor, or any corporal thing not for the sake of God) (*De doctrina Christiana*, 3.10.16). As human action, a "motum animi," Augustine's *caritas* seems synonymous with the "via prudentiae" of the advent antiphon, as well as the idea of *prudentia* Aquinas articulates in the thirteenth century: grounded in human behavior, both lead ultimately to God. In a sense, Sapientia of the antiphon and Amor of Boethius' poem in their ordering and harmonizing of the universe also originate prudence and love in the human soul.

The nexus of Sapientia and Amor touched on here forms the heart of the medieval sapiential tradition and finds expression in a range of medieval texts. Writing in the late eighth century as part of Charlemagne's effort to further liturgical reform, Alcuin of York (c.735–804) composed a votive *Missa de Sancta Sapientia*, an optional

---

[6] Feiss, general introduction to *On Love*, 51–61.

Mass for Wednesday, that became part of the Roman Missal until deleted in 1570 during the Tridentine reform.⁷ The Collect, or petitionary-gathering prayer chanted by the celebrant at the beginning of the Mass, reads: "Deus qui per coaeternam tibi sapientiam hominem, cum non esset, condidisti, perditumque misericorditer reformasti; praesti, quaesumus, ut eadem pectora nostra, inspirante te, tota mente amemus, et ad te toto corde curramus" (O God who has created man from nothing through your coeternal wisdom and has mercifully restored the lost: show forth, we ask, the same grace into our hearts that, by your in-breathing, we might love you with our entire mind and run to you with our entire heart).⁸ Echoing Jesus' reply to the question about the greatest commandment, the celebrant beseeches God through Sapientia *creatrix* to inspire love and active pursuit of God in himself and in all gathered to worship. This petitionary thread linking wisdom and love continues with the post-communion prayer: "Infunde, quaesumus, Domine per haec sancta quae sumpsimus, tuae cordibus nostris lumen sapientiae, ut te veraciter agnoscamus, et fideliter diligamus" (Through this holy communion we have taken on, pour into our hearts, we ask, O Lord, the light of your wisdom so that we might truly know and faithfully love you) (col. 451). From this desire for increased knowledge and love, the petitionary mode culminates in the prayer over the people preceding the final blessing: "Deus qui misisti Filium tuum, et ostendisti creaturae Creaturem; respice propitious super nos famulos tuos, et praepara agiae sophiae dignam in cordibus nostris habitationem" (O God, you who have sent your Son and have shown the Creator to the creature, look again favourably on us your family, and prepare in our hearts a worthy dwelling for holy wisdom) (col. 451). The fusion of wisdom and love in these prayers, expressing a desire to create Sapientia's dwelling in the congregants' hearts – an internal tabernacle for Hagia Sophia⁹ – is reminiscent of the advent antiphon in which again singers call forth Sapientia to show them the "via prudentiae."

Interest in Sapientia as developed and expressed in liturgy persisted throughout the Middle Ages. From prayers such as the advent antiphon and Alcuin's Mass to the annual round of lectionary readings taken from biblical sapiential literature, medieval Christians frequently encountered this figure as a creative, ordering force linked closely with love. The Benedictine abbess and liturgist Hildegard of Bingen (1098–179), for instance, offers a twelfth-century view of this link in her liturgical poetry. Implying Divine Wisdom's ordering, creative force, her antiphon "O virtus

---

7   Ellard, "Alcuin," 47–53; B. Newman, *Sister of Wisdom*, 44, and *God and the Goddesses*, 201. In *Liber sacramentarum*, Alcuin compiled or composed twenty-one votive masses to provide three devotional options per day: *Missa de Sancta Sapientia* falls on Feria IV, or Wednesday. It is one of seven unique compositions showing no borrowing. Ellard, "Alcuin," 53, 61.
8   Alcuin, *Liber sacramentorum*, ed. Migne, cols. 450–1.
9   This idea touches on the notion that believers make of themselves a holy tabernacle for the indwelling of the divine, which corresponds to churches as dwellings for the divine, which corresponds to the universe as dwelling for the divine (Mâle, *Gothic Image*, 27–63; von Simpson, *Gothic Cathedral*, 8–11, 37–9, 234–8). In his twelfth-century treatise *On Diverse Arts*, Theophilus draws all three levels together (77). On Holy Wisdom in art and architecture, see Meyendorff, "Wisdom – Sophia," 391–401.

Sapientie" shows a three-winged Sapientia "que circuiens circuisti, / comprehendo omnia / in una via que habet vitam" (who circling circled, encompassing all things in one path which possesses life): while "una in altum volat" (one wing flies on high), "altera de terra sudat / et tercia undique volat" (the second exudes from the earth and the third flies everywhere).[10] The image of circling echoes biblical Sapientia's act of circling heaven (Ecclus. 24:8), and the three wings, of course, suggest the Trinity: Father on high, Son on earth, and Holy Spirit everywhere.[11] Similarly, implying Divine Love's harmonizing impulse, her antiphon "Karitas" declares that Divine Love, most exalted and most loving, "habundat in omnia" (overflows into all things) (*Symphonia*, 140). Putting together these two ideas in "O ignis Spiritus Paracliti," a sequence praising the Holy Spirit as Love, she writes:

O iter fortissiumum,
Quod penetravit omnia
In altissimis et in terrenis
Et in omnibus abyssis,
Tu omnes componis et colligis,

De te nubes fluunt, ether volat,
lapides humorem habent, aque rivulos educunt,
et terra viriditatem sudat.

Tu etiam semper educis doctos
per inspirationem Sapientiae
letificatos.

(O mightiest way, which penetrated all things in the heights and on earth and in all depths, you gather and bring together all people. From you clouds pour out, ether flies, stones have moisture and pour forth streams, and the earth exudes greenness. You indeed always instruct the learned, gladdened through Sapientia's inspiration.) (*Symphonia*, 149–50)

In her praise here of the Holy Spirit, Hildegard expresses ideas of love and wisdom we have already encountered: a way or path, a wide-ranging divine force that harmonizes people, a life-bringing energy, and – linked to Sapientia in the final verse – an instructor of the learned. Hildegard wrote her liturgical texts for use in her own community.[12] Though they did not receive the widely distributed use that "O Sapientia" or even Alcuin's *Missa* enjoyed, they express her thought, including the link between love and wisdom, Sapientia-Amor, found in her other writings.[13]

---

[10] Hildegard, *Symphonia*, ed. B. Newman, 100.
[11] B. Newman, commentary to *Symphonia*, 268, and *Sister of Wisdom*, 65.
[12] B. Newman, introduction to *Symphonia*, 12–13.
[13] Hildegard's thought on Wisdom and Love is complex and variously manifest in her writing: for example, see *Scivias* 3.visio 9. For a full discussion, see B. Newman, *Sister of Wisdom*.

As she declares in *Explanatio Symboli Sancti Athanasii*, a treatise addressed to her community, "sapientia et charitas unum sunt" (wisdom and love are one).[14]

Hildegard draws on a rich and varied understanding of Sapientia-Amor when composing her liturgical poetry. In his treatise addressed to Cardinal Hameric, most commonly known as *Tractatus de diligendo Deo*, Hildegard's contemporary Bernard of Clairvaux (1090–153) draws on the same tradition when replying to Hameric's question "quare et quomodo diligendus sit Deo" (why and how much we ought to love God): an exploration of how to live wisely with love ruling one's heart.[15] His initial answer – "Causa diligendi Deum, Deus est; modus, sine modo diligere" (The cause of loving God is God; the manner, to love without measure) – sums up his treatise, but he elaborates: "Estne hoc satis? Fortassis utique, sed sapienti. Caeterum si et insipientibus debitor sum; ubi sat est dictum sapienti, etiam illis gerendus mos est. Itaque propter tardiores idem profusius, quam profundius repetere non gravabor" (Is this enough? Perhaps, at any rate, for a wise person. But if I am also debtor to the unwise then, where a word to the wise is enough, I ought also explain the practice to the unwise. And so because of their more profound slowness, I shall gladly repeat what I said in more depth) (col. 974–5). Bernard's play on "sapiens" and "insipiens" draws his reader – Hameric as well as any other – into the text for a fuller explication of his aphorism, part of which centers, as with Augustine before him, on Jesus' reply to the query about the greatest commandment. Bernard, however, explicates the love of self, neighbor, and God differently. He posits four degrees of love: (1) loving oneself for the sake of oneself, which begins in "amor carnalis" (carnal love) (col. 988) but through reason and virtue grows into social love of neighbor, that is, the natural world, in which one seeks the good of the other; (2) loving God for the sake of oneself, whereby acknowledging dependence on God leads to love of him through "prudentia" (col. 989); (3) loving God for His sake, whereby "diligit Deum propter Deum" (one loves God because He is God) (col. 990); and (4) loving oneself for God's sake, a degree unattainable in this life or by human effort (col. 990–2). This program of spiritual growth is, by implication, a "via prudentiae" for those "insipientes" (i.e., his readers) needing explication of his aphorism: a journey of love and wisdom through nature leading to contemplation of the Divine.

Writing in the fourteenth century, the Dominican friar Henry Suso draws on a similarly rich and varied understanding of wisdom and love in his devotional text *Horologium Sapientiae*. Widely and wildly popular with over 233 extant manuscripts, some 88 more known to have existed, and translations into Czech, Danish, Dutch, English, French, Hungarian, Italian, and Swedish, the *Horologium* was a late medieval bestseller among devotional texts.[16] Organized into two books of uneven length, and composed as a dialogue between Sapientia and a certain Discipulus, the *Horologium* is part vision text, part romance, part passion meditation, part *Brautmystic*

---

[14] Hildegard, *Explanatio Symboli*, ed. Migne, col. 1067.
[15] Bernard of Clairvaux, *Tractatus de diligendo Deo*, ed. Migne, col. 974.
[16] Colledge, introduction to *Horologium Sapientiae*, 15–16. Suso is among several medieval sapiential writers: see Francomano, *Wisdom and Her Lovers*, for discussion of Iberian sapiential writers.

treatise, part contemplative handbook, and all spiritual biography. Taken as a whole, the *Horologium* is a multi-dimensional treatise praising and exploring the human person's relationship with Sapientia-Amor.

In book one, chapter six (1.6), Suso particularly explores the connection between wisdom and love through a Song of Songs-infused mystical courtship between Sapientia and the Discipulus initially cast in the form of a first-person vision text.[17] Opening with a type of scene familiar to anyone who has read medieval love literature, the Discipulus recalls a spring season when he went out into flowering meadows to sport with friends and maidens, each of whom adopted a *carpe diem* attitude, gathered rosebuds, and "frenum concupiscentiae laxabant" (gave rein to concupiscence) (418). Noting how quickly his friends' blooms withered, he vowed never to grant his love to such perishable blossoms. Then one day he spied an incomparable flower high on a mountain top, rushed to gaze on it, and experienced an epiphanic moment when the flower transformed into a strikingly beautiful woman "quasi dea" (like a goddess) who "sole clarius rutilabat, et eloquia pulchritudinis dabat" (was glowing red more brightly than the sun and was offering words of beauty) (418): quoting Ecclesiasticus 24:24–8, she said "Transite ad me omnes qui concupiscitis me, et a generationibus meis adimplemini. Ego mater pulchrae dilectionis and timoris et agnitionis and sanctae spei" (Come over to me all you who desire me, and you will be filled by my generations. I am mother of beautiful love and of fear and of knowledge and of holy hope) (419). After an initial reticent moment, he responds: "O pulcherrima totius universitatis omnium creaturarum, quae ex animo laetabundo conditoris universorum prodiisti, edicito nobis nomen et progeniem tuam" (O most beautiful of all creatures in the entire universe, you who came forth from the mind of the creator of all, proclaim to us your name and lineage) (420).

A courtship dialogue follows in which the goddess self-identifies as "aeterna Sapientia," established before time and active at the creation, and the Discipulus – at points paraphrasing Ovid – professes his love, recounting how he had rejected other potential lovers in favor of her, and asks some share in her love. Sapientia's reply emphasizes the connection between wisdom and love when, assuring him he is loved in particular, she declares in part: "Dei sapientia amor est; unde sicut essentia sua in cunctis existens non partitur ... sic nec amor suus, licet cuncta diligat quae facit, minoratur" (the wisdom of God is love; where just as his essence existing in all things is not divided ... so too his love, though he loves all things that he has made, is not lessened) (428–9). God's wisdom and God's love are the same – Sapientia-Amor – and remain undiminished though shared singularly throughout creation. The Discipulus concludes the chapter in a rapturous prayer reminiscent of any lover's prayer to a beloved: "O mi dulcissima, felicissima sapientia, peto ut me a te nec vita nec mors, nec ulla fortunae sors separet, sed permaneat morte fortior noster amor in aevum (O my most sweet and most happy Sapientia: I beg that

---

[17] Suso, *Horologium Sapientiae*, ed. Künzle, 417.

neither life, nor death, nor any lot of fortune separate me from you but that our love persist stronger than death forever) (433).[18]

For Suso, the spiritual union between Sapientia and the Discipulus in the *Horologium*, finally achieved in 2.7, serves as an example to others much as Solomon intends his account of wooing and spiritual marriage to Wisdom to serve as an example to rulers (Wis. 6:1–8:20).[19] In a sense, Suso fleshes out what the "via prudentiae" of the "O Sapientia" antiphon might mean to his fourteenth-century audience when, from the outset of the *Horologium*, he closely ties Sapientia's path to reading.[20] In 1.1, his narrator recounts, it was reading biblical sapiential literature – alone and in hearing the lector read at table – that first sparked the Discipulus' love of Wisdom. Suso develops the theme of reading in 1.6 when, after the Discipulus encounters Sapientia in the meadow, she asks him about his response to nature, wondering why he does not consider the Creator when looking at, that is, reading, the creation: a consideration, she tells him, that leads to understanding her essence in all things and the universal concord she inspires. Suso continues the theme of reading in 1.8, after the Discipulus complains to Sapientia for behaving like an earthly beloved, coming and going at will. She replies rather cheekily that, if he wants to be in her presence, he need only read nature and sacred scripture, where she is found any time he troubles himself to look. Finally, Suso integrates reading in book two where he describes Sapientia's school: an education on living a life of wisdom, a "via prudentiae" resembling Bernard of Clairvaux's degrees of love that culminates in spiritual marriage in 2.7 between Sapientia and the Discipulus. Suso concludes with instruction in a series of exercises those seeking a similar union with Sapientia should practice throughout the year, including an appended daily round of prayers as well as the "O Sapientia" Advent antiphon. Sapientia's school in book two over which she presides, like the antiphon's "via prudentiae," is both means and end for Suso's Discipulus and any interested in following that path to wisdom.

Though Suso does not mention Minerva directly, he alludes to the Roman goddess in his visionary account in 1.6 when the Discipulus, recognizing Sapientia's divine origin, declares "ex animo laetabundo conditoris universorum prodiisti" (you came forth from the mind of the creator of all). This phrase – not found in biblical texts – suggests Minerva's birth from Jupiter's head and points to Sapientia's direct expression of the Divine Mind in Suso's text: lurking behind Suso's Sapientia in this descriptive moment, Minerva unveils herself briefly to any familiar with her origin story. Returning to the twelfth century, we find a poetic antecedent for

---

[18] 1.6 is, in part, an imaginative reworking of Wisdom 8:2–20 as well as a comment on the Song of Songs.

[19] See Horsley, "Spiritual Marriage with Sophia," 30–54, for discussion of spiritual marriage to Sophia in Hellenic Jewish and early Christian writing.

[20] A version in Brussels, Bibliothèque Royale, MS IV.111, fols. 13–133, illuminates this theme with thirty-two miniatures, nineteen of which depict at least one figure with open book reading, and many others figures holding or expressing scrolls with text signifying speech: see Monks, *Brussels Horologe de Sapience*, 1–130, 134–99, and Rozenski, "Henry Suso's *Horologium Sapientiae*," 364–80. On visual cues of oral performance in manuscript illuminations, see Camille, "Seeing," 27–9.

Minerva's association with Sapientia *creatrix* in Bernard Silvestris' *Cosmographia*. A teacher-scholar-poet contemporaneous with Hildegard, Bernard offers in his two-book prosimetric theogony an imaginative exploration of creation through the roles of Noys, Natura, Endelichia, Physis, and Urania in ordering the macrocosm and the microcosm.[21] Composed about 1147 and extant in some fifty manuscripts, the *Cosmographia* influenced later writers, including Alan of Lille, John of Hauvilla, Jean de Meun, Giovanni Boccaccio, who wrote out his own copy of the text, and Geoffrey Chaucer.[22] In "Megacosmus" (part one), having been called to action by Natura making her first figurative appearance in a medieval text,[23] Noys – the self-professed "dei ratio profundius exquisite" (profound and exquisite reason of God)[24] – gives shape to Silva, or primal matter, by separating the four elements; bringing forth Endelichia (world-soul) and marrying her to the cosmos; forming the heavens, angels, and stars; and then shaping earth and its inhabitants. Turning in "Microcosmus" (part two) to the culminating act of creation, the formation of humankind, Noys delegates the work to Urania to shape the soul, Physis to shape the body, and Natura to join the two. Following Urania and Natura's journey through the cosmos to join Physis in Granusion, an Edenesque garden on earth, where with further instruction from Noys they work to form the first man, the *Cosmographia* ends with the first man on the cusp of drawing breath: the moment of animation Hildegard recalls in a different context in her antiphon "O quam mirabilis."[25]

---

[21] Rooted in classical literature, prosimetrum – a hybrid genre integrating verse and prose – gained new life particularly in the twelfth century with works like *Cosmographia*. See Balint, *Ordering Chaos*, 1–9, 43–135; Dronke, *Verse with Prose*, 46–52; Heise, "Menippean Boethius," 111–26; Lerer, *Boethius and Dialogue*, 3–93; and Relihan, *Prisoner's Philosophy*, 1–33. On *Cosmographia*, see Balint, 63–7, 97–9; Stock, *Myth and Science*; and Wetherbee, *Platonism*, 158–86.

[22] Dronke, introduction to *Cosmographia*, 2, 9–15, 64–5.

[23] Bernard Silvestris offers the earliest known use of Natura as a complex, allegorical figure. Dronke, "Bernard Silvestris, Natura, and Personification," 16–31; Economou, *Goddess Natura*, 58–9. Her subsequent appearances in literature find their roots in *Cosmographia*. She continues to draw scholarly attention: see Economou's updated 2002 bibliography, xiii–xviii; and B. Newman, *God and the Goddesses*, 51–137. On the word "nature," see Lewis, *Studies*, 24–74.

[24] Bernard Silvestris, *Cosmographia*, ed. Dronke, *Meg.*2.1.

[25] Hildegard's antiphon reads:

> O quam mirabilis est
> prescientia divini pectoris
> que prescivit omnem creaturam.
> Nam cum Deus inspexit
> faciem hominis quem formavit,
> omnia opera sua
> in eadem forma hominis
> integra aspexit.
> quam mirabilis est inspiratio
> que hominem sic suscitavit

> (O how marvelous is the divine heart's foreknowledge that foreknew each creature. For when God gazed into the face of man, whom he formed, he beheld all his works,

In the twelfth-century Neo-Platonic universe evoked in the *Cosmographia*, Noys functions as *creatrix*: the "mens altissimi" (the mind of the most high) (1.2.13.2), she is mistress of ideal forms, "the chief shaping and vivifying agency," as Theodore Silverstein puts it, in the narrative.[26] The text opens with a sixty-six-line poem in elegiac verse in which Natura addresses Noys in *planctus* mode:

> "Vite viventis ymago,
> Prima, Noys – deus – orta deo, substantia veri,
> Consilii tenor eterni, michi vera Minerva:
> Si sensu fortasse meo maiora capesso –
> Mollius excudi Silvam, positoque veterno,
> Posse superduci melioris imagine forme –
> Huic operi nisi consentis, concepta relinquo"

(O Noys, foremost image of living life, God born from God, substance of truth, uninterrupted course of eternal counsel, my true Minerva: if I undertake perhaps a greater task than my ability – that Silva be made malleable, and having cast off old age, be led forth to take on a better form's image – I will give up my plan, unless you consent to do this work) (1.1.4b–10)

Calling on Noys as "deus – orta deo," "Consilii tenor eterni," and "michi vera Minerva," Natura invokes her as respectively the Second Person of the Trinity, biblical Sapientia, and the Roman goddess of wisdom. Natura then lodges her complaint in firm terms: Silva is chaotic, intractable, and conflicted – an amorphous mass without peace, law, or love, that needs Noys' ordering power to gain shape and achieve harmony. Adopting a slightly more humble tone, Natura identifies herself and concludes:

> "Pro Mundo Natura rogo. Satis est: nichil opto,
> Si rerum Munique suum natale videbo.
> Sed quid ego tibi plura? Pudet docuisse Minervam"

(I Natura ask on behalf of the Universe. It is enough: I wish nothing more if I may see the birth of the Universe and her creatures. But what more can I say to you? I am ashamed to have lectured Minerva) (1.1.64–6)

Stirring, Noys seems unbothered by Natura's tone of complaint and challenge; rather, like a parent to a child, she responds with loving words, naming her "uteri

---

integrated in that same human form. O how marvelous is the in-breathing that thus roused humankind!) (*Symphonia*, 100)

Recalling humankind's creation, this text encapsulates Hildegard's Christian humanism, which offers an instance of Southern's threefold interpretation of the concept as dignity of human nature, dignity of nature itself, and the intelligibility of the universe to human reason. *Medieval Humanism*, 31–3. See also Otten, *From Paradise to Paradigm*, 1–7, 9–44; and studies in Gersh and Roest, eds., *Medieval and Renaissance Humanism*, especially van Deusen, 31–53, and Pranger, 55–74.

26 Silverstein, "Fabulous Cosmogony," 107.

mei beata fecunditas" (blessed fruitfulness of my womb) and "filia Providentie" (daughter of Providence) (1.2.1.3–4). Fusing biblical Sapientia and Roman Minerva with the Platonic idea of a Divine Mind,[27] Bernard Silvestris creates a composite figure: Noys-Christ-Sapientia-Minerva who responds to Natura's request with loving action, "suaviterque disponens omnia" (ordering all things sweetly) in the manner of the "O Sapientia" antiphon and establishing universal harmony in the manner of Boethius' metrum 8.

Bernard Silvestris' "vera Minerva" is one instance of the Roman goddess' appearance in the twelfth century. As we shall see, she also appears in several other twelfth-century texts in a range of guises. Her direct relation to Sapientia in *Cosmographia*, however, links her in this instance to the medieval sapiential tradition of wisdom and love encapsulated respectively in "O Sapientia" and Boethius' metrum 8 and fused in a range of other texts from Alcuin's *Missa de Sancta Sapientia* to Suso's *Horologium*. Turning now to fifteenth-century England, we shift to John Lydgate's *Reson and Sensuallyte*, where Minerva appears again in the guise of Sapientia, a redemptress offering a path to wisdom through contemplation.

John Lydgate's *Reson and Sensuallyte*

John Lydgate (1371–1449), the prolific monk-priest from Bury St. Edmunds, wrote some 140,000 lines of English verse in his long poetic career.[28] *Reson and Sensuallyte*, likely written in the first decade of the fifteenth century, is Lydgate's unfinished translation of the anonymous French allegorical vision *Les Eschéz d'Amours*.[29] Early in *Reson and Sensuallyte* the dreamer-narrator encountered Minerva, Juno, Venus, and Mercury. After describing their appearance, he recounts being approached by Mercury, who retold the story of the Judgment of Paris and asked him whether or not Paris was correct. The narrator quickly assented to Paris' choice of Venus as the most beautiful, declaring "'I wold ha do the same / … Yif I hadde be arbitrour'."[30] Rejected, Minerva and Juno immediately left without a word, and Mercury, before taking flight, observed, "'Al this worlde goeth the same trace" (2107). Encompassing 1123 of the poem's 7042 lines, the Judgment of Paris scene is crucial to Lydgate's poetic agenda grounded in a desire for intelligent reading and proper judgment.

---

[27] Silverstein, "Fabulous Cosmogony," 107–12; Stock, *Myth and Science*, 87–97.
[28] See Pearsall, *John Lydgate (1371–1449): A Bio-bibliography*, 11–42, 53–80.
[29] A. Edwards, "Lydgate Manuscripts," 24–5, argues that no evidence other than Stow's sixteenth-century attribution supports Lydgate as author. While Simpson, "Economy of Involcrum," 392, reviews the question, J. Griffiths, *Diverting Authority*, 63–4 n.26, argues that the poem demonstrates poetic and thematic practices similar to Lydgate's other works. Along with most modern critics, I follow Stow's attribution to Lydgate here. Concerning date, most critics and the poem's modern editor date the work to Lydgate's early period, prior to 1412: see Ebin, *John Lydgate*, 35; Norton-Smith, introduction to *John Lydgate*, xiii; Pearsall, *John Lydgate*, 119–20; and *RS*, ed. Sieper, 2: 5–6.
[30] Lydgate, *Reson and Sensuallyte*, ed. Sieper, 2096, 98.

Minerva is central to this agenda, and examining Lydgate's poetics of translation and what we can glean of the poem's reception helps us understand his treatment of the Judgment of Paris scene and the goddess of wisdom's role in the poem.

Reson and Sensuallyte: Translatio and Reception

Composed between 1370 and 1380, *Les Eschéz d'Amours* is a poem of approximately 30,000 lines written in the tradition of *Le Roman de la Rose*. Lydgate translated only the first 4873 lines, or less than one-sixth of the original, expanding them to 7042 lines before discontinuing the project.[31] Lydgate's poem, along with Evrart de Conty's early fifteenth-century commentary *Livre des Eschez Amoureux Moralisés*, offer the earliest readings of *Les Eschéz*.[32] The current state of the manuscripts of *Les Eschéz*, however, has made it difficult to compare the Middle English poem with the French original, but with the recent edition of the poem's first 16,294 lines, we can begin to ascertain Lydgate's treatment of his source.[33] Like most medieval poets who composed translations, Lydgate used the opportunity for creative expression, and his translation differs from the original in its emphasis on the narrative's satirical thrust.

Any given text – whether Middle English poem or twenty-first-century film – is an artifact of its culture as well as the product of an author, director, poet, playwright. Translation involves, quite literally, the "carrying over" of such a text from its originating cultural group to another culturally different group so that an audience in the second group might access the text.[34] In medieval theory, the notion of *translatio* encompassed texts rendered both literally and freely, and from one medium or genre to another.[35] A play such as the York Crucifixion and a wood carving such as the Gero Crucifix, for example, translate the Gospel narratives of Jesus' death

---

[31] Ebin, *John Lydgate*, 35; Pearsall, *John Lydgate*, 116–19. *RS* is one of only two uncommissioned narratives, and it is Lydgate's only unfinished long narrative.

[32] Evrart de Conty's commentary on *Les Eschéz*'s first 5538 lines extends over 350 folios in its seven mss. (766 pages in its modern edition). See Guichard-Tesson and Roy, introduction to *Livre des Eschez*, xi–lxxiv, and Heyworth, introduction to *Les Eschéz*, 3–5, 26–8.

[33] An edition of *Les Eschéz d'Amours*, also known as *Les eschez amoureux*, is currently underway, with the first of two volumes in print. The poem is extant in two incomplete manuscripts: Dresden, Sachsische Landesbibliothek Oc 66 (c.1478); and Venice, Biblioteca Nazionale Marciana Fr. App. 23 (c.1400/10). Dresden contains 30,000+ lines, but seems to be missing a final quire. Greatly damaged during World War II, it has been nearly illegible until recent developments in photographic technology. Venice contains 13,269 lines and is missing sections of the poem, including the Judgment of Paris scene. See Ehrhart, *Judgment of the Trojan Prince Paris*, 151–3, 268 n.74; Galpin, "Les Echez Amoureux," 283–307; Heyworth, Introduction to *Les Eschéz*, 3–9, 41–7; D. O' Sullivan, Introduction to *Les Eschéz*, 81–4; and *RS*, ed. Sieper, 2:59–76.

[34] Lefevere calls this second group a "target culture" and argues a translator must carefully attend to both target-culture needs and the original text's "universe of discourse," or those elements implicit and explicit in the text that point to its originating culture. *Translating Literature*, 86, 120.

[35] Beer, introduction to *Medieval Translators*, 1–7; Copeland, *Rhetoric, Hermeneutics, and Translation*, 9–62, 151–78.

into active dramatic representation on the one hand and static visual representation on the other. Such a second text produced through an act of translation offers a reading, or interpretation, of the original text: a point Douglas Kelly emphasizes in his discussion of medieval *interpretatio*.[36] Frequently, this second text serves not as surrogate but more as replacement for the original. Thus, while many medieval writers followed Jerome and Boethius in their role as *fidus interpres* by translating "word-for-word" and "sense-for-sense," many also were concerned with the poetic invention translation could inspire.[37] Copeland argues that medieval rhetorical theory based on Augustine's *De doctrina Christiana* uses the term *inventio* to denote a method for discovering those things in a text which are meant to be understood.[38] In other words, *inventio* in such medieval theory takes on a hermeneutical tincture. When translating, poets who employ rhetorical *inventio* often amplify a source text by making explicit what it implies, which makes translation a unique product of the individual poet's reading.[39] Like many medieval poets, Lydgate bases much of his narrative poetry on sources, and he similarly uses rhetorical *inventio* to amplify them: a technique he begins to develop when translating *Les Eschéz d'Amours*.

Though interesting as a translation among Lydgate's early works, *Reson and Sensuallyte* has drawn little modern scholarly engagement. In the recent wave of critical interest in the poet, for instance, scholars have not paid much attention to this poem.[40] This present situation reflects the poem's critical history. With the exception of Ernst Sieper's introduction to the 1901, 1903 EETS ES edition and Margaret Ehrhart's somewhat negative assessment of the poem in her 1987 discussion of *Les Eschéz*, *Reson and Sensuallyte* had barely received passing notice in literary histories until James Simpson's and Jane Griffiths' recent studies.[41] Like his other

---

[36] D. Kelly, "*Fidus interpres*," 47–8.
[37] Burnett, "Translation and Translators," 138–40; Morse, *Truth and Convention*, 63–84, 179–230.
[38] Copeland, *Rhetoric, Hermeneutics, and Translation*, 154–8.
[39] Baltzell, "Rhetorical 'Amplification' and 'Abbreviation'," 32–9. Alexander Neckam, in *Novus Avianus*, ed. Hervieux, 463–4, illustrates how to amplify and abbreviate when translating: Hodapp, "Fables of Avianus," 17–19.
[40] Critiqued for decades as a prolix hack, Lydgate has gradually gained attention since Schirmer's, Renoir's, and Pearsall's re-assessments in 1961, 1967, and 1970 respectively, Ebin's studies in the mid- to late 1980s, and Pearsall's *Bio-bibliography* in 1997. Recent work re-examines Lydgate as a socio-literary poet (Barr, *Socioliterary Practice*, 188–98), as shaper of cultural expression (Strohm, *Politique*, 87–104; M. Nolan, *John Lydgate*; and the essays in Scanlon and Simpson, eds., *John Lydgate*, and in L. Cooper and Denny-Brown, eds., *Lydgate Matters*), as poet of reading the visual (Gayk, *Image, Text, and Religious Reform*, 84–122), and as post-Lollard poet of pilgrimage (L. Cooper, *Artisans and Narrative Craft*, 129–45).
[41] Ehrhart, *Judgment of the Trojan Prince Paris*, 167–8, critiques Lydgate's amplifications. Simpson, "Economy of Involucrum," 390–412, examines themes of idleness and reading. J. Griffiths, *Diverting Authorities*, 54–6, 63–80, studies the theme of authorship by examining glosses in Bodleian Library Ms. Fairfax 16. Lewis, *Allegory of Love*, 271–8, H. Bennett, *Chaucer and the Fifteenth Century*, 138–9, Schirmer, *John Lydgate*, 31–41, Pearsall, *John Lydgate*, 83–121, and Ebin, *John Lydgate*, 20–38, examine the poem as part of a literary tradition (Lewis) or of Lydgate's early canon (the others).

courtly poems, however, it enjoyed some popularity in the fifteenth and sixteenth centuries, as the manuscript tradition attests.[42] The poem survives today in two manuscripts, each offering evidence of other no-longer extant copies: Bodleian Library Ms. Fairfax 16, dating from the second quarter of the fifteenth century and compiled while the poet was still living, and British Library Ms. Additional 29729, dating from the mid-sixteenth century. As with similar fifteenth-century manuscripts, Fairfax 16 is a miscellany containing a number of poems including Thomas Hoccleve's *Letter of Cupid*, Chaucer's *Book of the Duchess*, *House of Fame*, and *Parliament of Fowls*, in which Nature appears prominently, and Lydgate's *Temple of Glas* and *Complaynt of a Lovers Lyfe* in addition to *Reson and Sensuallyte*. Although the manuscript has little decoration, its contents indicate an audience interested in courtly literature, dream vision, and allegory, and *Reson and Sensuallyte* itself is carefully decorated to facilitate oral or silent reading, including a rubricated subtitle ("her the auctour maketh a descripcion of pallas") marked with a blue paraph to emphasize the Minerva passages (fols. 216–19v).[43] The second manuscript, Additional 29729, originally compiled and owned by sixteenth-century antiquarian John Stowe, is a collection of Lydgate's poetry and poems attributed to him, bearing the title "Daune Lidgayt monke of burye his woorke" (fol. 1r). This anthology provides insights into the sixteenth-century reception of *Reson and Sensuallyte*: its material, selected and organized by author, demonstrates a humanistic concern for the integrity of a single author's works – a concern reinforced by its incomplete decoration plan.[44] Compared to Fairfax 16, Additional 29729 suggests a change in the literary context in which *Reson and Sensuallyte* was read, from a diverse miscellany of courtly poems and poets to a Lydgatian context, thereby evincing interest in the poet well into the sixteenth century.

The poem's subject matter, in addition to its manuscript tradition, further indicates its appeal to readers. It recounts the adventures of a young man who, in a dream, encounters not only Minerva, Juno, Venus, and Mercury but also Nature, Diana, Cupid, and Deduit. The attraction to Lydgate, his immediate audience, and

---

[42] Ebin, *John Lydgate*, 20.
[43] Fairfax 16 is a parchment ms. of 335 folios ruled in single columns for 38 or 39 lines. *RS* is on fols. 202–300 and is entitled "Reson and Sensualytte" in John Stowe's hand, which differs from that given in the table of contents: "The booke of þe autoure how he plaid at þe chesse and was mated of a Ferse" (2v). The title by which we know the poem today seems a sixteenth-century interpretation of the text. Designed to enhance reading, whether aloud or silently, its decorative program includes the following: the first letter of the text, "T," is blue with red scribal line decorations added; there is rubrication throughout (nearly every opening) with commentary, speaker tags, Latin marginal glosses, and light highlights on the first letter of each line to emphasize the line's beginning, thereby catching the reader's eye; each rubrication is accented with a blue paraph mark.
[44] Additional 29729 is a paper ms. codex ruled in single columns with 36 to 40 lines per folio depending on the text. The incomplete decoration plan, laid out for the whole, breaks off at two points: the final rubricated letter is on fol. 53; the final rubrication mark is on fol. 86. See *RS*, ed. Sieper, 1: xi–xvii, for a general description of the two manuscripts. See A. Edwards, "Fifteenth-Century Middle English Verse," 101–12, for a discussion of single-author verse collections in England.

subsequent fifteenth- and sixteenth-century readers of the allegorical journey as a spiritual narrative and the classical figures as "interiores animi potentias" is obvious in light of the *Roman de la Rose* tradition from which arose *Les Eschéz d'Amours*, this poem's chief source text. Lydgate accentuates the narrative's satire by amplifying his source through *inventio* while his audience enjoys the moral comedy of the narrator's self-proclaimed "Aventure" (46). Although he alters his source, Lydgate's amplification signals an important aspect of his poetics. For Lydgate, part of a poet's role was to "enlumyne" his matter. Ebin notes that "enlumyne" in Lydgate's critical vocabulary "draws together associations from the art of manuscript illumination and from the religious tradition of spiritual illumination."[45] Hence, for Lydgate, poetry both throws light upon and gives spiritual insight into its matter. A significant passage of the poem Lydgate "enlumynes" through *inventio* is the scene in which the narrator met Minerva.

Minerva: Iconography and the Judgment of Paris

As noted, Minerva appeared with Juno, Venus, and Mercury in a scene reminiscent of Paris' judgment. Before the narrator met Minerva, however, he encountered Dame Nature who, in the tradition of Alan of Lille's Natura from *De planctu Naturae*, encouraged him to pursue reason and wisdom. In its attention to the Judgment of Paris story, *Reson and Sensuallyte* offers a reading of Alan's text, where Natura refers to Paris and Helen five times as instances of love gone awry under the influence of "incestuose Cipridis" (unchaste Venus).[46] Part of the late medieval interest in Alan's *De planctu*,[47] *Reson and Sensuallyte* explores the tension in humankind between the rational and the sensual faculties, about which Alan's Natura observes: "Et sicut contra ratam firmamenti uolutionem motu contradictorio exercitus militat planetarum sic in homine sensualitatis rationisque continua reperitur hostilitas" (And just as the army of planets fights against the firmament's fixed turning, so in humankind is found the continuous hostility of reason and sensuality) (6.51–4). Lydgate's Nature commissioned the narrator to find work proper to humankind, and her relationship with the narrator provides insights into Minerva and her wisdom. Moreover, the narrator's psychological state, evident early in the poem and developed in his exchange with Nature, underscores the character of his later relationship with Minerva.

Like all first-person dream visions, *Reson and Sensuallyte* is the narrator's account of a remembered event. After a brief prologue but before any visionary encounters,

---

[45] Ebin, *Illuminator, Makar, Vates*, 20. See also J. Griffiths, *Diverting Authorities*, 63–80, for discussion of translation based on *Les Eschéz*'s Latin glosses and Evrart's commentary.

[46] Alan of Lille, *De planctu Naturae*, ed. Häring, 1.35, 1.51–2, 8.68–70, 9.27; quote from 18:87.

[47] The greater number of the 133+ *De planctu* manuscripts date from the fourteenth and fifteenth centuries (*De planctu*, 797, 804), following Jean de Meun's c.1270 continuation of Guillaume de Lorris' *Le Roman de la Rose* in which Jean directly draws on Alan's Natura. This sequence points to renewed late medieval interest in Alan's text. See B. Newman, *God and the Goddesses*, 73.

the narrator metaphorically describes his state of mind. In the delightful guise of a taverner, Fortune has two tuns "in her celler" (52) from which she serves delicious or bitter drink "To alle foolkys eve and morowe, / Some with Joye and some with sorowe" (75–6).[48] Having tasted both, the narrator found himself in bed one spring morning admiring blossoming flowers, budding trees, and singing birds outside his window all seeking to recover from winter through service to love (47–181). In a Boethian echo, this passage implies that, just as the creatures of nature had suffered winter's ravages, the narrator had suffered at Fortune's hands. The implicit correspondence – bad and good fortune; winter and spring seasons – underscores Fortune's and Nature's double-sidedness, yet their difference is fundamental: spring necessarily follows winter; good fortune does not necessarily follow bad. Though admiring the surrounding spring-time activity, the narrator languished in bed, "Nouther in slombre nor a-slepe" (194), content "To here the briddes chaunte and synge / On fresshe braunches in certayn" (196–7).[49] While he was in this state of mind, Dame Nature suddenly appeared, illuminating his chamber with so piercing a light and filling it with such a rich scent that he initially drew back from her, a distinct echo of the narrator's response in Alan of Lille's *De planctu* (4.14–17). Like a bell ringing lauds, she arrived to wake him up to the day and, as it turns out, to his duties as a human being. Although a bit stunned, he still recognized her as a "hevenly emperesse" (242): pausing in his narration, he then describes her attributes.

As the narrator reads Nature like a text, it becomes evident she resembles Alan of Lille's Natura in her relationship to God, her iconography, her role in sustaining the universe, and her particular concern with humanity's rational faculty. As "chefe goddesse" (256) under God, she rules the universe with celestial harmony and maintains earthly creatures, "Eche thinge in his ovne kynde" (302). Like Natura, Nature also wears clothing of her own making: a mantle woven from the four elements on which she depicted all of creation and which she continually re-weaves, repairing those threads severed by Atropos, the Fate who cuts the thread of life at death.[50] As in Alan, Nature's regenerative power seeks to inspire the common good, or what

---

[48] This image of Fortune as taverner with two tuns ultimately derives from Homer's Zeus, who dispenses good and ill from two jars (*Iliad*, 24.527), which Socrates quotes (Plato, *Republic*, 379d–e) and Boethius references (*CP* 2.pr.2.13–14). Jean de Meun, *Roman de la Rose*, ed. Langlois, 6813–54, expands on this reference, characterizing Fortune as tavern-hostess, an image the *Eschéz*-author references, *Les Eschéz d'Amours*, ed. Heyworth and O'Sullivan, 43–78, and Lydgate in turn uses.

[49] Although the narrator seems awake, he later states, "And thogh I slept, myn hert awook / Thus thoght I tho in my dremyng" (1834–5). This later reference indicates the narrator is dreaming throughout.

[50] Alan distinguishes Natura's clothing inscribed with images of creatures: her woolen robe of office contains birds; her muslin mantle, aquatic animals; and her linen tunic, terrestrial animals (*De planctu*, 2.138–278). Lydgate conflates the garments into one mantle on which he depicts all creatures. The rent-garment trope derives from Boethius' satire of philosophical schools rending bits from Philosophia (*CP* 1.pr.1.5), and Alan's satire against homosexuality (*De planctu*, 8.161–72). Lydgate universalizes the trope, making the wearing out of the garment an image of death.

Chaucer calls the "comoun profyt" (*PF*, 47), proper to a creature's "kynde" and necessary for ensuring universal order.⁵¹ And, her relation to man, depicted on her mantle in the highest place looking towards the heavens while other beasts "don enclyne / Her hedes to the erthe lowe" (400–1), accentuates humankind's place in the natural order and echoes Alan in emphasizing reason as humankind's distinguishing attribute (*De planctu* 2.232–5, 8.54–5). This association with Alan's Natura suggests a Nature figure in *Reson and Sensuallyte* concerned with humankind's ordered correspondence with the cosmos: like Alan's Natura, who advises, "intestino affectionis amore Prudentiam consecteris, ut penicius Sapientie matris cubiculum inoffenso intuitu valeas intueri" (pursue Prudentia with the internal love of affection so you may be able internally to gaze upon in unobstructed contemplation the inner room of mother Wisdom), Lydgate's Nature aligns with Sapientia.⁵²

As the narrative resumes, Nature chided the narrator for his sloth, told him to take a lesson from the birds who praise God in song, and charged him with offending "kynde" through "wilful ydelnesse, / The which ys lady and maistresse / Of vicys al[le]" (466–8). To address his wrong against "kynde" and avoid "ydelnesse," she suggested he travel the world to see its beauty so he may properly praise God as a man ought,⁵³ and she reminded him that, because he is endowed with reason, he is "'Lych to the goddys immortall'" (565) and should cultivate virtue and reject vice. The narrator responded that, though it is a good thing to be like God, self-governance and perfection are hard. Still, he said, he would try. Echoing

---

51   Natura in *De planctu* is complex and contradictory, drawing commentary over inconsistencies: see, for instance, Jordan, *Invention of Sodomy*, 67–91; and B. Newman, *God and the Goddesses*, 66–73.

52   Glosses reinforce this implied association between Nature and Sapientia. Rubricated marginal notes in Fairfax 16 at lines 393–5 – "Man was set in the hyest place / Towarde heven erecte hys face, / Clymynge hys diue herytage" – quote Ovid: "Vnde Ouidius de transformatis: prona q[ue] cum spectent etc." and "Os homini sublime dedit, celumque vi|dere / Iussit et erectos ad celum tendere vultus" (fol. 207v). Both citations are from the creation of humankind at the opening of *Met.*, 1.84–6 (and are also included in black ink in Additional 29729): "pronaque cum spectent animalia cetera terram, / os homini sublime dedit caelumque videre / iussit et erectos ad sidera tollere vultus" (and though other animals are prone and gaze on earth, he gave humankind an up-lifted face and ordered them to stand erect, turn their face to the stars and gaze on heaven). Part of the Venice ms. but not the later Dresden ms. of *Les Eschéz*, these Latin glosses indicate intertextual reading habits and the condition of Lydgate's source text, as he replicates many in his translation. See Coulson, "Latin Glosses of Venice," 95–104, for a discussion of glosses in *Les Eschéz*, and J. Griffiths for a discussion of how the translator "departs from both text and gloss in order to bring out *his own understanding* of the sense," *Diverting Authorities*, 64–76: 69. See also Simpson's discussion of the poem as "utterly familiar with and committed to a humanist tradition … confident in the possibilities of human improvement," "Economy of Involucrum," 393–6: 393: a tradition he delineates in *Sciences and the Self*.

53   Much as Nature's sudden appearance at dawn alludes to the call to lauds, her admonition to align with the natural order alludes to the Canticle of the Three Youths sung in litany at lauds on Sundays and feast days, in which all creation joins in praising God (Dan. 3:52–88; Collamore, "Prelude," 7). As a monk, Lydgate would have sung this chant as easily as breathing.

Alan's discussion of the essential opposition between Reason and sensuality, Nature then warned the narrator of two paths – sensuality, which leads to the west of false pleasure, and Reason, which leads to the east of heavenly joy[54] – and said:

"Begynne the weye, ech seson,
First at vertu and reson,
And fle ech thing that they dispreyse,
And vp to god thy herte reyse,
And love him over alle thinge,
Nat declynyng fro hys biddyng!
And her with al take good hede
Both to love him and to drede
As thy lorde most souereyne;
And to forn thyn eyen tweyne
Most enterly lat him be set!" (817–27)

In her advice and admonition, Nature implies Augustine's theory of the proper use of beauty: that it should be admired not for itself alone but for *The Beauty*, God, who is above it and who is its source.[55] She also echoes Bernard of Clairvaux's four degrees of love, where wise love of the natural world can lead to love of God (cols. 987–91), and Suso's *Aeterna Sapientia*, who instructs the Discipulus that delight in nature should lead to delight in the Creator (419). Alluding to the image of man depicted on her mantle, she emphasized the narrator's "kynde" when commanding "'Set thy desire and thyn entent / To thinges that be celestiall'" (830–1).

After Nature departed and the narrator began his journey, he almost immediately and rather comically forgot her advice to hold God before his eyes and, delighting alone in the beauties of the natural world, was shortly, in his own words, "disloggyd of my way" (928). As he progressed on his path, he first forgot his past, he then failed to recognize the true value of the beauty he was seeing, and finally, he reveals, he was pursuing "singular profit": "Whych was to me, y you ensure, / Ryght profytable to

---

[54] Latin glosses on "thorient" and "thoccident" (647, 648) indicate the east signifies "celestia et diuina" (heavenly and divine things) and the west "temporalia et terrena" (temporal and earthly things) with their respective paths – "via racionis" leading to the east and "via sensus" to the west: see J. Griffiths, *Diverting Authorities*, 73–5. In Christian buildings, architects built altars to face the east, the realm of light and paradise, and entrances to face the west, the realm of darkness and death. When entering a church, Christians progressed from the realm of darkness to the realm of light, from the realm of profane space to the realm of sacred space: movement east for Christians was moving towards Christ, whose second coming was anticipated with each day's sunrise: see Eliade, *Sacred and the Profane*, 20–67; and Mâle, *Gothic Image*, 5–7. Similarly, pilgrimage to Jerusalem was for Europeans a movement east, which took on a bellicose dimension with the crusades beginning in the eleventh century; and the movement east to west in the context of late medieval pilgrimage-crusade mentality perhaps signifies the threat of the exotic east exemplified by the Ottoman Turks. On pilgrimage and crusade, see Sumption, *Age of Pilgrimage*, 122–35, 194–207; on late medieval crusades, see Housley, *Later Crusades*, and essays in Housley, ed., *Crusading in the Fifteenth Century*.

[55] Augustine, *Confessions*, ed. O'Donnell, 10.34; Eco, *Art and Beauty*, 17–27.

my Norture" (987–8).⁵⁶ At this point, he met Mercury, Minerva, Juno, and Venus. Although he had forgotten Nature's advice, the narrator had not yet completely lost his reason, for he recognized the deities and luxuriates in descriptive detail as he reads each one for his narratee. These descriptions are key to the poem because the goddesses, who remained speechless during this encounter, metaphorically spoke through their iconography. Of the three goddesses, only Venus verbally addressed the narrator after this encounter. Beginning with Minerva, here under her name Pallas, he pauses the narration to read and describe the goddesses and Mercury in turn.

Minerva, he says, is Jupiter's "ovne doghtre dere" and "chef goddesse of sapience" (1042, 44) because wisdom descends directly from God. She is also the goddess of battle, takes idleness from men, leads them to prudent and virtuous lives, reveals divine secrets to them and, if they are willing, leads them to heavenly bliss (1089–94). After describing her attributes, the narrator describes her beauty: though old, her beauty and wisdom do not fade "For which she called ys Mynerve, / That ys to seyne in special / A thing that ys ay inmortal" (1112–14). Her eyes were like burning torches, and her height changeable,

> Somwhile amonge, I dar ensure,
> Comon she was of hir stature,
> And sommwhile she wex so long
> That to the hevene she raught amonge. (1125–8)

She wore a mantle of three colors representing the parts of philosopy,⁵⁷ which she had woven herself, and a helmet of temperance, and she carried a lance of righteousness in her right hand and a shield of patience in her left, on which was depicted

---

⁵⁶ The contrast between common and singular profit is a prevalent theme in late medieval literature, as Gower's *CA* and Chaucer's *PF* illustrate. In the latter, the narrator praises Scipio as a man "That lovede comoun profyt" (47) and then recounts Africanus' advice to Scipio to "'Know thyself first inmortal, / And loke ay besyly thow werche and wysse / To comoun profit'" (73–5). In the former, Genius contrasts communal demands of "comun profit" with selfish desires of "singulier beyete," *Confessio Amantis*, ed. Macauley, 7.1985–2002. See also Peck, *Kingship and Common Profit*.

⁵⁷ Presumably ethics, physics, and metaphysics, or what Augustine calls in *De civitate Dei*, ed. Latin Library, 8.4–9, moral, natural, and rational philosophy. The colors also could have a more specific reference. Hugh of St. Victor, inspired by Aristotle, divides philosophy into four areas – mechanical, practical, theoretical, and logical – and interestingly links Minerva to theoretical philosophy: "sunt qui has tres theoricae partes mystice quodam Palladis nomine, quae dea sapientiae fingitur esse, significari putant. dicitur enim Tritona, quasi tritoona, id est, tertia cognitio, videlicet Dei, quam intellectibilem nominavimus, et animarum, quam intelligibilem diximus, et corporum, quam naturalem appellavimus" (there are those who consider these three parts of the theoretical [theology, mathematics, physics] are mystically represented in one of the names of Pallas, who is depicted to be the goddess of wisdom. For she is called Tritona as if *tritoona*, that is, threefold apprehension of God, which we have named intellectible; of souls, which we have called intelligible; and of bodies, which we have called natural). *Didascalicon*, ed. Buttimer, 2.18.

Medusa's head. On her own head was a crown, signifying "That verray wysdam hath no delyt, / Ne no maner of appetyt / In worldly thing most transitorie" (1235–7). And around her head flew swans, whose song reminds reasonable men of the shortness of life.[58]

From this reading, we notice several links between Minerva and Nature. In her effort to rid men of "ydelnesse" (1076), Minerva aids Nature in her work of encouraging humans to find their true "kynde" in occupation directed towards praise of God. Minerva also supports Nature's desire for humans to remember they have been endowed with godlike immortality. The narrator states:

> And man, be kynde corumpable,
> She kan make pardurable,
> Yf she be vertu him gouerne,
> Lyk goddys for to be eterne. (1085–8)

Moreover, Minerva's relationship to the world, signified by her crown that has no "appetyt" for "transitorie" worldly things, resonates with Nature's advice to despise the transitoriness of earthly things. And their distinct relationships to Reason indirectly link the two. While Nature here claims Reason "'As myn ovne suster dere!'" (874), Minerva and Reason, represented in this poem by her path, are connected by a shared ability to lead humankind to eternal life.

In addition to Minerva's connection with Nature and the narrator's recognition of her ability to lead men to wisdom and eternal life, several of her iconographic details come from Minerva as explicated in mythographies.[59] In Fulgentius' *Mitologiae*, one of the early and more influential mythographic texts in medieval

---

[58] Occasionally, poets associate swans with Venus: in Ovid, *Metamorphoses* 10.718, for instance, swans pull Venus' chariot. Here, however, Lydgate uses swans and swan-song as portents of death. Again, Lydgate follows Alan of Lille, *De planctu*, 2.357–8. He also could be drawing on Chaucer's *PF* – "The jelous swan, ayens his deth that syngeth" (342) – his *Legend of Dido* – "'Ryght so,' quod she, 'as that the white swanne / Ayenst his deeth begynnthe for to synge'" (1355–6) – and his *Anelida and Arcite* – "But as the swan, I [Anelida] have herd seyde ful yore, / Ayeins his deth shal singe in his penaunce, / So singe I here my destany or chaunce" (346–8). Minerva's traditional bird, the owl, is also associated with warnings of death. In Virgil's *Aeneid*, Dido hears an owl sing shortly before Aeneas departs and she commits suicide (4.460–5). Similarly, in *The Owl and the Nightingale*, ed. Garbaty, 1151–2, the nightingale chides the owl for foretelling death, and in Lydgate's *Troy Book*, ed. Bergen, 2.2569–72, where Minerva does appear with an owl, the bird's song signifies death. In *RS*, Lydgate amplifies *Les Eschéz* by interpreting the reference.

[59] Lydgate read widely. As a monk of Bury St. Edmunds, he had access to both the large collection of books at the abbey and other monasteries' holdings through an interlibrary loan. In addition to a number of classical authors (Cicero, Virgil, Ovid, Horace, Juvenal), Bury St. Edmunds held or could access copies of Boethius' *CP*, Fulgentius' *Mit.*, Macrobius' *Saturnalia*, Bernard Silvestris' *Cosmographia*, Alan of Lille's *De planctu Naturae* and *Anticlaudianus*, and Richard de Bury's *Philobiblon*, among others listed in Henry of Kirkestede's *Catalogus*. See Summit, *Memory's Library*, 16–52, for Lydgate's involvement in re-organizing monastic holdings at the abbey and his use of Duke Humphrey's library before the Duke bequeathed it to Oxford University.

culture, Minerva's association with Medusa signifies the awe wisdom instills in its enemies, and she is helmeted and carries a spear and shield because wisdom is always armed and can strike at long range with its pronouncements.[60] While later mythographers echo many of Fulgentius' interpretations, they add other interpretive details Lydgate also employs in his poem. The twelfth-century Third Vatican Mythographer repeats much of Fulgentius but also draws on Martianus Capella and Ecclesiasticus to explain Minerva's descent from a high place when he writes: "Fingit Palladem Martianus de sublimiore et splendidiore loco descendisse [*De nuptiis* 1.39] quia videlicet in excelsis sapientia habitat, et omnem terrenae faecis supergraditur vilitatem. Habes ipsam dicentem: 'ego in altissimis habitavi, et thronus meus in columna nubis' [Ecclus. 24:7]" (Martianus imagines that Pallas descended from a more sublime and splendid place because clearly wisdom lives in the highest place and surpasses all worthlessness of earthly corruption. You know, she herself says: "I lived in the highest places, and my throne was on a column of cloud").[61] This passage sheds light on Lydgate's own explanation of Minerva and Jupiter's relationship, signifying "That alle wisdam descended is / Fro god a-bove" (1046–7). Similarly, Lydgate seems to develop his definition of "Minerva" as "immortal" from the mythographers. The late fourteenth-century monk Thomas Walsingham, repeating the Third Vatican Mythographer, writes: "Hinc et Minerva dici meruit, id est non mortalis; min enim non, erva mortalis interpretatur" (She deserves to be called Minerva, that is, not mortal; for *min* means not and *erva* means mortal).[62] Though erroneous, this etymology illustrates a tendency in medieval mythography to leave no detail unread. And, like Lydgate, the fourteenth-century professor-monk Pierre Bersuire – another of Walsingham's sources – describes Minerva's robe as three-colored; however, with Bersuire the colors signify "tres virtutes theologicas" (the three theological virtues) rather than the three parts of philosophy.[63]

We can trace other iconographic details of Minerva to Boethius' description of Philosophia or Guillaume de Lorris' description of Raison.[64] Philosophia's stature, for instance, is changeable: "Nam nunc quidem ad communem sese hominum

---

[60] Fulgentius, *Mit.*, 2.1. On Fulgentius, see Chance, *Medieval Mythography*, 1:95–101.
[61] TVM, *De diis gentium*, ed. Bode, 10.2.12–6. On authorship, see Chance, *Medieval Mythography*, 1:60, 486; and Pepin, introduction to *The Vatican Mythographers*, 9–10.
[62] Walsingham, *De archana deorum*, ed. van Kluyve, 1.10.6–8.
[63] Bersuire writes: "[Vir sapiens] Debet eciam habere scutum fortitudinis & patientiae ... triplicem vestem .i. tres virtutes theologicas" (The wise man also ought to possess a shield of fortitude and patience... and the triple-cloak of the three theological virtues), *De formis figuresque*, ed. Engels, 31. Bersuire gets Minerva's tripartite robe from earlier mythography. According to the SVM: "triplici etiam ueste fingunt hanc esse indutam quod sapientia tecta extrinsecus raro cognoscatur" (humans depict her clothed in a triple robe because wisdom is guarded, rarely recognized from the outside), *Mythographi Vaticani I et II*, ed. Kulcsar, 50. On Bersuire and Walsingham, see Chance, *Medieval Mythography*, 2:320. On Walsingham, see also J.G. Clark, *Monastic Renaissance at St. Albans*.
[64] Boethius' Philosophia is a literary precursor of Guillaume de Lorris and Jean de Meun's Raison. See Fleming, *Reason and the Lover*, 38–63.

mensuram cohibebat nunc ver pulsare caelum summi vertices cacumine videbatur; quae cum altius caput extulisset, ipsum etiam caelu penetrabat respicientiumque hominum frustrabatur intuitum" (For she seemed at one time to be confined to the common height of a man at another to strike her head on the highest peak of the heavens; and when she raised her head even higher she was penetrating heaven itself and frustrated the view of gazing men) (1.pr.1.8–14). This detail, also evident in other female wisdom figures such as Alan of Lille's Prudentia,[65] allegorically represents wisdom's ability both to range the earth and rise from it to heaven, as we see in Hildegard's antiphon "O virtus Sapientie." Similarly, Philosophia has burning eyes and a robe she has woven herself (*CP* 1.pr.1.13–16). Like Philosophia and Minerva, Raison has clear, bright eyes (*RR* 3199–200); however, unlike Philosophia, she wears a crown (*RR* 3201). While the features of the robe and crown further link Minerva with Nature, Nature does not have the same relationship to wisdom as Philosophia and Raison have. Like Minerva, Philosophia is involved in intellectual pursuits, and Raison is created directly by God, and in Lydgate's poem God directly forged Minerva's crown and crowned her in paradise (1230). Nature's connection to wisdom, on the other hand, centers on properly ordering creation: daughter of Noys in the *Cosmographia* and *vicaria Dei* in Alan of Lille, she calls forth and sustains creation's order through generation. Like Chaucer's Nature, who advises the formel eagle, "'If I were Resoun, certes, thanne wolde I / Conseyle you the ryal tersel take'" (*PF* 632–3), Lydgate's Nature encourages employing reason and pursuing wisdom, but she does not represent them.

A final element linking Minerva to Philosophia is the "Old Woman and Girl" topos Curtius discussed.[66] When the narrator describes Minerva as "fresh and nywe" yet "olde and of gret age" (1104, 1106), he incorporates a literary detail writers often use to suggest timelessness in female wisdom figures such as Philosophia, whom Boethius describes as having "colore vivido atque inexhausti vigoris, quamvis ita aevi plena foret ut nullo modo nostrae crederetur aetatis" (a complexion full of life and of untiring vigor, yet she seemed so full of years that in no way would any believe she was of our time) (1.pr.1.5–7). Likewise, Alan of Lille characterizes both Faith, in *Anticlaudianus* (6.66–72), and Temperance, in *De planctu* (16.77–88), as grey-haired and aged but with a youthful countenance. In the fifteenth-century *Court of Sapience*, once attributed to Lydgate, Sapyence herself declares, "'Though I seme yong, ful old my yeres bene'."[67] And, in the most significant link between the two goddesses in Lydgate's poem, Nature, too, seems "but yonge and tendir of age" though she is so old "That no man koude ... / Noumbre hir yeres euerychon" (393, 398–9). For Curtius, this topos connotes rejuvenation in vision literature with the ideal-woman figure acting as a potential redemptress for the visionary. In the examples cited, the ideal-woman figure offers the path of redemption characteristic to herself; thus, Nature's redemptive power lies in the proper ordering of "kynde,"

---

[65] Alan of Lille, *Anticlaudianus*, ed. Bossuat, 1.298–302.
[66] Curtius, *European Literature*, 101–5.
[67] *Court of Sapience*, ed. Harvey, 1.23.160.

Temperance's in "moderation," Faith's in "credal belief," and so on. Like others in the "Old Woman and Girl" tradition, Minerva in *Reson and Sensuallyte* embodies the redemptive power particular to her nature: the wisdom one finds in the "via prudentiae" – a life of love directed toward self, neighbor, and God for the sake of God, as Bernard of Clairvaux delineates.

While the "Old Woman and Girl" topos describes one aspect of Minerva's literary lineage, it also suggests in part her spiritual lineage from biblical wisdom literature. In Proverbs, Sapientia declares: "Dominus possedit me in initio viarum suarum, antequam quidquam faceret a principio. Ab aeterno ordinata sum, et ex antiquis antequam terra fieret" (The Lord possessed me in the beginning of his own ways, before he made anything at the beginning; I was ordained from eternity, and from of old before the earth was made) (Prov. 8:22–3). And, in the passage from Ecclesiasticus cited by the Third Vatican Mythographer above and quoted in part in the "O Sapientia" antiphon, she declares: "Ego ex ore Altissimi prodivi primogenita ante omnem creaturam: Ego feci in caelis ut oriretur lumen indeficiens, et sicut nebula texi omnem terram: Ego in altissimis habitavi, et thronus meus in columna nubis" (I proceeded from the mouth of the Most High, the first born before every creature; I made that a light unfailing appear in the heavens, and I covered all the earth as a cloud; I lived in the highest places, and my throne was on a column of cloud) (Ecclus. 24:5–7). As a wisdom figure, Minerva's "gret age" and descent "Fro god a-bove" resonate richly with Sapientia's own lineage and connect strongly to the spiritual life Sapientia offers to humankind.

After the narrator describes Minerva, he also describes Juno, Venus, and Mercury, indicating oppositional relationships between the three goddesses. Juno, clothed in a jewel-studded gold surcoat, wears a crown ringed by a rainbow, carries a scepter, and has peacocks at her feet. These details, as Fulgentius and later mythographers interpret them, signify Juno's concern with wealth and temporal rule: a concern that links her to Fortune (*Mit.*, 2.1).[68] Venus, on the other hand, is crowned with roses, has rings on every finger (as in "Vpon temse"), holds a fiery brand in her right hand and a golden apple in her left, and wears a skin-tight coat – "Lych as she had in soth be naked" (1564) – while doves fly around her head. The roses, doves, fiery brand, and near nakedness signify Venus' concern here with erotic love, as again Fulgentius and others suggest (*Mit.*, 2.1; TVM, 11.1; Bersuire, *De formis*, 7). Moreover, the narrator, by implication, also links Venus to Fortune when he declares her mood is forever changing (1549–54). Venus' iconographic details and association with Fortune

---

[68] In *RS*, Lydgate makes Juno's connection with Fortune explicit when the narrator states:

> For she is quene and eke goddesse
> Of worldly tresour and rychess,
> And hem gouerneth, sooth to say,
> For fortune doth hir lust obey,
> The gerful lady with hir whel,
> That blynd is and seth neuer a del ...
> For Iuno is the tresourere,
> And fortune hir awmonere. (1355–60, 1363–4)

suggest she is more the earthly than the celestial Venus in the framework Bernard Silvestris and later writers develop. The narrator underscores this suggestion when he recounts her birth from (as Lydgate has it) Saturn's castrated members flung into the sea (1443–64). As with her other iconographic details, the mythographers associate Venus' birth from the foamy sea with the carnal side of her nature (*Mit.*, 2.1; TVM, 11.1; Bersuire, *De formis*, 7; Walsingham, *De archana deorum*, 1.11.1–15).[69] After the goddesses, the narrator describes Mercury as the winged messenger of the gods, skilled in calculation, music, eloquence, and commerce. He carries a staff and wears the curved sword he used to slay Argus. Fulgentius and others link these details to Mercury as protector of merchants as well as messenger: the staff signifies control in commerce, and Argus and the sword signify cleverness in trading (*Mit.*, 1.18; TVM, 9.3; Bersuire, *De formis*, 25; Walsingham, *De archana deorum*, 1.22.1–17).[70] These associations point to Mercury's role here as mediator, if not almost panderer, between the narrator and the goddesses.

From mythographic interpretations of the deities' iconography and their roles in the Judgment of Paris story, we learn that the goddesses represent what Fulgentius describes as the threefold life of humankind: meditative, practical, and sensual. Minerva, as the contemplative life, represents the search for knowledge and truth without greed, rage, spite, or lust. Juno, as the active life, represents the acquisition of worldly advantages, wealth, and possessions. Venus, as the life of pleasure, represents the pursuit of lust (*Mit.*, 2.1).[71] Fulgentius concludes that Paris, "quia non ut sgitta certus et iaculo bonus et uultu decorus et ingenio sagicissimus, denique brutum quiddam desipuit et ut ferarum ac pecudum mos est ad libidinem limaces uisus intorsit quam uirtutem aut diuitias inquisiuit" (because he was not straight as an arrow, true as a spear, handsome of face, nor wise of mind, in short acted foolishly like a brute and, as is the custom of wild beasts and cattle, turned his snail eyes to lust instead of seeking virtue or wealth) (*Mit.* 2.1). In this comical passage in *Reson*

---

[69] Twycross, *Medieval Anadyomene*, 17–45, explicates medieval readings of Venus' associations with the sea, particularly Bersuire's interpretation.

[70] Concerning eloquence and trading, Hugh of St. Victor states: "haec rectissime quasi quaedam sui generis rhetorica est, eo quod huic professioni eloquentia maxime sit necessaria. unde et hic qui facundiae praeesse dicitur, Mercurius, quasi mercatorum kirrius, id est, Dominum appelatur. ([commerce] is most properly a particular kind of rhetoric because eloquence is absolutely necessary to this profession. Thus the one who has facility in speech is called a Mercury, as if a *mercatorum kirrius*, that is, he is called lord [among merchants]), *Didascalicon*, 2.23.

[71] Fulgentius, *Mit.*, 2.1; SVM, ed. Kulcsár, 248–9; Bernard Silvestris, *Commentum quod dicitur*, 6.64; Boccaccio, *Teseida*, 7.50; Bersuire, *De formis*, 30, and *Metamorphosis Ovidiana* 12, fols. 80v–81v; and Walsingham, *De archana deorum*, 1.24.9–13, and 12.1. In *Mit.*, 3.7, Fulgentius also implies the three lives when delineating the parts of human anatomy that the deities possessed: Minerva had the eyes, Juno the arms, Venus the kidneys and sex organs. These attributions are appropriate for the lives the goddesses represent: eyes to contemplate the truth; arms to pursue the active life; sex organs to pursue the sensual life. Juan Rodríguez del Padrón similarly engages this three-lives tradition in his *Siervo libre de amor* (c.1440), describing Minerva as "la vida contemplativa," ed. Dolz, 19: see also Francomano, *Wisdom and Her Lovers*, 1, 3.

and Sensuallyte, the narrator repeated Paris' judgment and became like one of the beasts on Nature's mantle that "don enclyne / Her hedes to the erthe lowe" (400–1). Considering the narrator's earlier disposition towards idleness, his assent to Paris' judgment is not surprising; considering Mercury's off-hand parting comment, he is not the first to do so. We can almost hear Mercury sigh and see Minerva and Juno shrug in resignation.

Still, Minerva's iconographic details and her role in the Judgment of Paris scene demonstrate she offers another way. As a representative of the contemplative life, Minerva offers the redemptive wisdom that biblical Sapientia and the medieval sapiential tradition encompass. In Proverbs, Sapientia advises, "Accipite disciplinam meam, et non pecuniam: doctrinam magis quam aurum eligite ... In viis justitiae ambulo, in medio semitarum judicii, Ut ditem diligentes me, et thesauros eorum repleam" (Receive my teaching and not money: choose instruction rather than gold ... I walk in the way of justice, and in the middle of the paths of judgment, so that I may enrich those loving me, and fill their storehouses) (Prov. 8:10, 20–1).[72] And, in Ecclesiasticus, quoted in part by Suso's Aeterna Sapientia (419), biblical Sapientia says:

> Ego mater pulcrae dilectionis, et timoris, et agnitionis, et sanctae spei. In me gratia omnis viae et veritatis, in me omnis spes vitae et virtutis. Transite ad me, omnes qui concupiscitis me, et a generationibus meis implemini ... Qui elucidant me, vitam aeternam habebunt.
>
> (I am the mother of beautiful love, fear, knowledge, and holy hope. In me is all grace of the way and the truth, and in me is the hope of all life and virtue. Come to me, all who desire me, and be filled by my fruits ... Those who reveal me, shall have eternal life. (Ecclus. 24:24–6)

Like Sapientia, Minerva offers the narrator a path of wisdom that includes knowledge, judgment, and truth, and her reward, too, is eternal life. Though the narrator encounters Minerva after he has chosen the path of sensuality, she is an allegory of redemptive wisdom's effort to draw him back to the path of reason. Opposed to the poem's sensual Venus, she represents the rejected life of wisdom in the narrator's assent to Paris' judgment.

The Poem's Primary Concerns and Minerva's Central Role

In the prologue to *Reson and Sensuallyte*, prior to the dream vision proper, Lydgate signals his two central concerns, intelligent reading and proper judgment, by expressing his apparent anxiety over the poem's reception. After identifying his audience as those "gentil ... and amerouse" folk who love to play chess, he summarizes

---

[72] Natura, *De planctu*, 12.126–48, similarly advises Alan's narrator to avoid riches and pursue wisdom.

the literal matter of his story, how through Fortune his narrator was checkmated by a queen (1–16), and he begs his audience not to pass a quick judgment on the poem or his name (17–24).[73] Like Chaucer, Lydgate is very much aware of an active audience here[74] and imagines this audience by constructing two kinds of readers who, in a sense, occupy opposite ends of a spectrum:

> For many oon, in metre and prose,
> That nouther kan the text nor glose,
> Wil ful oft at prime face
> Some thing hindren and difface,
> Or they can any lake espye,
> Oonly of malyce and envye
> Or collateral necligence;
> But who that of good dilligence
> Lyst bysye him to don his cure
> To sen and rede thys scripture,
> And feleth fully the sentence,
> Yif hee therin kan fynde offence,
> My wille is this, that he observe
> Me to repreve, as y desserve,
> Besechinge him for to directe
> Al that ys mys, and to correcte. (25–40)

Again like Chaucer, Lydgate recognizes that readers have power to make meaning from texts, to re-write them, and he invites such an affective engagement with his poem.[75] Yet he fears some will, like the first reader inscribed in the text, "difface" the poem (i.e., "produce a meaningless re-writing") based solely on a "prime face" understanding, so he inscribes a second reader who understands both text and gloss.[76]

---

[73] In *RS* chess functions as metaphor for wooing, a detail the *Eschéz*-poet draws from *RR*, 6620–726, where Jean de Meun uses it as metaphor for politics and battle. In *BD*, 618–84, Chaucer uses chess as metaphor for life and death, where Fortune takes the Black Knight's queen and checkmates him with a pawn. Interestingly, Fairfax 16 also includes a copy of the *BD*.

[74] In the prologue to the Miller's Tale, Chaucer constructs active reader-editors when his narrator says, "[W]hoso list it nat yheere / Turne over the leef and chese another tale" (3176–7).

[75] In *TC*, Chaucer recognizes readers contribute to meaning when he invites them to displace his narration with their own. His narrator states:

> For myne wordes, here and every part,
> I speke hem alle under correccioun
> Of yow that felyng han in loves art,
> And putte it al in youre discrecioun
> T'encresse or maken dyminucioun
> Of my langage, and that I yow byseche. (3.1331–6)

See Travis' discussion of this passage in "Affective Criticism," 203–4.

[76] This notion of inscribed readers comes from Prince's narratee ("Introduction à l'étude du narrataire," 177–96), Ong's fictionalized audience ("The Writer's Audience," 9–21), and W. Gibson's mock reader ("Authors, Speakers, Readers, and Mock Readers," 265–9).

Willing to accept correction (i.e., "meaningful re-writing") only from a reader who "feleth fully the sentence," Lydgate implicitly invites his audience to occupy the role of this second reader and concludes the prologue with a promise that, if they read the matter of the poem intelligently, they will be able to judge it properly (42–6). His expressed concern for intelligent reading and proper judgment, and their subsequent development in the poem, suggest that the Judgment of Paris scene is the poem's central allegorical action and Minerva its central allegorical figure.

In the dream vision itself, Nature reiterated Lydgate's concerns first, when she commissioned the narrator to read her Book, to judge its beauty, and to glean its wisdom as an antidote for his idleness (518–24). More importantly, she clearly articulated the purpose for pursuing the reading and judgment she orders:

"To fyn, that thou maist comprehende
The mater, and thy selfe amende,
To preyse the lorde eternal,
The whiche made and caused al." (525–8)

Reading the Book of Nature to understand the "mater," or *sententia*, of God's plan is a common idea in the Middle Ages, as numerous bestiaries, lapidaries, encyclopedias, and *specula* attest, and as Suso's Aeterna Sapientia counsels. For medieval Christians, as Nature implies, reading intelligently the Book of Nature leads to self-knowledge and to understanding of one's relationship to the universe and to God: as Bernard of Clairvaux might say, such reading is an act of love directed toward the Creator.

After giving the narrator this commission, Nature instructed him in effective reading methods, bestowing tools needed to fulfill his role in the order of creation. She suggested there are two methods of reading, sensual and rational. Using the common medieval "shell and kernel" metaphor for interpreting literary art, Nature attempted to dissuade the narrator from sensual reading alone, for it seeks only the "barke," disregarding the "pithe" hidden within (733–40). She then encouraged him to read rationally, which leads humans to know divine and spiritual truths (744–6), and advised him to follow the path of reason to heavenly joy rather than the path of sensuality to false pleasure. The narrator declared allegiance to Nature and, before parting, the goddess emphasized her advice with a final command, "'Do, as reson techeth the, / And thy wittis hool enclyne / To rewle the by hir doctrine'" (870–2). The narrator, as we have seen, forgot Nature's instruction and, inclined to sensual reading, misread the goddess' Book and misjudged the value of its flora, fauna, and

---

Lydgate's "text nor glose" resonates with the *BD*, where Chaucer's narrator describes stained glass illustrations of the Trojan story and *RR* – "bothe text and glose" – in his dream chamber (321–38: 333). Simpson also examines reading but in the context of idleness, noting "Reading *of* the poem, then, turns out to be potentially different from reading *in* the poem. *Reason and Sensuality*'s representation of readerly sloth can attract unslothful readings that reflect on sloth": "Economy of Involucrum," 393–404: 402.

firmament. Subsequently, he misread the value of Minerva, Juno, and Venus, and misjudged in favor of the latter.

Following the Judgment of Paris scene, Venus remained briefly to tell the narrator how to reach the garden of her sons Deduit and Cupid. In this passage, she secured his allegiance by promising him a lover "fairer than Helen" as a reward for service and by proclaiming her alliance with Nature, after he objected he cannot serve two goddesses (2257–97). Venus indicates throughout her discourse, however, that she serves a Nature quite different from the one the narrator encountered earlier. When describing Deduit's garden where he will find his promised lover, she advised him that the best way to gain entrance is to acquaint himself with Idleness, who is "the chefe porteresse, / Of the entre lady and maistresse" (2615–16). Though Venus undercut her claim "to serve" the Nature of this poem (2265), the narrator misread her discourse, taking her words "at prime face." Venus then pointed the way to Deduit's garden, saying with a touch of dramatic irony courtesy of the poet, "'Thow art wel onwarde on thy way'" (2648), and declared "'The wey[e] also brood and large'" (2652) that he should not miss it.[77]

Armed now with Venus' instruction, the narrator merrily commenced his journey to the garden and soon passed through a forest where he encountered the goddess Diana. By the time he met Diana, however, he had become a thoroughly sensual reader. When he first spied her, for instance, he was so taken by her physical beauty that he declared, "I dar afferme with-out[e] fage: / Of body, shappe, and of visage, / ... Ther was no fairer borne a-lyve" (2801–5), a judgment he had implicitly made about Venus earlier. Considering his total allegiance to Venus, his initial attraction to the goddess of chastity is outright funny, but more so it illustrates his inability to read intelligently. It is only later, when he realized her beauty was chaste and she attempted to dissuade him from the path of sensuality, that the narrator rejects Diana.

Like the descriptions of the other goddesses and Mercury, the narrator's iconographic description of Diana accentuates her moral significance in the poem. One detail in particular is important: her bow and arrows. Lydgate interjects a significant explanation of these when his narrator states that Diana's chief delight was to chase Idleness out of her forest by shooting arrows at her (2859–68). Because he ostensibly recognized her reason for carrying a bow and arrows before he even spoke to her, the narrator's abashed response to Diana's initial rebuke after he tried to make a pass at her (2879–936) is particularly ironic. Though the narrator fails to understand the implications of what he says, Lydgate's amplification of his source indicates Diana's true nature to the reader who "feleth fully the sentence," for Diana's frequent confrontations with Idleness link her with Nature and Minerva in their opposition here to Venus. Her discourse, which ultimately turned the narrator against her, substantiates this close relationship.

Diana raised the last voice in the dream on behalf of proper judgment. For example, when she admonished the narrator for confirming the Judgment of

---

[77] This latter line echoes the "broad" way "that leads to destruction" of Matthew 7:13–4 and of Sir John Clanvowe's *The Two Ways*.

Paris "'To hastely'" (3276–305) and he, again hastily, reconfirmed Paris' choice and seconded his own as reasonable (3307–14), Diana encouraged him to reconsider, declaring that quick judgments often lead to wrong decisions (3315–24). Diana's concern for careful judgment in moral decisions underscores Lydgate's own concern for careful judgment of his poem. Though the narrator fails to catch her message, Lydgate intends his inscribed audience to understand it, especially those who "haueth ... insight" (3321) to grasp his "sentence."

Diana also raised the last voice in the poem on behalf of intelligent reading when she indirectly warned the narrator of the garden's perils through a series of *exempla*. Like Genius in John Gower's *Confessio Amantis*, she recounted numerous tales, but perhaps the most important ones are those of love gone awry, including the adultery of Venus and Mars, the death of Narcissus, and the death of Pyramus and Thisbe. Then, like Raison in *Roman de la Rose*, she advised him to seek a "mean" in all activity (4193–4) and illustrated her point with tales of Icarus and Phaeton. She concluded her stories with an argument for their ethical value, saying that a wise man learns from others' mistakes (4244–51). The narrator, though, in defending Deduit's garden and Venus' love, critiqued her stories, arguing:

"But I me cast[e] nat to fle
With y-charus ouer the se,
Nor with Pheton al my lyve
The chere of Phebus for to dryve." (4603–8)

Following his sensual inclination, the narrator misread and misjudged Diana's tales, taking only the "barke" and leaving the "pithe" behind. As with Diana's argument for proper judgment, he again misunderstood her point regarding intelligent reading.

The narrator's comical inability to understand Diana's meaning, however, is not unexpected. A few lines before his literal reading of Diana's tales, he blatantly misinterpreted Nature's command when explaining his desire to see Deduit's garden. He emphatically declared: "'[Nature] bad me, as I kan report: / "Go se the world" and me disport, / And theryn oonly me delyte'" (4511–15). Diana challenged this misreading of Nature and refuted his claim that Nature ordered him to experience a place "'Wher ydelnesse bereth the key'" (4708). Realizing how the narrator is so completely of Venus' company that he even twists Nature's commission to justify his own desires, Diana left him with a final warning on free will (4768–72). The narrator, of course, followed his own discretion, but his choices, nevertheless, served his sensual appetite rather than wisdom, as Diana suggested.

Upon arrival at Deduit's garden, the narrator misread the garden and its inhabitants and sealed his moral downfall at the well of Narcissus. A carved message on the side of the well explained its danger, but the narrator, at possibly the only moment in the poem in which he should have read literally, ignored the message and, ravished by its outward beauty, sensually read the well itself, failing to understand it signified morally destructive self-love (5707–16). As an allegorical image of his moral state, the well defines the nature of Venus' love in this poem. More importantly, the well clarifies the nature of his desire for, like Amant in *Roman de la Rose*, he first saw Venus' promised lady reflected in its crystal bottom. Consequently, the lady represents more an object of the narcissistic narrator's self-centered desire than an actual or even imagined woman.

Reson and Sensuallyte ends with the narrator forever trapped in his own sensuality.[78] However, it offers a different end for Lydgate's inscribed audience. Diana's advice on rational reading – "'Prudently to taken hede / Of another mannys dede'" (4248–9) – resonates throughout the poem. For Lydgate's readers, the narrator's story, like Diana's many tales, serves as an *exemplum* of foolish love. His moral comedy stands in sharp relief against the poem's ethical message of the need for intelligent reading and proper judgment. Indeed, unlike many medieval writers who invite the audience to occupy affectively the "ego," or subject, position of the text, Lydgate here distances readers from his narrator by encouraging affective engagement with his poem through identification with the inscribed ideal reader rather than through the "ego" of the first-person narrative.[79]

Though the narrator seals his downfall at Narcissus' well, the position of the Judgment of Paris in the narrative, between Nature's and Diana's discourses on reading, emphasizes its significance as the poem's central allegorical scene. Moreover, Minerva's role in the scene suggests she is the poem's principal allegorical figure. Nature's attempt to prepare the narrator for the Judgment scene and Diana's attempt to persuade him to reconsider his choice serve as metaphorical bookends to the Judgment and Minerva herself. In a poem that draws on a rich intertextual tradition for its narrative and meaning, the Judgment of Paris story is the principal text within the poem. It demands intelligent reading and proper judgment. While the narrator misread the moral significance of the three goddesses, the poem's readers who diligently "rede thys scripture / And feleth fully the sentence" should not. Of the three goddesses, Minerva is to be preferred, as Lydgate indicates in the choices made when "illuminating" the scene through rhetorical *inventio*. Nature's and Diana's positive alliances with Minerva further underscore Lydgate's intent. Though verbally silent, Minerva speaks clearly through her iconography and role in the Judgment story. Her wisdom offers potential redemption to readers who, unlike the narrator, read the Judgment scene rationally and choose her life of wisdom: a life which seeks to know and love God; and the self, neighbors, and universe for His sake. Without a clear understanding of Minerva and her role in the poem, however, readers can misread *Reson and Sensuallyte* as Lydgate fears in his prologue and, like the narrator, mistake its "barke" for the "pithe" hidden within.

---

[78] The poem breaks off after the narrator began to prepare for a chess match with his promised heart's desire. In *Les Eschéz*, the narrator lost the match, Deduit counseled submission and Amor accepted him, and he prepared for a second match. At this point, Pallas appeared and, like Raison in *RR*, attempted to dissuade the narrator again from his pursuit. What follows is an extended encyclopedic discussion of proper education for the contemplative and the active lives (*RS* 2: 59–76; cf. Galpin, "*Les Echex Amoureux*," 288–307; Ehrhart, *Judgement of the Trojan Prince Paris*, 151–3). Based on *Les Eschéz*, we could reconstruct how Lydgate might have ended the poem, but he left *RS* unfinished, and readers, like the narrator, remain poised for the opening move of a chess match.

[79] For a discussion of how readers displace the particular self with the "ego" of lyric, see J.B. Allen, "Grammar, Poetic Form, and the Lyric Ego," 208.

Gavin Douglas and Wisdom's Path to Honor

Moving to Gavin Douglas' *Palice of Honoure* we shift from early fifteenth-century England to early sixteenth-century Scotland: some three or four generations, one country, and a linguistic skip north.[80] Douglas (c.1475–1522), a poet, priest, and younger contemporary of William Dunbar in Scotland and of Stephen Hawes and John Skelton in England, addresses in this poem the question, as C.S. Lewis succinctly put it, "'Where does true Honour lie?'"[81] Equally important, however, he also addresses the means and ends of poetic composition. Like Dunbar, Douglas – a younger son of Archibald "Bell-the-Cat," Fifth Earl of Douglas – was associated with the court of James IV of Scotland.[82] He wrote *The Palice of Honoure*, a tripartite dream vision with prologue and epilogue, dedicated it to James IV, and presumably first published it in manuscript at the court in about 1501.[83] Though no manuscript copies survive, three sixteenth-century printed editions, all published posthumously, give evidence of readership beyond the Scottish court.[84] In *The Palice*, Douglas draws on the tradition of Minerva as redemptress: a representative of contemplative wisdom. Though she does not appear in the fable of the Judgment of Paris, Minerva represents here, in conjunction with Diana, Venus, and Calliope, a potential path to a life of honor, which in Douglas' scheme has both mundane and eschatological purposes, as part three indicates.

The Palice opens with a prologue setting the frame for a dream vision in which the narrator encountered Minerva, Diana, Venus, Calliope, and their respective entourages. While wandering in a traditional May garden setting, noting the beauties of Flora's ornaments and Nature's tapestries, the narrator heard a locution in praise of the month and spring-time love. Frightened, he prayed to Nature and to May, seeking comfort. Unlike Lydgate's narrator, whose visit from Nature woke him

---

[80] J. Smith, *Older Scots*, 170–2.
[81] Lewis, *English Literature in the Sixteenth Century*, 77.
[82] Little is known about Douglas: he took a B.A. (1492) and M.A. at St. Andrew's University; he was a priest, holding various ecclesiastical posts including dean of Dunkeld (c.1497), provost of St. Giles in Edinburgh (c.1503), and bishop of Dunkeld (1515); following James IV's death at Flodden Field in 1513, he helped arrange Queen Margaret's re-marriage to his nephew in 1514 and seemed to be serving as Chancellor by November of that year; he was tried for treason and imprisoned in July 1515; released one year later, he regained his bishopric only to lose it again; he died in 1522 while in London working to restore his family's position in Scotland. See Bawcutt, *Gavin Douglas*, 1–22.
[83] Scholars date *The Palice* to about 1501, based on a note stating he finished the *Eneados* in July 1513, thereby fulfilling a promise to Venus (in *The Palice*) made twelve years before: see Spearing, *Medieval Poet as Voyeur*, 231, 300 n.1.
[84] Thomas Davidson published in Edinburgh the earliest surviving edition in about 1535. William Copland published it in London in 1553 with printed marginalia recording Scottish readership (nine copies survive). John Ros, working for Henry Charteris, printed the third – a version meant to correct earlier editions and revise the text for current Scots readership (see "To the Reidar") – in Edinburgh in 1579 (two copies survive). Both Copland and Charteris retain its dedication to James IV, suggesting perhaps they had manuscripts on hand as well as earlier printed editions. See Parkinson, introduction to *The Palice*, 2–4; and Ridley, "Middle Scots Writers," 1193.

76   THE FIGURE OF MINERVA IN MEDIEVAL LITERATURE

up into a dreamscape of beauty, or even Allan of Lille's narrator, whose visit from Natura turned into a tutorial of sorts, Douglas' narrator received "an impressioun" like an electromagnetic pulse: a flash that knocked him down and into a dazed ecstasy similar to Paul on the road to Damascus (Acts 9:3–9).[85] Amazed and nearly lifeless, he had a dream in which he found himself in a "desert place, / Amyd a forest by a hyddeous flude / With grysly fische" (122–4). Upon "waking" into this foul dreamscape, the narrator lamented against cruel Fortune and the inconstancy of the world, suggesting that the wasteland was also emblematic of his mental or moral condition as well as of the world itself. This wasteland is a place, as Antony Hasler notes, "where to be present at all is to be out of place": a displacement, I think, that echoes Augustine's observation about the human condition that "inquietum est cor nostrum donec requiescat in te" (our heart is restless until it rests in you [i.e., God]) (*Confessions* 1.1).[86] A noise soon interrupted the narrator's lament and, hiding himself in a hollow tree, he observed the approach of a group of "bestis rationall" (201) and read them as follows:

> Of ladyis fair and gudlie men arrayit
> In constant weid, that weil my spretis payit,
> With degest mind, quhairin all wyt aboundyt.
> Full soberlie thair haknais thay assayit
> Eftyr the feitis auld, and not forvayt.
> Thair hie prudence schew furth and nohyng roundit
> With gude effere quhare the wod resoundyt
> In stedfast ordour, to vysy onaffrayit
> Thay rydyng furth with stabylnes ygroundyt. (202–10)

A golden-haired, purple-robed queen rode in a chariot followed closely by twelve damsels amid a company "borne of hie estate and law degree" (225) that passed by his hiding place in an orderly fashion. Suddenly, out of the forest two wretches hurriedly passed by as well, one riding an ass, the other a nag. When the narrator accosted them, they stopped, identified themselves as Achitophel and Sinon and, as he requested, Sinon glossed the company. "'Yone is the Quene of Sapience,'" he shouted, the "'Lady Minerve'" (241–2) surrounded by the twelve "prudent

---

[85] Douglas, *Palice of Honoure*, ed. Bawcutt, 105. The language here recalls the narrator's response to being snatched by the eagle in *HF*, 2.549–53, and even more so Cresseid's collapse in *Testament of Cresseid*, 141–2, 538–9, when the *Palice*-narrator describes his own response, "As feminine so feebly fell I doun" (108). Note too Douglas' nod to Henryson's "hamelie language and ... termes rude" of the Fables, 36, in the narrator's promise "I shall descryve (as God wil geve me grace) / Myn avision in rurell termes rude" (125–6).

[86] Hasler, *Court Poetry*, 101. This restless condition finds further expression in Augustine's phrase "regio dissimilitudinis" (region of unlikeness) in *Confessions*, 7.10, which he adapts from Plato to describe humankind's spiritual state of alienation from God in this life. See Gilson, "*Regio Dissimilitudes* de Platon," 108. The listlessness we find Chaucer's narrator articulate in the opening of *BD*, 1–29, offers a poetic instance of a melancholic, depressive pose. In *The Palice*, 127–35, this pose reaches near self-flagellation in the narrator's opening stanza of part one, which sets up the poem's early nightmarish dreamscape.

Sibillais'" (243), Cassandra and Judith, and numerous "'Clerkis diuine'" (249), including Solomon, Aristotle, and Socrates: all going to the "Palice of Honour" (264). When pressed further, Achitophel accounted for their own exclusion from the group: "Richt sa we bene in tyll this company / Our wyt aboundit and vsyt was lewdy, / My wisdome ay fulfillit my desire" (274–6). He continued: while out of spite he had abused his wisdom by advising Jonathon to rebel against his father King David, leading to the son's death and his own suicide, Sinon had used his wisdom to persuade the Trojans to bring in the wooden horse, which led to Troy's fall. These political figures who abused their gifts of wisdom for personal gain suggest the kind of practical wisdom that concerns the narrator most: political counsel – a warning perhaps for Douglas' primary audience.[87] Before hastily parting, they informed the narrator that the courts of Diana and Venus would soon follow.

From the company's appearance, it becomes clear that Minerva here – though silent as in *Reson and Sensuallyte* – embodies the virtuous wisdom inherent in orderly, rational behavior: a path of wisdom out of the nightmare of worldly misfortune to the palace of honor should he decide to follow. Similarly, Diana who next appeared in company with a smaller group of virgin "fostaressys" (329) represented a path of "chastite" (331). Having just witnessed a re-enactment of Actaeon's death prior to the court's arrival (316–18), however, the narrator perhaps wisely remained silent and hidden in his hollow tree as they passed by. Shortly after Diana passed, Venus appeared in full-iconographic undress, attended by Mars, Cupid, and company, and the narrator experienced his first direct engagement in the dream with a deity. After reading the court as it passed by, listing a catalogue of lovers – some happy, some sad – the narrator responded perhaps unwisely to what he saw by singing a three-stanza love-complaint, ending: "'Wo worth Cupid and wo worth fals Venus, / Wo worth thaym bayth, ay waryit mot thay be! / Wo worth thair court, and cursit destane!'" (634–5).[88] Venus immediately called a halt and ordered a search, declaring "Quhare is yone poid that plenyeit" (641). Quickly discovered by the company, beaten by guards, and charged by Varius, the narrator in a Henryson-like moment was placed in the dock before Venus, Cupid, and Mars where he declared clerical exemption from Venus' secular court just as part one ends.[89] Part two opens with the

---

[87] Though he does not address Scotland directly, Strohm's assessment in *Politique* of language, political arts, and fortune in England is instructive for understanding how poetry reflects political concerns in the fifteenth and sixteenth centuries. Hasler, *Court Poetry*, takes a related approach to examine poetic identity tied to sources of authority within the context of fifteenth- and sixteenth-century English and Scottish courts.

[88] This extended "Wo worth" anaphora is a distinct Chaucerian echo (*TC* 2.244–7) though by this time it has become commonplace in love complaint. Chaucer uses anaphora elsewhere (e.g., "Swich fyn," *TC* 5.828–32, and "Lo here," *TC* 5.1849–54) to signal a heightened emotional response to a situation.

[89] In Henryson's *Testament of Cresseid*, 141–343, Cupid and the planetary deities convict Cresseid in a dream for her complaint against Venus and Cupid. She awakes from the nightmare trial a leper, condemned to live in the fatal disease's anonymous marginalization, her transformation so complete that neither Troilus nor she recognize the other later in the poem (484–539).

narrator's prayer for divine intervention and, as the narrative commences, a court of poets appeared led by the Muses. Calliope, the muse of epic poetry, intervened on the narrator's behalf and, after he composed a second song in praise of Venus and promised to do her bidding the next time she asked, he was freed, and Venus and court immediately departed. The narrator, led by a figure he calls "My Nymphe" (1078) – who thenceforth became his dream-guide – left the wasteland with Calliope and company and, for the remainder of part two, journeyed to the palace of honor, pausing briefly at Helicon on the way.

After opening part three by invoking the Muses for the gifts of eloquence and memory, the narrator describes his experience at the palace, which functions as an emblem of an afterlife of honor. The Nymphe first led the narrator up a mountain, from which he spied the world's vicissitudes, and then onto a broad "plane of peirles pulchritude" (1414), a paradisal setting in the midst of which stood the palace of honor: a shining gothic structure of walls, towers, gates, and halls. Upon entering the outer ward, the narrator encountered Venus again, holding court while many knights were tourneying in the goddess' service. Approaching Venus, the narrator gazed into her mirror and saw reflected the realm of the Muses: "The dedes and fetes of every erdly wight, / All thinges gone lyk as they wer present" (1496–7). He then narrates a catalogue of biblical, Greco-Roman, and English-Irish-Scottish figures and tales. Once finished gazing in the mirror, the narrator noticed Venus gazing at him. Recognizing him, Venus welcomed the narrator, handed him a book, recalled his promise to do her behest, and commissioned a translation of the book into "ryme" (1752): Douglas' translation of the *Aeneid* later published in 1513. The Nymphe then glossed the mirror as reflecting to beholders "the gret bewty of thir ladyis facis / Quaharin lovers thinkis thay behald all gracis" (1763–4).[90] Unlike Amant in *Roman de la Rose* or the narrator in *Reson and Sensuallytte*, who see their beloved reflected in the crystal bottom of a well, the narrator's beloved is comically all of biblical, classical, and British story – an encyclopedic synopsis of his engagement with texts. Douglas, here, comically twists the Ovidian expectation: instead of a Corinna or Laura inspiring the poet's verse, others' books and stories do. Moving then into the "cristall palyce" (1829) itself, the narrator lost himself for a time reading images of the universe – a bow to Minerva's contemplative wisdom – before approaching the closed door of the inner hall. At the Nymphe's prompting, he peered through a keyhole into the hall to see Honour himself, "a god armypotent" (1921). In this comical Dantean beatific vision, Honour's overwhelmingly bright gaze knocked him into a second swoon: a swoon within a swoon. Helping him recover, the Nymphe then glossed the palace, declaring emphatically that, compared to Honour's heavenly realm, "'Prosperite in erd is bot a dreme'" (1983): "Vertu," she continued further on, "is eik the perfyte sikkyr way, / And not ellis, til honour lestand ay'" (2008–9).

---

[90] On the twofold function of mirror imagery in medieval literature "to show us what we are and what we ought to be," see Bradley, "Backgrounds of the Title *Speculum*," 100–15: 111. The *speculum* image as metaphor or title for a text and its educative intent is evident in Vincent of Beauvais' encyclopedia *Speculum Maius* and in the popular *speculum principis* genre. See Bratu, "Mirrors for Princes," 1921–49.

Shortly after her discourse on true virtue, while crossing a tree-trunk bridge on the way to the court of rhetoric, the narrator slipped and fell into a moat, the shock of which caused him to wake in the garden of the poem's prologue: a now charmless arbor compared to Honour's paradise.

While Minerva, Diana, and Venus offer paths to the palace of honor through wisdom, chastity, and desire, Calliope and the "court rethoricall" (835) offer a path through poetic composition. As a poet, a singer of songs, the narrator – rescued from the power of an angry goddess by the court of poets – understandably chose to follow the Muses rather than wisdom or chastity or even desire alone: a choice that resonates with his experiences at the palace once he arrived and connects him through Fulgentius to the medieval Virgilian tradition.[91] Using Calliope and the Muses to represent the path his narrator follows, Douglas examines both the fundamentally human dilemma of choosing a way of life and the more specific issue of the means and ends of poetic composition. In its encyclopedic content reflected in Venus' mirror – perhaps an allusion to Vincent of Beauvais' *Speculum historiale* – and its intertextual engagement with courtly dream poetry, especially Chaucer's *House of Fame*, *The Palice of Honoure* as poem is a direct result of Douglas' reading, which serves in part as the means of poetic composition. Within the fictional world of the poem, the narrator not only read the courts as they passed by, and the catalogue of stories and figures in Venus' mirror, but also responded, producing the narrative itself as well as songs within the narrative, thereby offering poetic readings of what he experienced. And, after waking from the dream, he punctuated the whole narrative with a three-stanza song praising Honour, an encomium suggesting the ends of this poetic composition even as this poem sets up the poet's next one – the *Eneados*. Douglas develops his engagement with poetry, as Haydock delineates, within a Virgilian *cursus* culminating in his poetic translation of Virgil's epic mediated by Calliope and the Muses as guided by the Nymphe, commissioned by Venus, and executed by means of the *Palice* itself.[92]

Like Lydgate in *Reson and Sensuallyte*, Douglas explores the choice between ways

---

[91] In Fulgentius' *Mit.*, Calliope *magistra* recounted to her narrator-pupil the twenty-two fables making up book one. Though Calliope disappeared in books two and three, her role in book one establishes her as a keeper of myth and spinner of tales: recounting tales of the gods, the macrocosm, she set up the tales of the microcosm that appear in books two and three. In the context of Fulgentius' *oeuvres*, Calliope functions on the same diegetic level as Virgil, who explicated his *Aeneid* to the narrator in *Expositio Virgilianae*. See Chance, *Medieval Mythography*, 1:95–128; and *The Virgilian Tradition*, eds. Ziolkowski and Putnam, 660–72.

[92] Haydock, *Situational Poetics*, 66–8. As Haydock points out, "the verses at the end of Douglas's *Eneados* have a finality about them that suggests the summation of a life's work. Douglas claims that he has completed the Virgilian course of the poet's life, even though at this time he was still a relatively young man" (67). Hasler, *Court Poetry*, 99, on the other hand, sees *Palice* illustrating Douglas' move from allegorical Ovidian love poet – embedded in the text's themes, descriptions, and songs – to the promise of Virgilian epic poet. The Virgilian *cursus* Douglas appropriates for himself, however – a poetic path paralleling *Bucolics*, *Georgics*, and *Aeneid* – seems a clearer trajectory than an Ovidian-to-Virgilian *cursus*, even if he primarily articulated it at the end of his poetic career.

of life so strongly associated with the Judgment of Paris story. As with the Judgment story, he represents each way of life with a goddess: Minerva and the way of wisdom; Diana and chastity; Venus and desire. To these he adds a fourth: Calliope and the way of poetry. In this re-writing of the Judgment of Paris story, Douglas doubtless intends for his audience to enjoy with him the humor of introducing a fourth path, as well as substituting Diana for Juno. Advancing this fourth path over wisdom, chastity, or the earthly or heavenly Venus, Douglas knows the expected choice probably ought to be either wisdom or the more austere chastity: that the narrator chooses poetry instead is funny, even self-effacing for the poet. Although the narrator opts for Calliope, he does not reject Minerva, Diana, or even Venus in the end, and he encountered each again at the palace: Venus directly in the outer ward, where he discovers the object of his desire and the means to pursue it via the commission; Minerva indirectly in the crystal palace itself, as signified by images of the universe; Diana, I suggest, in the inner hall, where Honour's brightness shines throughout and overwhelms the narrator much as he fears gazing on Diana might do earlier in the dream; and Calliope in the sought-for court of rhetoric and in the text itself as he invokes her for eloquence and memory to compose this poem and look to the next. To the degree to which they lead people to Honour's palace, all these paths share virtue in common as a true way to honor.

Writing in the medieval sapiential tradition, Douglas uses Minerva to represent virtuous wisdom as he explores multiple paths to a life and afterlife of honor. A potential redemptress in the vein of Lydgate's Minerva in *Reson and Sensuallyte*, Minerva in the *Palice* offers the path of wisdom followed by such figures as Socrates, Cassandra, Judith, and Solomon and, by extension, any seeking to join such a court on the way to honor. Like Sapientia in the "O Sapientia" advent antiphon, and Amor in Boethius' metrum 8, Minerva offers here a "via prudentiae," a life lived with Love ruling the heart, that can lead to salvation should one choose it.

3

The Martianus Tradition: Minerva as Mistress of the Liberal Arts

Closely allied with Minerva-Sapientia, *creatrix* and redemptress offering a contemplative way to divine wisdom through love, Minerva the educator – *magistra artium*, the mistress of learning and skill – plays a central role in the liberal arts tradition of the Middle Ages. Medieval scholars and poets, largely through the influence of Martianus Capella, expand Minerva's ancient association with intelligence (*metis*) and the practical arts by giving her the role of mistress of the liberal arts as well.[1] While Minerva's relationship with the liberal arts comes to fruition in late antiquity and the Middle Ages, early hints of this relationship are evident in ancient and classical poetry. In Homer's *Odyssey* she is both weaver and wily wordsmith – a riddler or logician, even.[2] In the *Fasti*, 3.5–6, Ovid associates her with the arts as a civilizing force when he encourages Mars to rest from battle, saying "Ipse vides manibus peragi fera bella Minervae: / num minus ingenuis artibus illa vacat?" (You see that cruel wars are completed by Minerva's hands: is she now for those wars less free with the arts?). And later in *Fasti* 3.829–30, he implies her relationship with the liberal arts when, addressing her role in education, he states: "nec vos, turba fere censu fraudata, magistri, / spernite; discipulos attrahit illa novos" (do not reject [Minerva] you teachers, having been cheated as usual from pay by the crowd; she attracts new students). These examples suggest an early connection between Minerva and the *artes liberales*; however, writers most fully develop her direct association with them in the Middle Ages. As with the medieval sapiential tradition, the tradition linking Minerva and the seven liberal arts – what I call the Martianus tradition – proved productive for writers seeking to explore the relationship between wisdom

---

[1] In Greek literature, Pallas Athena (Minerva) as a goddess of technology oversees shipwrights (*Iliad* 5.61, 15.412), metalworkers (*Odyssey* 6.233), potters (*Homeric Epigram* 14.2), and joiners (*Homeric Hymn* 5.12–3), as well as weavers, and represents the skill or intelligence necessary for practicing these arts. Otto, *Homeric Gods*, 43–60; Seltman, *Twelve Olympians*, 54–63; Eliade, *History of Religious Ideas*, 1:280–2; Deacy, *Athena*, 50–4; and essays in Deacy and Villing, eds., *Athena in the Classical World*.

[2] On Ithaka, Athena remonstrates and praises Odysseus for his deceptive story-telling, declaring "let us no longer talk of this, being both well versed in craft, since you are far the best of all men in counsel and in speech, and I among all the gods am famed for wisdom and craft." *Odyssey*, 13.296–9.

and schooling, that is, formal education leading to literacy, intellectual development, and scientific knowledge. In this chapter, I explore Minerva *magistra artium liberalium* by first offering an overview of the arts in late antique and medieval education, with a particular focus on Martianus Capella (fl. 400). His fifth-century book *De nuptiis Philologiae et Mercurii* inspired commentary and poetic response in a range of texts, especially beginning in the ninth century. I then turn to her appearance in two English poems: the anonymous fifteenth-century *Court of Sapience* and John Skelton's 1523 *Garland of Laurel*. As mistress of the liberal arts, Minerva represents the wisdom one gains through study and intellectual development, fostering knowledge acquisition and critical thinking.

The Liberal Arts and the Martianus Tradition

In the mid-fifteenth century, the French Franciscan Nicolas de Orbellis penned this brief couplet:

> *Gram* loquitur, *Dia* vera docet, *Rhet* verba colorat,
> *Mus* canit, *Ar* numerat, *Ge* ponderat, *Ast* colit astra
>
> (*Grammatica* speaks, *Dialectica* teaches truths, *Rhetorica* colors words, *Musica* sings, *Arithmetica* enumerates, *Geometria* considers, *Astronomia* contemplates the stars)[3]

Likely intended as a mnemonic to help young scholars remember what they were studying, this poem sums up the medieval liberal arts curriculum fairly accurately. As the core of medieval education, these seven arts were part Greco-Roman inheritance and part means for translating that inheritance to and through the Middle Ages. The history of liberal learning in the West from Ancient Greece through the European Renaissance is a story of creative development, reception, and transformation. Adapted, adjusted, expanded, contracted, liberal arts education more than just survived from its early manifestations in Greek *paideia*; it thrived under multiple guises, in various places, at different times.[4] For our purposes, though, I begin with Cicero because medieval European thinkers accessed much of what they understood about Greco-Roman education through his works.

Liberal Arts in Classical and Medieval Cultures: A Brief Survey

Cicero considered education a means for preparing to be a member of society: to contribute to the common good by supporting oneself and one's dependents and by participating in public life. Not surprisingly, he had clear ideas about the kind of

---

[3] Rand, *Founders of the Middle Ages*, 223; Hicks, "Maritianus Capella," 307.
[4] See W. Jaeger, *Paideia*; Marrou, *History of Education in Antiquity*; and the essays in Too, ed., *Education in Greek and Roman Antiquity*.

preparation one could pursue for such work: *artes liberales*, those skills and knowledge, organized in particular ways (arts) suitable to a free person (liberal). In *De oratore*, published in 55 BCE, he argues that the *artes liberales* are foundational and identifies them as grammar, rhetoric, arithmetic, geometry, astronomy, and music, to which he later adds poetics, natural science, ethics, and politics.[5] And the sum of these arts, as he notes in *Tusculanae disputationes*, composed some ten years after *De oratore*, is philosophy, "ratio et disciplina studio sapientiae" (the order and eager knowledge of wisdom).[6] Following an educational program first taking shape in Greece four or five hundred years previously and developed extensively in Hellenistic culture, Cicero sought to integrate his own experiences with the knowledge and skill expressed in these arts in order to be an effective lawyer, senator, and public servant. Though difficult to be sure, it seems he considered such an education both suitable for all free persons and a means for helping a person become intellectually free, less bound by bias and ignorance. Summing up his thinking on education in *De officiis*, his epistolary treatise composed a year before his death and addressed to his son Marcus then studying in Athens, Cicero explores the themes of duties and ethics based in four key virtues: *cognitio* (thinking), *communitas* (community), *magnanimitas* (courage), and *moderatio* (moderation).[7] Offering advice from a father concerned over his son's future, he implicitly encourages Marcus to cultivate these virtues by applying his liberal arts learning, noting professions that free persons pursue "ut medicina, ut architectura, ut doctrina" (such as medicine, architecture, or teaching) benefit society or require intelligence more than labor or physical skill (1.42).

The program Cicero advocates in *De oratore* and elsewhere continued to take shape in the centuries of the Roman Empire. Writing a generation later, the architectural theorist Vitruvius argues liberal arts education forms the basis of training for an architect who simply cannot succeed without grounding in verbal and mathematical disciplines (*On Architecture*, 1.1). In *Institutio oratoria*, published some one hundred years after Vitruvius' *De architectura*, the Hispano-Roman professor of rhetoric Quintilian (c.35–100 CE) notes the education of an orator entails not only rhetorical art but also synthesis of grammar, interpretation, history, music, geometry, and astronomy.[8] And Galen (129–c.200 CE), fountainhead of medieval and early modern medical theory and practice, argues that study of the arts leads to full human development and a flourishing professional life.[9] As they lay out their advanced curricula for architects, rhetoricians, and physicians, these writers assume a system of primary and secondary education already at work in society: an education offered to all free persons, male and female, in the imperial schools.[10] By the

---

[5] Cicero, *De oratore*, eds. Sutton and Rackham, 1.16.72–3, 1.42.187, and 3.32.127 respectively.
[6] Cicero, *Tusculan Disputations*, ed. King, 1.1.1.
[7] Cicero, *De officiis*, ed. Miller, 1.43.152–3.
[8] Quintilian, *Institutio Oratoria*, ed. Butler, 1.4.
[9] Galen, "Exhortation to Study the Arts," trans. Walsh, 507–29.
[10] Marrou, *History of Education*, 358–80, 391–418. The Temple of Minerva complex in Assisium, for instance, included a *schola* as part of the larger civic project.

time the Empire reached its zenith in the fourth and fifth centuries CE, educators had sorted liberal learning into the seven arts of Nicolas de Orbellis' couplet: the *trivium*, or "three roads," consisting of grammar, logic/dialectic, and rhetoric; and the *quadrivium*, or "four roads," consisting of music, arithmetic, geometry, and astronomy. When the Empire in the West began to fragment in the fifth century, its physical and social infrastructure also began to deteriorate, creating a power vacuum filled by local Germanic war-leaders. Without support, the imperial schools, along with other social and administrative structures, began to shut down as well, creating an educational vacuum: a vacuum filled by local leaders of another kind.

In the fifth, sixth, and seventh centuries, monastic, presbyterial, and episcopal schools began to replace Imperial schools as centers of learning in those areas once part of the western Roman Empire.[11] Although general study of the liberal arts declined considerably during this time, teachers continued to use the arts as the basis for educational programs: two instances will suffice to illustrate, Augustine and Cassiodorus. Shortly after his conversion in August 386 and resignation from the professorship of rhetoric he held in Milan, Augustine entered a period of *otium liberale* (cultured retreat) at Cassiciacum near Milan.[12] While there, he composed a treatise entitled *De ordine*, a dialogue in which he explores Divine Providence's nature. In book two, Augustine traces human reason's development of the liberal arts as a progression from the arts of discourse to those of delight, from action to contemplation, and then discusses their place within an ordered, reasonable (*rationabile*) universe.[13] The arts underpin the educational program he later developed for his monastic-episcopal community and outlined in his most influential educational treatise *De doctrina Christiana*, completed near the end of his career in 427. Later, in the middle of the sixth century, Cassiodorus – a then retired Roman administrator also pursuing *otium liberale* – composed *Institutiones divinarum et humanarum lectionum* for the monks of Vivarium, the monastery he founded near Scyllacium in southern Italy.[14] In this treatise, Cassiodorus outlines an educational plan synthesizing Christian reading (the *divina* of the title) with liberal learning (the *humana*). While divine reading – theology, the Bible, church history – is most important for monastic education, Cassiodorus argues that training in the liberal arts – the *trivium* and the *quadrivium* – must precede divine reading if monks are to understand it. Book two, his summative treatment of the arts, disseminated widely and became an important schoolbook in medieval culture.[15]

Cassiodorus and Augustine, adapting liberal learning to Christianity, helped pass on the liberal arts in the west. Drawing on Cassiodorus in particular, Isidore of

---

[11] Marrou, *History of Education*, 443–63.
[12] Augustine, *Confessions*, 9.2–5; P. Brown, *Augustine of Hippo*, 108–20; Copleston, *Philosophy: Volume II*, 1:59.
[13] Augustine, *De ordine*, ed. Migne, 2.11–15.
[14] Duckett, *Gateway to the Middle Ages*, 17–33; O'Donnell, *Cassiodorus*, ch. 6; Rand, *Founders of the Middle Ages*, 240–8.
[15] Cassiodorus, *Institutiones divinarum et humanarum*, ed. Migne. See also L. Jones, introduction to *An Introduction*, 47–58.

Seville opened his seventh-century encyclopedia, *Etymologiae*, with three books on the arts that, in turn, proved highly influential throughout the medieval and early modern periods. Working in the northwest of Europe during the same centuries as Augustine, Cassiodorus, and Isidore, Irish monks similarly engaged liberal learning but in a wholly different context. Having never been conquered by Rome, Ireland also did not have Imperial schools.[16] Rather, Christianity itself was the source of Greco-Roman learning for the Irish: as it brought the culture of the book to Ireland, Christianity also brought books and the technology and skills for making them. At its height, Irish monasticism had schools at Aranmor, Clonard, Clonfert, Clonmacnoise, Glendalough, and elsewhere.[17] Columkille (521–97) epitomizes this drive for liberal learning integrated with Christian practice. Fired with missionary zeal, and exiled from Ireland for causing the Battle of Cúl Dreimhne in 561 over a copy of Finnian's psalter, Columkille settled in 563 on Iona just off the coast of Scotland, thereby inaugurating a one-hundred-year period of Irish missions spreading east and south into Europe, founding monasteries from Lindisfarne in northern England to Bobbio in northern Italy.[18] Later Romanized following the Synod of Whitby in 664, eventually adopting the Rule of St. Benedict, these Irish foundations integrated liberal arts education – particularly *grammatica* – into the context of monasticism much as Cassiodorus did in Italy. Though Benedict of Nursia (c.480–c.543) does not mention liberal education in his Rule establishing "domenici schola servitii" (a school for the Lord's service), his emphasis on reading assumes an education in *grammatica* and a need for books.[19] For practical reasons most Benedictine monasteries established schools to train youths and illiterate community members in *grammatica* so they might grow as monks.[20] The writings of Bede (673–735), for instance, demonstrate a rich liberal arts training, first learned as a child oblate in the monastic school of Wearmouth-Jarrow and developed through a lifetime of study and *lectio divina*.[21]

While during the fifth through seventh centuries religious and clergy integrated liberal studies as needed into educational life, the eighth and ninth centuries witnessed a resurgence in liberal arts education under Carolingian patronage.[22] Trained in the episcopal-monastic center at York, Alcuin of York developed a three-tiered educational program for Charlemagne's palace school: a basic course in *grammatica*, a basic course in liturgical chant, and intermediate and advanced sets

---

[16] Though unconquered, Ireland had experienced Roman culture through trade and perhaps Roman aggression prior to Christian conversion. N. Edwards, *Archaeology of Early Medieval Ireland*, 1–5; Di Martino, *Roman Ireland*.
[17] Ó Cróinin, *Early Medieval Ireland*, 169–224.
[18] Duckett, *Gateway to the Middle Ages*, 62–121; Farr, *Book of Kells*, 15–28. For studies of Irish monastic art, see the essays in Karkov, Ryan, and Farrell, eds., *Insular Tradition*.
[19] Benedict of Nursia, *Regula*, ed. Fry, Prologus, chs. 8–20, 38, 42, 47–8. See J.G. Clark, *Benedictines in the Middle Ages*, 203–12; Irvine, *Making of Textual Culture*, 189–92; and Rand, *Founders of the Middle Ages*, 239–40.
[20] J.G. Clark, *Benedictines in the Middle Ages*, 83–7, and "Monastic Manuscripts," 335–52; Leclerq, *Love of Learning*, 139–84.
[21] Irvine, *Making of Textual Culture*, 272–98.
[22] Riche, *Carolingians*, 325–38.

of courses in *litteratura*, Scripture, and the other arts.²³ He composed four *trivium*-related treatises: *Grammatica, De orthographia, Dialogus de rhetorica et virtutibus,* and *De dialectica*. In the preface to *Grammatica*, entitled *Disputatio de vera philosophia*, Alcuin presents in dialogue between a master and students an overview the seven liberal arts, which he links to the seven gifts of the Holy Spirit and to the seven columns of Sapientia's house from Proverbs 9:1.²⁴ While in *Grammatica* Alcuin uses a dialogue between a Saxon pupil, a Frankish pupil, and himself to explore *ars grammatica*, in *Dialogus* and *De dialectica* he uses dialogues between Charlemagne and himself to delineate not only the two arts respectively but also their function in teaching civic virtue and ethics. Together, these treatises articulate Alcuin's *trivium* curriculum promoted through the palace school, thereby influencing cathedral- and monastic-school curricula as well.²⁵

Courtly, cathedral, monastic, and presbyterial schools continued teaching the arts until well into the twelfth century.²⁶ Though emphases shifted where, for instance, we find in the tenth and eleventh centuries what C. Stephen Jaeger identifies as charismatic pedagogy, in which the teacher modeled behavior, developing *mores* (manners) was the focus, and "ethics colonized the other disciplines," the liberal arts remained foundational. Similar to the Carolingian period, the twelfth century saw a flourishing of liberal studies.²⁷ Twelfth-century scholars based pedagogical theories on two overlapping strands in the late antique liberal arts tradition, which Curtius identifies as patristic and secular.²⁸ Jerome, Augustine, and Cassiodorus were the most influential of the patristic writers, and Martianus Capella was of the secular. Both strands are evident in Hugh of St. Victor's (c.1096–141) *Didascalicon* and in John of Salisbury's (c.1120–80) *Metalogicon*. Building on Augustine's integration of the arts with the gifts of the Holy Spirit presented as seven steps to wisdom,²⁹ Hugh of St. Victor argues that study of the arts is an intellectual journey to wisdom:

---

²³ Duckett, *Gateway to the Middle Ages*, 73; Irvine, *Making of Textual Culture*, 315–17; C.S. Jaeger, *Envy of Angels*, 21–35.
²⁴ Alcuin, *Grammatica*, ed. Migne, cols. 849–54.
²⁵ *Medieval Grammar*, eds. Copeland and Sluiter, 272–5; C.S. Jaeger, *Envy of Angels*, 30–5.
²⁶ Black, *Humanism and Education*, 36–44, 64–9; Contreni, "Cathedral Schools," 59–63; Deanesly, "Medieval Schools," 765–79; Holmes, "Transitions in European Education," 15–38; C.S. Jaeger, *Envy of Angels*; R. Johnson, "Allegory and the Trivium," 81–121; Knowles, *Evolution of Medieval Thought*, 59–92; Riche, *Education and Culture*; Scheffler, "Education and Schooling," 384–90, 397–8; Wagner, "Seven Liberal Arts," 1–31.
²⁷ C.S. Jaeger, *Envy of Angels*, 36–179: 118.
²⁸ Curtius, *European Literature*, 39–41; Rand, *Founder of the Middle Ages*, 218–50.
²⁹ Isaiah 11:2–3, articulates the gifts of the Holy Spirit: "Et requiescet super eum spiritus Domini: spiritus sapientiae et intellectus, spiritus consilii et fortitudinis, spiritus scientiae et pietatis, Et replebit eum spiritus timoris Domini" (And the spirit of the Lord shall rest upon him: the spirit of wisdom and of understanding, the spirit of counsel and of fortitude, the spirit of knowledge and of piety, and the spirit of fear of the Lord will fill him). In *De doctrina Christiana*, 2.9–11, Augustine reverses Isaiah's order of the Spirit's gifts and presents their acquisition as a progressively upward movement. On Augustine's discussion of the arts, see *De ordine*, 2.12–15.

hoc ergo omnes artes agunt, hoc intendunt, ut divina similitudo in nobis reparetur, quae nobis forma est, Deo natura, cui quanto magis conformamur tanto magis sapimus. tunc enim in nobis incipit relucere, quod in eius ratione semper fuit, quodque in nobis transit, apud illum incommutabile consistit

(All the arts, then, lead to this point, they intend this end, that the divine likeness be restored in us, which is a form to us but nature to God: the more we are conformed to this likeness, the more we grow wise. For then there begins to shine forth in us what has always existed in God's reason, and what is transient in us stands unchanging in God) (*Didascalicon* 2.1.17–21)

Rooted in a sort of cultural nostalgia for a pre-lapsarian state, and founded on the Incarnation and Redemption, study of the arts in Hugh's program is an antidote to the fall of humankind. On the other hand, John of Salisbury emphasizes humanity's social sphere, arguing that the arts, especially the *trivium*, foster essential human nature. Alluding to Martianus Capella, he writes:

Mercurio Philolgiam inuidet, et ab amplexu Philologiae Mercurium auellet qui eloquentiae praeceptionem a studiis philosophiae eliminat ... Brutescent homines si concessi dote priuentur eloquii, ipsaeque urbes uidebuntur potius pecorum quasi saepta quam coetus hominum nexu quodam societatis foederatus, ut participatione officiorum et amica inuicem uicissitudine eodem iure uiuat

(The person who eliminates the teaching of eloquence from the studies of philosophy begrudges Philology to Mercury and snatches Mercury from Philology's embrace .... If deprived of their gift of speech, humans would become brutes, and cities would seem more like fences for livestock than communities of human beings united by the common bond of society so as to live under the same law, sharing duties and adjusting in turn as friends)[30]

John also argues that the arts help humans achieve wisdom, whose "fructus in amore boni at virtutum cultu consistat" (fruit consists in love of the good and cultivation of virtues) (2.1.5–6). The phrase *cultum virtutum*, as C.S. Jaeger shows, encapsulates a mode of education that taught virtues by integrating interior thought and understanding with exterior action and behavior.[31] By implication, study of the arts in John's scheme also aids in restoring fallen human nature.

The theories that studying the liberal arts can restore divine likeness and deepen understanding of human society had practical applications for medieval pedagogy. Like Cassiodorus, Hugh of St. Victor discusses the arts as necessary precursor to reading Scripture.[32] Scripture study, we should recall, is the root of theological studies in medieval Christian culture. Godfrey of St. Victor (c.1125–94), writing a generation

---

[30] John of Salisbury, *Metalogicon*, eds. Hall and Keats-Rohan, 1.1.63–6, 69–73.
[31] C.S. Jaeger, *Envy of Angels*, 76–117. Aristotle's ideas of virtue also affected medieval thinking, particularly beginning in the thirteenth century with the advent of the *Nicomachean Ethics* in Europe: Nederman, "Aristotelian Ethics," 55–75; Copleston, *Philosophy: Volume II*, 2:118–31.
[32] Smalley, *Study of the Bible*, 82–106; de Lubac, *Medieval Exegesis*, 3:211–67; Taylor,

later, epitomizes Hugh's ideas in his didactic poem *Fons philosophiae*, where he treats the liberal arts before summarizing theological wisdom.[33] And in the anonymous twelfth-century text *De septem septenis*, we find a similar movement as the liberal arts form the first step in a seven-fold way of the soul's journey to heaven.[34] Hugh's theory later bears practical fruit in the European university curricula developed in the thirteenth century, where liberal learning prepared students for advanced study in theology. Likewise, John of Salisbury's theory in the *Metalogicon* that the arts foster social responsibility by uniting reason and speech bears practical fruit as the foundation for advanced study in law.

From the later twelfth through the fifteenth centuries, during the rise and establishment of medieval universities, *grammatica* remained foundational to education and the remainder of arts central to preparation for advanced studies in theology, medicine, canon law, and civil law.[35] In the thirteenth century, Robert Grosseteste (c.1175–253) defended and wrote an exposition of the arts in *De artibus liberalibus*, Vincent of Beauvais organized his *Speculum doctrinale* around the liberal arts, and Bonaventure, who briefly held a chair in theology at Paris, demonstrated the relationship between the arts and theology in *De reductione artium ad theologiam*.[36] The arts also remained important at fourteenth- and fifteenth-century Oxford and Cambridge where students generally studied them for up to eight years, attaining the level of master, before advancing to doctoral study.[37] The liberal arts were the cornerstone of medieval academic learning; without firm training in them, a scholar could not pursue advanced studies.

This survey of the liberal arts in the medieval curriculum can be summed up visually by the wheel-shaped diagram illustrating education on folio 32r of Herrad of Hohenbourg's (c.1130–95) *Hortus deliciarum*, a late twelfth-century encyclopedic, multi-media text composed for interactive communal use in her convent at Ste.-Odile in Alsace (Fig. 3).[38] The diagram centers on a circle in which Philosophia sits

---

introduction to *The Didiscalicon*, 28–36; Wei, *Intellectual Culture in Medieval Paris*, 78–86; Wetherbee, *Platonism and Poetry*, 49–66.

[33] Godfrey's *Fons Philosophiae*, ed. Michaud-Quantin, falls into five parts: introduction (1–20), the mechanical arts (21–44), the liberal arts (45–464), theological wisdom (465–740), and history of the canons regular (741–836).

[34] *De septem septenis*, ed. Migne, col. 948.

[35] Black, *Humanism and Education*, 34–365; Janet Coleman, *Medieval Writers*, 26–41; Russell, *Chaucer and the Trivium*, 6–53; Sheffler, "Education and Schooling," 390–7, 399–403; Wei, *Intellectual Culture in Medieval Paris*, 87–124. On medieval universities, see Dunphy, "The Medieval University," 1705–34.

[36] On Grosseteste, see Southern, *Robert Grosseteste*, 63–82, 244–95, and Copleston, *Philosophy: Volume II*, 1:258–62; on Vincent of Beauvais, see Mâle, *Gothic Image*, 23–7, 64–97; on Bonaventure, see Copleston, *Philosophy: Volume II*, 1:269–79.

[37] In late medieval England, following training at song schools and grammar schools, students generally studied four to five years at university for a bachelor of arts and an additional three for a master of arts. Courtenay, *Schools and Scholars*, 30–48; Orme, *English Schools*, 79–86; Southern, *Robert Grosseteste*, 49–62; Wei, *Intellectual Culture in Medieval Paris*, 125–43.

[38] F. Griffiths, *Garden of Delights*, 1–8, 49–81; Monroe, "Dangerous Passages and Spiritual Redemption," 46–74. Though destroyed in the 1870 siege of Strasbourg, much survived

THE MARTIANUS TRADITION 89

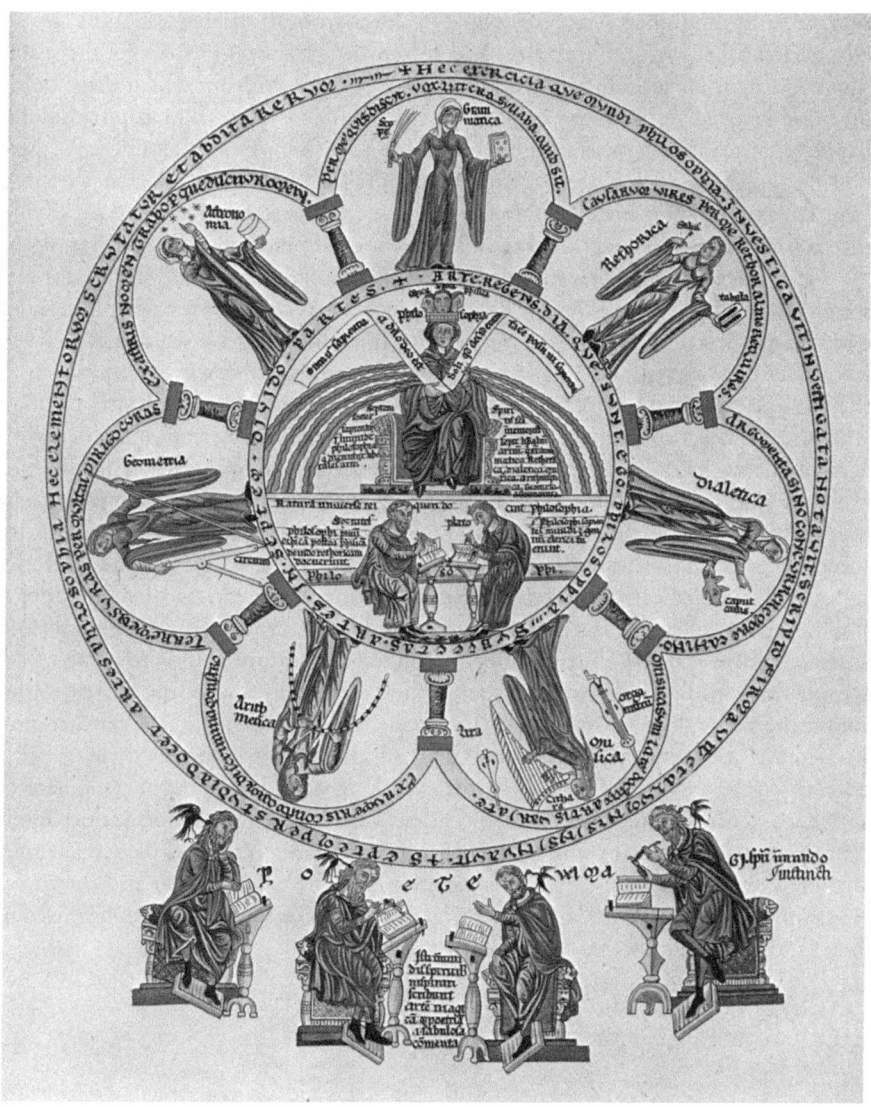

Figure 3. Herrad of Hohenbourg, *Hortus deliciarum*, fol. 32r.
By permission of the Warburg Institute.

in an 1818 copy. I base the following transcriptions on the 1979 facsimile, Herrad of Hohenbourg, *Hortus deliciarum*, eds. Green et al., 1:plate 18 and 2:104.

enthroned in the upper two-thirds while in the bottom third Socrates and Plato sit facing each other, writing in codices and accompanied by text identifying them and summarizing their teaching and studies. Wearing a crown from which three heads protrude labelled respectively "ethica," "logica," and "physica," Philosophia holds a banner that reads "Omnis sapientia a Domino Deo est soli quod desiderant facere possunt sapientes" (All wisdom is from God; only the wise can do what they desire). Four streams flow from Philosophia's right side and three from her left, signifying the seven liberal arts. In text ringing this inner circle, Philosophia states, "Arte regens dia que sunt ego philosophia subjectas artes in spetem divido partes" (I Philosophia, a goddess ruling by art all that is, divide subjected arts into seven parts). In a series of seven architectural arches laid out around this inner ring we see depicted seven female figures labeled and with iconographic detail, starting with Grammatica at the top and proceeding clockwise in the order Cassiodorus treats the arts through Rhetorica, Dialectica, Musica, Arithmetica, Geometria, and Astronomia, each with accompanying text. The text in the outer ring encompassing the whole reads "Hec exercicia que mundi philosophia investigavit investigata notavit scripto firmavit et alumnis insinuavit septem per studia docet artes philosophia hec elementorum scrutatur et abdita rerum" (Philosophia investigates these studies of the universe, notes and establishes her investigations in writing, and teaches them to pupils; Philosophia teaches the seven arts through study and scrutinizes the elements and secrets of things). Below the outer ring floating in the bottom margin four men sit at writing desks while black birds whisper in their ears: an image contrasting by implication the white dove whispering divine music in Gregory the Great's ear common in medieval iconography.[39] Text accompanying the images identifies them as poets and magicians taught by wicked spirits. Working outside Philosophia's sphere of influence, these "évangélistes du diable" (devil's evangelists) as Gérard Cames interprets them, warn against using liberal learning for negative ends.[40] Taken as a whole, this illumination and text serve as a mnemonic of the *artes liberales* and their relationship to philosophical education: a relationship also mnemonically epitomized in Martianus Capella's *De nuptiis Philologiae et Mercurii*.

---

[39] A tenth-century ivory book cover, for instance, entitled "HL. Gregor mit Schreibern," carved by the Meister der Wiener Gregorplatte, and now housed in Kunsthistorisches Museum, Vienna, illustrates the St. Gregory-dove iconography well. Framed by an acanthus-leaf border, the central image depicts Gregory the Great at his desk taking dictation from a dove – the Holy Spirit – perching on his right shoulder and whispering in his ear while in a panel below three monks copy in turn Gregory's writing. As a cover, the image authenticates the book's contents as divinely inspired, even if at least once removed from Gregory's pen. The *Hortus* image invokes this iconic moment in the negative as the black birds similarly perch on the magicians' shoulders and whisper in their ears.

[40] Cames, *Allégories et Symboles*, 16.

Martianus Capella in the Middle Ages

Writing about 1132 in a letter of consolation to a friend, Peter Abelard (1079–1142) describes his upbringing near Pallet, Brittany, stating in part:

> Ego vero quanto amplius et facilius in studio litterarum profeci, tanto ardentius eis inhaesi, et in tanto earum amore illectus sum ut, militaris gloriae pompam cum hereditate et praerogativa primogenitorum meorum fratribus derelinquens, Martis curiae penitus abdicarem ut Minervae gremio educarer. Et quoniam dialecticarum rationum armaturam omnibus philosophiae documentis praetuli, his armis alia commutavi et trophaeis bellorum conflictus praetuli disputationum

> (Truly the more fully and easily I progressed in the study of letters the more ardently I clung to them and increased in such great love of them that, relinquishing to my brother the trappings of military glory, along with the heredity and privilege of my first-born rights, I withdrew completely from Mars' court to study at Minerva's feet. And because I preferred the weapons of dialectic's methods over all other lessons of philosophy, I unhorsed others with these weapons and preferred the conflict of disputation rather than the trophies of war.[41]

Employing bellicose language in a witty play on Mars and Minerva's martial aspects as two ways of life open to him in his youth, a variation perhaps on the *sapientia et fortitudo* topos, Abelard treats education as battle in which he engages the opposition with intellectual weapons acquired at Minerva's court.[42] In another passage later in the letter, when Abelard recounts Heloise's arguments against marriage, she upholds pagan philosophers as models for emulation and says, "Quam sobrie autem atque continenter ipsi vixerint non est nostrum modo ex exemplis colliger ne Minervam ipsam videar docere" (But it is unnecessary for us to gather from examples how soberly and chastely they lived lest I seem to teach Minerva herself) (188). These allusions to Minerva – opaque to us in the twenty-first century – point directly to the fifth-century North African schoolmaster Martianus Capella's *De nuptiis Philologiae et Mercurii*, in which Minerva (Pallas) holds court as *magistra artium liberalium*.

In *De nuptiis*, Martianus offers a one-volume encyclopedic treatment of the seven liberal arts as understood in late antique Imperial Roman culture. Couching the whole in a mythic-allegorical setting, Martianus tells his son a story about Mercury god of eloquence seeking a bride. Considering several possibilities, and consulting the council of Olympian deities, he settled on Philology, or Love of Learning, who undertook a heroic journey from earth to the region of the fixed stars to marry the god. The balance of the text entails a presentation of wedding gifts, the seven liberal arts, to the divine newlyweds. Martianus organized the nine books of *De nuptiis* into three sections: the allegorical setting, books one and two; the *trivium*, books three to

---

[41] Abelard, "Abelard's Letter of Consolation," ed. Muckle, 175–6.
[42] Curtius, *European Literature*, 173–9. Solterer, *Master and Minerva*, 28–9, examines this same passage when explicating the feminization of wisdom and learning in the context of *disputatio*.

five; and the *quadrivium*, books six to nine.[43] As mistress of the arts, Minerva plays a crucial, often dramatic role in each section. In the first, even her initial appearance is a bit dramatic. As Jove bent to hear Juno's advice on the marriage, Minerva glided down from a high place of shimmering light – somewhere above Jove – and settled near his head: an allegory of divine wisdom engaging the issue at hand.[44] When Jove requested her advice on the marriage, however, Minerva declined to assent outright since she was unwed herself; she advised Jove to assemble the married gods, instead, because their support would be more advantageous to Mercury, Jove, and Philology (1.40). Before giving her advice, however, she unveiled her seven-rayed crown, which allegorically introduces the goddess' role as mistress of the arts.[45]

In the *trivium* section of *De nuptiis*, Minerva actively managed the maidens' discourses, adding comic touches to the frame story. Near the end of Grammatica's discourse, for instance, just as she moved to address elementary schoolroom issues and rhythm and meter, Minerva interrupted because the restless celestial court was showing signs of boredom and Grammatica was about to usurp Musica's rights. In a clever move of her own, Minerva summarized what Grammatica was about to say in an *occultatio*, the figure of speech that calls attention to a subject by summarily passing over it, thereby retaining the good will of all while bringing the discourse to a close (3.326).[46] Similarly, Minerva intervened when Dialectica was about to describe her art's deceptive side and return an insult Bacchus hurled at her earlier. Minerva's intervention suggests in the allegory that wisdom avoids logical fallacies, represented by Dialectica's intended *ad hominem* rebuttal to Bacchus. In this dramatic exchange, Dialectica remained obedient to the goddess, saying "uni famulandum est tibi, virgo; reticemus" (I must serve you alone, maiden; we shall be quiet) (4.424). Finally, Rhetorica, as the art of persuasion, kissed Minerva's breast before commencing her discourse: a gesture suggesting both her role as mover of the heart and submission to her mistress (5.434).

Minerva continued to play a dramatic role in the framing narrative of Martianus' *quadrivium* section, calling forth Arithmetica (7.725), discussing the presentation with Philology (8.803), and escorting Harmonia with Phoebus (9.909) among other interactions. But, more importantly, Martianus interrupts the narrative himself by opening book six with a thirty-four-line encomium to the goddess. This poem – a break in the narrative distinguishing the *quadrivium* section from the first two – emphasizes Minerva's role as mistress of the arts by explicating her nature as goddess of wisdom and detailing her iconographic attributes: she is knowledge bearer, mind

---

[43] R. Johnson, "Allegory and the Trivium," 83.
[44] Martianus Capella, *De nuptiis Philologiae*, ed. Willis, 1.39.
[45] Remigius of Auxerre allegorically interprets the rays as the seven liberal arts, stating: "CORONA SEPTEM RADIORUM aperitur ... septem liberalium artium scientia demonstratur" (the seven-rayed crown is uncovered ... [and] the knowledge of the seven liberal arts is demonstrated). *Commentum in Martianum*, ed. Lutz, 25.14.
[46] *Occultatio* seems appropriate for Minerva, who demonstrates a rhetorician's attention to audience as well as a *sapiens*' deep understanding of the subject (one cannot summarize without understanding).

of gods and men, guiding universal spirit, mentor of Jove, founder of learning; sculptors depict her with shield, spear, olive branch; and so on. He concludes the poem with a multi-layered invocation:

> O sacra doctarum prudentia fontigenarum,
> sola novem complens, Musis mens omnibus una,
> deprecor: ad proprium dignata illabere munus
> inspirans nobis Graias Latiariter artes
>
> (O holy wisdom of the learned spring-begetters, sole inspiration of the nine, one mind for all the Muses, I beseech you: deign to pour out your gift on your very own, inspiring us to present Greek arts in the Latin language) (6.574)

Calling on Minerva as the Muses' inspiration, and implicitly on the Muses in turn, he also implies the goddess *magistra artium*, for he employs the *trivium* arts himself to create the poem as well as the rest of the text. Coming at about the halfway point, this encomium meditates on Minerva's role in the entire text. As Remigius of Auxerre (c.841–908) observes in his ninth-century commentary:

> Invocatio ad Palladem et descriptio laudis et virtutis ipsius quam idcirco ad eandem agit Palladem quae est dea artium quia, descriptis tribus, Grammatica videlicet, Dialectica, atque Rhetorica, quae tantum in sermone sunt, ingressurus est ad describendum artium quattuor reliquarum quadruvium (sic) quae in intellectu consistunt. In his quippe mathematica constat, id est doctrinalis scientia
>
> (The invocation to Pallas and description of her praise and virtue therefore leads to the same Pallas who is the goddess of the arts because – with three having been described namely *Grammatica*, *Dialectica* and *Rhetorica*, who are only important in discourse – he is about to begin to describe the four remaining arts of the *quadrivium* that stand in the intellect. Indeed, mathematics consists of these, that is, theoretical knowledge) (6.265.6)

Minerva "dea artium" is figuratively and literally central to Martianus' text, linking its three sections through her role as mistress of the arts.

Popular in the Middle Ages, *De nuptiis Philologiae et Mercurii* offered the first presentation of the liberal arts in a single seven-part scheme, establishing fairly quickly what became liberal learning's dominant structure in medieval education.[47] Writing in the sixth century, for instance, Gregory of Tours (c.538–94) summarizes Martianus at the end of the *Historia Francorum* both to demonstrate his reading of the text and to control reader response to his own work.[48] With Boethius' *Conso-*

---

[47] Stahl, *Martianus Capella*, 55–6; *Medieval Grammar*, eds. Copeland and Sluiter, 148–51; Wagner, "Seven Liberal Arts," 19.
[48] Gregory of Tours writes: "Quod si te, o sacerdos Dei, quicumque es, Martianus noster septem disciplinis erudiit, id est, si te in grammaticis docuit legere, in dialecticis altercationum propositiones advertere, in rethoricis genera metrorum agnoscere, in geometricis terrarum linearumque mensuras colligere, in astrologiis cursus siderum contemplare, in arithmeticis numerorum partes colligere, in armoniis sonorum

latio Philosophiae, it modeled the prosimetrum form, influencing later writers such as Bernard Silvestris in *Cosmographia* and Alan of Lille in *De planctu Naturae*. *De nuptiis* also affected visual art, bequeathing some of its liberal arts iconography to the Middle Ages, including the attribution of noteworthy scholars to each art.[49] Martianus' descriptions of the arts are so visually striking that other poets, too, turned to *De nuptiis* when seeking to create verbally their visual impact. Theodulf of Orléans (c.760–821), the Carolingian educator and bishop, composed *De septem liberalibus artibus in quadam pictura depictis*, in which he describes the liberal arts iconographically following Martianus.[50] And, though Alcuin seems not to have known Martianus, the next generations of Carolingian commentators did, as we have already seen. In addition to Remigius of Auxerre, John Scotus Eriugena (c.815–77) composed *Annotationes in Marcianum*, a commentary and gloss on all nine books of *De nuptiis*; an anonymous glossator once thought to be a certain Dunchad composed a shorter set of glosses on books one, two, four, and five; and several glossators composed a set of interlinear and marginal glosses in the 820s and 830s related to the Dunchad text and referred to as the oldest gloss tradition: together, these comprise three distinct ninth-century strands of commentary on *De nuptiis*.[51] These commentary traditions, along with the nearly fifty extant full or partial ninth-century manuscript copies of *De nuptiis*, register a rising popularity of Martianus' text in Carolingian schools.[52]

Engagement with *De nuptiis* saw a pronounced spike in the twelfth century with the emphasis in cathedral schools on liberal learning. In the *Heptateucon*, for instance, Thierry of Chartres (c.1100–c.1155) compiled a massive anthology for teaching the seven liberal arts, including integrating books five and seven of *De nuptiis* in his

---

modulationes suavium accentuum carminibus concrepare; si in his omnibus ita fueris exercitatus, ut tibi stilus noster sit rusticus, nec sic quoque, deprecor, ut avellas quae scripsi. Sed si tibi in his quiddam placuerit, salvo opere nostro, te scribere versu non abnuo" (But even if our Martianus has taught you, o priest of God, whoever you are, the seven disciplines, that is, if he has taught you to read through grammar, to turn propositions in argument through dialectic, to recognize the types of meters through rhetoric, to mark the measurements of lands and boundary lines through geometry, to contemplate the courses of stars through astronomy, to gather the parts of numbers through arithmetic, to conceive the modulations of sounds with songs of sweet accents through music; if you have been so trained in all these studies that our pen seems rustic to you, I beseech you not to tear apart what I have written. But, if anything in these books will be pleasing to you, I do not forbid you to re-write it in verse, keeping our work intact). *Historia Francorum*, ed. Latin Library, 10.18. On Gregory, see Auerbach, *Literary Language*, 103–12.

[49] Katzenellenbogen, "Representations of the Seven Liberal Arts," 39–55; Mâle, *Gothic Image*, 77–90; Stahl and Johnson, *Martianus Capella*, 245–9. But see also Evans, "Allegorical Women and Practical Men," 307–9.

[50] Theodulf, *De septem liberalibus artibus*, ed. Migne, cols. 333–5. See Stahl and Johnson, *Martianus Capella*, 246; Deanesley, "Medieval Schools," 774–5; and Raby, *History of Christian Latin Poetry*, 171–7.

[51] S. O'Sullivan, introduction to *Glossae*, v–ix; Hicks, "Martianus Capella," 314–19.

[52] S. O'Sullivan, introduction to *Glossae*, v.n.1; McDonough, introduction to *Commentum*, xvii–xxiv; Stahl and Johnson, *Martianus Capella*, 65–70.

sections on rhetoric and arithmetic and using Martianus' marriage metaphor (here between the *trivium* and the *quadrivium*) in the prologue.⁵³ The text also continued to generate scholarly commentaries, including among others one attributed to Bernard Silvestris from the second quarter of the century and another by Alexander Neckam (1157–1217) on books one and two near century's end.⁵⁴ And, as indicated above, John of Salisbury wove references to *De nuptiis* into his *Metalogicon* that demonstrate a mind steeped in Martianus' text: a readiness and facility suggesting he retained it well in memory. In addition to inspiring new manuscript copies and commentaries, and informing full-blown treatises, Martianus' *De nuptiis* also generated new poems. Adelard of Bath's (c.1100–c.1142) *De eodem et diverso* centers on a debate between Philosophia and Philocosmia (Love-of-the-World), representing stability and change respectively, in which Philosophia explicates the liberal arts, who accompany her looking as though they had just stepped from Martianus' world into Adelard's. This view of the relationship between Philosophia and the arts is much the same as Herrard of Hohenbourg's later twelfth-century image in *Hortus deliciarium*, clearly an echo of Martianus as well.⁵⁵

Writing within a few years of Adelard, the anonymous poet of *Methamorphosis Golye episcopi*, a dream vision likely composed shortly after the Council of Sens, recasts Martianus' allegorical setting to address a topical issue in ecclesiastical politics.⁵⁶ The narrative begins as a remembered event in which one spring season the narrator fell asleep under a pine tree and had a dream. Wandering amid an idyllic

---

⁵³ Jeauneau, *Rethinking the School of Chartres*, 92; Stahl and Johnson, *Martianus Capella*, 68; Vignaux, *Philosophy in the Middle Ages*, 29. There is no modern edition of the *Heptateucon*, and the sole two-volume manuscript copy of the text, Chartres, Bibliothèque Municipale Ms. 497 and 498, was destroyed in an allied bombardment on May 26, 1944 (Jeauneau, *Rethinking the School of Chartres*, 68–71). Fortunately, copies exist on microfilm. Hill Museum and Manuscript Library owns a negative film copy of MS 497 I have consulted. Vignaux translated the preface (29).

⁵⁴ The commentary attributed to Bernard Silvestris is extant in one thirteenth-century ms.: Cambridge, University Library, Ms. Mm.1.18 (ff. 1–28r). The text offers commentary on book one, chapters 1–37, breaking off mid-sentence in the middle of line 32 of the first column on fol. 28r. This evidence, along with internal evidence, suggests the original covered books one and two of *De nuptiis* (*Commentary on Martianus*, 2–4, 17). See also Chance, *Medieval Mythography*, 1:463–78; and Wetherbee, *Platonism and Poetry*, 111–25. Alexander Neckam's commentary is extant in two fourteenth-century mss.: Oxford, Bodleian Library, Ms. Digby 222 (ff. 34v–88v) and Cambridge, Trinity College Ms. R.14.9 (ff. 38r–63r). Neckam's mythographic commentary synthesizes materials from sources like the TVM: *Commentum super Martianum*, ed. McDonough, xxiv–xxxiv. See also Chance, *Medieval Mythography*, 2:187–202; and Wetherbee, "Learned Mythography," 338–41.

⁵⁵ Cames, *Allégories et Symboles*, 16–18.

⁵⁶ Extant in two thirteenth-century mss. (London, British Library Ms. Harley 978 s.XIII, ff. 100v–102v; Saint-Omer Signatur 710, ff. 122v–124r), the poem does not evince wide readership though the mss. do suggest continued interest after its occasion for composition faded. See Benton, "Philology's Search for Abelard," 199–217; J.R. Clark, "Love and Learning," 156–71; C.S. Jaeger, *Ennobling Love*, 170–3; Raby, *History of Secular Latin Poetry*, 2:219–22; Synan, "Goliard Witness," 121–31; and Wetherbee, "Learned Mythography," 341–3, and *Platonism and Poetry*, 127–34.

forest glade and hearing the music of nature, he came upon a building in the midst of a meadow: the "domus ... universitatis" (palace of the universe) containing forms of all created things.[57] Entering this structure, he heard harmonious music of universal concord and observed in *tableau vivant* an enthroned king and queen with Minerva (Pallas) proceeding from the king's brow in a Martianus-like moment. Concerning Minerva, the narrator observes:

> Hec mens est Altissimi, mens divinitatis,
> que nature legibus imperat et fatis;
> incomprehensibilis res est deitatis,
> nam fugit angustias nostre parvitatis

> (She is the mind of the Most High, the mind of divinity, who commands with the laws of nature and divine oracles; she is the essence of the incomprehensible deity, for she flees the narrow ways of our puniness) (72–5)

This Minerva both embodies divine wisdom in the poem and glosses her role as *magistra artium* in Martianus. As the narrator continues, he next observed Mercury and his bride beside the king and queen, with the attendant Sun, Muses, and three Graces. With *De nuptiis* in mind, we have arrived at the moment of union between Mercury and Philology. The narrator's comment after introducing the god and his bride sums up Martianus' text as well:

> Nisi sapientie sermo copuletur
> vagus, dissolutus est, infirmus habetur,
> et cum parum proficit, parum promeretur,
> eget ut remigio eius gubernetur

> (Unless speech is joined to wisdom, it wanders, dissipates, grows ill, and when it advances little, it is little valued and flounders like a ship piloted by its oarsmen) (89–92)

The harmonious marriage of Philology and Mercury serves here and in Martianus as emblem of a key goal of liberal learning: to join love-of-learning with verbal expression. Either without the other remains fruitless. Yet, just as in Martianus when Pleasure and Venus (7.725–7) and Silenus and Cupid (8.804–5) seek to distract Mercury, this harmony in *Methamorphosis* is susceptible to comic disruption. Instead of an ordered parade of the liberal arts as we might expect, a drunken Silenus and crew of satyrs accompanied by Venus and Cupid burst onto the scene with raucous discord.

With this interruption, the dream veered suddenly in a different direction. While others seemed unable to respond, Minerva alone confronted Venus, thereby raising a question among all present as to which goddess was the worthier. A debate ensued, during which the narrator catalogues ancient and contemporary philosophers standing side-by-side: an allegory suggesting a then present-day re-birth of

---

[57] *Methamorphosis Golye*, ed. Huygens, 49.

liberal learning in the schools of Paris.⁵⁸ Though difficult to determine a winner, as the debate broke off when the unnamed bride sought out the absent Peter Abelard, Venus and Cupid perhaps gained a slight advantage by inspiring poets and philosophers alike with passion.⁵⁹ Abelard – the philosopher-lover-poet who in his own words studied at Minerva's feet – serves *in absentia* as emblem of passion united with learning.⁶⁰ After Abelard's students then complained of his condemnation by "cucullatus populi Primas cucullati" (the cowled leader of the cowled flock) (218) – that is, Bernard of Clairvaux – and of his absence from the gathering, the assembled deities banished this flock of monks from the marriage, declaring "ne philosophicum audiat secretum / studii mechanici teneat oletum" (lest they hear philosophical secrets let them hold to the stench of the mechanical arts) (231).⁶¹ Immediately following this revealing comment on both Cistercians and *artes machinales*, the narrator concludes with a petitionary prayer:

> Quicquid tante curie sanctione datur
> non cedat in irritum, ratum habeatur:
> cucullatus igitur grex vilipendatur
> et a philosophicis scolis expellatur. Amen

> (Let not whatever judgment given by sanction of so great a court be rendered null, let it be ratified; let the cowled flock, therefore, be vilified and expelled from philosophical schools. Amen) (233–6)

Methamorphosis Golye episcopi is a partisan poem redeploying imagery from Martianus' text to defend Abelard, Minerva's self-described student and – at least according to the poet – consummate practitioner of Philology and Mercury's wedded arts. Through this dreamscape, the poet imagines a council greater than the Council of Sens where he works out a revenge fantasy against those who condemned Abelard in 1141: apparently the poet was unaware that Abelard and Bernard of Clairvaux had reconciled before the former died.⁶² Underlying this poetic response to Abelard's condemnation is his equally strong concern for the state of humanism in the 1140s.⁶³ Under pressure from reformists such as William of St. Thierry and Bernard of Clairvaux, who feared a fractured Church, the humanism practiced by Abelard, Gilbert de la Porrée, and others increasingly came under ecclesiastical

---

⁵⁸ Southern, *Scholastic Humanism*, 221–5.
⁵⁹ C.S. Jaeger, *Ennobling Love*, 172–3.
⁶⁰ Abelard was also known for his love poetry though only some of his religious hymns and complaints survive. Luscombe, "Peter Abelard," 155–7; Mews, *Abelard and Heloise*, 164–73; Raby, *History of Christian Latin Poetry*, 319–26.
⁶¹ Bernard of Clairvaux opposed Abelard at the Council of Sens in 1141 and persuaded Pope Innocent II to condemn him and his teaching, which the Pope did in a letter promulgated July 16, 1141. Mews, "Bernard of Clarvaux," 133–68, and "Council of Sens," 342–80.
⁶² Mews, *Abelard and Heloise*, 242–3, "Bernard of Clairvaux," 167–8, and "Council of Sens," 374–5.
⁶³ Raby *History of Secular Latin*, 2:221–2; Wetherbee, *Platonism and Poetry*, 128.

scrutiny in this decade.[64] In a sense re-writing Martianus' allegory, updating it for his contemporary audience, the poet also employs humanistic learning *De nuptiis* helped make possible in defense of humanism itself by satirizing the "cucullatus populi" and even slightly the *artes machinales*.

Within a few years of *Methamorphosis Golye episcopi*, Bernard Silvestris likewise drew on Martianus' *De nuptiis* when composing *Cosmographia*. Having already discussed Minerva's role in this poem in some detail, I want only to mention here that one way to read *Cosmographia*, as C.S. Jaeger points out, is as an allegory of the educational process beginning with liberal learning.[65] In "Microcosmus," Noys instructs Natura, Urania, and Physis to fuse in humankind the mortal body with the immortal soul, by which the human person will be able to move through study of the cosmos from disorder and strife to a peace and harmony fully achieved after death when the soul assumes its place in the stars (10.1–54). This creative development of the human person projected in "Microcosmus" mirrors the journey Philology undertakes in *De nuptiis* to reach the council of the gods and marry Mercury; it also mirrors the process Noys undertakes in "Megacosmus" to order the cosmos itself. In this microcosm-macrocosm model, humans become co-creators of themselves through education. This developmental process projected in *Cosmographia* also mirrors the potential restoration of the human person through the arts that Hugh of St. Victor envisions in *Didascalicon* and John of Salisbury alludes to in *Metalogicon*. Twelfth-century poetic engagement with Martianus' *De nuptiis*, however, reaches perhaps its fullest expression in Alan of Lille's allegorical epic *Anticlaudianus de Antirufino*, which is as much a poetic response to *Cosmographia* as it is to Claudian's (c.370–404 CE) *Antirufinus*.

Composed between 1181 and 1184, *Anticlaudianus* is a nine-book, 4385-hexameter-line allegorical, cosmological epic in which Minerva as *magistra artium* helps advance the poem's main theme: the creation of the completely good man. Seeking to remedy past mistakes, Natura calls a celestial council of virtues, where she states her intention to make *novus homo*, a new man. Upon hearing Natura's plea, Prudentia (Phronesis/Sophia) replies first, supporting the goddess but noting only God can produce an immortal soul so the task at hand is impossible without his intervention. Prudentia's sister Ratio then rises and addresses the assembled virtues, arguing the value of Natura's cause and naming Prudentia to be their messenger to God. Though initially reluctant, Prudentia agrees (after Concordia speaks peace) to undertake a journey through the cosmos to secure an immortal soul for the new man. The liberal arts then build a four-wheeled chariot – drawn by five horses (the senses) and piloted by Ratio herself – that, much like Philology's "lectica" (litter) in *De nuptiis* (2.143), carries Prudentia through the spheres to the limits of the known universe. A second unnamed guide (though most scholars think she is Theologia) leads Prudentia to the heavenly court where, after experiencing the angelic choirs and saints, she swoons upon encountering Mary and Jesus. Fides, a third guide, helps her recover

---

[64] Knowles, *Evolution of Medieval Thought*, 122–30; Mews, "Council of Sens," 358–80; Jeauneau, *Rethinking the School of Chartres*, 57–8.
[65] C.S. Jaeger, *Envy of Angels*, 281–4.

and leads her to God, from whom she requests a soul: God agrees, Noys creates the soul, and Prudentia returns to earth as she had come. Natura then fashions a well-proportioned body from the four elements, Concordia joins the body to the soul, and the virtues, Ratio, and Prudentia – and Prudentia's handmaidens the liberal arts – give gifts to the new man. Even Fortuna, at her daughter Nobility's instigation and closely monitored by Ratio, grants gifts as well. The narrative then shifts to Allecto who, having heard a rumor of Natura's efforts, marshals an army of vices and attacks the new man. A psychomachia ensues in which the new man slays Allecto and Venus (an allegory it would seem of Patience over Wrath, on the one hand, and Chastity over Lust on the other) to usher in a new golden age of peace.

In her role as *magistra artium*, Minerva appears in *Anticlaudianus* at key junctures in the narrative. Imitating Natura in *Cosmographia* (1.1.66), who in turn seems to be imitating Heloise in Abelard's letter of consolation (188), Ratio offers the poem's first reference to the goddess when articulating her position of humility before Natura and the virtues, whom by implication she considers her superiors. Opening her first speech, she states: "'Plus quam posse meum posit me posse iubetis, / Dum uestram cogor indocta docere Mineruam'" (You ask that I display a power more than I am able when untaught I am pressured to teach your Minerva) (2.7–8). Ratio as human reason uses this modesty topos – collectively relating the virtues to Minerva as divine wisdom – in part to reassure this council of celestial beings that she knows her own place in the assembly.[66] After this address, and once Prudentia agrees to journey to God, Minerva appears in her role as mistress of the arts. While the liberal arts build Prudentia's chariot, Minerva directly supervises their work. The narrator a bit strenuously states:

> Ergo Minerua uidens tanto splendore Sophye,
> Tot donis tantisque datis splendore sorores,
> Ordinat, iniungit, iubet, imperat, orat ut instans
> Quelibet istarum comitum, comitante Sophia,
> Corpore, mente, fide studeat, desudet, anhelet,
> Instet et efficiat ut currus curat ad esse,
> Quo terre spacium, mare, sydera, nubile, celum
> Transeat et, trini superato cardine celi,
> Scrutetur secreta Noys sensusque profundos
> Hauriat et summi perquirat uelle magistri.

(Minerva, then, seeing that the sisters [i.e., the arts] are filled with Sophia's splendor and with so many great gifts, orders, joins, bids, commands, begs that pursuing the task in any way possible each of these companions, by accompanying Sophia, should in body, mind, and faith strive, sweat, pant, work hard and see to it that the chariot races to being, in which Prudentia could cross the space of earth, sea, stars, clouds, heavens and, having passed the axis of the triple heavens, scrutinize Noys' secrets, swallow her deep meaning, and examine carefully the will of the supreme master.) (2.363–72)

---

[66] Curtius, *European Literature*, 83–5.

Immediately, the maiden arts respond to Minerva's wishes, each bearing the tools of her art just as Martianus depicts: Grammatica appears with her sharp "scalprum" (pruning knife) (2.404; cf. *De nuptiis* 3.224), Astronomia carries her luminous "spera" (sphere) (4.11; cf. *De nuptiis* 8.810), and so on. And each has a particular task reflecting her art: Grammatica shapes the pole, the chariot's central element; Logica constructs the axles; Rhetorica finishes the frame; Arithmetica makes a granite wheel; Musica, a bronze wheel; Geometria, a lead wheel; and Astronomia, a golden wheel. With the chariot completed, Ratio harnesses and drives the five horses, and Prudentia ascends as far as Ratio, the arts, and the senses can take her. When Theologia takes over as guide, she wears a garment "Quam diuina manus et solers dextra Minerue / Texuit" (which Minerva's divine and skilled right hand had woven) (5.112–13). This garment seems an allegory of the liberal arts' integral relationship to theological study. Clothed by Minerva, Theologia pursues the highest studies: in a sense, "summi perquirat uelle magistri" (she examines carefully the will of the supreme master) (2.372) just as Minerva intends Prudentia herself will do when she meets Noys.

Alan weaves Minerva into the text of *Anticlaudianus*, drawing especially on her role as *magistra artium*. As in Martianus' *De nuptiis*, Minerva here represents wisdom gained through education. The product of Natura desiring to make amends for past mistakes, Prudentia questing to and through the heavens, Noys fashioning a soul and Natura a body, Concordia uniting the two, and the virtues and others bestowing gifts, the *novus homo* in *Anticlaudianus* is also the product of liberal learning. At Prudentia's behest, he receives the knowledge and skill of liberal training directly from each art: speech, writing, and poetics from Grammatica; rational thought and argument from Logica; style, balance, and ornamentation from Rhetorica; numbers and "secreta Minerue" (Minerva's secrets) (8.291) from Arithmetica; harmony and sound from Musica; measure and dimension from Geometria; and astral motions, heavenly laws, and self-governance from Astronomia (8.248–328). Though some scholars have argued the new man represents Christ, Adam, the artist, or historical personages such as Philip Augustus, the poem primarily sets out to articulate an optimistic view of education's effects.[67] Any person pursuing the path of education represented by Prudentia's journey and made possible by Minerva's arts has potential to become a *novus homo*, ready to engage challenges of human existence with knowledge, understanding, and virtue.

Surviving in over 100 manuscript copies, Alan of Lille's *Anticlaudianus*, like Bernard Silvestris' *Cosmographia*, was widely read, inspiring almost immediately a poetic response from John of Hauville (c.1150–c.1208) and influencing subsequent generations of scholars and poets.[68] As with other responses to *De nuptiis*,

---

[67] Chance, "Artist as Epic Hero," 238–47; L. Marshall, "Identity of the 'New Man'," 77–94; B. Newman, *God and the Goddesses*, 82–3. Simpson, *Sciences and the Self*, 116–33, cogently argues that the poem's hero is the reader, questing to know the self.

[68] Balint, *Ordering Chaos*, 152–5; *Medieval Grammar and Rhetoric*, eds. Copeland and Sluiter, 518–20; B. Newman, *God and the Goddesses*, 83–6. In *Architrenius*, John of Hauville recounts the journey of a young man seeking Natura to complain against vicious impulses he observes in others. Critiquing abuses at the court, the church, and

Anticlaudianus reinforces Martianus' personification of the arts and Minerva's role as *magistra artium liberalium*. Out of this tradition Nicolas de Orbellis, writing 1000 years after Martianus, composed the couplet with which I began this discussion of the arts: "*Gram* loquitur, *Dia* vera docet, *Rhet* verba colorat, / *Mus* canit, *Ar* numerat, *Ge* ponderat, *Ast* colit astra." Nicholas personifies the arts: each speaks, teaches, colors, sings, enumerates, considers, or contemplates as is appropriate to her discipline. This metaphorical way of viewing the liberal arts as active beings comes from Martianus' fantasy of the arts and Mercury's marriage to Philology. In their action, Nicholas' arts epitomize books three to nine of *De nuptiis* as well as serve as a student's mnemonic. Missing from the couplet, of course, is their *magistra*, Minerva herself. Like Nicholas de Orbilis, the anonymous poet who composed the Middle English *Court of Sapience* at about the same time in the mid-fifteenth century, draws on this scholarly and poetic tradition of personifying the arts, but he also includes their mistress Minerva in the poem's second book.

The Court of Sapience: A Fifteenth-Century Compendium of Learning

The poet of *The Court of Sapience* narrates an intellectual pilgrimage in the vein of twelfth-century philosophical poetry. E. Ruth Harvey, the poem's most recent editor, dates *The Court* to the middle third of the fifteenth century and characterizes it as encyclopedic, a poetic expression of a desire to encapsulate all knowledge.[69] Divided into two books, *The Court*, like *Reson and Sensuallyte*, is unfinished. The narrator recounts a dream in which he meets Dame Sapyence, learns of her most significant work through the "Four Daughters of God" story, and progresses to her home, where personifications of knowledge and virtue instruct him. Though the poem breaks off following Dame Hope's discourse, the poet evidently had in mind a larger plan. In the first prologue, after indicating the scope and subject of book one, the narrator states:

> Sone after this I shal Wysedom descryve,
> Her blessyd howshold, and her wonnyng place;
> And than retourne unto her actes blyve
> As she them wrought by tyme, processe, and space. (8–11)

Because lines 8–9 describe the subject of book two, we can speculate that lines 10–11 describe the subject of an intended third book. However, judging from manuscript

---

the schools, the poet satirizes twelfth-century culture until the hero arrives at Natura's abode, where he receives instruction in moral philosophy from ancient philosophers. Natura herself finally arrives and, after offering further instruction on the universe and marriage, matches him with Moderation, whom he marries at poem's end.

[69] Harvey, introduction to *The Court*, vii. Spindler's edition remains useful: he retains the Latin glosses in the text (Harvey notes them) and imitates Caxton's printed edition. Caxton's edition, of which three known copies exist (British Library; St. John's College, Oxford; John Rylands Library, Manchester), is also available in facsimile through EEBO's digitized microfilm of the British Library copy.

and print evidence, either the poet never completed this plan or the third book went missing.

Though incomplete, *The Court of Sapience* appealed to late medieval and early modern audiences. Its publication history, for instance, indicates a popularity that suggests early critical responses. Three of the poem's four manuscript copies date to the second half of the fifteenth century: British Library, Ms. Harley 2251 (ff. 287v–293v) and Cambridge, Trinity College Ms. R.3.21 (ff. 51–83) to the reign of Edward IV (1460–83); and Columbia University Library, Plimpton Ms. 256 to the last quarter of the century.[70] The fourth manuscript copy is in John Stowe's sixteenth-century compilation, British Library Ms. Additional 29729 (ff. 87–121v), which also includes the second known copy of *Reson and Sensuallyte*. Early manuscript association of the poem with Lydgate's poetry apparently codified for Stephen Hawes that Lydgate composed *The Court*: an assertion put to rest long ago.[71] Besides the four manuscript copies, two printed editions exist: Caxton's edition (*STC* 17015) printed between 1480 and 1483; and Wynken de Worde's 1510 edition (*STC* 17016), which closely follows Caxton's.[72] That Wynken de Worde reprinted the poem attests to its continued popularity in the early sixteenth century, likely reprinted in the wake of Hawes' 1509 *Pastime of Pleasure*.[73] This point leads to a second measure of early critical response to *The Court*: imitations it inspired such as Hawes' *Example of Virtue* and *Pastime of Pleasure*. Though popular in its day, *The Court of Sapience* has received little attention since the mid-sixteenth century.[74] Amid the paucity of criticism, it is not difficult to understand why Minerva's place in the poem remains unexamined, yet such an examination opens up the poem and presents an insight

---

[70] Harvey, introduction to *The Court*, x–xiii. See also Bühler, "Notes on the Plimpton Manuscript," 5–9.

[71] Hawes, *Pastime of Pleasure*, ed. Mead, 1357. In his edition of *The Court*, Spindler refuted Lydgate's authorship (46–105). Early attribution, however, emphasizes Lydgate's effect on later writers and compilers, who were quick to assign poems to him to increase his, and their own, authorial position. Interestingly, Stow also at one time owned Cambridge, Trinity College MS R.3.21, which he signed on folio 320v.

[72] Caxton used the five-stanza layout, apparently imitating the preferred fifteenth-century English and Scottish manuscript layout for poems written in rhyme royal evident in books like Cambridge, Corpus Christ College MS 61 and Oxford, Bodliean Library MS Arch. Selden. B.24. See Hodapp, "Visual Presentation," 238–49. De Worde's edition, on the other hand, evinces a shift away from this layout. See Harvey, introduction to *The Court*, xiii–xiv, for discussion of the printed editions.

[73] Wynkyn de Worde's 1510 edition offers evidence of early sixteenth-century interest. Perhaps the printer, seeing an opportunity following successful sales of Hawes' *Pastime*, brought out *The Court* as one of Hawes' sources much as contemporary publishers peddle Tolkien's sources, for instance.

[74] Modern critics predominantly concentrate on sources and on book one, in which Sapyence narrates the allegory of the "Four Daughters of God." On sources, see Bühler, *Sources of the* Court, 9; and Creek, "Four Daughters of God," 961–5. J. Murphy, "Caxton's Two Choices," 241–55, examines *The Court* as evidence of fifteenth-century attitudes towards rhetoric; H. Bennett, *Chaucer and the Fifteenth Century*, 154–5, sees it as encyclopedic; and Lewis, *Allegory of Love*, 262–4, praises its poetics.

into its appeal to fifteenth- and sixteenth-century audiences. In book two, Minerva represents wisdom gained through study of the arts, and the allegory represents the role the arts play as precursor to advanced studies in medieval curricula.

Dame Sapyence and the Four Daughters of God

While Minerva plays an important role in book two as *magistra artium liberalium*, Dame Sapyence is the unifying allegorical figure of the entire poem. Sapyence's role and wisdom illuminate Minerva's position in the poem and the educational wisdom she represents. As in *Reson and Sensuallyte*, Minerva does not directly address the narrator; rather, she indirectly communicates her wisdom in two distinct ways: through her iconography and through her relationships with other poetic figures, particularly Sapyence. Here, Sapyence represents the multi-layered medieval notions of divine wisdom we encounter in texts like Suso's *Horologium Sapientiae*, to which the poet may owe the use of dialogue between Sapyence and the narrator throughout and the idea of Sapyence's court in book two – a distinctive echo of Aeterna Sapientia's school in *Horologium* (2.1).

The narrator begins his account describing his pre-*somnium* psychological state before falling asleep, and in this description he presents the poem's central theme, the function of moral philosophy and knowledge in human life. He draws particularly on the Aristotelian division of practical philosophy into individual, economical, and political spheres. Fleeing "the stormy flode / Of fruteles worldly medytacyon" (71–2), the narrator went to bed one night but was unable to sleep because "thought" remained his guest.[75] Using chess as a "myrrour of polocye" (94) and, echoing Chaucer (*BD* 618–54), he describes how "in this bord eschekker of my mind" (106) Dame Fortune and the World had checkmated him. Reason came to the narrator and reproached him for playing the game with "moble Fortune and fals Worldlynesse" (114), whom no man can defeat.[76] Recognizing his dilemma, the narrator imitated Solomon, the biblical paragon of human wisdom, and prayed God to lead him to wisdom so that he might learn and practice discretion in his personal and public life; he then fell asleep.[77]

---

[75] Middle English "thought" – a descriptive word ubiquitous in English dream visions – carries several meanings, including sorrow, anxiety, and a state of anxiety or distress as well as vision, fantasy, remembrance, and more generally mental state. *MED*, "thought" 1.a.(c), 1.a.(f), 5.a, 5.b. When the narrator describes his condition using "thought," he implies a mental state we might call "the blues," "grief," "anxiety," or even "depression."

[76] Middle English "eschekker," or "cheker," comes from the Old French "éschequier," and has multiple meanings: a game board with sixty-four squares; a chess set; the game of chess or checkers; a checked design; a table covered with a checked cloth for counting money, counting table; the Crown's fiscal department; a register of accounts. *MED*, "cheker" 1.1a, b, c, 1.2.a; 2.1, 2.2. *The Court*-poet implies game and account, as well as politics and love, in his use of "eschekke" as a metaphor.

[77] In Wisdom, 9:1–5, the author prays: "Deus patrum meorum, et Domine misericordiae, qui fecisti omnia verbo tuo, et sapientia tua constituisti hominem, ut dominaretur creaturae, quae a te facta est, ut disponat orbem terrarum in aequitate et justitia, et in

The dream's opening stanzas mirror the narrator's pre-*somnium* state and represent allegorically his inability at the time to discern the good. Initially unable to see and terrified by pursuing wolves, he groped through a nightmarish landscape much as Gavin Douglas' poet-narrator would do in *Palice of Honoure*. A light eventually drew him onto a straight path and into a heavenly meadow with the fair river Quiet flowing through its middle. In this parallel to Dante's (1265–1321) opening canto of the *Inferno* and concluding cantos of the *Purgatorio*, the narrator met Dame Sapyence and her companions Dame Intelligence and Dame Scyence. Sapyence described herself as "the trewe propre knowlege certayne / Of ertheyly thyng, and eke of thyng dyvyne" and declared, "Though I seme yong, ful old my yeres bene" (157–8, 160). The narrator soon discovered that Sapyence, like himself, needed rest, having recently completed a great labor.

In addition to her name, Dame Sapyence's description immediately indicates her virtue and alliances with other literary wisdom figures including biblical Sapientia. Like Minerva in *Reson and Sensuallyte* and other texts, Sapyence is an "old woman and girl," an attribute suggesting her redemptive nature. Similarly, as a representative of divine and earthly knowledge, Sapyence is allied with those wisdom figures whose knowledge ranges the earth and reaches to the heavens, represented allegorically by their variable size. Finally, like biblical Sapientia, who invites the "parvulus" (little one) to her house in order to avoid the "illecebrae" (allurements) of the "mulier stulta" (foolish woman) (Prov. 9:4–17), Sapyence bid the narrator to leave "worldly occupacyon" and "duelle with me at home" (164). More able to distinguish the brightness of wisdom from the darkness of worldliness, the narrator then willingly offered his service and requested she tell him of her work. Assenting, Sapyence presented an allegory within the allegory – the Four Daughters of God story.

The Four Daughters allegory, popular in high to late medieval culture, parallels education's potentially restorative role, which Minerva *magistra artium liberalium* often represents. In a twelfth-century sermon on Psalm 84:11 ("Misericordia et veritas obviaverunt sibi: justitia et pax osculatae sunt" [Mercy and truth embraced each other; justice and peace kissed]), Bernard of Clairvaux personified Mercy, Truth, Justice, and Peace and wove an allegory of the fall and redemption.[78] The story recounts relationships between a father, his four daughters, his son, and a servant. The servant disobeys his master and, while Justice and Truth, two of the daughters,

---

    directione cordis judicium judicet: da mihi sedium tuarum assistricem sapientiam, et noli me reprobare a pueris tuis: quoniam servus tuus sum ego, et filius ancillae tuae, homo infirmus, et exigui temporis, et minor ad intellectum judicii et legum" (God of my fathers and Lord of mercy, You who made all things with your word and, by Your wisdom, established man so that he should have dominion over creation that was made by You; so that he should order the world in equity and justice and judge the sentence in straightness of heart: give me wisdom, standing by Your thrones, and do not reject me from your children: since I am Your servant, the son of Your handmaid, a weak man, and of short time, and weak in the understanding of judgment and laws).

[78] Bernard of Clairvaux, "In festo Annunciationis," ed. Migne, cols. 387–90. On the story in medieval culture, see Traver, *The Four Daughters of God*, and "Four Daughters of God," 44–92.

demand punishment, Mercy, a third, advocates on his behalf. In the subsequent row, the fourth daughter Peace leaves home unable to bear dissension, and four tormentors imprison the servant. After several thousand years, the son champions Mercy's cause, puts on the servant's clothes, defeats death, frees the servant, and returns victorious. Peace now returns because the son's actions satisfied her sisters. In addition to the highly popular Franciscan version of Bernard's allegory found in the *Meditationes vitae Christi*, the story attracted English playwrights and poets, including *The Court*-poet.[79] While retaining its outline, *The Court*-poet adds Sapyence's role and emphasizes the Trinitarian doctrine attributing Might to the Father, Wisdom to the Son, and Goodness to the Holy Spirit.[80] After the contention between the daughters, the Son called on Sapyence for counsel, who advised that, because the servant specifically offended the Wisdom of the Trinity, the Son was most suitable to redeem the servant. She then stated:

> "These sustres four who that shal pacyfye
> Must be the sone of man, and take mankynd,
> And for mannes gylt gyltles suffre to dye,
> And raunson man; than thynk I in my mynd,
> Syth but one Sone the Trynyte may find,
> Whiche Sone thou art, that by necessyte
> This solempne acte lyeth fynally in the." (561–7)

As she told the story to the narrator, Sapyence not only expressed first the plan for redemption, giving the Son the idea to offer Himself, but also began the process of restoring order both in heaven and on earth. This latter function mirrors the active role biblical Sapientia plays in ordering and maintaining the universe. Like her biblical counterpart, Sapyence in *The Court* performed her greatest work, what the poet calls "her moost notable cure" (4), by inspiring the Son, who saved the servant and restored peace.

In addition to characterizing Sapyence and emphasizing her role in the Redemption, book one serves an important function in the poet's larger plan, to which he alludes by introducing Dame Intelligence and Dame Scyence. The poet addresses three traditional aspects of wisdom: the wisdom of revelation, expressed in the Four Daughters allegory; the wisdom inherent in visible things, signified by Dame Scyence and familiar from Dame Nature's commission in *Reson and Sensuallyte*; and the wisdom inherent in speculation on invisible things, signified by Dame Intelligence. As Harvey suggests, Dame Sapyence has distinct connections with each

---

[79] *Meditations on the Life of Christ*, eds. Ragusa and Green, 6–9, and fig. 3; cf. Nicholas Love, *Mirrour of the Blessed Lyf*, ed. Hogg, 14–19. For Middle English narrative and dramatic adaptations, see Robert Grosseteste, *Chateau d'Amour*, or *The Castle of Love*, 275–554; William Langland, *Piers Plowman*, Passus 18.613–31; *The Castle of Perseverance*, 3129–649; and N-Town Cycle Play 11, 1–188.

[80] *Meditations on the Life of Christ*, 9, implies this doctrine: the Father is powerful; the Spirit, benign; the Son, a "median" between the two. *The Court* is closer to Nickolas Love, *Mirrour of the Blessed Lyf*, 18, who also includes Might, Wisdom, and Goodness as respective attributes of the Three Persons.

aspect of wisdom;[81] yet the poet considers revelation, which Sapyence alone signifies, to be wisdom's chief aspect in this poem. *The Court* recounts an intellectual pilgrimage to Sapyence's home beginning with the wisdom of revelation. Again, judging from the implied plan, the poet likely would have concluded *The Court* with revelation as well, thus rounding out his presentation. As a prominent member of Sapyence's court, and well within the Martianus tradition, Minerva represents the wisdom attained through study of the liberal arts. Though she makes only two appearances, her position in the poem and relation to other figures indicate she is a central allegorical figure in book two.

Minerva: Iconography and the Liberal Arts

The narrator opens book two invoking Minerva and alluding to her association with the liberal arts. After a Chaucer-like move requesting grace to avoid slander and to receive gratitude for his writing (*HF* 1.90–106), the narrator states:

> My style thou dresse, my langage thou depure,
> My wytte inforce, thou mynystre matere!
> For, syth I am moost symple creature,
> I nyl usurpe in thy palays t'apere
> But thou me guyde to shewe in what manere
> I shal pronounce thynges which thou dost me see;
> Thy refrendary only wyl I be.
>
> The pure knowlege and veray sentement
> Of thy wysedom was never my dower,
> But as the sonne, in lyght moost excellent,
> With his bemes the mone illumyneth clere,
> Soo done alday these wyse men fooles lere;
> Wherfor thy wysedom, as thou lust me teche,
> O lady myne, in my book wyl I preche. (911–24)

Again like Chaucer (*CT*, General Prologue 730–46), the narrator appropriates the role of reporter ("refrendary"), emphasizing this role through the rhetorical topos of affected modesty. His self-effacement accentuates Minerva as mistress of the arts: it is she who corrects his style, purifies his language, strengthens his wit, and furnishes the subject matter through her wise servants who, like the sun illuminating the moon, teach fools.

As book two proper begins, Sapyence repeated her invitation to the narrator, and they traveled in company to her home. When they proceeded onto the bridge spanning the river Quiet, the narrator read inscribed on a tower, "Who dredeth God, com in, and ryght welcome! / For drede of God is way of al wysedome" (944–5). Unlike the double message over Chaucer's gate in *The Parliament of Fowls*, this message is

---

[81] Harvey, introduction to *The Court*, xxvii.

clear.⁸² M. Smith argues that "Fear of the Lord," wisdom's most emphatic quality in the Bible, ennobles all other attributes of virtuous wisdom because it properly orients the creature to the Creator: "fear," in this context, means humble awe before the Otherness of God.⁸³ Similarly, it is the first of the seven gifts of the Holy Spirit, as reflected in the seven steps to wisdom that Augustine explicates in *De doctrina Christiana*. Armed with the proper attitude of wisdom, the narrator continued his journey and, for the next seventy-three stanzas, he details what he had observed: the various beautiful elements of the natural world, progressing up the chain of being from precious stones and flowers to trees, birds, and animals. Unlike the narrator in *Reson and Sensuallyte*, this narrator properly reads nature's beauty much in the way Suso's Sapientia instructs the Discipulus in *Horologium* (1.6 and 1.8), for Sapyence and "drede of God" guided him through the paradisal setting.

After traveling through the natural world, that is, Dame Scyence's arena and the second aspect of wisdom the poem examines, the narrator spied Sapyence's home. The poet reconstitutes biblical Sapientia's seven-pillared house (Prov. 9:1) as a medieval castle with seven towers – "The hyght of whiche astyed up to heven" (1477) – and a moat filled with water from the river Quiet. The castle was built upon a rock, an allusion to the wise man of the Gospel parable (Mt. 7:24–5) and to Jesus the living cornerstone (1 Peter 2:4–8), and elaborately decorated like a cathedral.⁸⁴ In an even closer echo of Chaucer, the castle gate had a second message, which read:

"This is the weye to vertu and to grace,
To connyng, knowledge, wyt, and al wysedome;
This is the wey unto that hevenly place
Ther storme ne stryfe, syn, vyce, ne evil may come;
This is the wey to that solempne kyngedome
Where rest, pees, blysse and comforte seceth never;
Come in who wyl, and ryght welcome forever!" (1492–8)

---

⁸² The double-message in *PF* reads:

"Thorw me men gon into that blysful place
Of hertes hele and dedly woundes cure;
Thorw me men gon unto the welle of grace,
There grene and lusty May shal evere endure.
This is the wey to al good aventure.
Be Glad, thow redere, and thy sorwe of-caste.
Al open am I; passe in, and sped the faste."

"Thorw me men gon," than spak that other side,
"Unto the mortal strokes of the spere,
Of which Disdayn and Daunger is the gyde,
There nevere tre shal fruyt ne leves bere.
This strem you ledeth to the sorweful were
There as the fish in prysoun is al drye –
Th'eschewing is only the remedye." (127–40)

⁸³ M. Smith, *Personification of Wisdom*, 6, 43–4.
⁸⁴ *The Court* seems to reverse dream images from Chaucer's poems: the court of Sapyence, not of Love or Nature; the house of Sapyence, firmly founded and well built, not of Fame, with its shaky foundations and flimsy structure.

This unambiguous message underscores the image of the seven-towered castle surrounded by water from the river Quiet. As with the earlier message on the bridge, this one reverberates with Augustine's presentation of the Holy Spirit's gifts, for his seventh step is wisdom itself, "qua pacatus tranquillusque perfruitur" (where one enjoys peace and tranquillity) (*De doctrina Christiana*, 2.7.11).

The narrator next met the seven virtues, each with seven attendants, Dame Theologye, in company with the seven liberal arts, and Dame Philosophy, with the seven sages. The dwelling had three courts: Dame Scyence's court, home of natural philosophy; Dame Intelligence's court, home of metaphysical philosophy; and Dame Sapyence's court, home of revealed and learned wisdom.[85] Minerva appeared in the latter court the second time, depicted on an "aras-werk in gold" (1737):

> And on the dayse Mynerve (that hyght Pallas)
> The goddesse of wysedom ful of all lyght
> On hevenly wyse portreyed and peynted was:
> A lady fayr, enarmed fresshe and bryght,
> Whoos hede was with the reynbowe bound and dyghte,
> A crest above, her ryght honde had a spere,
> The other syde a shyld of crystal clere;
>
> Her hede was ferful and eke monstruous
> For dyvers serpentes henge her hede aboute;
> Bryght eyen she had, and clothyng precious
> Of colours thre, delycyous and stoute;
> An olyve tree with braunches on a route,
> On whiche a nyght-crowe lustely was set
> Stode her besyde; it myght not be made bet. (1744–57)

Dame Sapyence glossed the portrait for the narrator: "'Thys is the goddesse of al wyt soverayne'" (1759), born of Jupiter's head, signifying "'That al wysedom commeth from God above / Whoome poetes clepen "Jubyter" and "Jove"'" (1763–4). The rainbow signified love and friendliness, and the crest, honor; the Gorgon's head represented fear of God, of death, and of the fiend's falsehood; the spear was correction and the shield, fortitude and patience; the olive tree represented peace while the owl ("nyght-crowe"), meekness and silence;[86] she had the eye of reason

---

[85] I suggested earlier a possible connection between Suso's *Horologium* and *The Court*. In Suso's text, the Discipulus has a vision of Aeterna Sapientia's school (2.1): a vast golden sphere adorned with gems and enclosing two mansions, one for liberal arts education and the other for theological study, over which Sapientia presides. The Discipulus studies the arts before proceeding to theology. The fifteenth-century French translation of *Horologium* in Brussels Royal Library MS IV III includes a half-page miniature depicting the school on fol. 90v. See Monks, *Brussels Horloge de Sapience*, 190–2, plate 28.

[86] The term "nyght-crowe" seems a literal rendition of the Latin *noctua* ("owl"). The twelfth-century monastic Hugh of Fouilloy distinguishes the *nycticorax* ("night raven") from the *bubo* ("owl"), giving the former a positive allegorical interpretation but the latter a negative one. *Aviarium*, ed. Clark, 39, 172–5 and 49, 216–19, respectively, and figs. 11, 12, and 46. By the late Middle Ages, however, bestiary writers equated *nycticorax* with the

and prudence, and the three colors of her clothing signified faith, hope, and charity (1758–78).

While much of this iconography is now familiar from the narrator's reading of Minerva in *Reson and Sensuallyte*, this passage integrates two additional iconographic details not already discussed: the olive tree and the owl. Aside from its significance glossed by Dame Sapyence, the owl, Fulgentius states, is Minerva's bird "quod saptientia etiam in tenebris proprium fulgorem possideat" (because wisdom also has its flash of lightning in darkness) (*Mit.* 2.1). Similarly, in his encomium to Minerva in *De nuptiis* Martianus combines the owl with the goddess' "Bryght eyen," connecting both with study in an image familiar to any scholar. He states:

> glaucam dant volucrem, quod lumina concolor igni es,
> tuque ignis flos es cluis et glaucopis Athene.
> an mage noctividae tibi traditur alitis usus,
> quod vigil insomnes ducat sollertia curas?

> (Artists give you the swift owl because you have bright eyes the color of fire, you are the peak of the flame and are called owl-eyed Athena. Or rather is the night-living bird given to you by custom because a study-vigil leads to sleepless efforts?) (6.571)

The olive tree comes from the story of the founding of Athens. Pallas Athena, contesting with Neptune over who should be the city's patron, presented Athens with the gift of an olive tree signifying peace: awarded the city, she named it for herself.[87] Both Fulgentius and Boccaccio connect the name *Athens* to immortality, "quia sapientia nec mori poterit" (because wisdom cannot die) (*Mit.* 2.1; *Teseida* 6.71). The olive tree, then, signifies not only peace but also wisdom's immortality, and the owl signifies not only meekness and silence but also wisdom's power to pierce darkness with its vision. The narrator acknowledges his debt to Fulgentius (1782) and invites the reader to turn to *Mitologiae*, where "shal he see whiche thyng I lete overgoo" (1785).[88]

---

owl, giving the latter positive allegorical attributes: "Nycticorax ipsa est noctua" (quoted in *Aviarum*, ed. Clark, n.1, 173).

[87] For medieval versions of this myth, see Remigius of Auxerre, *Commentum in Martianum*, 6.286.5, and Boccaccio's *Teseida*, 6.71.

[88] In several mythographies, Minerva's iconographic details evoke stories suggesting an ambivalent view of the goddess as well. Her association with Medusa offers a case in point: a rape victim of Neptune in Minerva's temple, Medusa seems further victimized by the goddess when Minerva first averted her gaze and then turned Medusa into a snaky-haired terror to punish the crime. Though Sapyence glosses the Gorgon's head as referencing "the parfyte drede / Of God, of deth, and of the highe falshede" (1768–9), readers of Perseus' account in Ovid, *Met.* 6.794–801, might also wonder at Minerva's justice. The Gorgon, however, remains associated with fear of the goddess even in Ovid, as Perseus glosses the tale "'nunc quoque, ut attonitos formidine terreat hostes, / pectore in adverso, quos fecit, sustinet angues'" (and now, so that she might frighten enemies dazed with terror, she wears the snakes that she made on her breast facing outward). *Met.* 6.802–3. The SVM, 50.6–7, for instance, reiterates this association, stating "Gorgonem huic addunt in pectore ut uir sapiens terrorem contra adversarios gestet in mente" (they

Sapyence's gloss of Minerva's birth fully armed from Jupiter's head, another detail important for understanding her wisdom, comes from overlapping interpretive strands in the mythographic and commentary traditions. One of the first interpretive strands in medieval mythography originates with Fulgentius, who states Minerva "de Iovis uertice natam dicunt, quia ingenium in cerebro positum sit" (was born from the head of Jove, they say, because intelligence is seated in the brain) (*Mit.* 2.1). Other mythographers repeat or elaborate Fulgentius' interpretation. For instance, while the First Vatican Mythographer simply repeats him (3.201.55–7), Bernard Silvestris expands Fulgentius in his *Aeneid* commentary by linking her origin to wisdom, saying "Minerva quasi media vel intima cogitatio est sapientia que in cerebro sedem habet" (Minerva, as if the middle or innermost thought, is wisdom which has its seat in the brain) (6.68). Pierre Bersuire (*De formis* 30) and Thomas Walsingham (*De archana deorum* 1.24.1) also link her birth with divine wisdom.

A related tradition developing the association between Minerva's and Sapientia's respective origins stems from Martianus Capella. In *De nuptiis*, as we have seen, Martianus hints at the fable of her origin when Minerva, descending from above, seems to rest on Jove's head while he and Juno confer about Mercury's marriage. Minerva then advises Jove from this position (1.39). Remigius of Auxerre states:

> Id est vertici Iovis, quia secundum fabulas de capite Iovis perhibetur fuisse nata. Quo figmento innuitur quia ex mente summi Dei sapientia progenita est. 'Ego,' inquit, 'ex ore Altissimi prodivi.' Nam et quod Pallas sine matre introducitur ostendit aeternam sapientiam non ex aliis exstantibus sed ex substantia Dei principium habuisse.

> (She is on Jove's forehead because according to fables it is asserted that she was born from the head of Jove, by which figment is signified that wisdom is begotten from the mind of the most-high God. She says, "I proceeded from the mouth of the Most High" [Ecclus. 24:5]. For the fact that Pallas was born without a mother demonstrates that eternal wisdom does not take its origin from other existences but from the substance of God.) (*Commentum in Maritianum*, 1.24.14)

Remigius adds the fable, implied in *De nuptiis*, to draw a connection between Minerva and Sapientia, and his reading influenced later interpreters. In particular, the Third Vatican Mythographer, though not commenting specifically on Martianus, repeats Remigius nearly verbatim when explaining the relationship between Minerva's birth and wisdom's divine origin (*De diis gentium*, 10.2). In another quite different commentary on this same passage from *De nuptiis*, Bernard Silvestris links the Capitoline trinity – Jove, Minerva, and Juno – with the Christian Trinity: "Hec ergo nomina trinitatis – pater, nois, anima mundi – ponit in aperto sermone philosophica pagina; in mistico autem Iovis est nomen divine potentie, Pallas divine sapientie, Iuno divine voluntatis" (Here, therefore, he places the names of the Trinity – Father, Noys, World Soul – in an open discourse on the philosophical page; in the

---

depict the Gorgon on her chest so that the wise man inspires in mind fear against his enemies).

mystical sense, however, Jove is the name of divine power, Pallas of divine wisdom, Juno of divine will) (*Commentary on Martianus*, 11.51–4). Bernard's commentary, like Remigius', illuminates Minerva's association with biblical Sapientia though without specifically addressing her origin. These two interpretive stems, growing from Martianus and Fulgentius, illuminate Sapyence's gloss in *The Court*: her explanation of Minerva's origin carries with it the full weight of medieval mythography and the Martianus tradition.

Positioned in the center of Sapyence's court, Minerva presided over the activities of the other figures the narrator encountered in this section of the poem. After describing her, the narrator examined the court's chapel and observed Dame Theologye, in company with Solomon, discoursing on holy Scripture and patristic texts. He then proceeded to examine the seven parlors adjacent to the court. In each he found one of the maiden liberal arts – Grammar, Dialectic, Rhetoric, Arithmetic, Geometry, Music, and Astronomy – discoursing on her subject. Historical figures famed for their connection to each particular art accompanied the maidens: he spied Cicero with Rhetoric (1919), Pythagoras with Arithmetic (1970), Euclid with Geometry (2015), Ptolemy with Astronomy (2199), and the like. While Dame Theologye's retinue echoes Suso's school of theology in the *Horologium* (2.1), the association of historical figures with each art comes from Martianus. When the tour of the liberal arts was complete, Dame Feyth led the narrator to her tower where she presented the articles of faith and her seven attendants sang a hymn of praise to God. The narrator then approached Dame Hope's tower where he similarly heard her discourse on hope and listened to her seven attendants sing God's praises. The poem breaks off at this point with a one-stanza summary of books one and two, but it seems the poet intended to continue with Charity. Minerva's tri-colored robe representing in this poem the three theological virtues (1777–8) – possibly following Bersuire's lead (*De formis* 31) – links her directly to Feyth, Hope, and Charity, the likely final stop on the virtues-leg of the tour.

Though she presides over all the activities of Sapyence's court, Minerva's central position is particularly significant in relation to the Martianus tradition. The catalog of poets whom the narrator observes attending Rhetoric, for instance, indicates that *The Court*-poet was familiar with both Bernard Silvestris' *Cosmographia* and Alan of Lille's *Anticlaudianus*, for he includes the poets by first name – "Alane, Bernard ..." (1932) – along with Prudentius among a list of classical authors (1931–2). The Latin gloss on this line in the Trinity College manuscript (possibly authorial) identifies Alane as "Alanus ab Insulis" and Bernard as "Bernardus Silvestris."[89] These textual references and interlinear glosses strengthen the intellectual and poetic relationship between *The Court* and its two twelfth-century predecessors, especially *Anticlaudianus*. While probably not a direct source for *The Court*-poet, Alan's allegory likely influenced his development of Minerva *magistra artium* as, in both poems, she influences the intellectual journey of the narrator or hero.

In addition to Minerva *magistra artium liberalium*, Martianus' *De nuptiis* gives

---

[89] See Harvey, introduction to *The Court*, 142; and Minnis, *Medieval Theory of Authorship*, xii.

another essential clue that aids in evaluating Minerva's wisdom in *The Court*. When Philology learns she is to wed Mercury, she attempts to ascertain if this will be a good marriage. She adds the numerical value of her name, four (the *quadrivium*), to that of Mercury's, three (the *trivium*), and arrives at seven, Minerva's number. Considering Philology (learning) coupled with Mercury (expression) equals Pallas (wisdom), Philology decides their marriage will be harmonious because seven, the heptad, is the only number in the series one through ten that is indivisible by two, three, four, or five; its parts demonstrate true proportion; and it represents celestial rationality (2.99–109). Arithmetica later echoes Philology, emphasizing Minerva's association with the number and underscoring her own relationship to the goddess:

> quid autem te, heptas, uenerandam commemorem? quae quod naturae opera sine feturarum contagione conformas, inter deos Tritoniae uirginis uocabulum possedisti. namque omnes numeri intra decadem positi aut gignunt alios aliisque gignunter aut procreantur: hexas, ogdoas, generantur tantummodo, tetras autem et creat et creatur, heptas uero quod nihil gignit, eo peruirgo perhibetur, sed quod a nullo nascitur, hinc Minerua est, et quod ex numeris tam masculinis quam femininis constet, Pallas uirago est appellate. nam ex tribus et quattuor septem fiunt

> (What things, now, shall I recount for honouring you, oh Heptad? Because you have fashioned nature's works without the touch of procreation, you have been given among the gods the name virgin Tritonia. For all other numbers placed within the dead either beget and are begotten by other numbers or produce other numbers: six and eight are only begotten; four, however, both creates and is created. But because seven begets no other number it is called virgin, because it is born from no number it is called Minerva, and because it consists of a masculine and a feminine number, it is named Pallas the female warrior. For seven comes to being from joining three and four) (7.738.)[90]

This explication of the heptad illustrates what Alan of Lille later calls Arithmetica's "secreta Minerue" (*Anticlaudianus* 8.291). Though the heptad alludes within *De nuptiis* to Minerva's role as *magistra artium liberalium*, the link in this passage between the heptad and creation also informs Natura's reading of Noys in *Cosmographia*, the creative wise "mens altissimi" (1.2.13.2), as "michi vera Minerva" (1.1.6). The

---

[90] Macrobius, citing the fable of her birth, also discusses Minerva's association with the number seven: "nulli enim aptius iungitur monas incorrupta quam uirgini. Huic autem numero, id est septenario, adeo opinio uirginitatis inoleuit ut Pallas quoque uocitetur. Nam uirgo creditur quia nullum ex se parit numerum duplicatus qui intra denarium coartetur, quem primum limitem constat esse numerorum; Pallas ideo quia ex solius monadis fetu et multiplicatione processit, sicut Minerua sola ex uno parente nata perhibetur" (for the incorrupt monad is joined to no number more than to the virgin. And for this number, that is, seven, the reputation of virginity has so grown that it is also called Pallas. Now, it is considered virgin because, when doubled, it produces from itself no number within ten, which establishes the first limit of numbers. It is Pallas, therefore, because it came forth as offspring only from the multiplication of the monad, just as Minerva alone is said to have been born of one parent). *In somnium Scipionis*, 1.6.10–11. See Remigius of Auxerre, *Commentum in Martianum*, 6.285.14, and the TVM, 10.2, for later discussions of seven and Minerva.

number seven, of course, is also central to *The Court*. It encompasses the totality of learning embodied in the liberal arts, the seven virtues, their seven attendants, and the seven sages the narrator encounters upon his arrival. Moreover, the dwelling itself, dominated by the seven towers derived from the pillars of biblical Sapientia's house, embodies in its architecture the wisdom the number represents, which, in Cassiodorus' scheme of the arts, is continuous, perpetual, and leads to eternal life.[91]

In this strongly Christian poem, Minerva's role as mistress of the arts suggests the poet knew the Martianus tradition well. Besides Clio, the muse of history whom the narrator invokes at the beginning of book one, the poet incorporates few other classical figures, and these are primarily planetary or stellar mentioned only in passing. Minerva, on the other hand, stands out as a poetic figure in book two. The invocation, her presiding position in the court, and her relation to the liberal arts and the number seven together indicate she is arguably the central allegorical figure of the second book next to Sapyence herself. As part of the Martianus tradition, Minerva is instrumental in the narrator's acquisition of wisdom's peace and tranquility. The pursuit of the intellectual perfection she represents here leads the narrator on a spiritual journey from "dredeful worldly occupacyon" to the peace of "wisdom of the spirit" – a path he must travel to reach divine wisdom in his effort to become a *novus homo* in the vein of Alan of Lille's *Anticlaudianus*.

John Skelton and *The Garland of Laurel*

Moving from *The Court of Sapience* to *The Garland of Laurel*, we shift from the efforts of an unknown poet to John Skelton, about whom in comparison we know a great deal. Considering the origin or occasion for each poem, we also shift from a general sense of time and place – mid-fifteenth-century England – to the more specific worlds of a 1490s provincial court and the 1520s Royal court and London printing scene. Skelton, whose professional and poetic career parallels somewhat his Scottish contemporary Gavin Douglas, was a priest, a Latin scholar, a laureate of

---

[91] Citing several biblical passages, including Proverbs 9:1, Cassiodorus opens book two of *Institutiones* with a discussion of the number seven, stating it signifies continuity and perpetuity. He then specifically links arithmetic with God, saying "Sic arithmetica disciplina dotata est, quando rerum opifex Deus dispositiones suas sub numeri, ponderis et mensurae quantitate, constituit ... Quapropter, opere Dei singularizato, magnificae res necessaria definitione conclusae sunt; ut sicut cum omni condidisse credimus, ita et quemadmodum facta sunt aliquatenus disceremus. Unde datur intelligi mala opera diaboli nec pondere, nec mensura, nec numero contineri: quoniam quidquid agit iniquitas, justitiae semper adversum est" (Thus, arithmetic is endowed with discipline since God the Creator established his orderly arrangements in quantity of number, weight, and measure ... On account of this disposition, God's singular and magnificent works are necessarily confined by definite limits so that just as we know he has created all things so may we discern in some measure the way they were made. Hence it is given to be understood that the evil works of the devil are not contained by weight or measure or number since whatever iniquity does is always opposed to justice). *Institutiones divinarum et humanarum, Praefatio*, cols. 1150–1.

three universities, and a poet attached to the courts of kings.⁹² *The Garland of Laurel*, first printed in 1523 by Richard Faques in London but composed in part during the final decade of the fifteenth century, illustrates Skelton's poetic process of continuous tinkering, revising, and adjusting, and his efforts to see his works into print.⁹³ Skelton is the earliest known living poet to be printed in England and, judging from the printing record, he worked with several printers at different times from Wynkyn de Worde and Richard Faques to John Rastall and Richard Pynson.⁹⁴ This evident interest in seeing works through the press and into readers' hands underscores a theme Skelton explores in a number of poems, including *The Garland*: the place of the poet and of poetry in society – in particular, his own.⁹⁵ In *The Garland*, Skelton examines this theme through an allegory of the relationship between wisdom and fame or notoriety, including a dialogue between Minerva (Pallas) and the Queen of Fame. This poem, in a sense, parallels Douglas' concerns in *Palice of Honoure*. Like Douglas' poem, *The Garland* is also Skelton's response to Chaucer's *House of Fame*; however, while recognizing Fame's fickle nature, the element of her personification Chaucer develops most fully, Skelton sees Fame's fickleness as less powerful than Chaucer does.⁹⁶ For Skelton, Fame's power is subject to forces outside her control and, though she may wish to eject the poet-narrator from her court, these forces thwart her ability to do so entirely in the audacious dream-fantasy Skelton imagines. Central to his claim to fame is his allegiance to Pallas as *magistra artium liberalium*.

Fame's limited power and Pallas' instrumental role in the dream narrative's action are first evident in their initial dialogue. The poem opens with the narrator describing a time when, musing on the heavens and on life's variableness, he leaned against an oak stump and – in true Macrobian fashion – had an enigmatic dreamlike experience "As one in a trance or in an ecstasy."⁹⁷ He spied a pavilion, inside which he observed "dame Pallas … / To whom supplied the royal Queen of Fame" (48–9):

---

92 Carpenter, *John Skelton*, 9–35; and Scattergood, *John Skelton*, 49–62, 127–39, 187–205. For reviews of Skelton scholarship, see J. Griffiths, *John Skelton and Poetic Authority*, 1–3, and Tonry, "John Skelton," 721–36.
93 Gingerich and Tucker, "Astronomical Dating," 207–20, first posed dating the poem to the 1490s based on astronomical reference, and Tucker, "Ladies in Skelton's 'Garland'," 333–45, further argued for an early date based on additional biographical and textual details. See also Boffey, "'Withdrawe Your Hand'," 73–6, who reviews recent scholarship on dating the poem, and J. Griffiths, *John Skelton and Poetic Authority*, 27–8 and n.30, who reviews its printing history. A facsimile of the British Library's copy of the 1523 edition is available on EEBO.
94 A. Edwards, "Circulation of English Verse," 70–2, and "Skelton's English Poems," 87–100.
95 A. Gillespie, "Caxton and the Invention of Printing," 23–8; Hasler, *Court Poetry*, 145–67; Lerer, *Chaucer and His Readers*, 176–80, 193–208; Scattergood, *John Skelton*, 356–75.
96 Skelton's engagement with Chaucer's *HF* has drawn critical comment. See Boffey, "'Withdrawe Your Hand'," 73–6; Ebin, *Illuminator, Makar, Vates*, 182–7; and Scattergood, "Skelton's *Garlande*," 122–38. For Skelton and medieval-modern periodization, see Breen, "Laureation and Identity," 347–62.
97 Skelton, *Book of the Laurel*, ed. Brownlow, 37. Macrobius, *In somnium Scipionis*, 3.1–20, classifies five types of dreams: *somnium* (enigmatic), *visio* (prophetic), *oraculum* (oracular),

Prynces moost pusaunt, of higth prehemynence,
Renowmmyd lady above the starry heven,
Alle other transcendinge of verey congruence:
Madame Regent of the Scyence Sevene,
To whos astate alle nobilnes most lene:
My supplicacioune to yow I arrecte,
Where of I beseke yow to tender the effect.

Not unremembred it is unto your grace
How ye yave me in roialle commaundment
That in my cowrte Skelton shuld have a place
By cause that his tyme he studiowsly hath spent
In your servyce: and to the accomplishment
Of your request, regesterd is his name
Withe Laureate Tryumphe in the Courte of Fame. (50–63)

Drawing on the tradition of Minerva *magistra artium liberalium* and her subsequent association with biblical Sapientia, Skelton presents a Pallas who, far from allying herself with Fame, rather had ordered the fickle goddess to admit the poet into her court. Though Fame "regesterd … his name" she remained unconvinced he belonged and wished to eject him for three reasons: Skelton was slothful, producing little; he failed to advocate for himself through his works as was ancient custom; and he had not worked "to purchase / The favour of ladys with wordis electe" (75–6). Later, citing Plato, Aristotle, Diogenes, and Aeschines among others, Fame particularly reiterated Skelton's lack of output as reason to excise his name from her roll. In response, Pallas challenged Aeschines' place in Fame's court, caught the goddess in a logical fallacy, charged her with fickleness, and stated:

For if ye laude hym whome honor hathe opprest,
Then he that dothe worst / is as goode as the best.

Bot whome that ye favor I se wele hathe a name
Be he never so litille of substance,
And whome ye love not ye wold put to shame:
Ye counterway not evynly youre balaunce:
As wele foly as wisdome ofte tyme ye avaunce. (174–80)

Pallas advocated for Skelton based on his service (he was, after all, once tutor to Prince Henry in addition to being laureate),[98] but Fame demanded documentation of his worthiness. Having earlier remarked on the lasting nature of writing, observing "'Beware, for wrytyng remayneth of recorde, / Displease not an hundreth for one mannes pleasure / Who wryteth wisely hath a grete treasure'" (89–91), Pallas assented and ordered Fame to summon a company of poets "'To se if Skelton dare put hym self in prece'" (239). Immediately, in a distinct echo from the *House of*

---

insomnium (nightmare), and *visum* (apparition). The first three are reliable, leading to divination; the last two are worthless.

[98] He even wrote a *speculum principis*, ed. Salter, for Henry when he was the Prince's tutor.

Fame, Eolus let out a horn blast, and a raucous crew rose up and sought Fame, each putting himself forward in a cacophony of shouts and shoves until a second blast from Eolus shivered them all to silence. This second blast also summoned the college of poets led by Orpheus and Amphion, whose harmonious song caused the oak trees to dance, including the narrator's oak stump. It jarred the narrator into action as well, who until this moment had remained leaning on the stump listening and observing but otherwise disengaged. He now "sprange up towarde the tent / Of noble Dame Pallas" (283–4) to where the college of "a thousand poetes" (286) approached.

Though silent for the next several stanzas, Pallas and Fame remained present for much of what followed. Phoebus, the college's laurel-headed lead poet, delivered a love complaint – the first embedded lyric in the narrative – in which he declared the origin of the poet's laurel, saying "'in remembraunce of Daphnes transformacyon / All famous poetis ensuying after me / Shall were a garlande of the laurel tre'" (320–2). The poet-narrator then catalogues classical and medieval poets he saw present, beginning with Quintiliane, Theocritus, Esiodus (Hesiod), and Homerus. Some nine stanzas later, he spied Gower, Chaucer, and Lydgate, who approached, embraced, and addressed him, each declaring Skelton's worthiness to be among them. Lydgate, in particular, declared that, on behalf of his fellow poets, "'I poynt yow to be prothonotory / Of Famys courte by alle oure hole assent, / Avaunsid by Pallas to laurelle preferment'" (432–4). Lydgate's reference to Pallas – presumably within earshot of the goddess – resonates with her as mistress of the arts, signaling that the college of poets was allied primarily to her rather than to Fame. The three English poets then led the reluctant poet-narrator to Pallas, who ordered the three to lead him to Fame's palace to prepare for his meeting with the fickle goddess. Next thing he knew, he arrived at Fame's palace where Occupacyon gave him a tour of the grounds and led him to the Countess of Surrey's chamber "at the heart of the poem," as Julia Boffey notes.[99] The Countess and her ladies-in-waiting proceeded to embroider a garland of laurel while Skelton – at Occupacyon's prompting – composed a set of thank you poems: eleven lyrics embedded in the narrative set to praise each lady in turn. Before commencing his compositions, however, the poet-narrator invoked Minerva "to vowche save me to enforme and ken" (825) and Mercury "To gyde and to governe my dredefulle tremlyng fyst" (828). Implied in this reference to the goddess is, again, her role as *magistra artium*: especially in conjunction with Mercury as god of eloquence. The poet-narrator's allegiance to Minerva mirrored that of his fellow poets, it inspired him to weave himself another kind of laurel crown – the chaplet of lyrics praising the ladies – and it protected him ultimately from Fame's fickleness. Noting Eolus' blast summoning the poet-narrator, Occupacyon punctuated his final poem, saying "'Withdrawe your hande'" (1080), and commanded him to "'Set on your hede this laurel whiche is wrought'" (1081): Gower, Chaucer, and Lydgate then led him to Fame's court to answer the Queen's summons.

Moving to resolution in a scene not unlike the trial scene in *The Palice of Honoure*, the end of Skelton's dream underscores the Queen of Fame's limited power. It also

---

[99] Boffey, "'Withdrawe Your Hand'," 77.

emphasizes Skelton's comic attitude towards fickle notoriety and what seems an underlying trust of a fame based in Pallas' wisdom, that is, knowledge and skill developed through liberal learning. As she did earlier in the dream, Fame again resisted claims on her when Gower, Chaucer, and Lydgate presented the poet-narrator crowned with the laurel made by the Countess of Surrey and company. Skeptically Fame demanded Occupacyon to enumerate from her "'boke of remembraunce'" (1143) his poetic efforts, declaring "'Let se now for hym how ye kan expownde, / For in oure courte ye wote wele his name kan not ryse / Bot if he wright oftener than onys or twyse'" (1147–9). Skelton undercuts Fame, here, for readers have just observed the poet-narrator compose nearly a dozen poems, far more than the one or two Fame expected. Occupacyon then cataloged Skelton's extensive "workkis" (1164–1497), concluding with *The Garland* itself. This final move – "a logical and chronological impossibility," as Jane Griffiths observes[100] – is audacious, ironic, and humorous in one, for his nearly overwhelming list of works indicating he has indeed written "oftener than onys or twyse" ends with the poem itself that lists his works. And the poem's Latin glosses at this point, quoting poets from among the college of poets as a type of marginal *florilegium*, further contextualize Skelton's works within poetic tradition.[101] The dream closes in a raucous round of acclaim in response to Occupacyon naming the laurel of poems embedded in the narrative. The narrator states:

Bot when of The Laurelle she made rehersalle,
Alle orators and poetis, with other grete and smalle,

A thowsand thowsand, I trow to my dome,
Triumpha, triumpha! they criyde alle abowte:
Of trumpettis and clariounis the noyce went to Rome:
The starry heven, me thowght, shoke with the showte:
The grownde gronid and trembild, the noyce was so stowte:
The Quene of Fame commaundid / shett fast the boke,
And there withe sodenly owte of my dreme I woke. (1497–505)

Though Fame herself sought to refuse Skelton the dreamer his place in her court, the numerous poets and orators constituting that court overturned her desires: her only recourse was to command "shett fast the boke." Fickle Fame was powerless in the face of Pallas' wisdom and the poets' overwhelming acceptance of Skelton, and she herself knew it, for earlier she admonished the poet's attempt to erase a work from his list, saying "whatso in this place / Of our noble courte is ones spoken out / It must needs after run all the world about" (1475–7). The word was out. All she

---

[100] J. Griffiths, *John Skelton and Poetic Authority*, 31.
[101] J. Griffiths states: "Claiming Skelton's works as part of a long tradition, the glosses become part of the way in which the poem establishes an opposition between the writer and the court [i.e., the corrupt court emblematized in *The Bowge of Court*]. Quotations from established *auctores* surround Skelton's works on the page just as their fictional selves surround and support the narrator. It swiftly becomes apparent that their support is contextual as well as visual." *John Skelton and Poetic Authority*, 118.

could do was order the book closed, leaving Skelton and his readers with minds "sumdele amasid" (1506) by the sound of his triumph.[102]

Yet, at poem's end, it seems, neither Fame nor the poet-narrator has her or his way completely. Fame sought to exclude the poet-narrator, and in the end seems to have failed to keep him out, but in the world of the poem she never assented to his presence at the court; rather, she did what many in power-positions do: simply closed the book. Like Chaucer and Dante, Skelton locates himself as poet-narrator in the company of poets from the past, but he does so through the fantasy acclamation of the poets themselves, thereby seeking to bridge classical and English traditions, as Breen concludes.[103] As a poet creating a dream world, however, he also seems fully aware of the situational irony into which he writes himself. Exploiting its comic possibilities, he creates a shy, self-effacing, and somewhat befuddled beneficiary of Pallas' advocacy, the Countess of Surrey's laurel, and the college of poets' praise who also bears his name and authored his works. The poet-narrator of *The Garland* is not so much John Skelton *orator regius* and *poet laureate* bent on securing patronage as he is Skelton's artful verbal construction: a poet-narrator "sumdele amasid" by the whole experience and not quite sure what it all meant.[104] Skelton the poet, however, composer of this fantastic response to Chaucer's dream poem, does not seem concerned merely with the notoriety of fame or with a gift of fortune in the Boethian sense. Rather, he seeks a fame grounded in a life of wisdom represented by mastery of the arts: the fame of a poet who lives on in his poetry, as do Gower, Chaucer, Lydgate, and the college of poets to which the poet-narrator is elected at dream's end. He must have known full well that determining such longevity was not up to him, for his Fame remains ever reluctant, thoroughly skeptical, and entirely capricious. No, his best chance was to throw in with Minerva *magistra artium liberalium* as poets before him did: to deploy liberal learning in an effort to establish a lasting fame within the context of a body of knowledge handed down within the Martianus tradition.

Although scholars do not consider Martianus' *De nuptiis* a direct source of either Skelton's *Garland of Laurel* or the anonymous *Court of Sapience*, both poets write within the Martianus tradition exemplified by the anonymous *Methamorphosis*

---

[102] Skelton's version of Chaucer's *HF* probably included Caxton's appended conclusion to the poem, which likewise ends with clamor awaking the dreamer immediately following the comic moment "lysing" and "soth sawe" (*HF* 2089) became stuck at a window, each trying to exit Fame's house. Caxton's conclusion cuts off the poem's final sixty-four lines and fragmented ending found in modern editions. Examining this conclusion, Haydock, "False and Sooth," 107–27, suggests that the print shop becomes a diligent version of Fame's house, ensuring an afterlife for poems and poets like Chaucer. Something similar might be argued for Skelton joining with the press to thwart fame's fickleness by printing both his poetry and the catalog of his poems listed in *The Garland*, though see Lerer, *Chaucer and His Readers*, 193–208, for discussion of Skelton's emphasis on oratorical performance.

[103] Chaucer, *TC* V.1791–2; Dante, *Divine Comedy: Inferno*, ed. Singleton, 4.78ff; Breen, "Laureation and Identity," 362–3.

[104] J. Griffiths, *John Skelton and Poetic Authority*, 18–37.

Golye episcopi, Alan of Lille's *Anticlaudianus*, and other poems. Just as *The Court*-narrator sought to leave "dredeful worldly occupacyon," Skelton's poet-narrator was troubled by life's variable nature. For *The Court*-poet, the answer to life's flux lies in the renewal and reformation Minerva's learning represents: Alan's *novus homo* that a journey through study to divine wisdom helps bring about. Skelton, on the other hand, deploys Pallas' learning for a different though fundamentally similar end. For Skelton, liberal learning exercised well leads to literary production – as Pallas said, "'Who wryteth wysely hath a grete treasure'" (91) – which in turn can lead to lasting fame grounded in the poetic inheritance acclaimed by the college of poets. Engaging the Martianus tradition, both poets explore the potential for transcendence to which learning, as understood within that tradition, might lead. This connection with Martianus' text might explain their respective post-sixteenth-century fortunes. Each poet composed his poem near what was to be the end of medieval culture and education in England. Similarly, Martianus, too, composed *De nuptiis* near the end of Greco-Roman culture as he knew it. In all three cases, each author articulated a particular view of the world and of education and its effects. However, *De nuptiis*, unlike *The Court* and *The Garland*, benefited from a culture that sympathetically assimilated it, breathing new life into the text as the text itself helped shape the medieval curriculum. Though *De nuptiis* enjoyed interest for about 1000 years and *The Court* and *The Garland* both held an appeal for some 100 years, all suffered similar fates after the sixteenth century.[105] Yet, when approached through Minerva *magistra artium liberalium*, they illuminate the cultures in which they flourished and are illuminated themselves.

[105] Concerning *De nuptiis*' post-medieval reception, see Stahl, *Martianus Capella*, 74–6.

4

The *Patrona* Tradition: Minerva as Protectress and Benefactor

The image of Minerva *patrona*, protectress and benefactor, is rooted in Greco-Roman culture much as Minerva *magistra artium liberalium*. As *patrona*, however, Minerva directly enters the political arena, manifesting in two key ways: patroness of the city-state and patroness of the prince. Greco-Roman stories of her patronage of city-states take three forms: her contest with Neptune over who would name Athens and be its chief benefactor, a role she secured with the gift of an olive tree; her protection of Troy in the form of the Palladium, with which Troy would never fall and without which it could never stand; and her ongoing protection of Rome, the new home of the Palladium, and by extension the Republic and subsequently the Empire. We see this role expressed generally in the brief Homeric hymn 11, where the poet invokes her as protectress of city and army in a prayer for future success (11.1–5). Her patronage of the prince, on the other hand – a sort of political microcosm of her macrocosmic protection of the state – is perhaps most familiar from Pallas Athena's role in the Homeric corpus. Again, as noted earlier, in the *Iliad* she takes a particular interest in Diomedes and Odysseus during their night raid on the Thracian camp, counseling moderation that leads to military success and personal survival (10.503–14).[1] And her direct interventions in the *Odyssey* – supporting

---

[1] Athena *patrona principis* helped Odysseus and Diomedes throughout the "Doloneia," book ten of the *Iliad*. Before their reconnaissance mission, both prayed to her for aid (277–94). Then, when chasing Dolon, whom Hektor had sent to spy on the Greeks, Athena infused Diomedes to catch the fleeing Trojan (365–8). After interrogating and executing Dolon, they stripped his body, and Odysseus offered the spoils to Athena in prayer (458–68). Later in the Thracian camp, as already noted, Athena intervened directly with Diomedes, counseling moderation as bloodlust threatened to overcome him (509–11). And, upon returning to the Greeks, they punctuated the experience with ritual cleansing and an offering to the goddess. In contrast, greed motivated Dolon, who confirmed from Hektor the promise of Achilles' chariot and horses as payment for undertaking his reconnaissance mission (319–32). Conspicuously, Dolon offered no prayer to Pallas Athena or any deity. Virgil's imitation of the "Doloneia" in the *Aeneid* 9.176–502 seems a response to Homer. Here, Nisus and Euryalus, ostensibly sent at night by Ascanius to retrieve the absent Aeneas when the Latins besieged the Trojan camp, got caught up rather in slaughtering and despoiling intoxicated Latins. Nowhere do they invoke Minerva's protection or guidance, and their greed and bloodlust betray them. Failing to elude capture, they fail in their mission to retrieve Aeneas.

Telemachos in his journey to seek his father and Odysseus in his return to Ithaka (passim) – help restore familial and political order to Odysseus' society. Writing circa 468 BCE, Aeschylus in the *Oresteia* offers yet another instance of her patronage of a prince when the goddess directly aids Orestes' cause by establishing the *areopagus* and placating the Erinyes with a new home near Athens (*Eumenides* 397–1031). As these stories suggest, her patronage of the prince, who under her tutelage rightly orders himself and performs his duties, can by extension affect the order of society as well. Though medieval writers exhibit interest in her patronage of city-states, they seem particularly keen on her involvement with princes. In this chapter, I explore Minerva as protectress and benefactor by first reviewing instances of the goddess' patronage of specific princes evident in Roman literature. This work offers a basis for exploring similar instances in medieval literature from Walter of Châtillon's *Alexandreis* to Christine de Pizan's *L'Epistre d'Othea*. I then turn to her appearance in two English poems: Stephen Hawes' *Example of Vertu* and the *Pastime of Pleasure* published in the first decade of the sixteenth century. As *patrona principis*, Minerva represents the wisdom one develops and uses in diplomatic and strategic interactions with others, prudence in addressing issues of justice and of peace. In Hawes' model, this wisdom underscores Christian knighthood exemplified by the prudent prince.

Minerva *Patrona* in Roman Literature

Writing in the first quarter of the second century CE, the Roman historian Suetonius (c.69–c.122) offers in *De vita Caesarum* a series of twelve biographies profiling Roman emperors from Julius Caesar (100–44 BCE) to Domitian (51–96 CE). In his profile of Domitian, who ruled from 81 to 96 CE, Suetonius notes the Emperor not only restored the Capitolium temple after fire had destroyed it but also regularly wore "coronam auream cum effigie Iovis ac Iunonis Minervaeque" (a golden crown with images of Jove, Juno, and Minerva) while attending games dedicated to the deities.[2] Domitian's devotion to the Capitoline triad centered especially on Minerva, for whom he also built two other temples, founded a college of priests, and established the Alban poetry contest to honor the goddess during her annual festival, the *Quinquatrus*.[3] Surviving coins from Domitian's reign on which an image of Minerva is cast opposite that of the Emperor underscore his devotion to the goddess.[4] Though as J.P. Sullivan notes it is difficult to know why Domitian chose Minerva as protectress,[5] one possible answer suggests itself from Greco-Roman mythology: her role as *patrona principis*. Minerva's direct interest in the political realm, and by extension the prince, manifests in Greek mythology, where she appears as Pallas Athena. These myths influence Roman poets, who integrate the goddess *patrona* in their own stories, where Minerva cares particularly for a number of princes.

[2] *De vita Caesarum*, *Domitian*, ed. Rolfe, 4.4.
[3] Quintilian, *Inst. ora.*, 10.1.91; Suetonius, *Dom.* 4.4; K. Coleman, "Emperor Domitian and Literature," 3095–111; Girard, "Domitien et Minerve," 233–44; B. Jones, *Emperor Domitian*, 100; Newlands, *Statius' Silvae*, 54–5; Sullivan, *Martial*, 138, 144.
[4] Moraweicki, "Symbolism of Minerva," 185–93.
[5] *Martial*, 144.

One of the older myths involving Minerva *patrona* centers on Cadmus founding Boeotia and the city of Thebes. As Ovid recounts the tale in *Metamorphoses* (3.1–137), King Agenor of Tyre sent his son Cadmus to search for his daughter Europa, whom Jove in the form of a white bull had seized (2.836–75). Unable to find his sister, Cadmus suffered exile by his father's decree and wandered until he arrived at Delphi, where Apollo told him to end his rootless journey by following a white heifer that would show him where to establish a new home. Doing as advised and finding the place – the future site of Thebes – Cadmus prepared a sacrifice to Jove when his companions were attacked and killed by a huge serpent, which he in turn killed in fierce combat. While he caught his breath and gazed on the dead serpent, a disembodied voice struck him with paralyzing fear, saying "'quid, Agenore nate, peremptum / serpentum spectas? et tu spectabere serpens'" (why, o child of Agenor, do you gaze on the slain serpent? You, too, shall become a serpent to gaze on) (3.97–8). The narrator continues,

> ille diu pavidus pariter cum mente colorem
> perdiderat, gelidoque comae terrore rigebant:
> ecce viri fautrix superas delapsa per auras
> Pallas adest motaeque iubet supponere terrae
> vipereos dentes, populi incrementa futuri
>
> (Trembling he stood a long time, his face drained of color, heart shaking, and hair standing on end in chilled terror: then behold the man's patroness, Pallas, descending from the upper air stood near and bid him to sow the serpent-teeth in plowed earth, the foundation of a future people) (3.99–103)

Combat-weary, entirely alone, and frightened by a prophetic voice he likely did not understand, Cadmus seemed at a loss until Minerva "fautrix" (patroness) coached him back into action. Again doing as a deity bid, he planted the serpent's teeth and witnessed an army of brothers, born of his labor, fight to the death until only five remained. Finally, Minerva intervened a second time, inspiring Echion – one of the five – to drop his weapons and seek peace with the remaining four (126–8): enthused by Minerva, these five in turn helped Cadmus secure a new home for himself and others by founding Thebes.

Cadmus' adventure founding Thebes illustrates the basic pattern of Greco-Roman stories in which Minerva *patrona principis* plays an important supporting role. The hero facing a challenge finds himself at a crucial moment of decision. While he considers the situation, Minerva appears in the guise of a disembodied voice or thought, as with Diomedes in the *Iliad* (10.503–14); in the guise of another person, as with Telemachos when she disguised herself first as Mentes (*Odyssey* 1.105–324) and then as Mentor (*Odyssey* 2.267–3.373); or in her own guise, as we have just seen with Ovid's Cadmus. Through this epiphany, the goddess directly intervenes, guiding or protecting the hero who resolves the situation with thought and action.[6]

---

[6] In epic and elsewhere, an epiphany is a manifestation or appearance of a divine or superhuman being. See Risden, *Heroes, Gods and the Role of Epiphany*, 9–36, for an overview.

A number of these stories reinforce or lend certain elements to Minerva's iconic attributes. The goddess' half-brother Perseus, for instance, relied on Minerva at key moments in his adventures before establishing the first Danaan dynasty in Argos. Chief of these adventures was his defeat of the Gorgon Medusa, whose gaze petrified living creatures and whose snaky-haired head became part of Minerva's iconography. Challenged by Polydectes of Seriphus to bring him Medusa's head, Perseus enlisted the aid of Mercury and Minerva. As Perseus himself told her tale in Ovid's *Metamorphoses* (4.793–801), Medusa was once beautiful with many suitors until Neptune ravished her in Minerva's temple. The ever-chaste goddess averted her gaze from the act but later punished the Gorgon for violating her temple by changing Medusa's hair into snaky locks: "'nunc quoque,'" as Perseus continued, "'ut attonitos formidine terreat hostes, / pectore in adverso, quos fecit, sustinet angues'" (and now, so that she might terrify her thunderstruck enemies with fear Minerva sustains upon her breast the snakes she made) (802–3). As Lucan (39–65 CE) recounts Perseus' Medusan adventure in *De bello civili*, Minerva's active support was crucial to the hero's success.[7] Armed with Mercury's scimitar and winged sandals, and Minerva's bronze shield, Perseus flew backwards to Medusa's abode, coached by his half-sister to use the shield as a sort of rear-view mirror to avoid the Gorgon's direct gaze. Once there, he approached the sleeping Medusa with trepidation. Lucan's narrator continues: "Ipsa regit trepidum Pallas dextraque trementem / Perseos aversi Cyllenida derigit harpen, / Lata colubriferi rumpens confinia colli" (Pallas herself ruled the jumpy, gaze-averted Perseus, and her right hand directed Mercury's shaking scimitar, cutting through the broad confines of Medusa's snaky neck) (9.675–7). In Ovid's earlier version of the story (*Met.* 4.609–5.249), which focuses on the aftermath of his Medusan adventure, Perseus found himself in three more difficult situations: freeing Andromeda from a sea monster (4.669–734), after which he offered sacrifice to Jove, Mercury, and Minerva (4.753–6); defending himself at his wedding feast from Phineus' jealous attack (5.1–235), at which "bellica Pallas adest et protegit aegide fratrem / datque animos" (warlike Pallas was present, protected her brother with the aegis, and gave him courage) (5.46–7); and establishing with Andromeda the Danaan line in Argos and slaying Polydectes of Seriphus (5.236–49). "Hactenus," Ovid's narrator concludes, "aurigenae comitem Tritonia fratri / se dedit" (in all of these adventures, Minerva presented herself as companion to her gold-begotten brother) (5.250–1).

Minerva *patrona principis*, evident in the Homeric corpus and in these two foundation stories of Thebes and of the Danaan line, surfaces with other heroes as well. In the *Thebaid*, for instance, Statius' (c.45–c.96 CE) version of the Seven against Thebes story, Minerva particularly takes the side of Tydeus, Polynices' brother-in-law. Though initially at odds, Tydeus and Polynices became friends in the house of their mutual father-in-law Adrastus, King of Argos: a friendship serving as foil to Polynices and Eteocles' fratricidal relationship. Early in the epic, after Eteocles refused Polynices his turn on the throne of Thebes, Tydeus approached Eteocles

---

[7] *De bello civili*, ed. Houseman, 9.619–99.

on embassy to explore a peaceful resolution, which Eteocles refused outright. After Tydeus left Thebes, Eteocles rashly sent fifty men to ambush him on the road, all but one of whom died at Tydeus' hands. Flushed with battle rage and covered in gore, Tydeus would have returned to Thebes showing his triumph, Statius' narrator states,

> ... ni tu, Tritonia virgo,
> flagrantem multaque operis caligine plenum
> consilio dignata virum: 'sate gente superbi
> Oeneos, absentes cui dudum vincere Thebas
> annuimus, iam pone modum nimiumque secundis
> parce deis: huic una fides optanda labori.
> Fortuna satis usus abi'.

(if you, Tritonian virgin, had not thought it worthy to counsel the man, enflamed and oppressed by the blinding fog of war: "enough, offspring of proud Oeneos, to whom I just granted victory while Thebes was absent; mark out now an end and spare the too favourable gods; you ought wish only that this feat be believed; Fortuna has been used enough – go".)[8]

Much as with Cadmus, Minerva intervened after battle, counseling the prince to prudent action. In this prequel-like event, both anticipating and repeating his son Diomedes' experience with the goddess in the *Iliad*, Tydeus regained his senses, spared the lone survivor Maeon, and charged him to return to Thebes with news of this battle and a message to prepare for war.[9] He then offered the spoils of the combat to Minerva before returning to Argos.

In a similar way, Minerva on occasion watches over Theseus, legendary leader of Athens. Statius, for instance, concludes the *Thebaid* with Theseus defeating Creon in battle and restoring the dead – Tydeus included – to their families: that portion of the story familiar to medievalists through Boccaccio's *Teseida* and Chaucer's Knight's Tale. Just prior to the poem's final battle, after Theseus had verbally confronted Creon, Statius' narrator notes:

> ipsa metus Libycos servatricemque Medusam
> pectoris incussa movit Tritonia parma.
> protinus erecti toto simul agmine Thebas
> respexere angues

---

[8] *Thebaid*, ed. Shakleton Bailey, 2.684–90.
[9] The *Thebaid* recounts events happening a generation prior to those of the *Iliad*. In that sense, Tydeus' actions and relationship with Minerva anticipate his son Diomedes' subsequent engagement with the goddess. Within the context of literary history, however, the reverse is true. Writing eight or nine centuries after the Homeric corpus was written, Statius likely shaped Tydeus based on Homer's account of Diomedes, who recounts his father's adventure at Thebes in his prayer to Athena (*Iliad* 10.285–90). Lewis, *Allegory of Love*, reads this moment in *Thebaid* as allegory, noting Minerva is "undisguisedly a state of Tydeus' mind" (52). Feeney, *Gods in Epic*, 365–7, on the other hand, argues she is more than allegory alone if we consider the whole scene.

(striking her shield, Tritonia herself roused the Libyan menace, Medusa, protectress of her heart; immediately, the serpents stirred into action, turned as one like a herd to gaze on Thebes) (12.606–9)[10]

Minerva is certainly on Theseus' side here. Ovid, too, notes the goddess' particular protection of Theseus in that part of the *Metamorphoses* where he recounts the Trojan War (12–13.428). During a long truce near the war's end, Nestor entertained the Greeks with tales of past adventures, including the marriage feast of Pirithoüs and Hippodame at which a fight broke out between centaurs and men (12.210–535). As Nestor recounted the story, Theseus led much of the attack and defense; at one point, a centaur threw a tree at him "'sed procul'," Nestor noted, "'a telo Theseus veniente recesset / Pallados admonitu: credi sic ipse volebat'" (but as Pallas advised him, Theseus dodged the weapon coming from afar: at least that was what he wished us to understand) (12.359–60). Though Nestor introduces some doubt as to whether or not Pallas directly intervened, Theseus avoided death in the moment, and none of Nestor's auditors questioned the possibility of her aid. Just as with Cadmus and Tydeus, Minerva's aid to Theseus seems almost an allegory for presence of mind as the hero recognized a need for action, a sort of cooperative moment with the goddess.

This idea of cooperation, though mostly implicit in the stories, seems key to a given prince's success, for once coming under Minerva's protection the prince must employ his own talents – his gifts of mind and physical prowess – as well. Returning to Tydeus in Statius' *Thebaid*, we find a clear instance of what can happen when a Minerva-protected prince forgets himself and, what is worse, the goddess. At the battle's height in book eight, Tydeus and Melanippus mortally wounded each other. Knowing Tydeus' fate, Minerva ascended to Jove, seeking apotheosis for her favored prince. Meanwhile, seized by battle rage and knowing death was imminent, Tydeus ordered his companions to decapitate the still-alive Melanippus and bring his head to him. Statius' narrator continues:

> ... iamque inflexo Tritonia patre
> venerat et misero decus immortale ferebat,
> atque illum effracti perfusum tabe cerebri
> aspicit et vivo scelerantem sanguine fauces
> (nec comites auferre valent): stetit aspera Gorgon
> crinibus emissis rectique ante ora cerastae
> velavere deam; fugit aversata iacentem,
> nec prius astra subit quam mystica lampas et insons
> Elisos multa purgavit lumina lympha.

(And now Tritonia had come from her compliant father and was bearing immortal honor for the wretched warrior. But she looked at him, drenched in the rot of broken brain and desecrating his jaws with living blood {nor could his friends

---

[10] This passage echoes snake-haired Tisiphone's appearance in book one, where the Fury gazed toward Thebes in response to Oedipus' curse (56–122). Framing the poem's recurring imagery of sight and forming a ring of malevolent gazes, books one and twelve underscore the recursive viciousness that is a central theme of the epic.

snatch away the head}; the rough Gorgon stood with hair on end, and the serpents rising before her face veiled the goddess. Turning her gaze from the doomed man, the goddess fled; she did not ascend to the stars before the mystic light and sinless Elisos purged her eyes with much water.) (8.758–66)

Tydeus' vicious cannibalism – a direct result of war-rage's attendant forgetfulness – counters strategic Minerva's warfare, and the goddess, who moments before gloried in his battle prowess, rejected her hero because of this final thoughtless, rash act: a *nefas* that pollutes the goddess' eyes and excludes Tydeus from apotheosis.[11]

Statius was Domitian's contemporary, winning several poetry contests sponsored by the Emperor and developing what Carole E. Newlands calls a poetics of Empire. His use of Minerva *patrona principis* in presenting Tydeus and Theseus likely reflects the Emperor's own attachment to the goddess, serving perhaps as a *speculum* for Domitian even as Statius offers the poem to him (12.814).[12] We find this association in other poems as well. In *Silvae* 1.1, Statius uses one art form to describe another, the *Equus Domitiani*: the Emperor's bronze equestrian statue dedicated and installed at the west end of the Roman Forum in 91.[13] Addressing the poem to Domitian, Statius notes:

dextra vetat pugnas, laevam Tritonia virgo
non gravat et sectae praetendit colla Medusae
ceu stimulis accendit equum; nec dulcior usquam
lecta deae sedes, nec si pater ipse teneres

(Your right hand bans battles; the virgin Tritonia does not burden your left, and she brandishes the head of decapitated Medusa as if with spurs she goads the horse; nor could there ever be a sweeter seat chosen by the goddess, not even if the father [i.e., Jove] himself held her)[14]

In this ekphrasis, Statius describes an icon – a statuette of Minerva in Medusan warrior-mode – as part of a larger icon, the Emperor's statue showing forth his Minerva-like role as warrior-diplomat. As he interprets the statue and statuette in this subtle interplay between plastic and verbal art, Statius reads the Emperor's function to be Minerva's throne itself: her "sedes" when with her *princeps* Domitian.[15] Statius' fellow poet Martial (40–c.102) also drew on Minerva *patrona principis* for

[11] On hatred in *Thebaid*, see Fantham, *Roman Readings*, who considers Tydeus' boundless *furor* as breaking "the bonds of human decency in victory over an enemy warrior who has not offended him or the code of battle" (596–7). On the choice between bestial and divine, see Hardie, *Epic Successors*, 66–9, who connects a beast-man-god triad to the epic's cosmic structure of Hell-Earth-Heaven, a structure Feeney, *Gods in Epic*, 344–64, explores at length. On battle more generally, see B. Gibson, "Battle Narrative in Statius' *Thebaid*," 85–109.
[12] Newlands, *Statius'* Silvae, 26–7, suggests as much. On Statius' references to Domitian and Virgil, *Thebaid* 12.810–19, see Rosati, "Statius, Domitian and Acknowledging Paternity," 175–93.
[13] Varner, *Mutilation and Transformation*, 113.
[14] *Silvae*, ed. Shakleton Bailey, 1.1.37–40.
[15] For a full discussion of this poem, see Newlands, *Statius'* Silvae, 46–73.

some epigrams addressed to Domitian. In epigram 7.1, he links the Emperor to Perseus implicitly and to Minerva directly, stating:

> Accipe belligerae crudum thoraca Minervae,
> ipsa Medusaeae quem timet ira comae.
> dum vacat, haec, Caesar, poterit lorica vocari:
> pectore cum sacro sederit, aegis erit

(Take up the rough breastplate of bellicose Minerva, she whom the wrath of Medusa's hair fears. While unworn, O Caesar, this can be called a breastplate: when worn on a sacred breast it will be the aegis)[16]

Engaging Domitian's relationship with Minerva, Martial implies that once the Emperor dons the "belligerae crudum thoraca Minervae" he becomes Minerva herself as bearer of the aegis, Jove's protective garment. Later, in epigram 9.3, the poet re-emphasizes Domitian's close association with the goddess when praising the Emperor's generosity to the gods, all of whom are indebted to him except Minerva. He writes simply: "Pallada praetereo: res agit illa tuas" (But I skip over Pallas: she manages your affairs) (9.3.10).

Domitian's affiliation with Minerva *patrona principis* was so strong that, when Suetonius writes about him some twenty years after courtiers assassinated him on September 18, 96, he decides to account for Minerva's conspicuous absence in the Emperor's hour of need.[17] Within the context of recounting Domitian's fearful and suspicious nature, Suetonius writes: "Minervam, quam superstitiose colebat, somniavit excedere sacrario negantemque ultra se tueri eum posse, quod exarmata esset a Iove" (He dreamed that Minerva, whom he superstitiously worshipped, departed from her shrine and denied that she could defend him any longer because she had been disarmed by Jove) (*Dom*. 15.3). Withdrawing her protection, no longer functioning as *patrona principis*, Minerva's abandonment in this dream is key.[18] Oliver Hekster refers to such an event as a "reversed epiphany," a moment in which a deity appears to a favorite only to declare he or she is leaving, and links it to the Roman notion of *evocatio*: the calling forth of tutelary deities from a city before it is sacked.[19] Even though skeptical of Domitian's veneration of the goddess, Suetonius apparently felt a need to explain Minerva's absence, which seems partly responsible for the Emperor's deposition. Much as with Tydeus in Statius' epic, Minerva sets aside her role as *patrona principis* in Domitian's dream, rejecting him in the end. The goddess' abandonment underscores the cooperative nature of the relationship between the prince and his patroness: it is not enough to be Minerva's favorite; the prince, too, must use his talents to fulfill his duties. For Suetonius, Minerva's

---

[16] *Epigrams*, ed. Ker, 7.1.1–4.
[17] B. Jones, *Emperor Domitian*, 193–6.
[18] See Harris, "Roman Opinions," 18–34, for attitudes towards dreams. Minerva's action here mirrors the prophesied protection or abandonment of the State over the retention of the Palladium, which was part of the Roman *pignora imperii* (pledges of rule) that included the sacred fire of Vesta and the *ancilia*, or twelve shields, of Mars.
[19] Hekster, "Reversed Epiphanies," 604, 611–13.

departure reinforces his reading of Domitian as a lustful, overly superstitious tyrant who ultimately failed to work for the common good.

One final text merits a glance before we turn to Minerva *patrona principis* in medieval literature: the *Ilias Latina* attributed to Baebius Italicus and composed during Nero's reign around 60 CE. In a type of translation Maria-Kristiina Lotman identifies as equiprosodic, where the translator reflects the original's system of versification, the *Ilias*-poet writes an epyllion, or little epic, in the vein of Catullus and Ovid, in which he recounts Homer's *Iliad*.[20] Reducing Homer's 15,693 Greek lines to 1070 Latin dactylic hexameters, the poet streamlines the narrative, offering a synopsis of the *Iliad* focused on the epic's main theme and action: Achilles' wrath over Briseis, the deaths of Patroclus and Hector, and the momentary reconciliation between Priam and Achilles.[21] The *Ilias Latina* illustrates on a grand scale the kind of paraphrase exercise Quintilian recommends a generation later as suitable for grammatical training (*Inst. ora.* 1.9.2–6). It also demonstrates the Trojan story's popularity in Roman culture in the 50s and 60s CE, during which Nero himself composed *Troica*, a no-longer extant epic.[22]

Though in translating the *Iliad* the poet reduces the action of deities almost to nil, for instance jettisoning the account discussed earlier of Athena's aid to Diomedes and Odysseus, he retains Minerva's role as *patrona principis* when Achilles confronts Hector. While Homer recounts the fight between the two heroes in 235 lines (22.131–366), the *Ilias*-poet reduces the scene to 24 (or about one-tenth of the original), adding a detail important to his account. At the moment in Homer when Achilles first approached Hector, the latter grew inexplicably afraid and ran, leading the Greek hero on a three-lap race around Troy's walls (22.136–8). The *Ilias*-poet maintains the outline of this action but writes:

> Quem procul ut uidit tectum caelestibus armis,
> ante oculos subito uisa est Tritonia Pallas
> pertimuit clausisque fugit sua moenia circum
> infelix portis, sequitur Nereius heros.

> (At a distance, as he saw Achilles guarded with celestial weapons, Hector suddenly had a vision of Tritonia Pallas before his eyes and gave in to fear; the unhappy man fled around his own walls with their closed gates; Achilles followed.) (934–7)

Offering a cause for Hector's sudden fear, that is, Minerva's armed presence at Achilles' side, the *Ilias*-poet introduces Minerva *patrona principis* into this scene

---

[20] Lotman, "Equiprosodic Translation Method," 452–3. The epyllion is a short narrative in dactylic hexameters; Catullus 64 and Ovid's *Metamorphoses*, a linked series of epyllia, offer key instances. Later poets also adapt the form, for example, Christopher Marlowe, *Hero and Leander*, and William Shakespeare, *Venus and Adonis*. See Baumbach and Bär, *Brill's Companion to Greek and Latin Epillion*.

[21] Baebius Italicus' synopsis of the *Iliad* covers books 1–9 in lines 1–685 and books 10–24 in lines 686–1070.

[22] Freudenburg, *Satires of Rome*, 154–8.

from its beginning.²³ Homer, on the other hand, interrupts the narrative, inserting a council-of-deities episode in the middle of the fight (22.166–87) that set up Pallas Athena's subsequent intervention. The goddess only entered the fight later when she approached Achilles directly, advising him to take a breather (22.214–23), before disguised as Deiphobus she encouraged Hector to stand and fight (22.226–47). The *Ilias*-poet, though, writes:

> Huic subito ante oculos similes Tritonia fratri
> occurens iuuenem simulato decipt ore;
> nam cum Deiphobi tutum se credidit armis,
> transtulit ad Danaos iterum sua numina Pallas
>
> (Suddenly before Hector's eyes, Tritonia running in the guise of his brother deceived the youth with simulated speech; though he believed that he would be protected by Deiphobus' arms, Minerva revealed her divine power to the Greeks) (946–9)

In this epiphany, Minerva indirectly aided her favored prince Achilles by emboldening Hector to stand ground, a move leading to his own death. Adding Minerva's role in frightening Hector, the *Ilias*-poet maintains the goddess' role as *patrona* on Achilles' behalf while deleting the council of the gods entirely from his epitome of Homer's epic.

The *Ilias*-poet's use of Minerva *patrona principis* differs from others we have considered here. Rather than appearing directly to her favored prince as she did in Ovid, Lucan, Statius, or even in the *Iliad* itself, she revealed herself in *Ilias Latina* to her prince's enemy. Setting up the Trojan prince to seem a coward by frightening him and a fool by tricking him into standing fast, Minerva appeared to Hector in order to emphasize Achilles' heroism: Hector's Minerva-inspired cowardice and folly serve as a foil to Achilles' bravery and strategic wisdom. Though Minerva's epiphany tricked Hector rather than inspired Achilles, the goddess' behavior in *Ilias Latina* offers yet another instance of her role as *patrona principis*. Such patronage evident in Latin literature also finds expression in several medieval texts where poets seek to explore the relationship between wisdom and the prince.

Minerva *Patrona* in Medieval Literature

Near the end of *Troilus and Criseyde*, Chaucer famously concludes his long narrative poem, stating in part:

> Go, litel bok, go, litel myn tragedye,
> Ther God thi makere yet, er that he dye,
> So sende myght to make in som comedye!

---

²³ In this gaze that strikes fear we find some intimation of Medusa's image on the goddess' *caelestibus armis*: an image of Minerva's battle mode adopted from the Gorgon's powerful gaze.

> But litel book, no making thow n'envie,
> But subgit be to alle poesye;
> And kis the steppes where as thow seest pace
> Virgile, Ovide, Omer, Lucan and Stace. (5.1786–92)

This "go little book" envoi has a long literary ancestry reaching back through Boccaccio, Petrarch (1304–74), Dante, Italian lyric, and troubadour and trouvere poetry to Statius, Martial, and Ovid themselves.[24] Chaucer's homage to his Roman predecessors Virgil, Ovid, Lucan, and Statius reminds us of the central place Latin literature held in the medieval curriculum: students read these authors and several others, including Martial, as part of their training in *grammatica*.[25] And Chaucer's "Omer," I should add, also most likely refers to the *Ilias Latina*, which was frequently titled "Homerus Latinus" in manuscripts and offered the Latin Middle Ages its primary glimpse at Homer's *Iliad* until long after copies and translations of the Greek epic began to appear later in the fourteenth century.[26] It, too, was a standard school text.[27] Chaucer's selection of these authors seems tied to subject and genre as he closes out his "tragedye"; his move places his own effort at telling a classical story within the textual community shaped by these earlier texts. Works of four of these authors, as explicated above, served in part as literary vehicles translating Minerva *patrona* to medieval authors who, in turn, took up the image for their own purposes.

Although the Latin poetry Chaucer evokes helped shape Latinity in the Middle Ages, as it had also done in late antiquity, the advent in medieval Europe of narratives retelling and reshaping Greco-Roman stories is largely a twelfth-century

---

[24] Young, *Origin and Development*, 178–9, first advanced Boccaccio's *Filocolo* 2.376–8 as the likely source of details in the "Go, litel book" stanza; Tatlock, "Epilog of Chaucer's *Troilus*," 627–30, traced its literary history back to Ovid's *Tristia* 1.1.1.

[25] Curtius, *European Literature*, 48–54; Hunt, *Teaching and Learning Latin*, 1:59–79; Irvine, *Making of Textual Culture*, 355–64; Copeland, "The Curricular Classics," 21–33, and "The Trivium and the Classics," 53–76; Woods, "Experiencing the Classics in Medieval Education," 35–52.

[26] Petrarch acquired a Greek copy of the *Iliad* in 1354 (Milan Bibl. Ambrose. I 98 inf.); later, Boccaccio commissioned Leontius Pilatus to translate the poem into Latin. Solomon, "Vacillations of the Trojan Myth," 506. These are the earliest known copies of Homer's poem in the West since late antiquity.

[27] Extant in some 100 mss., *Ilias Latina* was widely read. P. Marshall, "*Ilias Latina*," 191; Hunt, *Teaching and Learning Latin*, 1:67. Cologny, Foundation Martin Bodmer, Cod. Bodmer 86, fols. 1r–13v, offers one instance of medieval readership. A fourteenth-century Italian copy of the poem, the text is in a clear semi-cursive Gothic script with marginal and interlinear glosses indicating readership over time. Cologny, Foundation Martin Bodmer, Cod. Bodmer 87, fols. 1r–22v, also Italian and produced about 100 years later (dated 1469 on fol. 22v), has a copy of the poem in clear humanist script with rubrics marking book divisions. Though it has no glossing, this copy indicates continued interest in the text. National Library of Scotland, Advocates Ms. 18.4.8, fols. 57r–86v, offers yet another instance. Bound with a copy of Dares' *De excidio Troiae historia*, *Ilias Latina* shows reader use from interlinear to marginal glosses, including records of royal secretary Archibald Whitelaw's late fifteenth-century reading. See Mapstone, "Origins of Criseyde," 131–2, 147.

phenomenon.[28] The Matter of Rome, which Jean Bodel (fl. 1200) describes as a subject for narrative, encompasses stories set in ancient cities such as Thebes, Athens, or Rome as well as stories about particular figures from Achilles to Aeneas.[29] The French genre of roman antique like Benoît de Saint-Maure's *Roman de Troie*, the *Roman de Thébes*, and the *Roman d'Eneas*, offers twelfth-century instances of this kind of narrative; Chaucer's *Troilus and Criseyde*, focusing on a love story set in wartime Troy, is a fourteenth-century English instance. In a number of these texts, Minerva appears in various guises, including her role as *patrona principis*.

Twelfth-Century Epic: Walter of Châtillon and Joseph of Exeter

Our first medieval text is Walter of Châtillon's (c.1135–c.1200) *Alexandreis*: a ten-book epic in 5500 Latin-hexameter lines recounting the life, military campaigns, and death of Alexander of Macedon (356–323 BCE). According to his prologue, Walter spent five years composing the epic, likely completing it between 1176 and 1181.[30] Though he dedicated it to his chief patron William of the White Hands, Archbishop of Rheims, Walter clearly had a wider readership in mind as well.[31] His peers noticed the epic almost immediately, and within a short time masters adopted it into school curricula, placing it alongside Virgil's *Aeneid*, Ovid's *Metamorphoses*, Lucan's *Bellum civile*, Statius' *Thebaid* and *Achilliad*, and Claudian's *De raptu Proserpinae* as an instance of Latin epic.[32] Walter himself also claims this place, noting that none of the antique poets had dared take up this subject matter (Prologue 35–6), that is, he is filling a gap left by the ancients. And *Alexandreis* seems to have held pride of place as perhaps the Alexander story's most widely read version from the late twelfth century until well into the early modern period, as attested by some 209 extant

---

[28] Ziolkowski, "Epic," 547–51, notes that early medieval epic treated biblical and historical subjects, but the twelfth century saw a turn to classical stories.

[29] *La Chanson des Saxons*, ed. Francisque, 6–14. Bodel also identifies the Matter of France, i.e., stories touching on Charlemagne, and the Matter of Britain, i.e., stories touching on Arthur.

[30] Colker, introduction to *Galteri*, xv; Kratz, *Mocking Epic*, 61–2; Lafferty, *Walter of Châtillon's* Alexandreis, 14; Townsend, introduction to *The Alexandreis*, 14–15. Born near Lille and educated in Paris, Walter taught at Castellio and Laon before studying law in Bologna; he then served William, Archbishop of Rheims, who named him canon at a cathedral; and, according to medieval *vitae*, he died of leprosy. Lafferty, *Walter of Châtillon's* Alexandreis, 3–12, and "Chapter Eight," 177–80. His medieval *vitae* provide a number of details about his life (see editions in Colker). On the poem's date, see Dionisotti, "Walter of Châtillon," 74–5; and Lafferty, *Walter of Châtillon's* Alexandreis, 183–9, and "Chapter Eight," 182–3.

[31] In addition to in-text references to Archbishop William (1.12–26, 5.510–20, 10.461–9), the first letter of each book spells out the acrostic GUILLERMUS, the Latin form of his name.

[32] Alan of Lille attacks the poem in his c.1182 *Anticlaudianus* (1.166–70), and John of Hauville frequently echoes it in his 1184 *Architrenius* (passim; xxv). See Curtius, *European Literature*, 50; Colker, introduction to *Galteri*, xviii–xx; and Townsend, introduction to *The Alexandreis*, 15–16.

manuscript copies from across Europe and four early printed editions.[33] Drawing primarily on Quintus Curtius Rufus' *Historiae Alexandri Magni Macedonis*, a first-century Latin history, Walter abbreviates the detailed Latin prose in several places while at the same time amplifies it in others so as to match Latin epic form and convention such as extended similes, councils of deities, invocations, ekphrases, and the like. He also draws on Roman epics for model scenes. Near the end of book one, for instance, Alexander tours Troy's ruins, visits Achilles' tomb, and reflects on poetry's memorial power to secure lasting fame for its subject.[34] This episode, as Maura Lafferty notes, echoes Lucan's account of Julius Caesar's visit to Troy (*De bello civili*, 9.961–99) in structure, theme, and subject – if not actual verbal construction.[35] In addition to addressing the demands and opportunities of epic form and convention, Walter amplifies his sources to emphasize themes important in the final quarter of the twelfth century: heroism and irony, political power and personal glory, fate and fortune, memory and interpretation.[36]

Developing these themes, all of which concern right rule, Walter amplifies his source in part by integrating the image of Minerva *patrona* in three distinct ways.[37] The earliest mention of the goddess, occurring in book one, alludes to her role as patroness of the city-state Athens. Upon the death of Philip of Macedon and Alexander's subsequent coronation, both Athens and Thebes separately withdrew from their alliances with Macedon. In response, Alexander quickly marshalled troops to quell the rebellions, besieging first Athens where the city's leaders, safe "in Palladis arce" (in Pallas' stronghold) (1.276), debated what to do. Aeschines' proposal of peaceful cooperation won the day, and Alexander reintegrated the city under his rule, leaving Athenians to pursue freely their civic life "artibus ingenuis studiisque" (with native arts and studies) (1.282). The implication of the allusion, that is, Athenians adopting a wise course of action under Minerva's patronage, serves as foil to Thebes' belligerent response, which led to that city's utter destruction in

---

[33] Colker, introduction to *Galteri*, xxxiii–xxxviii. On the medieval Alexander, see Cary, *Medieval Alexander*, 77–225; essays in Noble, Polak, and Isoz, eds., *Medieval Alexander Legend*; essays in Maddox and Sturm-Maddox, eds., *Medieval French Alexander*; essays in Zuwiyya, ed., *Companion to Alexander Literature*; and Ross, *Alexander Historiatus*. Printed editions attest to early modern interest in the *Alexandreis*, including the *editio princeps* published by Guillaume de Tailleur (Rouen c.1487) and three sixteenth-century editions published by J. Adolphus (Strassburg 1513), O. von Eck (Ingolstadt 1541), and R. Granjon (Lyon 1558) respectively. See Colker, xxxviii.

[34] *Galteri de Castillione Alexandreis*, ed. Colker, 1.452–92.

[35] Lafferty, *Walter of Châtillon's* Alexandreis, 15. Though Curtius' text is missing its first two books, Walter seems to have had on hand a version that interpolated the missing material. Smits, "Medieval Supplement," 89–124. Colker's bottom-page notes are informative.

[36] See Raby, *History of Secular Latin Poetry*, 2.72–9; Kratz, *Mocking Epic*, 1–13, 61–155; Dionisotti, "Walter of Châtillon," 78–90; and Lafferty, *Walter of Châtillon's* Alexandreis, 31–182.

[37] Though he does not develop Minerva *patrona* in his history, Quintus Curtius Rufus references the goddess as recipient of Alexander's worship and sacrifice. *History of Alexander*, ed. Rolfe, 3.7.3, 3.12.27, 4.13.15, 8.2.32, 8.11.24.

spite of Cleades' song reminding Alexander of Aristotle's teaching on mercy to the vanquished (1.284–348).

Having re-conquered Greece, Alexander sailed east to face Darius and the Persian Empire, in the context of which Walter alludes to Minerva *patrona* a second time. Following Alexander's encounter with Darius at the Battle of Issus, where Macedonian troops captured the Persian Emperor's family, the narrator recounts how Darius' wife later died in captivity, prompting the Persian to sue for peace. Darius sent ten captains on embassy "cum Palladis arbore" (with Pallas' branch) (4.70), offering land, his daughter's hand in marriage, his son as hostage, and 30,000 talents in gold if Alexander would agree to a treaty and ransom the Emperor's family. Minerva's branch, the olive, serving in this poem as a universal sign of peace and diplomacy, stems directly from the goddess' role as patroness of Athens. Just as the Athenians wisely sued for peace in book one from within Minerva's protective stronghold so did Darius in book four under her diplomatic patronage. In spite of the field commander Parmenion's advice to accept the offer, however, Alexander scornfully rejected it in favor of winning personal glory in battle and taking the whole empire.

We find the third image of Minerva *patrona* within the context of the subsequent Battle of Arbela. As with earlier battle descriptions, Walter depicts this final defeat of Darius using the epic convention of serial single combats, moving narrative attention from one warrior to another and lingering occasionally on Alexander himself in his single-minded pursuit of the Persian Emperor. Amid this description, Walter interjects a council between Mars and his sister Bellona, the goddess of war. Noting Darius was fated for another end and Alexander wasted himself pursuing the Persian while his own troops were being slaughtered, Mars sent Bellona to the Macedonian leader with orders to break off his futile chase and aid Parmenion's forces. In response to her brother's wish, as the narrator continues:

> … imbrifero Bellona citatior Austro
> Fertur et ad dextrum pertransit stridula cornu
> Induiturque genas horrendaque Palladis arma,
> Gorgonis anguicomos pretendens egide uultus,
> Commemoransque dei breuiter mandata recessit
> Infecitque diem ferali nube recedens

(Bellona bore herself more swiftly than the rain-filled south wind, crossed to the right with a shrill sound, and clothed herself in Pallas' likeness and horrendous weapons, holding the aegis with the Gorgon's snake-haired face. Rehearsing briefly Mars' commands, she then vanished and, leaving, poisoned the day with a deadly cloud) (5.235–40)

Adopting Minerva's Medusan-warrior mode, Bellona assumed the goddess' role as *patrona prinicipis*, seeking to call Alexander back to right order as commander of the army. In un-epic fashion, however, Alexander not only rejected the goddess' message but also declared his own view of the field superior to any other, deity or otherwise, saying "Ex Dario pendet nostri spes unica voti, / Quem si perdidero, parui michi cetera parui / Perdita momenti" (our wish's only hope hangs on Darius whom, if I shall have destroyed, other losses will be of very little importance to me) (5.452–4).³⁸ Alexander, though, was wrong: his army won the day in spite of heavy losses and Darius escaped – their victory, it seems, came from hard-fighting troops under capable field commanders rather than from securing Darius as he declared. Though he may have counted the losses as nothing compared to killing or capturing the Persian Emperor, Alexander's generals and men bore the burden of his choices, including his decision to reject the command of Bellona quasi Minerva *patrona principis*. Alexander's pattern of glory-seeking behavior – emphasized in this scene through the Minerva *patrona* image and his rejection of the deity – continues throughout the epic, which in part explores possibilities and examines limitations of princely power.³⁹

Writing in the wake of the *Alexandreis*, and perhaps directly following Walter of Châtillon's lead, Joseph of Exeter (fl. 1180–90) – an English cleric serving Baldwin, Archbishop of Canterbury (1186–90) – completed *Frigii Daretis Yliados*, a six-book epic in 3673 dactylic hexameter lines, in about 1185.⁴⁰ Offering what A.G. Rigg calls "the first full-fledged medieval epic on Troy," covering the story from the Argonauts' voyage to the aftermath of the city's second sacking, Joseph translates the prose of Dares Phrygius' *De excidio Troiae historia*, along with a small section of Dictys Cretensis' *Ephemeridos belli Troiani*, into epic verse.⁴¹ These two late antique texts, purporting to be translations into Latin of eyewitness accounts from the Trojan and the Greek sides respectively, gave what medieval readers considered legitimate historical accounts of the Trojan War. Sparse in detail, Dares' account particularly

---

[38] As Dionisotti, "Walter of Châtillon," 80–1, points out, Alexander does not behave as expected in the presence of a deity, i.e., with awe and action as directed. Rejecting Bellona and Mars, he unknowingly alludes to *Aeneid* 4.556–70, one of Walter's models for this scene, declaring he would not change course even if Mercury himself came. Lafferty, *Walter of Châtillon's Alexandreis*, 51–4, argues that this scene indicates Alexander's inability to perceive his own limitations.

[39] In his effort to shape his own fate, Alexander ultimately lost. When dying, he turned prophet, declaring he was summoned "Consilio Iouis et superum" (by counsel of Jove and the gods) (10.416) to help rule Olympus. At the moment of death, however, the narrator describes Alexander's spirit "erumpens tenues exiuit in auras" (bursting forth expired into thin air) (10.427). Unlike Pompey in Lucan's *Bellum civile*, 9.1–18, Walter's likely model for this scene, there is no apotheosis in the *Alexandreis*; once dead "cui non suffecerat orbis, / Sufficit exciso defossa marmore terra / Quinque pedum fabricate domus" (he for whom the world was insufficient had only five feet of tunneled earth, carved from cut marble, for his abode) (10.448–50). Though Walter's attitude towards his subject remains ambivalent, this ending is dramatically ironic: Alexander's minuscule bit of earth starkly contrasts with his world-conquering ambition.

[40] Joseph knew the *Alexandreis*. As Lafferty notes, *Walter of Châtillon's Alexandreis*, 11 n.46, he drew on *Alexandreis* 1.2–4 as a model for young King Henry. *Frigii Daretis Yliados*, ed. Gompf, 5.533–5. Regarding Joseph's life, we know few details: from Exeter, he was Baldwin's nephew and accompanied the Archbishop to the Holy Land on the Third Crusade, where Baldwin died in 1190. A friend of Guibert, Abbot of Fleury, Joseph authored poems on virginity, St. Martin, and a crusade epic (*Antiocheis*, of which only twenty-five lines survive) as well as the *Ylias*. Raby, *History of Secular Latin Poetry*, 2:132–3; and Rigg, *History of Anglo-Latin Literature*, 99.

[41] Rigg, *History of Anglo-Latin Literature*, 99, and "Appendix A," 142. Dares, *De excidio Troiae*, ed. Meister, and Dictys, *Ephemeridos Belli Troiani*, ed. Eisenhut.

provided Joseph a narrative platform from which to adapt the story's imaginative potential through *amplificatio* and *abbrevatio*.⁴² Joseph, for instance, translates Paris' dream, which takes a mere sentence of prose in Dares' brief account (*De excidio* 7), into a 415-line dream vision complete with debating goddesses seeking Paris' favorable judgment (2.198–613). He particularly amplifies the role of Minerva, whom Dares mentions only twice (*De excidio* 7, 41) but who plays key roles in the *Ylias*.⁴³

Joseph integrates Minerva *patrona* into his epic in the same three ways Walter does in the *Alexandreis*. After Priam rebuilds Troy at the end of book one, Minerva *patrona urbis* appears, much as we saw with Athens in the *Alexandreis*, when the narrator comments, "Arces Pallas habet et habetur Pallade fatum" (Pallas holds the citadel, and its destiny is held by the Palladium) (1.544). The narrator alludes to Minerva *patrona urbis* twice more: when Astur "custos Tritonidis" (the guardian of the Palladium) (5.116) spied the Greek invasion and raised the alarm; and when the Greeks piled their loot "in arce Minerve" (in Minerva's stronghold) (6.856) following the city's second sacking. Both allusions assume the audience's understanding of the goddess as Troy's protectress, a position Minerva abandoned as the war got underway. Minerva *patrona* also appears in her diplomatic guise. In book one, when Hercules returned to Troy to punish Laomedon for his earlier inhospitality to the Argonauts, he charged the king as "'spreta pacis cum fronde Minerva'" (having scorned Minerva with her branch of peace) (1.434). Minerva's branch of peace – the olive we saw in *Alexandreis* 4.70 – surfaces again when Trojan Antenor carried it on embassy to Telamon to request the return of Priam's sister Hesione (2.156) and when the Greeks later sued for a truce in the midst of the second war (5.394). While these instances of the image point to a message of peace under Minerva's patronage, the image surfaces once more in a slightly different context. Near the end of the second war, both sides, weary after fighting nearly ten years, received fresh troops: Penthesilia led her Amazon army to Troy's aid while Achilles' son Pyrrhus led reinforcements to the Greeks. Both sides, the narrator notes, proclaimed their allegiances to deities on their shields and armor: Trojans and their allies declared for Cybele, Venus, and Jupiter, and the Greeks showed forth Mars, Juno, and Minerva, particularly on the Athenian shield that "Palladie pacem mentitur olive" (feigned the peace of Pallas' olive) (6.580). Minerva's branch of peace depicted on Athenian war shields – an image enemy warriors would see in combat – is an ironic bit of grim humor in place of what one perhaps might expect, an image of Minerva's aegis. Though peace may result from war, such peace only comes at a cost in human life and material damage.

These two images of Minerva *patrona* frame the third, her role as *patrona principis*. In this role, the goddess played to both sides, but, as in the *Ilias Latina*, she

---

⁴² On Joseph's reworking of Darius, see Raby, *History of Secular Latin Poetry*, 2.132–7; Sedgewick, "*Bellum Troianum*," 66–9; Riddehough, "Forgotten Poet," 254–9; Roberts, "Worthy of Their Envy," 16–22; and Rigg, *History of Anglo-Latin Literature*, 102, and "Calchas, Renegade and Traitor," 176–8.

⁴³ On Joseph's addition of deities to the narrative, see Dunkle, "Satirical Themes," 208–10; Parker, "Pagan Gods," 273–8; and Rigg, "Joseph of Exeter's Pagan Gods," 19–28.

primarily supported the Greeks. We first see Minerva *patrona principis* in book two during the Judgment of Paris scene. After Antenor returned from his failed attempt to regain Hesione, Priam called a council at which Paris argued for leading a military expedition to recoup Trojan honor. Recounting a dream he had experienced when sleeping on Mount Ida while resting midday from a hunt, Paris told what he declared was a "'mira ... sed vera'" (wondrous but true) tale familiar from Lydgate's *Reson and Sensuallyte*: Mercury led Juno, Minerva, and Venus to Paris to judge the goddesses' beauty; each offered him a gift should he choose her; and the prince picked Venus as most beautiful.[44] In the *Ylias*, however, the action centers on the goddesses' debate – Joseph's greatest amplification of his source – where each in turn presented her own attributes while critiquing the others'. Though weaving in her *patrona* role throughout her discourse, Minerva summed it most clearly when she concluded her argument declaring:

"Maxime Priamidum, nostra est si gloria, quicquid
Mars audet, quod Clio docet, quod tractat Aragne,
Si tibi mixta manus et partitura, Minervam,
Si tutoris agent artes et in arce triumphat
Palladium, forme titulum si virgo meretur,
Annue et Yliacum, iudex, ne despice fatum"

("O Priam's greatest son, if my glory lies in what Mars dares, Clio teaches, and Arachne practices, if the company gathered to you will take part in Minerva's wisdom, if the guardian's arts protect and the Palladium triumphs in Troy's citadel, if a virgin merits beauty's title, vote for me, O judge, and despise not Ilium's destiny") (2.449–54)

In this series of conditional statements, recapping three chief spheres of influence (war, education, craft), Minerva emphasized her strategic and political wisdom, cautioning the prince to consider the City's good in making his choice: as ever, she implied, the prince's microcosmic action affects the city-state's macrocosmic outcome. Venus, of course, won Paris' judgment, but not without first promising the prince Helen of Sparta before performing what Gildas Roberts calls "a quick strip tease," baring her breasts as a type of visual aid to conclude her argument (2.600–9).[45] Though the narrator later notes that Helenus and Deiphebus, two Trojan princes, were particularly devoted to the goddess (4.59), Minerva rejected Trojan interests following Paris' decision and leaned to the Greeks.

---

[44] A figure's appearance during a midday nap taken while out hunting would likely raise a number of issues for Joseph's audience were they somehow unaware of the Judgment story itself. When associated with Venus, hunting was a common metaphor for sexual activity, deriving in part from Ovid, *Ars am.*, 1.45–50; napping in this context, then, suggests sloth; and a midday appearance evokes the "daemonium meridianum" (midday demon) tradition. On hunting, see Robertson, *Preface*, 263–4, and Thiébaux, *Stage of Love*, 89–142; on the midday demon, see Ehrhart, *Judgment of the Trojan Prince Paris*, 46–9.
[45] Roberts, "Worthy of Their Envy," 15.

As we have also seen in *Ilias Latina*, Joseph's Minerva particularly supported Achilles on the battlefield.[46] Her patronage of this prince first becomes evident moments before Achilles and Hector fight. Abbreviating and amplifying his source, Joseph creates an Achilles initially reluctant to confront the Trojan hero, who was annihilating Greek warriors in his battle rage (5.470–82). The narrator notes:

> … non ille quidem certamina tanto
> temptasset conferre viro, sed Iuno negantem
> Sollicitat, stimulat Pallas pariterque precantes
> Prebent hec animos, hec iras, utraque vires
>
> (Achilles would not have attempted to enter a contest with such a man, but Juno probed his reluctance and Minerva equally inspired his desires: they provided him courage – the one, wrath; the other, strength) (5.486–9)

Compared to Dares' Achilles, who considered the situation and unhesitatingly fought Hector (*De excidio* 24), Joseph's hero needed divine help: Juno's rage and Minerva's fortitude moved him to act. Once he joined the fight, however, Achilles directly confronted Hector, whom he dispatched after fierce single combat – a fight punctuated by a truce to bury and mourn Troy's fallen hero. With Hector dead, and following the year-long truce, Troilus became the chief Trojan hero once battle resumed. Meanwhile, having recused himself from fighting out of deference to the Trojan princess Polyxena, with whom on Venus' instigation he had fallen in love during her brother Hector's funeral (6.84–5), Achilles remained disengaged until Troilus killed Yparcus, leader of the Myrmidons. Achilles re-entered the fray; the narrator states:

> Frendit atrox, quantumque ingens dabat ira, lacertum
> Erigit Eacides ac toto robore nisus
> Iam responsuros parat ictus. Venerat ante
> Lancea Priamide levosque invaserat armos
> Hostis, at innocuum fallit Tritonia telum.
> Sentit et adversos incusat Palladis astus
> Troilus
>
> (His wrathful spirit giving a great roar, fierce Achilles raged, raised up his shoulder, and then prepared with all his might a painful blow in response. Troilus' spear had come first and struck his left shoulder, but Minerva deflected the harmless dart. Troilus perceived Minerva's cleverness and cursed her) (6.304–10)

Once more the goddess intervened on behalf of a favored prince and, though Troilus fought well, Achilles killed him and Memnon soon after. Then, turning from Minerva and giving himself over to battle rage, the Greek hero rampaged through the Trojan army, indiscriminately killing soldiers until "cedit vix exorante

---

[46] Though difficult to draw a direct link between *Ilias Latina* and *Ylias*, Joseph's portrayal of Minerva's relationship with Achilles suggests a possible relationship.

Minerva" (with difficulty Minerva persuaded him: he withdrew) (6.369). Inspired by the goddess, Achilles retreated from war-rage madness and returned to a more rational, strategic approach to battle: unlike Tydeus in Statius' *Thebaid*, he did not entirely succumb to wrath. Not long after this battle, however, Achilles himself died when attempting to meet and secretly marry Polyxena in Apollo's temple. Here again Minerva sought to aid the prince, much as she aided her brother Perseus when ambushed at his wedding feast, but Jupiter prevented it (6.454–6), allowing Paris and his troop to slaughter the Greek prince and his companion, Nestor's son Antilochus. In these three instances, Minerva *patrona principis* aided – or sought to aid – Achilles by inspiring fortitude, defensive tactics, and strategic thinking.[47]

Writing the *Ylias*, Joseph of Exeter contributed to a growing twelfth-century interest in the matter of Troy seen in texts from Geoffrey of Monmouth's account of the war's aftermath and Brutus' founding of Britain and *Troia Nova* (*Historia regum Britanniae*, c.1136) to Benoît de Sainte-Maure's expansive and influential *Le Roman de Troie* (c.1155/60).[48] Joseph, as Francine Mora-Lebrun suggests, perhaps even wrote *Ylias* as a response to Benoît's highly-charged version of the city's destruction.[49] Though a gripping account in its own right, Joseph's *Ylias* seems not, however, as influential as other texts considered here. Still, its manuscript history demonstrates interest in the poem, and Chaucer certainly read it.[50] Along with the *Alexandreis*, then, the *Ylias* offered medieval readers three images of Minerva *patrona* as protectress of the city, of peaceful diplomacy, and of the prince: a set of images that continued to appear in later versions of classical stories.

---

[47] Though we might expect her to aid Achilles' son Pyrrhus once he arrived, she refused to help him defeat Penthesilia (6.636–7), presumably because she did not want to fight against a female warrior.

[48] On the medieval Troy story, see Benson, *History of Troy*, 3–6; Hodapp, "Geoffrey of Monmouth," 17–22; Ingledew, "Book of Troy," 670–704; and Solomon, "Vacillations of the Trojan Myth," 504–14.

[49] Mora, "L'*Ylias* de Joseph d'Exeter," 199–213; Mora-Lebrun, "D'une esthétique à l'autre," 31–3.

[50] Joseph of Exeter's *Ylias* survives in five copies, with eleven known to have existed, and as quotes in *florilegia*. Rigg, *History of Anglo-Latin Literature*, 349 n.116. One ms. copy, Cambridge, Corpus Christi College, Ms. 406, hints at the context in which people read the poem. Comprised of 144 folios, this thirteenth-century anthology includes Seneca's tragedies (1r–39v), John of Hauville's *Architrenius* (41r–64v), Bernard Silvestris' *Cosmographia* (65r–74r), Joseph's *Ylias* (74v–86v), Alan of Lille's *Anticlaudianus* (86v–100v), Geoffrey of Vinsauf's *Poetria nova* (102r–112v), and Walter of Châtillon's *Alexandreis* (113r–142r). Six scribes, writing in a two- or three-column format, contribute to the book, which suggests it is a reader's anthology rather than a patron's (i.e., a reader gathered under one binding a series of texts executed separately). Three texts, however – *Cosmographia*, *Ylias*, and *Architrenius* – seem intended together as two scribes write them (hands and format change in the *Ylias* at 77r). Abbreviated throughout, the texts require readers steeped in both Latin and its abbreviations to read them well. Likely used as a school text, CCCC Ms. 406 also evinces multiple readers over time in its marginal comments and glosses. On Chaucer reading *Ylias*, see Root, "Chaucer's Dares," 1–22.

Guido delle Colonne, John Lydgate, and the Matter of Troy

Though Joseph of Exeter's *Ylias* may not have been widely read, the Trojan story itself found audiences via Benoît's (c.1210–c.1290) French verse and its many adaptations and translations, including Guido delle Colonne's circa 1287 Latin prose rendering *Historia destructionis Troiae*.[51] In Guido's popular version of the Troy story, which he declared corrected Virgil, Ovid, and Homer, Minerva *patrona principis* appears again in Paris' account of his judgment dream.[52] Unlike in Joseph, with his loquacious and comical exchange between the goddesses and the Trojan prince, Guido's goddesses remained silent while Mercury addressed Paris, detailing the cause of their disagreement (the prized apple), their willingness to submit to his judgment, and the gift each promised: Juno would grant him magnificence; Pallas, all human knowledge; and Venus, the most beautiful and noble Greek woman (6.61–3). Interestingly, Guido added a detail that critics have argued emphasizes Paris' sensual nature: the prince required the goddesses to present themselves naked to him so he might render "uerum … iudicium" (a true judgment) on their beauty (6.62)[53.] They did, Venus of course won, and Paris bypassed Minerva (and Juno) as a potential patroness for himself and his city-state. Though frequently mentioned, deities take no active part in Guido's narrative other than in this dream moment. Minerva herself appears again in her role as *patrona urbis*, but only through yet another story-within-the-story: Antenor's account of Troy's safety being tied to the Palladium, which he then helped Ulixes steal so the Greeks could win the war (29–30.226–9). Synthesizing sources and jettisoning the more fantastic and amorous elements of Benoît's *Roman de Troie*, Guido wrote what he and his readers deemed a historical account of the Trojan experience.

As with Benoît's *Roman*, Guido's chief source, the *Historia destructionis Troiae* proved influential in turn throughout Europe, inspiring numerous vernacular translations including John Lydgate's *Troy Book*, in which Minerva also appears as *patrona principis* in the context of Paris' judgment.[54] Commissioned by Henry, Prince of Wales, in 1412 and completed and presented to him as Henry V in 1420, *Troy Book* is now extant in twenty-three manuscript copies and in two sixteenth-century editions

---

[51] Benson, *History of Troy*, 1–29; Solomon, "Vacillations of the Trojan Myth," 511–13.
[52] Guido delle Colonne, *Historia destructionis Troiae*, ed. Griffin, 35.276. Guido was a poet, chronicler, lawyer, judge, and member of the Sicilian School of poetry, whom Dante cites in *De vulgari eloquentia*, ed. Rajna, 2.5.4. Guido's reference to Homer most likely is to *Ilias Latina*. Griffin, introduction to *Historia*, xi–xv, mentions consulting ninety-four manuscript copies and locating an additional forty-two before choosing five on which to base his edition; these 136 mss., a list Griffin thought incomplete, and the text's seven pre-1500 printed editions suggest its popularity through the fifteenth century.
[53] Ehrhart, *Judgment of the Trojan Prince Paris*, 49.
[54] In addition to *TB*, Guido's text inspired two other Middle English poems: the alliterative *Gest Historiale of the Destruction of Troy* (c.1385/1400) and the *Laud Troy Book* (c.1400/1410) – both exist in single ms. copies. Benson, *History of Troy*, 42–129. That Lydgate draws on other sources has been evident at least since Atwood, "Some Minor Sources," 27–42, teased out borrowings from Ovid and Chaucer.

by Pynson (1513) and Marshe (1555) respectively.[55] This evidence suggests relatively wide readership and, along with William Caxton's *Recuyell of the Historyes of Troye* (1473), *Troy Book* influenced subsequent English and Scottish writers from Robert Henryson and Stephen Hawes to Thomas Kyd, Christopher Marlowe, and William Shakespeare.[56] Like Guido, Joseph, and other writers basing accounts of Troy on Dares, Lydgate casts Paris' judgment as a dream. Following the outline of Guido's account, including his beauty pageant of naked goddesses, Lydgate amplifies his source considerably, expanding the dream experience into a love vision set "among the bowes glade" beside "a crystal welle"[57] and adding mythographic iconography for each deity much as we have seen in his earlier *Reson and Sensuallyte* (2.2467–792). Recounting his dream vision, Paris turned into a learned schoolmaster, explicating mythographic details and even citing Fulgentius as his interpretive-authoritative guide to reading the deities (2.2486–9). Rationalizing Paris' experience with the divine by casting it as a dream, Lydgate also allegorizes it, as Ehrhart notes.[58] Like his Lydgatian predecessor the *Reson and Sensuallyte* narrator, Paris understood fully each deity's significance: he also presumably understood the ramifications of his choice. Rejecting Minerva *patrona* in *Troy Book*, as he inevitably must have done to maintain the story's trajectory, Paris serves again as a negative *exemplum* for the prince: a lesson in what not to do. Though the theme may seem worn by Lydgate's time – no one familiar with the Trojan story need be reminded Paris made a bad choice – the poet infuses the story with new life and comic potential as he casts Paris'

---

[55] Some consider *TB* part of Henry V's effort to foster an English language standard. See Fisher, *Emergence of Standard English*, 25–33, and *Importance of Chaucer*, 145–7; and Machan, *English in the Middle Ages*, 161–5. Others consider it an effort to elevate the language's prestige. See Baswell, "*Troy Book*," 217–37. Both seem to have happened as aristocratic patrons commissioned and owned several of the poem's ms. copies. The Carent family of Somerset, for instance, initially owned John Rylands University Library English Ms. 1: a single-text, carefully planned and decorated copy dating c.1450 (executed by two scribes in 174 folios and ruled in two columns of approximately eighty lines per folio side). Similarly, in c.1457, Sir William Herbert, 1st earl of Pembroke, likely commissioned the early portion of British Library Ms. Royal 18 D.ii, constituting carefully planned (two-column layout with 100 lines per folio side) and decorated copies of *TB* (fols. 6r–146r) and *Siege of Thebes* (fols. 147v–162r), as a presentation gift either to Henry VI or Edward IV. R.F. Green, *Poets and Princepleasers*, 155. For a fuller discussion of the mss., see L. Lawton, "Illustration of Late Medieval Secular Texts," 41–69. Pynson's 1513 printed edition of *TB* mirrors the ms. tradition in its two-column layout with 100 lines per page, two-to-four-line initial letters and paragraph marks to signal minor text breaks, and woodcut illustrations (thirty-eight woodcuts) to signal major text breaks. Marshe's 1555 edition, on the other hand, is much plainer. Though he uses a two-column layout with ninety-eight lines per page and two-to-four-line initial letters and one-line paragraph marks to signal text breaks, he does not incorporate woodcuts; rather, he emphasizes major text breaks at books three, four, and five with large-font titles (148, 208, 280). Perhaps the shift away from woodcuts reflects a shift from oral/aural to silent reading habits.
[56] Benson, *History of Troy*, 97.
[57] *TB*, 2.2447, 56.
[58] Ehrhart, *Judgment of the Trojan Prince Paris*, 58–60.

dream as a first-person medieval love vision complete with authorial mythographic commentary.[59]

Lydgate sets out in *Troy Book* to translate Guido for an English-reading audience, offering a versified history – what he insistently calls in the Prologue "trouthe" (153) – so they might remember and take example from the past.[60] As with any translation, *Troy Book* reveals Lydgate's sense of his target audience and their concerns, interests, and preoccupations.[61] Writing what he deems history, he also integrates conventions from other genres in his 30,117-line narrative: the dream-vision love poem, as we have just seen; the encomium in dedicating the poem to Henry V (Lenvoye 1–91); the envoy itself as he takes leave of the poem by integrating directly Chaucer's "Go, litel bok" phrase (Lenvoye 92); and the five-book structure of Chaucer's *Troilus and Criseyde*.[62] Similarly, he weaves in epic conventions throughout the narrative, but particularly in the Prologue's opening sixty-two lines where he invokes Mars as patron of chivalry (1–37); Othea as goddess of prudence and mistress of the Muses, especially Clio patroness of history (38–45); and Calliope as mother of Orpheus and patroness of musicians (46–62). These epic invocations initially seem out of place for a history based on what Lydgate's audience considered eyewitness accounts (why not, for instance, invoke Dares and Dictys instead?). But Lydgate seems unbothered by the apparent incongruity; perhaps, steeped in mythographic

---

[59] As Ehrhart details, the Judgment of Paris was a popular narrative and mythographic subject throughout the Middle Ages. It also appeared occasionally in royal civic ritual. When James IV and the City of Edinburgh welcomed the King's betrothed, Princess Margaret Tudor, on August 7, 1503, the Judgment was staged alongside pageants depicting the Annunciation and the Marriage of the Blessed Virgin, a staging perhaps modeled on similar performances in Lille, 1469, Antwerp, 1494, and Brussels, 1496. Gray, "Royal Entry," 18–19. In addition to *patrona principis* in the Judgment dream, Minerva appears as *patrona urbis* in *TB* when the narrator notes Athenian devotion to the goddess (2.5676–706) and Antenor notes Trojan (4.5570–657). In each instance, though, she is more object of veneration than agent in narrative action. Benson, *History of Troy*, 106, considers such uses of classical material evidence of Lydgate's effort "to create a believable picture of the ancient world for his readers." In one instance, however, the narrator gives the goddess narrative agency when he explains the destruction of Greek ships and Ajax's near drowning as a result of Minerva's anger at the Greek leader for seizing Cassandra at her altar in Troy (5.657–96).

[60] Benson, *History of Troy*, 97–129.

[61] Scholars pushing beyond the standard critique of Lydgate's prolixity have discussed a range of issues evident in the text from humanism (Schirmer, *John Lydgate*, 42–51), classicism (Simpson, "Other Book of Troy," 397–423), and medievalism (Pearsall, *John Lydgate*, and "Lydgate as Innovator," 5–13) to poetics (Ebin, *Illuminator, Makar, Vates*, 15–17), Lancastrian politics (Baswell, "Troy Book," 215–37; Benson, *History of Troy*, 116–20; R.F. Green, *Poets and Princepleasers*, 155, 187–90; D. Lawton, "Dullness and the Fifteenth Century," 779–82; Patterson, "Making Identities," 69–107), and more broadly prudence (Benson, *History of Troy*, 124–9; Fewer, "John Lydgate's *Troy Book*," 230–41). See the essays in Scanlon and Simpson for wider discussions of Lydgate's poetics in relation to Lancastrian England.

[62] On the intertextual relationship between Chaucer's *TC* and Lydgate's *TB*, see Atwood, "Some Minor Sources," 27–42; Benson, "Critic and Poet," 23–33; and Baswell, "*Troy Book*," 216.

and allegorical reading and eager to align his poem with Chaucer's, he sees none. Rather, using the deities as thematic figures, he integrates each topic these deities represent – chivalry, prudence, history, and poetry-performance respectively. His particular use of Othea to introduce the theme of prudence, as C. David Benson noted, points to his reading of Christine de Pizan's *Epistre d'Othea*.[63]

Christine de Pizan's *L'Epistre d'Othea*

The first European woman known to have made her living as an author and publisher, Christine de Pizan (1364–c.1431) wrote and initially produced *L'Epistre d'Othea* in about 1400, dedicating the text to Louis, Duc d'Orleans and brother to France's King Charles VI.[64] Extant in forty-eight manuscript copies, seven early printed French editions, and three English translations, *L'Epistre* found its readers on both sides of the English Channel until well into the sixteenth century.[65] In *L'Epistre*, a carefully illustrated prosimetrum work, Christine creates a multi-layered, multi-genre fiction in which Othea, the goddess of prudence, addresses a verse letter of advice to the Trojan prince Hector when he is fifteen.[66] She invents Othea, a Minerva-Athena-Sapientia-like wisdom figure, and employs Hector, a budding knight and prince, to emphasize a central concern for prudent, well-ordered chivalric conduct: as the prince rules himself, Christine suggests, so shall he rule the state – a theme we have seen elsewhere.[67] To this verse letter, Christine appends mythographic and allegorical commentary, thereby creating another fictive layer to lend the

---

[63] Benson, *History of Troy*, 124–9.
[64] She also gave copies to Charles VI, Philip Duc de Burgundy, Jean Duc de Berry, Henry IV, and Isabeau Queen of France among others. Chance, *Medieval Mythography*, 3: 246. These recipients underscore Christine's milieu. Daughter of Thomas de Pizan, Charles V's astrologer-physician, she was associated with the court of France from a young age. At fifteen she married Etienne du Castel, a royal secretary, and had three children. Widowed and without independent means in 1390, she took up the pen to support her household, working as a scribe as well as writing her own works. *L'Epistre* is one of her early works. Chance, introduction to *Christine*, 1–8, 31, and *Medieval Mythography*. 3: 206–10; and Hindman, *Christine de Pizan's* Epistre Othéa, 1–19.
[65] On the mss., see Parussa, introduction to *Epistre*, 87–101, and Ouy, Reno, and Villela-Petit, *Album Christine de Pizan*, 131–42, 345–56. The USTC lists three French editions: Philippe Pigouchet (Paris, c.1499), Philippe Le Noir (Paris, 1522), and Raulin Gaultier (Rouen, n.d.). Bühler, introduction to *The Epistle*, xii n.2, lists four more sixteenth-century editions. There are two fifteenth-century English translations, one by Stephen Scrope (c.1396–1472), completed circa 1440–59 and extant in three mss., and another by Anthony Babyngton (fl. 1450–1500) completed in the century's second half and extant in one ms. Bühler, introduction to *The Epistle*, xi–xix; Gray, "'Fulle Wyse Gentyl-Woman'," 237. The printer Robert Wyer (fl. 1530–56) offered a third translation in 1549, suggesting resurging interest.
[66] Hindman, *Christine de Pizan's* Epistre Othéa, 25–33; Willard, *Christine de Pizan*, 91–4.
[67] Abray, "Imagining the Masculine," 133–47; Chance, *Medieval Mythography*, 3: 258–9, 357–62; Hindman, *Christine de Pizan's* Epistre Othéa, 33–51; Willard, *Christine de Pizan*, 94.

letter authority; as with classical texts it imitates, she seems to be saying, the letter merits interpretation, which she seeks to direct through the accompanying Glose and Allegorie.[68] While her creation of Othea underscores the role of wise women throughout *L'Epistre*, she roots her choice of Hector in France's ethnogenic myth of its origins from Francion, Hector's son. Like the British, who viewed themselves as Aeneas' descendants through his grandson Brutus, the French considered themselves descendants of Hector, who was also one of the nine worthies.[69] As Christine implies through Othea's instruction, however, *translatio imperii* is not a simple matter. The Trojan story and Hector's role in it carry a warning to anyone wishing to re-create Trojan culture: such culture is fragile – Achilles, after all, killed Hector, and the Greeks sacked Troy. But death and destruction are in the future within the fictive world Christine creates in the letter, even as Othea writes of both.

Though the form of Othea's name has suggested to some that Christine means her to be Minerva herself, the goddess rather functions as an overarching notion of "sagace de femme" (the wisdom of woman), as Christine notes in Glose I.[70] Other female figures, including Minerva, represent aspects of wisdom and virtue in Christine's effort, as Chance argues, to counter the worldly wisdom of Ovid's Dipsas and Jean de Meun's Vieille by emphasizing *sapientia et fortitudo*, the wisdom and courage Christine "believes both chevalier and *miles Christi* should inculcate."[71] The structure of *L'Epistre* reinforces the implication that, though fictively addressed to Hector, Christine intends the letter for her contemporaries. She organizes the letter into 100 short chapters, each with four parts: an image depicting an event from classical mythology; a verse Texte working in tandem with the image; a Glose expanding the event, applying it to individual behavior, and punctuating the application with a philosophical saying; and an Allegorie offering a spiritual application punctuated by a saying or observation from a Church Father and a biblical quote.[72] Each chapter works as an *aide-mémoire*. While the image supplies a visual cue for memory and the verse a pithy poetic statement related to the image, the Glose develops the story's ethical application, and the Allegorie presents a spiritual understanding. Working

---

[68] Tuve, *Allegorical Imagery*, 33–45.
[69] Abray, "Imagining the Masculine," 136–7; Hindman, *Christine de Pizan's* Epistre Othéa, 35–7. In the c.1312 Alexander romance *Les Vœux du Paon*, Jacques de Longuyon developed the nine worthies trope, which included three worthies from Jewish culture – Joshua, David, Judas Maccabeus – three from pagan culture – Hector, Alexander, Julius Caesar – and three from Christian culture – Arthur, Charlemagne, Godfrey of Bouillon. Extract from "Les Vœux," ed. Gollancz, 48–147; Hindman, *Christine de Pizan's* Epistre Othéa, 34–5. Though most frequently held up for admiration, the worthies were not flawless and, as Elde observes in *Parlement of the Thre Ages*, ed., Offord, 295–583, they were limited: each lost all he had when he died.
[70] *Epistre Othea*, ed. Parussa, 1.73–4. The name Othea, likely from Greek "O Thea," has puzzled scholars. Chance, introduction to *Christine*, 25–6.
[71] *Medieval Mythography* 3: 258–71: 259.
[72] For discussions on form and structure, see Chance, *Medieval Mythography*, 3: 253–8; Ignatius, "Christine de Pizan's *Epistre*," 127–42, and "Manuscript Format," 121–4; and Tuve, *Allegorical Imagery*, 34–43. For a review of Christine's sources, with a focus on the *Chaplet des vertus*, see Rouse and Rouse, "Prudence, Mother of Virtues," 185–228.

with chapter one in the Queen's manuscript (British Library Harley Ms. 4431), the holograph anthology Christine presented to Queen Isabeau of France in 1414, we can parse how this reading process works (Fig. 4).[73] Christine formatted the manuscript in two columns. The illumination on folio 95v, painted in the bottom third of the first column, depicts Othea in the upper left quadrant sitting on a blue cloud and hovering over a tree as she leans down to deliver a letter to a youth standing in the bottom center, wearing a blue garment, bearing a falcon in his left hand, and reaching for the letter with his right. Three men, standing behind and to the right of the youth, witness the exchange. In fifty-eight verses following the image, Othea identifies herself, salutes Hector by name, and explains her purpose. Advancing a euhemerist reading, Christine then writes the prose Glose in the voice of a Christian scholar, explicating ancient Greek religion, Othea's origin as a wise woman who helped Hector, and her significance as "la vertu de prudence et sagece" (the virtue of prudence and wisdom) (1.102–3). After a prologue to the Allegorie, explaining its purpose to array the soul with virtue, Christine concludes by explicating that "prudence et sagece soit mere et conduisarresse de toutes vertus" (prudence and wisdom are mother and founder of all virtues) (1.146–7): one needs prudence for both chivalric and spiritual knighthood. Organizing the whole, Christine groups the chapters as follows: cardinal virtues and Perseus as their epitome (1–5), planets (6–12), theological virtues (13–15), seven deadly sins (16–22), twelve articles of the creed (23–34), ten commandments (35–44), miscellaneous stories (45–59), stories of Troy and Thebes (60–99), and Caesar Augustus and the Cumean Sibyl (100). Christine designed *L'Epistre*, as Rosamond Tuve noted years ago, like a summa.[74]

Minerva plays a key role in *L'Epistre* as Christine weaves her into image, Texte, and Glose at various points. We first meet her almost immediately when Othea, in formal epistolary fashion, addresses Hector in part as "Filz de Mars, le dieu de bataille /... Et de Minerve, la deese / Puissant qui d'armes est maistresse" (son of Mars, the god of battle ... and of Minerva, the goddess, who is the powerful mistress of arms) (1.18, 20–1). In naming Minerva's relationship to Hector, Christine transforms her

---

[73] In addition to a color plate in Hindman, *Christine de Pizan's* Epistre Othéa, iii, and digital images in Laidlaw, Grout, Mansfield, and Clegg, *Christine de Pizan*, "Images," a digital facsimile of the Queen's ms. is available at the British Library Digital Manuscripts website. For a description, see Ouy, Reno, and Villela-Petit, *Album Christine de Pizan*, 317–43. Christine organized a scriptorium in Paris, producing fifty of her extant mss. between 1399 and 1418. Laidlaw et al., "Research Context." Among these mss. are three holograph copies of *L'Epistre*, one of which is part of the Queen's manuscript. Desmond and Sheingorn, *Myth, Montage, and Visuality*, 17; Hindman, 15–16; and Laidlaw et al., "Introduction." This anthology and the Duke's manuscript, an anthology completed some years before and acquired by Jean Duc de Berry in about 1408 (now BnF 835, 606, 836, 605, 607), offer insight into how Christine worked; she not only wrote the text but also planned the illumination. See Desmond and Sheingorn, passim; Hindman, 61–99; and Laidlaw et al., passim. Interestingly, the English translator and printer Wyer also includes woodcuts throughout his 1549 edition: a hint he was working from a similar manuscript as he translated and prepared the text.

[74] Tuve, *Allegorical Imagery*, 43.

Figure 4. British Library, Harley Ms. 4431, fol. 95v.
© The British Library Board (Harley Ms. 4431).

from *patrona* to *mater principis*.⁷⁵ As Mars *pater principis* offers Hector prowess, Minerva *mater principis* offers him strategic wisdom: Hector has the potential to unite both in his person as he matures if he attends to Othea's lessons and acts accordingly. When Minerva next appears in chapter thirteen, Othea reminds the prince of this relationship. Turning again to the Queen's manuscript, the framed illumination on the bottom half of the first column of folio 102v depicts Minerva in the top half of the painting (Fig. 5). Armed in plate with sword girt and shield on her back, she is bare-headed with flowing blond tresses and, like Othea on folio 95v, floats on a blue cloud while passing down armor to a group of men in various stages of arming themselves. With this image in mind, the reader moves to the Texte:

> Armeüres de toutes sortes,
> Pour toy armer bonnes et fortes,
> Te livrera assez ta mere
> Minerve, que ne t'est amere

> (Armor of every kind, to arm yourself well and strong, your mother offers to deliver you, Minerva, who is not bitter to you) (13.2–5)

Othea's playful aural pun on "mere" and "amere" expresses the goddess' wit and underscores Minerva's role as Hector's "not bitter" mother. We then learn from Christine's euhemeristic Glose that Minerva, a lady of great intelligence, first devised armor and, because of her great knowledge, "l'appellerent deesse" (they called her a goddess) (13.10): a reading Christine likely derives from Boccaccio.⁷⁶ Othea names her Hector's mother, Christine continues, to refer to Minerva's association with those who practice arms, especially the Trojan prince. In the Allegorie, then, Christine implies the armor of faith metaphor, linking Minerva to the first theological virtue without which, quoting Paul, "impossible est placere Deo" (it is impossible to please God) (13.28).

Minerva next appears immediately in chapter fourteen with her Greek counterpart Pallas Athena. The illumination from the Queen's manuscript – in the same opening as chapter thirteen – is instructive. Located in the top half of the first column on folio 103r, and introduced with the rubric "La deesse Minerve et la deesse Pallas ensemble" (the goddess Minerva and the goddess Pallas together), the illumination depicts an armed Minerva in the upper left quadrant, with drawn sword leaning on her left shoulder, while a robed Athena holding a book in her left hand occupies the upper right quadrant: both again float on blue clouds and each gazes down on two groups of standing men, chevaliers on the left and clerics on the right. The Texte reads:

> Adjouste Pallas la deesse
> Et mes aveucques ta prouece

---

⁷⁵ Chance, "Interpretive Essay: Christine's Minerva," 126–33, examines Christine's view of Minerva as Hector's mother.
⁷⁶ *De mulieribus claris*, ed. and trans. Brown, 6.

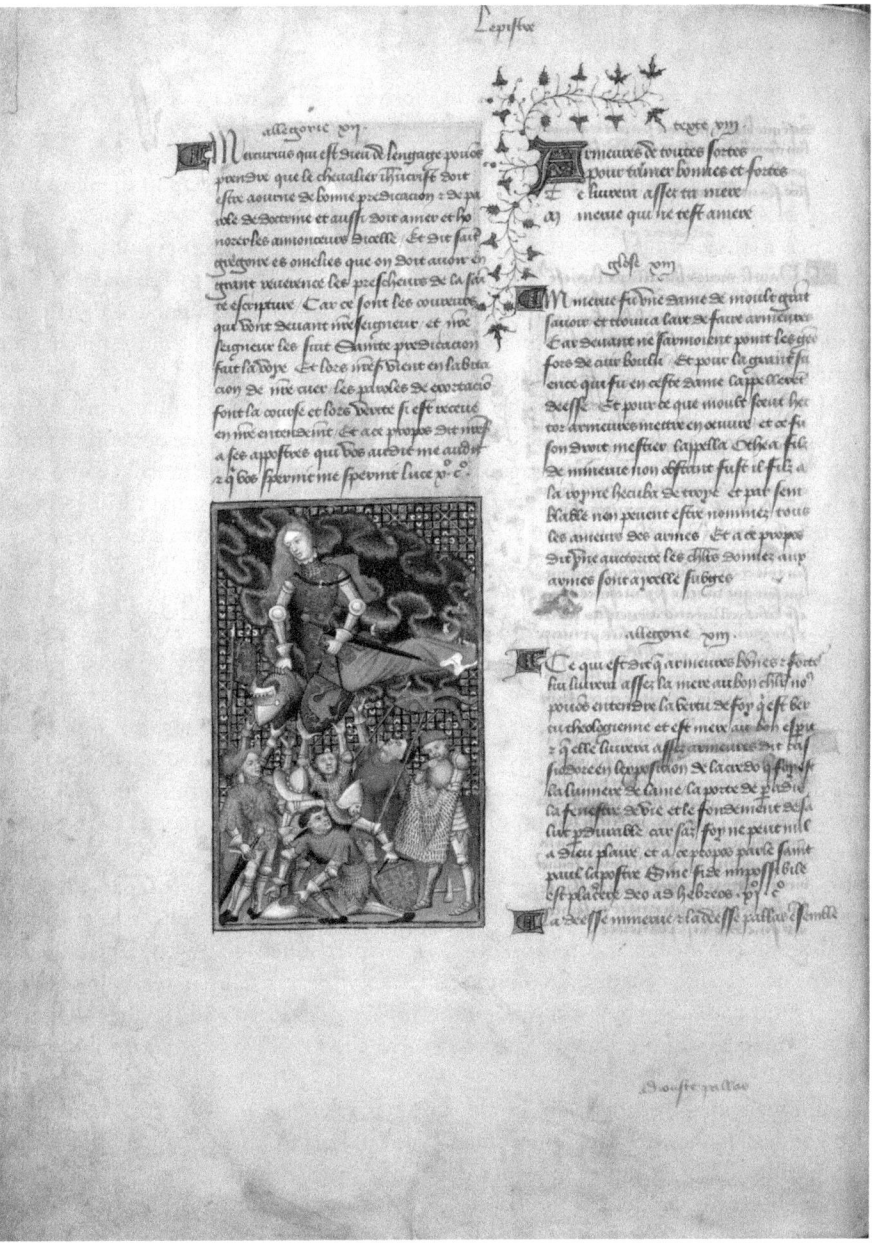

Figure 5. British Library, Harley Ms. 4431, fol. 102v.
© The British Library Board (Harley Ms. 4431).

> Tout bien te venra se tu l'as
> Bien siet o Minerve Pallas
>
> (Join Pallas the goddess to yourself and more so together with your prowess. All good will come to you if you have her; Pallas sits well with Minerva) (14.3–6)

As the quatrain's final line directly reflects on the goddesses' position in the illumination, Christine explains that "Pallas et Minerve est une mesmes chose, mais les noms sont pris a .ij. entendemens" (Pallas and Minerva is one same thing, but the names are taken as two understandings") (14.9–11): Minerva pertains to "chevalerie" and Pallas to "sagace" (wisdom) (14.17–18). Thus, Christine notes, a good knight joins wisdom to chivalry. And, as Minerva represents Faith in the Allegorie of chapter thirteen, Pallas represents Hope here.

Minerva-Pallas appears again in *L'Epistre* (60–99) in events familiar from stories of Thebes and Troy. In chapter sixty, for instance, in which Othea cautions against discord, Christine glosses the image and Texte by recounting the marriage of Peleus and Thetis and the great debate between Pallas, Juno, and Venus that ultimately led to Hector's death and the second sack of Troy. Similarly in chapter sixty-four, where Othea cautions Hector against boasting, Christine retells in the Glose the story of Pallas and Arachne and the latter's punishment of ceaseless spinning and weaving. In seventy-three, as Othea addresses wise judgment by Paris' negative example, Christine recounts the Judgment of Paris episode in the Glose, giving voice to each goddess in turn. Here, Pallas does not solely represent the way of contemplation familiar from *Reson and Sensuallyte*; rather, because she is writing for a chivalric milieu, Christine rehearses her theme from chapter fourteen when Pallas says: "'Je suis deesse de chevaleries et de sagece et par moy sont departies armes aux chevaliers et sciences aux clercs, et se tu la pomme me veulx donner saches que sur tous te feray chevalereux et tous passeras en toutes sciences'" (I am the goddess of chivalry and wisdom, and through me arms are granted to chevaliers and knowledge to clerics; if you wish to give me the apple you hold I shall make you chivalrous, and you shall excel in all knowledge) (73.15–20). And, in chapter ninety-six, when Othea warns Hector not to allow enemies to offer sacrifice at Minerva's temple, Christine glosses her cryptic comment by recounting the Trojan horse story and, in the Allegorie, links Minerva's temple to the Church, where she argues prayer alone should be offered.

Although chapter ninety-six holds the final reference to Minerva in *L'Epistre*, the goddess makes her last appearance in the Glose to chapter ninety. Placed in the middle of a five-chapter sequence detailing Hector's death (88–92), this chapter works directly in tandem with chapter eighty-eight, in which Othea hints at and Christine recounts the story of Andromache's dream that opens the sequence: both draw the lesson not to reject a wise woman's counsel (implicitly including their own). Following a warning in chapter eighty-nine not to rely solely on strong city walls in time of war, as the Babylonians did, Othea in chapter ninety reluctantly begins to tell Hector of his death, warning him it will be imminent "quant le roy Priant / Ne croiras" (when you do not trust King Priam) (90.4–5). Christine, then, glosses the reference, recounting details of Andromache's dream as she had told it to Priam: that "Mars, le dieu de bataille, et Minerve, deesse d'armes" had revealed Hector's death to her while she slept so she might warn her husband. Though Priam tried to stop him, Christine continues, Hector slipped out of the city, fought, and died that day. In this final appearance within Andromache's account of her dream vision, Mars and Minerva reprise their roles as Hector's parents from the opening lines of *L'Epistre* and their early chapters (11 and 13 respectively). Unlike other versions of Hector's death where Minerva aids Achilles in combat against the Trojan, Minerva here remains *matrem principis*. To thrive as a warrior-prince, however, Hector would need to cooperate with the goddess (and with Othea for that matter) were her wisdom and chivalry to aid him. Like Statius' Tydeus before him, but not with similar gruesome results, the Hector Christine glosses in chapters eighty-eight and ninety ignores his wife's and his father's pleas, forgets Othea's warnings, and rejects Mars and Minerva's aid. Though Othea continues to advise the Trojan prince by warning him particularly not to be caught unprotected in battle (91) and to avoid coveting Polibetes' armor (92), Christine again tells the story for her readers, recounting in the Glose to ninety-two that, preoccupied with stripping Polibetes' armor Hector opened himself to Achilles' fatal attack: the exposure was imprudent, and despoiling Polibetes unchivalric.[77] In the moment of his death, as image, Glose, and even Texte imply, Hector forgot Othea's lessons and the Minerva-Pallas message of joining *sapientia et fortitudo*. His forgetfulness serves as a foil to Christine's effort to offer readers a memorial text designed in form and content to reflect on chivalry. Worthy though he might be, Christine seems to say, Hector's mistake had far-reaching consequences. Leaving Troy without its chief champion, the prince's un-chivalric folly – his self-centered personal action on the battlefield – affected Troy's security and peace, and the common good suffered.

Reading Christine's *Epistre d'Othea*, John Lydgate offers an early response to the text in his *Troy Book*, exemplifying again the dynamic intertextual processes of medieval poetics. Like Christine, Lydgate emphasizes throughout the narrative the theme of prudence, wisdom's ethical dimension expressed in the moral and practical sphere of human action: the "via prudentiae" that, grounded in love, leads to right living in relation to the Divine and other creatures. As C. David Benson notes, *L'Epistre* "affects the entire *Troy Book* and seems responsible for the poem's emphasis on the value of Prudence."[78] Taking Christine's lead of critiquing Hector for his imprudent, un-chivalric action the day he died, Lydgate amplifies Hector's death scene in Guido's *Historia* from three Latin sentences (21, 175) to sixty-eight English lines. Beginning the episode by pausing in the battle to describe a nameless Greek king's armor and surcoat, the narrator sets up Hector's death with a focus on this single warrior's wealth. The Greek catches Hector's eye; the narrator continues:

---

[77] Images in the Queen's manuscript are, again, instructive. Both appear in the same opening – folios 136v and 137r – and depict first (91) Hector in the midst of a mêlée gripping a dead knight and exposing himself to attack, and second (92) Achilles' fatal attack, thrusting a spear into Hector's lower back. On this image in relation to gender and violence, see Desmond and Sheingorn, *Myth, Montage, and Visuality*, 184–9.

[78] Benson, *History of Troy*, 125.

Of whos array, whan Hector taketh hede,
Towardis hym faste gan hym drawe.
And firste, I fynd how he hath him slawe;
And after that, by force of his manhede
He rent hym up aforn him on his stede
And faste gan with hym for to ride
From the wardis a litel oute aside,
At good leiser pleynly, yif he may,
To spoillen hym of his riche array,
Ful glad and light of his newe emprise. (3.5344–53)

Unlike in Guido, where he takes the Greek prisoner, Hector kills him outright here. The narrator's comment, "I fynd how he hath hym slawe," suggests a readerly gesture towards a source. Perhaps we see here a record of the moment Lydgate read Christine's chapter ninety-two, where we, too, find this detail. As he rides off with his booty, the dead man's armor-clad body, however, Hector's callous light-hearted gladness over his prize is as short-lived as he at this narrative moment. Seeing Hector has exposed his chest "Al unwarly" to bear off the body to despoil it, Achilles slays him with a spear (3.5392–9: 5395).[79] Compared to the Homeric version of Hector's death, or even Joseph of Exeter's, there is little heroic in this moment for either Hector or Achilles: as the one loses his life over mere glitz, the other takes it in a workmanlike fashion. Reviewing some of these changes and others, Benson argues Lydgate developed the theme of prudence to counter Guido's pessimistic view of the Trojan experience as purely random, driven by fate and fortune; sharing *L'Epistre*'s "celebration of prudence," as Benson puts it, Lydgate interjects into the poem the prince's agency leading to his own death, thereby making it possible to examine his actions.[80] Though Minerva *mater principis* is absent from Hector's experience in the *Troy Book*, she is intertextually present through Lydgate's reading of *L'Epistre d'Othea*. The union of wisdom with chivalry, Minerva's key message as *mater principis*, comes through particularly in the negative example of Hector, who forgets himself and his responsibilities in his desire for booty.

The Minerva *patrona* image appearing in a range of medieval texts, from Walter of Chatillon's *Alexandreis* to Christine de Pizan's *Epistre d'Othea*, can work to protect the city, sponsor diplomacy and strategic war, and inspire the prince. Regarding right rule, the realm of the prince, a common theme emerges: the prince's microcosmic decisions can have macrocosmic effects concerning the state's

---

[79] This detail of despoiling a dead warrior recalls Hector's killing of Patroclus and twice-thwarted attempts to strip his armor (*TB* 3.344–899). Chaucer's version of Hector's death in *TC* is similar, stressing Hector's unwariness to the Boethian "indiscretus ictus" (*CP* 2.pr.2.13), which Chaucer translates in *Boece* as "unwar strook" (2.pr.2.69) – note the use of "unwar."

> For as he drough a kyng by th'aventaille,
> Unwar of this, Achilles thorugh the maille
> And thorugh the body gan hym forto ryue;
> And thus the worthi knyght was brought of lyve. (5.1558–61)

[80] Benson, *History of Troy*, 124–9: 128.

health. Turning now to Stephen Hawes, we move forward in time from Christine de Pizan and John Lydgate some eighty to one hundred years, and we shift from the third-person narration of epic-chronicle and mythographic commentary to the first-person of dream vision and allegorical pilgrimage. In *The Example of Vertu* and *The Pastime of Pleasure*, Hawes draws on Minerva *patrona* to articulate the role wisdom plays in fostering Christian knighthood, a concern we have seen in the Allegories of *L'Epistre* but which Hawes places at the center of his allegorical fictions. Concerned with eschatology in both poems, Hawes – like John Skelton and Gavin Douglas – also explores the issues of fame and honor in the Christian knight's spiritual quest.

Stephen Hawes and Minerva *patrona principis*

Active early in the sixteenth century, Stephen Hawes (c.1474–c.1523) produced a number of shorter poems in addition to his more ambitious narratives *The Example of Vertu* and *The Pastime of Pleasure*. Like Skelton, Hawes was a member of Henry VII's *familia regis*, being by 1502 a groom of the King's chamber, one of Henry's courtier-servants. In 1503, the royal account records a grant to Hawes of four yards of black cloth for the funeral of Henry's wife, Elizabeth of York, and on January 10, 1506, it shows a payment of ten shillings to Hawes for a "ballet that he gave to the king's grace."[81] Aside from these details, we know with surety little else about him except that he was also a poet.[82] According to colophons preceding each poem, Hawes composed *Vertu* in the nineteenth year of Henry's reign (August 1503–August 1504), and *Pastime* in the twenty-first year (August 1505–August 1506). As a groom of the chamber, Hawes would have first published these poems in manuscript for consumption at court. Fashioning himself as a sort of second Lydgate, Hawes in fact presents *The Pastime of Pleasure* to Henry VII by alluding to Lydgate's dedication of *Troy Book* to Henry V (26–35). The poem's dedication manuscript, unfortunately, is

---

[81] Gluck and Morgan, introduction to *Stephen Hawes*, xiii
[82] Other details also may pertain to the poet. Possibly born in Suffolk, Hawes may have matriculated at Magdalen College, Oxford, in 1493 (an SH is mentioned in the College's roll but could have easily been someone else). Hawes likely left the court at Henry VII's death on April 21, 1509, but may have left as early as January 1507 to serve as rector at Withern, Lincolnshire, where a Stephen Hawes was installed (if so, he was dead by January 10, 1510). He was not noted as present for Henry's funeral, but we cannot make too much of absence in records such as these. The next royal record of a Hawes occurs in 1521 with an account payment of £6, 13s. 4d. for a play. Apart from court records, on January 16, 1523, the will of a Stephen Hawes was proved in the arch-diaconal court of Suffolk. In it the testator left all his property to his wife Katherine. See Cannan, "Stephen Hawes," 188–90; A. Edwards, *Stephen Hawes*, 2–3, and "Stephen Hawes," 166; Gluck and Morgan, introduction to *Stephen Hawes*, xi–xiv; Hasler, "Stephen Hawes," 6, and *Court Poetry*, 108–9; Mead, introduction to *The Pastime*, xiii–xv; and Wakelin, "Stephen Hawes," 54–5. R.F. Green, *Poets and Princepleasers*, 13–70, discusses the *familia regis* and the *camera regis* in late medieval England, shedding light on the place in court of poets like Hawes, Skelton, and others.

not extant nor are any complete manuscript copies of Hawes' poetry. Other than a few manuscript fragments, Hawes' poems are now extant only in printed editions. By 1509, the year of transition between Henry VII and Henry VIII, Hawes had entered an arrangement with Wynkyn de Worde to publish his poetry, a relationship that continued until after Hawes' death.[83] This move indicates the poet was seeking an audience wider than the court. And, as it progressed, 1509 became an *annus mirabilis* of sorts not only for a nation both grieving the loss of an old king and rejoicing at the rise of a new one but also for Wynkyn de Worde and his poet-collaborator Stephen Hawes. That summer London experienced an influx of visitors as British subjects converged on the city to join festivities marking Henry VIII's coronation. Ever the businessman, and presumably sensing an opportunity, de Worde published twenty-four separate titles that year, including five from Hawes' pen: *The Example of Vertu*, *The Pastime of Pleasure*, *The Conversion of Swearers*, *An Elegy on the Death of Henry VII*, and *A Joyful Meditation*, the poet's celebratory poem marking Henry VIII's coronation.[84]

The Example of Vertu

In *The Example of Vertu*, a 2129-line poem in rhyme royal, Hawes uses dream vision and personification allegory to explore the education of the Christian knight, during which Minerva plays a small part related to her role as *patrona*. Youth, his dreamer-narrator, undertakes an educational journey guided initially by Morpheus, god of sleep, and then by Dame Discretion, whom he met in a "medowe amorous."[85]

---

[83] A. Edwards, "Poet and Printer," 82–8, and "Stephen Hawes," 170. Unlike his master Caxton, who in addition to others' works printed many of his own texts in a sort of self-publishing venture, Wynkyn de Worde printed only works written or translated by others. His business method involved in part entering into relationships with poets like Hawes, presumably when he thought he could market a text. Coldiron, "William Caxton," 160–9; A. Edwards, "Marketing of Printed Books," 119–20. De Worde's hunch about Hawes must have been sound as the 1509 edition of *Vertu*, a print run of something like 700–1200 copies, has only one extant copy today, located at Pepys Library, Magdalene College, Cambridge; similarly, the 1509 edition of *Pastime* exists only in fragments of two copies in the Bodleian Library, Oxford. On early print runs, see Gaskell, *New Introduction to Bibliography*, 160–3.

[84] On this 1509 publication history, see the *STC* as well as EEBO. Six years later, in 1515, Wynkyn de Worde published Hawes' *Comfort of Lovers* for the first time; sometime before 1517, he published a second edition of *The Pastime of Pleasure*, and then second and third editions of *Vertu* in 1520 and 1530 respectively. De Worde was Hawes' sole publisher until 1531 when John Skot printed an edition of *The Conversion of Swearers*. In the early to mid-1550s, William Copland printed another edition of *The Conversion of Swearers*, and John Wayland and Richard Tottel brought out separate editions of *The Pastime of Pleasure*. In each case, the publication record attests to continued and renewed interest in Hawes' works. See also Duff, "Introduction of Printing," par. 44; A. Edwards, *Stephen Hawes*, 2–3, 20–5; Gluck and Morgan, introduction to *Stephen Hawes*, xv–xxii; and Mead, introduction to *The Pastime*, xxix–xl.

[85] *The Example of Vertu*, ed. Gluck and Morgan, 48.

During the early stage of this journey, he sailed over stormy seas to a fair island where Discretion introduced him to four ladies – Dame Nature, Dame Fortune, Dame Hardiness, and her own "syster" (177) Dame Sapience – dwelling together in "a fayre castell / Besyde a ryuer moche depe and clere" (183–4). We are squarely in an allegorical dreamscape familiar to us from poems like *The Court of Sapience*, which Hawes knew well: the stormy sea and island signify the world; the castle, it would seem, humankind or the human soul.[86] Upon arrival, Youth learned the four ladies disagreed as to whom among them most benefited humankind and observed their debate before Dame Justice: Hardiness declared she gives courage; Sapience, prudence and understanding; Fortune, success in the world; and Nature, life. Unlike the Four Daughters of God story in *The Court of Sapience*, the debate here ended in an apparent draw: Justice simply enjoined them all to help humankind. Still, Sapience is pre-eminent throughout. Of the four ladies, she alone directly addressed Youth on his arrival (366–490), and he chose to dwell with her prior to the debate. During the debate itself she declared, "I am grounde of the artes seuen / And of all good werkes in communyon / For no man without me can go to heuen" (716–18). And then later, among other points, she noted, "I Sapyence am of the kynges counsayll" (879). In addition to her association here with the liberal arts, Hawes' Sapience relates to biblical Sapientia: the way-and-means to heaven familiar from texts such as the first "O" antiphon, and the guide of kings in imitation of King Solomon (1 Kings 3:4–28).

Following the debate and Justice's ruling, during which Youth learned how each lady contributes to human life, the dreamer-narrator's role began to shift from observation to action, from didactic to experiential learning. Sapience tarried with Youth and Discretion, joining with her sister in discussing a suitable partner for the dreamer-narrator. They settled on Dame Cleanness, and Youth and Discretion resumed the journey. Sapience later rejoined the hero and her sister on the road and helped lead him to meet Cleanness and the King of Love, who commissioned Youth to defeat a three-headed dragon so as to win Cleanness' hand in marriage. Sapience again aided Youth directly, arming the hero (1380–1401) and accompanying him throughout his fight. Though the narrator does not mention the other three ladies at this juncture, they are implicitly present as Justice demanded. With their aid, Youth vanquished the three-headed dragon (representing the Three Temptations: The World, The Flesh, and The Devil), the King of Love renamed him Vertu, and he married Dame Cleanness, with whom he shared a beatific vision at poem's end. In an epilogue, a narrative voice other than Vertu's concludes the poem, addressing King Henry, Princess Margaret, and Prince Henry "our second treasure" (2095) before taking leave of Gower, Chaucer, and Lydgate. For her part, Minerva briefly appeared early in the narrative accompanying Dame Hardiness (i.e., Courage or Fortitude) in the latter's dwelling when the narrator observed "A noble vyrgyn there did her serue / That first made harnes called Mynerue" (286–7). Drawing on the euhemeristic reading of Minerva as the inventor of armor, familiar from Christine de Pizan and her source Boccaccio, Hawes' passing reference sets up the later

---

[86] Wells, "Stephen Hawes and *The Court*," 285–94.

arming scene: the "fayre armure" (1380) Sapience buckled onto the hero, which he glosses as Paul's "armure for the soule" (1394), echoes Christine's allusion in *L'Epistre* 13 to Paul's armor of faith.[87] Here in *The Example*, as Minerva *patrona*'s invention, the armor, by synecdoche, represented her aid when Youth fought the dragon.[88] Again, with help from Discretion, the four ladies (particularly Sapience who alone can lead to heaven), and indirectly Minerva *patrona*, Youth achieved the ends of his educational journey: defeat of the dragon, transformation into Vertu, union with Cleanness, and beatific vision.[89]

The Pastime of Pleasure

Returning to ideas worked out in *The Example*, Hawes further and more fully develops the theme of education proper to the active life of a Christian knight in his 5816-line *Pastime of Pleasure*, an extended exploration of not only education but also death and the Boethian idea of the second death when one's fame dies. The poet

---

[87] Though he might have known Christine's *Epistre* through Scrope's translation, Hawes likely knew Christine's *Epistre* directly as the royal library owned a copy that is now in the British Library: Royal Ms. 14.E.ii. See Downes, "A 'Frenche book called the Pistill of Othea'," 457–68; Kekewich, "Edward IV, William Caxton," 481–7; and Nievergelt, *Allegorical Quests*, 74.

[88] Those familiar with Spenser's *Faerie Queene* note connections when reading Hawes' *Example* and *Pastime*. See C. Kaske, "How Spenser Really Used Stephen Hawes," 119–36; J. King, "Allegorical Pattern," 57–67; Lewis, "Edmund Spenser," 130–1; Nievergelt, *Allegorical Quests*, 169; and Zander, *Stephen Hawes*.

[89] It is tempting to try lifting the veil of allegory and speculate whether events at court prompted *The Example*'s composition. Written six to eighteen months after Elizabeth of York's death on February 11, 1503, *The Example* is perhaps a consolation poem. Though initially a political arrangement, Henry and Elizabeth's marriage turned out well: Henry evidently loved his wife and grieved deeply when she died. Alexander, *First of the Tudors*, 42–3, 185–6; Chrimes, *Henry VII*, 65–7, 93. Youth-Vertu's journey to Cleanness, their marriage, and their subsequent beatific vision suggest an implicit parallel to the King and Queen. If Youth-Vertu functions as an allegorical figure for Henry and Cleanness for Elizabeth, the poem itself, then, would function on one level as an allegory for their marriage and, perhaps, on another as a consolatory gesture to a grieving husband. The opening stanza of *Pastime*, addressed to Henry VII, underscores this hunch:

> Ryght myghty prynce / & redoubted souerayne
> Saylynge forthe well / in the shyppe of grace
> Ouer the wawes / of this lyfe vncertayne
> Ryght towarde heuen / to haue dwellynge place
> Grace dothe you guyde / in euery doubtfull cace
> Your gouernaunce / dothe euermore eschewe
> The synne of slouthe / enemy to vertewe. (1–7)

Setting aside the commonplace nature of the imagery – a ship on the sea of life journeying toward heaven – we see a possible allusion to *The Example*, where Youth-Vertu undertook this same journey. The stanza, of course, also leans forward into *Pastime*, in which Graunde Amoure undertook much the same: like Henry, both heroes "euermore eschewe / The synne of slouth / enemy to vertewe."

opens with a fifty-six-line prologue addressed to Henry VII, where he presents his "lytell boke" (24) containing a "fayned fable" (44) under which "a truthe maye aryse" (50), before moving into the fable itself: a forty-five-chapter narrative with a forty-sixth as epilogue. Writing in the vein of first-person literary pilgrimage literature, what Marco Nievergelt calls allegorical quests,[90] Hawes organizes *The Pastime*'s chapters around a journey punctuated by eight key sites of action: a meadow (chs. 1–2), the Tower of Doctrine (chs. 3–25), the Tower of Chivalry (chs. 26–8), the Temple of Venus (chs. 29–31), the Tower of Chastisement (chs. 32–5), the Temple of Pallas (chs. 36–7), the Palace of La Belle Pucell (chs. 38–41), and an old temple (chs. 42–5). Like his literary antecedent Youth-Vertu, the poem's narrator-protagonist, Graunde Amoure, recounts his adventure in the past tense: a remembered journey he undertook to achieve union with his beloved La Belle Pucell. Graunde Amoure closes the narrative with the journey's aftermath – married life, old age, death, and afterlife – and Hawes concludes the whole with the three-stanza epilogue addressed to fellow poets, the book itself, and God. Composing *The Pastime*, Hawes does not merely rehash or amplify his theme of education proper to the Christian knight; rather, he revises for narrative emphases. One such revision centers on how he develops and integrates the Minerva *patrona* image he inherited from Lydgate and Christine de Pizan. While the goddess only appears briefly and by implication in *The Example*, she plays a recurring role foundational to the hero's success in *The Pastime*'s narrative action.

Following Hawes' dedicatory prologue, Graunde Amoure opens his story with an astrological reference siting the initial narrative action in a late May morning when he journeyed "In to a medowe / bothe gaye and glorious" (8). Minerva makes her first appearance, albeit indirectly, in the narrative's subsequent commissioning scene. Initially wandering among the meadow's May flowers, Graunde Amoure discovered "By sodayne chaunce / a fayre path" (71), down which he meandered. Like several literary ancestors, including the *Reson and Sensuallyte* narrator, Graunde Amoure soon faced another choice when the path led "Vnto two hye wayes" (83) with road signs indicating "the streyght waye / of contemplacyon" (85) to the right and "the waye / of worldly dygnyte / Of the actyfe lyfe" (93–4) to the left. He mused over the decision but finally chose the latter and "went / The actyfe waye / with all my hole entent" (111–12) until he encountered, at day's end, a copper portrait with a message declaring this the way to the Tower of Doctrine. Exhausted and a bit puzzled, he slept under it and woke next morning to the sound of a horn and the arrival of a lady in flames: Fame accompanied by the hounds Governance and Grace. Establishing her credentials, Fame recalled the golden age of antiquity and recounted a catalog of noteworthy figures, including Saturn, king of Crete and inventor of agriculture; Melyzyus, king of Thessaly and horse tamer; and Hercules, noble hero

---

[90] Nievergelt, *Allegorical Quests*, 1–22. Similarly, Wenzel, "Pilgrimage of Life," 377–8, places Hawes' narratives in what he calls the pilgrimage of life genre. The only known copy of a key text for Wenzel's argument, Jean de Courcy's *Chemin de Vaillance* (374–7, 383–7), is in BL Royal MS 14.E.ii, which also includes the copy of Christine's *Epistre* Hawes likely read: perhaps Hawes knew de Courcy's poem, too. For a general discussion of the pilgrimage of life theme in art and literature, see Chew, *Pilgrimage of Life*.

of the commonwealth. Graunde Amoure first heard of Minerva in this catalog when Fame declared:

> "Also Mynerue / the right hardy goddess
> In the same tyme / of so hyghe renowne
> Vaynquysshed Pallas / by her grete worthynesse
> And fyrste made harnyes / to leye his pryde adowne
> Whose grete defence / in euery realme and towne
> Was spredde aboute / for her hye chyualry
> Whiche by her harneys / wanne the vyctory" (225–31)

Fame's recollection of Minerva's invention of armor invokes Minerva *patrona*, "Whose grete defence" and "hye chyualry" underscore her role as protectress and benefactor later in the poem. And along with these other figures from antiquity, Fame noted, Minerva worked for "the comyn proffet" (241). Turning back to Graunde Amoure, she then mentioned La Belle Pucell, and described her surpassing beauty, wisdom, and virtue. Graunde Amoure immediately fell in love in response to Fame's report. Before she departed, leaving her two greyhounds as his companions, Fame specifically commissioned him to journey to the Tower of Doctrine to learn the "seuen scyences" (305) and meet La Belle Pucell in person.

Though with mention of the "seuen scyences" we might expect Minerva to appear in the Tower of Doctrine, Hawes focuses on the Minerva *patrona* image alone in *The Pastime*, and the goddess next appears at the Tower of Chivalry. Prior to Graunde Amoure's training in chivalry, however, he undertook training in the liberal arts at the Tower of Doctrine as Fame commissioned. Here he met the seven ladies familiar to us from the Martianus tradition and encountered La Belle Pucell in Music's train, where he danced with his beloved and declared his love. Initially reluctant, La Belle Pucell eventually accepted Graunde Amoure's advances, swore him to secrecy, told him she must depart for "a ferre nacyon" (2279), and warned him of perils on his journey to join her. After parting with his beloved, and completing his liberal education, Graunde Amoure journeyed for advanced training to the Tower of Chivalry where, upon arrival, he made a false start. Entering the nearby Temple of Mars, he read depicted on the walls the story of Troy's fall and Hector and Troilus' fates in a clear reference to the Temple of Juno ekphrasis in Virgil's *Aeneid*, which also works to puzzle and delude the wandering Aeneas, who "animum pictura pascit inani" (feeds his soul on lifeless paintings) (1.464, 495). Spying Mars standing "On a whele top with a lady of pryde" (3034), who "had two faces" (3036), he beseeched the god's aid. Mars agreed to help but said Graunde Amoure needed to enlist Venus' aid first, at which Fortune "with the faces twayne" (3111) interrupted and debate ensued about who had pre-eminence in this case. Graunde Amoure states:

> To here of Mars the meruaylous argument
> And of fortune I was sore amased
> Tyll that I sawe a lady excellent
> Clerely armed vpon whome I gased
> And her armes full preuely I blased

> The sheld of golde as I wel vnderstande
> With a lyon of asure through passande
>
> To me she came with lowely countenaunce
> And bad me welcome vnto that mancyon
> Ledynge me forthe with Ioy and plesaunce
> Into an hall of meruaylous facyon (3221–31)

The lady who rescued him from Mars and Fortune's fruitless debate was Minerva, and the hall she led him into was also adorned but with "The sege of Thebes depaynted fayre and clere" (3240–1). For Hawes, the stories of Troy and Thebes underscore the contrast between Mars and Minerva: the former, it would seem, driven by hot passion and Fortune's caprice; the latter fostering cool reason and strategic thinking. Under Minerva *patrona principis*, Theseus, after all, sacked Thebes and restored right order while Troy fell in part as a result of Paris rejecting the goddess and Hector setting her aside.[91]

Following Minerva's lead, and by implication Theseus' as well, Graunde Amoure approached King Melyzyus, tamer of horses and first knight, and requested admission to the court for training.[92] The narrator continues:

> Welcome [Melyzyus] sayd to this courte ryall
> Mynerue shall arme you with grete dylygence
> And teche you the feastes of armes all
> For she them knoweth by good experience
> In the olde tyme it was her scyence
> And I my selfe shall gyue you a worthy stede
> Called galantyse to help you in your nede
>
> I humbly thanked his grete hyenes
> And so to Mynerue I dyde than applye
> Whiche dyde me teche with syker perfytness
> For to haunt armes right well and nobly
> Sapyence me ruled well and prudently
> Thus amonge knyghtes for to Iust and tourney
> Mynerue me taught in sundry wyse all day (3319–32)

Instructed by Minerva to be ruled by "Sapyence," Graunde Amoure by his own account progressed in training, saying again "Mynerue me taught my strokes and defence / That in shorte space was no resystence / Agaynst my power and myghty

---

[91] The Troy-Thebes distinction feels odd because Greeks sacked both cities; still, Hawes seems to use the stories as emblems of confusion (Troy) and of clear thinking (Thebes). The sack of Thebes came about when Theseus with Minerva's aid intervened to correct Creon's tyranny in the wake of civil war; that of Troy when Greeks also with Minerva's aid attempted to restore Helen to her husband. As with Virgil's ekphrasis, Hawes depicts the sack of Troy from the Trojan perspective, hence Graunde Amoure's Aeneas-like confusion.

[92] On Melyzyus, see Bühler, "'Kynge Melyzyus'," 438–40.

puyssaunce" (3338–40). Melyzyus soon recalled him to the court, instructed him to defend the commonwealth, and knighted him, all of which Graunde Amoure "dyde well regystre in my remembraunce" (3396). Minerva then led him back to the hall where, he notes, she

> ... armed me as she coude deuyse
> And brought vnto me my fayre barbed stede
> On whome I mounted in all godly guyse
> With shelde and spere as nothynge to drede
> In ryght to fyght for to attayne my mede (3410–14)

Accompanied by a fairly exhaustive list of personified knightly virtues, Graunde Amoure rode out of the Tower, "And dame Mynerue the chyualreous goddess / Dyde me endue then with herty hardynes" (3429–30). The fellowship accompanied Graunde Amoure to "a goodly playne" (3431), where he took his license and they prepared to part ways. He continues:

> And good dame Mynerue vnto me than sayde
> Be not adredde of your hye entreprise
> Be bolde and hardy and nothynge afrayde
> And rather deye in ony maner of wise
> To attyne honoure and the lyfe dyspyse
> Than for to lyue and to remayne in shame
> For to dye with honoure it is a good name
>
> Fare well she sayde and be of good chere
> I must departe I may no lenger tary
> Ryde on your way the weder is full clere
> Seke your aduenture and loke ye not vary
> Frome your hye ordre by ony contrary
> And therwithall forthe on her way she rode
> Ryght so dyde I whiche no lenger abode (3445–58)

Educated in liberal and chivalric arts, and embracing Minerva's commission "To attyne honoure," Graunde Amoure continued his journey to La Belle Pucell accompanied by the greyhounds and a page. In episodic fashion germane to allegorical quest literature, he encountered a range of adventures from a stop at Venus' Temple to combat with giants.[93] Each episode contributed to his experiential learning and growth, represented by personified virtues like Comfort and Perseverance who join

---

[93] The full list of episodes includes a comic interlude with an anti-feminist dwarf, Godfrey Gobelyue; the visit to Venus' Temple; a visit to the Tower of Chastisement, where he witnessed the punishment of false lovers; combat with the three-headed giant Falsehood-Imagination-Perjury, whom he defeated with his sword Claraprudence; medical treatment from three corresponding personified virtues – Verity, Good Operation, Fidelity – and aid from Perseverance and Comfort; combat with and defeat of the seven-headed giant Dissimulation-Delay-Discomfort-Variance-Envy-Detraction-Doubleness; and again aid from seven corresponding personified virtues: Steadfastness, Amorous Purveyance, Joy, Continuance, Pleasaunce, Report Famous, and Amity.

in his journey, until after long travels he and his company of virtues finally spied La Belle Pucell's palace.

At this point in the narrative, Minerva *patrona* appears a third time but in the guise of Pallas Athena. Seeing the way to the palace blocked by a fire-breathing "fende fallacious" (4939), which Disdain and Strangeness had made of seven metals through necromancy, Perseverance recommended they retire to a nearby temple dedicated to "wyse dame Pallas" (4965) to seek the goddess' advice "How we may scape the brennynge violence" (4969). Upon entering the temple, "Prostrate we fell mekely to the grounde / And sodaynly we were caste in a swounde" (4975–6). Graunde Amoure continues:

> Thus as we lay in a deedly chaunce
> We thought to her we made petycyon
> And all in englysshe with longe cyrcumstaunce
> She shewed vs all the hole condycyon
> Of the meruaylous serpents operacyon
> And dyde shewe vs a perfyte remedy
> To withstande all the craft of sorcery (4977–83)

During this visionary experience, curiously noting it transpired in English, Graunde Amoure learned both how the metal dragon operated and how to defeat it. He continues:

> But that dame pallas of her gentyll mynde
> Of meruaylous herbes a remedy dyde fynde
> And anone a boxe of meruaylous oyntemente
> She toke to me to withstonde the serpent
>
> Thus all esmeruayled we dyde than awake
> And in my hande I had the oyntemente
> Closed in a boxe of whiche I should take
> To anoynte my harneys for the serpent
> Whiche schall deuoyde his fyre so seruente
> And my swerde also to cause to departe
> Astroth the fende so sette with Magyckes arte. (5008–18)

The next day, armed with Pallas' ointment and instructions and Minerva's training and armor, Graunde Amoure faced the dragon: a creature with a maid's face, scorpion-like tail, and metallic body – a sort of futuristic, for Hawes, mechanized weapon named "malyce preuy" (5111). Graunde Amoure prepared for combat, as he says:

> I toke my boxe as Pallas commaunded
> And my swerde and shelde with all my armure
> In euery place I ryght well anointed
> To hardynes I toke my herte in cure
> Makynge me redy / and whan I thought me sure
> I toke my swerde and with an hardy herte
> Towarde the dragon I began to sterte (5117–23)

In presenting both Minerva and Pallas in *The Pastime*, Hawes implies Christine de Pizan's distinction and fusion of the two in *L'Epistre* 14 and uses the distinction to underscore for Graunde Amoure the fusion of wisdom with fortitude. Protected by Pallas-Minerva, he defeated the dragon, piercing it and causing a blast of smoke that covered the land, after which the ladies in his company declared, "Blyssed be Pallas the goddes glorious / Which that thou taught a perfyte remedy / For to deuoyde the crafte of sorcery" (5163–5). Having achieved this final success on his long quest, Graunde Amoure entered La Belle Pucell's palace, where he married his beloved, lived to old age, and died.

Buried in an old temple, Graunde Amoure continues to narrate the fable until the epilogue, and his comments underscore Hawes' larger eschatological project to consider the end as well as the ends of life. As Graunde Amoure recounts it, Remembrance made his epitaph, with a *memento mori* reflection on the seven deadly sins addressed to any passing by his tomb. In light of life's precariousness, and the losses Henry VII experienced directly, one stanza of the epitaph seems particularly poignant:

> O mortall folke / you may beholde and se
> How I lye here / somtyme a mighty knyght
> The ende of Ioye / and all prosperyte
> Is dethe at last / through his course and myght
> After the day there cometh the derke nyght
> For though the day be neuer so longe
> At last the belles ryngeth to euensonge (5474–80)

The parting image of evensong bells reminds Hawes' audience not to forget that death is the final action for every person.[94] It also sets up Graunde Amoure's concluding meditation. Just as Remembrance finished the epitaph, Fame in flames reappeared and promised Graunde Amoure to spread his name; like the nine worthies, to whom she devoted a stanza each, Graunde Amoure, she claimed, "shall dure and be eternall" (5590). Then winged and feathered, carrying a horologe in one hand and flame in the other, and wearing a girt sword and the planets, Time entered and corrected Fame's claim, saying he alone provided humans the opportunity for action, and he brought about that opportunity's end. In a Boethian moment, he noted that though God exists outside of time, humankind does not: a human's second death – the death of one's name on which Boethius also reflects (*CP* 2.m7) – is inevitable and complete when Time's own end marks the coming of eternity. At this point, Eternity – "Of heuen queen and of hell empress" (5753) – entered and explained that heaven and hell, like God, also exist outside time. Echoing Remembrance, she then called on "mortall folke" to recognize the transitory state of the world: "Set not your mynde vpon worldly welthe / But euermore regarde your soules helthe" (5780–1). Unlike Skelton, who moves to thwart Fame's efforts to discount him in his audacious comic-fantasy *A Garlande of Laurel*, Hawes draws a different conclusion

---

[94] See Lewis, *Allegory of Love*, 283–5, and Hasler, *Court Poetry*, 118–24, for other discussions of Hawes' meditation on death.

about this fickle figure who claims for herself "Infenyte I am nothynge can me mate" (5604). In spite of her boasts otherwise, Hawes' Fame ends in time, and his Time ends in Eternity.

Graunde Amoure's closing mediation on fame, time, and eternity again reinforces Hawes' larger project, which centers on the question what is the end of the dignified active life lived with honor in the world.[95] His principal characters serve allegorically as motive and goal for his concept of this life. La Belle Pucell (i.e., the Beautiful Maid), with her connection to Music – the liberal art that sets all the arts "in concorde" (1550) – functions in part as goal. In a sense, as object of Graunde Amoure's desire, she helps harmonize his learning in the liberal and chivalric arts by inspiring his quest at least as much as Fame instigates it. Graunde Amoure (i.e., Great Love) is desire itself: love of learning, honor, the dignified active life, harmony, balance, and ultimately eternity. Fostering Graunde Amoure's education at a key moment in the Tower of Chivalry, and later offering advanced training at the Temple of Pallas, Minerva *patrona* helped him prepare to face the gravest challenges on his quest.

Minerva *patrona* in Hawes' poems represents strategic and defensive warfare – a fusion of wisdom and fortitude – in service of Christian knighthood as played out within dream-vision and allegorical pilgrimage literature. In *The Example of Vertu*, she served Dame Hardynes as armor-maker and, by synecdoche, protected Youth-Vertu in his battle with the three-headed dragon. In *The Pastime of Pleasure*, she served as inspiration at the beginning of Graund Amoure's journey, as teacher at the Tower of Chivalry, and as mentor-protectress when he prepared to face his greatest challenge, the metallic dragon Malyce Preuy. Already educated in the liberal arts, Graunde Amoure received his advanced education at Minerva's hands. Ruling himself, he defeated his enemies, won La Belle Pucell's hand in marriage and, at poem's end, attained salvation in a judgment scene presided over by Eternity. In both poems, Hawes examines the ends of education for the active life and offers an answer. For layman and prince alike in early sixteenth-century England, the poet seems to say, the ends of education were moral and intellectual freedom and ultimately salvation: ends achieved through uniting wisdom and fortitude exemplified by Minerva *patrona*. Addressing both poems primarily to Henry VII and Prince Henry, he associates the goddess with princely rule and, like Minerva *patrona principis* in classical and medieval literature, she allegorically represents here the prudence a warrior-prince-knight needs to rule himself and others wisely.

---

[95] Again it is tempting to speculate whether events at court inspired Hawes to compose *Pastime*. If prior to spring 1502 Prince Henry was indeed preparing for a career in the Church as some have thought (though there seems to be no real evidence for it), Prince Arthur's death changed Henry's trajectory, and by the time Hawes wrote the poem the Prince was being groomed for the crown. Graunde Amoure's choice at poem's beginning between the contemplative life and the active could perhaps be a veiled hint at what might have happened to Henry; regardless, the poet's effort to fuse liberal and chivalric learning within the narrative mirrors somewhat Henry's educational experience. Scarisbrick, *Henry VIII*, 4–7. More generally, see Wakelin, "Stephen Hawes," on Hawes and education at Henry VII's court.

5

The Patristic Tradition: Minerva as Idol

The image of Minerva as idol finds its earliest expression in late antique Roman culture. Religious practice in the pre-Constantine Roman world was multi-form and various but with three key features: it tended to encapsulate religious ideas through deities associated with places and human activities; it employed a syncretic approach to religious expression, synthesizing ideas and practices encountered elsewhere with traditional Roman expression; and it emphasized public worship and respect for the city-state's ancestral deities – the *pax deorum*, or harmony between human and divine maintained through religious practice. As they encountered local religions through conquest, Romans typically allowed subjugated people to continue their religious practices if they did not challenge the *pax deorum*. Even Judaism *sans* political insurrection, for instance, though it rejected Roman polytheism, received a measure of toleration from the state because of its antiquity and ethnicity.[1] In the main, pre-Constantine Roman religion was an eclectic, fairly tolerant, cultural phenomenon tied to public life. Universalistic monotheism challenged this multicultural approach to religion.[2] With its advent in the Empire's early years and especially with its later ascendancy during the fourth and fifth centuries, Christianity particularly became a transformative force in Roman culture. Initially a marginalized sect of Judaism, Christianity separated from Judaism early in its development as Christians sought to proselytize among non-Jews, a mission that occasionally brought them into direct conflict with the state. Following the end of the Great Persecution (303–13) with the Edict of Milan in 313 and a period of civil conflict from which Constantine emerged as sole emperor in 324, Christianity moved from

---

[1] Corcoran, "Unholy Madness to Right-Mindedness," 67–8; Lim, "Christian Triumph and Controversy," 198. I am glossing over political tensions between Jews and Romans, which began in 63 BCE when Rome brought the region into its orbit as a client state. At the request of Jewish leaders frustrated by Herod Archelaus' lack of leadership, Augustus established *Provincia Iudaea* in 6 CE. The following 129 years were marked by deep tension and three major rebellions in 66–73 (the Great Jewish Revolt), 115–17 (Kitos War), and 132–5 (Bar Kokhba's Revolt), leading to a final destruction of the Temple. Hadrian changed the name of the province to *Syria Palaestina* in part to efface Jewish ties to the region, and the Jewish diaspora was more-or-less complete. Josephus' *Bellum Judaicum* offers a contemporary account of the Great Jewish Revolt; see also essays in Popović, ed., *Jewish Revolt against Rome*.

[2] Lim, "Christian Triumph and Controversy," 196.

the margins to the center of the Empire: as they gained access to power, Christian leaders initially sought to marginalize in turn and then ultimately, and aggressively at times, to ban ancient religious beliefs and practices, diminishing and eradicating them in an effort to foster their religion's position within the state. In the context of this official shift from a pluralistic religious culture to the universalistic monotheism of Nicene Christianity, Minerva along with the other deities of the Roman pantheon became classified as an idol. From this early Christian viewpoint, the goddess as idol is possibly the most easily recognizable facet of the five-fold paradigm of Minerva imagery examined here. In this chapter, I explore Minerva as she appears in early Christian Latin poetry and fourth- and fifth-century apologetics. Patristic writers construct the goddess within an anti-pagan discourse where she represents either a demon or human intellectual powers used in pursuit of worldly or self-centered ends. Steeped in this patristic tradition, medieval writers occasionally use Minerva as idol within an anti-pagan discourse, as is evident in a range of texts. Addressing this tradition, I then turn again to two late medieval poems – the anonymous *Assembly of Gods* and William Dunbar's *The Golden Targe* – to explore the patristic tradition's continued influence in English and Scots poetry where Minerva's alliances with other deities particularly inform her idolatrous imagery. Though articulated in patristic literature and later used by medieval poets, the concept of idolatry in Christian thought is rooted in Jewish and Christian scripture. To set the context for understanding Minerva as idol, I shall first review this concept before turning to patristic and medieval writing.

Idols and Idolatry in Jewish and Christian Cultures

The notion of idolatry in Jewish and Christian cultures – the worship of some mortal creature or object, an idol, rather than the Creator – coalesces, if not originates, with the Israelites' experience of God on Mount Sinai as recounted in Exodus 20–32.[3] Following their escape from Egypt, Moses led the people to a meeting with God on Mount Sinai in which God gave a series of commands, the first ten of which have remained prominent in Jewish and Christian thinking. The Decalogue begins with two statements key to understanding idolatry. Stating "ego sum Dominus Deus tuus qui eduxi te de terra Aeypti" (I am the Lord your God who brought you out of Egypt) (Ex. 22:2),[4] the first of the Ten Commandments, God declares his active role in delivering the Israelites from bondage and then states:

> non habebis deos alienos coram me non facies tibi sculptile neque omnem similitudinem quae est in caelo desuper et quae in terra deorsum nec eorum quae sunt in aquis sub terra non adorabis ea neque coles ego sum Dominus Deus tuus fortis zelotes visitans iniquitatem patrum in filiis in tertiam et quartam generationem

---

[3] See Camille, *Gothic Idol*, 27–49.
[4] Though perhaps I should refer here to the Tanakh, I follow the Latin Vulgate because medieval writers examined later would have read the Latin version.

eorum qui oderunt me et faciens misericordiam in milia his qui diligunt me et custodiunt praecepta mea

(You shall not have strange gods before me. You shall not make for yourself a graven image, nor the likeness of anything that is in heaven above or in the earth below, nor of those things that are in the waters under the earth. You shall not adore them, nor serve them; I am the Lord your God: mighty, jealous, visiting the iniquity of fathers upon their children unto the third and fourth generation of those who hate me, and showing mercy unto the thousandth generation to those who love me and keep my commandments) (Ex. 20:3–6)

Beginning with a prohibition in this second commandment, God elaborated on what having "deos alienos" meant – adoring and serving images or likenesses – delineated the punishment for any who so erred, and promised mercy to those "qui diligent me et custodiunt praecepta mea." This final message of love of God and keeping his commandments is central to the concept of idolatry in Jewish and Christian cultures. Within this cultural framework, and not unlike the *pax deorum* of Roman culture, religious behavior, that is, keeping God's commandments, seems to be the means by which believers live out love of God, thereby assuring his mercy unto the thousandth generation.

As the story goes, though, the people of Israel almost immediately broke these first two commandments. While Moses spent forty days and nights on Sinai receiving further instruction and two stone tablets containing all the laws, the people denied God and demanded of Moses' brother Aaron to fashion a golden statue of a calf to worship. The Exodus narrator continues: "surgentesque mane obtulerunt holocausta et hostias pacificas et sedit populus comedere ac bibere et surrexerunt ludere" (and rising in the morning they offered burnt offerings and peace sacrifices, and the people sat down to eat and drink, and then they rose up to play) (Ex. 32:6). This religious behavior contrary to divine command irritated God, who determined to destroy the people, until Moses prevailed on their behalf. Returning to the camp, Moses disrupted the celebration, broke the stone tablets in wrath, melted the golden calf, and punished the people by executing some three thousand. Moses returned to the mountain and confessed the people's sin, saying to God, "obsecro peccavit populus iste peccatum magnum feceruntque sibi deos aureos aut dimitte eis hanc noxam aut si non facis dele me de libro tuo quem scripsisti" (I beseech you: this people has sinned a great sin and have made for themselves golden gods; either forgive them this offense or, if you do not, erase me from your book that you have written) (Ex. 32:31). Responding he would only remove from the book the names of those who sinned, God commanded Moses to lead the people out from Sinai and promised retribution "in die ultionis" (on the day of revenge) (32:34). Removing idolaters' names signifies their ultimate exclusion from the people of Israel and illustrates idolatry's stark effects: as they forgot God in their idolatry, God will forget them. The narrator concludes: "percussit ergo Dominus populum pro reatu vituli quem fecit Aaron" (the Lord therefore struck the people for the crime of the calf that Aaron had made) (32:35). The centerpiece of this story is the Decalogue, which served as foundation text for the Israelite people: it articulated who they were – a people of God led out from Egypt – and how they should behave in relation to God and others. We can read much of what follows in Jewish scripture in light of Exodus 20–32.

As this story's pattern – prohibition, falling away, correction, confession, restitution – underlies much of the subsequent Israelite experience, it also illustrates the prevalent competitive religious environment between monotheism and polytheism in the ancient world. Even God's prohibition in the second commandment, "you shall not have strange gods before me," implicitly acknowledges the presence, at least culturally, of "deos alienos." Setting up the theme of idolatry and its results, this story also offers a model of right religious behavior directed toward God in love by following his commandments and worshipping him alone. Living within a richly pluralistic religious environment, not all Israelites managed to remain free of idolatry, however, and this particular sin seems to have been a major concern within the cultural milieu articulated in several books in the Hebrew Bible. From King Solomon's apostasy and its effects (1 Kings 11:1–43) to Daniel's idol-smashing during the Babylonian Exile (605–539 BCE), Jewish story-tellers and audiences admired heroic fidelity to the God of Israel, particularly when facing pressure from a dominant culture to conform through idolatry.

Two Jewish texts, both of which inform Christian attitudes, encapsulate this anti-idolatrous sentiment. In Psalm 113 (Vulgate), after recounting moments of divine intervention in the Israelite experience from exodus journey to promised-land settlement, the psalmist turns to God and states: "non nobis Domine non nobis sed nomini tuo da gloriam / super misericordia tua et veritate tua nequando dicant gentes ubi est Deus eorum" (Not to us, O Lord, not to us but to your name give glory for your mercy and truth lest gentiles say, where is their god?) (9–10).[5] Turning then to fellow Israelites, the psalmist draws together the community by answering this question: "Deus autem noster in caelo omnia quaecumque voluit fecit" (Our God, however, is in heaven: he has done all things, whatsoever he wished) (11). Incorporating all Israelites with the simple plural pronoun ("noster" in Latin), the psalmist then instructs the community of Israel on the nature of gentile gods:

simulacra gentium argentum et aurum opera manuum hominum
os habent et non loquentur oculos habent et non videbunt.
aures habent et non audient nares habent et non odorabuntur
manus habent et non palpabunt pedes habent et non ambulabunt non
    clamabunt in gutture suo
similes illis fiant qui faciunt ea et omnes qui confidunt eis

(The idols of the gentiles are silver and gold, the works of human hands: they have mouths, but they will not speak; they have eyes, but they will not see; they have ears, but they will not hear; they have nostrils, but they will not smell; they have hands, but they will not feel; they have feet, but they will not walk; they will not

---

[5] Likely composed during the postexilic period (c.430 BCE), Psalm 113 admonishes Israelites to remain faithful to God. See R. Clifford, *Psalms*, 54–5; Dahood, *Anchor Bible*, 139; Sabourin, *Psalms*, 320–1. For the Psalms in medieval culture, see the case studies in Van Deusen, ed., *Place of the Psalms*.

cry out from their own throat. Let those who make these become like them, and all who confide in them) (10–16)

A reminder, perhaps, not to stray, Psalm 113 also functions as lyric commentary on the first and second commandments and the notion of idolatry articulated in the story of the Sinai experience. In contrast to the living creative God of mercy and truth, according to the psalmist, such human-made deities – like the golden calf of Exodus 32 – lack power and life, as do their makers and followers.

Similarly, sapiential writers examined idolatry, finding it the antithesis of divine wisdom through which God created the universe and virtuous wisdom through which humans participate harmoniously in that universe. In Wisdom 14:8–21, the author describes in euhemeristic fashion the origin of idols and idolatry in the improper use and veneration of created things: a use that underscores the antithetical relationship between virtuous wisdom and idolatry as human practices. While "timor Dei" is the beginning of wisdom in Jewish scriptures, "infandorum enim idolorum cultura omnis mali causa est et initium et finis" (the worship of abominable idols is the cause, the beginning and the end of all evil) (Wisdom 14:27), according to the Wisdom-author. Indeed, as the Wisdom-author continues, idolatry destroys the social fabric divine wisdom establishes and virtuous wisdom maintains; it leads to a series of crimes against self, neighbor, and God, including murder, adultery, theft, and deception; and perhaps most serious of all it leads practitioners to "Domini immemoratio" (forgetfulness of the Lord) (Wisdom 14:26). This last phrase sums up the experiences of Israelites who, like the golden-calf worshippers in the Sinai, forget the first and second commandments. As idolaters forget the Lord, the phrase implies, so again the Lord will forget them.

Early Christianity, with its origins as a sect of Judaism, inherited this notion of idolatry as well. Like their Jewish ancestors and contemporaries, early Christians participated in a pluralistic and competitive religious environment, which they entered with missionary zeal. Paul's experience in Athens recounted in Acts of the Apostles, for instance, illustrates early Christian engagement with Greco-Roman religious pluralism. While there, Paul was moved, as the Acts-narrator says, "videns idolatriae deditam civitatem" (seeing the city given to idolatry) (17:16). Consequently, he disputed with Jews in the synagogue and gentiles in the forum, who then brought him to the Areopagus where he preached:

> viri athensienses per omnia quasi superstitiosiores vos video praeteriens enim et videns simulacra vestra inveni et aram in qua scriptum erat ignoto deo quod ergo ignorantes colitis hoc ego adnuntio vobis Deus qui fecit mundum et omnia quae in eo sunt hic caeli et terrae cum sit Dominus non in manufactis templis in habitat nec manibus humanis colitur indigens aliquo cum ipse det omnibus vitam et inspirationem et omnia

> (Men of Athens, I see in all things that you act as if very superstitious, for passing through and seeing your idols, I also found an altar on which was written "To an unknown god." What you worship, therefore, without knowing, that I preach to you. God who made the world and all things that are in it is Lord of heaven and earth: he does not dwell in human-made temples nor is he adorned by human

hands as though in need of anything. He gives to all life, breath, and all things) (17:22–5).

Deftly using Athenian religious and philosophical culture as entrée, Paul preached God the creator much the same as we see in Jewish scripture: faithful Jews would probably have found Paul's teaching acceptable and might even have admired his clever reading of "ignoto deo." Paraphrasing Job 12:10 and quoting the Greek poet Aratus (fl. 300 BCE) from his *Phaenomena*, Paul continued: "in ipso enim vivimus et movemur et sumus sicut et quidam vestrum poetarum dixerunt ipsius enim et genus sumus genus ergo cum simus Dei non debemus aestimare auro aut argento aut lapidi sculpturae artis et cogitationis hominis divinum esse simile" (for in him we live and move and exist, and as one of these your poets said, we too are his children; therefore, as we are God's children, we ought not hold that divinity is like gold, or silver, or stone, shaped by the art and design of a human) (17:28–9).[6] Contrasting God the all-powerful creator with a limited human maker of images, Paul had some success converting Athenians, including Dionysius the Areopagite (17:34). Later, in his letter to the Romans, Paul addresses idolatry again when characterizing non-believers as willfully ignoring God's truth revealed in creation:

> cum cognovissent Deum non sicut Deum glorificaverunt aut gratias egerunt sed evanuerunt in cogitationibus suis et obscuratum est insipiens cor eorum dicentes enim se esse sapientes stulti facti sunt et mutaverunt gloriam incorruptibilis Dei in similitudinem imaginis corruptibilis hominis et volucrum et quadrupedum et serpentium propter quod tradidit illos Deus in desideria cordis eorum in inmunditiam ut contumeliis adficiant corpora sua in semet ipsis qui commutaverunt vertatem Dei in mendacio et coluerunt et servierunt creaturae potius quam creatori qui est benedictus in saecula amen
>
> (Although they have known God, they have not glorified him as God nor thanked him, but they have grown vain in their thinking and their foolish heart has darkened, for declaring themselves wise they became fools. And they changed the glory of the incorruptible God into the likeness of an image of a corruptible man and of birds and of animals and of serpents. Therefore, God handed them over to the desires and impurity of their heart to dishonor their own bodies among themselves. They changed the truth of God into a lie, and they worship and serve the creature rather than the creator, who is blessed forever. Amen.) (1:21–2)

Sounding like the Wisdom-author, Paul implies that idol making and idolatry underpin non-believers' willful ignorance of God. Both source and result of vain error, idolatry has led them, as he notes a few verses later, to a perverted life of wickedness, greed, vice, and so on (1:26–32). In both Jewish and Christian cultures, then,

---

[6] Aratus, *Phaenomena*, ed. Mair and Mair, 5. *Phaenomena* opens by acknowledging Zeus as omnipresent father of all (1–18). The half-line Paul quotes declares humanity to be Zeus' offspring. Paul quoting *Phaenomena* is both sound rhetorical strategy and an instance of re-purposing a Greco-Roman cultural artifact similar to converting Assisi's Temple of Minerva into a church.

idolatry undermines the Jewish-Christian formulation of right living to love God with one's mind, heart, and soul (Deut. 6:5) and to love one's neighbor as oneself (Lev. 19:18). Rather, like *cupiditas* in Augustine's discussion on love, idolatry fosters using the intellect to pursue worldly rather than spiritual goals. In early Christian and patristic literature, writers treat classical deities, Minerva included, as idols and their worship as idolatry; moreover, they ally her and all other divinities with demons in the Christian view of good and evil spirits.

Minerva and the Fathers: The Goddess in Patristic Writing

In 242 CE, Persian armies of the Sassanid Empire were pressuring the Roman Empire's eastern frontier, taking cities and territories.[7] The Emperor Gordian III, then but sixteen years old, chose to meet the threat in part by joining the defensive campaign. Before leaving Rome, he performed two distinct religious actions in an effort to invoke patronage from the gods: he opened the gates of Janus' temple, the ancient sign of war in Roman culture, and he proclaimed athletic games to honor Minerva. Drawing on the goddess' role as *patrona*, thereby recalling Athena's defense of Athens against earlier Persian threats (499–49 BCE), Gordian III invoked the goddess' protection and aid as he prepared to lead Roman armies to defend the Empire. Though he died on campaign in 244, Gordian III initially succeeded in regaining lost territory, re-establishing Roman control of the eastern frontier, and stemming the Persian threat. About 100 years later (c.350) in the far-flung north-western province of Britannia at the Temple of Sulis-Minerva, geographically opposite to Gordian III's theater of action, a Roman citizen invoked the goddess' aid in recovering property of another kind when he wrote on a curse tablet:

> seu gen(til)is seu C-h(r)istianus quaecumque utrum vir [u]trum mulier utrum puer utrum puella utrum s[er]vus utrum liber mihi Annia[n]-o ma<n>tutene de bursa mea s(e)x argente[o]s furaverit tu d[o]mina dea ab ipso perexi[g]e [eo]s
>
> (Whether pagan or Christian, whosoever, whether man or woman, whether boy or girl, whether slave or free, has stolen from me, Annianus son of Matutina, six silver coins from my purse, you, Lady Goddess, exact them from him)[8]

Expressing, as John G. Gager notes, "a formalized wish to bring other persons or animals under the client's power," *defixiones*, or curse tablets, open a window onto an intriguing aspect of Roman religious and cultural practice.[9] In this case, believing Sulis-Minerva exercises power over all, Annianus demands the goddess directly intervene on his behalf. Though six stolen pieces of silver hardly compare to the loss of lands, cities, and people, both the Emperor Gordian III and Annianus the

---

[7] See Eutropius, *Breviarium*, ed. Droysen, 9.2.2; *Historia Augusta*, ed. Magie, *Gord.* 26.3; and Lane Fox, *Pagans and Christians*, 11–13.
[8] *Tabellae Sulis*, ed. Tomlin, 98.232–4.
[9] Gager, *Curse Tablets*, 21.

Romano-Celt assume Minerva's benevolent interest in their affairs and her ability to render aid. As R.S.O. Tomlin, Peter Brown, and John Gager suggest, however, Annianus' tablet is particularly interesting in his addition "seu gentiles seu christianus quaecumque" to the standard curse formula, thereby attempting an inclusive sweep of all potential suspects.[10] Where Gordian III gave Christianity no consideration when invoking Minerva, Annianus clearly thought it necessary to remind the goddess she held sway over all, Christian as well as pagan. What happened in the years between Gordian III and Annianus was, as we know, Constantine's emperorship (312–37) and the beginning of Christianity's move from the margins to the center of Roman culture: a move that eventually led to demonizing the gods and charging them with powerlessness in affecting positively human affairs.

The story of this move – what Peter Brown calls the Christianization of the Roman world – is complex, multifaceted, and fascinating, and it illuminates how Minerva became an idol in patristic discourse.[11] From the time of the Apostles (c.33–100) through the patristic period (c.100–c.450), a mix of deep tension and relative calm marked Christianity's relationship to and eventual alliance with the dominant Roman culture. In this period, whether polytheistic pagan or monotheistic Christian, state-sponsored religion was central to Roman experience, and Romans considered non-participants in the state religion to be atheists. In the pre-Constantine Roman world, the Roman attitude toward religion tended to be, as Béatrice Caseau writes, "encompassing and inclusive."[12] A pluralistic ever-expanding polytheism marked this culture: a syncretic, inclusive practice about which the poet Prudentius (c.348–c.405) observed later in his *Contra Symmachum*, with the possible exaggeration of an apologist mustering polemical fire, that pre-Christian Rome "facta est terrigenae domus unica maiestatis / et tot templa deum Romae quot in orbe sepulcra / heroum numerare licet" (was made the single home of all earth-born divinity where one may number as many temples of gods as tombs of heroes in all the world).[13] In the context of an Imperial policy fostering polytheism rooted in bellicose patriotism, Christianity's universalistic and exclusive monotheism with its message of love and mercy was suspect and at key moments unwelcome. Until Constantine, Roman emperors and citizens periodically persecuted Christians, occasionally using them

---

[10] *Tabulae Sulis*, ed. Tomlin, 233; P. Brown, *Authority and the Sacred*, 3–4; Gager, *Curse Tablets*, 195.

[11] The phrase comes from the subtitle to P. Brown's *Authority and the Sacred*. In addition to Brown's *Authority* for what follows here, see Cameron, *Christianity and the Rhetoric of Empire*; Gregory, *Vox populi*; C. Jones, *Between Pagan and Christian*; Kahlos, *Debate and Dialogue*; Krautheimer, *Rome*, 3–58; Lane Fox, *Pagans and Christians*; Lim, "Christian Triumph and Controversy," 196–218; MacMullen, *Christianity and Paganism*, and *Christianizing the Roman Empire*; the essays in Papaconstantinou, McLynn, and Schawartz, eds., *Conversion in Late Antiquity*; Rapp, *Holy Bishops in Late Antiquity*; Rebillard, *Christians and Their Many Identities*; and Stark, *Rise of Christianity*.

[12] Caseau, "Sacred Landscapes," 21.

[13] *Contra Symmachum*, ed. Cunningham, 1.189–9, in *Aurelii Prudentii Clementis Carmina*. Hereafter, I cite references to this edition of Prudentius' poems in the text.

as scapegoats for deeper problems in the Empire.[14] Co-emperors Constantine in the west and Licinius (c.263–325) in the east radically changed Christianity's political standing when they granted it and all religions in the Empire full tolerance with the Edict of Milan in 313.

In spite of this recognition by the state, the Church's fortunes vacillated throughout the next two centuries as it solidified its position within society. The most crucial problems the Church faced during this period involved definition, which is not surprising given that pre-Constantine Christianity was marked by localized variety: "a plurality of Christianities," as Lim describes it.[15] Constantine convened the First Council of Nicea in 325 to attain consensus on issues affecting Christian belief and practice, from the nature of Jesus as Son of God to the uniform observance of Easter.[16] Not all Christians, however, accepted the Council's compromises and decisions, and many chose to continue defining Christianity locally, causing deep division and argument exemplified by the Alexandrian priest Arius (c.256–336) and his followers but including a number of other factions. As the century unfolded and Nicene Christianity became identified as orthodox, with its formulation of the Trinity at its center, Emperor Theodosius I (347–95) in 380 decreed it the only legitimate Imperial religion and the only catholic, or universal, form of Christianity, thereby denying legitimacy to polytheism and heterodox, that is, non-Nicene, varieties of Christianity. The centripetal and centrifugal effects of Theodosius I's declaration shifted ecclesiastical method away from consensus-building compromise based in persuasion to authoritative statement and required obedience. By the turn of the fifth century, some church leaders like Augustine were hard at work developing what Lim describes as "a taxonomy of Judeo-Christian sects" so as to identify heresies: a stage in the effort to define orthodox belief by contrast.[17] As a result, orthodox leaders declared heretical over the next decades several non-conforming alternative beliefs and practices. Tensions arising in the fourth and fifth centuries between orthodox and heterodox teachings encouraged Church intellectuals, notably Augustine, to formulate a blueprint of sorts for belief, practice, and ecclesial structure that served the western Church for the next 1000 years.

While internal competition for definition and uniformity, and thus for the hearts and minds of believers, was a hallmark of ecclesiastical development in the post-Constantine era of the patristic period, the Church also faced pressure from without in two forms: civil strife caused by external invasion and internal political intrigue, and continued engagement in non-Christian religious beliefs and practices. It might

---

[14] A popular impression that in the first 250–300 years of the church Christians lived under a constant shadow of harassment and threat does not reflect accurately the situation. Periods of persecution occurred but were infrequent with perhaps as few as 1000 victims in total. If Romans wanted to eradicate or suppress Christianity, they went about it the wrong way. See Stark, *Rise of Christianity*, 163–89.
[15] Lim, "Christian Triumph and Controversy," 200. See also Rebillard, *Christians and Their Many Identities*, 9–33.
[16] Bokenkotter, *Concise History*, 51–2; Bowder, *Age of Constantine and Julian*, 70–5; Lim, "Christian Triumph and Controversy," 200–1.
[17] Lim, "Christian Triumph and Controversy," 201–11: 208.

seem from early church historians of generations past that Christian hegemony in the Roman world was inevitable and complete by the end of the patristic period, but non-Christian religious beliefs and practices did not die quick deaths with Constantine's conversion nor did Christianity dominate western Roman culture overnight: Christianization, rather, was a gradual, at times contested and at others accommodated, process. Although the Emperor Julian's (330–63) brief attempt in 361–3 to reinvigorate traditional Roman polytheism as the state religion failed, most pagans, including the conservative majority of the Roman senate in the late fourth century, continued to reject Christianity, considering it a new progressive religion with shallow roots. At the same time as Nicene Christians competed with heterodox Christians to define orthodoxy, they also competed with non-Christians as they advanced universalistic monotheism.[18] In the context of traditional attitudes of religious tolerance, the Christian demand of religious conformity – a sort of reverse *pax deorum* compliance with an exclusionary twist – was simply not in good form.[19] Within this climate of internal and external pressures, following the sack of Rome in 410, Augustine composed *De civitate Dei*, which incorporates his most influential polemic against paganism in general and Minerva in particular.

Begun at the request of his disciple Marcellinus, but addressed to the cultured aristocratic class of pagans for whom Christianity held little appeal, *De civitate Dei* took Augustine thirteen years to complete (413–26): truly "magnum opus et arduum" (a great and difficult work) (1.praefatio) on many levels.[20] As detailed in a letter to a Carthaginian named Firmus covering a gift copy, he organized the text into twenty-two books divided into five parts.[21] In parts one and two, Augustine engages detractors of Christianity with a sharply argued construction of polytheism and pagan philosophy in which he recasts the Roman gods as demons rather than as divinities who protect Rome and ensure eternal life. To grasp this argument, we need to understand his use of the term "demon." In Greek, *daemon* can mean both divine power and knowledge. Following Christian thought of the day, however, Augustine

---

[18] Occasionally, Christians and non-Christians alike were caught up in tensions brought on by the Theodosian Christianization of the Empire as late fourth- and early fifth-century Alexandria illustrates. From Theophilus of Alexandria's (c.350–412) destruction of the Temple of Serapis in 392 to Cyril of Alexandria's (c.376–444) suppression of Nestorian Christianity in 412 and expulsion of Jews in 415, rising Nicene Christian hegemony produced internal tensions in the city. Haas, *Alexandria in Late Antiquity*, 161–3, 295–312; Hahn, "Conversion of the Cult Statues," 335–65. One of the most notorious events during this period was the brutal murder of the neoplatonic mathematician and philosopher Hypatia in March, 415. Following a Cyril-sanctioned smear campaign, desert monks publicly tortured Hypatia to death for supporting the Christian Imperial Prefect Orestes. Though many have considered Hypatia's story an instance of ignorant, intolerant Christianity attacking enlightened, tolerant non-Christianity, evidence points more to power-brokering as cause: Cyril desired political power, Orestes tried to check him, Hypatia was squashed in the middle. See Dzielska, "Hypatia," 502–3; Bowersock and Grabar *Hypatia of Alexandria*, 66–100; and Haas, *Alexandria in Late Antiquity*, 312–16.

[19] O'Donnell, "Demise of Paganism," 45–62.

[20] P. Brown, *Augustine of Hippo*, 297–329.

[21] Augustine, "Letter 1*A," trans. Eno, 15.

revises this definition, emphasizing a growing pejorative sense of the term. Citing Apuleius' (c.123–c.180) use of the term in *De deo Socratis* (13), Augustine defines demons as a species of beings superior to humans, immortal, and endowed with bodies of air, rational faculty, and emotions. However, instead of functioning as mediators between gods and humans, he considers them enemies to humankind (9.8–9). Then, placing the Greek meaning of *daemon* as "knowledge" beside Paul's assertion to the Corinthians that "scientia inflat charitas vero aedificat" (knowledge inflates, charity truly edifies) (1 Cor. 8:1), Augustine amplifies the term's significance as follows:

> quod recte aliter non intellegitur, nisi scientiam tunc prodesse, cum caritas inest; sine hac autem inflare, id est in superbiam inanissimae quasi uentositatis extollere. Est ergo in daemonibus scientia sine caritate, et ideo tam inflati, hoc est tam superbi sunt, ut honores diuinos et religionis seruitutem, quam uero Deo deberi sciunt

> (this saying is not rightly understood except that knowledge is only valuable when charity infuses it; but without charity it puffs up, that is, it exalts in an arrogance of emptiness, as it were, of bombast. In demons, there is knowledge without charity, and therefore they are so puffed up, that is, excessively proud to receive divine honors and devout service, which they know ought to be given to the true God) (9.20)

Implying their particularly deceptive nature, for they know worship is due to God alone, Augustine syncretizes the notion of demons from Apuleius with those whom Jesus confronts in the gospels (e.g., Mt. 4:1–11, 8:28–34; Mk. 1:12–3, 1:21–7; Lk. 4:1–13, 31–7). Knowing and fearing Jesus, these demons were powerless before him, unable to resist his commands (9.21).

Though he presents and exemplifies this definition of demon near the end of part two, Augustine links pagan deities with demons earlier when he calls the gods "maligni spiritus" (malignant spirits) who, through fables, "humanas ... retibus induant et a praedestinatum supplicium secum trahant" (ensnare people in nets and drag them with them to their predestined punishment) (2.10). Later, in the preface to Book 6, when summarizing the import of Books 1–5, he states:

> Quinque superioribus libris satis mihi aduersus eos uideor disputasse, qui multos deos et falsos, quos esse inutilia simulacra uel inmundos spiritus et perniciosa daemonia uel certe creaturas, non creatorem ueritas Christiana conuincit, propter uitae huius mortalis rerumque terrenarum utilitatem eo ritu ac seruitute, quae Graece latreia dicitur et uni uero Deo debetur, uenerandos et colendos putant.

> (It seems to me that in the first five books I sufficiently argued against those who think that, on account of their usefulness in worldly affairs and this mortal life, many false gods ought to be venerated and worshipped by rite and humble service, which is called *latreia* in Greek but ought to be given to the true God alone. Christian truth proves these gods are useless images or unclean spirits and pernicious demons: creatures at any rate, not the creator.) (6.praefatio)

Augustine would have found biblical precedent for his synthesis of the gods and demons in Psalm 95 (Vulgate), a lyric attributed to David but likely composed in the postexilic period (fifth century BCE). Calling together the community of Israelites, the psalmist says in Jerome's Latin translation of the Greek Septuagint:

> Cantate Domino canticum novum cantate Domino omnis terra
> cantate Domino benedicite nomini eius adnuntiate diem de die salutare eius
> adnuntiate inter gentes gloriam eius in omnibus populis mirabilia eius
> quoniam magnus Domninus et laudabilis valde terribilis est super omnes deos
> quoniam omnes dii gentium daemonia at vero Dominus caelos fecit

> (Sing to the Lord a new song; sing to the Lord all the earth; sing to the Lord and bless his name; make known his salvation from day to day. Proclaim his glory among the nations, his marvels among all peoples. For the Lord is great and greatly to be praised: he is to be feared above all gods. For all the gods of the gentiles are demons, but the Lord made the heavens) (1–6)

Jerome's use of "daemonia" to transliterate the Greek word δαιμόνια emphasizes the created nature of the gentile gods in contrast to the creator God of Israel.[22] In the Jewish-Christian understanding of right worship reserved for the creator alone that Augustine implies in the preface to Book 6, these "inutilia simulacra uel inmundos spiritus et perniciosa daemonia" not only do not merit veneration as gods but also are spiritually dangerous to humans, for they lead them astray into idolatry of the kind Moses confronted in Sinai, the psalmists in Jerusalem, the Wisdom-author in Palestine, and Paul in Athens.

For Augustine, demons take their most pernicious form as Rome's "select" divinities, a pantheon of twelve gods and eight goddesses, including Minerva, Venus, Mars, Diana, Neptune, Jupiter, and other Romanized Greek deities. He asserts their malignancy when he states:

---

[22] The history of psalms and their translations is complex. Psalm 95:5/Tehillim 96:5 in Hebrew reads from right to left:

כִּי ׀ כָּל־אֱלֹהֵי הָעַמִּים אֱלִילִים וַיהוָה שָׁמַיִם עָשָׂה׃

(For all the gods of the peoples are things of nought; but the LORD made the heavens).

The Septuagint Bible, the third-first century BCE Greek version of the Hebrew Bible, translates Psalm 95.5 as "ὅτι πάντες οἱ θεοὶ τῶν ἐθνῶν δαιμόνια, ὁ δὲ Κύριος τοὺς οὐρανοὺς ἐποίησεν" (for all the gods of nations are demons, but the Lord made the heavens). Jerome produced three versions of the psalms, basing *Versio Romana* (completed 384) and *Versio Gallicana* (completed 391), both revisions of the *Vetus Latina*, on the Septuagint, and *Versio juxta Hebraicum* (ca. 400) on the Hebrew. For the latter, Jerome translates Psalm 95.5 "omnes enim dii populorum sculptilia Dominus autem caelos fecit" (for all the gods of the peoples are engraved things but the Lord made the heavens). His earlier close translation of the Septuagint is slightly, but importantly, different: "quoniam omnes dii gentium daemonia; Dominus autem caelos fecit" (for all the gods of the nations are demons, but the Lord made the heavens). Though his translation of the Hebrew text is closer to the original, his translation of the Greek was more widely known in the Middle Ages through use in the Gallican and Roman rites.

> Per hanc ergo religionem unam et ueram potuit aperiri deos gentium esse inmundissimos daemones, sub defunctarum occasionibus animarum uel creaturarum specie mundanarum deos se putari cupientes ... hi, de quibus nunc agimus, tamquam in senatum deorum selecti; sed plane selecti nobilitate criminum, non dignitate uirtutum.
>
> (Through this one and true religion [i.e., Christianity], therefore, it can be proven that the gods of the pagans are most unclean demons. Under the guise of dead souls or the form of creatures of the world, they desire to be thought gods ... These divinities, about which we are now discoursing, have been selected as a sort of senate of gods; but clearly they have been selected for the notoriety of their crimes not the worthiness of their virtues.) (7.33)

Constructing, or again perhaps deconstructing, the traditional gods as "inmundissimos daemons," Augustine seeks both to undercut polytheism and reinforce orthodox Christian belief and practice. He, of course, is not alone in his efforts to demonize the gods.[23] Paulinus of Nola (c.354–431), for example, a poet, monk, bishop and contemporary of Augustine, writes in a poem honoring Nola's Christian patron St. Felix that, like stars in the heavens, the holy tombs of saints are scattered about the Empire.[24] He continues:

> inlustrant totum superis virtutibus orbem
> et toto antiquum detrudunt orbe draconem,
> qui genus humanum per nomina mille deorum,
> quae tamen ex obitis mortalibus et sibi sumpsit
> ipse suisque dedit coluber, quatit arte nocendi,
> princeps in uacuo taetrum gerit aere regnum
> daemonibusque caput nobis inimicus oberrat
>
> (they illuminate the entire world with heavenly virtues and dislodge from that whole world the ancient dragon who controlled the human race under the names of a thousand gods; for that snake had assumed these names from dead mortals and gave them to himself and his servants, whom he leads in the art of harming; the prince wields a foul tyranny: the head of the demons and enemy to us wanders through the empty air)[25]

Paulinus, implying a euhemeristic understanding of the gods' origins "obitis mortalibus," links the gods to demons, who are defeated in turn through the agency of other dead mortals, the saints. As the poem continues, Paulinus celebrates Felix's defeat particularly of Venus and Bacchus – Nola's pre-Christian patrons – through the cleansing medicine of his martyrdom (19.164–248). His tomb, like other saints' tombs in the new monotheistic world of Christian Roman culture, replaces shrines

---

[23] See Brakke, *Demons and the Making of the Monk*, 213–39; and Kahlos, *Debate and Dialogue*, 172–84. On demonization in medieval art, see Camille, *Gothic Idol*, 73–128.
[24] Raby, *History of Christian Latin Poetry*, 101–7. On the origin of the cult of saints, see Bartlett, *Why Can the Dead Do Such Great Things?*, 3–26.
[25] Paulinus of Nola, *Carmina*, ed. de Hartel, 19.157–64.

to the gods, thereby concurrently de-sacralizing and re-sacralizing the landscape.[26] As Paulinus declares, saints' tombs defeat "antiquum ... draconem," the chief of the demons who ruled the pagan world "per nomina mille deorum."

Within the context of this polemical impulse to demonize the gods, Minerva of course is one of those thousand names the ancient dragon assumed. Sulpicius Severus (c.360–425), for instance, friend of Paulinus and disciple-hagiographer of Martin of Tours, directly ties Minerva and other of Augustine's select divinities with the devil in his *Vita beati Martini*. He writes:

> Frequenter autem diabolus, dum mille nocendi artibus sanctum virum conabatur illudere, visibilem se ei formis diversissimis ingerebat. Nam interdum in Jovis persona, plerumque Mercurii, persaepe etiam se Veneris ac Minervae transfiguratum vultibus offerebat: adversus quam semper interritus, signo se crucis et orationis auxilio protegebat.
>
> (Often, however, while trying to ridicule the holy man by a thousand injurious arts, the devil would make himself visible to Martin in a great variety of forms. For sometimes he presented himself under the mask of Jove, and often of Mercury; he also often presented himself transfigured by the features of Venus or Minerva, against whom the always undaunted Martin protected himself with the sign of the cross and help of prayer.)[27]

Martin (c.336–97) was what we might consider a first-generation Christian; both parents remained pagan, though his mother converted later in life according to Severus (2.161, 6.164). His story illustrates elements of religious transition in the fourth-century Empire. As in Paulinus and Augustine, where demons "deos se putari cupientes" disguise themselves, the pagan deities in this passage, including Minerva, are demonic disguises the devil uses. Winning his battles with the devil by relying on his spiritual armor, "signo ... cruces et orationis auxilio," Martin demonstrates for Severus' audience the devil's powerlessness in the face of Christian truth. Attempting to check potential backsliding among his Christian audience, Severus implicitly warns against idolatry, suggesting that though he failed to overcome Martin, the devil's deceptive shape-shifting abilities under the guise of pagan gods can seduce the unwary.

The issue of true power and who has it is implicit in the demonization of the gods and explicit in stories of Jesus and his followers confronting demons. Just as Jesus confronted the devil in the desert (Mt. 4:1–11; Mk. 1:12–13; Lk. 4:1–13), Martin overcame him in his many guises as pagan deities. A common charge that pagan deities were powerless idols reverberates throughout early Christian apologetics. Citing the story of Troy in the opening argument of *De civitate Dei*, for instance, Augustine particularly illustrates this point through Minerva, stating:

---

[26] Caseau, "Sacred Landscape," 30–6.
[27] Severus, *De vita beati Martini*, ed. Migne, 22.172.

Nec ideo Troia periit, quia Mineruam perdidit. Quid enim prius ipsa Minerua perdiderat, ut periret? an forte custodes suos? Hoc sane uerum est; illis quippe interemptis potuit auferri. Neque enim homines a simulacro, sed simulacrum ab hominibus seruabatur. Quomodo ergo colebatur, ut patriam custodiret et ciues, quae suos non ualuit custodire custodes?

(And Troy was not destroyed because it lost Minerva. What, indeed, had Minerva herself first lost so that she might be lost in turn? Was it perhaps her guards? This is no doubt true; obviously, by killing them it was possible to bear her away. For the men were not preserved by the image, but the image was being preserved by the men. Why then was she worshipped to protect the country and its citizens when she could not protect her own guards?) (1.2)

According to Augustine, Troy fell not because Trojans lost the Palladium but because they misguidedly relied on Minerva's image in the first place. Minerva, as an ineffectual demon inhabiting a mere image, simply was powerless to protect her worshippers. Prudentius, too, argues in *Contra Symmachum* that pagan deities are powerless. In answer to Symmachus' plea to restore the Altar of Victory to the senate, Prudentius declares that strength, hard work, and trust in God assure victory to Rome, not reliance on an altar dedicated to an illusory female warrior (2.17–38). Such assertions in the fifth century echo earlier ones. In his euhemeristic discussion of polytheism, for instance, Lactantius – Christian apologist and councilor to Constantine – argued the gods are mere mortals who, though deified through erroneous belief and practice, exercise no real power in the world (*Divinarum Institutiones*, 1.15–18).

Drawing on these themes, Prudentius presents Minerva as a powerless demonic idol in two of the fourteen martyr tales that constitute his *Liber Peristephanon*. In *Peristephanon* 14, which recounts the Roman Agnes' (c. 291–304) martyrdom, Minerva functioned as an idol linked with a brothel. During Agnes' trial, her prosecutor declared:

> ... "Si facile est ...
> poenam subactis ferre doloribus
> et vita vilis spernitur, at pudor
> carus dicatae virginitatis est.
> Hanc in lupananr trudere publicum
> certum est, ad aram ni caput adplicat
> ac de Minerva iam veniam rogat,
> quam virgo pergit temnere virginem"

> (If having considered the suffering she is willing to bear the penalty, and spurns life as cheap but holds virginity's modesty dear, then I am certain to drive her into a public brothel unless she bows her head to the altar and asks for favor from the virgin Minerva whom she, a virgin herself, continues to offend) (21–8)

Agnes of course refused to worship Minerva and, though he did not place her in a brothel, the prosecutor ordered her stripped and put on public display. All present averted their gaze, the narrator continues, except one lustful young man, who was struck blind; God then cured him through Agnes' intercessory prayer. In response to this miraculous cure, her prosecutor grew more hard-hearted and ordered her death. After her martyrdom, in an early literary antecedent to Boccaccio's Arcita and Chaucer's Troilus, Agnes laughed at the folly of the world and, most importantly, as the narrator notes, "quod malorum taetrius omnium est / gentilitatis sordida nubila" (what is the foulest of all evils, the vile gloom of paganism) (110–11) as she ascended into heaven to receive her double-crown of martyrdom and virginity.[28]

The prosecutor in *Peristephanon* 14 invoked Minerva as the offended deity; however, as with the devil-Minerva in *De vita beati Martini* or even Troy's Minerva in *De civitate Dei*, the goddess remained powerless. Though stripped of life in Minerva's name, Agnes received her reward in heaven from the true God. A similarly idolatrous Minerva appears in *Peristephanon* 10. As Prudentius recounts Romanus of Caesarea's (d. 303) torture-trial, the saint confronted his oppressors by patient suffering and sheer volume of words, even after losing his tongue. Romanus particularly invoked Minerva in a catalog of Rome's select divinities as one of several idols, declaring:

Ars seminandis efficax erroribus,
barbam rigentem dum Iovis circumplicat,
dum defluentem leniter flectens comam
limat capillos et corymbos Liberi,
et dum Minervae pectus hydris asperat,
iniecit atram territis formidinem,
ut fulmen aeris ceu Tonantis horreant,
tremant venenum sibilantis Gorgonae,
putent ephebum post triumfos Indicos
ferire thyrso posse, cum sit ebrius

(Art produced the begetting of errors. While it curled Jove's rigid beard, polished Liber's gently curving hair and flowing locks and ivy-berry clusters, and made Minerva's breast fierce with the hydra, it imposed dark fear on terrified people so they might shudder at the thunderbolt of the air as if it was the Thunderer's, tremble at the hissing Gorgon's venom, and think a young man after Indian triumphs can strike them with a thyrsus, though he is drunk) (271–80)

In this section of his diatribe against pagan belief and practice, Romanus argued that artistic representation of the gods was really an idolatry of terror. Giving voice to his martyr hero, Prudentius implies the three theories of divinity familiar from Cicero's *De natura deorum* to demonstrate the folly of pagan belief: euhemerism (Bacchus); naturalism (thunder); and allegorism (effects of artistic representation). Though

---

[28] In *Teseida*, 11.3, Arcita's spirit rises to the eighth sphere whence he looks upon the world and laughs, censuring human vanity and blindness. Boccaccio's Arcita is most probably Chaucer's source for Troilus' behavior when his spirit similarly proceeds to the eighth sphere, looks down upon the world, laughs, and condemns "al oure werk that foloweth so / The blyde lust, the which that may not laste, / And shulden al oure herte on heven caste" (*TC* V.1823–5).

Romanus' mortal life ended in a grisly execution, he only died after having delivered his extensive, anti-pagan polemic from the dock, much of it miraculously without a tongue. He, too, achieved eternal reward, as the narrator says, when "anima absoluta vinculis caelum petit" (freed from the chains, his soul sought heaven) (1110).

Roman authorities executed Agnes and Romanus early in the final persecutions of Christians begun under Diocletian in 303 because, as Prudentius recounts, they refused to honor the Empire's traditional gods. These Roman authorities considered religious action, such as Gordian III performed when preparing to defend the Empire in 242, key to maintaining *pax deorum*: to refuse was a capital offense. By the time Annianus the Romano-Celt wrote his curse tablet invoking Sulis-Minerva's aid, reminding her she also held sway over Christians, these persecutions were a few decades in the past. As he placed the tablet, he could not have known his beloved goddess would be rendered a powerless, ineffectual demon within four or five decades as the Theodosian Christianization gained ascendancy. Though patristic writers did not find dislodging Minerva and her fellow select divinities from their position in Roman culture particularly easy, they were largely successful in time. And, as Nicene Christianity secured its cultural position and external pressures on the Church brought about by polytheism waned, Lactantius, Prudentius, Paulinus of Nola, Sulpicius Severus, Augustine, and other patristic writers continued to influence subsequent Christian poetics and thought,[29] in part bequeathing to the Middle Ages an attitude towards polytheism and idolatry that affected certain poetic uses of classical figures, including of course Minerva.

Minerva as Idol in Medieval Literature: The Catalog of Deities

Writing nearly 1000 years after Prudentius, Geoffrey Chaucer inserts this stanza near the end of *Troilus and Criseyde*:

> Lo here, of payens corsed olde rites!
> Lo here, what alle hire goddes may availle!
> Lo here, thise wrecched worldes appetites!
> Lo here, the fyn and guerdon for travaille
> Of Jove, Appollo, of Mars, of swich rascaille!
> Lo here, the forme of olde clerkis speche
> In poetrie, if ye hire bokes seche. (5.1849–55)

---

[29] Prudentius and Paulinus became part of the medieval canon of writers to read and study. See Curtius, *European Literature*, 48–54; Irvine, *Making of Textual Culture*, 315–16, 355–8; and Raby, *History of Christian Latin Poetry*, 68–71, 101–7. Selections from the Fathers and from saints lives, such as Sulpicius, were frequently read in religious houses in matins, in community, and during "lectio divina." See Collamore, "Prelude," 4–7; Heffernan, "Liturgy and the Literature," 88–97; Pfaff, *Liturgy in Medieval England*, 7–8; and Szendrei, "On the Prose Historia," 430–43. On the influence of *De civitate Dei*, see P. Brown, *Augustine of Hippo*, 297–311; Rand, *Founder of the Middle Ages*, 266–77; and O'Meara, *Charter of Christiandom*.

Not based on his source text, Giovanni Boccaccio's *Filostrato*, this stanza has puzzled readers for, in the wake of Troilus' post-mortem ascent through the spheres and the end of narrative action, the narrator's denunciation of "payens corsed olde rites" and "what alle hire goddes may availle" seems superfluous. Benson aptly sums up the puzzlement, stating, "No conceivable medieval or modern audience of the poem has ever needed to be warned against the pagan gods": a denunciation, he continues, that is "somewhat irrelevant" to the narrative.[30] A key effect of the passage, however, is to remind the poem's audience of the historical and cultural distance between the poem's imagined world and their own so as to draw out similarities and differences between the two, a point John P. McCall suggests.[31] Just as Prudentius' Romanus invoked a catalog of deities in his anti-pagan diatribe from the dock, thereby sharply distinguishing his true Christian belief from false pagan practice, Chaucer's narrator invokes a similar – albeit smaller – catalog "Of Jove, Appollo, of Mars, of swich rascaille." Chaucer, it seems, is here alluding to the anti-pagan discourse developed in patristic writing as he closes out his poem set in ancient Troy.

Though writing after the Christian ascendancy in late Roman culture, medieval writers continued on occasion to tap into the anti-pagan discourse of the Fathers when seeking to emphasize historical and cultural difference between their present and the past. One such early medieval writer, Isidore of Seville, draws on the patristic point of view when reviewing pagan belief and practice in *Etymologiae*. Tracing the development of image making and deification, he describes this phenomenon matter-of-factly:

> Fuerent etiam et quidam viri fortes aut urbium conditores, quibus mortuis homines, qui eos dilexerunt, simulacra finxerunt, ut haberent aliquod ex imaginum contemplatione solacium; sed paulatim hunc errorem persuadentibus daemonibus ita in posteris inrepsisse, ut quos illi pro sola nominis memoria honoraverunt, successors deos existimarent atque colerent

> (And there were also certain strong men or founders of cities for whom, after they died, people who loved them had likenesses made so they might have some comfort in contemplating the image; but, through persuading demons, this error gradually crept into later generations in such a way that those whom people had honoured only for the memory of their name their successors esteemed as gods and worshipped) (8.11.4)

Fusing the euhemeristic theory of the pagan divinities' origins with the Jewish-Christian idea of idolatry, Isidore links the gods of polytheistic belief to biblical demons much as we have seen in Augustine and elsewhere (8.11.1–22). He then catalogs the deities from Saturn to Faunus (8.11.29–104), and his discussion of Minerva illustrates his method. As he explicates the goddess, he writes in the present tense as though describing an image of her. In particular, he focuses on Minerva's

---

[30] Benson, *Chaucer's Troilus and Criseyde*, 199.
[31] McCall, *Chaucer among the Gods*, 103–4.

associations with the mind, noting Greeks and Romans "hanc enim inventricem multiorum ingeniorum perhibent, et inde eam artem at rationem interpretantur, quia sine ratione nihil potest contineri" (maintain she indeed was an inventor of many talents, and so they interpret her as art and reason because without reason nothing can be comprehended) (8.11.71). He continues:

> In cuius pectore ideo caput Gorgonis fingitur, quod illic est omnis prudentia, quae confundit alios, et inperitos ac saxeos conprobat: quod et in antiquis Imperatorum statuis cernimus in medio pectore loricae, propter insinuandam sapientiam et virtutem
>
> (And the Gorgon's head is depicted on her chest because all prudence – which confuses others and proves them ignorant and stony – is located there; and we also see this image in the middle of the breastplate on ancient statues of Emperors because it insinuates wisdom and virtue) (8.11.73)

As this passage unfolds, it becomes evident that Isidore and his immediate seventh-century audience remain directly aware of the old culture, the detritus of which seems available to their gaze "in antiquis Imperatorum statuis": an allusion, perhaps unintended, to Minerva *patrona principis* in the form of the Gorgon's head depicted on the Emperors' breastplates. Examining two other names associated with Minerva, Tritonia and Pallas, he then traces her origins either to Triton, a swamp in Africa, or the island Pallane in Thrace, noting "unde et tanto proclivius dea credita, quanto minus origo eius innotuit" (thus the less her origin is known the more likely she is believed a goddess) (8.11.74). Isidore's need to explicate pre-Christian Roman polytheism and his desire for origins in that explication are palpable in his discussion of Minerva, for with that knowledge – like his patristic forebears – he puts in its cultural place pagan belief and practice: a misguided idolatry of the past.

Where Isidore incorporates his discussion of the pagan deities within a larger project of seeking to encompass all knowledge, later writers employ the patristic view of polytheism and idolatry in other ways. In the thirteenth century, for instance, we find Guido delle Colonne integrating a discussion of pagan belief and practice into his reworking of the Trojan story. Guido seeks in *Historia destructionis Troiae* to set the historical record straight by basing his Trojan narrative in Dares' and Dictys' accounts and deliberately discounting poetic versions in Virgil, Ovid, and Homer (prologus.3–5; 35.276). In Book 10, as the Greeks prepared to sail to Troy, Agamemnon decided to consult the oracle of Apollo at Delos before proceeding: the Greek leaders assented and chose Achilles and Patroclus as messengers. The two journeyed to Delos and entered the temple that had "maxima ymago tota ex auro composita" (a great image entirely made of gold) (10.93), a reference for Guido's Christian audience signaling an idolatrous situation in its echo of the Sinai golden calf. As the Greek heroes approached to consult the image, Guido interrupts the narrative with a fairly long digression on the origin of idolatry based largely, as he notes, on Isidore's account (10.96). In the midst of the digression he includes a catalog of twelve divinities beginning with Saturn and the other planetary deities and concluding with a list of noteworthy founders and patrons of cities, including Minerva, patroness of Athens (10.95). Resuming the narrative, Guido continues where he left off with Achilles and Patroclus standing before the golden image. Quoting a verse from Psalm 95, he writes:

> Per demonum igitur ingressum in ydola surda et muta eliciebantur ab eis petita responsa que tunc gentilitas excolebat. Vnde Dauid: "Quoniam omnis dii gencium demonia; dominus autem celos fecit." Et per hanc dyabolice decepcionis astuciam deus Appollo responsa sua in dicta insula Delos petentibus exhibebat

> (The sought-after responses, therefore, were elicited by them from the demon possessing the deaf and mute idol the pagans were then worshipping. Whence David said: "for all pagan gods are demons: but the lord made the heavens" [Ps. 95:5]. And through this cunning of diabolical deception, the god Apollo offered his response to the seekers on the said island Delos) (10.97)

As with Isidore and patristic writers, Guido undercuts Greek religious practice in the story by demonizing the oracle of Apollo at Delos. His digression, too, reiterates the marginal cultural position pre-Christian polytheism holds: a pernicious cultural artifact from a time long past. For Guido's thirteenth-century audience inscribed in the text such practice elicits interest primarily as a foil contrasting their own Christian belief and practice.

A catalog of deities similar to that invoked by Romanus and Guido, and in a different way Isidore, becomes a stock image in medieval literature for poets who, like Chaucer, deal in some way with the subject of idolatry. John Gower (c.1330–1408) – Chaucer's contemporary and dedicatee of *Troilus and Criseyde* – incorporates such a catalog in *Confessio Amantis*.[32] Organized around the seven deadly sins, with a *speculum principis* digression on the education of Alexander the Great, *Confessio Amantis* is a substantial eight-book 33,444-line dream vision modeled on Boethius' *Consolatio Philosophiae*. In the poem's frame narrative, the Roman god Genius, priest of Venus and story-teller extraordinaire, functioned as confessor-interlocutor to the troubled, somewhat naïve, narrator-lover Amans.[33] In book five, where Genius examined avarice through illustrative narratives, the priest-god digressed from the book's main topic by discussing world religions, during which he introduced a catalog of deities. Amans sparked this digression in response to Genius' story of Vulcan, Venus, and Mars, told to exemplify the dangers of jealousy in love, when he stated:

> Mi fader, this ensample is hard,
> Hou such thing to the heveneward
> Among the goddes myhte falle:

---

[32] Chaucer dedicates *TC* to "moral Gower" and "philosophical Strode" (5.1856, 57) in the stanza following the anti-pagan diatribe. On Chaucer and Gower's friendship, see Carlson, "Gower *Agonistes*," 391–3; Fisher, *John Gower*, 26–34, 285–92; and Pearsall, "Gower's Narrative Art," 483–4.

[33] Genius and Amans, with Venus at the end, are the frame-narrative's characters. See Barrington, "Personas and Performance," 414–33; Bennett, "Gower's 'Honeste Love'," 107–21; Simpson, *Sciences and the Self*, 134–271; and Wetherbee, "Genius and Interpretation," 241–60. I hold with Simpson that they function as "faculties of the same soul" (135).

> For ther is bot o god of alle,
> Which is the lord of hevene and helle. (5.729–33)

Genius' answer to Amans' incredulity linked polytheism with folly when he replied,

> Mi Sone, it is thus overal
> With hem that stonden misbelieved
> That suche goddes ben believed
> In sondri place sondri wise
> Amonges hem whiche are unwise. (5.738–42)

In a curious move, then, considering he was a priest of Venus in this poem and a god himself in Roman religion (he is one of the "select divinities" Augustine attacks), Genius subsequently traced the history of polytheism and debunked it before addressing Judaic monotheism and Christianity's salvific message.[34]

Gower's examination of classical deities here implicitly follows anti-pagan arguments by patristic writers. In opening the discussion of Greek religion, Genius associated belief in the gods with irrationality and the gods themselves with vice, stating:

> Among the Greks, out of the weie
> As thei that reson putte aweie,
> Ther was, as the Cronique seith,
> Of misbelieve an other feith,
> That thei here goddes and goddesses,
> As who seith, token al to gesses
> Of suche as weren full of vice,
> To whom thei made here sacrifice. (5.835–42)

Beginning with Saturn, Genius then discussed the more significant classical deities from a euhemeristic position, discounting their divinity because of their mere humanity. In this section, demonstrating his debt to Isidore of Seville, Gower presents a clear example of a trend to distinguish Minerva from Pallas Athena within a catalog of deities.[35] Genius traced Minerva's history and stated that

---

[34] Genius' "In sondri place sondri wise" line echoes Chaucer's narrator commenting on Trojan ritual honoring Minerva: "In sondry wises shewed, as I rede, / The folk of Troie hir observaunces olde, / Palladiones feste for to holde" (*TC* 1.159–61). Both emphasize cultural distance. Genius subsequently asserted Christian truth as though a priest of the Church and summarized salvation history before tracing Christian doctrine (5.1733–45). Shutters, "Confronting Venus," 38–65, examines Gower's "continuity and inclusion" and "severance and exclusion" (39) as an instance of a Christian poet's simultaneous engagement with/disengagement from the classical past.

[35] Isidore of Seville writes: "Quos pagani deos asserunt, homines olim fuisse produntur, et pro uniuscuiusque vita vel meritis coli apud suos post mortem coeperunt" (Those whom the pagans claim as gods are shown to have been humans once; after death they began to be cherished among their own people for their life or merits"). *Etymologiarum*, 8.11.1–3. On Gower's debt to Isidore, see Cooke, "Euhemerism," 402–4.

> ... sche was so wys
> That sche fond ferst in hire avis
> The cloth makinge of wolle and lyn,
> Men seiden that sche was divin,
> And the goddesse of Sapience
> Thei clepen hire in the credence. (5.1201–6)

Gower gives the traits of wisdom and weaving to Minerva while Pallas is "The goddesse of batailles hote" (5.1218), as Genius described her.

Finally, Gower colors this digression with a closing statement on idolatry that associates the deities with demons. Following the general argument of the impetus behind idolatry outlined in Jewish-Christian scriptures and early Christian writers, Genius traced the origins of idolatry in which Prometheus, the first idol-maker in classical tradition, made an image of Syrophanes' dead son that people worshipped in the market-place.[36] Genius concluded this discussion by linking idolatry with the devil, saying:

> And thus the fend fro dai to dai
> The worschipe of ydolatrie
> Drowh forth upon the fantasie
> Of hem that weren thanne blinde
> And couthen noght the trouthe finde. (1586–90)

Minerva and Pallas Athena, as members of Genius' catalog of classical deities, are by association in league with the "fend" in opposition to the Christian "trouthe" Genius subsequently advocated.

Gower examines classical deities in relation to idolatry within the framework of a dream-vision poem. However, as evident from Lydgate's *Troy Book*, the tradition of idolatrous pagan deities in an assembly or catalog is found in historical-epic narratives as well. Just as in Guido's *Historia*, *Troy Book*'s main source, Lydgate's Agamemnon sent Achilles and his companion to consult the oracle of Apollo at Delos before sailing for Troy. Lydgate, following his source in outline, similarly uses this narrative action as a springboard for the digression on idolatry and significant classical deities. After describing Apollo's temple and its location, the narrator says:

---

[36] In Jewish and patristic literature, the origin of idolatry is often linked to a father's grief. Making an image of his dead son, the father honors the son as a god and encourages this practice among his dependants and descendants. See Wisdom 14:12–21; Lactantius, *Divinarum Institutiones*, 1.16. Fulgentius, *Mit*. 1.1, apparently is Gower's source for the Syrophanes story of idolatry's origin though Gower adds the detail of Prometheus' role. Cooke, "Euhemerism," 405. Regarding the first idol-makers, Lydgate later writes in *TB*:

> But as the Iewes recorde of Ysmael,
> That he was first that mawmetrie fonde,
> And made of clay an ydole with his honde,
> And as peynymys write & tellen vs
> That aldirfirst was Promotheus
> That fond ydolis, schortly to conclude. (2.5510–15)

> And in his temple large, longe, and olde,
> Ther was a statue al of purid golde,
> Ful gret and highe, & of huge weighte,
> And ther-in was, thorugh the deuels sleighte,
> A spirit vnclene, be false illusioun,
> That gaf answere to euery questioun –
> Nat the ydole, dovmbe as stok or stoon.
> And thus the peple, deceyued euerychon,
> Were by the fend brought in gret errour,
> To done worschip & swyche false honour,
> With sacrifise & cursed mawmentrie.
> And in this wyse began ydolatrie. (2.5469–80)

Asserting the demonic nature of pagan deities who inspire false worship, and alluding to both patristic writing and Isidore of Seville, Lydgate amplifies Guido and then traces the genealogy of classical divinities, beginning with Saturn, by following closely Lactantius' association of pagan deities with certain peoples.

Minerva, whom Lydgate does not distinguish from Pallas, appears in this section of *Troy Book* as the founder of Athens. While her description in part suggests virtuous wisdom, Minerva's association with other deities in the catalog and her place within Lydgate's polemic against idolatry indicate a demonic nature at this point in the poem. Lydgate amplifies Guido considerably, who just mentions "apud Athenas Minerva" (at Athens Minerva) (10.95), by recounting the story of the dispute between Neptune and Minerva over the naming of the city, in which Apollo granted the privilege to the goddess. The narrator states:

> And sche anon gaf name to the toun,
> And callid it, be highe discrecioun,
> Athenes, the whiche in special
> Is to seyn, a cite in-mortal:
> For wisdam first ther be-gan to floure.
> And for this skile, this cite dide honour
> Mighty Pallas, goddesse of science,
> And had hir ay moste in reuerence. (2.5699–706)

As demonstrated in chapter three, mythographers and commentators associate the story of Athens' founding with wisdom's immortality (e.g., Fulgentius, *Mit.* 2.1; SVM, 50.10–3). For mythographers, the wisdom Minerva represents in an Athenian context carries a positive connotation, as it seems to do here with Lydgate; yet Lydgate continues to be aware of his larger argument against idolatry.

Minerva as an object of worship in ancient Athens remains an idol in the Christian context of Lydgate's discussion: a context shaped in part by Augustine's *civitas Dei*, the "cite in-mortal" *nonpareil*. The poet, moreover, like Severus in *De vita beati Martini*, underscores her idolatrous nature by associating her with Venus in his catalog of deities. Like his Minerva, Lydgate draws his Venus, "ful of doubilnes" (2.1509), from mythographies: she is naked, floating on a sea, and is attended by doves, the three graces, and blind Cupid. This familiar iconography, according to mythographers, indicates a cupidinous and, by association, idolatrous Venus (e.g., Fulgentius, *Mit.* 2.1; TVM, II.1; Bersuire, *De formis figurisque*, 22–3). That Lydgate places Minerva next to Venus suggests an intention to question her wisdom; his conclusion of the digression verifies this suggestion. Again amplifying Guido, his narrator states:

> And thus the fend, first whan that he toke
> Forme of a snake & a woman loke,
> And made the tonge in hir hed to meve,
> By fals engyn mankynde for to greve …
> The same serpent, he Levyathan,
> Contynvyng ay falsly as he gan
> In cursid ydoles dovmbe, defe, & blynde,
> Ful ofte spekith be spirites, as I fynde,
> Whiche ar but fendis, Dauid writ certeyn,
> The goddis alle, whom folkis so in veyn
> Honour with ritis superstycious. (2.5907–10, 5915–21)

Linking pagan deities to the "fend" of Eden, and alluding to Psalm 95:5, which Guido quotes, Lydgate declares all gods and goddesses in his catalog demonic.[37] In this context, Minerva seems especially pernicious, to borrow a term from Augustine, for her wisdom here deceives. In spite of virtuous connotations suggested by her association with Athens, she remains in Lydgate's *Troy Book* an idol in the tradition of Christian patristic writing.

Gower and Lydgate, tapping into the patristic tradition, use classical gods and goddesses to exemplify the notion of idolatry before discounting them as powerless idols and malignant spirits: the objects of misguided worship following, to borrow Chaucer's phrase, "corsed olde rites." While each poet uses the patristic tradition for slightly different purposes and in slightly different ways, the catalog of deities becomes a topos in late medieval English poetry that connotes a deeply felt and recognizable concept of spiritual idolatry. Writing in the wake of Chaucer, Gower, and Lydgate, *The Assembly of Gods*-poet also invokes this concept in his dream vision, to which we now turn.

---

[37] Lydgate's derives his fiend of Eden – the devil in the form of a snake with a woman's face – from Guido as well. See Camille, *Gothic Idol*, 59–60, and fig. 30, for a discussion of Guido and a ms. image of the female-faced serpent.

The Assembly of Gods and Minerva as Idol

The anonymous Middle English poem *The Assembly of Gods* presents an illuminating fifteenth-century example of classical figures as idols and of the worldly wisdom Minerva represents as an idolatrous image.[38] In late medieval English poetry, Minerva can take on an idolatrous connotation when she appears in a large assembly of gods and goddesses; and occasionally, as we see in Gower's *Confessio Amantis*, poets distinguish between Minerva and Pallas Athena in this context, presumably to increase their catalogs of divinities, to ensure complete coverage when denouncing pagan idols, or simply to account for the kind of distinction between the two names that we find in writers like Boccaccio and Christine de Pizan. Though the Church had long-since neutralized the external threat of Greco-Roman polytheism, the internal threat of moral idolatry, a threat against an individual's spiritual health, remained a concern.[39] The *Assembly*-poet, implicitly following the outline of Prudentius' *Psychomachia*, translates Christian polemics against idolatry from the external realm of society, where patristic writers waged their battles for the hearts and minds of believers, to the internal landscape of the soul through the use of dream vision.

In *The Assembly of Gods*, a 2107-line narrative in 301 rime royal stanzas, the first-person narrator recounts a dream vision in which he had undertaken an eschatological spiritual journey into the soul guided by the dream-god Morpheus, who was dwelling in "a lytyll corner callyd 'Fantasy'" (35).[40] We can divide the narrative's action into a prologue, a tripartite dream report, and an epilogue: three sections that together emphasize the poem's didactic thrust. In the dream report's first two parts – what we might call "the trial of Eolus" and the "psychomachia" – the narrator observed and listened to various personifications and figures. The narrator's role here was much like an audience member at a play: he neither participated in nor commented on the action.[41] This narrative technique differs from participant narrators found in *Reson and Sensuallyte*, *The Court of Sapience*, *The Palice of Honour*, *The Pastime of Pleasure*, and elsewhere, and the poet seems to use it for two key reasons.

---

[38] Triggs, introduction to *The Assembly*, xi–xiv, dated *The Assembly* to c.1420 based on early reception attributing it to Lydgate: printed editions include colophons naming Lydgate as author, and Hawes, *Pastime* 1362–4, considered it so. The poem's meter and language, however, discount Lydgate's authorship. See Lewis, *Allegory of Love*, 262; and Baugh, *Literary History of England*, 290. Chance, introduction to *The Assembly*, 2–3, dates it to the third quarter of the fifteenth century.

[39] The concern about internal idolatry received increased attention following the Fourth Lateran Council of 1215, which codified in Canon 21 cumpulsory annual confession. This internalization also affected visual art. See Camille, *Gothic Idol*, 10–11, 57–72.

[40] The poet's choice of Morpheus as dream-guide mirrors Gower's choice of Genius as confessor-guide in *CA*. The poet also seems to be alluding to Chaucer's use of Morpheus in recounting the tale of Ceyx and Alcione in *BD*, 62–214, as well as the god's role in Ovid, *Metamorphoses*, 11.444–748.

[41] We see this kind of approach in *The Parlement of the Thre Ages* and in *The Debate of the Body and Soul*, where the narrator observes but does not directly participate in the dream's action, thereby allowing the audience access to the dream unmediated by narrative commentary.

First, by refusing narrative comment, the poet draws readers into the narrator's position of observer and listener so they in a sense also experience the vision directly. And second, the lack of narrative comment in the first two parts prepares more vividly for the third in which Dame Doctryne, a female wisdom-figure in the vein of Philosophia and Sapientia, instructed the narrator about the significance of his experience. Though some critics may think the poet's emphasis on Dame Doctryne's role typifies allegory's waning power in fifteenth-century poetics, the poem's didacticism and the comic moments of Doctryne's instruction presumably appealed to an audience enmeshed in the religiously tumultuous and politically unstable scene of late medieval England.[42]

Like much fifteenth-century poetry, *The Assembly* has received little notice from modern critics.[43] The lack of modern interest in *The Assembly* belies its poetic and philosophical merits, and the poem's obvious popularity in its day suggests a need to re-evaluate it.[44] Populated with gods, goddesses, and personifications, the poem's principal action depicts Christianity's overthrow of polytheism through a psychomachic battle between Vertu, aided by the Lord of Light, and Vyce, aided by classical deities. The poet draws on Christine de Pizan's *Epître d'Othéa* when presenting Minerva and Pallas Athena. As in Christine, Minerva is goddess of war; for Pallas, on the other hand, the poet fuses the goddess' traits of wisdom with Christine's Othea, who here serves as both prudent Othea and Athena *patrona* found in *L'Epître*.[45]

---

[42] See H. Bennett, *Chaucer and the Fifteenth Century*, 96–217; Lewis, *Allegory of Love*, 232–3, and *English Literature*, 120–56. For an overview of more recent attitudes, see Kuskin, "The Fourth Generation," 171–8.

[43] See Baugh, *Literary History of England*, 190; Bühler, "Assembly of Gods," 251–4; Chance, introduction to *The Assembly*, 2–17; Lewis, *The Allegory of Love*, 259–64; and Stearns, "Note on Henryson and Lydgate," 101–3.

[44] The poem's manuscript and printing history attests to its popularity in England until about 1540. Its earliest extant copy in Cambridge, Trinity College Ms. R.3.19 (67v–97v) dates c.1468–80. Wynkyn de Worde printed it in 1498, and twice in 1500; Richard Pynson c.1505; and John Skot c.1530. De Worde's 1498 edition is extant in three copies, his first 1500 edition in three copies, and his second 1500 edition in one copy; Pynson's 1505 edition and Skot's 1530 edition are each extant in one copy. A second manuscript copy extant in British Library Royal Ms. 18.D.ii (167r–180v), dating c.1516–23, is a copy of de Worde's first 1500 edition. See Chance, introduction to *The Assembly*, 2–17. Royal Ms. 18.D.II has 211 parchment folios in thirty gatherings copied in two phases: the early portion (fols. 1r–162v), including Lydgate's *Testament*, *TB* and *Siege of Thebes*, dates c.1457–60; the later portion (fols. 163r–211v), including *The Assembly*, dates c.1516–27. In the context of English book-production, this manuscript copy of *The Assembly* illustrates an uncommon practice where a scribe produces a unique version of a text based on a mass-produced printed text. This evidence, and the low survival rate of the early printed copies, suggests people enjoyed reading *The Assembly* and considered it within a Lydgatian context as Hawes, the printers' colophons, and the Royal Ms. copy itself attest.

[45] Triggs assumes "Othea" was a scribal error and states "I am confident that Athena is the right reading" (68, n. to line 249). Presumably, he was unfamiliar with Christine's *L'Epistre* though the poet draws on it for *The Assembly*, including most likely Othea's name and attributes. Bühler, "Assembly of Gods," 251–4. The poet may also have Lydgate's *TB* in mind. Regardless, he fuses Athena's attributes with Othea's; Triggs is not mistaken in thinking of Athena here though he does not account for the name.

Minerva and Othea function within an assembly of deities and derive idolatrous connotations largely from their relationships to the group.

Minerva-Othea and Idolatry

Othea appears three times and Minerva once in "the trial of Eolus" section of the poem (36–609). We can subdivide this section by location into "Minos' court" (36–189) and "Apollo's banquet" (190–609) and, though Minerva and Othea appear only at the banquet, the court scene begins to establish the nature of the divinities in this poem. In the opening hearing of Eolus' trial, held before Minos and Pluto in hell, Diana and Neptune accused Eolus, the god of wind, of overstepping his prerogative. The charges against Eolus, as is often the case in court-room drama, illuminate the plaintiffs' characters as much as the defendant's. Diana, after complaining that Eolus destroyed sections of her forest, stated "'Whyche to my name a reproche syngler / Shuld be for ever whyle the world last'" (71–2). Similarly, Neptune, upon accusing Eolus of usurping his jurisdiction over the sea, complained that travelers now curse "'the tyme that ever they me fande. / Thus among the pepyll lost ys my name, / And so by hys labour put I am to shame'" (131–3). Both Diana and Neptune were primarily concerned with their reputations: yet, they seemed to lack the power either to curb Eolus' behavior or assert control over their respective dominions.[46]

This implicit characterization of Diana and Neptune reverberates with the common charge leveled against pagan deities. When *The Assembly*-poet presents a Diana and a Neptune more concerned with reputation than with exercising control over their domains, he suggests, along with the psalmists, the Daniel-author, Paul, Augustine, Prudentius, and other Jewish and Christian writers, that pagan deities lack power though they wish to retain its appearance and benefits. The poet emphasizes this theme of powerlessness and reputation when his narrator describes a messenger interrupting the trial the moment Pluto called on Eolus to answer the charges. Expressing outright his intention of postponing judgment, the messenger invited all to a banquet at Apollo's home. Surprisingly, perhaps, Diana and Neptune quickly agreed, and Eolus' sole comment in the poem, "'I am well pleysd'" (180), draws out the moment's humor. We can almost perceive between the lines the god of wind's ironic smile as, the narrator notes, "Pluto commaundyd the court to be broke" (182) and all retired to dinner.

Upon arrival at Apollo's home, Diana to her credit insisted on a judgment before sitting down to the banquet; yet, the recompense she received underscores the poet's suggestion she was not so much concerned with true dominion as with its

---

[46] Readers familiar with Virgil's *Aeneid*, 1.50–156, would likely find the Eolus-Neptune conjunction in *The Assembly* puzzling, if not amusing, in light of this Neptune's complaint and powerlessness over the god of wind. Aeolus, to whom Juno promised the nymph Deiopea in payment for his aid, unleashed his winds to destroy Aeneas' Trojan fleet. Disturbed in the deeps by the storm, Neptune rose to the water's surface, rebuked the winds, sent them scurrying back to Aeolus, and instantly calmed the seas, thereby saving the remnants of the fleet. In Virgil Neptune holds sway over Aeolus' winds.

appearance. Apollo pled Eolus' case and offered a divine out-of-court settlement, promising that "For every tree that he maketh fall, / Out of the erthe, an hundred aryse shall" (230–1). Diana, in accepting the settlement, seemed to abdicate her claim of dominion over woodlands. As goddess of woodlands, she should have had power herself to raise replacement trees, it would seem. This comic exchange illustrates a type of compromise familiar to any with experience of parliamentary processes, and certainly to the poet's fifteenth-century audience. Apollo, wishing to commence the banquet, also interceded in Neptune's case, suggesting he accept Phebe as arbiter. Neptune acquiesced, Apollo called the deities to feast, and the answer to Neptune's charge was again postponed.[47]

The characterization of Diana and Neptune as powerless and acquiescent sheds light on Othea and Minerva as members of their assembly. Othea first appeared to the narrator in an exchange with Apollo when he called for the feast immediately after Neptune acquiesced:

"Well, then," quod Apollo, "I pray you, goddes all,
And goddesses eke, that be heere present,
That ye compaygnably wyll aboorde fall."
"Nay, then," seyde Othea, "hit ys nat conuenyent.
A dew ordre in every place ys expedyent
To be had, wherfore ye may nat let
To be your owne marchall at your owne banket." (246–52)

Fulfilling her role as goddess of wisdom, Othea asserted the need for due order as the deities assembled. Aside from introducing the subsequent catalog of the goddesses and the gods, an important narrative function itself, Othea's assertion hints at her own concern to maintain proper balance of power. However, it also suggests that, like the deities involved in the lawsuit, she was quick to intercede when she perceived another divinity usurping her prerogative.

Even though she maintained her authority among the deities by insisting on an orderly approach to dining, in itself not a bad thing, Othea's wisdom becomes ultimately suspect because she allied herself and Minerva with morally questionable gods. As the order of the deities at table unfolded, Othea sat between Cupid and Pluto with Fortune next in line. The narrator recalls:

Next to Cupido in ordyr, by and by,
Of worldly wysdom sate the forteresse
Callyd Othea, chyef grounde of polyty,
Rewler of knyghthode, of Prudence the goddesse.
Clad all in purpur was she, more and lesse;

---

[47] The poet is writing during a period of political instability and violence in England. Perhaps this concern in the poem for prerogatives, due order, and power hints at societal unrest. Keen, *English Society*, 187–214, describes three levels of violence that contributed to this unrest: common felony and trespass, private wars between magnates, and open rebellion to royal authority.

> Safe on her hede a crowne ther stood,
> Cowchyd with perles oryent fyne and good.
>
> And next to her was god Pluto set,
> With a derke myst envyrond all aboute;
> Hys clothing was made of a smoky net.
> Hys colour was, bothe withyn and withoute,
> Foule, derke, and dymme; hys eyen, gret and stoute.
> Of fyre and sulphure all hys odour wase,
> That wo was me whyle I beheld hys fase. (302–15)

Unlike Minerva's crown and robe in *Reson and Sensuallyte*, which signify her relation to Sapientia, Philosophia, and Raison, Othea's purple attire and crown of pearls reinforce the adjective "worldly" modifying her "wysdom" in this poem. While the attribute of worldliness might be construed positively as the prudence proper to right management of the state as in the *patrona* tradition, her association with Cupid on one side, with his "kerchyef of plesaunce" (299), and Pluto on the other, "Foule, derke and dymme" whose stage-devilish appearance and odor caused the narrator woe, raises doubts about Othea's prudence. The association next in line with Fortune, as "Varyaunt" and "Changeable" as ever (318, 321), reinforces the doubts. Moreover, on reflection at poem's end, her placement at table with Pluto, whose son Vyce battles Vertu later in the narrative, especially suggests a negative, if not demonic, dimension to her worldly wisdom at this point in the poem.

Minerva, for her part, made her only appearance within the catalog of deities; yet, like Othea, her placement at table and description call into question her character. As the narrator recounts the setting, she appeared immediately following Neptune, the god with the postponed lawsuit:

> Then toke Mynerve, the goddesse, her sete,
> Joyntly to Neptunus, all in curas clad,
> Gauntlettes on hyr handys and sabatouns on hyr fete.
> She loked ever about as though she had be mad.
> An hamer and a sythe on her hede she had.
> She weryd two bokelers, oone by her syde,
> That other, ye wote where; thys was all her pryde. (344–50)

Minerva is strictly the goddess of war, here, and her bellicose attire and demeanor indicate not the strategic and defensive warfare she represents in earlier literature but a more crazed, possibly bloodthirsty, warfare in the tradition of Mars. Like Mars, Minerva was irascible and unsettled rather than calm and rational. Her association with the inebriated Bacchus, who sits next to her "Holdyng in hys hande a cup full of wyne" (352), emphasizes her madness; drunkenness, like madness itself, indicates lack of self-control and moderation: a loss, if temporary, of rational faculty. This detail recalls Romanus' diatribe in *Peristephanon* 10. Though not necessarily a direct source for *The Assembly*-poet, Romanus also associated Minerva with a drunken Bacchus (278–80).

Their iconongraphy, association with the litigious divinities, and placement within an assembly of corrupt gods indicate Othea and Minerva are morally questionable, too. Like their Greco-Roman ancestors in patristic writing, they function as idolatrous images in *The Assembly*, and Othea's final appearance exemplifies this aspect of her nature and her worldly wisdom in this poem. After the deities were seated, Discord tried to enter the banquet hall, but the assembly barred her because the gods and goddesses remembered the rift she caused at Peleus' wedding feast. Seeking redress, the offended Discord enlisted aid from Attropos, who declared "'Ones yet for your sake shall I make hem wrooth'" (427). Attropos, who is male in this poem, entered the hall, reminded the deities of his function to bring death to all, and issued a complaint against them, saying:

> "Thus have I brought every creature
> To an ende, bothe man, fysshe, foule, and beste,
> And every thyng in whom Dame Nature
> Hath any jurysdiccion, owther most or leste.
> Except oonly oon, in whom your beheste
> Ys to me broke, for ye me promysyd
> That my myght of noon shuld haue be dyspysyd." (477–83)

Declaring there was "oon" being over whom he had no power, in spite of the deities' "beheste" he have dominion over all creatures of Nature, Attropos challenged their authority and demanded their aid, stating:

> "And yef ye so have, then do ye nat as goddys,
> For a goddes wrytyng may nat reversyd be.
> Yef hit shuld I wold nat geve two pesecoddys
> For graunt of your patent of offyce, ner of fee.
> Wherfore in thys mater do me equyté
> Accordyng to my patent, for tyll thys be do,
> Ye have no more my servyce nor my good wyll, lo!" (491–7)

Without knowing Attropos' enemy, identified later as Vertu (591), the deities, sensing a threat to their divine reputations, immediately pledged to destroy the "oonly oon" Attropos could not kill: Apollo will burn him, Neptune drown him, Saturn freeze him, and so on. At this point, Othea stepped in:

> "Ye," quod Othea, "yet may he well be
> In the eyre where he woll, and ax yow no leve.
> Wherfore, my counsell ys that all we
> May entrete Neptunus hys rancour to forgeve,
> And then I dowte not Eolus wyll him myscheve,
> So may ye be sewre he shall yow nat escape.
> And elles of all your angre woll he make but a jape." (519–25)

Othea intervened in Neptune's case with Eolus to restore order among the gods so they might fight Attropos' enemy as a group. Though a prudent military strategist, she exercised her wisdom here for worldly ends: to protect the deities' reputation with Attropos. Not surprisingly, considering the patristic tradition, the gods and goddesses became more inclined to fight the enemy when Attropos identified him as Vertu. Pluto called forth his son Vyce, the gods and goddesses allied themselves with him, and the forces of evil prepared for battle.

The next section of the poem is a psychomachia in the tradition of Prudentius. Unlike Alan of Lille's *Anticlaudianus*, however, where Minerva aids the *novus homo* in his fight against the Vices of hell, Othea and Minerva here were on Vyce's side, though they did not take an active part in the battle.[48] Sensualyté, however, played a key role in Vyce's strategy, sowing weeds on the field of microcosm, or the human soul, "Whyche made the grounde as slepyr as an yele" (1026), while Reson serves Vertu. The Minerva-Othea alliance with Sensualyté is an important detail in distinguishing the idolatrous tradition of Minerva imagery. Vertu, of course, won the battle against Vyce and set the soul in proper order, placing Reson over Free Will (1254–60), who had sided with Sensualyté and Vyce early in the battle before converting to Vertu's side. Attropos, disgruntled with the deities, sought a new master, the Lord of Light, who through his agent Ryghtwysnes, changed Attropos' name to Dethe and gave him possession of microcosm (1380–1421). Concerning the pagan deities, Ryghtwysnes said to Attropos:

"And as for theym whom thow dedyst serve,
For as moche as they presume on hem to take
That hygh name of God, they shall as they deserve
Therfore be rewardyd, I dare undyrtake,
With peyn perpetuell among fendes blake,
And her names shall be put to oblyuyon –
Among men, but hit be in derysyon." (1408–14)

In an echo of a passage from Prudentius' *Contra Symmachum*, the pagan deities, including Minerva and Othea, were cast with Vyce into hell where, now supplanted by Christian truth, they suffer for their presumption in "oblyuyon," remembered if at all as a mere joke.[49] As with Gower and Lydgate, *The Assembly*-poet follows here the patristic tradition associating the pagan deities with "fendes," which he emphasizes later when Dame Doctryne declares them to be idols (1737–43).

---

[48] Minerva does not directly appear in the psychomachic section of *Anticlaudianus*; however, as *magistra artium* she sides with the *novus homo*'s forces as each liberal art helps arm him before his epic battle (7.245–328). In the battle, however, his education is hardly used. See Trout, *Voyage of Prudence*, 125.

[49] In response to those who encourage polytheism in Rome, Prudentius writes: "Heu, male de populo meriti, male patribus ipsis / blanditi, quos praecipites in tartara mergi / cum Iove siuerunt multa et cum plebe deorum!" (Alas! They have been served evilly by the people, coaxed evilly by the senators themselves whom they allowed to be plunged headlong into hell with Jove and with many common gods!). *Contra Symmachum*, 1.25–7.

The Poem's Primary Concerns and Minerva-Othea's Worldly Wisdom

The classical deities as a group of idolatrous images serve important narrative and philosophical functions in the poem's didactic plan. Three concerns pervade *The Assembly*: the "acorde" of Reson and Sensualyté (6), the affirmation of the new (i.e., Christian) religion, and the necessity to learn from Doctryne. The poet uses the classical deities differently to address each of these concerns. In affirming the new religion, for example, the classical deities act as a foil: they represent a limited system of belief over which Christianity triumphs. Again, while polytheism no longer poses an external threat to the Christian Church of the fifteenth century, the idolatry it represents poses an internal threat to individual Christians. Similarly, regarding the need to learn from Doctryne, the classical deities play an important function in Doctryne's discourse. They exemplify "paynym lawe" and "How false idolatry ledeth [pagans] by the sleve" (1679, 1680). Further, they represent the period of Deviation, the first in Doctryne's four-part division of salvation history, which also includes periods of Revocation, Reconciliation, and Pilgrimage (1744–85).

Although the functions the deities serve in affirming the new religion and the need to learn from Doctryne seem obvious from the narrative, their function regarding the poet's primary concern is less obvious. The "acorde" of Reson and Sensualyté is the poem's ostensible theme, as the narrator says in the opening stanza:

> Whan Phebus in the Crabbe had nere hys cours ronne
> And toward the leon his journé gan take,
> To loke on Pictagoras speere I had begonne,
> Syttyng all solytary alone besyde a lake,
> Musyng on a maner how that I myght make
> Reson and Sensualyté in oon to acorde.
> But I cowde nat bryng about that monacorde. (1–7)

In a general sense, the poet sets out to comment on the medieval notion of discord between the rational and the sensual faculties of the human soul. More specifically, considering the poem's provenance and relation to fifteenth-century dream visions, the poet wishes to respond to his master Lydgate, who separates the rational from the sensual in *Reson and Sensuallyte*. What Lydgate insists on leaving asunder, however, *The Assembly*-poet proposes to make "acorde." Like his master, though, who uses satire to emphasize the discord between Reson and Sensuallyte, *The Assembly*-poet uses comedy to "bring about that monacorde."[50]

---

50 The Middle English noun "monacorde" or "monocorde" refers specifically to a "musical instrument consisting of a sounding board and a single string stretched over a moveable fret or bridge; also, an instrument with several strings and bridges," or figuratively to "agreement, harmony." *MED*, "mono-corde" 1.a, b. In addition to two citations in *The Assembly*, the *MED* cites Chilston's fifteenth-century treatise on musical proportions, in British Library, Ms. Lansdowne 763, as another known use of the term: "Þu shalt fynde more pleynli in þe makyng of þe monacorde þat is callid þe jnstrument of plain-song." Meech, "Three Musical Treatises," 265–9: 269. In her edition of the poem, n.7, 91–2, Chance notes that "monocorde" as agreement suggests a desired movement towards the

The three sections of the poem work together to demonstrate the issue on which Reson and Sensualyté agree, though initially the poem merely seems to reinforce their traditional discord. In the "psychomachia," the poet articulates the usual relationship between Reson and Sensualyté: the former fought for Vertu while the latter for Vyce. The result of the battle, too, in which Ryghtwysnes placed Reson as lord over Free Will, emphasizes the ideal victory of the rational over the sensual faculty and reinforces common medieval ideas about the human soul. Throughout this visually dramatic section of the narrative, the continued opposition between the two faculties and the cause for the narrator's quandary – how to bring about their union – remains. It is with the deities and Attropos, however, that the potential for "acorde" is born. The deities' primary role regarding this concern is to provide a context for Attropos' activity and a reason for his conversion. When the self-absorbed deities failed to defeat Vertu, Attropos changed his allegiance and his name. As Dethe, he is the only classical figure in this poem to adjust to Christianity and transform into an active, powerful member of the new religion. This part of the poem, in a sense, recounts an intriguing, possibly unique, origin myth of death as a poetic and psychological figure, and Dethe plays a crucial role in addressing the narrator's primary concern.

The final answer the narrator received regarding the "acorde" of Reson and Sensualyté was presented again dramatically in the manner of the earlier "trial of Eolus" (36–609) and "psychomachia" (610–1468). After Doctryne interpreted his visionary experience (1618–1868), the narrator again raised his initial question. Dethe immediately entered Doctryne's chapel and, while the narrator cowered in fear behind Morpheus, Reson and Sensualyté followed. When the narrator refused to appear after Doctryne called for him, Reson and Sensualyté excused him, saying:

"Blame hym nat … alwey that to use,
When he seeth Dethe so neere at hys hande.
Yet ys hys part hym to wythstande."

"Or at the leste way, ellys fro hym flee
As long as he may; who dothe otherwyse
Ys an ydiote." Quoth Sensualyté.
"Who dredyth nat Dethe wyse men hym dyspyse."
"What!" seyde Doctryne, "how long hath thys gyse
Be holdyn and usyd thus, atwyx yow tweyne?
Yee were nat wont to acorede, certeyne." (1958–67)

And, as Reson declared in answer to Doctryne's incredulity, "'To every man have wee geven our counsayll, / Dethe for to flee as long as they may. / … In that poynt oonly dyscordyd we never'" (1969–70, 1973). Half-mockingly Doctryne again called forth the still frightened and confused narrator from behind Morpheus and quizzed

---

One, a Pythagorean and Boethian idea about which Philosophia sings in *CP* 3.m9 and Boethius writes in his *De musica*. See Teviotdale, "Music and Pictures," 187, for a twelfth-century illumination of Boethius holding a monochord while explaining musical theory.

him, saying "'Herdest thow nat Reson and Sensualyté / Declare thy dowte here before thee?'" The narrator acknowledged hearing but, for lack of wit and fear of Dethe, admitted not understanding them. Clarifying for him, then, what lesson he should draw, Doctryne's final word of her closing direct statement frames the entire narrative:

> "Bothe Sensualyté and Reson applyeth,
> Rather Dethe to fle then with hit to be tane.
> Loo, in that point accorde they holly thane,
> And in all other they clerely dyscorde.
> Thus ys trewly set thy doutfull monacorde" (2014–16).

Reson and Sensualyté achieved "monacorde" in the fear of Dethe and, in doing so, emphasize the centrality of the Attropos-Dethe myth to this narrative. In Doctryne's repetition of "monacorde," we perhaps also see a subtle distinction drawn between polytheism and monotheism. The pagan deities dissemble the oneness of knowledge in this poem where feeling and reason only come together in Christian thought. Interestingly, too, the poet, though surely familiar with the great emphasis in Christian theology and literature on the negation of death by the Redemption, exemplified in Prudentius' *Peristephanon* 14, chooses not to develop this theme. Rather, he suggests that human reason, limited in its comprehension of Christian mysteries, naturally fears death; and he implies that faith, above all, is necessary to face it fearlessly.

While the idolatrous deities provide the general context of false belief from which Attropos is transformed into Dethe, Minerva-Othea imagery represents specifically worldly wisdom, as she does in Guido delle Colonne's *Historia destructionis Troiae*, Gower's *Confessio Amantis*, Lydgate's *Troy Book*, and especially in patristic writing. In a catalog of deities such as we find in *The Assembly*, Minerva assumes an idolatrous nature through her alliance with other more obviously corrupt deities. The Assembly-poet uses Minerva-Othea imagery to suggest the nature of the wisdom she represents as an idolatrous image. This wisdom, though apparently prudent, is deceptive, for its motive and end are both spiritually false. Othea exercises her prerogative to establish order among the gods at the banquet and before battle so they can better aid in the attempted destruction of Vertu. Her ends in relation to the Christian thought pervading this poem cast a shadow over her wisdom; her motive for achieving these ends contradicts and ultimately discounts any positive trait implied in her description. Turning to the Scots poet, William Dunbar, we find a similar use of Minerva imagery in his courtly dream vision *The Golden Targe*.

William Dunbar's Minerva-Athena Imagery in *The Golden Targe*

Writing in late fifteenth- and early sixteenth-century Scotland, William Dunbar (c.1460–c.1513/20) composed poems ranging in subject and genre that demonstrate mastery of short forms: even his narratives, where we might expect the poet to stretch, exhibit concise economy of style and sharp control of meter and rhyme.[51] He identified himself as a "mackar" (70: 22), but in court documents and colophons to several other poems scribes referred to him as "maister," that is, a university graduate: likely the William Dunbar who graduated from the University of St. Andrews in 1479.[52] Attached to King James IV's court by 1500, Dunbar was ordained a priest in 1504, granted raises in his royal pension in 1507 and 1510, and received the final known payment of his pension on May 14, 1513. We know little else about the poet beyond occasional additional payments and his involvement in two legal actions in 1502 and 1509. He may have died in the Battle of Flodden on September 9, 1513, but was certainly dead by 1530 when Sir David Lyndsay (c.1490–c.1555) lamented his passing.[53] Though Dunbar's sparse historical record stops with the May 1513 pension payment, his poetry reveals a lively engagement with "the flux of actual life," as Priscilla Bawcutt aptly puts it, including life at the court of King James IV.[54] In light of poetic uses of Minerva as idol, we find a similar use of Minerva-Athena imagery in *The Golden Targe*: a courtly dream vision Dunbar probably composed in the 1590s or early in the first decade of the sixteenth century while in residence at James IV's court.[55]

In the *Targe*, Dunbar uses Minerva as idolatrous image to help develop themes of love, human perception and psychology, microcosmic-macrocosmic correspondence, and poetic composition, for the *Targe* is a poetic celebration of style, form, and tradition that Dunbar underscores particularly at poem's end. Composed of 279 iambic pentameter lines in thirty-one nine-line stanzas rhyming a-a-b-a-a-b-b-a-b, a stanza Chaucer uses for Anelida's complaint in *Anelida and Arcite* (211–350), the *Targe* is a brief narrative in which the narrator recounts a dream vision he experienced one unusually glorious May morning. As the poetic landscape, infused by Phebus' morning light, sparkled and gleamed in jewel-like grandeur, the narrator's enthusiasm for the natural world and spring – presumably in the wake of the "doolie sessoun," as Henryson describes winter (*Testament of Cresseid*, 1) – shines as brightly as the sun-draped landscape. Lulled by sensory experiences of stunning

---

[51] Modern editors generally accept eighty-four poems as genuine, the longest of which is *The Flyting of Dumbar and Kennedie* at 552 lines. *Poems of William Dunbar*, ed. Bawcutt, 65. The next longest is *The Tretis of the Tua Mariit Wemen and the Wedo* at 530 lines (3); *The Golden Targe* is a distant third at 279 lines (59). On Dunbar's use of rhyme, see Burrow, "Dunbar and the Accidents of Rhyme," 20–8; on style, see Ebin, *Illuminator, Makar, Vates*, 74–89; Haydock, "Dunbar's Perfection," 72–87; and Ramson, "Aureate Paradox," 93–103.

[52] See Bawcutt, *Dunbar the Makar*, 5–8, and Introduction to *The Poems*, 1–4; Burrow, "William Dunbar," 133; and Parkinson, "William Dunbar" 226–8.

[53] Lyndsay, *Papyngo*, 17–18, in *Works of Sir David Lyndsay*, ed. Hamer.

[54] Bawcutt, *Dunbar the Makar*, 39. See also Hasler, *Court Poetry*, 63–86; Hepburn, "William Dunbar," 95–112; Parkinson, "William Dunbar," 226–8; Robinson, *Court Politics, Culture and Literature*, 23–4, 116–18.

[55] It is difficult to date Dunbar's *Golden Targe*. Like many of his poems, the *Targe* appears written for a courtly audience; thus, we might assume he composed it sometime during his stay at court or earlier. See Bawcutt's notes in Dunbar, *The Poems*, 413–14; and Reiss, *William Dunbar*, 105–9. Citing Bawcutt, Burrow, "William Dunbar," thinks an early date "likely, for it has all the air of a 'masterwork', in the old sense of that term, the piece of work by which a craftsman gained the recognized rank of 'master'" (137).

visual beauty, harmonious birdsong, and running water in the natural world, he fell asleep by a rosebush and river and entered a dreamscape where he observed a golden ship approach "As falcoun swift desyrouse of hir pray" (54) and conduct what seems an amphibious landing nearby. One hundred ladies, who made up the court of Venus and Nature "quene and quene" (73), disembarked, and the narrator interrupts the narrative to catalog them from memory, including "Thetis, Pallas, and prudent Minerua" (78). A second court, led by "Cupide, the king, wyth bow in hand ybent / And dredefull arowis grundyn scharp and square" (110–11), also disembarked, and he again catalogs this group of classical deities, including "Mars the god armypotent / ... crabbit Saturn, ald and haire / ... [and] Bacus, the gladder of the table" (112, 114, 124). As the courts joined together in song and dance, the narrator indulged his curiosity, like Acteon creeping forward for a better look, and Venus saw him. The goddess immediately ordered her fierce archers to arrest him, much as her literary counterpart arrested the dreamer-narrator in *Palice of Honoure*. In the *Targe*, four different groups of personified ladies attacked him, but Reson, a "plate and maille"-wearing "cheuallere" (152, 153), repulsed each onslaught with his "goldyn Targe" (157), a possible allusion to Solomon's golden shields (1 Kings 10:16–17) and to biblical Sapientia.[56] In a final attack, Presence blinded Reson with a powder, Dissymulance and company "banyst hym amang the bewis grene" (206), and the dreamer yielded "To lady Beautee in a moment space" (210). Though with Reson blinded and banished the dreamer now thought his beloved "seymt lustier of chere / ... Than of before, and lufliare of face" (211, 213), the narrator soon interrupts the dream again, lamenting in the present tense of narration "Quhy was thou blyndit, Reson, quhi, allace? / And gert ane hell my paradise appere, / And mercy seme quhare that I fand no grace" (214–16). As quickly as he succumbed to Presence and Beautee, who with Dissymulance, Fair Calling, Cherishing, and New Acquyntance favored him briefly ("quhill men mycht go a myle" [221]), the dreamer saw Dangere approach, and finally Departing "me delyverit vnto Hevynesse / For to remayne, and scho in cure me toke" (227–8). With the dreamer sunk in melancholy, the dream swiftly closed when Eolus, the questionable culprit in *The Assembly of Gods*, "his bugill blew" (230), blasting the dreamscape into a nightmarish "wildernes" (233). Summoned, the courts embarked and swiftly sailed away to raucous noise of cannon fire, which awakened the dreamer into the natural world of his pre-*somnium* experience. With the dream now over, the poet concludes again in the present tense with two stanzas praising Chaucer, Gower, and Lydgate before addressing in the final stanza his own "lytill quair" (257), which he implies is worthy, if humbly, to join company with the poets' "fresch anamalit termes celicall" (257) that "Oure rude langage has clere illumynate" (266).[57]

---

[56] Foran, "Dunbar's Broken Rainbow," 54–5.
[57] The poem's final stanza literally suggests otherwise. Addressing the poem, the poet says

> Thou lytill quair, be ewir obedient,
> Humble, subiect and simple of entent
> Before the face of ewiry connyng wight.
> I knaw quhat thou of rethorike hes spent.

This courtly poem allegorising a seduction and subsequent brief love affair seems to have made Dunbar's poetic reputation at least in part. As early as 1501, Dunbar was known for his poetry: in *The Palice of Honoure* his fellow courtier Gavin Douglas lists him among a catalog of poets that, perhaps cued by the *Targe*'s final stanzas, includes Chaucer, Gower, and Lydgate as well as two other then-living Scots poets.[58] Although it is presently impossible to know if he had the *Targe* in mind, Douglas' inclusion of Dunbar in the list suggests the poem's original literary and courtly milieu. It is also presently impossible to know specifics of what Jon Robinson would call the *Targe*'s "initial performance," or what we might call its first publication, but the *Targe* itself suggests a few points worth reviewing.[59] Its dream-vision form, love-story psychomachia, and classical detail inscribe an audience steeped in medieval classicism and the allegorical love vision of the *Roman de la Rose* tradition: a learned-courtly audience that appreciates Dunbar's distinctive shift, turning the *Roman*'s traditional first-person narrator-wooer into the wooed. Not the subject-agent of the affair, Dunbar's dreamer-narrator was the object whom, once conquered, Lady Beautee quickly dismissed. The poem's lack of direct discourse and focus on sight, on what the narrator observed as well as experienced in a mime-like performance accompanied by sound but no words, also points to another courtly form developing in England and Scotland: the masque. As Enid Welsford and Frank Shuffleton suggest, and Pamela King carefully explicates, the movement to-and-fro of the ship, the disembarkation and embarkation of the deities, the battle itself, even the cannon fire point to an allegorical masque-like performance familiar to James

---

> Off all hir lusty rosis redolent
> Is non in to thy gerland sett on hicht.
> Eschame tharof and draw the out of sicht.
> Rude is they wede, disteynit, bare and rent,
> Wele aucht thou be aferit of the licht. (277–9)

In this carefully-constructed poem attentive to sight and perception and infused with light imagery, the poet telling his "lytill quair" it has no art and counseling it to stay "out of sicht" and "be aferit of the licht" is self-deprecatingly funny. If Dunbar literally meant what he wrote, and likely recited at its first publication, we would not have the poem. One can almost hear a "connyng wight," in the brief silence following the recited final line, mumble in his cup or shout from the back of the hall: "Too late!"

[58] Douglas writes:

> 3it thare I saw of Brutus Albion
> Goffryd Chaucere, as a per se, sance pere
> In his wulgare and morell Iohn Gowere.
> Lydgat the monk raid musand him allone
> Of this natioun I knew also anone
> Gret Kennedy and Dunbar 3it vndede,
> And Quyntyne with ane huttok on his hede. (*Palice*, 918–24)

Kennedy likely refers to Walter Kennedy of the *Flyting*, and Quyntyne to Quintin, another poet also mentioned in the *Flyting* (65: 2). On Dunbar and Douglas, see Lyall, "Stylistic Relationship," 69–84.

[59] Robinson, *Court Politics, Culture and Literature*, 2–5.

and his court.[60] If not an actual masque-poem composed for a specific occasion, as Shuffleton argues, the *Targe* certainly shows forth that type of courtly entertainment: it is not a poem for the tavern.

Although no known autograph or scribal manuscripts of the poem are extant from Dunbar's lifetime, other external evidence provides a sense for the poem's early reception outside the court as well. Some six years following Douglas' Dunbar reference in *The Palice*, Walter Chepman and Andrew Myllar received on September 15, 1507, the first Royal patent to print books in Scotland. Once established, they almost immediately turned to Dunbar for material, bringing out six of his poems – the most from their press of any single known poet – including the earliest extant copy of the *Targe* in April 1508.[61] Among the known authors Chepman and Myllar printed, Dunbar and Walter Kennedy were likely the only living poets at the time of printing.[62] As with John Skelton and Stephen Hawes in England, printing Dunbar's poetry in Scotland made it available to a wide audience, giving readers in Edinburgh and elsewhere access to literary texts initially produced in and for James IV's court, thereby opening a window of sorts for them into the King's courtly world. And the printers must have succeeded to some degree as the few surviving copies of their printed texts – the Chepman and Myllar prints in the National Library of Scotland – represent several hundred other no-longer extant copies that were likely read to tatters.[63]

---

[60] Welsford, *Court Masque*, 74–5; Shuffleton, "Imperial Flower," 201–5; King, "Dunbar's *The Golden Targe*," 115–31.

[61] Mapstone, introduction to *The Chepman and Myllar Prints*, 3; van Buuren, "Chepman and Myllar Texts," 24–5. In addition to *The Golden Targe*, the Chepman and Myllar prints include *The Tretis of the Tua Mariit Wemen and the Wedo* (*Poems* 3), "I that in heill was" (*Poems* 21), "I maister andro kennedy" (*Poems* 19), *The Flyting of Dunbar and Kennedie* (*Poems* 65), and "The Ballade of Barnard Stewart" (*Poems* 56).

[62] Although in "I that in heill was" (*Poems* 21), or *The Lament for the Makars*, Dunbar mentions "Gud maister Walter Kennedy / In point of dede lyis veraly" (89–90), Kennedy lived until 1518. Bawcutt, "Religious Verse," 124. This poem, dated c.1505–8, is among the Chepman and Myllar prints.

[63] The poem drew attention throughout the sixteenth century. The single surviving copy of the Chepman and Myllar *Targe* – Edinburgh, National Library of Scotland – includes an inscription, giving evidence of one such reader: "Liber florentini mertyne … borthwick" (the book of Florentine Martin … Borthwick). Chepman and Myllar, *Chepman and Myllar Prints*, 89. A minor Scottish landowner from Gibliston in Fife, Martin appears in historical records between 1511 and 1568 (Bawcutt, introduction to *The Poems*, 5). This single inscription hints at perhaps the kind of owner-reader Chepman and Myllar sought to reach and offers, as Mapstone notes, "interesting and important evidence of how Scottish literature of this ilk was reaching a non-courtly community in the first half of the sixteenth century." Introduction to *The Chepman and Myllar Prints*, 8. Scotsmen like Martin, however, were not the poem's only readers. In his 1530 reference to Dunbar noted above, the courtier-poet Sir David Lyndsay mentions the *Targe* specifically, writing "Dunbar, quhilk language had at large, / As maye be sene in tyll his *Goldin Targe*." *Papyngo*, 17–18. Two important later sixteenth-century manuscript anthologies also include copies of the poem, offering instances of continued interest: the Bannatyne Manuscript – Edinburgh, National Library of Scotland MS Adv.1.1.6 – compiled by Edinburgh merchant George Bannatyne in 1568; and the Maitland

Turning back to the poem, its masque-like qualities remind us of the classical deities' presence in the dream. As silent as every other character in the poem and as seemingly inactive as the narrator himself, the deities at first glance perhaps seem more forgettable than formidable, and I suspect some readers do forget them as the narrator focuses on Venus and on Lady Beautee and company's attack. Yet, in their supporting role, they remain ever-present to the poem's action from disembarkation to embarkation much like in a *tableau vivant*, allegorical painting, or dramatic performance. Once on stage, so to speak, they do not leave until Eolus cues their exit with his landscape-devastating bugle blast: a reminder perhaps on first reading the poem that they have been there with Venus the whole time.[64] Though mentioned only once, Minerva and Athena along with their companion deities remain supporting players in the *Targe*'s larger allegorical scheme.

Dunbar's treatment of Pallas and Minerva as separate goddesses, however, has proven problematic for critics. Linking Dunbar's catalog of deities to Lydgate's use of "Pallas" and "Minerva" to name the goddess in *Reson and Sensuallyte*, R.D.S. Jack and R.J. Lyall separately argue that Dunbar misreads Lydgate and thinks these are two deities rather than two names for one.[65] E. Allen Tilley, citing the Third Vatican Mythographer and John of Garland, argues that Dunbar's distinction is valid based on medieval etymology, concluding "Dunbar seems to be suggesting two very different loci of signification, enduring Wisdom (or Fame) and Battle, with essentially the same goddess."[66] Walter Scheps also considers the two names represent one goddess but argues that Dunbar separates the one into two to signal ironically his narrator's limited powers of observation.[67] And David DeVries speculates that the two names contribute to the dream's enigmatic status within Macrobian dream taxonomy.[68] While engaging discussions, these readings overlook Dunbar's use of the classical deities as rooted in the patristic tradition. In addition to *Reson and Sensuallyte*, Dunbar may have read *The Assembly of Gods*, where we have seen another such crowd complete with a distinct Othea and Minerva similarly engaged within the psychomachic action of a dream vision. Regardless, writing his own

---

Folio – Cambridge, Pepys Library, Magdalene College MS 2553 – compiled 1570–86 for Sir Richard Maitland. See Bawcutt, "Scottish Manuscript Miscellanies," 46–7, 60–4; MacDonald, "Sir Richard Maitland and William Dunbar," 134–49; Ramson, "Aureate Paradox," 94; van Heijnsbergen, "Dunbar, Scott and the Making of Poetry," 108–33; and J. Williams, "Dunbar and His Immediate Heirs," 85–107.

[64] As in *The Assembly*, Eolus again is a disruptive force. Mindful of Eolus' role in Chaucer's *HF* where he serves Fame, Fortune's sister (3.1547), by blasting his horns Clere Laud or Sklaundre as she capriciously orders (3.1567–867), I suspect Dunbar alludes here to ill-fame for the narrator over the short-lived love affair. Is Dunbar perhaps suggesting Eolus' blast is a metaphor for the *Targe* itself as it broadcasts an illicit affair? In the epithalamium *Thrissll and the Rois*, 52:64–6, on the other hand, Nature pre-emptively enjoined Eolus to be still so as not to disturb her May morning gathering, the harmonious garden, and the birdsong celebration of the Rois.

[65] Jack, "Dunbar and Lydgate," 215–27; Lyall, "Moral Allegory in Dunbar's *The Golden Targe*," 47–65.

[66] Tilley, "Meaning of Dunbar's *The Golden Targe*," 225.

[67] Scheps, "*The Golden Targe*," 349.

[68] DeVries, "The Pleasure of Influence," 123–4.

psychomachia, Dunbar does not make a mistake when naming "Pallas and prudent Minerua" (78); rather, likely having read Gower's *Confessio*, he intentionally treats Pallas and Minerva separately not only to suggest distinct loci, as Tilley observes, but also to articulate the idolatrous nature of his assembly of deities.

In poetic catalogs of classical goddesses and gods, the deities' associations with each other and their individual and collective behavior indicate their nature. As chief among the group in this dream, Venus orients our understanding of Dunbar's deities in the *Targe*. Though associated with the goddess Nature, whom by implication the narrator praises through his description of the May-morning, the Venus of the dream seems more allied to Alan of Lille's post-lapsarian Venus in *De planctu Naturae* than to the heavenly goddess of love, who inspired the "birdis" to sing "as Venus chapell clerkis" (20, 21) in the narrator's pre-*somnium* experience. Venus' indirect relationships with the male deities, especially Cupid, Mars, Saturn, and Bacchus, suggest further that she represents here erotic sensuality rather than celestial love: invoking their names invites auditors to recall intertextually her association with Bacchus' inebriation, her foamy birth from Saturn's severed testicles, her adulterous liaison with Mars, and her alliance with an armed Cupid, all of which point to a sensual Venus. And the narrative's action reinforces the worldly nature of her love, for celestial love – the love Boethius describes (*CP* 2.m8) – binds the universe through harmonious rational order: an order evident in Nature's pre- and post-*somnium* "Halesum" (248) landscape.[69] Celestial love surely would not oppose Reson in a psychomachic battle as Venus does. The deities' presence, arrayed opposite the narrator, supports Venus and her efforts to seduce him. With the subsequent battle between Reson with his defensive golden targe and Venus with her offensive minions, Dunbar returns us to the conflict between reason and sensuality that both Lydgate and the *Assembly*-poet explore. Venus functions in the *Targe*'s dream as a figure for the narrator's own sensual faculty. Pallas and Minerva, as members of Venus' court, then, indeed represent warfare and wisdom, but in the service of disorienting sensuality. Though they do not participate directly in the battle, Pallas and Minerva oppose the Boethian ideal of reasonable love figured by pre- and post-*somnium* Nature. Like other gods and goddesses in the poem, they function as idolatrous images in the vein of classical deities found in the patristic tradition. From a patristic point of view, they are demons helping to draw the narrator into an inordinate relationship with creation: both with himself and other creatures. The beauty Venus and company offer, though initially attractive to the narrator, ends in a cacophonous wind-blasted wilderness of unrequited love that contrasts sharply with Nature's harmonious pre- and post-*somnium* beauty. The narrator states:

And as I did awake of my sueving,
The ioyfull birdis merily did syng
For myrth of Phebus tender bemes schene.
Suete war the vapouris, soft the morowing,

---

[69] Bawcutt, *Dunbar the Makar*, 314. *DOST* defines Dunbar's use of "halesum" under 1.a, "Conducive to health; health-giving, salubrious."

> Halesum the vale depaynt with flouris ying,
> The air attemperit, sobir and amene.
> In quhite and rede was all the felde besene,
> Throu Naturis nobil fresch anamalyng
> In mirthfull May of ewiry moneth queen. (244–52)

The narrator's palpable relief on waking is evident in his description of Nature's illuminated, peaceful, "Halesum," and harmonious May-time world: a Nature allied with Sapientia of the first "O" antiphon and Boethius' Amor (*CP* 2.m8), who order and harmonize the universe and originate prudence and love in the human soul.[70]

The Golden Targe, Dunbar's tightly-constructed, artful poem, sparkles with gold-infused light. Just as he praises Nature for her "nobil fresch anamalyng" (251), he implicitly claims for poets a similar ability to create a verbal perception of the world and human experience with "anamalit termes celicall" (257) using "angel mouthis most mellifluate" (265).[71] In offering the *Targe* as an instance of his own "anamalit" performance, he synthesizes a wide range of poetic traditions, devices, forms, and materials to explore themes of love and perception, thereby celebrating the *makar*'s craft through his own poetic creation. The patristic tradition of Minerva as idolatrous image – a tradition he would have known from reading the Fathers as well as Gower, Lydgate, and perhaps Isidore of Seville, Guido delle Colonne, and *The Assembly of Gods* – is part of Dunbar's synthesis as he seeks to illuminate relationships between rational and sensual faculties in the microcosmic human soul and the macrocosmic universe.

---

[70] The poem's attention to the natural world and to Nature and Venus as figures has drawn scholarly comment. See Bawcutt, *Dunbar the Makar*, 310–15; Foran, "Dunbar's Broken Rainbow," 47–61; and Strong, "Supra-Natural Creation," 149–63.

[71] Dunbar has long been recognized for his aureate poetics. See, for instance, Lewis, *Allegory of Love*, 251–3, and *English Literature*, 90–8; Hyde, "Primary Sources," 481–92; Fox, "Dunbar's *The Golden Targe*," 312–14; Ramson, "Aureate Paradox," 93–104; Ebin, *Illuminator, Makar, Vates*, 74–90.

6

The Ovidian Tradition: Minerva as Venus' Ally

Mutual indifference if not outright conflict tends to characterize the relationship between Athena-Minerva and Aphrodite-Venus in Greco-Roman literature. In Homer's *Iliad* 5.1–430, for instance, Athena as *patrona principis* directly inspired Diomedes, granting power to distinguish deities from men and commanding him to avoid fighting the former – except Aphrodite. When he saw the goddess of love rescue her son Aeneas, Diomedes as Athena's agent wounded Aphrodite's wrist, causing her to drop Aeneas, bleed ichor, and flee the field. The goddess of wisdom subsequently mocked Aphrodite on Olympus, prompting Zeus to remind the goddess of love to stick to what she knows and leave warfare to Ares and Athena. Homeric Hymn 5, 8–32, underscores their opposition when the poet includes Athena among the three goddesses (including Artemis and Hestia) whom Aphrodite cannot conquer. Hymns 10 and 11 similarly express fundamental distinctions: while 10 praises Aphrodite's honeyed gifts, 11 celebrates Athena *patrona urbis* and war goddess. Athena's aversion to Aphrodite's realm is particularly evident in Apollodorus' first-century BCE account of Erichthonius' birth.[1] Their conflict, based on their distinctive arenas of action, is perhaps clearest at the Judgment of Paris, which led to Troy's destruction and the Trojan diaspora. Medieval writers, too, take up this theme of conflict, but they also treat another less prevalent theme of alliance where Minerva serves Venus in the latter's work of promoting love. Considering the patristic tradition, this mythological theme of alliance between the goddesses perhaps seems simply an extension of their roles as idols. Yet, while Minerva's role as idol comes from early Christian culture, her alliance with Venus derives from classical antiquity, particularly Ovid.[2] In this chapter, I explore the contrasting themes of tension and union between these two goddesses evident in Ovid and the medieval Ovidian tradition. In

---

[1] Hephaestus, rejected by Aphrodite, became sexually aroused when Athena tried to order weapons from him. She resisted his advances, and the lame god ejaculated on her leg. Disgusted, she wiped off the semen with wool, throwing it on the ground, from which Erichthonius was born. Athena raised the boy in secret; he became king, set up an image of the goddess, and established the Panathenaea festival. Apollodorus, *The Library*, ed. Frazer, 3.14.6. See Deacy, "Vulnerability of Athena," 43–64.

[2] The theme of alliance between the goddesses has received little attention beyond Wittkower's brief discussion of instances where artists fuse Minerva-Venus imagery in late fifteenth- and sixteenth-century art. See "Transformations of Minerva in Renaissance Imagery," 202–3.

many respects, the medieval Ovidian tradition of Minerva imagery draws on the four other traditions explicated thus far. When allied with Venus, Minerva can represent, in Clanvowe's terms, "wisdom of the spirit" as she does in the sapiential, Martianus, and *patrona* traditions; she can also represent "wisdom of the flessh" as she does in the patristic tradition. Interpretation of any given instance, then, depends on assessing both the goddess' relationship to Venus and her means and ends. Following Horace (65–8 BCE), medieval writers wanted to entertain and instruct their audiences.³ In their focus on means and ends regarding decisions and actions, they invite readers to engage their poetry attentively as they play with the Ovidian tradition of Minerva imagery: a tradition that informs particularly the goddess' appearances in John Lydgate's *Temple of Glas*, James I of Scotland's *The Kingis Quair*, and the third narrative of Charles d'Orléans' *Fortunes Stabilnes*.

Ovid's Venus and Minerva

Much of what we know of Publius Ovidius Naso (43 BCE–17 CE) comes from his writing, particularly *Tristia* 4.10: an exile elegy in which he recounts details of his life.⁴ In a career spanning approximately forty years, Ovid published in rough chronological order *Amores, Heroides, Medea, Medicamina faciei femineae, Ars*

---

3   In *Ars poetica*, 333–4, ed. Fairclough, Horace states: "Aut prodesse volunt aut delectare poetae / aut simul et iucunda et idonea dicere vitae" (Poets wish either to benefit or delight or in other words speak things both pleasing and helpful to life). He continues: "omne tulit punctum qui mscuit utile dulci, / lectorem delectando pariterque monendo" (the poet who has mixed usefulness with sweetness, equally instructing and delighting the reader, carries every vote) (343–4). Boccaccio echoes this double intent when he states: "tanti quidem sunt fabule, ut earum primo contextu oblectentur indocti, et circa abscondita doctorum exerceantur ingenia, et sic una et eadem lectione proficient et delectant" (fictions are of such worth, then, that the unlearned are delighted by their outer coherence, and the minds of the learned are exercised by obscurities, and so they progress and are delighted by one and the same reading). *Genealogie deorum gentilium*, 14.9.709.

4   *Tristia; Ex Ponto*, ed. Wheeler, rev. Goold, 196–207. The younger of two sons, Ovid was born in Sulmo (Sulmona, Abruzzi) on the second day of Minerva's *Quinquatrus*, March 20. Intended for public careers, Ovid and his brother were educated in Sulmo and Rome. Recalling their school days, Seneca the Elder notes Ovid's predilection for verse over prose, clever delivery, preference for deliberative orations, and love for his own verse. *Declamations, Volume I*, ed. Winterbottom, 2.2.8–1. Following a brief foray into public service, he pursued poetry instead. Twice married briefly, he found a suitable partner in his third wife, of and to whom he writes with affection from exile. He addresses *Tristia* 5.14, for instance, to "mihi me coniunx carior" (wife dearer to me than myself) and, in a consolatory move, says, "dumque legar, mecum pariter tua fama legetur, / nec potes in maestos omnis abire rogas" (and as long as I shall be read, your reputation will be read equally with me, nor can you pass away entirely into the sad pyre) (5–6). His references to her in his exile poetry seem an attempt to invoke her presence through language: a means to span distances of time and space much as poetry itself promises immortality to both poet and subject "dum legatur." Other letters to her include *Tristia* 1.6, 3.3, 4.3, 5.2, 5.5, 5.11, and *Ep. ex. Pon.* 1.4, 3.1. For these and other biographical details, see Armstrong,

amatoria, Remedia amoris, Metamorphoses, Fasti, Tristia, Ibis, and *Epistulae ex Ponto*: all survive in medieval manuscripts except *Medea*.[5] Wit marks his poetry. Even in his exile elegies following banishment and the removal of his works from Rome's public libraries for "carmen et error" (a song and a mistake) (*Tristia* 2.207), he remains playfully elusive. In *Tristia* 2, a poetic defense addressed to Augustus, he writes:

> crede mihi, distant mores a carmine nostri –
> vita verecunda est, Musa iocosa mea –
> magnaque pars mendax operum est et ficta meorum:
> plus sibi permisit compositore suo.
> nec liber indicum est animi, sed honesta voluptas;
> plurima mulcendis auribus apta feret.
> Accius esset atrox, conviva Terentius esset,
> Essent pugnaces quo fera bella canunt

(Believe me, my character differs from my poetry – my life is upright, my Muse is jocular – and most of my work is false and fictitious; it has permitted for itself more license than its author has had. A book is not an indictment of a writer's mind, but is an honest pleasure; it will offer many things for sweetening the ears. Otherwise, Accius would be cruel, Terence convivial, or those who sing fierce wars pugnacious) (353–60)

Arguing for distinguishing his literary personae from himself as poet, Ovid underscores the misinterpretation possible when readers confuse the two: readers not poets are responsible, he declares earlier in *Tristia* 2 (277–312), for their own interpretations. Whether or not he read Ovid's poetry, Augustus' condemnation of both poet and works was, Ovid implies, a misreading. This audacious, comical implication – an attempt, perhaps, to illustrate the point – failed if it registered at all: neither Emperor Augustus nor Tiberius who followed him pardoned the poet.

If the personae Ovid adopted in his "mendax operum … et ficta" indeed permitted more for themselves than their author did for himself, they also licensed him to take "a comprehensive approach" to his subjects, as Richard Tarrant observes, by exploring various poses and perspectives.[6] Adopting again the position of literary theorist, Ovid writes in one of his later verse epistles:

Ovid and His Love Poetry, 1–3; Mack, *Ovid*, 12–52; Rand, *Ovid and His Influence*, 3–9; Tarrant, "Ovid and Ancient Literary History," 13–33; and Wilkinson, *Ovid Recalled*, 1–16.

5 Ovid mentions a non-extant poem he composed on Augustus following his death in 14 CE (*Ep. ex. Pon.* 4.6.15–18). Quintilian cites or quotes Ovid twelve times, including references to three non-extant works: *Liber in malos poetas*, two quotes from *Medea*, and one quote from *Epigrammata* (*Inst. ora.* 6.3.96, 8.5.6, 10.1.98, and 9.3.70 respectively). And Lactantius quotes Ovid's non-extant translation of Aratus' *Phaenomina* (*Divinarum institutionum* 2.5.24). On Ovid's medieval manuscripts, see McKinley, "Manuscripts of Ovid in England 1100 to 1500," 41–85; and Tarrant, "Ovid," 257–84.

6 Tarrant, "Ovid and Ancient Literary History," 18. On his many poses and perspectives in the *Amores*, for example, see Stapleton, *Harmful Eloquence*, 1–37; and Armstrong, *Ovid and His Love Poetry*, 21–52.

scripta ferunt annos. scriptis Agamemnona nosti,
et quisquis contra vel simul arma tulit.
quis Thebas septemque duces sine carmine nosset,
et quicquid post haec, quidquid et ante fuit?
di quoque carminibus, si fas est dicere, fiunt,
tantaque maiestas ore canentis eget

(Writing endures the years. Through writing you know Agamemnon and those who bore arms either with or against him. Without verse, who would know Thebes and the seven leaders, or anything that happened before or after these events? Even the gods, if this is right to say, come to life in verses, and their great majesty needs the singer's voice) (*Ep. ex. Pon.* 4.8.51–6)

The poet declares for himself if not the role of creator or priest at least the role of medium for the gods who live through his verses.[7] Part of Ovid's comprehensive approach to his subjects and his function as *cantor deorum* includes his treatment of Minerva and her relationship to Venus.

Ovid's Minerva is multifaceted. In *Fasti*, as we have seen, Romans celebrate Minerva as mistress of arts and artisans, schoolmasters and students, physicians and poets and flute players. Similarly, in the exile poetry, she takes on various roles with which we are familiar from *patrona principis* (*Tristia* 1.2.9–10) and *patrona urbis* (*Tristia* 3.1.29) to the goddess of weaving (*Ep. ex Pon.* 3.8.9), ship-craft (*Tristia* 1.10), and the olive (*Tristia* 4.5.4). In *Heroides*, she represents battle-prowess in the three accounts of the Judgment of Paris (5.33–40, 16.53–88, 17.115–30). In *Metamorphoses*, where she appears in fourteen particular stories, Minerva functions as protectress of virgins (2.550–95), goddess of weaving (4.1–415), goddess of learning and mind-craft (8.236–59), *patrona principis* (12.360), *patrona urbis* (2.708–13), and of course divine wisdom itself, where she frequently opposes Venus in her disruptive game of love. Often in these poems her roles overlap. In the story of Arachne recounted in *Metamorphoses* (6.1–145), she represents both the craft of weaving and divine wisdom, which mortals should attend with humility. She also illustrates Ovid's maxim "tangit et ira deos" (anger can even touch the gods) (8.279), becoming a wrathful deity by story's end.[8] After hearing the mortal Arachne's proud denial of the goddess' gifts,

---

[7] See McGowan, *Ovid in Exile*, 25–36.
[8] Modern scholars discuss *Met*. 6.1–145 as an exploration of art, divine power, and Ovid's reflection on poets and poetry. See Fantham, *Ovid's* Metamorphoses, 51–60; P. Johnson, *Ovid before Exile*, 74–95; and Pavlock, *Image of the Poet*, 3–8. Medieval scholars, too, found the episode important. Walsingham, for example, interprets Pallas as the wisdom of age and Arachne as the folly of youth, saying: "Sed quia tela eius arida est et sine succo sapientie, suspenditur et a vento utpote res vana ventilatur et in vermem mutatur, id est a terrena respicit quod est proprie verminum. Sed in araneam potius quam in aliam quia quemadmodum aranea ex se ipsa fila elicit, sic et insipientia seipsam seducit" (But because her [Arachne's] loom is dry and without the juice of wisdom, she is suspended and blown about by the wind as a vain thing and is changed into a worm; that is, she gazes from the earth, which is a property of worms. But she is changed into a spider more than into something else because as the spider herself elicits children from herself, so folly leads herself astray). *De archana deorum*, 6.2.82–6.

saying "'certet ... mecum: nihil est, quod victa recusem'" (let her compete with me: there is nothing that I would object to if conquered) (25), Minerva approached the girl humbly disguised as an old woman and cautioned her against hubris, saying in part:

"consilium ne sperne meum: tibi fama petatur
inter mortals faciendae maxima lanae;
cede deae veniamque tuis, temeraria, dictis
supplice voce roga: veniam dabit illa roganti"

(Do not spurn my counsel: great fame for working wool should be sought by you among mortals; yield to the goddess and, with humble voice, o thoughtless girl, ask forgiveness for your words: the goddess will grant pardon if you ask) (30–3)

With unconcealed disdain and near violence, the youthful Arachne rejected the disguised goddess as a doting old fool; Minerva then revealed her divinity, accepted the challenge, and the contest began. Both produced flawless narrative tapestries: Minerva's celebrated divine majesty by recounting her own victory over Neptune in becoming Athens' *patrona*, framed by four cautionary tales of human presumption against the gods; Arachne's critiqued divine dissimulation through an Ovid-like series of twenty-one tales marked, as Ovid's narrator interjects twice (104, 121–2), by graphic verisimilitude depicting disguised lustful male gods ravishing females. Arachne executed her tapestry so well that "non illud Pallas, non illud carpere Livor / possit opus" (neither Pallas nor Envy could criticize the work) (129–30). Offended, though, Minerva's response was immediate: she destroyed the tapestry, struck Arachne on the head with a shuttle, and transformed her into a spider. Though the goddess' wrath seemed motivated by her envy of Arachne's skill, Minerva was also responding to Arachne's near pornographic depiction of the gods when under Venus' influence.[9] Absent in person, Venus manifested through Arachne's tales of divine sexual misbehavior the love goddess inspired: as Arachne's tale telling invoked

---

[9] This decidedly slippery tale suggests a range of interpretations. Placed amid a series of three tales in which human or semi-divine artists contend with divine artists and lose (*Met*. 5.250–678, 6.1–145, 6.382–400), Arachne's story indicates a capricious side to Minerva: seemingly unable to best the mortal outright in skill, she exercised divine power and transformed her tapestry to tatters and her human life of artful weaving – after Arachne herself attempted suicide – to a nonhuman life of unending spinning. Still, though Arachne evidently matched the goddess in technical performance, she was no match in wisdom. Having denied the goddess and ignored her warnings, she might have at least read her own lessons more carefully: mortals lose when contending with divinity. In addition to product and graphic subject matter, Arachne's unrepentant arrogance born of a refusal to acknowledge her own humanity also offended Minerva. Instead of celebrating the mortal's weaving success, the goddess exercised divine power, destroying Arachne's tapestry and humanity: the "nihil" she blithely surrendered when issuing her challenge (25). To overreach is to surrender one's humanity and transform into something else, be it magpies or spiders. Though Ovid likely did not know Jewish wisdom literature, his tale resonates with the maxim in Eccl. 1:16: "initium sapientia timor Domini" (the beginning of wisdom is fear of the Lord).

the absent goddess, Minerva's aggressive response sought to erase both the goddess and her artistic medium.[10]

Whether or not the goddess of love is directly present, then, Minerva's anger rises in *Metamorphoses* when she opposes Venus or her effects. In the story of Mercury, Aglauros, and Herse (*Met.* 2.708–835), Venus again makes no direct appearance, but her influence is evident throughout. Flying over Athens on a festival day dedicated to Minerva, Mercury spied a group of maidens returning from the temple following religious rites honoring the virgin goddess. The narrator describes the action in a series of extended similes. Circling like a swift kite approaching a newly slain sacrifice, Mercury saw Herse standing out from the company like the moon outshining Lucifer and, as a bullet thrown by a Belearic sling gains heat in flight, he burned increasingly with passion while moving through the air. The god's instant passion signals he has entered Venus and Cupid's arena. Descending, Mercury decided on direct tactics – no disguise this time – and, in a comic narrative moment, primped himself before approaching the maid's bedchamber. Spying the god, Herse's sister Aglauros intercepted him, asking his name and mission. Sticking to plan, Mercury identified himself, declared he had come to woo Herse, and asked for Aglauros' aid. Seizing the opportunity, Aglauros extracted a promise of payment in gold for her pandering service before coaxing him to leave for the time being. Minerva, meanwhile, saw the transaction. It was her festival day, after all: presumably she had attended the procession and expected participants to be mindful of her rather than prostituting virgins. Offended at Aglauros' pimping, "vertit ad hanc torvi dea bellica luminis orbem" (the warrior goddess turned her fierce-bright eyes on her) (752). Recalling the girl's earlier betrayal of trust in the matter of Erichthonius, and knowing her greedy temperament, Minerva sought out Envy and commanded the vile deity to infect the girl.[11] Thoroughly given over to the vice, Aglauros refused Mercury help on his return and – in a moment straight out of the love-elegy tradition – guarded Herse's shut door, saying "'hinc ego me non sum nisi te motura repulso'" (I am not moving from here myself until I have repulsed your advances) (817): obliging her, Mercury turned her into stone and opened the door himself. In a final simile comparing the process to the spread of "immedicabile cancer" (incurable

---

[10] The form of Arachne's transformation and the destruction of her work underscore this point about art and Venus. Such images and stories can entrap audiences in lust, deceiving the unwary and encouraging illicit behavior – a conclusion that Socrates also draws in Plato's *Republic*, 2.377b–3.398b, 10.600a–698b. Dante's account of Paolo and Francesca, *Divine Comedy: Inferno*, 5.73–142, is a recognizable medieval instance of this idea, where reading a Lancelot tale led to adultery and ultimately murder. The punishment here, then, seems poetically just from Minerva's perspective. Arachne's art weaves webs that can trap the unwary. It also, perhaps, suggests a metacritical stance on his own poetics by Ovid himself.

[11] These moments in the episode – Minerva's journey to Envy's cave, the deity's foulness, her quick command and exit, Envy's journey to Athens and infection of Aglauros, and the girl's subsequent madness (2.760–815) – illustrate both the psychology of envy and Erich Auerbach's insight into Greco-Roman epic's externalized narration. *Mimesis*, 1–23. Along with the extended similes punctuating the story, these moments demonstrate Ovid's command of epic style and convention.

cancer) (825), the narrator lingers on Aglauros' lapidification, hardening to a lifeless statue stained by her soul, before concluding the tale with the god's swift exit "has ubi verborum poenas mentisque profanae / cepit Atlantiades" (when Mercury enforced these punishments for her wicked words and thought) (833). Countering the Venerian impulses in the tale, Minerva thwarted Aglauros and perhaps even Mercury, though Ovid is not wholly clear.

Minerva reacted angrily in other Venerian moments in *Metamorphoses* as well. As her half-brother Perseus told the tale (*Met.* 6.793–803), the goddess punished Medusa, turning her beautiful hair into snakes, following her rape by Neptune in Minerva's temple. Similarly, in Diomedes' account of his post-Trojan War wanderings (*Met.* 14.463–511), she punished the Greeks, whom she had favored in the war, after Locrian Ajax raped the suppliant Cassandra in her temple. In Ovid's metamorphic epic, whenever Venus or her effects were at play and Minerva was near, she stood opposed. And Venus herself acknowledged this animosity. During Minerva's visit with the Muses on Helicon (*Met.* 5.250–678), Urania recounted how Calliope defeated the Emathides in a contest by singing the tale of Proserpine.[12] In Urania's account of Calliope's song, which she sings for Minerva, Venus noted to Cupid that, as he ruled Jove and the heavens and Neptune and the sea, so should he rule Dis and the underworld. She then complained: "'Pallade nonne vides iaculatriceque Dianam / abscessisse mihi? Cereis quoque filia virgo, / si patiemur, erit'" (Do you not see that Pallas and huntress Diana have rejected me? And now Ceres' daughter will be a virgin if we allow it) (5.375–7), thus sparking the events leading to Proserpine's rape. Once Dis fell to Cupid's arrow, Minerva and Diana remained the sole Olympians opposed to Venus' empire-building scheme. Turning again to Diomedes' account of his wanderings, we see this direct opposition further develop when he said "'me ... armiferae servatum cura Minervae'" (the care of well-armed Minerva saved me) as Venus repeatedly punished him for wounding her on the battlefield. Along with the Judgment of Paris accounts in *Heroides*, Ovid presents the theme of opposition between the two goddesses most clearly in *Metamorphoses*, where parameters of inherited mythological stories govern his tales. He develops his theme of alliance between the goddesses, on the other hand, in the less-constrained context of love poetry. Here, his playful wit dominates, and through his poetry the theme enters medieval literary culture, where it receives its fullest development.

Ovid first hints at an alliance between Minerva and Venus in *Amores* 1.1. Alluding to Virgil and poetic composition, he begins:

Arma gravi numero violentaque bella parabam
edere, materia conveniente modis.
par erat inferior versus – risisse Cupido
dicitur atque unum surripuisse pedem.
"Quis tibi, saeve puer, dedit hoc in carmina iuris?
Pieridum vates, non tua turba sumus.

---

[12] See Fantham, *Ovid's* Metamorphoses, 51–3; and P. Johnson, *Ovid before Exile*, 41–73.

quid, si praeripiat flavae Venus arma Minervae,
ventilet accensas flava Minerva faces?"

(Arms and violent wars I was just now preparing to declare, with appropriate matter in weighty measures. The second verse was equal to the first – Cupid laughed, it is said, and pilfered one foot. "Who gave you, cruel boy, this authority over poetry? We are the poets of the Pierides, not of your crowd. What if Venus should carry off the weapons of golden-haired Minerva or if golden-haired Minerva should fan the kindled flames of love?")[13]

Yes, indeed: what if? The witty implication in Ovid's conditional sentence is that Venus may have, after all, drawn Minerva into her game of love through Cupid's usurpation of poetic composition, changing the dactylic hexameters of epic to the alternating hexameter and pentameter of elegiac lyric. The elegiac meter itself becomes throughout the *Amores* a metaphor for Cupid's power. Disordering epic meter, usurping its "material," shooting *amans*, Ovid's poetic persona, with "in exitium spicula facta meum" (arrows made for my ruin) (22), Cupid created an upside-down world through meter and content. Though later in Ovid's poetic career Venus would complain about Minerva's opposition (*Met.* 5.375–7), here in the first poem of his first publication Ovid implicitly aligns Minerva's wisdom with Venus: in the love poetry "ventilat accensas flava Minerva faces." This opening elegy, serving as prologue to the entire sequence, sets the tone for Minerva's appearances in the remainder of the *Amores* and in *Ars amatoria* as well. Unlike with Athena in ancient Greek poetry, or in her appearances elsewhere in Ovid's *oeuvres*, Minerva's weapons here serve Venus.

Just as he later develops the theme of opposition in *Metamorphoses*, Ovid subtly allies Minerva with Venus in the love poetry. In *Amores* 1.7 – perhaps the collection's most disturbing poem – *amans* recounts physically abusing his beloved, stating "furor in dominam temeraria bracchia movit; / flet mea vaesana laesa puella manu" (madness moved rash hands against my mistress; the girl cries from the violence of my raging blows) (3–4). Using personification to distance himself from the act – "furor" beat her – *amans* raises his domestic abuse to mythic levels, equating his mad actions with Telamon Ajax and Orestes before asking "ergo ego digestos potui laniare capillos?" (was I then right to mangle her well-arranged hair?) (11).[14] He answers by directly addressing Minerva:

nec dominam motae dedecuere comae.
sic formosa fuit ...
sic, nisi vittatis quod erat Cassandra capillis,
procubuit templo, casta Minerva, tuo

---

[13] *Heroides; Amores*, ed. Showerman, rev. Goold, 1.1–8.
[14] In a double movement similar to mock-heroic, the persona's equation of his domestic abuse to the mythic affects both: while it inflates his base behavior with overstated importance, it deflates the mythic to basely human levels.

(Disturbed hair did not dishonor the lady. She was beautiful thus ... In the same way, Cassandra – except that she was wearing fillets in her hair – laid stretched out in your temple, O chaste Minerva) (12–13, 17–18)

Amans here associates Minerva's suppliant with his own object of desire and implicitly claims for himself Locrian Ajax's destructive role. Apparently legitimizing abusive behavior, beauty associated with Minerva serves Venus and Cupid in this instance: enlisting "casta Minerva" to justify himself, he invokes the goddess of wisdom to see his bashed beloved, recall Cassandra, and approve. As stand-in for Locrian Ajax, however, his assault ought to incur Minerva's wrath rather than approval, so he later equates his actions with Minerva's protégé Diomedes, saying "ille deam primus perculit – alter ego" (he was the first to strike a goddess – I, the second) (32), and his beloved becomes a stand-in for Venus herself. Admittedly hyperbolic, perhaps indicating the whole episode is more fantastic than representational, the language of *Amores* 1.7 – his rending and scratching; her silent weeping; the mythic allusions – nonetheless links Minerva to Venerian madness in the topsy-turvy world of Ovid's love elegies.[15]

Another suggestive example is found in *Amores* 3.3 which opens aggressively "Esse deos, i, crede – fidem iurata fefellit, / et facies illi, quae fuit ante, manet!" (Go, believe gods exist – having sworn, she broke her oath, but her appearance remains as it was before) (1–2). As *amans* invites his addressee into another round of hyperbolic discourse, inveighing against the gods because his unfaithful beloved has sworn by them yet remains unpunished, he declares: "scilicet aeterni falsum iurare puellis / di quoque concedunt, formaque numen habet" (evidently even the eternal gods pardon falsehood sworn by girls, and beauty has divine privilege) (11–12). He continues:

aut sine re nomen deus est frustraque timetur
et stulta populos credulitate movet;
aut, siquis deus est, teneras amat ille paellas
et nimium solas omnia posse iubet.
nobis fatifero Mavors accingitur ense;
nos petit invicta Palladis hasta manu ...
formosas superi metuunt offendere laesi (11–12, 23–8, 31)

(Either god is a name without substance and it is feared in vain and it moves people with foolish credulity; or, if god exists, he loves tender girls and judges too much that they alone can do all things. Against us men Mars is armed with a fatal sword; the unconquered spear of Pallas attacks us from her hand ... [But] the high gods fear to offend beautiful women with a blow) (23–8, 31)

---

[15] The poem's mock-heroic inclination, which certainly helped inspire Alexander Pope's *Rape of the Lock*, leads some critics to conclude the high-pitched rhetoric is entirely hyperbolic, reading the final couplet as undercutting the whole: "neve mei sceleris tam tristia signa supersint, / pone recompositas in statione comas" (so that the sad signs of my crime not survive put your ordered locks back in place), *Am.*, 1.7.67–8, i.e., fix your hair, dear, and let's move on. See Mack, *Ovid*, 59–60. On this poem's relation to *Ars. Am.*, 2.169–74, where the *praeceptor amoris* reflects on a time when he upset his mistress' hair and it cost him a new tunic, see Armstrong, *Ovid and His Love* Poetry, 33–4.

Overturning Minerva's usual associations with reason and order, *amans* accuses her of siding with other deities to pardon unjustly the beloved's false oath out of fear. Again, under Ovid's pen, Minerva implicitly joins with Venus in her game of love.[16] Though these allusions to Minerva in the *Amores* make little sense in light of her traditional opposition to Venus, they indicate another tradition in which the two ally. Turning to *Ars amatoria*, we find similar points of juncture where Ovid's *praeceptor amoris* further develops the theme.

In *Ars amatoria*, the poet's troublesome book that contributed to Augustus' disfavor, Ovid's persona audaciously claims to be Cupid's teacher – *praeceptor Amoris* (1.17) – who, as Chiron taught Achilles the lyre, can likewise tame the boy-god through art, the craft and discipline he mastered experientially. His tripartite book aims to teach men how to find, gain, and maintain love (books one and two) and women to do the same (book three). Minerva makes six direct appearances in the text. In book one, for instance, where the *praeceptor* instructs how to talk to the beloved, he refers to the Judgment of Paris to illustrate that even an honest, chaste woman enjoys praise, asking rhetorically "Nam cur in Phrygiis Iunonem et Pallada silvis / Nunc quoque iudicium non tenuisse pudet?" (for why do you think Juno and Pallas even now are ashamed they did not win the judgment in Phrygian woods?) (1.625–6). Stroking her ego, telling her she is beautiful like Venus, it seems, might seduce even Minerva. Addressing seduction again in book two, he draws on Minerva in conjunction with Venus, stating:

Nominibus mollire licet mala: fusca vocetur,
Nigrior Illyrica cui pice sanguis erit:
Si straba, sit Veneri similes: si rava, Minervae:
Sit gracilis, macie quae male viva sua est;
Dic habilem, quaecumque brevis, quae turgida, plenam,
Et lateat vitium proximitate boni

(It is all right to soften faults with names: let her be called tawny whose bloodline is blacker than Illyrian pitch: if a squinter, let her be likened to Venus; if gray-haired, Minerva: let her be slender whose thinness is bad for her health; call her nimble who is short, and who is fat, full-bodied: let the defect lie hidden in its nearness to a good) (2.657–61)

---

[16] The motif of false oaths appears elsewhere as well. In his advice to the student-lover, the *praeceptor amoris* of *Ars amatoria* states:

Nec timide promitte: trahunt promissa paellas;
Pollicito testes quoslibet adde deos.
Iuppiter ex alto periuria ridet amantum,
Et iubet Aeolios inrita ferre natos

(Do not promise timidly: promises win over girls; by a promise call whatever gods as witnesses. Jupiter from on high laughs at the lovers' perjuries and orders Aeolian winds to carry them away)

The Art of Love *and Other Poems*, ed. Mozley, rev. Goold, 1.631–4. Though he complains of being victimized by false oaths in 3.7, *amans* also freely offers and breaks oaths, as *Am.*, 2.7 and 2.8 illustrate.

The *praeceptor*, much like a marketing or propaganda strategist today, advises veiling truth in euphemistic language: the student-lover is to use whatever terms mask, including naming Venus or Minerva, to achieve his ends. In a different but related masking move, Achilles indirectly uses Minerva's art to seduce Deidamia in the *praeceptor*'s brief account of their story (1.681–706), which he tells to illustrate the use of force as a wooing technique. Achilles attempted to avoid the Trojan War by disguising himself among a group of female weavers. The *praeceptor* interrupts the narrative, asking: "Quid facis, Aeacide? non sunt tua munera lanae; / Tu titulos alia Palladis arte petas" (What are you doing Aeacides? Woolens are not your honors; you will seek reknown by Pallas' other art) (1.691–2), that is, warfare rather than weaving. He then describes how Achilles raped Deidamia, by implication under the guise of Minerva's weaving arts, before trading in the distaff for weapons. He justifies Achilles' actions by asking Deidamia in turn: "Vis ubi nunc illa est? Quid blanda voce moraris / Auctorem stupri, Deidamia, tui?" (Where is that assault now? Why, Deidamia, did you seek with coaxing voice to delay the author of your violation?) (1.703–4). The *praeceptor* cynically concludes: "Scilicet ut pudor est quaedam coepisse priorem, / Sic alio gratum est incipiente pati" (evidently just as there is some shame to begin first, so when another begins it is pleasing to submit) (1.705–6). Turning Achilles' affair with Deidamia into a rape story, the *praeceptor* presents Minerva, implied in her weaving arts, not as the goddess of vengeance we have seen when she opposes Venus, but as a helper, if indirect, to the hero's sexual assault.[17]

Though she apparently opposes Venus when the *praeceptor* contrasts the sun-tanned athlete seeking Minerva's crown with the pale lover (1.727–8), Minerva in *Ars amatoria* primarily aids the goddess of love, or is used by the *praeceptor* to advance love's game.[18] Minerva's fundamental help, though, comes in the text's genre. Ostensibly an instruction manual for would-be lovers of both sexes, the *Ars* is Minervan as much as Venerian, for it purports to be a wisdom text, teaching an art – the skill and knowledge of a subject – just the same as the arts of sailing or rowing a ship or driving a chariot: both Minervan arts associated with the goddess as ship builder and horse tamer respectively (1.1–4).[19] In the *Ars*, the *praeceptor* advances a mode of loving wise lovers adopt, saying at one point, for instance, "Ludite, si sapitis, solas impune paellas: / Hac minus est una fraude tuenda fides" (deceive only girls with impunity, if you are wise: defend fidelity except this one little fraud) (1.643), at another "Quis sapiens blandis non misceat oscula verbis?" (who that is wise would not mix kisses with winsome words?) (1.663), and at yet a third "Quisquis sapienter amabit / Vincit, et e nostra, quodpetet, arte feret" (whosoever will love wisely

---

[17] Other versions cast the affair as a love-match, producing Neoptolemus. See Apollodorus, *The Library*, 3.13.8.
[18] The two other allusions underscore this association: a reference to "bacas Palladis" (Pallas' berries, i.e., olives) (2.518) to illustrate lovers' innumerable pains; and the goddess' story of the flute as exemplar for women to control passionate facial expression (3.503–8).
[19] With *Ars. am.* and *Rem. am.*, Ovid taps into a long tradition of didactic literature. See Armstrong, *Ovid and His Love Poetry*, 16–19; Dalzell, *Criticism of Didactic Poetry*, 132–64; and Watson, "Praecepta Amoris," 141–65. For Athena's associations with the sea and horses, see Deacy, *Athena*, 47–50.

conquers, and by my art carries off what he seeks) (2.511–12).[20] The *praeceptor* teaches the student-lover how to be wise: "to give the appearance of being an elegiac lover without fully being one," as Rebecca Armstrong argues.[21] Ovid underscores this Minervan element with two key metaphors for the game of love that he inherited from the love-poetry tradition, the hunt and the battlefield.[22] With tongue in cheek, he implies in these metaphors Venus' two arch-enemies, Diana and Minerva: their craft implicitly girds his *praeceptor*'s method. In book two, where he teaches how to keep a finally-captured beloved, the hunter's prey and the soldier's prisoner, the *praeceptor* rejects drugs and magic, declaring aphoristically "ut ameris, amabilis esto / Quod tibi non facies solave forma dabit" (so that you might be loved, be lovable, which neither face nor figure alone will give you) (2.107–8). He continues:

> Ut dominam teneas, nec te mirere relictum,
> Ingenii dotes corporis adde bonis ...
> Iam molire animum, qui duret, et adstrue formae:
> Solus ad extremos permanet ille rogos.
> Nec levis ingenuas pectus coluisse per artes
> Cura sit et linguas edidicisse duas.
> Non formosus erat, sed erat facundus Ulixes,
> Et tamen aequoreas torsit amore deas.
>
> (That you might keep your lady, nor wonder at yourself abandoned, add endowments of mind to bodily goods ... Now make a soul that endures and add it to your beauty: that alone will survive to the final pyre. Nor let your care be slight to cultivate your character through liberal arts and to learn two languages. Ulysses was not handsome, but he was eloquent, and he nevertheless enflamed two sea-goddesses with love) (2.111–12, 121–6)

In this advertisement for the value of liberal learning, the *praeceptor* implicitly enlists Minerva *magistra artium* and *patrona principis* to underscore the worldly wit a lover needs to maintain his affair in the face of time's ravages. His self-claimed position as worldly wise, experienced lover – a male version of the poet's Dipsas in *Amores* 1.8 – comically engages Ovid's inscribed reader through the *praeceptor*'s satiric, at times ironic and cynical, art of love. After recounting the price he paid for physically mistreating his beloved (2.169–72), he notes: "At vos, si sapitis, vestri peccata magistri / Effugite, et culpae damna timete meae" (But you, if you are wise, flee from the errors of your master and fear the penalties of my fault) (2.173–4). The practical wisdom the *praeceptor* offers implicitly under Minerva's aegis centers on using reason to advance a Venerian love affair. Though he wrote primarily for a Roman audience, Ovid's love poetry exercised a broad and deep influence on Western poetics in

---

[20] Ovid subtly weaves in this wisdom theme throughout, using *sapiens* or its derivatives at ten points in the text (1.65, 1.643, 1.663, 1.760, 2.173, 2.501, 2.511, 3.369, 3.565, 3.655).
[21] Armstrong, *Ovid and His Love Poetry*, 16.
[22] Murgatroyd, "Amatory Hunting, Fishing, and Fowling," 362–8, and "*Militia amoris*," 59–79.

subsequent generations. His two themes of Minerva's opposition to and aid of Venus allow us a focused look into the Ovidian tradition in medieval culture.

The Ovidian Tradition

In a prophetic-like moment at the end of *Metamorphoses*, Ovid punctuates his epic, declaring:

> Iamque opus exegi, quod nec Iovis ira nec ignis
> nec poterit ferrum nec edax abolere vetustas.
> cum volet, illa dies, quae nil nisi corporis huius
> ius habet, incerti spatium mihi finiat aevi:
> parte tamen meliore mei super alta perennis
> astra ferar, nomenque erit indelebile nostrum,
> quaque patet domitis Romana potentia terries,
> ore legar populi,perque omnia saecula fama,
> siquid habent veri vatum praesagia, vivam.

(And now I have finished my work, which neither Jove's anger nor fire nor sword nor devouring time shall be able to erase. When it wishes, that day, which has no right except over this body, will complete the length of my uncertain time: yet, in my better part I shall be borne above the high stars on wings and my name shall be indelible, and wherever Roman power extends to conquered lands, I shall be read by the lips of people and, if poets' prophecies have any truth, I shall live in fame through all ages.) (15.871–9)

Ovid likely would be delighted and amused at his post-mortem reception, for his poetry and name have long outlasted even the Empire itself: "vivam," he concludes, in a self-claimed apotheosis borne largely by his own indelible verses mouthed "ore ... populi." And he was right: this audacious prophecy is largely accurate, and his poems, if they have not assured his immortality among the stars, have certainly influenced subsequent literary and artistic efforts in the West to this day. No doubt as purveyor-celebrator of metamorphoses he would particularly enjoy their medieval reception and transformation.

The history of Ovid's reception in the West, however, is complex.[23] From the time of his banishment his popularity waxed and waned, yet people consistently read his poetry, and writers and artists drew on it in their own work: a practice he himself mastered.[24] This intertextual influence, the Ovidian tradition, richly and deeply

---

[23] For an overview beginning with Seneca, see A. Elliott, "Ovid and the Critics," 9–20. For thematic and case-study surveys, see the essays in Hardie, ed., *Cambridge Companion to Ovid*; Martindale, ed., *Ovid Renewed*; and Miller and Newlands, eds., *Handbook to the Reception of Ovid*.
[24] Tarrant, "Ovid and Ancient Literary History," 13–33.

registers in medieval culture.²⁵ Though Virgil and Horace seem to have been more influential than Ovid in the earlier medieval period, poets studied and imitated him throughout the Middle Ages.²⁶ By the ninth century, teachers were using his poems as standard texts in medieval grammar schools;²⁷ by the eleventh century, scholars began to develop fully-fledged commentaries, interpreting them allegorically within an ethical framework to, in a sense, tame this seemingly anti-*auctoritas auctor*; and by the twelfth century, his place in medieval culture was assured.²⁸ Medieval poets

25 See Akbari, "Ovid and Ovidianism," 187–208; P. Allen, *Art of Love*, 38–58, 111–17; Born, "Ovid and Allegory," 362–3; Clark, introduction to *Ovid*, 1–6; Dimmick, "Ovid in the Middle Ages," 264–87; Dwyer, "Ovid in the Middle Ages," 312–14; Fumo, *Legacy of Apollo*, 23–75; H. Kelly, *Love and Marriage*, 73–160; Rand, *Ovid and His Influence*, 112–49; Robathan, "Ovid in the Middle Ages," 191–209; Sadlek, *Idleness Working*; Sowell, Introduction, in *Dante and Ovid*, 1–8; and Wilkinson, *Ovid Recalled*, 366–98.
26 Discussing Medieval Latin metrics, Traube described the eighth and ninth centuries as *aetas Vergiliana*, the tenth and eleventh centuries as *aetas Horatiana*, and the twelfth and thirteenth centuries as *aetas Ovidiana* because of these Roman poets' respective influence on verse during these centuries. *Vorlesungen und Abhandlungen*, 2:113. See also P. Allen, *The Art of Love*, 47; Rand, *Ovid and His Influence*, 112–13; and Wheeler, "Before the 'aetas Ovidiana'," 9–26.
27 Theodulf of Orleans offers a glimpse of Ovid's place in eighth- and ninth-century Visigoth and Carolingian cultures. After cataloging several classical poets, including Ovid, in his poem *De libris quos legere solebam*, Theodulf argues for their educational merits, saying:

> In quorum dictis quanquam sint frivola multa
> Plurima sub falso tegmine vera latent.
> Falsa poetarum stylus affert, vera sophorum,
> Falsa horum in verum vertere saepe solent

> (Although there are many frivolous things in their words, many more truths lie hidden under a false covering. The pen expresses poets' errors and wise men's truths; they [i.e., readers] are often in the habit of turning poets' errors into truth) (*Carmina*, ed. Duemmler, 45.19–22)

In an Ovid-like gesture, Theodulf places interpretive responsibility on the reader, who finds truth "sub falsa tegmine." Theodulf imitated Ovid's poetry throughout his life but perhaps most poignantly near the end in an elegiac epistle exchange with Modoin (c.770–840/3), then Bishop of Autun whom Alcuin had nicknamed Naso to Theodulf's Pindar during their courtly days. Exiled to Angers by Louis the Pious in 817, Theodulf wrote to his friend, adopting the pose of the unjustly accused Ovidian exile: Modoin's reply illustrates how steeped both were in Ovid as he consoles his friend by affirming his pose (*Carmina*, 72 and 73). As Theodulf and fellow Carolingian poets illustrate, Ovid was being read in the eighth century and earlier in parts of the former Empire. On Theodulf, see Raby, *History of Christian-Latin Poetry*, 171–9, and *History of Secular-Latin Poetry in the Middle Ages*, 180–1. On Modoin as Naso and Theodulf as Pindar, see Raby, *A History of Christian-Latin Poetry*, 157 and 173 respectively. On Alcuin's nicknaming habit, see Garrison, "Social World of Alcuin," 59–79.
28 For case studies, see essays in Clark, Coulson, and McKinley, eds., *Ovid in the Middle Ages*, and in Desmond, ed., "Ovid in Medieval Culture." See Stapleton, *Harmful Eloquence*, 39–132, on medieval receptions of *Amores*. Extant in four mss. the anonymous *L'Art d'Amours*, ed. Roy, a French prose translation of *Ars am.* punctuated with glosses, illustrates thirteenth-century reception and transformation that flattens Ovid's satiric wit in favor of narrative commentary and occasional amplification cued to perceived audience needs.

who composed mythological and amatory poems in vernacular languages and in Latin mined Ovid's poetry for stories, themes, and images, and they patterned much of their poetic diction on Ovid's language. Peter Dronke observes that themes common in medieval love lyrics, such as surrender to the god of love, love-service to the beloved, love-worship of the beloved, and love as source of virtue, find their roots in Ovid's poetry.[29] Similarly, the lovesickness trope – a pose *amans* adopts (*Am.* 1.2.1–8), and the *praeceptor amoris* counsels (*Ars am.* 1.729–38) and remedies (*Rem. am.*) – gains new literary life with the advent in Europe of Constantine the African's (d. 1098/99) *Viaticum*, a medical treatise explicating the disease "eros" and its treatments.[30] Moreover, we often can trace classical allusions, motifs, images, and references to Ovid or Ovidian influence. For instance, in "Parce continuis," an early twelfth-century Latin lyric, the poet invokes Ovid's tales of Pyramus and Thisbe (*Met.* 4.55–166), Hero and Leander (*Her.* 18 and 19), and Orpheus and Eurydice (*Met.* 10.1–85) to illustrate the theme of love's overwhelming bonds.[31] In the late twelfth century, Andreas Capellanus patterns his treatise *De arte honeste amandi*, or *De amore*, on Ovid's *Ars amatoria* and *Remedia amoris*.[32] Jean de Meun, in the thirteenth century, directly cites Ovid several times and uses his poetry as sources in his portion of *Le Roman de la Rose*, and of course the entire 21,780-line poem, with its mythographical and amatory themes, is Ovidian.[33] In the fourteenth century, Chaucer draws on Ovid in much of his love poetry, translating from *Heroides* in the *Legend of Good Women* and, as noted in chapter one, using Ovid's tale of Ceyx and Alcione (*Met.* 11.410–748) in *The Book of the Duchess*.[34] As these examples suggest,

---

[29] Dronke, *Medieval Latin*, 163–81.
[30] Wack, *Lovesickness in the Middle Ages*, 14–16, 179–93. As Wack notes, "readers of Constantine's chapter on lovesickness sometimes jotted down lines from Ovid in the margins" (15): a practice that continued into the thirteenth century.
[31] "Parce continuis," in Dronke, *Medieval Latin*, 341–52. Extant in two ms. versions, the poem was, Dronke posits, "designed for solo performance to an intellectual clerical audience" (347).
[32] The first two books of *De amore* correspond to *Ars am.* and the third to *Rem. am.* That Andreas had Ovid in mind is evident from his twofold treatment of love outlined in the preface though he does not fully carry through with it. *De amore*, ed. and trans. Walsh, 30, 12–15. Concerning Andreas and Ovid, see P. Allen, *Art of Love*, 59–78. On *De amore*'s position in medieval culture, see Cherchi, *Andreas and the Ambiguity of Courtly Love*; Karnein, *"De amore" in volksprachlicher Literatur*; Leclercq, *Monks on Marriage*, 63–8; Lewis, *The Allegory of Love*, 32–43; Moi, "Desire in Language," 11–33; Monson, *Andreas Capellanus, Scholasticism, and the Courtly Tradition*; Robertson, *A Preface to Chaucer*, 391–448; and Roy, "A la Recherche des Lecteurs Médiévaux," 45–73.
[33] In his advice to avoid poverty, for instance, Amis says, "Car povres n'a don s'amour paisse, / Si come Ovides le confesse" (for the poor man has nothing to feed his love just as Ovid declares). Guillaume de Lorris and Jean de Meun, *Le Roman de la Rose*, ed. Langlois, 7985–6. See also the God of Love's (10522–5) and Genius' (20175–84) respective discussions of Ovid as literary authority on love, as well as the poem's numerous references to Ovid's poetry (passim). Concerning Ovid and the *Roman de la Rose*, see P. Allen, *Art of Love*, 79–110.
[34] The *Legend of Cleopatra*, alone, is not a translation of Ovid. Scholars have long recognized Chaucer's debt to Ovid. For a range of responses, see Calabrese, *Chaucer's Ovidian Arts of Love*; Cooper, "Chaucer and Ovid," 71–81; Fumo, *Legacy of Apollo*; Fyler, *Chaucer and*

relationships between Ovid's poetry and the poetry, treatises, and commentaries it inspired are varied and multifaceted. Ovid's works invite interpretation and creative response: a key set of themes medieval writers inherit from Ovid and transform in their work is his treatment of Minerva and Venus.

As in *Metamorphoses* and elsewhere, we find the theme of opposition in a range of Medieval Latin texts. In the early twelfth-century spring-time lyric, "Dant ad veris honorem," Minerva fights Venus' attempt to dominate nature: a precursor to Venus' role in Alan of Lille's *Planctus Naturae* and to their animosity in *Anticlaudianus*. In the lyric, Minerva represents reason, aided by universal order and learning (Jupiter, the Fates, Apollo, Mercury, and Philology), while Venus represents disruptive, cupidinous love, aided by gluttony and lust (Ceres, Bacchus, Pan).[35] The opposition between Minerva as reason and Venus as sensuality implied in this poem receives similar treatment in Walter Map's (1140–c.1210) twelfth-century *De nugis curialium*, where a woman seduced an intoxicated man in the afternoon sun. Map observes, "Sic nimirum semper assurgunt Veneri Phebus et Pan, Ceres et Cacus, a quorum ubique conuentu celebri Pallas excluditur" (It is ever thus, of course, that Phoebus and Pan, Ceres and Bacchus, defer to Venus, and from their meetings Pallas is always excluded).[36] In another passage comically analogous to Dunbar's *Golden Targe*, Map incorporates the goddesses in a tale where a queen, attempting to seduce her chamberlain, starts a bedroom brawl: "Nam hec assilit, hic defendit; hec tela proteruie mittit, hic clipeo modestie suscepit; hec intentat Uenerem, hic Mineruam obiicit" (For she jumped him, he fended her off; she brazenly sent darts, he modestly received them with a targe; she directed Venus at him, he sent forth Minerva) (3.2, 110). Unlike the *Targe*-narrator, the chamberlain managed to avoid the queen's unwanted advances, thanks to Minerva's help. Likewise, in *Metamorphosis Goliae*, as we saw in chapter three, Minerva's learning and wisdom alone oppose Venus, while deities, philosophers, and poets fall under her influence. The Ovidian theme of the goddesses' opposition also suggests tension between learning and sexual desire in "Ianus annum circinat," a lyric in *Carmina Burana*. In a moment of choice similar to the Judgment of Paris, a student of Pallas forgoes the goddess to enter Venus' school, where he spies a girl with the face of Helen and declares in the poem's refrain, "Amor cuncta superat, / Amor dura terebrat" (Love conquers all, Love drills hard things).[37] Though the student does not attain his beloved, he

---

Ovid; Hanning, "Chaucer's First Ovid," 121–63; Hoffman, *Ovid and the Canterbury Tales*; Sadlek, *Idleness Working*, 208–58; and Shannon, *Chaucer and the Roman Poets*. Of parallel interest is Harbert, "Lessons from the Great Clerk," 83–97.

[35] "Dant ad veris honorem," in Dronke, *Medieval Latin*, 367–9.
[36] *De nugis curialium*, ed. Rhodes, 4.11, 180–1.
[37] Stanza three reads:

   Dum alumnus Palladis
      Cytheree scolam
   introissem, inter multas
      bene cultas
   vidi unam solam
      facie

remains hopeful and in a final prayer to Cupid and Venus says, "olim tiro Palladis / nunc tuo iuri cedo" (once a student of Pallas, now I believe in your law) (5.8–9), before launching into the final refrain, "Vincit Amor omnia / regit Amor omnia" (Love conquers all, Love rules everything). And, in Petrarch's unfinished epic *Africa*, Laelius observed relief sculptures on Syphax's palace depicting the gods in action. In one ekphrasis, Minerva directly opposed Venus accompanied by Cupid, and their familiar iconography characterizes Minerva as goddess of virtuous wisdom and Venus as goddess of lust.[38]

While the theme of conflict between the goddesses is prominent in Latin texts, it often appears in vernacular literature as well. Lydgate's *Reson and Sensuallyte* is an obvious example of this opposition, but Chaucer also draws on this theme. In the Physician's Tale, for instance, the Physician describes Virginia as modest and eloquent, as "Though she were wis as Pallas" (49), and later, in a passage that reverberates with Ovid, Map, and others, he declares, "Bacus hadde of hir mouth right no maistrie; / For wyn and youthe dooth Venus encresse / As men in fyr wol casten oille or greesse" (57–9).[39] As in Map's tale of the inebriated lover, the deities here are metonyms for virtuous wisdom, cupidinous love, and inebriation, and Virginia, by implication, adheres to wisdom (Pallas), thereby avoiding cupidity (Venus) and drunkenness (Bacchus).

Poets play against this theme of opposition when they follow Ovid's lead and ally Minerva with Venus. Writing in the sixth century, the poet Maximianus composed elegies in which he echoes Ovid's theme of alliance between the goddesses. In the six elegies of his corpus that remain, Maximianus develops a comic persona of an aged lover, based partly on *Amores* 3.7. The aged lover recounts in Elegy 3 his first youthful affair with a girl named Aquilina. Both burning with lovesickness, their passion initially increased when his guardian and her parents forbade the relationship, but Boethius pandered for the lover and Aquilina, finally securing parental consent through gifts. Once granted, "permissum fit vile nefas, fit languidus ardour" (wicked permission made it vile, and passion became weak).[40] They did not consummate their affair, Aquilina quickly lost desire, and the lovesick youth recovered from his misery. He continues:

> Tyndaridi
> ac Veneri
> secundam,
> plenam elegantie
> et magis pudibundam.
> *Refr.* Amor cunta superat,
> Amor dura terebrat.

Carmina Burana, ed. Hilka and Schumann, 56, 1.
[38] *Africa*, ed. Pingaud, 3.204–23, 138–9.
[39] The trope of wine aiding sex comes from *Ars. am.*, 1.229–44, 565–4, and *Rem. am.*, 803–10. Boccaccio, for instance, incorporates the trope in *Teseida*, 6.66, and its accompanying gloss.
[40] *Elegies of Maximianus*, ed. Webster, 3.77.

> quae postquam perlata viro sunt omnia tanto
> meque videt fluctus exuperasse meos,
> 'macte' inquit 'iuvenis, proprii dominator amoris,
> et de contemptu sume trophaea tuo.
> arma tibi Veneris cedantque Cupidinis arcus,
> cedat et armipotens ipsa Minerva tibi.'
> sic mihi peccandi studium permissa potestas
> abstulit atque ipsum talia velle fugit

> (After all was reported to that great man [Boethius], and he saw that I had escaped from my passions, he said, "Magnify, young man, the ruler of your love, and take up the trophies of your scorn. Let the weapons of Venus and the bow of Cupid yield to you, and let warrior Minerva herself yield to you." Thus, the power of sinning granted carried away my desire, and the very wish to do so fled) (3.85–92)

Maximianus' larger comic theme in this elegy, the death of passion upon receipt of permission, implies Ovid's notion that denial of fulfillment increases passion.[41] He also subtly presents the theme of alliance between Venus and Minerva, who seems to signify here the *realpolitik* wisdom of using bribery to attain ends. Sorting his own *remedium amoris*, Boethius assumed that lust, once assented to, would quickly burn out. When "pudica" (a modest life) (3.94) replaced lust, the lover overcame, in Boethius' words, not only Venus and Cupid but also Minerva's worldly-wise weapons. As in Ovid, Minerva is initially part of the youth's group of deities who encourage *cupiditas*. His mastery over passion, however, transforms lust to love and, in turn, the deities from worldly to virtuous. The end to which Minerva's wisdom led ultimately helped the persona rightly order his love for Aquilina. Maximianus' development of this theme influenced medieval poets, for his elegies, alongside Ovid's poetry, were standard grammar-school texts in the Middle Ages.[42]

---

[41] In *Amores* 2.29.1–4, for instance, the persona addresses his beloved's guardian:

> Si tibi non opus est servata, stulte, puella,
> at mihi fac serves, quo magis ipse velim!
> quod licet, ingratum est; quod non licet acrius urit.
> ferreus est, siquis, quod sinit alter, amat"

> (If you do not need to protect the girl for yourself, O fool, at least see that you protect her for me, so that I may desire her more. What is permitted is unappreciated; what is not permitted burns more keenly. He is iron if he loves what another allows).

Chaucer also develops this theme in *Anelida and Arcite* when, after describing Arcite's betrayal of Anelida and the "daunger" he endures for his "new lady," the narrator says:

> Ensample of this, ye thrifty wymmen alle,
> Take here of Anelida and fals Arcite …
> The kynde of mannes hert is to delyte
> In thing that straunge is, also God me save!
> For what he may not gete, that wold he have (197–8, 201–3)

[42] Curtius, *European Literature*, 48–54. Not all reception was positive. Alexander de Villedieu (c.1175–240) disparages Maximianus, saying "quamvis haec non sit doctrina satis generalis, / proderit ipsa tamen plus nugis Maximiani" (although this teaching

In the high to late Middle Ages, love-poets following Ovid and Maximianus develop further Minerva's alliance with Venus. Two Latin poems from *Carmina Burana* illustrate well how poets subtly employ this theme. The first, "Ecce, chorus virginum," is a seven-stanza lyric with a refrain "Cypridis in voto / fronde pausa tilie, / Cyridis in voto!" (In devotion to Venus pause under the green bough of the lime tree, in devotion to Venus) (59.1.9–11). Punctuating each stanza, this refrain suggests the poet's comic tone throughout toward Venus' game of love. The lyric's persona, a male lover led by Fortune into a flowery grove and influenced by Cupid's bow, observes his beloved among a group of girls, dancing "Cypridis in voto." In the fifth stanza, a debate ensues among the girls concerning whether it is better to be chaste or unchaste. Flora pronounces: "'caste non est similis / turpiter amata'" ('the chaste one is not the same as one loved shamelessly) (5.7–8). The recurring refrain, "Cypridis in voto," immediately follows Flora's statement, comically contextualizing her ambiguous proverbial wisdom. In the sixth stanza, Juno, Pallas, Calliope, and Venus – an unusual conjunction in light of the Judgment of Paris story – "affirmant interprete / Flore verbi iura" (affirm the word's lasting authority by the interpreter Flora) (6.3–4), saying

"flagrabit felicius
   nectare mellito
castam amans potius
   quam in infinito."
Refr. Cypridis in voto
   fronde pausa tilie,
   Cypridis in voto.

(happier, he will burn in honeyed nectar loving a chaste girl rather than a boundless number. In devotion to Venus pause under the green bough of the lime tree, in devotion to Venus.) (6.5–11)

The refrain following the goddesses' affirmation again provides a comical twist, for Venus seemingly pronounces against herself. However, the lover recognizes this humorous incongruity in stanza seven, when he says:

Iura grata refero
   puellarum ludis.
vigeant in prospero
   pudice futuris!
actibus emeritas
   nulla salutaris,
contingat iocunditas
   spes adulta caris!
Refr. Cypridis in voto

---

may not be entirely thorough, nevertheless it is more useful than Maximianus' trifles). *Doctrinale*, ed. Reichling, 24–5.

fronde pausa tilie,
Cypridis in voto! (7.1–11)

(I ascribe pleasant laws to girls' games. Let them flourish with favorable modesty in future times. No beneficial delight or mature hope touches worn out women with affectionate actions! In devotion to Venus pause under the green bough of the lime tree, in devotion to Venus!

Labelling the girls' "iura grata" as games, the lover minimizes them as incidental to Venus' larger game of love. Then riffing on the *carpe diem* theme, he suggests that, while willing for girls to be modest when they are "emeritae," he intends to pursue delight now by pausing with his beloved "fronde ... tilie." Minerva, affirming Flora, endorses Venus' game of love: her wisdom legitimizes it and becomes part of the girls' and the lover's play, danced "Cypridis in voto."

The second poem from *Carmina Burana*, "De Phyllide et Flora," is a seventy-nine-stanza debate between Phyllis and Flora concerning who is the better lover: a knight or a cleric. Phyllis, whose lover is Paris, argues forcefully for the knight, while Flora, whose lover is Alcibiades, argues eloquently for the cleric. Upon reaching an impasse in the debate, they agree the god of love should decide and prepare to journey to his grove. In a passage comically echoing epic arming-of-the-hero scenes, the poet describes Phyllis' mule and Flora's horse and accoutrements (stanzas 44–57). In the midst of making Achilles' shield, the poet says, Vulcan laid aside his work to make Flora's engraved saddle and bridle, fashioning the bridle's reins from strands of Venus' hair. Minerva, too, laid aside her work to make the saddle's purple covering, and "acantho texuerat et flore narcisso" (wove it from acanthus and narcissus in bloom) (57.3). Once described, the two mount up and travel swiftly to "Cytheree natus" (Venus' son) (72.1) who, in mythographic fashion, is "pennatus" (winged) with "arcum" (bow) in hand and "sagittas" (arrows) at side (72.3, 4). After venerating him, they present their debate, Cupid's judges declare in favor of the cleric, and his court confirms the judgment (stanzas 73–9). The poem, of course, is an elaborate joke, a clerical fantasy, relying on classical allusion for much of its humor – a medieval cleric's version of the athlete-versus-intellectual theme in popular culture today. Though the description of Minerva's saddle covering is brief, the poet allies her with Venus through references to the love goddess' hair, which Flora also uses, and the flower of narcissus, the emblem of destructive self-love. Minerva weaving the saddle's covering represents allegorically the use of worldly wisdom seeking sensual ends. As patroness of clerks, Minerva competes for honor in the world of this poem, and her wisdom helps Flora win the debate for cleric-lovers who, like Ovid's *praeceptor amoris*, use their intellect to pursue Venus' rewards.

Poets writing in vernacular languages also develop the theme of alliance between the goddesses. In his encyclopaedic continuation of Guillaume de Lorris' dream vision *Le Roman de la Rose*, Jean de Meun links the goddesses in Genius' sermon to the barons (19491–20667). After the God of Love vested him as bishop and Venus placed a torch in his hand, Genius pronounced anathema against all who reject the acts "Par cui Nature est soutenue" (by which Nature is sustained) (19532). In Jean's parody of a medieval bishop's sermon, Genius preached against celibacy and homosexuality, using stylus and tablet, hammer and anvil, and especially plow and field as metaphors for heterosexual acts.[43] "'Arez, pour Dieu, baron, arez,'" he declared, "'E voz lignages reparez'" (plow, by God, barons, plow, and you will repair your lineages) (19701–2). To fix his point in their minds, like a good preacher should, he told a story – an *exemplum* with which we are familiar: the foundation myth of Thebes where "Cadmus, au dit dame Palas, / De terre ara plus d'un arpent / E sema les denz d'un sarpent" (Cadmus, as Dame Pallas ordered, plowed more than an arpent of ground and sowed the teeth of a serpent) (19736–8). Genius then offered his sexualized reading of the *exemplum* for his audience in an *epimythium*:

> Mout fist Cadmus bone semence,
> Qui son people ainsinc li avance:
> Se vous ausinc bien comenciez,
> Voz lignages mout avanciez
>
> (Cadmus' sowing was very good, by which he advanced his people: if you [barons] also start well, you will greatly advance your lines) (19749–51)

Just as Minerva *patrona principis* inspired Cadmus, Genius deployed the Theban foundation myth to spur his audience, underscoring Raison's earlier assertion that love always should seek fruition according to the law of "Kynde," as Chaucer's translation has it (*RR*, 4845–55). However, his metaphoric language also undercut somewhat his association with her. Earlier in the poem, when Amans objected to Raison's use of the term "coilles" (testicles) (6929) on the grounds that the God of Love forbade bawdy speech, Raison defended her language, saying

> N'encor ne faz je pas pechié
> Se je nome les nobles choses
> Par plain texte, senz metre gloses,
> Que mes peres en paradis
> Fist de ses propres mains jadis
>
> (Again, I do not commit a sin if I name noble things in plain text, without gloss, because my father in paradise made them of old with his own hands) (6956–60)

While Raison's "plain texte" declares the natural end of love by highlighting God's intention, Genius' metaphoric text playfully hides procreative sex under the cloak of euphemism, as the God of Love prescribed.[44] Though Genius' use of metaphor and *exemplum* mirrors contemporary preaching practice and philosophical arguments advancing allegorical language, Genius' praise of Cadmus' lineage rings hollowly.

---

[43] Genius follows the model of a *sermo*, where a preacher develops and expands on a theme rather than explicates a text. See Wenzel, *Preaching in the Age of Chaucer*, ix–xi. On social parody as entertainment, see Bayless, *Parody in the Middle Ages*, 1–7.

[44] Chaucer too plays with this distinction between plain and metaphoric text in the Wife of Bath's Prologue, especially 26–9, 119–34, and 508–14.

In an Ovidian move, he told only half the tale.[45] Cadmus' line was unhappy: his four daughters and grandchildren, with the exception of Bacchus, suffered terribly, and Cadmus himself despaired. In the end, the gods transformed him and his wife Harmonia into serpents (*Met.* 3–4.603). Moreover, poets associated Thebes with Venus and Bacchus in opposition to Athens, Minerva's city and home of philosophy. Athens, then, became a metonym in mythography for virtuous wisdom and the rational faculty, and Thebes for appetitive passion and the sensual faculty.[46] An auditor knowing the whole Cadmus story might think twice about Genius' half-told tale. Originally part of an ancient foundation myth, Minerva's advice to Cadmus as Genius uses the story links her wisdom to Venus' agenda in *Le Roman de la Rose*.

Chaucer also draws on the theme of alliance in his Trojan romance *Troilus and Criseyde*, where each of the three principal characters link Minerva with Venus in the early stages of the poem's two love affairs. She first appeared with Venus in Book 2 when Pandarus swore by "'the goddesse Mynerve ... / And by the blysful Venus that I serve'" (232, 234) that he intended no harm to Criseyde as he began to pander like Ovid's *praeceptor amoris* on Troilus' behalf. Shortly thereafter Criseyde, too, invoked the goddess when, unsure of herself following Pandarus' revelation of Troilus' love, she said: "'O lady myn, Pallas, / Thow in this dredful cas for me purveye'" (425–6). As Venus' ally, Minerva aided both characters, for Pandarus' argument succeeded as the goddess implicitly guided Criseyde to grant Troilus friendship, her first step towards entering the affair.[47] Later in Book 2, while composing his initial love letter

---

[45] Ovid partially tells tales often enough in his love poetry as to suggest it is a feature of his *preceptor*'s pedagogical style. In *Rem. am.*, 465–86, arguing for taking a new love to get over a break-up, he recounts Agamemnon autocratically replacing Chryseis with Achilles' bedmate Briseis and concludes: "Ergo adsume novas auctore Agamemnone flammas, / Ut tuus in bivio distineatur amor" (Therefore, by Agamemnon's example, share new flames so that your love may be separated at the fork in the road) (485–6). He suppresses from the story, as anyone familiar with the *Iliad* knows, that Agamemnon's actions led to Achilles' wrath, withdrawal from battle, and the deaths of hundreds of Greeks in the Trojan War. Agamemnon, in the end, returned Briseis to Achilles untouched, or so he swore (*Iliad*, 19.261–3). Though the *preceptor* tells a bit more at 777–84, he does not tell the full tale in *Rem. am.* This partial tale telling is deliberate: Ovid playfully invites readers to complete the tales, thereby casting an ironic, even skeptical gaze on his *praeceptor amoris*. I suspect this joke illustrates the kind of thing Augustus and other subsequent readers of serious bent miss or ignore.

[46] The opposition between Athens (Minerva) and Thebes (Venus and Bacchus) is evident in Statius' *Thebaid*, 12.464–796, in which Theseus defeats Creon and restores the Argive dead to their widows. In the century after Jean completed the poem, Boccaccio and Chaucer take up the story in *Teseida* (2.25–84) and the Knight's Tale (893–1000), respectively. Boccaccio's mythographic glosses in *Teseida* demonstrate his moral readings of Athens (1.60) and Thebes (7.50). One way to read the *Teseida* and Knight's Tale sees Athens' victory over Thebes and the tale's concluding marriage as an allegory of the proper ordering of sensuality to reason, a reading Robertson advances, saying "the marriage of Palamon and Emelye establishes Thebes, the city of Venus and Bacchus, in a position of 'obeisance' to Athens, the city of Minerva" (*Preface to Chaucer*, 265). See Chance, *Mythographic Chaucer*, 184–213, for a multifaceted mythographic reading of the Knight's Tale.

[47] Criseyde apparently recognized Pandarus' *ars amatoria* when critiquing his "reed" (422)

to Criseyde, Troilus also invoked the goddess: "'thow, Mynerva the white, / Yef thow me wit my lettre to devyse'" (1062–3). Again by implication, Minerva helped Troilus in his pursuit, for his letter's "wit" led to early success.[48] Chaucer repeats this pattern of Minerva furthering Venus' ends when Criseyde begins to accept Diomede's advances in Book 5. On the evening of her tenth day in the Greek camp, the day on which she was to return to Troilus, she recounted her marriage and swore to Diomede that "'other love, as help me here Pallas, / Ther in myn herte nys, ne nevere was'" (977–8). Through this Ovidian oath (*Ars am.* 1.631–4), dramatically ironic for both narrator and narratee, Criseyde used Minerva (Pallas) to legitimize her denial of Troilus, which paves the way for the affair with Diomede. This service to Venus becomes clear a few lines later when she invoked Minerva again:

"And er ye gon, thus muche I sey you here:
As helpe me Pallas with hire heres clere,
If that I sholde of any Grek han routhe,
It shulde be yourselven, by my trouthe.

"I sey not therfore that I wol yow love,
Ne say not nay; but in conclusion,
I mene wel, by God that sit above!" (998–1004)

Neither denying nor accepting Diomede as a lover here, Criseyde employed Minerva's strategic wisdom to begin developing a relationship with him. And, in a sense, Diomede himself – Minerva's darling in other stories – seems more Criseyde's match than Troilus as the Greek also employed strategic wisdom in wooing her from the moment they met (5.85–175) to this juncture in the tale. It comes as no surprise when, in the next stanza, she gave Diomede her glove as a token of attachment and their relationship soon developed fully.

Underlying these instances, in which characters directly invoke Minerva to advance the love affairs, we find *Troilus and Criseyde*'s fundamental expression of the Minerva-Venus alliance in a scene where, though neither was directly invoked by name, both goddesses were implicitly present. Early in the poem the narrator recounts a religious ritual: Troy's festival of the Palladion – a service honoring the city's patroness, Pallas Athena, and her sacred statue. It was April, Venus' month in the classical calendar, freshened with spring-time growth and blooming flowers: the temple was abuzz with "many a lusty knight, / ... lady fresh and mayden bright"

---

and "paynted process" (424). While Pandarus sophistically collapsed Venus and Minerva, Criseyde's appeal to Minerva seems an effort to distinguish the two by requesting protection from the Venerian Pandarus. Minerva's invoked protection that soon led Criseyde to assent to friendship, though, further suggests the goddess' alliance with rather than opposition to Venus in this poem.

[48] Erotic letter writing, too, is an Ovidian theme as *amans* and the *praeceptor amoris* attempt to use eloquence to advance eros (*Am.*, 1.11 and 1.12; *Ars am.*, 1.437–58). The *praeceptor* also counsels mastering "bonas artes" (honest arts) not for public service or the common good but, as we would expect, for effective wooing (*Ars. am.*, 1.459–86: 459).

(1.165–6), all in their best array "bothe for the seson and the feste" (1.168).⁴⁹ Criseyde was there in widow's black, yet "In beaute first so stood she, makeles" (1.172), as the narrator observes. Troilus for his part guided "his yonge knyghtes" (1.184) throughout the temple, observing and mocking lovers, saying "'O veray fooles, nyce and blynde be ye!'" (1.202). Not surprisingly, "the God of Love gan loken rowe" (1.206) at Troilus for his arrogance, and "sodeynly he hitte hym atte fulle" (1.209). In an instance similar to Mercury's first-sight passion for Herse at Minerva's Athenian festival (Ovid, *Met.* 2.708–835), Troilus fell the moment his gaze fixed on Criseyde, and he surreptitiously observed her "whil that servyse laste" (1.315).⁵⁰ And so his lovesickness began in Minerva's temple and within the context of a religious service devoted to the virgin goddess of wisdom, *patrona urbis*. We might wonder why Cupid was inside Minerva's temple during her service, but it was held during the Venerian month of April: both goddesses were implicitly present, and where Venus is present Cupid often hovers nearby. If Minerva did not directly promote Venus' cause, her festival provided the occasion and temple the space, just as Ovid's *praeceptor* claimed such public spaces and gatherings would do (*Ars am.* 66–176). In a sense, the temple episode functions as poetic commentary on Ovid's lines "Spectatum veniunt, veniunt spectentur ut ipsae: / Ille locus casti damna pudoris habet" (they come to see, they come so they might be seen: that place renders loss of modest chastity) (*Ars am.* 99–100).⁵¹ Turning now to Lydgate's *Temple of Glas*, we take up the theme of Minerva as Venus' ally within the context of dream vision: a discussion that will expand to include two of Lydgate's contemporaries – James I of Scotland and Charles d'Orléans.

---

⁴⁹ On April as Venus' month see Ovid, *Fasti*, 4.1–19.
⁵⁰ For similar scenes, see Guido delle Colonne, *Historia destructionis Troiae*, 7.69–74; Boccaccio, *Il Filostrato*, trans. Gordon, 1.16–30; and Petrarch, *Rerum Vulgarium Fragmenta*, ed. Contini, trans. Cook, 2 and 3. The motif of sexual attraction or seduction during religious services is a source of farcical humor as well. See Chaucer's Miller's Tale (3339–51), and the Middle English carol "Jolly Jankin," in *Secular Lyrics*, ed. Robbins, 21–2.
⁵¹ In Boccaccio's *Il Filostrato*, 1.16–30, Criseida seems more in line with Ovid's remark, a heroine who comes to be seen. Henryson, *Testament of Cresseid*, 106–22, offers a near parody of this scene by emphasizing Cresseid's effort to avoid notice and by shifting the action from public to private worship and place from Pallas' to Venus' temple. In Lydgate's version of the temple scene with Paris and Helen, based on Guido's account, the narrator makes Ovid's comment explicit:

> But as the maner is of women alle
> To draw thider, platly to conclude
> Where as thei be sure that multitude
> Gadrid is, at liberte to se,
> Where thei may finde opportunyte. (*TB*, 2.3536–40)

Paris' subsequent decision to steal everything from the temple, including Helen, seems to mix Minervan and Venerian aspirations. Approaching the Minerva-Venus relationship from another perspective in "Pallas Athena and the Three-fold Choice," 159–76, Orr offers a compelling reading of *TC* in light of the Aristotelian threefold life represented by the two goddesses and Juno.

John Lydgate's *Temple of Glas*

Composed in the first quarter of the fifteenth century, *The Temple of Glas* evinces Lydgate's deep reading of Chaucer, particularly *House of Fame*, *Parliament of Fowls*, and *Troilus and Criseyde*.[52] Writing a mix of rhyming couplets and rhyme royal stanzas, and casting the whole within a first-person dream-vision frame, Lydgate organizes the narrative's 1403 lines into three parts: the first centered on a lady's complaint to Venus, the second on a man's, and the third on their union. The poem opens with the narrator recounting his own state of mind "þis oþer ny3t" (3): it was mid-December and, in Ovidian fashion, he suffered from lovesickness-induced insomnia (*Am.* 1.2.1–8), noting

> Wiþin my bed for sore I gan me shroude,
> Al desolate for constreint of my wo,
> The long[e] ni3t waloing to and fro,
> Til at[te] last, er I gan taken kepe,
> Me did oppresse a sodein dedli slepe,
> Wiþin þe which me þou3t[e] þat I was
> Rauysshid in spirit in [a] temple of glas. (10–16)

Finding himself at a temple built "on a craggy roche, / Like ise ifrore" (19–20), the narrator details his remembered experience in the narrational present tense. As with *Metamorphosis Goliae* and *The Assembly of Gods*, however, Lydgate's dreamer-narrator participates minimally in the poem's action. Though he moved through the dreamscape, he functioned as listener-observer, or like a voyeur as Spearing aptly describes this narrative effect, never interacting directly with other characters.[53] The dreamer's voyeurism gives readers the impression that they – again as though viewing a play – directly access the poem's central action, scanning the space and overhearing conversations through the narrator's eyes and ears. This move allows Lydgate freedom to present an open, enigmatic *somnium* in the Macrobian sense, a dream text that invites readers to enter the dreamer's perspective.

The dream's action is fairly simple as the narrator leisurely unfolds his recollected experience. Initially blinded by sunlight reflecting off the glassy temple, the dreamer's vision cleared when a cloud covered the sun: reminiscent of *Le Roman de la Rose*, he spied a circular space "compaswise, round b'entaile wrou3t" (37), which he entered through a little gate. Inside, he saw painted on the walls "full many a faire image / Of sundri louers" (45–6) in various poses presenting bills to Venus "as she sate fleting in þe se" (53). From Dido to Canace, he registered a range of literary figures, each brief iconic reference invoking a love story. Moving further into the temple, he then saw many thousands of lovers "redi to complein / Vnto þe goddess" (145–6), including oblates vowed to religious life before the age of discretion (196–208) and wives

---

[52] Norton-Smith notes sixty-five allusions to Chaucer's poems in *The Temple of Glas*, including five to *HF*, ten to *PF*, and twenty-one to *TC*. *John Lydgate*, ed. Norton-Smith, 179–91. Hereafter, I cite references to this edition of *Temple* in the text.

[53] Spearing, "Medieval Poet as Voyeur," 57–86, and *Medieval Poet as Voyeur*.

married too young against their will (209–14), before his gaze fell on a lady kneeling near the statue of Venus.[54] The variety of lovers and love situations rehearsed to this point serve as narrative setting for the poem's central love story. A superlative figure, the lady drew the narrator's focus and, listening, he overheard her complain, admit to a secret love, and ask for help.[55] Venus replied, counseling patience and promising "'That ʒe shal haue ful poss[ess]ion / Of him þat ʒe cherish nov so wel'" (427–8), for Cupid "'shal him so distres / Vnto your hond[e] wiþ þe arow of gold, / That he ne shal escapen þouʒ he would'" (444–6). The poem's *prima pars* closes with the lady's prayer of gratitude and Venus' gift of a chaplet to be worn as a sign of constancy.[56] Reminding the narratee "Thus euer sleping and dremyng as I lay" (531), the narrator then opens "le secund parti de la song" by recalling the "Gret pres of folk" (533) vying for Venus' attention. The dreamer moved apart, spied a man – "The most passing þat euir ʒit Nature / Made in hir werkes" (558–9) – and in turn overheard his lament. As with Troilus, Cupid's sudden attack had surprised the man, who said:

> "O god of Loue, hov sharp is nov thin arowe,
> Hou maist thou nov so cruelli and narowe
> Withoute cause hurt[e] me and wound,
> And ta[k]e non hede my soris forto sound?" (599–603)

Seeking redress, the man proceeded through the temple to "an oratorie" (696), where kneeling "Tofore þe goddess" (698) he promised fidelity and requested Venus' aid to attain his beloved who is "'exemplaire to al þat wil be stable, / Discrete, prudent, of wisdom suffisaunce / Mirrour of wit, ground of gouernaunce'" (752–4). The goddess replied, promising help with his lady "'Whan she seþ tyme þuruʒ oure purueaunce'" (862). In the meantime, Venus counseled among other points "'Lete reson bridel lust bi buxumnes / Without grucching or rebellioun'" (878–9) before sending him to the lady. Pausing, the narrator recounts his own difficulty writing about the man's sorrow: this move sets up the poem's third part (not indicated as such in the manuscripts), centering on the lovers' union. After the man declared his

---

[54] Early critics wondering why a monk would pose as an Ovidian lover and write a love allegory argued that these two passages indicated the poem's historical occasion, linking the petitioning lady to the second group and Lydgate to the first. See Crockett, "Venus Unveiled," 205–7; MacCracken, "Additional Light," 133–9; Mitchell, "Queen Katherine," 54–76; and Pearsall, *John Lydgate*, 107–9.

[55] The manuscripts evince multiple versions of the text, with key differences centered on the lady's complaint. In the earliest version, edited by Boffey, she complains generally against envious tongues, jealousy, and oppression; in the latest version, edited by Norton-Smith, she complains that "'I am bounde to þing þat I nold: / Freli to chese þere lak I liberte'" (335–6). Critics have taken these and subsequent lines in the second version as indicating the lady is married, and thus the poem's love affair as adulterous or potentially so. See, for example, Crockett, "Venus Unveiled," 205–7; Lewis, *Allegory of Love*, 241–3, Pearsall, *John Lydgate*, 104–6; and Wilson "Poet and Patron," 27–32. On the revisions, see Norton-Smith, "Lydgate's Changes," 166–72.

[56] The chaplet is another detail Lydgate revises from the earlier "roses whyte and rede" (Boffey ed., 525) to the later "braunchis white and grene / Of haw[e]thorn" (Norton-Smith ed., 504–5).

love and promised his service, the lady granted his request, saying as long as "'ȝoure entent is sette / Oonli in vertu'" (1061–2) and Venus approves. And the goddess did approve, for she joined them in a betrothal-like ceremony, wrapping their hearts with "a golden cheyne" (1106) and offering instruction to pursue virtue, practice patience, and remain faithful "'That nouȝt but deþ shal þe [k]not vnbynd'" (1270). With the sermon finished, the lady sealed the ritual with a kiss, Venus confirmed "This tweyn in oon, and neuere forto varie" (1298), the assembly in the temple completed the ceremony with a three-stanza ballade praising Venus as planetary and celestial goddess, and this "heuenli melodie" (1362) startled the dreamer from sleep.[57] Recounting his initial "heuynes" over loosing "siȝt / Of hir þat I, all þe long[e] nyȝt, / Had dremed of in myn auisioun" (1372–4), and his struggle to recall the dream, the narrator concludes with a promise

> Forto expoune my foresaid visioun;
> And tel in plein þe significaunce,
> So as it comeþ to my remembraunce,
> So þat herafter my ladi may it loke. (1389–92)

He then punctuates the whole with an eleven-line envoy addressed to "þou litel rude boke" (1393), sending it to the lady for revision.

Though the narrator never expounds "in plein þe significaunce" of the vision, Lydgate invites his audience to do so, that is, to re-read the text like grammarians, paying careful attention to detail. One such detail is Minerva's appearance as Pallas. After describing the extensive crowd of lovers waiting for a hearing in Venus' temple, the narrator says,

> But alderlast as I walk and biheld,
> Biside Pallas wiþ hir cristal sheld,
> Tofore þe statue of Venus set on height
> Hov þat þer knelid a ladi in my siȝt. (247–50)

Focusing his and his narratee's vision on the lady, the narrator gazes past Pallas so quickly that she could be easily overlooked yet, as with a silent character on stage, the goddess of wisdom remains "Biside" the lady through the remainder of *prima pars* as she registers her complaint and request. Thoroughly steeped in mythographic and Chaucerian poetics, Lydgate wants readers to catch this single line describing "Pallas wiþ hir cristal sheld": it cannot be a toss off or simply an instance of Lydgate's prolixity. Minerva's appearance at this point in the dream carried some weight for the lady, and the weight she herself carried, her "cristal sheld," invokes mythographic detail Lydgate invites his audience to carry into their intertextual reading of the goddess of wisdom.[58] Supporting the lady as she makes her case to Venus, Minerva functions allegorically as wisdom in service to love, particularly through the verbal

---

[57] H. Kelly, *Love and Marriage*, 291–3, considers this union a clandestine marriage in light of medieval civil and canon law. See also Tinkle, *Medieval Venuses and Cupids*, 154–9.

[58] The "cristal sheld" phrase translates "scutum crysallinum," which Minerva carries in mythographic descriptions (e.g., *De deorum imaginibus libellus*, 8.913; Bersuire, *De formis*

arts for the lady argued effectively. In the second and third parts, then, Venus herself advocated a wise approach to love, counseling the man to control desire with reason and both lovers to pursue virtue through their love. As Dronke and C.S. Jaeger argue, and Dante demonstrates in *Commedia*, love seeking virtuous ends could ennoble lovers, raising them above the mundane or base.[59] Though when the narrator first described the goddess painted on the wall as depicted "fleting in the se" (53), a familiar iconographic detail indicating in mythography an earthly Venus, the goddess of love in this poem primarily acted as Venus *concordia*: the goddess of Chaucer's hymn (*TC* 3.1–44) and of this poem's final ballade.[60] As suggested by her shield and her influence in the narrative, Minerva leavens both the lady's discourse and the love Venus represents in the poem: a love redolent of Boethius' harmonious cosmic force (*CP* 2.m8). Minerva's alliance with Venus here parallels the nexus of Sapientia-Amor underpinning the goddess' redemptress role in the sapiential tradition.

The poem's story and the intertextual interpretations it encourages apparently appealed to fifteenth- and early sixteenth-century readers. Offering evidence of multi-stage revision, *The Temple of Glas* survives in one fragmentary and seven complete manuscript copies dating from the end of the first quarter to the end of the fifteenth century.[61] In addition, printers brought out at least five editions before 1530, including Caxton's copy printed shortly after he established his press in Westminster, two by Wynkyn de Worde, one by Richard Pynson, and one by Thomas Berthelet.[62] That prolific letter-writing and social-climbing family the

---

    figurisque, 30). Boccaccio, *Genealogie deorum gentilium*, 5.48.2–4, includes this detail to connote wise strategic forethought.
[59] Dronke, *Medieval Latin*, 57–97; C.S. Jaeger, *Ennobling Love*, 27–35, 145–54. On Dante, see Mazzeo, "Plato's Eros and Dante's Amore," 315–37.
[60] Crockett, "Venus Unveiled," 201–30, posits an ironic treatment of love in *TC*, grounding his reading in a lustful, idolatrous Venus. Yet, Lydgate includes celestial as well as earthly elements: his Venus is multivalent as might be expected in her own temple. On Venus *concordia*, see Chance, *Mythographic Chaucer*, 95–104; and Tinkle, *Medieval Venuses and Cupids*, 198–210.
[61] As Norton-Smith, *John Lydgate*, 176, delineates the poem's stages in the mss., the earliest version is in Cambridge, University Library, Ms. Gg. 4. 27, fols. 491r–509v, and London, British Library, Ms. Additional 16165, fols. 206v–241v. An intermediate version is in Oxford, Bodleian Library, Ms. Fairfax 16, fols. 63r–82v, and Oxford, Bodleian Library, Ms. Bodley 638, fols. 16v–38r. The final version is in Oxford, Bodleian Library, Ms. Tanner 346, fols. 76r–97r; Longleat, Warminster, Library of the Marquis of Bath, Ms. 258, fols. 1r–32r; and Cambridge, Magdalene College, Ms. Pepys 2006, pp. 17–52. London, British Library, Ms. Sloane 1212, fols. 1, 2, 4, is fragmentary, with a pastiche on fol. 1 of sixteen lines and revisions of 736–54 and 762–3 suggesting an adaptation of direct petition to a lady rather than Venus. See MacCracken, "Additional Light," 128. For *Temple of Glas* mss., see *NIMEV*, 851.
[62] *The temple of glas*, Westminster: William Caxton, 1477. *STC* 17032; *Here begynneth the Temple of glas*, Westminster: Wynkyn de Worde, 1495. *STC* 17032a; *Here begynneth the Temple of glas*, London: Wynkyn de Worde, 1506. *STC* 17033.7; *The temple of glas*, London: Rycharde Pynson, 1503. *STC* 17033.3; *This boke called the Te[m]ple of glasse, is in many places amended, and late diligently imprinted*, London: Thomas Berthelet, 1529. *STC* 17034; see also *STC* 12955.

Pastons owned a manuscript copy, to which Sir John Paston refers specifically in a letter to his brother.[63] And other poets read and responded to the poem in various ways. Whether or not James I of Scotland directly knew Lydgate's poem, as modern editors surmise, he developed a similar yet more fully realized association between the goddesses in *The Kingis Quair*, which he composed around the same time a scribe wrote the earliest extant copy of *The Temple of Glas*.[64]

Minerva and Venus in James I's *Kingis Quair*

Minerva's alliance with Venus in King James I of Scotland's (1394–1437) *Kingis Quair* underscores the key theme of this chapter: the relationship between love and wisdom. Though the poem has garnered critical and scholarly attention since the eighteenth century, material evidence suggests the *Quair* was relatively unknown in the fifteenth and early sixteenth centuries: we do not find the usual evidence of multiple manuscripts or early printings to suggest wide appeal, as with *The Temple of Glas* and other poems in this study.[65] Surviving in a unique manuscript copy compiled in Scotland during the fourth quarter of the fifteenth century (c.1489–1505), the *Quair* consists of 197 rhyme royal stanzas totaling 1379 lines. The story, through first-person narration, centers on the love adventures of a prisoner who spied a lady in a garden through a window in his prison tower, immediately fell in love with her and, after she left his sight, passed the day in torment. Weary from lovesickness, he fell asleep, dreamed he in turn met and interacted with the goddesses Venus, Minerva, and Fortune, and woke in the tower still imprisoned. In his immediate post-*somnium* state, anxious about the dream's possible causes or significance, he received a message from a dove flying in through the tower's window, assuring him all would be well. Fusing the Ovidian *personae* of the exile and the lover, the poet frames this love story and dream vision with a prologue of nineteen stanzas and an epilogue of fifteen, in which the narrator discusses respectively how he came to write the story and how his fortune changed for the good after the dream: he is now – in the present tense of narration – happily living under "lufis yoke that esy is and sure," as he notes near poem's end.[66]

---

[63] Attempting to trace the poem's occasion, MacCracken, "Additional Light, 133–4, reviews the Paston association with Lydgate's poetry.

[64] The earliest extant copy is in Cambridge, University Library, Ms. Gg.4.27, fols. 491r–509v, c.1420–5.

[65] For studies through 1978, see Scheps and Looney, *Middle Scots Poets*, 16–51. Possibly the poem's earliest paratext is a c.1460–80 epitaph in a ms. copy of John Bower's *Scotichronicon* in Edinburgh, National Library of Scotland, Adv. Ms. 35.6.7, fols. 270v–271r. Referring to James I as a love poet, the comment also mentions Venus, Minerva, and Fortune: a likely reference to the *Quair*. See Summers, *Late-Medieval Prison Writing*, 63. In his 1521 discussion of James, John Major records a notice to "artificiosum libellum de Regina dum captiuus erat composuit" (an artful little book on the queen he composed when he was a captive). *Historia Maioris Britanniae*, 6.13. Major likely means the *Quair* and, if so, offers its earliest known printed paratext. The poem's first printed edition appeared in 1783 in *Poetical Remains of James the First, King of Scotland*, ed. Tytler, 67–162.

[66] James I of Scotland, *The Kingis Quair*, ed. Norton-Smith, 1346. On reception of Ovid's exile and lover *personae*, see Lyne, "Love and Exile after Ovid," 288–300. Though Lyne

In the prologue, the narrator also recounts details of his capture as a youth and life as a prisoner that parallel James I's experience as a Scottish exile-prisoner of the English from 1406 until his release and marriage to Lady Joan Beaufort in February 1424.[67]

Though external evidence for the popularity of *The Kingis Quair* in its own day is lacking, the manuscript book of which the poem is part provides insight into its late fifteenth- and early sixteenth-century reception. Written by two main Scottish scribes on 231 paper folios, the book, Bodleian Library Ms. Arch. Selden B.24, is a miscellany of courtly and religious poems, including Chaucer's *Troilus and Criseyde*, *Parlement of Fowls*, and *Legend of Good Women*, as well as Lydgate's *Complaynt of a Loveres Life*, Clanvowe's *Boke of Cupid*, and Hoccleve's *Mother of God* and *Letter of Cupid*. The *Quair* (fols. 192r–211r) is embedded in the manuscript between Chaucer's *Legend* and Hoccleve's *Letter*: an order suggesting the manuscript's commissioner perceived and read the *Quair* in an Ovidian as well as a Chaucerian literary context.[68] Chaucer's use of Ovid's Minerva-Venus alliance is, in a sense, intimately connected physically as well as thematically with James' development of the theme, for *Troilus and Criseyde* is the first poem in the book. Were the anthology read cover-to-cover, Minerva and Venus' relationship in *Troilus* could suggest a reading of their relationship in the *Quair*. That James had read *Troilus* is evident by his more than thirty allusions, echoes, and paraphrases of Chaucer's poem.[69] He also read much of Chaucer's other works, including *The Parlement of Fowls* and the Knight's Tale.

Like his master Chaucer, James also uses the motif of reading as a springboard for narrative. Unlike Chaucer, who in the *Parlement* (17–21) and *The Book of the Duchess* (44–9) describes reading as a precursor to dreaming, James describes it as a precursor to writing.[70] Recalling a sleepless, star-gazing night in the past when he

---

sees a fusion of these *personae* first in George Chapman's 1595 *Ovids Banquet of Sence* (294), we begin to see hints of it earlier here and in Charles d'Orléans.

[67] James I was captured as a boy of eleven and held by the English for nearly eighteen years; as part of his ransom agreement, he married Lady Joan Beaufort before returning to Scotland. See Balfour-Melville, *James I*, 28–105; and M. Brown, *James I*, 9–39. On the poem's language, see Craigie, "The Language of the *Kingis Quair*," 22–38; Jeffrey, "Anglo-Scots Poetry and *The Kingis Quair*," 207–21; Boffey and Edwards, "Bodleian MS Arch. Selden.B.24 and the 'Scotticization' of Middle English Verse," 166–85.

[68] See *The Works of Geoffrey Chaucer and* The Kingis Quair, intro. Boffey and Edwards, app. Barker-Benfield. Boffey and Edwards posit a three-stage development of the ms.: (1) fols. 1r–118v; (2) fols. 118v–209v; (3) fols. 209v–231v. See "Bodleian MS Arch. Selden. B.24: The Genesis and Evolution of a Scottish Poetical Anthology," 32–46.

[69] Norton-Smith notes thirty-two such intertextual references to *TC*.

[70] Since Preston's 1956 article, "'Fortunys Exiltree'," 339–47, several critics have concentrated on the poem's Chaucerian, Macrobian, and Boethian aspects, with particular focus on Fortune. See J. Bennett, "A King's Quire," 13–14; I. Brown, "The Mental Traveller," 246–52; Carretta, "*The Kingis Quair*," 14–28; Cherniss, *Boethian Apocalypse*, 193–210; Ebin, "Boethius, Chaucer and *The Kingis Quair*," 321–41; James, "*The Kingis Quair*," 95–118; MacQueen, "Tradition and the Interpretation," 117–31; Markland, "Structure of *The Kingis Quair*," 273–86; Petrina, *The* Kingis Quair *of James I of Scotland*, 131–7; Rohrberger, "*The Kingis Quair*," 292–302; Scheps, "Chaucerian Synthesis," 143–65; Spearing, "Dreams in *The Kingis Quair*," 126–34, and *Medieval Dream Poetry*, 185; Summers, *Late-Medieval Prison Writing*, 169–74; and von Hendy, "The Free Thrall," 141–51.

"toke a boke to rede apon a quhile" (14) in an effort to "borowe a slepe" (30), the narrator describes reading Boethius' *Consolatio Philosophiae*. Instead of the desired effect, however, reading woke him further. In the present tense of narration, he summarizes Boethius' loss of good fortune and subsequent recovery at the hands of Philosophia, noting the Roman's turn from "unsekir warldis appetitis" (40) to self-sufficient virtue. Still unable to sleep, the narrator received a fantastic locution when the matin bell, he notes, "Said to me: 'tell on, man, quhat thee befell'" (77). Reflecting on what he read about the workings of Fortune, and on this strange command, he decided to write his own experience with the fickle goddess and thus commences his story, which amusingly centers on a time when he did fall asleep. Reading leads the narrator not to a dream, as with Chaucer, but to recalling and interpreting a dream he had some time before.

Again, Minerva, Venus, and Fortune appear in the *Quair* within the framework of the narrator's dream. Though they appear serially as the narrator visits each in turn, together they articulate the relationship between wisdom and love within the human condition. In his dream, a light came in the prison-tower window, a disembodied voice proclaimed, "'I bring thee confort and hele, be noght affrayde'" (518), and he walked out the door. He was then taken into the heavens on a crystal cloud and passed swiftly through the spheres to the "Signifer" (529), the region of fixed stars and location of Venus and Minerva's houses. The narrator first arrived at Venus' house where he encountered "mony a mylioun" (543) lovers in various conditions. Another locution glossed four groups in particular: those who died old, content in love; those who died young serving love; those religious who served love secretly rather than openly; and those who, as in *The Temple of Glas*, were unwillingly cloistered or matched (575–644). This variety suggests Venus' house here in the heavens was a purgatorial or paradisal place for lovers, depending on their conduct while living. Following the locution and a glance at a group grieving the sudden loss of their beloved from Fortune's "variance" (646), the narrator spied Cupid, sitting "in a chiere of estate besyde / With wingis bright, all plumyt bot his face" (652–3). In mythographical fashion, Cupid was also blind and held a "bent full redy" (655) bow and three arrows tipped respectively in gold, silver, and steel. Each arrow, the narrator pauses to gloss, caused a different degree of love: the gold had an "esy cure" (660); the silver caused a "harder auenture" (662); the steel was "schot without recure" (663). According to Bersuire, Cupid's wings, blindness, and arrows signify *cupiditas*' arbitrary and swift nature: a fairly accurate description of how the narrator understood his "chance" (310) experience falling in love.[71] The arrows' effects, then, function allegorically for a beloved's response in any given love situation, ranging from gold (requited) to steel (unrequited) with silver (partially or reluctantly requited?) somewhere in the middle. The narrator then approached Venus who, lying "vpon hir bed" (670), was clothed with a "mantill cast ouer hir schuldres quhite" (671) and a chaplet of "rede rosis full suete" (678) on her head. "With quaking hert astonate of that sight" (680), a not unreasonable response in an epiphanic moment, he courteously petitioned the goddess, apologizing for

---

[71] Bersuire, *De formis figurisque*, 23–4.

ignorance of her law, requesting a "'remedye'" (712) for his lovesickness, and calling on her mercy to "'do me nought to deye'" (721). Noting his inexperience and her own prior knowledge of his case, "'Sen of my grace I haue inspirit thee'" (733), Venus instructed the narrator to be patient in his "'auenture'" (736) and delineated the division of labor she shared with Cupid, saying "'He can the stroke, to me langis the cure / Quhen I se tyme'" (738–9).

While Venus claimed for herself the power to cure lovers of their malady, and we see this action in Gower's *Confessio Amantis* (8.2816–19), she seems unable to act unilaterally. Time, that is, opportunity, mattered, and though she had "'by ordynance eterne'" (746) authority "'In lufis lawe the septre to gouerne'" (744), she relied on others "'to discerne / Quhilum in thingis bothe to cum and gone'" (747–8).[72] To that end, she continued:

> "As I haue said, vnto me belangith
> Specialy the cure of thy seknesse, –
> Bot now thy mater so in balance hangith
> That it requerith to thy sekernesse
> The help of other mo tha[t] bene goddes,
> And haue in tham the menes and the lore
> In this mater to schorten with thy sore." (771–7)

Recognizing his precarious condition, Venus then sent him to Minerva who, as she stated, would counsel him regarding the best way to "'Atteyne vnto that glad and goldyn floure / That thou wold haue so fayn with all thy hart'" (796–7). With Gude Hope as guide, the narrator took his leave and proceeded quickly "Vnto Mineruis palace fair and bryght" (868).

The narrator's exchange with the goddess of wisdom explicates the poem's *sapientia-amor* theme as Minerva led this novice in "lufis dance" (312) to deeper understanding of love properly ordered by virtuous wisdom. Upon their arrival at Minerva's palace, where Patience the porter ushered them in, Gude Hope led the narrator into the presence of "the pacient goddesse" (877), and he recounted "with dredefull humylnesse" (879) the cause for his visit. Upon hearing his tale, Minerva initially counseled him to ensure his end was set not on "'nyce lust'" (899) but on "'vertew'" (902) and to orient his love in relation to God. She said:

> "Tak him before in al thy gouernance,
> That in his hand the stere has of you all,
> And pray vnto his hye purueyance
> Thy lufe to gye, and on him traist and call
> That corner-stone and ground is of the wall
> That failis noght; and trust (withoutin drede)
> Vnto thy purpose sone he sall thee lede" (906–10)

---

[72] Lines 745–7 are difficult to decipher in the ms. I follow Boffey's emendations here (*TKQ*, 129).

Counseling trust in God, Minerva began to introduce Philosophia's discourse on "hye purueyance," that is, divine providence as worked out in *Consolatio* (4.pr.6–m.6), where "alternus amor" (reciprocal love) (4.m.6.17) harmonizes the cosmos under the creator's guidance: "Hic est cunctis communis amor," Philosophia sang, "Repetuntque boni fine teneri" (this is love common to all, and they seek to be embraced by their goal, the good) (4.m.6.44–5). Trust in divine providence as guide, Minerva noted, for "'Vnto thy purpose sone he sall thee lede.'" She continued:

> "For, lo, the werk that first is foundit sure
> May better bere a pace and hyar be
> Than other-wise, and langer sall endure
> Be monyfald, this may thy resoun see,
> And stronger to defend aduersitee.
> Ground thy werk therefore vpon the stone,
> And thy desire sall forthward with thee gone." (911–17)

Using architecture as a metaphor for a love relationship, Minerva Christianized Philosophia's creator by encouraging the narrator to trust the "'corner-stone'" and to ground his "'werk vpon the stone'": both biblical allusions.[73] To do so would ensure a steady, strong, and higher love able to endure life's adversities. She then encouraged him to remain true, meek, steadfast, and diligent and to integrate word, thought, and action through moderation for,

> "'All thing has tyme', thus sais Ecclesiaste
> And wele is him that his tyme w[e]l abit.
> Abyde thy tyme, for he that can bot haste
> Can noght of hap, the wise man it writ;
> And oft gud fortune flourith with gude wit:
> Quharefore, gif thou will be wele fortunyt
> Lat wisedom ay [vn]to thy will be iunyt. (925–31)

Minerva *magistra*, like an English tutor, not only alluded to the Bible but also quoted and explicated a passage from a sapiental book. Reinforcing Venus' message to be patient, Minerva wittily punned her way to her own message – behave, exercise wit, join wisdom to will, and things will sort out well.[74] Her emphasis on "gude wit" alludes to prudence, wisdom's ethical and practical dimension and the first element of Bernard Silvestris' tripartite "sapientiam perfectam" (perfect wisdom) attributed to the goddess.[75] She then framed a query by attacking those who feigned love and

---

[73] E.g., Ps. 118:22; Eph. 2:20; 1 Peter 2:6.
[74] The poem includes verbal play passim. Here, James puns with meaning and sound on "wele" (health or state of being)/"wel" (adverb), "will" (future)/"will" (faculty), and "wit" (intellect, prudence)/"wisdom" to reinforce Minerva's emphases.
[75] In his commentary on *Aeneid* 6.68, Bernard writes: "Minerva quasi media vel intima cogitatio est, sapientia que in cerebro sedem habet. Tria namque sunt que sapientiam perfectam reddunt, ingenium, scilicet vis inveniendi, ratio vis discernendi inventa, memoria vis conservandi" (Minerva, as if the central or innermost thought, is wisdom, which has her seat in the brain. For there are three things that constitute perfect

declaring that their deceit spoiled things for those "'That menen wele and ar noght variant'" (957). But, she said, if his love were grounded in God's law, she promised help, saying "'Opyn thy hert, therefore, and lat me se / Gif thy remede be pertynent to me'" (965–6).

In the subsequent exchange, Minerva offered a tutorial in love grounded in wisdom. To her invitation to open his heart, the narrator replied "'I lufe that flour abufe all othir thing: / And would bene he that to hir worschipping / Myght ought auaille'" (970–2). Furthermore, he said, he would protect "'hir gude fame'" (978) and, declaring his sincerity, concluded: "'Bot so desire my wittis dooth compace, / More ioy in erth kepe I noght bot your grace'" (986–7). Picking up on this final point, and perhaps suspecting shallowness on his part, Minerva responded that desire is good if grounded in "'Cristin wise / And therefore, son, opyn thy hert playnly'" (989–90). To her further prodding, the narrator replied:

"Madame ... trew withoutin fantise,
That day sall I neuer [se] vp-rise
For my delyte to couate the plesance
That may hir worschip putten in balance.

"For ouer all thing, lo, this were my gladnesse:
To sene the fresche beautee of hir face.
And gif it might deserue, be processe,
For my grete lufe and treuth to stond in grace,
Hir worschip sauf, lo, here the blissful cace
That I would ask, and [eke] thereto attend,
For my most ioye vnto lyfis end." (991–1001)

Satisfied his desire was oriented to the lady's good, and "'That in vertew thy lufe is set with treuth'" (1003), she promised to pray on his behalf to Fortune, "'that has the cuttis two / In hand – bothe of your wele and of your wo'" (1014–15). She then launched into a discussion of necessity and free will, alluding to Boethius (*CP* 5.pr.1–pr.6), noted Fortune's power depended upon foreknowledge, and comically said, "'Sen thou are wayke and feble, lo, therefore, / The more thou art in dangere and commune / With hir that clerkis clepen so Fortune'" (1041–3). For Venus' sake and out of compassion, then, she advised him "'Pray Fortune help, for mich vnlikly thing / Full oft about sche sodeynly dooth bring'" (1049–50). Minerva's advice to pray to Fortune seems startling at first as it contrasts with Philosophia's early lesson on the fickle goddess (*CP* 2.pr.1–pr.8), yet it fits within a full reading of Boethius' text.[76]

---

wisdom: wit, that is to say, the power of discovering; reason, the power of discerning the discovered; memory, the power of preserving). *Commentum quod dicitur*, 47. On "wit" as equivalent of "ingenium," see Lewis, *Studies in Words*, 86–110.

[76] Describing Fortune, Philosophia reminded the prisoner-narrator: "aequo animo toleres oportet quidquid intra fortunae aream geritur, cum semel iugo eius colla submiseris ... Fortunae te regendum dedisti; dominae moribus oportet obtemperes. Tu vero volventis rotae impetum retinere conaris? At, omnium mortalium stolidissime, si manere incipit, fors esse desistit" (when once you have submitted your neck to her yoke, it is right that

In her discussion of divine providence, Philosophia delineated terms: divine providence is divine reason and pertains only to God; fate is divine providence working in time and pertains to mutable things; fortune is fate pertaining to humans in their earthly existence (*CP* 4.pr.6). God the first cause, Philosophia sang, orders the universe through love and harmony (*CP* 4.m.6). Thus, she explained further, since it is either just or useful, all fortune is good for those seeking virtue: just as a brave man ought not shirk the sound of war in his quest for glory, she continued, a wise man ought to embrace Fortuna's struggles on his path to wisdom (*CP* 6.pr.7).[77] This idea of Fortuna as agent of divine providence informs Dante's formulation of her in *Commedia*, and Chaucer's reflection in his ballade "Fortune" (65–72).[78] In the *Quair*, it undergirds Minerva's lesson on "hye purueyance" and the virtuous path of moderation to rightly ordered love: *saptientia-amor*. Even Minerva's final admonition to pray finds its source in Boethius when Philosophia concludes the *Consolatio* with a similar admonition to prayer: "'Auersamini igitur uitia, colite uirtutes, ad rectas spes animum sublevate, humiles preces in excelsa porrigite'" (Turn away, therefore, from vices, cultivate virtues, lift up your mind to righteous hopes, offer humble prayers on high) (5.pr.6.47). Taking his leave from Minerva, the narrator returned to earth "als straught as ony lyne / Within a beme, that fro the contree divine, / Sche percyng throw the firmament, extendit" (1054–6).

Finding himself "in a lusty plane," the narrator proceeded through an earthly paradise, an emblem of Natura's realm, to Fortune's abode, where he received a

---

you bear with equanimity whatever is offered to you on Fortune's ground … You have given yourself to Fortune's rule; it is proper that you comply with the lady's customs. Will you, in fact, try to stop the rush of her revolving wheel? But, o most foolish of all mortals, if it begins to stop, she ceases to be fortune). *CP*, 2.pr.1.16, 18–19. Though most critics perceive Minerva favorably, some do not. On the positive side, see J. Bennett, "A King's Quire," 12–13; I. Brown, "Mental Traveller," 246–7; Cherniss, *Boethian Apocalypse*, 204; Ebin, "Boethius, Chaucer and *The Kingis Quair*," 336; MacQueen, "Tradition," 121; Quinn, "Memory and the Matrix of Unity," 344–6; Scheps, "Chaucerian Synthesis," 150–1; von Hendy, "The Free Thrall," 147. On the negative, see Carretta, "*The Kingis Quair*," 22; and James, "*The Kingis Quair*," 105–6.

[77] Joining the brave and the wise man, Boethius implies the heroic ideal of *saptientia et fortitudo* in this passage. See Curtius, *European Literature*, 167–82. On Boethian Fortuna, see Patch, *Goddess Fortuna*, 17–20; Pickering, *Literature and Art*, 192–91; and Relihan, *Prisoner's Philosophy*, 21–4.

[78] Dante, *Divine Comedy: Inferno*, 7.61–96. A précis of Boethian Fortune, from purveyor of random suffering and joy to agent of God, Chaucer's "Fortune" is a dialogue between a plaintiff and the goddess, in which the former – though recognizing she sorts good from bad friends and drives him toward self-sufficiency – complains of Fortune's "errour" (4) and "adversitee" (49), to which she replies:

Lo, th'execucion of the majestee
That al purveyeth of his rightwysenesse,
That same thing "Fortune" clepen ye,
Ye blinde bestes ful of lewednesse.
The hevene hath propretee of sikernesse,
This world hat ever resteles travayle;
Thy laste day is ende of myn intresse.
In general, this reule may nat fayle. (65–72)

final lesson regarding providence.[79] The narrator's journey and catalog of creatures (1059–106) allowed him to meditate on his experience as he approached Fortune's garden that, like the stream for fish and earth for plants and animals, functioned allegorically as the place of human action. Entering her round-walled place, he saw Fortune in its midst with her wheel, on which were clambering "A multitude of folk" (1113). Hesitating, he observed the goddess exhibiting frowns and smiles "ay in variance" (1127), and watched in fear as the multitude climbed, spun, and fell until Fortune called him by name and asked his intent. In the ensuing exchange, the narrator requested her aid in his love quest, and she, observing his "'deadly colour pale'" (1178), said "'Thou art to feble of thy self to streche, / Upon my quhele, to clymbe or to hale / Withouten help'" (1179–81). She led him herself to the wheel and, as he stepped on to it, said:

> "Now hald thy grippis ... for thy tyme,
> An hour and more it rynnis ouer prime:
> To count the hole, the half is nere away –
> Spend wele, therfore, the remnanant of the day." (1194–7)

Reinforcing the theme of time, of spending it well, she gave him a final warning that "'my quhele be rollit as a ball / ... After ane hicht, to vale and geue a fall – / Thus, quhen me likith, up or doune to fall'" (1199, 1201–2). As she prepared to spin the wheel, Fortune bid farewell, tweaked his ear, and the dreamer woke to his imprisoned state.

Though initially agitated until he received assurances, as noted above, the narrator returns to the present tense of narration as he recognizes his change in fortune and begins to conclude the poem. Among a series of prayers, he expresses gratitude for "the goddis mercifull virking" (1310). The narrator's experiences with Venus, Minerva, and Fortune function like a triptych: each exchange explores aspects of his inner state as he aligns himself with divine love, wisdom, and providence. As projections of Bernard Silvestris' "interiores animi potentias" (inner powers of the soul) (*Commentum quod dicitur*, 47), Venus represents the soul's sensual faculty and Minerva, the soul's rational faculty: together they advocate for reasonable love, *sapientia-amor*, desire grounded in virtue and tempered by wisdom. The narrator's progress through his dream, moving from one epiphany to the next, indicates also a growing if limited human understanding of love, wisdom, and providence. For her part, Minerva serves as a bridge between love and providence and is the central panel in the verbal triptych: without her wisdom, the narrator would be less able to ground his love in virtue and recognize providence in his life. What seemed "chance" when he spied the lady in the garden before the dream he recognized as divine gift near poem's end, declaring:

---

[79] On Natura and the ideal landscape topos, see Curtius, *European Literature*, 106–27, 183–202. See also Economou, *Goddess Natura*; and Dronke, "Bernard Silvestris, Natura, and Personification," 16–31. Nature, mentioned elsewhere in *TKQ* (135, 297, 350, 460, 704), is implicitly present here as well.

"Blissit mot[en] be the goddis all,
So fair that glateren in the firmament;
And blissit be thare myght celestiall
That haue convoyit hale with one assent
My lufe, and to so glade a consequent.
And thankit be fortunys exil[tr]ee
And quh[e]le, that thus so wele has quhirlit me." (1317–23)[80]

Turning to Charles d'Orléans, we find another though dissimilar engagement with these three goddesses acting in the course of a love affair. With Charles, as with James I, we are again in the context of a prisoner-exile writing from confinement: a literary and historical position not unlike Ovid's in his final years.[81]

Charles d'Orléans, Venus, Fortune, and Minerva's Bird

Born the same year as James I of Scotland, Charles de Valois, duc d'Orléans (1394–1465), coincidentally also spent a good portion of his life as a prisoner of the English, perhaps even meeting James when both were held at the Tower of London in 1416–17.[82] Sometime during his twenty-five-year prisoner-of-war experience (October 25, 1415 to 1440), Charles composed, or adapted from his own French, numerous Middle English lyrics, which he organized into two ballade sequences separated by a

---

[80] The phrase "fortunys exil[tr]ee" merits comment. Here, I follow Norton-Smith's reading of Fortune's "axle-tree" though the ms. reads "exilte," which Boffey glosses in her edition as "the exile imposed by Fortune" (*TKQ* 154). Though quite different, with Boffey's suggesting the narrator's exile as a prisoner or the Boethian idea that the further one is from the Prime Mover the more Fortune holds sway, either reading works for my interpretation of the passage.

[81] On prison writing in James I and Charles d'Orléans, see Boffey, "Chaucerian Prisoners," 84–99; Epstein, "Prisoners of Reflection," 159–98; Spearing, "Prison, Writing, Absence," 83–99; and Summers, *Late-Medieval Prison Writing*, 60–107.

[82] Charles de Valois, the oldest surviving son of Louis I duc d'Orleans and Valentina Visconti, was born into great wealth and educated in the arts. With his father's assassination on November 23, 1407, Charles assumed his title. His mother died in December 1408 and his wife, Isabelle of France, died in childbirth in September 1409, leaving Charles a widower, orphan, and father before the age of fifteen. Captured at Agincourt on October 25, 1415, he remained a prisoner of the English until released on October 28, 1440. His second wife, Bonne d'Armagnac, died during his captivity. He married Marie de Clèves on his return to France; their son was Louis XII, King of France. Charles died in Amboise on January 5, 1465 and was buried at Saint-Denis Abbey outside Paris. Charles and his brother Jean d'Angoulême, also a prisoner of the English, were bibliophiles: approximately two hundred of their books are extant today. Charles' reading was wide-ranging – medicine, philosophy, devotional writing, Chaucer – and he composed in Latin as well as French and English. See Arn, introduction to *Fortunes Stabilnes*, 12–27; Fox and Arn, introduction to *Poetry of Charles d'Orléans*, xxviii–xl; and essays in Arn, ed., *Charles d'Orléans in England*. On connections between Charles and James I, see Askins, "The Brothers Orléans and Their Keepers," 30; and Spearing, "Dreams in *The Kingis Quair* and the Duke's Book," 123–44. On Charles and his brother Jean, see Askins, passim; and Ouy, "Charles d'Orléans and His Brother," 47–60.

sequence of roundels.[83] Following continental models, he linked the lyric sequences with three allegorical narratives to develop a plot: together Charles' 6531 lines of mixed verse-forms delineate two love affairs from the lover's perspective, the first terminated by the beloved's death.[84] The third allegorical narrative (4638–5351) – an account of a dream vision and its prologue and aftermath – functions not only structurally as a link between the roundels and the second group of ballades but also thematically as a transition between the love affairs. As with Lydgate and James I, Charles' dream vision involves an exchange with Venus. Similarly invoking Boethius' *Consolatio*, though not directly like James, Charles also draws on the conventions of medieval mythography to explore comically the relationship between love, fortune, and wisdom, represented respectively by Venus, Fortune, and an owl.[85] This owl, a bird not typically associated with Venus, signifies Minerva through synecdoche. Though never uttering a single hoot or screech, much less word, the owl plays a central role in the narrator's psychomachia as a figure for wisdom in Venus' service.

As in *The Temple of Glas* and *The Kingis Quair*, the third narrative's opening indicates the dreamer-narrator's mental and emotional state, setting the stage for his later meeting with Venus, the owl, and Fortune. By this point in the plot, we sense that Charles' narrator, self-named "Charlis Duk of Orlyaunce" (2720) in the text, had become a comic figure, who misunderstands his experiences even in the present tense of narration. In the first narrative, he pledged service to the God of Love on St. Valentine's Day, met his beloved, and began their mostly distant affair: the first sequence of seventy-four ballades. Having heard she had taken ill, then recovered, he learned by ballade 57 (1994–2025) that his beloved had died; he grieves in the sequence's remaining seventeen ballades. In the second narrative, exhausted with grief at day's end, he fell asleep and dreamed "Bifore me stoned a man with lokkis gray / Which y not knew" (2552–3): Age had come abruptly and by surprise – an echo no doubt of Gower's *Confessio Amantis* (8.2745–970), a poem Charles knew.[86] Age introduced himself to the baffled narrator, recounted how Resoun complained to Nature about the narrator and his mistress "'Of wrong doon'" (2567), and advised him to leave Love's service honourably before he grew too old and became a target for mockery. Though the God of Love tried to dissuade him, Charlis Duk of Orlyaunce successfully regained his heart, retired to the castle of No Care, and

---

[83] The English poems survive in London, British Library Ms. Harley 682; several of the poems correspond to poems in Charles' French manuscript, Paris, BnF, MS fr. 25458. See Arn, introduction to *Fortunes Stabilnes*, 32–9, 93–5. Hereafter, I cite references to Arn's edition of *Fortunes Stabilnes* in the text.

[84] Harley 682 lacks its first quire, approximately 200 lines. In the French text, the opening narrative details how the first-person narrator came to serve the God of Love: the extant English text opens with the lover's letter patent from Love. See *Poetry of Charles d'Orléans and His Circle*, eds. Fox and Arn; and *Fortunes Stabilnes*, ed. Arn. On the French manuscript, see Arn, *The Poet's Notebook*.

[85] Owning five copies of *CP*, including two he had with him in England, Charles knew Boethius' text. He also owned Suso's *Horologium* and knew Chaucer's poetry and reworking of Boethius. See Askins, "The Brothers Orléans," 33, 36–40.

[86] Askins, "The Brothers Orléans," 40.

performed a sequence of ninety-six roundels:[87] a jubilee marking his retirement from Love's service. The third narrative – what Julia Boffey calls *Love's Renewal* – opens with the narrator recounting his time in No Care, praying for his dead beloved and composing ballades and roundels on request. One such request, a ballade "Forto biwayle fortunes stabilness" (4660), leads to the poem's single embedded lyric: a lament composed while sitting by the sea and addressed to Fortune, blaming the fickle goddess for her stability in adversity (4680–735). Though ostensibly composed on behalf of a friend, this lyric summarizes the dominant theme about Fortune he articulated in the earlier ballades and roundels, that is, his ever-steady negative treatment at the fickle goddess' hands encapsulated in this ballade's refrain "So that y may biwayle thi stabilnes" (4695). In this lament, the narrator inhabited Boethius' lyric persona bewailing his own misfortune at the opening of the *Consolatio* (1.m.1). Charlis Duk of Orlyaunce was primed for a visit from Philosophia.

While reading led to dreaming in Chaucer's dream poems, and reading led to writing about a dream in *The Kingis Quair*, writing led to dreaming in Charles' third narrative when, after composing the lament, the narrator fell asleep where he was on a cliff by the sea. He continues:

> Ovir the see, where that the roryng wawes
> Did ouyrcast the gravell here and there,
> As that y slepe in sweven y saw this:
> A lady nakid alle thing saue hir here,
> And on hir hed lijk as a crowne she were
> Of dowfis white, and many a thousand payre
> Hie ouyr hir gan fletter in the ayre.
>
> Abowt hir wast a kercher of plesaunce,
> And on hir hond an Owle y sigh sittyng.
> Vpon the wawes owt more suffisaunce,
> Me thought afer she came to me fletyng,
> And verily it semyd me waking,
> And went me downe vnto the bank apace
> To vndirstonde of hir what that she was. (4757–70)

Failing to recognize this naked lady floating on the sea with doves fluttering around her head, the dreamer greeted and attempted to kiss her. Blushing, she waved him away, saying "'Knowe ye not me?'" "'No – yes!'," the narrator confusedly replied, "'… Nay, certes, nay!'" (4781). In this Boethian moment, comically mirroring the *Consolatio*-narrator's description and failure to recognize Philosophia (*CP* 1.pr.1 2), the dreamer here "stood so masid in that stound / That y not koude oon sely word abreide" (4784–5). Shocked to speechlessness, he did not recognize his visitor until she called him by name, "'Charlis'" (4788), and he "wel had lokid on hir face" (4793). Though it took Charlis a second hard look, the poem's fifteenth-century

---

[87] The ms. has numbered spaces for roundels 95–101 with roundels 102 and 103 closing the sequence, leaving a total of ninety-six roundels extant.

courtly audience would have immediately recognized her from the descriptive details Charles the poet provided. She was, of course, not Boethius' Philosophia as perhaps expected: rather, Venus had arrived and, like Philosophia, her iconographic details were telling. Medieval mythographers gloss these details as follows: her nakedness signifies the inability to conceal lust; her association with the raging sea signifies immersion in sensual delights, the shipwreck of lust, and her birth from Saturn's castrated members; and her doves represent lechery because of their fervid love-making.[88] Unlike with James I's narrator, and even Lydgate's, Charlis is not in the realm of the celestial Venus.

One detail of the goddess' iconography here has puzzled critics: the "Owle."[89] For a poet who obviously drew on the mythographic tradition for Venus, however, his inclusion of the owl seems, like Lydgate's Pallas in *The Temple of Glas*, no mere accident. Drawing on Minerva's classical association with the owl, such as we have seen in the Pompeiian graffiti discussed in Chapter 1, poets and mythographers throughout the Middle Ages consistently retained Minerva's link with the bird, using it to indicate the goddess' wisdom. As noted in Chapter 3, Fulgentius invokes this association when detailing the goddess' iconography (*Mit.* 2.1, 65) – an association later mythographers reiterate[90] – and Martianus Capella connects the owl with study (*De nuptiis* 6.571). Middle English poets, too, incorporate the owl in Minerva's iconography. In both *The Wars of Alexander* (4530–1) and Lydgate's *Troy Book* (2.2555–6), for instance, the owl underscores Minerva's traditional association with contemplative wisdom in the Judgment of Paris story, and again as we have seen in Chapter 3, Minerva appears in *The Court of Sapience* (2.1756) much like Venus here with owl in hand. Charles, on the other hand, in his parody of the *Consolatio*, plays with the mythographic association between the owl and Minerva both to suggest the goddess' presence in the poem and to connect her wisdom with Venus' sensuality.

Although it did not speak directly, Minerva's owl expressed the goddess' wisdom through Venus, who held the bird throughout her discourse. In a sense, the owl gave Venus license to assume the role of a wisdom figure, asking a series of questions to probe his condition. The narrator's responses, revealing depression over the loss of his beloved, culminated in a series of Troilus-like remembrances (*TC* 5.561–81, 603–16) sparked by seeing places where they talked, danced, bathed, slept, played post and pillar, made love (4822–40). Like Philosophia, Venus recognized that the narrator suffered from the loss of a gift of Fortune, in this case his beloved.

---

[88] For example, see Fulgentius, *Mit.* 2.1; TVM, 11.1; Bersuire, *De formis figurisque* 22–5; and Walsingham, *De archana deorum* 1.11.

[89] In the introduction and notes to their edition, *The English Poems of Charles of Orléans*, 1: xxxii, 2: 32, Steele and Day only mention the owl as Minerva's bird. Goodrich, *Charles of Orléans*, 123–4, interprets the bird as a messenger of death, as we see for instance in Chaucer's *TC* 5.319 (123–4). Arn, in a series of articles, does not examine its presence: "Structure of the English Poems," 17–23; "'Fortunes Stabilnes'," 1–18; and "Poetic Form as a Mirror of Meaning," 13–29. And in the introduction to *Fortunes Stabilnes*, 63, she argues against the owl here as Minerva's bird. As I also argued elsewhere, however, the owl seems primarily to represent Minerva ("Minerva's Owl," 3–7).

[90] See also TVM, 10.2, Bersuire, *De formis figurisque*, 30, and Walsingham, *De archana deorum*, 1.10, who include an owl as one of the goddess' iconographic details.

Unlike Lady Philosophia, however, who administered reason's medicine to the ailing *Consolatio*-narrator, or even Age who acts on Resoun's behalf in this poem's second allegorical narrative, Venus badgered the narrator to seek a new love. In a humorous discourse couched in religious and Boethian language, she said:

> "Remembre must ye that ye ar a man
> And haue of nature als youre lymys goode,
> So ought ye kyndely, thenk me, spend it than,
> Or ellis ye were to moche to blame, bi the roode,
> Though that yowre hert so trewly stonde or stode
> Yowre ladi to. O, what! Now she is goo,
> What vaylith here to stroy yowre silf in woo?
>
> "Ye may as wel chese yow a lady newe
> And for hir sowle as dayly forto pray
> And ben in hert to hir as verry trewe
> As wilfully to doon youre silf to day
> And forto spende in vayne yowre tyme away,
> For, though ye take a lady in yowre arme,
> God wot, as now hit doth hir litille harm!" (4869–82)

Venus' advice to the narrator parodies Philosophia's early admonition to remember that, as a man, the *Consolatio*-narrator was a rational creature and should rise above Fortune's influence (*CP* 1.pr.6). Noting rather that Charlis' natural physical endowments remained intact ("lymys" means both limbs and genitalia), Venus not surprisingly advocated that he behave "'kyndely'," set aside memory of his dead beloved, and "'chese yow a lady newe'."[91] Implicitly invoking the *Consolatio* in this passage, Charles the poet undercuts Venus' counsel, the wisdom represented by Minerva's owl, and Charlis the inscribed lyric-narrative lover who, if he truly remembered he was a man endowed with reason, would likely not follow Venus' advice.[92] His initial resistance, based on realization that a new love too could die and reluctance to re-enter the courtly game, signaled he recognized Venus' advice was suspect.

Venus applied pressure, though, and launched into counterargument, interrupted in the narrative by a ring composition of what is arguably the most elaborate description of the goddess Fortune in Middle English literature (4965–5050). Looking past Venus while she spoke, Charlis saw the fickle goddess in all her changeable detail

---

[91] Although Venus seems intent on convincing the dreamer he remains capable of being a lover, the lines "'For, though ye take a lady in yowre arme, / God wot, as now hit doth hir litille harm!'" also suggest a joke about his current state not leaving much for him to offer anyway.

[92] Charlis is no more a human being than Boethius' narrator in the *CP*: both are linguistic constructs given attributes resembling a human being by their human authors, Charles d'Orléans and Boethius respectively. Unlike human beings, these constructs cannot "behave" otherwise than as inscribed in the text: humans engaging the texts, however, can assess actions and words of such verbal constructs. See Spearing, *Medieval Autographies*, for an insightful discussion of what he calls in the book's subtitle, "The 'I' of the Text." He particularly mentions James I of Scotland and Charles d'Orléans on 100–1.

descend in a chariot. His gaze drawn to the crowd on the wheel in the goddess' hand, he mistook a woman on the wheel's height for his beloved and interrupted Venus, saying "'Allas! ... But lyvith my lady yet? / Nys she not she that y se yondir sitt?'" (5056–7). Registering his amazement, Venus said "'Where loke ye, doty fon?'" In an outrageously funny exchange, he then explained what he saw, Venus responded he must be dreaming (a dream within a dream?), and he counseled Venus

> "I pray yow turne abowt – not hastily
> But as it were who <sekith> for othir thing –
> And loke where so that ye kan ought aspy
> What that she is or gesse to yowre semyng." (5079–83)

Venus turned, saw Fortune, blushed, and said in part: "'A Seynt Antone, but turne yow! hide, hide, hide / Allas, that ther nar ny of hir sum boch!'" (5088–9). The poet's comedy of a sensual Venus embarrassed at being caught with a man is rich. Once the dreamer calmed her down, Venus explained the lady was Fortune and said "'How, knowe ye hir not?'" (5100). Again baffled by what he saw and unable to identify the being he was encountering, Charlis said:

> "O no, Madame – whi yes! bi god, now ... now ...
> Y am ... y am right wel on hir bethought.
> She stale with deth my lady, wot ye how,
> Which yonder sitt! Bi god, y make a vow:
> Might y hir reche, anoon y shulde hir slee!" (5101–5)

As with Venus, and Age for that matter, Charles' audience knew Fortune almost as soon as the narrator began to describe her. The dreamer's inability to identify her in the world of the poem underscores his folly: indeed, as Venus said, he was a "'doty fon'." Correcting his perception and clarifying that the lady was not his beloved, saying in part "'O trouthe, me thynke ye ought wel borrow wit!'" (5110), Venus still capitalized on his obsession, promised a chance with this new lady, and ordered "'Hange hir vpon my hercher of plesaunce, / And y shal brynge thee vp to hir aloft'" (5170–1). Grasping her kerchief and crying out in fear during his flight to the height of Fortune's wheel, he woke where he had fallen asleep, but with Venus' "pese of plesaunce" (5191) in hand. Puzzling over the experience, he began to walk, soon spied the lady among a group playing post and pillar, entered the game, and began wooing her in the second ballade sequence with language ironically mirroring that of his first love affair. Though we do not know whether or how this second affair ends, Charlis' ongoing pose of the unrequited lover – even complaining against Fortune again in ballade 118 – suggests little has changed.[93] Still, he seems less invested this second time around, and composes fewer poems: knowing Fortune's fickleness – or rather "stabilnes" – perhaps Charlis had gained a little wisdom after all and approached the "lady newe" with reservation. Regardless, Charles the poet satirized courtly

---

[93] Though the persona bids the lady farewell in the final lyric, ballade 121, the last lines – "Albe y fer forget me nevyr / To eft sone þat y may yow more biwray" (6530–1) – suggest more verses may yet come as if the poet cannot quite conclude this literary relationship.

convention by targeting himself or rather the literary narrator-persona named "Charlis Duk of Orlyaunce," who remained imprisoned in the cyclical, if stable because literary, role of an abject, unrequited lover.

For all its humor, *Fortunes Stabilnes* does not seem to have been widely read beyond its original milieu. Charles d'Orléans composed the poems for courtly, perhaps even private, entertainment while in captivity. As with *The Kingis Quair*, *Fortunes Stabilnes* exists in a single manuscript copy: British Library Ms. Harley 682. Charles likely had a hand in producing this book (c.1439–40), but left it in England when he returned to France.[94] Extant fragments of another copy made from Harley 682 indicate interest beyond its immediate audience, and the author of *The Assembly of Ladies* (c.1470–80) apparently based the poem's portrait of Attemperaunce on Charles' description of Fortune.[95] Still, *Fortunes Stabilnes* garnered little notice until the nineteenth century. This apparent lack of interest belies Charles' poetic craft and sense of humor evident throughout the work but particularly in the third narrative's parody of Boethius' *Consolatio*.

Minerva's owl, though small and silent, was central to this portion of the poem. As it presided over the dialogue between the narrator and Venus, the owl allied with sensuality and fickle fortune rather than reasonable love, *sapientia-amor*. This association qualified the wisdom the bird represented just as the bird lent its authority to Venus in the love goddess' efforts to recall Charlis to a life of sensual pleasure. As in the *Quair*, the goddesses here are on one level "interiores animi potentias," with Venus representing the soul's sensual faculty and Minerva's owl the soul's rational faculty. Together they work to justify Charlis' actions. Though Charlis seemed earnest about the "lady newe," the poet treats his behavior comically as he assented to another gift of Fortune in spite of previous loss. His "lady newe" was not really new; rather, she was more an allegory of desire within the inner landscape of his soul. As Minerva's bird, the owl tempered Venus' speech and signaled the validity of pursuing sensual desire not as grounded in "'Cristin wise'," like James I's Minerva argued, but as an end in itself: an end likely leading to dissatisfaction at best.[96] The owl's alliance with

---

[94] Arn, "Two Manuscripts, One Mind," 61–78.
[95] The two fragments are Bodleian Library Ms. Hearne's Diaries 38, fols. 261–4, and Cambridge University Library Ms. Additional 2585(1). Arn, introduction to *Fortunes Stabilnes*, 38–9, 122–3; *The Assembly of Ladies*, ed. Pearsall, 519–39.
[96] In Ovid's version of the myth of Proserpina, *Met.*, 5.345–571, Proserpina transformed the tattle-tale Ascalaphus, "foedaque fit volucris, venturi nuntia luctus, / ignavus bubo, dirum mortalibus omen" (and he became a vile bird, a messenger of coming distress, a listless owl, a fearful omen to mortals). Distinguishing "bubo" from "ulula" (screech owl), "noctua" (night owl), "nycticorax" (night raven), and "strix" (screech owl again), Isidore of Seville quotes these lines from Ovid to support his interpretation of "bubo" as a sluggish harbinger of disaster. *Etymologiae*, 12.7.38–42: 39. Citing Isidore and following Rabanus Maurus (*De Universo*, ed. Migne, 8.6, cols. 246–7), Hugh of Fouilloy describes "bubo" in similarly negative terms, interpreting the bird as an image for indolent sinners. *Aviarum*, 49, 217–19. In posing as Minerva-Philosophia in *Fortunes Stabilnes*, perhaps Venus and her owl together also serve as a mock ominous "venturi nuntia luctus" in the vein of Ovid's listless owl. This reading could link to Goodrich's interpretation of the owl as harbinger of death.

this Venus indicates its wisdom is suspect, underscoring Charles d'Orléans' playful treatment of his dreamer-narrator and his debt to Ovid's comic development of the alliance between Venus and Minerva and to the medieval Ovidian tradition.

Conclusion

Drawing this study to a close, I would like to return briefly to "Vpon temse," the short dream vision in Leiden, University Library Vossius Germ. Gall. Q.9, folio 112r, with which I began this book:

> Vpon temse fro London myles iij
> jn my chambir riht as j lay slepyng
> me thought I sawe apperyng vn to me
> the fresh venus mercifully lokyng
> vpon her fyngris many a strange Ring
> of which the stonys gaf so gret clernesse
> that neuer sawe j so fresh a brithnesse
>
> And in her hand me semed that she helde
> depeynted vpon a skyn of velem whiht
> the Resemblance of a floury felde
> and in the meddis a woman stod vp right
> of which the figure so fayre was to my siht
> that neuer in gravyng nor in portrature
> sawe j depict so fayre A creature

The word "venus," as I argued in the Introduction, is crucial to understanding the poem's subject: the narrator assumes his narratee understands fully the reference; without it, the narratee (and we ourselves) would not necessarily know the poem is about love. This particular reference illustrates poetics and reading practices at the heart of medieval classicism. In naming the dream's central figure "venus," the poet invites the poem's audience to read intertextually, which as Jo-Marie Claassen describes the practice is "a form of 'literary *anamnesis*'": a recollective interpretive exercise relying on previous reading experiences.[1]

As with any first-person dream-vision narrative, readers base resulting interpretations of "Vpon temse" on an assumption about the narrator recollecting the dream event; that is, we assume the narrator is correct when naming the poem's female vision figure. This assumption leads to yet another fundamental question in this case: how did the dreamer-narrator know that this vision figure in the first stanza,

---

[1] Claassen, "Literary *Anamnesis*," 3.

whom he describes in the second stanza as holding a painting, was indeed Venus? This appearance of a female vision figure in "Vpon temse" joins, as we have seen, a long line of such appearances stretching back to biblical and classical texts. When considering visionary literature, though, we also note a trend in which narrators describe vision figures in some detail as well as, and often prior to, identifying the figure. To illustrate we need only recollect Boethius' *De consolatione Philosophiae*, in which the narrator broke off his opening complaint when a woman suddenly appeared. With fiery eyes, an aged yet youthful countenance, and variable stature, she wore a self-woven robe bearing letters and symbols, carried books in one hand, and held a scepter in the other. Though able to describe her various attributes, the narrator failed to recognize her until she wiped his teary eyes with her robe. Blurred vision cleared, the narrator declared "respicio nutricem meam cuius ab adulescentia laribus obversatus fueram Philosophiam" (I recognized my nurse Philosophia, in whose home I had lived since youth) (1.pr.3.2). The pattern underlying Boethius' treatment of Philosophia, in which authors describe as well as identify the figure, became a generic element for subsequent treatments of vision figures.

Unlike the dreamer-narrator "Charlis" in Charles d'Orléans' third allegorical narrative, who described Venus without recognizing her, the dreamer-narrator in "Vpon temse" apparently had little trouble identifying the female figure with portrait in hand. Though he describes her as fresh and bright, qualities that seem to be long-standing attributes of the goddess as the late antique poem *Pervigilium Veneris* attests, freshness and brightness are also attributes of other dream-vision figures – again Boethius' Philosophia for one.[2] The dreamer-narrator offers nothing else here by way of recognition. And so, I find myself returning to the question: how does he know she is Venus? The answer, I think, lies in an intertextual reading of the noun "venus" – an exercise in literary *anamnesis* that draws on iconographic descriptions such as those found in mythographers like Fulgentius and Boccaccio and in poets like Chaucer (e.g., *House of Fame* 128–39; Knight's Tale 1955–62) and Charles d'Orléans (*Fortunes Stabilnes* 4757–70). A distinctive iconographic attribute for Venus is her nakedness; I would argue this dreamer-narrator, paradoxically perhaps, knows Venus not so much by what he sees but by what he does not see, namely, clothing. And when the dreamer-narrator declares that the female vision figure is Venus, those who read the poem intertextually imagine the Roman goddess of love much as described by other writers.

As noted in the Introduction, "Vpon temse" illustrates how one medieval poet uses a classical figure within a dream vision to explore an aspect of the human condition, that is, love. The poem also illustrates intertextual poetics and reading practices fostered by medieval classicism: the reception and transformation of the antique in the Middle Ages. The figure of Minerva examined in this study offers similar glimpses into the multivalent ways medieval writers develop and deploy classical imagery. Like classical and antique writers preceding them, medieval poets use the traditions of Minerva imagery in illuminating ways to develop their various interests in wisdom as a human and divine attribute, often with a particular concern for

---

[2] *Pervigilium Veneris*, ed. MacKail, 346–67.

ethical, at times eschatological, concerns that engage narrators and readers alike. In drawing on these traditions of Minerva imagery, medieval poets express confidence in their conventions as well, for they minimize interpretive commentary to guide their audience and take for granted allegorical significances of their Minerva images. Placing themselves within poetic traditions by intertextually engaging previous poets and writers, they develop Minerva within medieval classicism through playful reception and transformation of imagery. Readings of late medieval poets indicate that each tradition teased out in this study implies particular interpretations of the wisdom Minerva can represent in allegorical and dream-vision poems.

Minerva's role as redemptress, for instance, implies specifically a contemplative wisdom based on love: *sapientia-amor*. Like the biblical Sapientia, who informs liturgical and devotional texts from Alcuin of York's *Missa de Sancta Sapientia* to Henry Suso's *Horologium Sapientiae*, Minerva as redemptress offers to narrators (or receptive audiences) a life of virtuous wisdom in which one loves God as a creature ought, that is, through the proper understanding of Him and of one's relationship to Him and to other created things. Though Bernard Silvestris articulates Minerva's connection to Sapientia in *Cosmographia*, the implications of this tradition are especially clear in *Reson and Sensuallyte*, where John Lydgate emphasizes Minerva's redemptive nature through her iconography and role in the Judgment of Paris story and through his own expressed concerns for careful reading and judgment. In this poem, Nature and Diana instructed the narrator to read and judge intelligently, but he failed to do so and, like Paris before him, misread Minerva's life of wisdom and misjudged in favor of Venus' life of sensuality. Though the narrator failed to engage properly the Judgment of Paris story, careful readers who seek the "sentence" Lydgate advocates in the prologue do not. Lydgate's development of his narrator serves as a comic *exemplum* of foolish love, emphasizing by contrast the *sapientia-amor* undergirding Minerva's contemplative wisdom. In *The Palice of Honoure*, Gavin Douglas also uses Minerva to represent virtuous wisdom as he examines multiple paths to a life and afterlife of honor. As a potential redemptress, Minerva in *The Palice* offered a path of wisdom: a "via prudentiae," or life lived with *sapientia-amor*, in which one might join the likes of Socrates and Solomon in an honorable, wise mode of living that could ultimately lead to salvation.

Similarly, Minerva's role as *magistra artium liberalium*, mistress of the liberal arts, implies a wisdom of *caritas* based on the proper use of knowledge. Here, however, knowledge refers specifically to the school curricula of the arts that, as Hugh of St. Victor argues, restore humans to their divine likeness.[3] This tradition, stemming from Martianus Capella but rooted in ancient and classical literature, finds expression in several medieval texts, including the anonymous *Methamorphosis Golye episcopi* and Alan of Lille's *Anticlaudianus*. It is also central to book two of *The Court of Sapience*, in which the narrator undertook an intellectual journey to Sapience's house where Minerva presided over the maiden liberal arts as they served Theology in pursuit of knowledge and truth. Through this journey, *The Court*-poet articulates ethical and eschatological implications of Minerva's wisdom, saying that "the ordre of the artes

---

[3] Hugh of St. Victor, *Didascalicon*, 2.1.17–21.

seven, / Styre folk to leve the world and drawe to heven" (2204–5). As mistress of the arts, Minerva in *The Court* offered a path to divine wisdom that resonates with Hugh's notion of the arts as an antidote to the fall of humankind. In his *Garland of Laurel*, John Skelton later draws on this tradition to explore the issue of poetic fame. For Skelton, fame grounded in a life of wisdom represented by mastery of the arts, like the wisdom practiced by Gower, Chaucer, Lydgate, and the college of poets at poem's end, offered his best chance to establish a lasting name when confronting Fame's reluctant, skeptical, capricious response to his poetic efforts. Life's variable nature troubled both *The Court*-narrator and Skelton's poet-narrator, and both poets explore the transcendence to which Minerva's learning might lead: a wisdom of potential renewal and reform or lasting poetic fame grounded in liberal learning.

As *patrona principis*, a role related closely to Athena *polis* from classical Greece, Minerva enters the political sphere, attempting to help particular heroes achieve self-rule in order to serve the common good. Appearing in a range of medieval narrative texts, from Walter of Châtillon's *Alexandreis* to Christine de Pizan's *Epistre d'Othea*, Minerva as patroness fosters right rule, the realm of the prince, from which emerges a common theme: the effect of the prince's microcosmic decisions on the macrocosm of the community. Stephen Hawes draws on this tradition in his dream-vision poem *Example of Vertu* and his allegorical narrative *The Pastime of Pleasure*. While in *The Example* Sapience declared "I am grounde of the artes seuen" (716) and played the leading role in Vertu attaining heaven, Minerva represented an aspect of Christian knighthood as the armor-making servant of Hardiness. Hawes develops Minerva's *patrona* role further in *Pastime*, where the goddess provided advanced education and aid in Grand Amoure's effort to win La Belle Pucell's hand in marriage. Minerva in Hawes' poems represents wisdom in the tradition of Christian knighthood. Examining the ends of a dignified active life in both poems, Hawes engages Minerva *patrona principis* to foster the prudence needed to rule, and when necessary battle, wisely and well.

The virtuous "wisdom of the spirit" expressed in Minerva's roles as redemptress, *magistra artium liberalium*, and *patrona principis* encourages narrators to be other-centered by contemplating or seeking to understand divine wisdom manifested in creation and revelation and to act accordingly; the worldly "wisdom of the flessh" underlying her role as an idolatrous image, on the other hand, can lead to pursuing self-centered desires. Rooted in early Christian Latin poetics and apologetics, Minerva's role as idol stems from the anti-pagan polemics of the Church Fathers. In place of the early debates Augustine and others waged publicly with non-Christian thinkers, later writers like Isidore of Seville and Guido delle Colonne use Greco-Roman gods as a foil for Christian belief and practice, thereby emphasizing the cultural distance between their present and the non-Christian past. Engaging this sentiment, and following Prudentius, some medieval poets move the deities to an internal landscape where they participate in a psychomachia. In *The Assembly of Gods*, the anonymous poet develops Minerva's role as idol through the goddess' iconography and activities in the poem. Here, the double-image of Minerva-Othea represents a deceptive wisdom that, though apparently prudent in its strategic planning and desire for order, is ultimately undermined by the goddesses' opposition to

Vertu and their alliance with other, more obviously corrupt, deities. William Dunbar also employs Minerva as idol in his psychomachic *Golden Targe* to examine themes of love, perception, and poetic composition itself. Similarly articulating Minerva and Pallas, Dunbar joins the goddesses with Venus in her attack on Reson, an allegory of seduction that quickly turns into a nightmare of unrequited love. The narrator's palpable relief upon waking from this stark dream into a harmonious, golden May landscape underscores the negative significance in the dream of the entire catalog of deities. Though they did not participate directly in the battle, Pallas and Minerva, like the other gods and goddesses in the poem, functioned as idolatrous images in the vein of classical deities in the patristic tradition.

Primarily opposed to each other in much classical and medieval literature, Minerva and Venus also come together as allies in Ovid's love poetry under the poet's guidance as *cantor deorum*. In her role as an earthly Venus' ally, Minerva can manifest a worldly wisdom serving self-centered, or perhaps self-deceptive, *cupiditas* as she does in her idolatrous tradition. But, depending on her ends, she can also help a celestial Venus foster ennobling love: *sapientia-amor*. Medieval writers from the *Carmina Burana* love poets to Chaucer play with this theme of alliance to examine the relationship between love and wisdom in human heterosexual relations. While John Lydgate's *Temple of Glas* offers an instance of Minerva helping a lady petition Venus, and later leavening the goddess of love's discourse as she joined the lovers in a betrothal ceremony, James I's *Kingis Quair* examines more fully the relationship between celestial Venus, sapiential Minerva, and providential Fortune as agents in the narrator's quest for union with his beloved, an ennobling love achieved by poem's end. Shifting from ennobling love, the third narrative of Charles d'Orléans' *Fortunes Stabilnes* illustrates a comic use of the alliance in the form of Minerva's owl, held in hand as Venus seduced a gullible dreamer into pursuing a less worthy love affair after his first beloved died. Playing off Boethius' *De consolatione Philosophiae*, an Ovidian text in its own right, both James I and Charles d'Orléans examine Ovidian poetics of exile, imprisonment, and love in part through Ovid's theme of alliance between Minerva and Venus.

Minerva's role as Venus' ally intertextually, if subtly, integrates the other traditions. As the lady addressed Venus in *The Temple of Glas*, for instance, she successfully used Minerva *magistra*'s verbal arts to make her case. Implying her redemptress, *magistra*, and *patrona* traditions, Minerva's instruction and advice in *The Kingis Quair*, serving as a middle panel of sorts in a verbal triptych, fused Venus' celestial love with Fortune's sub-lunar providence to offer the prisoner-dreamer-narrator a path to fruitful union and freedom, which also implicitly gave him a chance at self-rule following years of exile and imprisonment. As worldly ally to an earthly Venus in *Fortunes Stabilnes*, the goddess in the form of her owl supports, albeit silently, Venus' argument to remedy Charlis' grief by replacing his dead beloved with another woman: any woman, it would seem. Though initially resistant, he falls for a second beloved when he mistakes her for the first, just as Venus here seems to be masquerading as Minerva. In the third narrative, Venus and Minerva's owl function much like idols in the patristic tradition as they seduce the narrator into pursuing an unrequited relationship leading ultimately nowhere. Collectively, the five traditions of Minerva imagery illustrate the poetics of medieval classicism. In dream-vision and allegorical texts examined in this study, poets use classical figures to illustrate in part "interiores animi potentias," or aspects of their narrators' souls. Minerva particularly illustrates the rational faculty, and the wisdom she represents – whether virtuous or worldly – bears on ethical choices medieval writers encourage audiences to consider.

Though the latest texts read in this study date from the early sixteenth century, Minerva – as and aspect of the inheritance early modern humanists sought to engage – continued to appear in later texts. Jasper Heywood (1535–98), sometime Oxford scholar, member of Gray's Inn, and eventual Jesuit priest, for example, published three translations of Seneca plays while still in Oxford: *Troas* (1559), *Thyestes* (1560), and *Hercules Furens* (1561). In the 884-line preface to *Thyestes*, the translator recounts a dream vision he had on a rainy November 24 in which a garlanded, robed, shining-eyed figure appeared with book in hand. Self-identifying as Seneca, the figure commissioned the dreamer – having already translated *Troas* – "agayne to take thy pen" and translate "My other works."[4] Adopting an affected-modesty stance in the presence of his muse-like predecessor,[5] the narrator demurred, saying in part:

> goe where Minervaus men,
> And finest witts doe swarme: whome she
> hath taught too passe with pen.
> Jn Lyncolnes Jnne and Temples twayne,
> Grayes Jnne and other mo,
> Thou shalt them fynde whose paynfull pen
> thy verse shal florishe so. (256–62)

The clerks and lawyers of the Inns of Court at the time Heywood penned these lines were, as Laurie Shannon argues, "the hub of new, sixteenth-century intellectual networks of textual production and exchange."[6] Naming them "Minervaus men ... whome she / hath taught," and later suggesting they were "begotten as Pallas was, / of myghtie Joue his brayne" (277–8), Heywood taps into the goddess' *magistra* and redemptress roles to characterize their wisdom and ability. Seneca, however, insisted he take up the charge, promising the narrator for his labor a place in the Muses' Parnassian paradise where,

> Jn fulgent seate dothe fleeying fame,
> There syt full hyghe from grounde,
> And prayse of Pallas poets sends
> To starres with trumpets sounde. (595–8)

With an eye likely on Skelton in this brief reference, Heywood again alludes to Minerva *magistra* in a similarly audacious move to set the intellectual and artistic context in which he produced his translation: a "Christmas tyme" (455) exercise as gift for Sir John Mason, then Chancellor of Oxford University. Seneca opened his

---

[4] *Thyestes*, in *Jasper Heywood and His Translations*, ed. De Vocht, 196, 198.
[5] On the affected-modesty topos, see Curtius, *European Literature*, 83–5.
[6] Shannon, "Minerva's Men," 438.

book, the authentic manuscript copy of his plays made on Parnassus with fawn-skin parchment and Helicon ink, "chaunced" (677) upon *Thyestes*, and began to read, thereby authorizing Heywood's translation of this Parnassian, Minerva-inspired, version of the text.

Just as Jasper Heywood plays with Minerva imagery, knowing his audience will recognize his intertextual allusions to the goddess' redemptress and *magistra* roles, Henry Peacham (1578–c.1644) draws on the goddess fifty-two years later to frame his 1612 *Minerva Britanna*, an emblem book dedicated to Henry, Prince of Wales. In a brief verse narrative following dedicatory letters and a poem, the narrator recounts Minerva's birth from Jove's brain before glossing *Minerva Britanna* itself as another "vera MINERVA" (true Minerva) born from Peacham's "ingenium" (genius).[7] Casting Peacham in the role of Jove, and implicitly the printer Dight in the role of Vulcan, the narrator-commentator promises *Minerva Britanna* will bring "aurea sec[u]la" (a golden age) for readers. The playwright Thomas Heywood (c.1575–1641) subsequently continues to play with the imagery in his dedicatory poem "Vpon the Avthor and his Minerva." Invoking Minerva *patrona* in a direct address to the goddess, Heywood declares Peacham a second champion "As great in Artes, as was stout DIOMED / In Armes" ([xiii]) and, after summarizing Diomede's battlefield successes, concludes,

> Thy champion too, whose Artes are fam'd as farre,
> As was TYDIDES for his deedes of warre,
> We know thou art MINERVA that alike
> Hold'st Artes and Armes, canst speake as well as strike. ([xiii])

And in the book's final dedicatory poem, "To Master Henry Peacham. A Vision Vpon This His Minerva," a certain D.S. offers two rhyme royal stanzas recounting a dream vision in which he saw the Genius of Troy weeping:

> So grieu'd to see that BRITAINE should enjoy
> Her PALLAS, whom she held and honour'd so:
> And now no little memorie could show
> To eternize her, since she did infuse,
> Her Enthean soule, into this English Muse. ([xv])

As with Thomas Heywood, D.S. draws on Minerva *patrona*, and implicitly on London as *Troia Nova*, in his conceit that Troy's divinely-inspired ("Enthean") Genius realized Pallas now dwells in Peacham's soul. Together, as these paratextual-dedicatory poems act as advertisements for the book, they also reinforce Peacham's frame of *Minerva Britanna* itself, which he revisits in the emblem titled "Omnis a Deo Sapientia."[8] Recounting again in image and text Minerva's birth from Jove's head, Peacham glosses the emblem's significance:

---

[7] Peacham, *Minerva Britanna*, [ix]. Peacham's "vera Minerva" seems a direct quote from Bernard Silvestris' *Cosmographia*, 1.1.6, but it is difficult to know whether or not Peacham knew Bernard's text directly.

[8] In the 206 emblems constituting *Minerva Britanna*, Peacham rigorously follows the

> By PALLAS, is all heavenly wisdome ment,
> Which not from Nature, and our selues proceedes,
> But is from God, immediately sent,
> (For in our selues, how little goodness breedes)
> That threefold power of the Soule againe
> Resembling God, resideth in our braine. (188)

Invoking Minerva redemptress as an image of divine wisdom, Peacham implies the "via prudentiae" of the medieval sapiential tradition: the infusion or "inspirationem Sapientiae" (the in-breathing of Sapientia), as Hildegard of Bingen puts it in her sequence "O ignis Spiritus Paracliti." We perhaps also catch an intertextual glimpse – fleeting though it may be – of the medieval theory of the arts as restorative of the divine likeness in the human soul.

These appearances of Minerva in Peacham's *Minerva Britanna* and Jasper Heywood's preface to *Thyestes* reflect the medieval and classical traditions from which they derive. Like many of their medieval predecessors, neither Peacham and company nor Heywood felt compelled to explicate the imagery *per se*: they assumed readers would understand the references. In a similar way, and as a final instance, Philip Ayres (1638–1712) plays off the Ovidian theme of Minerva's alliance with Venus in his 1683 *Cupids addresse to the Ladies*, an emblem book explicating love through a series of images and brief verse epigrams in Latin, English, Italian, and French. In Emblem 1, entitled "The Marvellous Seed of Love," we find an opening with a full-page image depicting Cupid sowing seeds in a field with little heads sprouting from the ground on the left page and an allusion to Minerva *magistra* and redemptress in the text on the right, the English version of which reads,

> Strange Power of Love thus to transforme our Parts!
> It gives new Souls & does our wits improve;
> Confesse hereafter that the Queen of Arts
> Sprung from Love's seed not from ye Brain of Jove.[9]

Addressing the reader directly, and explicating the image (clarifying, anyway, that the little sprouting heads depict souls), the text's persona demands a confession from the addressee: Minerva *magistra* and redemptress did not come from Jove's head but from Love's seed. In an Ovid-like gesture, this strange text insistently turns Minerva topsy-turvy as it celebrates Love's equally strange power. Together Peacham, Heywood, and Ayres demonstrate yet another set of intertextual iterations of Minerva's post-classical reception and transformation.

Similar to these later English writers briefly discussed here, the medieval writers examined in this study did not compose in a cultural or literary vacuum. Their intertextual reading practices informed and shaped their compositions. As they examined and developed ideas about wisdom through Minerva imagery, they

---

tri-partite emblem structure: *superscriptio* (motto or title), *pictura* (image), *subscriptio* (epigram or text). See Chardin, "A New Historicist Reading," 637–41; and Stritmatter, "Triangular Numbers," 89–90.

[9] Ayres, *Cupids addresse to the Ladies*, [9–10].

received multivalent aspects of the goddess from antique culture and transformed them for their own uses, collectively presenting several facets of Minerva to their audiences: presentations that likewise invited careful reading and engagement. And their invitation to their primary audience to read intertextually extends to us today as we engage in reception ourselves. Minerva's multifaceted appearances, the variety of her imagery, suggest a need for attentive reading and careful analysis when encountering the goddess of wisdom in medieval literature. If not attentive and careful, we twenty-first-century readers may stumble in the same way Ovid suggested of Augustus and misread her appearances in the literature. Being sensitive to the distinct, at times competing, traditions of Minerva imagery in medieval texts helps us examine closely her role in a given tradition as well as her specific appearance in each text. Such careful intertextual readings foster a fuller understanding of her various poetic meanings. This analysis of Minerva as redemptress, mistress of the liberal arts, patroness of princes, idol, and Venus' ally deepens our understanding of the figure of Minerva in the unique contexts of the several medieval texts examined here, from Bernard Silvestris' *Cosmographia* to Charles d'Orléans *Fortunes Stabilnes*, even as they in turn help inform and shape our understanding of medieval classicism.

Bibliography

Primary Sources

Manuscripts

Cambridge, Corpus Christi College Ms. 61
Cambridge, Corpus Christi College Ms. 406
Cambridge, Trinity College Ms. R.3.19
Cambridge, Trinity College Ms. R.3.21
Cambridge, Trinity College Ms. R.14.9
Cambridge, University Library Ms. F.f.6.33
Cambridge, University Library Ms. Gg.4.27
Cambridge, University Library Ms. K.k.6.26
Cambridge, University Library Ms. Mm.1.18
Chartres, Bibliotheque Municipale Ms. 497. HMML microfilm
Cologny, Foundation Martin Bodmer, Cod. Bodmer 86. http://www.ecodices.unifr.ch/en/fmb/cb-0086
Cologny, Foundation Martin Bodmer, Cod. Bodmer 87. http://www.e-codices.unifr.ch/en/fmb/cb-0087
Edinburgh, National Library of Scotland, Adv. Ms. 35.6.7
John Rylands University Library English Ms. 1
Leiden, Leiden University Vossius Germ. Gall. Q.9
London, British Library Ms. Additional 29729
London, British Library Ms. Harley 682
London, British Library Ms. Harley 2251
London, British Library Ms. Harley 4431
London, British Library Ms. Royal 18 D II
Oxford, Bodleian Library Ms. Arch. Selden. B.24
Oxford, Bodleian Library Ms. Digby 222
Oxford, Bodleian Library Ms. Fairfax 16

Printed Books and Editions

Abelard, Peter. "Abelard's Letter of Consolation to a Friend (*Historia calamitatum*)." Edited by J.T. Muckle. *Mediaeval Studies* 12 (1950): 163–213.
Adelard of Bath. *Conversations with His Nephew: On the Same and the Different, Questions on Natural Science, and On Birds*. Edited and translated by Charles Burnett et al. CMC 9. Cambridge: Cambridge University Press, 1998.

Aeschylus. *Oresteia: Agamemnon; Libation Bearers; Eumenides*. Edited and translated by Alan H. Sommerstein. LCL 146. Cambridge, MA: Harvard University Press, 2009.

Alan of Lille. *Anticlaudianus*. Edited by R. Bossuat. Textes Philosophiques du Moyen Age 1. Paris: Libraire Philosophique J. Vrin, 1955.

—. *De planctu Naturae*. Edited by Nikolaus M. Häring. *Studi Medievali* ser. 3 (1978): 797–879.

Alcuin of York. *De Dialectica*. In *Opera Omnia*, vol. 2, cols. 949–75. Edited by J.-P. Migne. PL 101. Paris: Migne, 1863.

—. *De orthographia*. In *Opera Omnia*, vol. 2, cols. 902–19. Edited by J.-P. Migne. PL 101. Paris: Migne, 1863.

—. *Dialogus de rhetorica et virtutibus*. In *Opera Omnia*, vol. 2, cols. 919–49. Edited by J.-P. Migne. PL 101. Paris: Migne, 1863.

—. *Grammatica*. In *Opera Omnia*, vol. 2, cols. 849–902. Edited by J.-P. Migne. PL 101. Paris: Migne, 1863.

—. *Liber sacramentarum*. In *Opera Omnia*, vol. 2, cols. 445–65. Edited by J.-P. Migne. PL 101. Paris: Migne, 1863.

Alexander de Villedieu. *Doctrinale*. Edited by Theodore Reichling. Monumenta Germaniae Paedagogica 12. Berlin: A. Hofmann, 1893.

Andreas Capellanus. *De arte honeste amandi (On Love)*. Edited and translated by P.G. Walsh. London: Duckworth, 1982.

Apollodorus. *The Library*. Edited and translated by J.G. Frazer. LCL 121, 122. Cambridge, MA: Harvard University Press, 1976, 1979.

Apuleius. *De deo Socratis*. The Latin Library. http://www.thelatinlibrary.com/apuleius.html.

Aquinas, Thomas. *Summa Theologiae*. 3 vols. Edited by Peter Caramello. Rome: Marietta, 1952–6.

Aratus. *Phaenomena*. *Callimachus:* Hymns and Epigrams; *Lycophron:* Alexandra; *Aratus:* Phaenomena. Edited and translated by A. W. Mair and G. R. Mair. LCL 129. Cambridge, MA: Harvard University Press, 1921.

Aristotle. *Poetics*. In *Aristotle:* Poetics. *Longinus:* On the Sublime. *Demetrius:* On Style, 27–141. Edited and translated by Stephen Halliwell; W. Hamilton Fyfe and Donald A. Russell; Doreen C. Innes and W. Rhys Roberts. LCL 199. Cambridge, MA: Harvard University Press, 1995.

The Assembly of Gods. Edited by Jane Chance. Kalamazoo, MI: Medieval Institute, 1999.

The Assembly of Gods. Edited by Oscar Lovell Triggs. English Studies 1. Chicago: University of Chicago Press, 1895.

The Assembly of Gods. London: Wynkyn de Worde, c.1498. *STC* 17005. EEBO.

The Assembly of Gods. London: Wynkyn de Worde, c.1500. *STC* 17007. EEBO.

The Assembly of Gods. London: Wynkyn de Worde, 1500. *STC* 17006. EEBO.

The Assembly of Gods. London: Richard Pynson, c.1505. *STC* 17007.5. EEBO.

The Assembly of Gods. London: John Skot, c.1530. *STC* 17007a. EEBO.

The Assembly of Ladies. In *The Floure and Leaf, The Assembly of Ladies, The Isle of Ladies*, 29–62. Edited by Derek Pearsall. Kalamazoo, MI: Medieval Institute, 1990.

Augustine. *Confessions*. Edited by James J. O'Donnell. Oxford: Oxford University Press, 1992. *The* Confessions *of Augustine: An Electronic Edition*. http://www.stoa.org/hippo/.

—. *De civitate Dei*. The Latin Library. http://www.thelatinlibrary.com/august.html.

—. *De doctrina Christiana*. In *Omnia Opera*, vol. 3, cols. 16–121. Edited by J.-P. Migne. PL 34. Paris: Migne, 1865.

—. *De Ordine*. In *Omnia Opera*, vol. 1, cols. 977–1020. Edited by J.-P. Migne. PL 32. Paris: Migne, 1877.

—. *De Trinitate. The Trinity.* Translated by Stephen McKenna. Fathers of the Church 45. Washington, DC: Catholic University of America Press, 1963.

—. "Letter 1*A." In *Letters*, 14–16. Vol. 6. Translated by Robert B. Eno. Fathers of the Church 81. Washington, DC: Catholic University of America Press, 1989.

Ayres, Philip. *Cupids addresse to the Ladies. Emblemata Amatoria, Emblems of Love, Embleme d'Amore, Emblemes d'Amour.* London: R. Bently, S. Tidmarch, 1683.

[Baebius Italicus]. *Ilias Latina.* The Latin Library. http://www.thelatinlibrary.com/ilias.html.

Benedict of Nursia. *Regula. RB 1980: The Rule of St. Benedict in Latin and English.* Edited and translated by Timothy Fry. Collegeville, MN: Liturgical Press, 1981.

Benjamin Minor. In The Cloud of Unknowing *and Related Treatises on Contemplative Prayer*, 129–45. Edited by Phyllis Hodgson. Analecta Cartusiana 3. Exeter: Catholic Records, 1984.

Bernard of Clairvaux. *Tractatus de diligendo Deo.* In *Opera Omnia*, vol. 1, cols. 973–99. Edited by J.-P. Migne. PL 182. Paris: Migne, 1859.

—. "In festo Annunciationis Beatae Mariae Virginis: Sermo I." In *Opera Omnia*, vol. 2, cols. 383–90. Edited by J.-P. Migne. PL 183. Paris: Migne, 1859.

Bernard Silvestris. *The Commentary on Martianus Capella's De Nuptiis Philologiae et Mercurii Attributed to Bernard Silvestris.* Edited by Haijo Jan Westra. Studies and Texts 80. Toronto: PIMS, 1986.

—. *Commentum quod dicitur Bernardi Silvestris super sex libros Eneidos Virgilii.* Edited by Julian Ward Jones and Elizabeth Frances Jones. Lincoln: University of Nebraska Press, 1977.

—. *Cosmographia.* Edited by Peter Dronke. Textus Minores 53. Leiden: Brill, 1978.

Bersuire, Pierre. *Reductiorium morale, Liber XV: Ovidius maralizatus, cap. I: De formis figurisque deorum.* Edited by J. Engels. Utrecht: Instituut voor Laat Latijn der Rijksuniversiteit, 1966.

—. Metamorphosis Ovidiana Moraliter ... Explanata *and* Libellus. New York: Garland, 1979.

Biblia Sacra: Iuxta Vulgatam Versionem. 4th ed. Edited by Robert Weber et al. Stuttgart: Deutsche Bibelgesellschaft, 1994.

Boccaccio, Giovanni. *Amorosa Visione.* Bilingual edition. Translated by Robert Hollander, Timothy Hampton, and Margherita Frankel. Introduced by Vittore Branca. Hanover, NH: University Press of New England, 1986.

—. *De mulieribus claris* [*On Famous Women*]. Edited and translated by Virginia Brown. Cambridge, MA: Harvard University Press, 2001.

—. *Il Filostrato.* In *The Story of Troilus.* Translated by R.K. Gordon. MART 2. Toronto: University of Toronto Press, 1978.

—. *Genealogie Deorum Gentilium Libri.* 2 vols. Edited by Vincenzo Romano. Bari: Gius Laterza & Figli, 1951.

—. *Teseida.* Edited by Salvatore Battaglia. Firenze: G.C. Sansoni, 1938.

Bodel, Jean. *La Chanson des Saxons.* Edited by Michel Francisque. Paris: Techener, 1839.

Boethius. *De consolatione Philosophiae (Philosophiae consolationis).* Edited by William Weinberger. CSEL 67. Vindobonae [New York]: Hoelder-Pichler-Tempsky, 1934.

Bonaventure. *Commentaria in quatuor libros sententiarum Magistri Petri Lombardi Tomus I: in primum librum Sententiarum. Opera Omni*, vol. 1. Quaracchi: Ex typographia Collegii S. Monaventurae, 1882.

—. *De reductione artium ad theologiam*, 319–25. *Opera Omnia*, vol. 5. Quaracchi: Ex typographia Collegii S. Monaventurae, 1891.

Carmina Burana. Edited by Alfons Hilka and Otto Schumann. Vol. 1. Heidelberg: Winter, 1941.
Cassiodorus, Marcus Aurelius. *Institutiones divinarum et humanarum. Opera Omnia*, vol. 2, cols. 1105–219. Edited by J.-P. Migne. PL 70. Paris: Migne, 1865.
—. *Variarum libri XII*. The Latin Library http://www.thelatinlibrary.com/cassiodorus.html.
The Castle of Perseverance. In *The Macro Plays*. Edited by Mark Eccles. EETS OS 262. London: Oxford University Press, 1969. 1–111.
Caxton, William, trans. *The Recuyell of the Historyes of Troye*. By Raoul Lefevre. Bruges: William Caxton, 1473. EEBO.
Charles d'Orléans. *Fortunes Stabilnes: Charles of Orleans's English Book of Love*. Edited by Mary-Jo Arn. MRTS 138. Binghamton, NY: Center for Medieval and Early Renaissance Studies, 1994.
—. *The French Chansons of Charles D'Orleans: with the corresponding Middle English chansons*. Edited and translated by Sarah Spence. Garland Library of Medieval Literature 46, ser. A. New York: Garland, 1986.
—. *Love's Renewal. Fifteenth-Century English Dream Poems*, 158–94. Edited by Julia Boffey. Oxford: Oxford University Press, 2005.
—. *Poetry of Charles d'Orléans and His Circle: A Critical Edition of BnF MS. fr. 25458, Charles d'Orléans's Personal Manuscript*. Edited by John Fox and Mary-Jo Arn. Translated by R. Barton Palmer. Contribution by Stephanie A.V.G. Klamath. MRTS 383/ASMAR 34. Tempe: ACMRS; Turnhout: Brepols, 2010.
Chaucer, Geoffrey. *The Riverside Chaucer*. 3rd ed. Edited by Larry D. Benson et al. Boston: Houghton Mifflin, 1987.
Chepman, Walter, and Androw Myllar. *The Chepman and Myllar Prints: Digitised Facsimiles with Introduction, Headnotes, and Transcriptions*. General editor Sally Mapstone. Edinburgh: Scottish Text Society and the National Library of Scotland, 2008. DVD-ROM.
Christine de Pizan. *Epistre Othea*. Edited by Gabriella Parussa. Geneve: Droz, 1999.
Cicero. *De natura deorum; Academica*. Edited and translated by H. Rackham. LCL 268. Cambridge, MA: Harvard University Press, 1933.
—. *De officiis*. Edited and translated by Walter Miller. LCL 30. London: Heinemann, 1968.
—. *De oratore*. 2 vols. Edited and translated by E.W. Sutton and H. Rackham. LCL 348, 349. Cambridge, MA: Harvard University Press, 1988, 1982.
—. *Tusculan Disputations*. 2nd ed. Edited and translated by J.E. King. LCL 141. London: Heinemann, 1950.
Clanvowe, Sir John. *The Two Ways*. In *The Works of Sir John Clanvowe*, 57–80. Edited by V.J. Scattergood. Totowa, NJ: Rowman and Littlefield, 1975.
Copeland, Rita, and Ineke Sluiter, eds. *Medieval Grammar and Rhetoric: Language Arts and Literary Theory, AD 300–1475*. Oxford: Oxford University Press, 2009.
The Court of Sapience. Edited by E. Ruth Harvey. Toronto Medieval Texts and Translations 2. Toronto: University of Toronto Press, 1984.
The Court of Sapience. Edited by Robert Spindler. Beitrage zur Englischen Philologie 6. Leipzig: Verlag von Bernhard Tauchnitz, 1927.
The Court of Sapience. London: William Caxton, 1480. EEBO.
The Court of Sapience. London: Wynkyn de Worde, 1510. EEBO.
Dante Alighieri. *The Divine Comedy*. 6 vols. Edited and translated by Charles S. Singleton. Bollingen Series 80. Princeton: Princeton University Press, 1970.

—. *De vulgari eloquentia*. Edited by Pio Rajna. Florence: Soceità Dantesca Italiana, 1960. Digital copy at Princeton Dante Project: http://etcweb.princeton.edu/dante/pdp/vulgari.html.
—. "The Letter to Can Grande." In *Literary Criticism of Dante Alighieri*, 95–111. Translated by Robert S. Heller. Lincoln: University of Nebraska Press, 1973.
Dares Phrygius. *De excidio Troiae historia*. Edited by Ferdinand Meister. Leipzig: Teubner, 1873.
The Debate of the Body and Soul. In *Medieval English Literature*, 603–19. Edited by Thomas J. Garbaty. Lexington, MA: Heath, 1984.
De deorum imaginibus libellus. In *Auctores Mythographi Latini*, 896–938. Edited by Augustino van Staveren. Amsterdam: J. Wetstenium and G. Smith, 1742.
De septem septenis. In *Johannes Saresberiensis: Opera omnia*, cols. 945–64. J.-P. Migne. PL 199. Paris: Migne, 1855.
Dictys Cretensis. *Ephemeridos Belli Troiani*. Edited by Werner Eisenhut. Leipzig: Teubner, repr. 1973.
The Didache, The Epistle of Barnabas, The Epistles and the Martydom of St. Polycarp, The Fragments of Papias, The Epistle to Diogenetus. Translated by James A Kleist. Ancient Christian Writers: The Works of the Fathers in Translation 6. Westminster, MD: Newman Press, 1948.
Douglas, Gavin. *The Palice of Honoure*. In *The Shorter Poems of Gavin Douglas*, 1–133. 2nd ed. Edited by Priscilla Bawcutt. STS 4th ser. 3. Edinburgh: STS, 2003.
—. *The Palis of Honoure*. London: William Copland, 1553. EEBO.
—. *Ane Treatis callit the Palice of Honour*. London: Henry Charteris, 1579. EEBO.
Dunbar, William. *The Poems of William Dunbar*. Edited by Priscilla Bawcutt. The Association for Scottish Literary Studies 27 and 28. Glasgow: Association for Scottish Literary Studies, 1998.
Dunchad. *Glossae in Martianum*. Edited by Cora E. Lutz. Philological Monographs 12. Lancaster, PA: American Philological Association, 1944.
Eutropius. *Breviarium ab urbe condita*. In *Eutropi breviarium ab urbe condita cum versionibus Graecis et Pauli Landolfique*, 8–182. Edited by H. Droysen. MGH. Berlin: Wiedmannnos, 1979.
Evrart de Conty. *Livre des Eschez Amoureux Moralisés*. Edited by Françoise Guichard-Tesson and Bruno Roy. Bibliothèque de Moyen Français 2. Montréal: Ceres, 1993.
Excidium Troiae. Edited by E. Bagby Atwood and Virgil K. Whitaker. MAAP 44. Cambridge, MA: Medieval Academy of America, 1944.
Fulgentius. *Expositio Virgilianae continentiae secundum philosophos moralis*. The Latin Library. http://www.thelatinlibrary.com/fulgentius.html.
—. *Mitologiae (Mitologiarum libri tres)*. The Latin Library. http://www.thelatinlibrary.com/fulgentius.html.
Galen. "Exhortation to Study the Arts (*Exhortatio ad Artes Addiscendas*)." Translated by Joseph Walsh. *Medical Life* 37 (1930): 507–29. E-copy available at *Medicina Antiqua*: http://www.ucl.ac.uk/~ucgajpd/medicina%20antiqua/tr_GalExhort.html.
Geoffrey of Monmouth. *The Historia regum Britannie of Geoffrey of Monmouth, I: Bern, Burgerbibliothek, Ms. 568*. Edited by Neil Wright. Cambridge: D.S. Brewer, 1984.
Geoffrey of Vinsauf. *Poetria Nova*. In *Les Artes Poétiques du XIIe et du XIIIe Siècle*, 194–262. Edited by Edmond Faral. Paris: Libraire Honoré Champion, 1962.
Glossae aevi Carolini in Libros I–II Martiani Capellae De nuptiis Philologiae et Mercurii. Edited by Sinéad O'Sullivan. CCCM 237. Turnhout: Brepols, 2010.
Godfrey of St. Victor. *Fons Philosophiae*. Edited by Pierre Michaud-Quantin. Analecta mediaevalis Namurcensia 8. Louvain: Namur, 1956.

Gower, John. *Confessio Amantis*. In *The English Works of John Gower*. 2 vols. Edited by G.C. Macauley. EETS ES 81, 82. London: Kegan Paul, 1900, 1901.
Gregory of Tours. *Historia Francorum (Libri Historiarum)*. The Latin Library. http://www.thelatinlibrary.com/gregorytours.html.
Grosseteste, Robert. *The Castle of Love*. In *The Minor Poems of the Vernon Manuscript*, 355–94. Edited by Carl Horstmann. EETS OS 117, part 1. London: Kegan Paul, 1892.
Guido delle Colonne. *Historia destructionis Troiae*. Edited by Nathaniel Edward Griffin. MAAP 26. Cambridge, MA: Medieval Academy of America, 1936.
Guillaume de Lorris and Jean de Meun. *Le Roman de la Rose*. 5 vols. Edited by Ernest Langlois. Paris: Librairie de Firmin-Didot, 1914, 1920, 1921, 1922, 1924.
Hawes, Stephen. *The Example of Vertu*. In *The Minor Poems*, 1–71. Edited by Florence W. Gluck and Alice B. Morgan. EETS OS 271. London: Oxford University Press, 1974.
—. *The Example of Vertu*. London: Wynkyn de Worde, 1504. EEBO.
—. *The Example of Vertu*. London: Wynkyn de Worde, 1530. EEBO.
—. *The Pastime of Pleasure*. Edited by William Edward Mead. EETS OS 173. London: Oxford University Press, 1928.
—. *The Pastime of Pleasure*. London: Tottel, 1555. EEBO.
—. *The Pastime of Pleasure*. London: Wayland, 1554. EEBO.
Hebrew Bible. Ancient Hebrew Research Center. https://www.ancient-hebrew.org/hebrewbible/Psalms_96.html.
Henry of Kirkestede. *Catalogus de libris autenticis et apocrifis*. Edited by Richard H. Rouse and Mary A. Rouse. London: British Library, 2004.
Henryson, Robert. *The Poems and Fables of Robert Henryson*. Edited by H. Harvey Wood. Edinburgh: Mercat Press, 1978.
Herrad of Hohenbourg (Landsberg). *Hortus deliciarum*. 2 vols. Edited by Rosalie Green et al. Studies of the Warburg Institute 36. London: Warburg Institute, 1979.
Hesiod. *Theogony; Works and Days; Testimonia*. Edited and translated by Glenn W. Most. LCL 57. Cambridge, MA: Harvard University Press, 2007.
Heywood, Jasper. *The Seconde Tragedie of Seneca entituled Thyestes faithfully Englished by Jasper Heywood fellow of Alsolne College in Oxforde*. London: Thomas Betthelettes, 1560. EEBO.
—. *Thyestes*. In *Jasper Heywood and His Translations of Seneca's Troas, Thyestes, and Hercules Furens*, 89–196. Edited by H. De Vocht. Louvain: A Uystpruyst, 1913.
Hilary of Poitiers. *De Trinitate (The Trinity)*. Translated by Stephen McKenna. Fathers of the Church 25. Washington, DC: Catholic University of America Press, 1954.
Hildegard of Bingen. *Explanatio Symboli Sancti Athanasii*. Opera Omnia, cols. 1066–81. Edited by J.-P. Migne. PL 197. Paris: Migne, 1855.
—. *Scivias*. Edited by Adelgundis Führkötter and Angela Carlevaris. CCCM 43–43a. Belgium: Turnhout, 1978.
—. *Symphonia: A Critical Edition of the Symphonia armonie celestium revelationum*. Edited and translated by Barbara Newman. Ithaca, NY: Cornell University Press, 1988.
Historia Augusta. 3 vols. Edited and translated by David Magie. LCL 139, 140, 263. London: Heinemann, 1921, 1924, 1932.
Homer. *The Iliad*. 2 vols. Edited and translated by A.T. Murray. LCL 170, 171. London: Heinemann, 1924, 1925.
—. *The Odyssey*. 2 vols. Edited and translated by A.T. Murray; revised by George E. Dimock. LCL 104, 105. Cambridge, MA: Harvard University Press, 1995.
Homeric Epigrams. In *Hesiod, The Homeric Hymns, and Homerica*, 465–77. LCL 57. Edited and translated by Hugh G. Evelyn-White. London: Heinemann, 1920.

Homeric Hymns, Homeric Apocrypha, Lives of Homer. Edited and translated by Martin L. West. LCL 496. Cambridge, MA: Harvard University Press, 2003.
Horace. *Ars poetica.* In *Horace Satires, Epistles, Ars Poetica,* 442–89. Edited and translated by H.R. Fairclough. LCL 194. Cambridge, MA: Harvard University Press, 1929.
Hugh of Fouilloy. *Aviarium.* Edited by Willene B. Clark. MRTS 80. Binghamton, NY: Center for Medieval and Early Renaissance Studies, 1992.
Hugh of St. Victor. *Didascalicon: De studio Legendi.* Edited by Charles Henry Buttimer. Washington, DC: Catholic University of America Press, 1939.
Isidore of Seville. *Etymologiarum sive Originum Libri XX.* Edited by W.M. Lindsay. Oxford: Clarendon Press, 1911.
Jacques de Longuyon. Extract from "Les Vœux du paon." In *The Parlement of the Thre Ages,* 121–5. Edited by Israel Gollancz. Roxburghe Club. London: Nichols, 1897.
James I of Scotland. *The Kingis Quair.* Edited by John Norton-Smith. Oxford: Clarendon Press, 1971.
—. *The Kingis Quair.* In *Fifteenth-Century English Dream Visions,* 90–157. Edited by Julia Boffey. Oxford: Oxford University Press, 2005.
—. *Poetical Remains of James the First, King of Scotland.* Edited by William Tytler. Edinburgh: J. & E. Balfour, 1783.
John of Hauville. *Architrenius.* Edited and translated by Winthrop Wetherbee. CMC 3. Cambridge: Cambridge University Press, 1994.
John of Salisbury. *Metalogicon.* Edited by J.B. Hall, with K.S.B. Keats-Rohan. CCCM 98. Turnholt: Brepols, 1991.
John Scotus Eriugena. *Annotationes in Marcianum.* Edited by Cora E. Lutz. MAAP 34. Cambridge, MA: Medieval Academy of America, 1939.
Joseph of Exeter. *Frigii Daretis Yliados libri sex.* In *Joseph Iscanus: Werke und Briefe,* 77–211. Edited by Ludwig Gompf. Mittellateinische Studien und Texte 4. Leiden: Brill, 1970.
Juan Rodríguez del Padrón. *Siervo libre de amor.* Edited by Enric Dolz. Anexos de la Revista Lemir, 2004. http://parnaseo.uv.es/Lemir/Textos/Siervo/Completa.pdf.
Lactantius. *Divinae Institutiones.* In *Opera Omnia: Pars I,* 1–672. Edited by Samuel Brandt. CSEL 19. Prague: Tempsky, 1890.
[Lactantius]. *De ave phoenice.* The Latin Library. http://www.thelatinlibrary.com/ave.phoen.html.
Langland, William. *Piers Plowman: The B-Version.* Edited by G. Kane and E.T. Donaldson. London: Athlone, 1975.
L'Art d'Amours: Traduction et commentaire de l'"Ars amatoria" d'Ovide. Edited by Bruno Roy. Leiden: Brill, 1974.
Les Eschéz d'Amours: A Critical Edition of the Poem and Its Latin Glosses. Edited by Gregory Heyworth and Daniel E. O'Sullivan, with Frank Coulson. MRAT 10. Leiden: Brill, 2013.
Liber Usualis. Edited by the Benedictines of Solesmes. Tournai: Desclée, 1953; republ. Great Falls, MT: St Bonaventure, 1997.
Love, Nicholas. *The Mirrour of the Blessed Lyf of Jesu Christ.* Edited by James Hogg and Laurence F. Powell. Analecta Cartusiana 91. Salzburg: Institut fur Anglistik und Amerikanistik, 1989.
Lucan. *De bello civili.* Edited and translated by A.E. Houseman. LCL 220. Cambridge, MA: Harvard University Press, 1928.
Lydgate, John. *This boke called the Te[m]ple of glasse, is in many places amended, and late diligently imprinted.* London: Thomas Berthelet, 1529. EEBO.
—. *Here begynneth the Temple of glas.* Westminster: Wynkyn de Worde, 1495. EEBO.

—. *Here begynneth the Temple of glas*. London: Wynkyn de Worde, 1506. EEBO.
—. *The History, Sege, and Destruction of Troy*. London: Thomas Marshe, 1555. EEBO.
—. *The History, Sege, and Destruction of Troy*. London: Richard Pynson, 1513. EEBO.
—. *Reson and Sensuallyte*. Edited by Ernst Sieper. EETS ES 84, 89. London: Kegan Paul, 1901, 1903.
—. *The Temple of Glass*. In *Fifteenth-Century English Dream Visions: An Anthology*, 15–89. Edited by Julia Boffey. Oxford: Oxford University Press, 2003.
—. *The Temple of Glas*. In *John Lydgate: Poems*, 67–112. Edited by John Norton-Smith. Oxford: Clarendon Press, 1966.
—. *The temple of glas*. Westminster: William Caxton, 1477. EEBO.
—. *The temple of glas*. London: Rycharde Pynson, 1503. EEBO.
—. *Troy Book*. Edited by Henry Bergen. EETS ES 97, 103, 106. London: Kegan Paul, 1906, 1908, 1910.
Lyndsay, David. *The Works of Sir David Lindsay of the Mount 1490–1555*. Edited by Douglas Hamer. 4 vols. STS ser. 3. Edinburgh: Scottish Text Society, 1931–6.
Macrobius. *In somnium Scipionis commentarii*. Edited by Valentia Rinaldi and Simona Rota. DigilibLT Project, 2014. http://digiliblt.lett.unipmn.it/xtf/view?query=;brand=default;docId=dlt000338/dlt000338.xml.
Major, John. *Historia Maioris Britanniae*. Paris: Iodocus Badious Ascensius, 1521.
Map, Walter. *De Nugis Curialium*. Edited by M.R. Rhodes. Anecdota Oxoniensia: Texts, Documents, and Extracts, Medieval and Modern Series 14. Oxford: Clarendon Press, 1914.
Martial. *Epigrams*. 2 vols. Edited and translated by Walter C.A. Ker. LCL 94, 95. London: Heinemann, 1925, 1920.
Martianus Capella. *De nuptiis Philologiae et Mercurii*. Edited by James Willis. Leipzig: Teubner, 1983.
Maximianus. *The Elegies of Maximianus*. Edited by Richard Webster. Princeton: Princeton University Press, 1900.
Medieval Literary Theory and Criticism c.1100–c.1375: The Commentary-Tradition. Edited by A.J. Minnis and A.B. Scott. Oxford: Clarendon, 1988.
Meditations on the Life of Christ: An Illustrated Manuscript of the Fourteenth Century. Edited and translated by Isa Ragusa and Rosalie B. Green. Princeton: Princeton University Press, 1961.
Meister der Wiener Gregorplatte. "HL. Gregor mit Schreibern." Vienna: Kunsthistorisches Museum. https://www.khm.at/objektdb/?query=Gregorplatte.
Methamorphosis Golye episcopi. Edited by R.B.C. Huygens. *Studi Medievali* 3/3 (1962): 764–72.
Neckam, Alexander. *Commentum super Martianum*. Edited by Christopher J. McDonough. Millennio Medievale 64, Testi 15. Firenze: SISMEL, 2006.
—. *Novus Avianus*. In *Les fabulists Latins, 3: Avianus et ses anciens imitateurs*, 222–34, 462–7. Edited by Leopold Hervieux. Paris, 1895.
The N-Town Play. Edited by Stephen Spector. EETS SS 11, 12. Oxford: Oxford University Press, 1991.
Ovid. *The Art of Love and Other Poems*. Edited and translated by J.H. Mozley, revised by G.P. Goold. LCL 232. Cambridge, MA: Harvard University Press, 1979.
—. *Fasti*. 2nd ed. Edited and translated by James G. Frazer, revised by G.P. Gould. LCL 253. Cambridge, MA: Harvard University Press, 1989.
—. *Heroides; Amores*. 2nd ed. Edited and translated by Grant Showerman, revised by G.P. Gould. LCL 41. Cambridge, MA: Harvard University Press, 1977.

—. *Metamorphoses*. 2nd ed. Edited and translated by Frank Justus Miller, revised by G.P. Gould. LCL 42, 43. Cambridge, MA: Harvard University Press, 1984.

—. *Tristia; Ex Ponto*. 2nd ed. Edited and translated by A.L. Wheeler, revised by G.P. Gould. LCL 151. Cambridge, MA: Harvard University Press, 1988.

The Owl and the Nightingale. In *Medieval English Literature*, 556–602. Edited by Thomas J. Garbaty. Lexington, MA: Heath, 1984.

Parlement of the Thre Ages. Edited by M.Y. Offord. EETS OS 246. London: Oxford University Press, 1959.

Paulinus of Nola. *Carmina*. Edited by G. de Hartel. CSEL 30.2. Prague: Tempsky, 1894.

Peacham, Henry. *Minerva Britanna or a Garden of Heroical Deuises, furnished, and adorned with* Emblemes *and* Impresa's *of sundery natures, Newly devised*, moralized, and published. London: Wa. Dight, 1612.

Pervigilium Veneris. In *Catullus, Tibullus, Pervigilium Veneris*, 341–67. Edited and translated by J.W. MacKail. LCL 6. Cambridge, MA: Harvard University Press, 1976.

Petrarch, Francesco. *Africa*. Edited by L. Pingaud. Paris: Apud Ernest Thorin, 1872.

—. *Rerum Vulgarium Fragmenta. Petrarch's Songbook*. Edited by Gianfranco Contini; trans. James Wyatt Cook. Binghamton, NY: Medieval and Renaissance Texts and Studies, 1996.

Plato. *Lysis; Symposium; Gorgias*. Edited and translated by W.R.M. Lamb. LCL 166. Cambridge, MA: Harvard University Press, 1925.

—. *Republic*. 2 vols. Edited and translated by Chris Emlyn-Jones and William Preddy. LCL 237, 276. Cambridge, MA: Harvard University Press, 2013.

Prosper of Aquitaine. *Prosperi Aquitani Opera*. Edited by P. Callens and M. Gastaldo. CCSL 68a. Turnholt: Brepols, 1972.

Prudentius. *Aurelii Prudentii Clementis Carmina*. Edited by Maurice P. Cunningham. CCSL 126. Turnholt: Brepols, 1966.

Quintilian. *The Institutio Oratoria of Quintilian*. 4 vols. Edited and translated by H.E. Butler. LCL 124, 125, 126, 127. London: Heinemann, 1920, 1921, 1922.

Quintus Curtius Rufus. *History of Alexander*. 2 vols. Edited and translated by J.C. Rolfe. LCL 368, 369. Cambridge, MA: Harvard University Press, 1946.

Rabanus Maurus. *De Clericorum Institutione*. In *Omnia Opera*, vol. 1, cols. 297–420. Edited by J.-P. Migne. PL 107. Paris: Migne, 1864.

—. *De Universo libri viginti duo*. In *Omnia Opera*, vol. 5, cols. 9–614. Edited by J.-P. Migne. PL 111. Paris: Migne, 1864.

Remigius of Auxerre. *Commentum in Martianum Capellam*. Edited by Cora E. Lutz. Vol. 2. Leiden: Brill, 1962.

Richard de Bury. *Philobiblon*. The Latin Library. http://www.thelatinlibrary.com/debury.html.

"The Ruin." In *The Anglo-Saxon Poetic Records: A Collective Edition. III: The Exeter Book*, 227–9. Edited by George Philip Krapp and Elliott Van Kirk Dobbie. New York: Columbia University Press, 1936.

Scrope, Stephen, trans. The Epistle of Othea*: Translated from the French Text of Christine de Pisan*. Edited by Curt F. Buhler. EETS OS 264. London: Oxford University Press, 1970.

Second Vatican Mythographer. *Mythographi Vaticani I et II*, 93–345. Edited by Peter Kulcsar. CCSL 91c. Turnholt: Brepols, 1987.

Secular Lyrics of the XIVth and XVth Centuries. 2nd ed. Edited by Rossell Hope Robbins. Oxford: Clarendon Press, 1955.

Sedulius, Caelius. *Carmen Paschale. Sedulii Opera Omnia*. Edited by J. Huemer. CSEL 10. Vindobonae: C. Gerolidi, 1885.

Seneca the Elder. *Declamations, Volume I: Controversiae, Books 1–6*. Edited and translated by Michael Winterbottom. LCL 463. Cambridge, MA: Harvard University Press, 1974.
Septuagint Bible. Elpenor. http://www.ellopos.net/elpenor/greek-texts/septuagint/.
Sidney, Sir Philip. "Defense of Poesie." In *Literary Criticism from Plato to Dryden*, 406–61. Edited by Allan H. Gilbert. Detroit: Wayne State University Press, 1967.
Skelton, John. *The Book of the Laurel*. Edited by F.W. Brownlow. Newark: University of Delaware Press, 1990.
—. *A Goodly Garlande or Chapelet of Laurell*. London: Richard Faukes, 1523. EEBO.
—. *Speculum Principis*. Edited by F.M. Salter. "Skelton's *Speculum Principis*." *Speculum* 9 (1934): 33–7.
Statius. *Silvae*. In *Statius I*. 1 vol. Edited and translated by D.R. Shakleton Bailey. LCL 206. Cambridge, MA: Harvard University Press, 2003.
—. *Thebaid*. In *Statius II* and *III*. 2 vols. Edited and translated by D.R. Shakleton Bailey. LCL 207, 498. Cambridge, MA: Harvard University Press, 2003.
Suetonius. *De vita Caesarum*. In *Suetonius I* and *II*. 2 vols. Edited and translated by J.C. Rolfe. LCL 31, 38. London: Heinemann, 1924.
Sulpicius Severus. *De vita beati Martini liber unus*. In *Quinti Saeculi Scriptorum Ecclesiasticorum: Opera Omnia*. Edited by J.-P. Migne. PL 20. Paris: Migne, 1845. Cols. 159–76.
Super Thebaiden. In *Fabii Planciadis Fulgentii: Opera*, 180–6. Edited by Rudolf Helm. New York: Teubner, 1898.
Suso, Henry. *Horologium Sapientiae*. Edited by Pius Künzle. Freiburg: Universitätsverlag, 1977.
Tabellae Sulis: Roman Inscribed Tablets of Tin and Lead from the Sacred Spring at Bath. Part 4: *The Temple of Sulis Minerva at Bath, II: Finds from the Sacred Spring*. Edited and translated by R.S.O. Tomlin. OUCA Monograph 16. Oxford: Oxford University Committee for Archaeology, 1988.
Theodulf of Orleans. *Carmina*. In *Poetae Latini aevi Carolin*, vol. 1, 437–581. Edited by Ernest Duemmler. MGH. Berlin: Apud Wiedmannos, 1881.
—. *De libros quos legere solebam*. In *Opera Omnia*, col. 331–3. Edited by J.-P. Migne. PL 105. Paris: Migne, 1851.
—. *De septem liberalibus artibus in quadam pictura depictis*. In *Opera Omnia*, col. 333. Edited by J.-P. Migne. PL 105. Paris: Migne, 1851.
Theophilus. *On Divers Arts*. Translated by John G. Hawthorne and Cyril Stanley Smith. New York: Dover, 1963, 1979.
Third Vatican Mythographer. *De diis gentium et illorum allegoriis*. In *Scriptores rerum mythicarum Latini tres Romae nuper reperti*, 152–256. Edited by George H. Bode. Repr. Hildesheim: Olms, 1968.
Virgil. *Aeneid*. 2 vols. Edited and translated by H.R. Fairclough. Revised by G.P. Gould. LCL 63, 64. Cambridge, MA: Harvard University Press, 1999, 2000.
The Virgilian Tradition: The First Fifteen Hundred Years. Edited by Jan M. Ziolkowski and Michael C.J. Putnam. New Haven: Yale University Press, 2008.
Vitruvius. *On Architecture*. Edited and translated by Frank Granger. LCL 251, 280. Cambridge, MA: Harvard University Press, 1931, 1934.
Walsingham, Thomas. *De Archana Deorum*. Edited by Robert A. van Kluyve. Durham, NC: Duke University Press, 1968.
Walter of Châtillon. *Galteri de Castillione Alexandreis*. Edited by Marvin L Colker. Padua: Antenore, 1978.

Walton, John, trans. *Boethius: De Consolatione Philosophiae*. Edited by Mark Science. EETS OS 170. London: Oxford University Press, 1927.
Wisdom. In *The Macro Plays*, 113–52. Edited by Mark Eccles. EETS OS 262. London: Oxford University Press, 1969.
The Works of Geoffrey Chaucer and The Kingis Quair: *A Facsimile of Bodleian Library, Oxford, MS Arch.Selden.B.24*. Introduced by Julia Boffey and A.S.G. Edwards, with an appendix by B.C. Barker-Benfield. Cambridge: D.S. Brewer, 1997.
Wyer, Robert, trans. *Here foloweth the L. Hyctoryes of Troye: Lepistre de Othea deesse de prudence*. London: Robert Wyer, 1549. EEBO.

Secondary Sources

Abate, Giuseppe. *La Medievale "Piazza Grande" di Assisi*. A cure di Francesco Santucci. Assisi: Accademia Properziana del Subasio, 1986.
Abbott, H. Porter. *The Cambridge Introduction to Narrative*. Cambridge: Cambridge University Press, 2002.
Abray, Lorna Jane. "Imagining the Masculine: Christine de Pizan's Hector, Prince of Troy." In *Fantasies of Troy: Classical Tales and the Social Imaginary in Medieval and Early Modern Europe*, 133–48. Edited by Alan Shepard and Stephen D. Powell. Toronto: Centre for Reformation and Renaissance Studies, 2004.
Adolf, Helen. "The Figure of Wisdom in the Middle Ages." In *Arts libéraux et philosophie au moyen âge: Actes de quatrime contres international de philosophei médiévale*, 429–43. Montréal: Institut d'Etudes Médiévale; Paris: Libraire Philosophique J. Vrin, 1969.
Akbari, Suzanne Conklin. "Ovid and Ovidianism." In *The Oxford History of Classical Reception in English Literature: Volume 1 (800–1558)*, 187–208. Edited by Rita Copeland. Oxford: Oxford University Press, 2016.
—. *Seeing Through the Veil: Optical Theory and Medieval Allegory*. Toronto: University of Toronto Press, 2004.
Alexander, Michael Van Cleave. *The First of the Tudors: A Study of Henry VII and His Reign*. Totowa, NJ: Rowman and Littlefield, 1980.
Allen, Judson B. *The Ethical Poetic of the Later Middle Ages*. Toronto: University of Toronto Press, 1982.
—. "Grammar, Poetic Form, and the Lyric Ego: A Medieval *A Priori*." In *Vernacular Poetics in the Middle Ages*, 199–226. Edited by Lois Ebin. SMC 16. Kalamazoo: Medieval Institute, 1984.
Allen, Peter. *The Art of Love: Amatory Fiction from Ovid to the* Romance of the Rose. Philadelphia: University of Pennsylvania Press, 1992.
Alton, E.H. "Ovid in the Mediaeval Schoolroom." *Hermathena* 94/95 (1960/1): 21–38, 67–82.
The American Heritage Dictionary. 3rd ed. Edited by Anne H. Soukhanov. Boston: Houghton Mifflin, 1992.
The American Heritage Dictionary of Indo-European Roots. 3rd ed. Edited by Calvert Watkins. Boston: Houghton Mifflin, 2011.
Amodio, Mark C. *Writing the Oral Tradition: Oral Poetics and Literate Culture in Medieval England*. Notre Dame: University of Notre Dame Press, 2004.
Anscombe, G.E.M. "The First Person." In *Mind and Language*, 45–65. Edited by Samuel Guttenplan. Oxford: Clarendon Press, 1975.
Armstrong, Rebecca. *Ovid and His Love Poetry*. London: Bloomsbury Academic, 2005.

Arn, Mary-Jo, ed. *Charles d'Orléans in England (1415–1440)*. Cambridge: D.S. Brewer, 2000.
—. Introduction to *Fortunes Stabilnes: Charles of Orleans's English Book of Love*, 1–129. Edited by Mary-Jo Arn, MRTS 138. Binghamton, NY: Center for Medieval and Early Renaissance Studies, 1994.
—. "'Fortunes Stabilness': The English Poems of Charles of Orleans in Their English Context." *Fifteenth-Century Studies* 7 (1983): 1–18.
—. "Poetic Form as a Mirror of Meaning in the English Poems of Charles of Orleans." *Philological Quarterly* 69 (1990): 13–29.
—. *The Poet's Notebook: The Personal Manuscript of Charles d'Orléans (Paris, BnF, MS fr. 25458)*. Texts and Transcriptions: Studies in the History of Manuscripts and Printed Books 3. Turnhout: Brepols, 2008.
—. "The Structure of the English Poems of Charles of Orleans." *Fifteenth-Century Studies* 4 (1981): 17–23.
—. "Two Manuscripts, One Mind: Charles d'Orléans and the Production of Manuscripts in Two Languages (Paris, BN MS fr. 25458 and London, BL MS Harley 682." In *Charles d'Orléans in England (1415–1440)*, 61–78. Edited by Mary-Jo Arn. Cambridge: D.S. Brewer, 2000.
Askins, William. "The Brothers Orléans and Their Keepers." In *Charles d'Orléans in England (1415–1440)*, 27–45. Edited by Mary-Jo Arn. Cambridge: D.S. Brewer, 2000.
Atwood, E. Bagby. "Some Minor Sources of Lydgate's 'Troy' Book." *Studies in Philology* 35 (1938): 25–42.
Auerbach, Erich. "Figura." In *Scenes from the Drama of European Literature*, 11–76. Translated by Ralph Manheim. Theory and History of Literature 9. Minneapolis: University of Minnesota Press, 1984.
—. *Literary Language and Its Public in Late Latin Antiquity and the Middle Ages*. Translated by Ralph Mannheim. Bollingen Series 74. Princeton: Princeton University Press, 1965.
—. *Mimesis: The Representation of Reality in Western Literature*. Translated by Willard R. Trask. Princeton: Princeton University Press, 1968.
Balfour-Melville, E.W.M. *James I, King of Scots 1406–1437*. London: Methuen, 1936.
Balint, Bridget. *Ordering Chaos: The Self and the Cosmos in Twelfth-Century Latin Prosimetrum*. MRAT 3. Leiden: Brill, 2009.
Baltzell, Jane. "Rhetorical 'Amplification' and 'Abbreviation' and the Structure of Medieval Narrative." *Pacific Coast Philology* 2 (1967): 32–9.
Barney, Stephen A., W.J. Lewis, J.A. Beach, and Oliver Berghof. Introduction to *The Etymologies of Isidore of Seville*, 3–28. Translated by Barney et al., with Murial Hall. Cambridge: Cambridge University Press, 2006.
Barnish, S.J.B. "Maximian, Cassiodorus, Boethius, Theodahad: Literature, Philosophy and Politics in Ostrogothic Italy." *Nottingham Medieval Studies* 34 (1990): 16–32.
Barr, Helen. *Socioliterary Practice in Late Medieval England*. Oxford: Oxford University Press, 2001.
Barrington, Candace. "Personas and Performance in Gower's *Confessio Amantis*." *The Chaucer Review* 48 (2014): 414–33.
Bartlett, Robert. *Why Can the Dead Do Such Great Things? Saints and Worshippers from the Martyrs to the Reformation*. Princeton: Princeton University Press, 2013.
Baswell, Christopher. "*Troy Book*: How Lydgate Translates Chaucer into Latin." In *Translation Theory and Practice in the Middle Ages*, 215–37. Edited by Jeanette Beer. SMC 38. Kalamazoo, MI: Medieval Institute, 1997.

Baugh, A.C. *A Literary History of England*. 2nd ed. New York: Appleton-Century-Crofts, 1967.
Baumbach, Manuel, and Silvio Bär, eds. *Brill's Companion to Greek and Latin Epillion and Its Reception*. Leiden: Brill, 2012.
Bawcutt, Priscilla. *Dunbar the Makar*. Oxford: Clarendon Press, 1992.
—. *Gavin Douglas: A Critical Study*. Edinburgh: Edinburgh University Press, 1976.
—. Introduction to *The Palice of Honoure*." In *The Shorter Poems of Gavin Douglas*, xv–lii. 2nd ed. Edited by Priscilla Bawcutt. STS, 5th series 2. Edinburgh: Scottish Text Society, 2003.
—. Introduction to *The Poems of William Dunbar*. Edited by Priscilla Bawcutt. 2 vols. The Association for Scottish Literary Studies 27 and 28. Glasgow: The Association for Scottish Literary Studies, 1998.
—. "Religious Verse in Medieval Scotland." In *A Companion to Medieval Scottish Poetry*, 119–31. Edited by Priscilla Bawcutt and Janet Hadley Williams. Cambridge: D.S. Brewer, 2006.
—. "Scottish Manuscript Miscellanies from the Fifteenth to the Seventeenth Century." In *English Manuscript Studies: 1100–1700*, 46–73. Vol. 12. Edited by Peter Beal and A.S.G. Edwards. London: The British Library, 2005.
Bayless, Martha. *Parody in the Middle Ages: The Latin Tradition*. Ann Arbor: University of Michigan Press, 1996.
Beckwith, John. *Early Medieval Art: Carolingian, Ottonian, Romanesque*. New York: Thames and Hudson, 1969.
Beer, Jeanette. Introduction to *Medieval Translators and Their Craft*, 1–7. Edited by Jeanette Beer. SMC 25. Kalamazoo, MI: Medieval Institute, 1989.
Bennett, H.S. *Chaucer and the Fifteenth Century*. OHEL 2.1. Oxford: Clarendon, 1947.
Bennett, J.A.W. "Gower's 'Honeste Love'." In *Patterns of Love and Courtesy: Essays in Memory of C.S. Lewis*, 107–21. Edited by John Lawlor. London: Arnold, 1966.
—. "A King's Quire." *Poetica* 3 (1975): 1–16.
Benson, C. David. "The Ancient World of John Lydgate's *Troy Book*." *The American Benedictine Review* 24 (1973): 299–312.
—. *Chaucer's* Troilus and Criseyde. London: Unwin Hyman, 1992.
—. "Critic and Poet: What Lydgate and Henryson Did to Chaucer's *Troilus and Criseyde*." *Modern Language Quarterly* 52 (1992): 23–40.
—. *The History of Troy in Middle English Literature: Guido delle Colonne's* Historia Destructionis Troiae *in Medieval England*. Cambridge: D.S. Brewer, 1981.
Benton, John F. "Philology's Search for Abelard in the *Metamorphosis Goliae*." *Speculum* 50 (1975): 199–217.
Black, Robert. *Humanism and Education in Medieval and Renaissance Italy: Tradition and Innovation in Latin Schools from the Twelfth to the Fifteenth Century*. Cambridge: Cambridge University Press, 2001.
Blagg, T.F.C. "The Temple at Bath (Aquae Sulis) in the Context of Classical Temples in the Western European Provinces." *Journal of Roman Archaeology* 3 (1990): 419–30.
Bloomfield, Morton and Charles Dunn. *The Role of the Poet in Early Societies*. Cambridge: D.S. Brewer, 1989.
Boffey, Julia. "Chaucerian Prisoners: The Context of *The Kingis Quair*." In *Chaucer and Fifteenth-Century Poetry*, 84–102. Edited by Julia Boffey and Janet Cowen. King's College London Medieval Studies 5. Exeter: Short Run Press, 1991.
—. "From Manuscript to Print: Continuity and Change." In *A Companion to the Early Printed Book in Britain 1476–1558*, 13–26. Edited by Vincent Gillespie and Susan Powell. Cambridge: D.S. Brewer, 2014.

—. "'Withdrawe Your Hande': The Lyrics of 'The Garland of Laurel' from Manuscript to Print." *Trivium* 31 (1999): 73–85.

—, and A.S.G. Edwards. "Bodleian MS Arch. Selden. B.24: The Genesis and Evolution of a Scottish Poetical Anthology," *Poetica* 60 (2003): 32–46.

—. "Bodleian MS Arch.Selden.B.24 and the 'Scotticization' of Middle English Verse." In *Rewriting Chaucer: Culture, Authority, and the Idea of the Authentic Text, 1400–1602*, 166–85. Edited by Thomas A. Prendergast and Barbara Kline. Columbus: Ohio State University Press, 1999.

—. *A New Index of Middle English Verse*. London: British Library, 2005.

Bokenkotter, Thomas. *A Concise History of the Catholic Church*. Rev. ed. Garden City, NY: Image, 1979.

Bond, Gerald A. "Composing Yourself: Ovid's *Heroides*, Baudri of Bourgeueil and the Problem of Persona." *Mediaevalia* 13 (1989 for 1987): 83–117.

—. "'Iocus Amoris': The Poetry of Baudri of Bourgueil and the Formation of the Ovidian Subculture." *Traditio* 42 (1986): 143–93.

Born, Lester K. "Ovid and Allegory." *Speculum* 9 (1934): 362–79.

Bowder, Diana. *The Age of Constantine and Julian*. New York: Harper, 1978.

Boyarin, Daniel. "Origen as Theorist of Allegory: Alexandrian Contexts." In *The Cambridge Companion to Allegory*, 39–54. Edited by Rita Copeland and Peter T. Struck. Cambridge: Cambridge University Press, 2010.

Bradbury, Nancy Mason. *Writing Aloud: Storytelling in Late Medieval England*. Urbana: University of Illinois Press, 1998.

Bradley, Ritamary. "Backgrounds to the Title *Speculum* in Mediaeval Literature." *Speculum* 29 (1954): 100–15.

Brakke, David. *Demons and the Making of the Monk: Spiritual Combat in Early Christianity*. Cambridge, MA: Harvard University Press, 2006.

Bratu, Christian. "Mirrors for Princes (Western)." In *Handbook of Medieval Studies: Terms – Methods – Trends, 1921–49*. 3 vols. Edited by Albrecht Classen. Berlin: De Gruyter, 2010.

Breen, Dan. "Laureation and Identity: Rewriting Literary History in John Skelton's *Garland of Laurel*. *Journal of Medieval and Early Modern Studies* 40 (2010): 347–71.

British Library. Description of Royal MS 18.D.II. Digitised Manuscripts Catalogue. http://www.bl.uk/manuscripts/FullDisplay.aspx?ref=Royal_MS_18_D_II.

Brockliss, William, Pramit Chaudhuri, Ayelet Haimson Lushkov, and Katherine Wasdin, eds. *Reception and the Classics*. Yale Classical Studies 36. Cambridge: Cambridge University Press, 2012.

Brown, Ian. "The Mental Traveller – A Study of the *Kingis Quair*." *Studies in Scottish Literature* 5 (1968): 246–52.

Brown, J.T.T. *The Authorship of* The Kingis Quair: *A New Criticism*. New York: Macmillan, 1896.

Brown, Michael. *James I*. The Stewart Dynasty in Scotland 2. Edinburgh: Canongate Academic, 1994.

Brown, Peter. *Augustine of Hippo: A Biography*. New ed. Berkeley: University of California Press, 2000.

—. *Authority and the Sacred: Aspects of the Christianisation of the Roman World*. Cambridge: Cambridge University Press, 1995.

Bühler, Curt F. "The Assembly of Gods and Christine de Pisan." *English Language Notes* 4 (1967): 251–4.

—. Introduction to *The Epistle of Othea* by Stephen Scrope, xi–xxxvii. Edited by Curt F.

Bühler. EETS OS 264. London: Oxford University Press, 1970.
—. "'Kynge Melyzyus' and *The Pastime of Pleasure.*" *Review of English Studies* 10 (1934): 438–41.
—. "Notes on the Plimpton Manuscript of the *Court of Sapience.*" *Modern Language Notes* 59 (1944): 5–9.
—. *The Sources of the* Court of Sapience. Leipzig: Verlag von Bernhard Tauchnitz, 1932.
Burnett, Charles S.F. "Astrology." In *Medieval Latin: An Introduction and Bibliographical Guide*, 369–82. Edited by F.A.C. Mantello and A.G. Rigg. Washington, DC: Catholic University of America Press, 1996.
—. "Translation and Translators, Western European." In *Dictionary of the Middle Ages*, vol. 12, 136–42. New York: Scribner's, 1989.
Burrow, J.A. "The Alterity of Medieval Literature." *New Literary History* 10 (1979): 385–90.
—. "Dunbar and the Accidents of Rhyme." *Essays in Criticism* 63 (2013): 20–8.
—. "William Dunbar." In *A Companion to Medieval Scottish Poetry*, 133–48. Edited by Priscilla Bawcutt and Janet Hadley Williams. Cambridge: D.S. Brewer, 2006.
Calabrese, Michael. *Chaucer's Ovidian Arts of Love*. Gainesville: University of Florida Press, 1994.
Cameron, Averil. *Christianity and the Rhetoric of Empire: The Development of Christian Discourse*. Berkeley: University of California Press, 1991.
—. "Remaking the Past." In *Late Antiquity: A Guide to the Postclassical World*, 1–20. Edited by G.W. Bowersock, Peter Brown, and Oleg Grabar. Cambridge, MA: Belknap Press of Harvard University Press, 1999.
Cames, Gérard. *Allégories et Symboles dans l'Hortus Deliciarum*. Leiden: Brill, 1971.
Camille, Michael. *The Gothic Idol: Ideology and Image-Making in Medieval Art*. Cambridge: Cambridge University Press, 1989.
—. *Image on the Edge: The Margins of Medieval Art*. Essays in Art and Culture. London: Reaktion, 1992.
—. "Seeing and Reading: Some Visual Implications of Medieval Literacy and Illiteracy." *Art History* 8 (1985): 26–49.
Cannan, Edwin. "Stephen Hawes." In *The Dictionary of National Biography*, vol. 25, 188–90. Edited by Leslie Stephen and Sidney Lee. New York: Macmillan, 1891.
Carlson, David R. "Gower *Agonistes* and Chaucer on Ovid (and Virgil)." *Modern Language Review* 109 (2014): 931–52.
Carpenter, Nan Cooke. *John Skelton*. TEAS 61. New York: Twayne, 1967.
Carretta, Vincent. "*The Kingis Quair* and *The Consolation of Philosophy*." *Studies in Scottish Literature* 16 (1981): 14–28.
Carruthers, Mary. *The Book of Memory: A Study of Memory in Medieval Culture*. CSML 10. Cambridge: Cambridge University Press, 1990.
—. *The Craft of Thought: Meditation, Rhetoric, and the Making of Images, 400–1200*. CSML 34. Cambridge: Cambridge University Press, 1998.
—. *The Experience of Beauty in the Middle Ages*. Oxford–Warburg Studies. Oxford: Oxford University Press, 2013.
—. ed. *Rhetoric beyond Words: Delight and Persuasion in the Arts of the Middle Ages*. Cambridge: Cambridge University Press, 2010.
—. and Jan M. Ziolkowski. *The Medieval Craft of Memory: An Anthology of Texts and Pictures*. Philadelphia: University of Pennsylvania Press, 2002.
Cary, George. *The Medieval Alexander*. Cambridge: Cambridge University Press, 1956.
Caseau, Béatrice. "Sacred Landscapes." In *Late Antiquity: A Guide to the Postclassical*

World, 21–59. Edited by G.W. Bowersock, Peter Brown, and Oleg Grabar. Cambridge, MA: Belknap Press of Harvard University Press, 1999.

Chance, Jane. "The Artist as Epic Hero in Alan of Lille's *Anticlaudianus*." *Mittellateinisches Jahrbuch* 18 (1983): 238–47.

—. Introduction to *The Assembly of Gods*, 1–26. Edited by Jane Chance. Kalamazoo, MI: Medieval Institute, 1999.

—. Introduction to *Christine de Pizan's Letter of Othea to Hector*, 1–32. Translated by Jane Chance. Cambridge: D.S. Brewer, 1990.

—. "Interpretive Essay: Christine's Minerva, the Mother Valorized." In *Christine de Pizan's Letter of Othea to Hector*, 121–33. Translated by Jane Chance. Cambridge: D.S. Brewer, 1990.

—. *Medieval Mythography, Volume 1: From Roman North Africa to the School of Chartres, A.D. 433–1177*. Gainesville: University Press of Florida, 1994.

—. *Medieval Mythography, Volume 2: From the School of Chartres to the Court at Avignon, 1177–1350*. Gainesville: University Press of Florida, 2000.

—. *Medieval Mythography, Volume 3: The Emergence of Italian Humanism, 1321–1475*. Gainesville: University Press of Florida, 2015.

—. *The Mythographic Chaucer: The Fabulation of Sexual Poetics*. Minneapolis: University of Minnesota Press, 1995.

—. ed. *The Mythographic Art: Classical Fable and the Rise of the Vernacular in Early France and England*. Gainesville: University of Florida Press, 1990.

Chance Nitzsche, Jane. *The Genius Figure in Antiquity and the Middle Ages*. New York: Columbia University Press, 1975.

Chardin, Jean-Jacques. "A New Historicist Reading of Henry Peacham's *Minerva Britanna*." *Poetics Today* 35 (2014): 635–58.

Charon, Jean. *Cosmology: Theories of the Universe*. Translated by Patrick Moore. New York: McGraw-Hill, 1970.

Cherchi, Paolo. *Andreas and the Ambiguity of Courtly Love*. Toronto: University of Toronto Press, 1994.

Cherniss, Michael D. *Boethian Apocalypse: Studies in Middle English Vision Poetry*. Norman, OK: Pilgrim, 1987.

Chew, Samuel C. *The Pilgrimage of Life*. Port Washington, NY: Kennikat, 1962.

Chrimes, S.B. *Henry VII*. New Haven: Yale University Press, 1999.

Christie, Neil. *From Constantine to Charlemagne: An Archaeology of Italy, AD 300–800*. Aldershot: Ashgate, 2006.

Chuvin, Pierre. *A Chronicle of the Last Pagans*. Cambridge, MA: Harvard University Press, 1990.

Claassen, Jo-Marie. "Literary *Anamnesis*: Boethius Remembers Ovid." *Helios* 34 (2007): 1–35.

Classical Reception Studies Network. "Classics in Dialogue across Time and Culture." *The Open University: CRSN*. http://www.open.ac.uk/arts/research/crsn/.

Clanchy, M.T. *From Memory to Written Record: England 1066–1307*. 2nd ed. Oxford: Blackwell, 1993.

Clark, James G. *The Benedictines in the Middle Ages*. Woodbridge: Boydell Press, 2011.

—. Introduction to *Ovid in the Middle Ages*, 1–25. Edited by James G. Clark, Frank T. Coulson, and Kathryn L. McKinley. Cambridge: Cambridge University Press, 2011.

—. "Monastic Manuscripts and the Transmission of the Classics in Late Medieval England." In *Vehicles of Transmission, Translation, and Transformation in Medieval Textual Culture*, 335–52. Edited by Robert Wisnovsky, Faith Wallis, Jamie C. Fumo, and Carlos Fraenkel. Turnhout: Brepols, 2011.

—. *A Monastic Renaissance at St Albans: Thomas Walsingham and His Circle c.1350–1440*. Oxford: Clarendon Press, 2004.
—, Frank T. Coulson, and Kathryn L. McKinley, eds. *Ovid in the Middle Ages*. Cambridge: Cambridge University Press, 2011.
Clark, John R. "Love and Learning in the 'Metamorphosis Golye Episcopi'." *Mittellateinisches Jahrbuch* 21 (1986): 156–71.
Clifford, Gay. *The Transformations of Allegory*. London: Routledge, 1974.
Clifford, Richard J. *Psalms 73–150*. Collegeville Bible Commentary 23. Collegeville, MN: Liturgical Press, 1986.
Coldiron, A.E.B. "William Caxton." In *The Oxford History of Literary Translation in English*. Vol. 1 to 1550, 160–9. Edited by Roger Ellis. Oxford: Oxford University Press, 2008.
Coleman, Janet. *Medieval Readers and Writers: 1350–1400*. New York: Columbia University Press, 1981.
Coleman, Joyce. "Interactive Parchment: The Theory and Practice of Medieval English Aurality." *Yearbook of English Studies* 25 (1995): 63–79.
—. *Public Reading and the Reading Public in Late Medieval England and France*. CSML 26. Cambridge: Cambridge University Press, 1996.
—. "Where Chaucer Got His Pulpit: Audience and Intervisuality in the *Troilus and Criseyde* Frontispiece." *Studies in the Age of Chaucer* 32 (2010): 103–28.
Coleman, K.M. "The Emperor Domitian and Literature." *ANRW* 2.32.5 (1986): 3087–115.
Colker, Marvin L. Introduction to *Galteri de Castellione Alexandreis*. In *Galteri de Castellione Alexandreis*, ix–xlv. Edited by Marvin L. Colker. Padua: Antenore, 1978.
Collamore, Lila. "Prelude: Charting the Divine Office." In *The Divine Office in the Latin Middle Ages: Methodology and Source Studies, Regional Developments, Hagiography*, 3–11. Edited by Margot E. Fassler and Rebecca A. Baltzer. Oxford: Oxford University Press, 2000.
Colledge, Edmund. Introduction to *Wisdom's Watch Upon the Hours*, by Henry Suso, 1–50. Translated by Edmund Colledge. Fathers of the Church, Medieval Continuation 4. Washington, DC: Catholic University of America Press, 1994.
Collins, John J. *Daniel with an Introduction to Apocalyptic Literature*. The Forms of the Old Testament 20. Grand Rapids, MI: Eerdmans, 1984.
Conley, K. "Wisdom." In *New Catholic Encyclopedia*, vol. 14, 967–71. New York: McGraw, 1967.
Contreni, John J. "Cathedral Schools." In *Dictionary of the Middle Ages*, vol. 11, 59–63. New York: Scribner's, 1988.
Cooke, John Daniel. "Euhemerism: A Mediaeval Interpretation of Classical Paganism." *Speculum* 2 (1927): 396–410.
Cooper, Helen. "Chaucer and Ovid: A Question of Authority." In *Ovid Renewed: Ovidian Influences on Literature and Art from the Middle Ages to the Twentieth Century*, 71–81. Edited by Charles Martindale. Cambridge: Cambridge University Press, 1988.
Cooper, Lisa H. *Artisans and Narrative Craft in Late Medieval England*. CSML 82. Cambridge: Cambridge University Press, 2011.
—. and Andrea Denny-Brown, eds. *Lydgate Matters: Poetry and Material Culture in the Fifteenth Century*. New York: Palgrave, 2008.
Copeland, Rita. "The Curricular Classics in the Middle Ages." In *The Oxford History of Classical Reception in English Literature: Volume 1 (800–1558)*, 21–33. Edited by Rita Copeland. Oxford: Oxford University Press, 2016.
—. "Introduction: England and the Classics from the Early Middle Ages to Early

Humanism." In *The Oxford History of Classical Reception in English Literature: Volume 1 (800–1558)*, 1–20. Edited by Rita Copeland. Oxford: Oxford University Press, 2016.
—, ed. *The Oxford History of Classical Reception in English Literature: Volume 1 (800–1558)*. Oxford: Oxford University Press, 2016.
—. *Rhetoric, Hermeneutics, and Translation in the Middle Ages: Academic Traditions and Vernacular Texts*. Cambridge: Cambridge University Press, 1991.
—. "The Trivium and the Classics." In *The Oxford History of Classical Reception in English Literature: Volume 1 (800–1558)*, 53–76. Edited by Rita Copeland. Oxford: Oxford University Press, 2016.
—, and Peter T. Struck. Introduction to *The Cambridge Companion to Allegory*, 1–11. Edited by Rita Copeland and Peter T. Struck. Cambridge: Cambridge University Press, 2010.
Copleston, Frederick. *A History of Philosophy: Volume I: Greece and Rome*. Rev. ed. 2 parts. Garden City, NY: Image, 1962.
—. *A History of Philosophy: Volume II: Mediaeval Philosophy*. Rev. ed. 2 parts. New York: Image, 1962.
Corcoran, Simon. "From Unholy Madness to Right-Mindedness: Or How to Legislate for Religious Conformity from Decius to Justinian." In *Conversion in Late Antiquity: Christianity, Islam, and Beyond*, 67–94. Edited by Arietta Papaconstantinou, Neil McLynn, and Daniel L. Schwartz. Farnham, UK: Ashgate, 2015.
Coulson, F. "The Latin Glosses of Venice Fr. App.123." In *Les Eschéz d'Amours: A Critical Edition of the Poem and Its Latin Glosses*, 95–104. Edited by Gregory Heyworth and Daniel E. O'Sullivan, with Frank Coulson. MRAT 10. Leiden: Brill, 2013.
Courtenay, William J. *Schools and Scholars in the Fourteenth Century*. Princeton: Princeton University Press, 1987.
Craigie, W.A. "The Language of the *Kingis Quair*." *Essays and Studies* 25 (1939): 22–38.
Creek, Sr. Mary Immaculate. "The Four Daughters of God in the *Gesta Romanorum* and the *Court of Sapience*." *PMLA* 57 (1942): 951–65.
Crockett, Bryan. "Venus Unveiled: Lydgate's *Temple of Glass* and the Religion of Love." *Mediaevalia* 14 (1991 [for 1988]): 201–30.
Croon, J.H. "The Cult of Sul-Minerva at Bath." *Antiquity* 27 (1953): 79–83.
Crosby, Ruth. "Chaucer and the Custom of Oral Delivery." *Speculum* 13 (1938): 413–32.
—. "Oral Delivery in the Middle Ages." *Speculum* 11 (1936): 88–110.
Curry, Walter Clyde. "The Wife of Bath." In *Chaucer: Modern Essays in Criticism*, 166–87. Edited by Edward Wagenknecht. London: Oxford University Press, 1959.
Curtius, Ernst R. *European Literature and the Latin Middle Ages*. Translated by Willard R. Trask. Bollingen Series 36. Princeton: Princeton University Press, 1983.
Dahood, Mitchell. *The Anchor Bible: Psalms III 101–150*. Garden City, NY: Doubleday, 1970.
Dalzell, Alexander. *The Criticism of Didactic Poetry: Essays on Lucretius, Virgil, and Ovid*. Toronto: University of Toronto Press, 1996.
Davenport, Tony. *Medieval Narrative: An Introduction*. Oxford: Oxford University Press, 2004.
Davis-Weyer, Caecilia. *Early Medieval Art 300–1150: Sources and Documents*. MART 17. Toronto: University of Toronto Press, 1986.
Deacy, Susan. *Athena*. Gods and Heroes of the Ancient World. London: Routledge, 2008.
—. "The Vulnerability of Athena: *Parthenoi* and Rape in Greek Myth." In *Rape in Antiquity: Sexual Violence in the Greek and Roman Worlds*, 43–64. Edited by Susan Deacy and Karen F Pierce. London: Duckworth, 1997.

—, and Alexandra Villing, eds. *Athena in the Classical World*. Leiden: Brill, 2001.
Deanesly, Margaret. "Medieval Schools to c. 1300." In *The Cambridge Medieval History*, vol. 5, 765–79. New York: Macmillan, 1926.
de Ghellinck, J. "Neotericus, Neoterice." *Archivum Latinitatis Medii Aevi* 15 (1940): 113–26.
de Lubac, Henri. *Medieval Exegesis: The Four Senses of Scripture*. 3 vols. Translated by Mark Sebanc. Grand Rapids, MI: Eerdmans, 1998.
Depres, Denise. *Ghostly Sights: Visual Meditation in Late Medieval Literature*. Norman, OK: Pilgrim, 1989.
Desmond, Marilynn, ed. "Ovid in Medieval Culture: A Special Issue." *Mediaevalia* 13 (1989 [for 1987]): 1–307.
—, and Pamela Sheingorn. *Myth, Montage, and Visuality in Late Medieval Manuscript Culture: Christine de Pizan's* Epistre Othea. Ann Arbor: University of Michigan Press, 2006.
DeVries, David N. "The Pleasure of Influence: Dunbar's *Golden Targe* and Dream Poetry." *Studies in Scottish Literature* 27 (1992): 113–27.
A Dictionary of the Older Scots Tongue (up to 1700). *Dictionary of the Scots Language*. http://www.dsl.ac.uk/.
Dierkens, Alain. "Evidence of Archaeology." In *The Pagan Middle Ages*, 39–64. Edited by Ludo J.R. Milis and translated by Tanis Guest. Woodbridge: Boydell, 1998.
Di Martino, Vittorio. *Roman Ireland*. Cork: Collins Press, 2003.
Dimier, Anselm. *Stones Laid before the Lord: A History of Monastic Architecture*. Translated by Gilchrist Lavigne. Cistercian Studies Series 152. Kalamazoo, MI: Cistercian Publications, 1999.
Dimmick, Jeremy. "Ovid in the Middle Ages: Authority and Poetry." In *The Cambridge Companion to Ovid*, 264–87. Edited by Philip Hardie. Cambridge: Cambridge University Press, 2002.
Dionisotti, A.C. "Walter of Châtillon and the Greek." In *Latin Poetry and the Classical Tradition: Essays in Medieval and Renaissance Literature*, 73–96. Edited by Peter Godman and Oswyn Murray. Oxford: Clarendon Press, 1990.
Donovan, Stephen. "Assisi." *The Catholic Encyclopedia*, vol. 1. New York: Appleton, 1907. http://www.newadvent.org/cathen/01801a.htm.
Downes, Stephanie. "A 'Frenche booke called the Pistill of Othea': Christine de Pizan's French in England." In *Language and Culture in Medieval Britain: The French of England, c. 1100–c.1500*, 457–68. Edited by Jocelyn Wogan-Browne et al. York: York Medieval Press, 2009.
Dronke, Peter. "Bernard Silvestris, Natura, and Personification." *Journal of the Warburg and Courtauld Institutes* 43 (1980): 16–31.
—. *Fabula: Explorations into the Uses of Myth in Medieval Platonism*. Mittellateinische Studien und Texte 9. Leiden and Koln: E.J. Brill, 1974.
—. Introduction to *Cosmographia*, by Bernard Silvestris, 1–91. Edited by Peter Dronke. Textus Minores 53. Leiden: Brill, 1978.
—. *Medieval Latin and the Rise of the European Love Lyric*. 2nd ed. Oxford: Clarendon, 1968.
—. *Verse with Prose from Petronius to Dante: The Art and Scope of the Mixed Form*. Cambridge, MA: Harvard University Press, 1994.
DuBois, Thomas A. *Lyric, Meaning, and Audience in the Oral Tradition of Northern Europe*. Notre Dame: University of Notre Dame Press, 2006.
Duckett, Eleanor Shipley. *The Gateway to the Middle Ages: Monasticism*. Ann Arbor: University of Michigan Press, 1938, 1966.

Duff, E. Gordon. "The Introduction of Printing into England and the Early Work of the Press: Wynken de Worde." In *The Cambridge History of English and American Literature*, vol. 2, para. 41–50. Edited by A. W. Ward and A.R. Waller. New York: Putnam, 1907. Bartleby.com. http://www.bartleby.com/212/1315.html.

Dumézil, Georges. *Archaic Roman Religion with an Appendix on the Religion of the Etruscans*. 2 vols. Translated by Philip Kapp. Chicago: University of Chicago Press, 1970.

Dunkle, J.R. "Satirical Themes in Joseph of Exeter's *De bello Troiano*." *Classica et Medievalia* 38 (1987): 203–13.

Dunphy, Graeme. "The Medieval University." In *Handbook of Medieval Culture: Fundamental Aspects and Conditions of the European Middle Ages*, 1705–34. 3 vols. Edited by Albrecht Classen. Berlin: De Gruyter, 2015.

Dwyer, Richard A. "Ovid in the Middle Ages." In *Dictionary of the Middle Ages*, vol. 9, 312–14. New York: Schribner's, 1987.

Dzielska, Maria. "Hypatia." In *Late Antiquity: A Guide to the Postclassical World*, 502–3. Edited by G.W. Bowersock, Peter Brown, and Oleg Grabar. Cambridge, MA: Belknap Press of Harvard University Press, 1999.

—. *Hypatia of Alexandria*. Translated by F. Lyra. Revealing Antiquity 8. Cambridge, MA: Harvard University Press, 1995.

Ebin, Lois A. "Boethius, Chaucer and *The Kingis Quair*." *Philological Quarterly* 53 (1974): 321–41.

—. *Illuminator, Makar, Vates: Visions of Poetry in the Fifteenth Century*. Lincoln: University of Nebraska Press, 1988.

—. *John Lydgate*. TEAS 407. Boston: Twayne, 1985.

Eco, Umberto. *The Aesthetics of Thomas Aquinas*. Translated by Hugh Bredin. Cambridge, MA: Harvard University Press, 1988.

—. *Art and Beauty in the Middle Ages*. Translated by Hugh Bredin. New Haven: Yale University Press, 1986.

—. *The Role of the Reader: Explorations in the Semiotics of Texts*. Bloomington: Indiana University Press, 1979.

Economou, George D. *The Goddess Natura in the Middle Ages*. Cambridge, MA: Harvard University Press, 1972; reprint Notre Dame: University of Notre Dame Press, 2002.

—. "The Two Venuses and Courtly Love." In *Pursuit of Perfection: Courtly Love in Medieval Literature*, 17–50. Edited by Joan M. Ferrante and George D. Economou. Port Washington, NY: Kennikat Press, 1975.

Edwards, A.S.G. "The Circulation of English Verse in Manuscript after the Advent of Print in England." *Studia Neophilologica* 83 (2011): 67–77.

—. "Fifteenth-Century Middle English Verse Author Collections." In *The English Medieval Book: Studies in Memory of Jeremy Griffiths*, 101–12. Edited by A.S.G. Edwards, Vincent Gillespie, and Ralph Hanna. London: British Library, 2000.

—. "Lydgate Manuscripts: Some Directions for Future Research." In *Manuscripts and Readers in Fifteenth-Century England: The Literary Implications of Manuscript Study*, 15–26. Edited by Derek Pearsall. Cambridge: D.S. Brewer, 1983.

—. "The Marketing of Printed Books in Late Medieval England." *Library* 15 (1993): 95–124.

—. "Poet and Printer in Sixteenth Century England: Stephen Hawes and Wynkyn de Worde." *Gutenberg Jahrbuch* (1980): 82–8.

—. "Skelton's English Poems in Print and Manuscript." *Trivium* 31 (1999): 87–100.

—. *Stephen Hawes*. TEAS 354. Boston: Twayne, 1983.

—. "Stephen Hawes." In *Sixteenth-Century British Nondramatic Writers*, 166–71. Edited

by David A. Richardson. Dictionary of Literary Biography 132. Detroit: Gale Research, 1993.
Edwards, Nancy. *The Archaeology of Early Medieval Ireland*. Philadelphia: University of Pennsylvania Press, 1989.
Ehrhart, Margaret J. *The Judgment of the Trojan Prince Paris in Medieval Literature*. Philadelphia: University of Pennsylvania Press, 1987.
Eliade, Mircea. *A History of Religious Ideas: Volume 1*. Translated by Willard R. Trask. Chicago: University of Chicago Press, 1978.
—. *The Sacred and the Profane*. Translated by Willard R. Trask. New York: Harcourt, 1959.
Ellard, Gerald. "Alcuin and Some Favored Votive Masses." *Theological Studies* 1 (1940): 37–61.
Elliott, Alison Goddard. "Ovid and the Critics: Seneca, Quintilian, and 'Seriousness'." *Helios* 12 (1985): 9–20.
Elliott, Robert. C. *The Literary Persona*. Chicago: University of Chicago Press, 1982.
English Short Title Catalogue. British Library. http://estc.bl.uk/F/?func=file&file_name =login-bl-estc.
Epstein, Robert. "Prisoners of Reflection: The Fifteenth-Century Poetry of Exile and Imprisonment." *Exemplaria* 15 (2003): 159–98.
Evans, Michael. "Allegorical Women and Practical Men: The Iconography of the *Artes* Reconsidered." *Studies in Church History, Subsidia* 1 (1978): 305–29.
Ewald, Marie Liguori. *Ovid in the* Contra orationem Symmachi *of Prudentius*. Catholic University of America Patristic Studies 66. Washington, DC: Catholic University of America Press, 1942.
Fantham, Elaine. *Ovid's* Metamorphoses. Oxford: Oxford University Press, 2004
—. *Roman Readings: Roman Response to Greek Literature from Plautus to Satius and Quintilian*. Berlin: de Gruyter, 2011.
Farr, Carol. *The Book of Kells: Its Function and Audience*. London: British Library, 1997.
Federico, Sylvia. *New Troy: Fantasies of Empire in the Late Middle Ages*. Medieval Cultures 36. Minneapolis: University of Minnesota Press, 2003.
Feeney, D.C. *The Gods in Epic: Poets and Critics of the Classical Tradition*. Oxford: Clarendon Press, 1991.
Feiss, Hugh. General Introduction to *On Love: A Selection of Works of Hugh, Adam, Achard, Richard, Godfrey of St. Victor*, 33–112. Edited by Hugh Feiss. Victorine Texts in Translation 2. New York: New City Press, 2012.
Fewer, Colin. "John Lydgate's *Troy Book* and the Ideology of Prudence." *The Chaucer Review* 38 (2004): 229–45.
Fisher, John H. *The Emergence of Standard English*. Lexington: University Press of Kentucky, 1996.
—. *The Importance of Chaucer*. Carbondale: Southern Illinois University Press, 1992.
—. *John Gower: Moral Philosopher and Friend of Chaucer*. London: Methuen, 1965.
Fleming, John V. *Reason and the Lover*. Princeton: Princeton University Press, 1984.
Foley, John Miles. *Traditional Oral Epic: The* Odyssey, Beowulf, *and the Serbo-Croatian Return Song*. Berkeley: University of California Press, 1990.
Foran, Gregory A. "Dunbar's Broken Rainbow: Symbol, Allegory, and Apocalypse in 'The Golden Targe.'" *Philological Quarterly* 86 (2007): 47–65.
Fox, Denton. "Dunbar's Golden Targe." *ELH* 26 (1959): 311–34.
Fox, John, and Mary-Jo Arn. Introduction to *Poetry of Charles d'Orléans and His Circle: A Critical Edition of BnF MS. fr. 25458, Charles d'Orléans's Personal Manuscript*, xxviii–xl.

Edited by John Fox and Mary-Jo Arn, translated by R. Barton Palmer, contribution by Stephanie A.V.G. Klamath. MRTS 383/ASMAR 34. Tempe: ACMRS; Turnhout: Brepols, 2010.

Franciscanum.it. "Tempio di Minerva, Assisi." http://www.franciscanum.it/tempio-di-minerva/.

Francomano, Emily C. *Wisdom and Her Lovers in Medieval and Early Modern Hispanic Literature*. New York: Palgrave, 2008.

Freudenburg, Kirk. *Satires of Rome: Threatening Poses from Lucilius to Juvenal*. Cambridge: Cambridge University Press, 2001.

Friedman, John B. *Orpheus in the Middle Ages*. Cambridge, MA: Harvard University Press, 1970.

Frisch, Teresa G. *Gothic Art 1140–1450: Sources and Documents*. MART 20. Toronto: University of Toronto Press, 1987.

Fumo, Jamie C. *The Legacy of Apollo: Antiquity, Authority, and Chaucerian Poetics*. Toronto: University of Toronto Press, 2010.

Fyler, John M. *Chaucer and Ovid*. New Haven: Yale University Press, 1979.

Gager, John G. *Curse Tablets and Binding Spells from the Ancient World*. Oxford: Oxford University Press, 1992.

Galpin, Stanley L. "*Les Echez Amoureux*: A Complete Synopsis with Unpublished Extracts." *Romanic Review* 11 (1920): 283–307.

Galway, Margaret. "The 'Troilus' Frontispiece." *Modern Language Review* 44 (1949): 161–77.

Garrison, Mary. "The Social World of Alcuin: Nicknames at York and at the Carolingian Court." In *Alcuin of York: Scholar at the Carolingian Court*, 59–79. Edited by L.A.J.R. Houwen and A.A. MacDonald. Groningen: Egbert Forsten, 1998.

Gaskill, Philip. *A New Introduction to Bibliography*. New Castle, DE: Oak Knoll Press, 2009.

Gayk, Shannon. *Image, Text, and Religious Reform in Fifteenth-Century England*. CSML 81. Cambridge: Cambridge University Press, 2010.

Gersh, Stephen, and Bert Roest, eds. *Medieval and Renaissance Humanism: Rhetoric, Representation and Reform*. Brill's Studies in Intellectual History 115. Leiden: Brill, 2003.

Gibson, Bruce. "Battle Narrative in Statius' *Thebaid*." In *The Poetry of Statius*, 85–109. Edited by Johannes J.L. Smolenaars, Harm-Jan van Dam, and Ruurd R. Nauta. MGRLL 306. Leiden: Brill, 2008.

Gibson, Walker. "Authors, Speakers, Readers, and Mock Readers." *College English* 11 (1950): 265–9.

Gillespie, Alexandra. "Caxton and the Invention of Printing." In *The Oxford Handbook of Tudor Literature, 1485–1603*, 21–36. Edited by Mike Pincombe and Cathy Shrank. Oxford: Oxford University Press, 2009.

Gillespie, Vincent. "The Study of Classical Authors from the Twelfth Century to c. 1450." In *The Cambridge History of Literary Criticism: Volume 2*, 145–235. Edited by Alastair Minnis and Ian Johnson. Cambridge: Cambridge University Press, 2005.

Gingerich, Owen, and Melvin J. Tucker. "The Astronomical Dating of Skelton's 'Garland of Laurel'." *Huntigton Library Quarterly* 32 (1969): 207–20.

Girard, J.-L. "Domitien et Minerve: une predilection imperiale" *ANRW* 2.17 (1981): 133–45.

Gluck, Florence W., and Alice B. Morgan. Introduction to *Stephen Hawes: The Minor Poems*, xi–xlvii. Edited by Florence W. Gluck and Alice B. Morgan. EETS OS 271. London: Oxford University Press, 1974.

Godman, Peter, and Oswyn Murray, eds. *Latin Poetry and the Classical Tradition: Essays in Medieval and Renaissance Literature*. Oxford: Clarendon Press, 1990.
Gompf, Ludwig. Einleitung [introduction]. *Joseph Iscanus: Werke und Briefe*, 3–73. Mittellateinische Studien und Texte 4. Leiden: Brill, 1970.
Goodrich, Norma. *Charles of Orleans: A Study of Themes in His French and in His English Poetry*. Geneve: Libraire Droz, 1967.
Graf, Fritz. "Athena and Minerva: Two Faces of One Goddess." In *Athena in the Classical World*, 127–39. Edited by Susan Deacy and Alexandra Villing. Leiden: Brill, 2001.
Grafton, Anthony, Glenn W. Most, and Salvatore Settis, eds. *The Classical Tradition*. Cambridge, MA: Belknap Press of Harvard University Press, 2010.
Grant, Edward. "Astronomy, Cosmology, and Cosmography." In *Medieval Latin: An Introduction and Bibliographical Guide*, 363–8. Edited by F.A.C. Mantello and A.G. Rigg. Washington, DC: Catholic University of America Press, 1996.
Gray, Douglas. "'A Fulle Wyse Gentyl-Woman of Fraunce': The *Epistre d'Othea* and Later Medieval English Literary Culture." In *Medieval Women: Text and Contexts in Late Medieval Britain: Essays for Felicity Riddy*, 237–49. Edited by Jocelyn Wogan-Browne, Rosalynn Voaden, Arlyn Diamond, Ann Hutchison, Carol M. Meade, and Lesley Johnson. Turnhout: Brepols, 2000.
—. "The Royal Entry in Sixteenth-Century Scotland." In *The Rose and the Thistle: Essay on the Culture of Late Medieval and Renaissance Scotland*, 10–37. Edited by Sally Mapstone and Juliette Wood. East Lothian: Tuckwell, 1998.
Green, Richard Firth. *Poets and Princepleasers: Literature and the English Court in the Late Middle Ages*. Toronto: University of Toronto Press, 1980.
Green, Richard Hamilton. "Classical Fable and English Poetry in the Fourteenth Century." In *Critical Approaches to Medieval Literature*, 110–33. Edited by Dorothy Bethurum. New York: Columbia University Press, 1960.
Greenblatt, Stephen. "Culture." In *Critical Terms for Literary Study*, 225–32. Edited by Frank Lentricchia and Thomas McLaughlin. Chicago: University of Chicago Press, 1990.
Greenhalgh, Michael. *Marble Past, Monumental Present: Building with Antiquities in the Mediaeval Mediterranean*. Leiden: Brill, 2009.
Gregory, Timothy E. *Vox populi: Popular Opinion and Violence in the Religious Controversies of the Fifth Century A.D.* Columbus: Ohio State University Press, 1979.
Griffin, Nathanial Edward. Introduction to *Historia destructionis Troiae* by Guido delle Colonne, ix–xvii. Edited by Nathaniel Edward Griffin. MAAP 26. Cambridge, MA: Medieval Academy of America, 1936.
Griffiths, Fiona J. *The Garden of Delights: Reform and Renaissance for Women in the Twelfth Century*. Philadelphia: University of Pennsylvania Press, 2007.
Griffiths, Jane. *Diverting Authorities: Experimental Glossing Practices in Manuscript and Print*. Oxford: Oxford University Press, 2014.
—. *John Skelton and Poetic Authority: Defining the Liberty to Speak*. Oxford: Clarendon Press, 2006.
Gros, Pierre. *L'architecture Romaine de Début du IIIe Siecle á la Fin du Haut-Empire: 1 Les Monuments Public*. Paris: Picard, 1996.
Guichard-Tesson, Françoise, and Bruno Roy. Introduction to *Livre des Eschez Amoureux Moralisés*, by Evrart de Conty, xi–lxxiv. Edited by Françoise Guichard-Tesson and Bruno Roy. Bibliothèque de Moyen Français 2. Montréal: Ceres, 1993.
Haas, Christopher. *Alexandria in Late Antiquity: Topography and Social Conflict*. Baltimore: Johns Hopkins University Press, 1997.

Hagen, Susan K. *Allegorical Remembrance: A Study of* The Pilgrimage of the Life of Man *as a Medieval Treatise on Seeing and Remembering*. Athens: University of Georgia Press, 1990.

Hahn, Johannes. "The Conversion of the Cult Statues: The Destruction of the Serapeum 392 A.D. and the Transformation of Alexandria into the 'Christ-Loving' City." In *From Temple to Church: Destruction and Renewal of Local Cultic Topography in Late Antiquity*, 335–65. Edited by Ulrich Gotter, Stephen Emmel, and Johannes Hahn. Religions in the Greco-Roman World 163. Leiden: Brill, 2008.

—, Stephen Emmel, and Ulrich Gotter, eds. *From Temple to Church: Destruction and Renewal of Local Cultic Topography in Late Antiquity*. Religions in the Greco-Roman World 163. Leiden: Brill, 2008.

Hamilton, George L. *The Indebtedness of Chaucer's* Troilus and Criseyde *to Guido delle Colonne's* Historia Trojana. New York: Columbia University Press, 1903.

Hanning, Robert W. "Chaucer's First Ovid: Metamorphosis and Poetic Tradition in *The Book of the Duchess* and *The House of Fame*." In *Chaucer and the Craft of Fiction*, 121–63. Edited by Leigh A. Arrathoon. Rochester, MI: Solaris, 1986.

Hanson, Maria Fabricius. *The Spolia Churches of Rome: Recycling Antiquity in the Middle Ages*. Translated by Barbara J. Haveland. Aarhus: Aarhus University Press, 2015.

Harbert, Bruce. "Lessons from the Great Clerk: Ovid and John Gower." In *Ovid Renewed: Ovidian Influences on Literature and Art from the Middle Ages to the Twentieth Century*, 83–97. Edited by Charles Martindale. Cambridge: Cambridge University Press, 1988.

Hardie, Philip, ed. *The Cambridge Companion to Ovid*. Cambridge: Cambridge University Press, 2002.

—. *The Epic Successors of Virgil: A Study of the Dynamics of a Tradition*. Cambridge: Cambridge University Press, 1993.

Hardwick, Lorna, and Christopher Stray, eds. *A Companion to Classical Receptions*. Oxford: Blackwell, 2011.

Harris, W.V. "Roman Opinions about the Truthfulness of Dreams." *The Journal of Roman Studies* 93 (2003): 18–34.

Hartman, Louis F., and Alexander A. Di Lella. *The Anchor Bible: The Book of Daniel*. Garden City, NY: Doubleday, 1978.

Harvey, E. Ruth. Introduction to *The Court of Sapience*, ix–xlv. *The Court of Sapience*. Edited by E. Ruth Harvey. Toronto: University of Toronto Press, 1984.

Hasler, Antony. *Court Poetry in Late Medieval England and Scotland: Allegories of Authority*. CSML 80. Cambridge: Cambridge University Press, 2011.

—. "Stephen Hawes." In *The Oxford Encyclopedia of British Literature*, vol. 3, 6–9. Edited by David Scott Kastan. Oxford: Oxford University Press, 2006.

Haydock, Nickolas A. "Dunbar's Perfection: The Still Movement of Aureate Poetics in The Thistle and the Rose." *Atenea* 29 (2009): 69–90.

—. "False and Sooth Compounded in Caxton's Ending of Chaucer's House of Fame." *Atenea* 26 (2006): 107.

—. *Situational Poetics in Robert Henryson's* Testament of Cresseid. Amherst, NY: Cambria Press, 2010.

Heffernan, Thomas J. "The Liturgy and the Literature of the Saints' Lives." In *The Liturgy of the Medieval Church*, 73–105. Edited by Thomas J. Heffernan and E. Ann Matter. Kalamazoo, MI: Medieval Institute, 2001.

Heinrichs, Katherine. *The Myths of Love: Classical Lovers in Medieval Literature*. University Park: Pennsylvania State University Press, 1990.

Heise, William. "The Menippean Boethius in the Personification Allegories of the

Middle Ages." In *The Prisoner's Philosophy: Life and Death in Boethius's Consolation*, by Joel C. Relihan, 111–26. Notre Dame: University of Notre Dame Press, 2007.
Hekster, Oliver. "Reversed Epiphanies: Roman Emperors Deserted by Gods." *Mnemosyne* 63 (2010): 601–15.
Henderson, John. *The Medieval World of Isidore of Seville: Truth from Words*. Cambridge: Cambridge University Press, 2007.
Hepburn, William. "William Dunbar and the Courtmen: Poetry as a Source for the Court of James IV." *The Innes Review* 65 (2012): 95–112.
Herman, Luc, and Bart Vervaeck. *Handbook of Narrative Analysis*. Lincoln: University of Nebraska Press, 2005.
Heyworth, Gregory. Introduction to *Les Eschéz d'Amours: A Critical Edition of the Poem and Its Latin Glosses*, 3–80. Edited by Gregory Heyworth and Daniel E. O'Sullivan, with Frank Coulson. MRAT 10. Leiden: Brill, 2013.
Hicks, Andrew. "Martianus Capella and the Liberal Arts." In *The Oxford Handbook of Medieval Latin Literature*, 307–34. Edited by Ralph J. Hexter and David Townsend. Oxford: Oxford University Press, 2012.
Highet, Gilbert. *The Classical Tradition: Greek and Roman Influences on Western Literature*. Oxford: Oxford University Press, 1976.
Hiley, David. *Western Plainchant: A Handbook*. Oxford: Clarendon Press, 1993.
Hindman, Sandra L. *Christine de Pizan's Epistre Othéa: Painting and Politics at the Court of Charles VI*. Toronto: PIMS, 1986.
Hodapp, William F. "Conquered by Babylon: Fate, Fortune, and Reward in Walter of Châtillon's *Alexandreis*." *Enarratio* 16 (2009): 64–78.
———. "The Fables of Avianus." In *Medieval Literature for Children*, 12–28. Edited by Daniel T. Kline. New York: Routledge, 2003.
———. "Geoffrey of Monmouth and the *Gawain* Poet: Remembering Troy." In *Sir Gawain and the Classical Tradition: Essays on the Ancient Antecedents*, 17–29. Edited by E.L. Risden. Jefferson, NC: McFarland, 2006.
———. "The Judgement of Paris and Methods of Reading in John Lydgate's *Reson and Sensuallyte*." *Enarratio* 3 (1995): 110–23.
———. "Minerva's Owl in Charles d'Orléans's English Poems: A Mythographic Note on Line 4765," *ANQ* 9 (1996): 3–7.
———. "The Visual Presentation of Chaucer's *Troilus and Criseyde* in Three Fifteenth-Century Manuscripts." *Manuscripta* 38 (1994): 237–52.
Hoffman, Richard L. *Ovid and the Canterbury Tales*. London: Oxford University Press, 1966.
Hollander, Robert. *Boccaccio's Two Venuses*. New York: Columbia University Press, 1977.
Holmes, Urban T., Jr. "Transitions in European Education." In *Twelfth-Century Europe and the Foundations of Modern Society*, 15–38. Edited by Marshall Clagett et al. Madison: University of Wisconsin Press, 1961.
Horsley, Richard A. "Spiritual Marriage with Sophia." *Vigiliae Christianae* 33 (1979): 30–54.
Hoskin, Michael, and Owen Gingerich. "Medieval Latin Astronomy." In *The Cambridge Illustrated History of Astronomy*, 68–97. Edited by Michael Hoskin. Cambridge: Cambridge University Press, 1997.
Housley, Norman, ed. *Crusading in the Fifteenth Century: Message and Impact*. Basingstoke: Palgrave, 2004.
———. *The Later Crusades, 1284–1580: From Lyons to Alcazar*. Oxford: Oxford University Press, 1992.

Howard, D.R. *The Three Temptations: Medieval Man in Search of the World.* Princeton: Princeton University Press, 1966.
Hume, Robert D. "The Aims and Limits of Historical Scholarship." *Review of English Studies* 53 (2002): 399–422.
—. *Reconstructing Contexts: The Aims and Principles of Archaeo-Historicism.* Oxford: Oxford University Press, 1999.
Hunt, Tony. *Teaching and Learning Latin in Thirteenth-Century England: I Texts, II Glosses, III Indexes.* 3 vols. Cambridge: D.S. Brewer, 1991.
Hyde, Isabel. "Primary Sources and Associations of Dunbar's Aureate Imagery." *Modern Language Review* 51 (1956): 481–92.
Ignatius, Mary Ann. "Christine de Pizan's *Epistre Othea*: An Experiment in Literary Form." *Medievalia et Humanistica* 9 (1979): 127–42.
—. "Manuscript Format and Text Structure: Christine de Pizan's *Epistre Othea*." *Studies in Medieval Culture* 12 (1978): 121–4.
Ingledew, Francis. "The Book of Troy and the Genealogical Construction of History: The Case of Geoffrey of Monmouth's *Historia regum Britanniae*." *Speculum* 69 (1994): 665–704.
Irvine, Martin. *The Making of Textual Culture: 'Grammatica' and Literary Theory 350–1100.* CSML 19. Cambridge: Cambridge University Press, 1994.
—. and David Thomson. "*Grammatica* and Literary Theory." In *The Cambridge History of Literary Criticism: Volume 2*, 15–41. Edited by Alastair Minnis and Ian Johnson. Cambridge: Cambridge University Press, 2005.
Jack, R.D.S. "Dunbar and Lydgate." *Studies in Scottish Literature* 8 (1971): 215–27.
Jaeger, C. Stephen. *Ennobling Love: In Search of a Lost Sensibility.* Philadelphia: University of Pennsylvania Press, 1999.
—. *The Envy of Angels: Cathedral Schools and Social Ideals in Medieval Europe, 950–1200.* Philadelphia: University of Pennsylvania Press, 1994.
Jaeger, Werner. *Paideia: The Ideals of Greek Culture.* 3 vols. Translated by Gilbert Highet. Oxford: Oxford University Press, 1943–5.
James, Clair. "*The Kingis Quair*: The Plight of the Courtly Lover." In *New Readings of Late Medieval Love Poems*, 95–118. Edited by David Chamberlain. Lanham, MD: University Press of America, 1993.
Jauss, Hans Robert. "The Alterity and Modernity of Medieval Literature." Translated by Timothy Bahti. *New Literary History* 10 (1979): 181–227.
—. "Literary History as a Challenge to Literary Theory." Translated by Elizabeth Benzinger. *New Literary History* 2 (1970): 7–37.
Jeauneau, Édouard. *Rethinking the School of Chartres.* Translated by Claude Paul Desmarais. Rethinking the Middle Ages 3. Toronto: University of Toronto Press, 2009.
Jeffrey, C.D. "Anglo-Scots Poetry and *The Kingis Quair*." In *Actes de se colloque de langue et de littérature écossaises (Moyen Age et Renaissance)*, 207–21. Edited by Jean-Jacques Blanchot and Claude Graf. Strasbourg: Institute d'etudes anglaises de Strasbourg et l'Association des médiévistes anglicistes de l'enseignement supérieur, 1979.
Jeffrey, David L. "Reference and Recognition in Medieval Thought." In *By Things Seen: Reference and Recognition in Medieval Thought*, 1–17. Edited by David L. Jeffrey. Ottawa: University of Ottawa Press, 1979.
Johnson, Patricia. *Ovid before Exile: Art and Punishment in the* Metamorphoses. Madison: University of Wisconsin Press, 2008.
Johnson, Richard. "The Allegory and the Trivium." In *Martianus Capella and the Seven Liberal Arts*, vol. 1, 81–121. New York: Columbia University Press, 1971, 1991.

Jones, Brian W. *The Emperor Domitian*. London: Routledge, 1992.
Jones, Christopher P. *Between Pagan and Christian*. Cambridge, MA: Harvard University Press, 2014.
Jones, Leslie W. Introduction to *An Introduction to Divine and Human Readings* by Cassiodorus, 1–64. Translated by Leslie W. Jones. New York: Columbia University Press, 1946.
Jordan, Mark. *The Invention of Sodomy in Christian Theology*. Chicago: University of Chicago Press, 1997.
Kahlos, Maijastina. *Debate and Dialogue: Christian and Pagan Cultures c.360–430*. Aldershot: Ashgate, 2007.
Kallendorf, Craig W., ed. *A Companion to the Classical Tradition*. Oxford: Blackwell, 2010.
Karkov, Catherine E., Michael Ryan, and Robert T. Farrell, eds. *The Insular Tradition*. Albany: SUNY Press, 1997.
Karnein, Alfred. *De amore in volksprachlicher Literatur: Untersuchungen zur Andreas-Capellanus-Rezeption in Mittlealter und Renaissance*. Germanisch-Romanische Monatsschrift, Beiheft 4. Heidelberg: Winter, 1985.
Kaske, Carol V. "How Spenser Really Used Stephen Hawes in the Legend of Holiness." In *Unfolded Tales: Essays on Renaissance Romance*, 119–36. Edited by George M. Logan, Gordon Teskey, and Northrop Frye. Ithaca, NY: Cornell University Press, 1989.
Katzenellenbogen, Alfred. "The Representations of the Seven Liberal Arts." In *Twelfth-Century Europe and the Foundations of Modern Society*, 39–55. Edited by Marshall Clagett et al. Madison: University of Wisconsin Press, 1961.
Keen, Maurice. *English Society in the Later Middle Ages: 1348–1500*. Harmondsworth, UK: Penguin, 1990.
Kekewich, Margaret. "Edward IV, William Caxton, and Literary Patronage in Yorkist England." *Modern Language Review* 66 (1971): 481–7.
Kelly, Douglas. "The *Fidus interpres*: Aid or Impediment to Medieval Translation and *Translatio*?" In *Translation Theory and Practice in the Middle Ages*, 47–58. Edited by Jeanette Beer. SMC 38. Kalamazoo, MI: Medieval Institute, 1997.
Kelly, Henry Ansgar. *Love and Marriage in the Age of Chaucer*. Ithaca, NY: Cornell University Press, 1975.
King, John N. "Allegorical Pattern in Stephen Hawes's *The Pastime of Pleasure*." *Studies in the Literary Imagination* 11 (1978): 57–67.
King, Pamela. "Dunbar's *The Golden Targe*: A Chaucerian Masque." *Studies in Scottish Literature* 19 (1984): 115–31.
Klibansky, Raymond, et al. *Saturn and Melancholy*. London: Thomas Nelson, 1964.
Knowles, David. *The Evolution of Medieval Thought*. New York: Vintage, 1962.
Kratz, Dennis M. *Mocking Epic: Waltharius, Alexandreis, and the Problem of Christian Heroism*. Madrid: Studia Humanitatis, 1980.
Krautheimer, Richard. *Rome: Profile of a City, 312–1308*. Princeton: Princeton University Press, 1980.
Kruger, Steven F. *Dreaming in the Middle Ages*. CSML 14. Cambridge: Cambridge University Press, 1992.
Kuskin, William. "The Fourth Generation: Figuring Literary History out of the Long Fifteenth Century." *Reformation* 14 (1009): 171–8.
Lafferty, Maura. "Chapter Eight: Walter of Châtillon's *Alexandreis*." In *A Companion to Alexander Literature in the Middle Ages*, 177–99. Edited by Z. David Zuwiyya. BCCT 29. Leiden: Brill, 2011

—. *Walter of Châtillon's* Alexandreis: *Epic and the Problem of Historical Understanding*. Publications of the Journal of Medieval Latin 2. Turnhout: Brepols, 1998.

Laidlaw, J.C. "Christine de Pizan – An Author's Progress." *Modern Language Review* 78 (1983): 532–50.

—. "Christine de Pizan – A Publisher's Progress." *Modern Language Review* 82 (1987): 35–75.

—, Andrew Grout, Charlie Mansfield, and Justin Clegg. *Christine de Pizan: The Making of the Queen's Manuscript London, British Library, Harley MS 4431*. University of Edinburgh, 2014. https://eserve.org.uk/pizan/index.html.

Lamberton, Robert. "Language, Text, and Truth in Ancient Polytheistic Exegesis." In *Interpretation and Allegory: Antiquity to the Modern Period*, 73–88. Edited by Jon Whitman. Leiden: Brill, 2000.

Lane Fox, Robin. *Pagans and Christians*. New York: Knopf, 1986.

Lawton, David. "Dullness and the Fifteenth Century." *ELH* 54 (1987): 761–99.

Lawton, Lesley. "The Illustration of Late Medieval Secular Texts, with Special Reference to Lydgate's Troy *Book*." In *Manuscripts and Readers in Fifteenth-Century England: The Literary Implications of Manuscript Study*, 41–69. Edited by Derek Pearsall. Cambridge: Cambridge University Press, 1983.

Leclerq, Jean. *The Love of Learning and the Desire for God: A Study of Monastic Culture*. New York: Fordham University Press, 1961.

—. *Monks on Marriage: A Twelfth-Century View*. New York: Seabury, 1982.

Lefevere, André. *Translating Literature: Practice and Theory in a Comparative Literature Context*. New York: MLA, 1992.

Le Goff, Jacques. *The Medieval Imagination*. Translated by Arthur Goldhammer. Chicago: University of Chicago Press, 1988.

Leicester, H. Marshall, Jr. "Oure Tonges *Differance*: Textuality and Deconstruction in Chaucer." In *Medieval Texts and Contemporary Readers*, 15–26. Edited by Laurie Finke and Martin Schichtman. Ithaca, NY: Cornell University Press, 1987.

Lenz, Tanya S. *Dreams, Medicine, and Literary Practice: Exploring the Western Literary Tradition through Chaucer*. Cursor Mundi 18. Turnhout: Brepols, 2014.

Lerer, Seth. *Boethius and Dialogue: Literary Method in* The Consolation of Philosophy. Princeton: Princeton University Press, 1985.

—. *Chaucer and His Readers: Imagining the Author in Late-Medieval England*. Princeton: Princeton University Press, 1993.

Lewis, C.S. *The Allegory of Love*. Oxford: Oxford University Press, 1936.

—. *The Discarded Image: An Introduction to Medieval and Renaissance Literature*. Cambridge: Cambridge University Press, 1964.

—. "Edmund Spenser, 1552–1599." In *Studies in Medieval and Renaissance Literature*, 121–46. Edited by Walter Hooper. Cambridge: Cambridge University Press, 1966.

—. *English Literature in the Sixteenth Century Excluding Drama*. OHEL 3. Oxford: Clarendon Press, 1953.

—. *Studies in Words*. 2nd ed. Cambridge: Cambridge University Press, 1967.

Lim, Richard. "Christian Triumph and Controversy." In *Late Antiquity: A Guide to the Postclassical World*, 196–218. Edited by G.W. Bowersock, Peter Brown, and Oleg Grabar. Cambridge, MA: Belknap Press of Harvard University Press, 1999.

Lord, Albert Bates. *Epic Singers and Oral Tradition*. Ithaca, NY: Cornell University Press, 1991.

Lotman, Maria-Kristiina. "Equiprosodic Translation Method in Estonian Poetry." *Sign Systems Studies* 40 (2012): 447–72.

Luscombe, David. "Peter Abelard and the Poets." In *Poetry and Philosophy in the Middle Ages: A Festschrift for Peter Dronke*, 155–71. Edited by John Marenbon. Mittellateinische Studien und Texte 29. Leiden: Brill, 2001.
Lyall, R.J. "Moral Allegory in Dunbar's *The Golden Targe*." *Studies in Scottish Literature* 11 (1974): 47–65.
—. "The Stylistic Relationship between Dunbar and Douglas." In *William Dunbar, 'The Nobill Poyet': Essays in Honour of Priscilla Bawcutt*, 69–84. Edited by Sally Mapstone. East Linton, UK: Tuckwell Press, 2001.
Lynch, Kathryn. *Chaucer's Philosophical Visions*. Chaucer Studies 27. Woodbridge: D.S. Brewer, 2000.
—. *The High Medieval Dream Vision: Poetry, Philosophy, and Literary Form*. Stanford: Stanford University Press, 1988.
Lyne, Raphael. "Love and Exile after Ovid." In *The Cambridge Companion to Ovid*, 288–300. Edited by Philip Hardie. Cambridge: Cambridge University Press, 2001.
MacCracken, Henry Noble. "Additional Light on the *Temple of Glass*." *PMLA* 23 (1908): 128–40.
MacDonald, A.A. "Sir Richard Maitland and William Dunbar: Textual Symbiosis and Poetic Individuality." In *William Dunbar, 'The Nobill Poyet': Essays in Honour of Priscilla Bawcutt*, 134–49. Edited by Sally Mapstone. East Linton, UK: Tuckwell Press, 2001.
Machan, Tim William. *English in the Middle Ages*. Oxford: Oxford University Press, 2003.
Mack, Sara. *Ovid*. New Haven: Yale University Press, 1988.
MacMullen, Ramsay. *Christianity and Paganism in the Fourth to Eighth Centuries*. New Haven: Yale University Press, 1997.
—. *Christianizing the Roman Empire (A.D. 100–400)*. New Haven: Yale University Press, 1984.
MacQueen, John. "Tradition and the Interpretation of the *Kingis Quair*." *Review of English Studies* ns 12 (1961): 117–31.
Maddox, Donald, and Sara Sturm-Maddox, eds. *The Medieval French Alexander*. Albany: University of New York Press, 2002.
Mâle, Emile. *The Gothic Image*. Translated by Dora Nussey. New York: Harper, 1972.
Mapstone, Sally. Introduction. *The Chepman and Myllar Prints: Digitised Facsimiles with Introduction, Headnotes, and Transcriptions*, 1–10. General editor Sally Mapstone. Edinburgh: Scottish Text Society and the National Library of Scotland, 2008. DVD-ROM.
—. "The Origins of Criseyde." In *Medieval Women: Texts and Contexts in Late Medieval Britain*, 131–47. Edited by Jocelyn Wogan-Browne, Rosalynn Voaden, Arlyn Diamond, Ann Hutchison, Carol M. Meale, and Lesley Johnson. Medieval Women: Texts and Contexts 3. Turnhout: Brepols, 2000.
Marcattili, Francesco. "Templum Castorum et Minervae (Chron. 354, P. 146 M) Il Tempio di Minerva ad Assisi Il Culto Romano Dei Dioscuri." *Archeologia Classica* 64 (2013): 263–94.
Markland, Murray F. "The Structure of *The Kingis Quair*." *Research Studies of the State College of Washington* 25 (1957): 273–86.
Marks, Diane R. "Poems from Prison: James I of Scotland and Charles of Orleans." *Fifteenth-Century Studies* 15 (1989): 245–58.
Marrou, H.I. *A History of Education in Antiquity*. Translated by George Lamb. New York: Mentor NAL, 1956.

Marshall, Linda E. "The Identity of the 'New Man' in the *Anticlaudianus* of Alan of Lille." *Viator* 10 (1979): 77–94.
Marshall, P.K. "*Ilias Latina*." In *Texts and Transmission: A Survey of the Latin Classics*, 191–4. Edited by Leighton D. Reynolds and N.G. Wilson. Oxford: Clarendon Press, 1983.
Martindale, Charles, ed. *Ovid Renewed: Ovidian Influences on Literature and Art from the Middle Ages to the Twentieth Century*. Cambridge: Cambridge University Press, 1988.
Mazzeo, Joseph Anthony. "Plato's Eros and Dante's Amore." *Traditio* 12 (1956): 315–37.
McCall, John P. *Chaucer among the Gods: The Poetics of Classical Myth*. University Park: Pennsylvania State University Press, 1979.
McDonough, Christopher J. Introduction to *Commentum super Martianum*, by Alexander Neckam, ix–xliii. Edited by Christopher J. McDonough. Firenze: SISMEL, 2006.
McFarlane, K.B. *Lancastrian Kings and Lollard Knights*. Oxford: Oxford University Press, 1972.
McGowan, Matthew M. *Ovid in Exile: Power and Poetic Redress in the* Tristia *and* Epistulae Ex Ponto. Mnemosyne Supplements 309. Leiden: Brill, 2009.
McKinley, Kathryn L. "Manuscripts of Ovid in England 1100 to 1500." In *English Manuscript Studies 1100—1700*, vol. 7, 41–85. Edited by Peter Beal and Jeremy Griffiths. London: British Library, 1998.
Mead, William Edward. Introduction to *The Pastime of Pleasure*, xiii–cxvi. Edited by William Edward Mead. EETS OS 173. London: Oxford University Press, 1928.
Meech, Sanford B. "Three Musical Treatises in English from a Fifteenth-Century Manuscript." *Speculum* 10 (1935): 235–69.
Mews, Constant J. *Abelard and Heloise*. Oxford: Oxford University Press, 2005.
—. "Bernard of Clairvaux and Peter Abelard." In *A Companion to Bernard of Clairvaux*, 133–68. Edited by Brian Patrick McGuire. BCCT 25. Leiden: Brill, 2011.
—. "The Council of Sens (1141): Abelard, Bernard, and the Fear of Social Upheaval." *Speculum* 77 (2002): 342–80.
Meyendorff, John. "Wisdom–Sophia: Contrasting Approaches to a Complex Theme." *Dumbarton Oaks Papers* 41 (1987): 391–401.
Middle English Dictionary. Electronic edition. University of Michigan, 2001, 2013. https://quod.lib.umich.edu/m/med/.
Miller, J. Hillis. "Narrative." In *Critical Terms for Literary Study*, 66–79. Edited by Frank Lentricchia and Thomas McLaughlin. Chicago: University of Chicago Press, 1990.
Miller, John F., and Carole E. Newlands, eds. *A Handbook to the Reception of Ovid*. Hoboken, NJ: Wiley Blackwell, 2014.
Minnis, A.J. *Chaucer and Pagan Antiquity*. Totowa, NJ: Rowman and Littlefield, 1982.
—. *Medieval Theory of Authorship*. 2nd ed. Philadelphia: University of Pennsylvania Press, 1988.
Miskimin, Alice. "Patterns in *The Kingis Quair* and the *Temple of Glas*." *Papers on Language and Literature* 13 (1977): 339–61.
Mitchell, J. Allen. "Queen Katherine and the Secret of Lydgate's *Temple of Glas*." *Medium Aevum* 77 (2008): 54–76.
Moi, Toril. "Desire in Language: Andreas Capellanus and the Controversy of Courtly Love." In *Medieval Literature: Criticism, Ideology, and History*, 11–33. Edited by David Aers. Sussex: Harvester, 1986.
Monks, Peter Rolfe. *The Brussels Horloge de Sapience: Iconography and Text of Brussels, Bibliothèque Royale, MS. IV 111*. Leiden: Brill, 1990.

Monroe, Elizabeth. "Dangerous Passages and Spiritual Redemption in the *Hortus deliciarum*." In *Push Me, Pull You: Imaginative, Emotional, Physical, and Spatial Interaction in Late Medieval and Renaissance Art*, vol. 1, 39–74. Edited by Laura Gelfand and Sarah Blick. Leiden: Brill, 2011.
Monson, Don A. *Andreas Capellanus, Scholasticism, and the Courtly Tradition*. Washington, DC: Catholic University of America Press, 2005.
Mooney, Linne R. "Chaucer's Scribe." *Speculum* 81 (2006): 97–138.
Mora, Francine. "L'*Ylias* de Joseph d'Exeter: Une Réaction Cléricale au *Roman de Troiae* de Benoît de Sainte-Maure." In *Progrès, Réaction, Décadence dans L'Occident Médiéval*, 199–213. Edited by Emmanuèle Baumgartner and Laurence Harf-Lancner. Publications Romanes et Françaises 231. Geneva: Droz, 2003.
Mora-Lebrun, Francine. "D'une esthétique à l'autre: la prole feminine dans l'*Iliade* de Joseph d'Exeter et le *Roman de Troie* de benoît de Sainte-Maure." In *Conter de Troie et l'Alexandre*, 31–50. Edited by Laurence Harf-Lancner, Laurence Mathey-Maille, and Michelle Szkilnik. Paris: Sorbonne Houvelle, 2006.
Morawiecki, L. "The Symbolism of Minerva on the Coins of Domitianus." *Klio* 59 (1977): 185–93.
Morse, Ruth. *Truth and Convention in the Middle Ages: Rhetoric, Representation, and Reality*. Cambridge: Cambridge University Press, 1991.
Most, Glenn W. "Hellenistic Allegory and Early Imperial Rhetoric." In *The Cambridge Companion to Allegory*, 26–38. Edited by Rita Copeland and Peter T. Struck. Cambridge: Cambridge University Press, 2010.
Murgatroyd, Paul. "Amatory Hunting, Fishing, and Fowling," *Latomus* 43 (1984): 362–8.
—. "*Militia amoris* and the Roman Elegists," *Latomus* 34 (1975): 59–79.
Murphy, James J. "The Arts of Poetry and Prose." In *The Cambridge History of Literary Criticism: Volume 2*, 42–67. Edited by Alastair Minnis and Ian Johnson. Cambridge: Cambridge University Press, 2005.
—. "Caxton's Two Choices: 'Modern' and 'Medieval' Rhetoric in Traversgni's *Nova Rhetorica* and the Anonymous *Court of Sapience*." *Medievalia et Humanistica* ns 3 (1972): 241–55.
—. *Rhetoric in the Middle Ages: A History of Rhetorical Theory from Saint Augustine to the Renaissance*. Berkeley: University of California Press, 1974.
Murphy, R.E. "Wisdom (in the Bible)." In *New Catholic Encyclopedia*, vol. 14, 971–4. New York: McGraw, 1967.
Newlands, Carole E. *Statius' Silvae and the Poetics of Empire*. Cambridge: Cambridge University Press, 2002.
Newman, Barbara. *God and the Goddesses: Vision, Poetry, and Belief in the Middle Ages*. Philadelphia: University of Pennsylvania Press, 2003.
—. Introduction and commentary to *Symphonia: A Critical Edition of the Symphonia armonie celestium revelationum*, 1–67, 267–319. Edited and translated by Barbara Newman. Ithaca, NY: Cornell University Press, 1988.
—. *Sister of Wisdom: St. Hildegard's Theology of the Feminine*. Berkeley: University of California Press, 1987.
—. "What Did It Mean to Say 'I Saw'? The Clash between Theory and Practice in Medieval Visionary Culture." *Speculum* 80 (2005): 1–43.
Newman, Jonathan M. "Narratology and Literary Theory in Medieval Studies." In *Handbook of Medieval Studies: Terms – Methods – Trends*, 990–8. 3 vols. Edited by Albrecht Classen. Berlin: De Gruyter, 2010.
Niederwimmer, Kurt. *The Didache: A Commentary*. Edited by Harold W. Attridge. Translated by Linda M. Maloney. Minneapolis: Fortress Press, 1998.

Nievergelt, Marco. *Allegorical Quests from Deguileville to Spenser*. Cambridge: D.S. Brewer, 2012.
Niles, John D. *Homo Narrans: The Poetics and Anthropology of Oral Literature*. Philadelphia: University of Pennsylvania Press, 1999.
Noble, Peter, Lucie Polak, and Claire Isoz, eds. *The Medieval Alexander Legend and Romance Epic: Essays in Honour of David J.A. Ross*. Millwood, NY: Kraus, 1982.
Nolan, Barbara. *The Gothic Visionary Perspective*. Princeton: Princeton University Press, 1977.
Nolan, Maura. "Historicism after Historicism." In *The Post-Historical Middle Ages*, 63–85. Edited by Elizabeth Scala and Sylvia Federico. New York: Palgrave, 2009.
—. *John Lydgate and the Making of Public Culture*. CSML 58. Cambridge: Cambridge University Press, 2005.
Norton-Smith, John. Introduction to *John Lydgate: Poems*, ix–xv. Edited by John Norton-Smith. Oxford: Clarendon Press, 1966.
—. "Lydgate's Changes in the 'Temple of Glas'." *Medium Aevum* 27 (1958): 166–72.
Obbink, Dirk. "Early Greek Allegory." In *The Cambridge Companion to Allegory*, 15–25. Edited by Rita Copeland and Peter T. Struck. Cambridge: Cambridge University Press, 2010.
Ó Cróinin, Dáibhi. *Early Medieval Ireland, 400–1200*. London: Longman, 1995.
O'Donnell, James J. *Cassiodorus*. Berkeley: University of California Press, 1979. *Georgetown.edu*. http://faculty.georgetown.edu/jod/texts/cassbook/toc.html.
—. "The Demise of Paganism." *Traditio* 35 (1979): 45–88.
Ogilvie, R.M. *The Romans and Their Gods in the Age of Augustus*. London: Chatto and Windus, 1974.
Olson, Paul A. *The Journey to Wisdom: Self-Education in Patristic and Medieval Literature*. Lincoln: University of Nebraska Press, 1995.
O'Meara, John J. *Charter of Christendom: The Significance of the City of God*. New York: Macmillan, 1961.
Ong, Walter. "The Writer's Audience Is Always a Fiction." *PMLA* 90 (1975): 9–21.
Orme, Nicholas. *English Schools in the Middle Ages*. London: Methuen, 1973.
—. *Medieval Schools: From Roman Britain to Renaissance England*. New Haven: Yale University Press, 2006.
Orr, Patricia R. "Pallas Athena and the Three-fold Choice in Chaucer's *Troilus and Criseyde*." In *The Mythographic Art: Classical Fable and the Rise of the Vernacular in Early France and England*, 159–76. Edited by Jane Chance. Gainesville: University of Florida Press, 1990.
Ostia: Ancient Harbour City of Rome. "The Fullers (fullonicae)." http://www.ostia-antica.org/.
—. "Regio I – Forum – Capitolum." http://www.ostia-antica.org/.
O'Sullivan, David E. Introduction to *Les Eschéz d'Amours: A Critical Edition of the Poem and Its Latin Glosses*, 80–94, 105–14. Edited by Gregory Heyworth and Daniel E. O'Sullivan, with Frank Coulson. MRAT 10. Leiden: Brill, 2013.
O'Sullivan, Sinéad. Introduction to *Glossae aevi Carolini in Libros I–II Martiani Capellae De nuptiis Philologiae et Mercurii*, v–clxxxi. Edited by Sinéad O'Sullivan. CCCM 237. Turnhout: Brepols, 2010.
Otten, Willemien. *From Paradise to Paradigm: A Study of Twelfth-Century Humanism*. Brill's Studies in Intellectual History 127. Leiden: Brill, 2004.
Otto, Walter F. *The Homeric Gods: The Spiritual Significance of Greek Religion*. Translated by Moses Hadas. New York: Pantheon, 1954.

Ouy, Gilbert. "Charles d'Orléans and his Brother Jean d'Angoulême in England: What Their Manuscripts Have to Tell." In *Charles d'Orléans in England (1415–1440)*, 47–60. Edited by Mary-Jo Arn. Woodbridge: D.S. Brewer, 2000.

—, Christine Reno, and Inès Villela-Petit. *Album Christine de Pizan*. Texte, Codex & Contexte 14. Turnhout: Brepols, 2012.

Palmer, Robert E.A. "Juno in Archaic Italy." In *Roman Religion and Roman Empire: Five Essays*, 3–56. Philadelphia: University of Pennsylvania Press, 1974.

Papaconstantinou, Arietta, Neil McLynn, and Daniel L. Schwartz, eds. *Conversion in Late Antiquity: Christianity, Islam, and Beyond*. Farnham, UK: Ashgate, 2015.

Papadopoulou, Thalia. "Representations of Athena in Greek Tragedy." In *Athena in the Classical World*, 293–310. Edited by Susan Deacy and Alexandra Villing. Leiden: Brill, 2001.

Parker, Hugh C. "The Pagan Gods in Joseph of Exeter's 'De bello Troiano'." *Medium Aevum* 64 (1995): 273–8.

Parkinson, David J. Introduction to *The Palis of Honoure*, by Gavin Douglas, 1–14. Kalamazoo, MI: Medieval Institute, 1992.

—. "William Dunbar." In *The Oxford Encyclopedia of British Literature*, vol. 2, 226–9. Edited by David Scott Kastan. Oxford: Oxford University Press, 2006.

Parussa, Gabriella. Introduction to *Epistre Othea* by Christine de Pizan, 1–193. Edited by Gabriella Parussa. Geneva: Droz, 1999.

Patch, Howard R. *The Goddess Fortuna in Mediaeval Literature*. Cambridge, MA: Harvard University Press, 1927.

Patterson, Lee. "Making Identities in Fifteenth-Century England: Henry V and John Lydgate." In *New Historical Literary Study*, 69–107. Edited by Jeffrey N. Cox and Larry J. Reynolds. Princeton: Princeton University Press, 1993.

Pavlock, Barbara. *The Image of the Poet in Ovid's* Metamorphoses. Madison: University of Wisconsin Press, 2009.

Paxson, James J. *The Poetics of Personification*. Literature, Culture, Theory 6. Cambridge: Cambridge University Press, 1994.

Pearsall, Derek. "Gower's Narrative Art." *PMLA* 81 (1966): 475–84.

—. *John Lydgate*. Charlottesville: University Press of Virginia, 1970.

—. *John Lydgate (1371–1449): A Bio-bibliography*. English Literary Studies, monograph series 71. Victoria, BC: University of Victoria Press, 1997.

—. "Lydgate as Innovator." *Modern Language Quarterly* 53 (1992): 5–22.

—. "The 'Troilus' Frontispiece and Chaucer's Audience." *Yearbook of English Studies* 7 (1977): 68–74.

Peck, Russell A. *Kingship and Common Profit in Gower's* Confessio Amantis. Carbondale: Southern Illinois University, 1978.

Pedersen, Olaf. *Early Physics and Astronomy: A Historical Introduction*. Rev. ed. Cambridge: Cambridge University Press, 1993.

Pepin, Ronald E. Introduction to *The Vatican Mythographers*, 1–12. Translated by Ronald E. Pepin. New York: Fordham University Press, 2008.

Petrina, Alessandra. *The* Kingis Quair *of James I of Scotland*. Padova: Unipress, 1997.

Pfaff, Richard W. *The Liturgy in Medieval England: A History*. Cambridge: Cambridge University Press, 2009.

Pickering, F.P. *Literature and Art in the Middle Ages*. Coral Gables, FL: University of Miami Press, 1970.

Piehler, Paul. *The Visionary Landscape: A Study in Medieval Allegory*. Montreal: McGill-Queen's University Press, 1971.

Popović, Mladen, ed. *The Jewish Revolt against Rome: Interdisciplinary Perspectives*. Leiden: Brill, 2011.
Preston, John. "'Fortunys Exiltree': A Study of *The Kingis Quair*." *Review of English Studies* ns 7 (1956): 339–47.
Prince, Gerald. *A Dictionary of Narratology*. Lincoln: University of Nebraska Press, 1987.
—. "Introduction à l'étude du narrataire." *Poetique* 14 (1973): 177–96.
Quinn, William. "Memory and the Matrix of Unity in *The Kingis Quair*." *The Chaucer Review* 15 (1981): 332–55.
—. *Olde Clerkis Speche: Chaucer's* Troilus and Criseyde *and the Implications of Authorial Recital*. Washington, DC: Catholic University of America Press, 2013.
Raby, F.J.E. "*Amor* and *Amicitia*: A Medieval Poem." *Speculum* 40 (1965): 599–610.
—. *A History of Christian Latin Poetry from the Beginnings to the Close of the Middle Ages*. 2nd ed. Oxford: Oxford University Press, 1953.
—. *A History of Secular Latin Poetry in the Middle Ages*. 2 vols. Oxford: Clarendon Press, 1934.
Ramson, W.S. "The Aureate Paradox." *Parergon* 1 (1983): 93–104.
Rand, E.K. *Founders of the Middle Ages*. New York: Dover, 1957.
—. *Ovid and His Influence*. New York: Cooper Square, 1963.
Rapp, Claudia. *Holy Bishops in Late Antiquity: The Nature of Christian Leadership in an Age of Transition*. The Transformation of the Classical Heritage 37. Berkeley: University of California Press, 2005.
Rebillard, Éric. *Christians and Their Many Identities in Late Antiquity, North Africa 200–450 CE*. Ithaca, NY: Cornell University Press, 2012.
Reiss, Edmund. *William Dunbar*. TEAS 257. Boston: Twayne, 1979.
Relihan, Joel C. *The Prisoner's Philosophy: Life and Death in Boethius's Consolation*. With a contribution by William E. Heise. Notre Dame: University of Notre Dame Press, 2007.
Renoir, Alain. *The Poetry of John Lydgate*. Cambridge, MA: Harvard University Press, 1967.
Reynolds, L.D. Introduction to *Texts and Transmission: A Survey of the Latin Classics*, xiii–xliii. Edited by L.D. Reynolds. Oxford: Clarendon Press, 1983.
—, and N.G. Wilson. *Scribes and Scholars: A Guide to the Transmission of Greek and Latin Literature*. 4th ed. Oxford: Oxford University Press, 2013.
Reynolds, Suzanne. *Medieval Reading: Grammar, Rhetoric and the Classical Text*. CSML 27. Cambridge: Cambridge University Press, 1996.
Riche, Pierre. *The Carolingians*. Translated by Michael Idomir Allen. Philadelphia: University of Pennsylvania Press, 1993.
—. *Education and Culture in the Barbarian West: Sixth through Eighth Centuries*. Translated by John J. Contreni. Columbia: University of South Carolina Press, 1976.
Riddehough, Geoffrey B. "A Forgotten Poet: Joseph of Exeter." *JEGP* 46 (1947): 254–9.
Ridley, Florence H. "Middle Scots Writers." In *A Manual of the Writings of Middle English 1050–1500*, vol. 4, 961–1060, 1121–284. Edited by Albert E. Hartung. Hamden: Connecticut Academy of Arts and Sciences, 1973.
Rigg, A.G. "Appendix A: Correspondences between Joseph's *Ylias* and Its Sources." In *Joseph of Exeter: Iliad*, 141. Translated by A.G. Rigg. Toronto: Centre for Medieval Studies, 2005. http://medieval.utoronto.ca/ylias/.
—. "Calchas, Renegade and Traitor: Dares and Joseph of Exeter." *N&Q* 45 (1998): 176–8.
—. *A History of Anglo-Latin Literature 1066–1422*. Cambridge: Cambridge University Press, 1992.

—. "Joseph of Exeter's Pagan Gods Again." *Medium Aevum* 70 (2001): 19–28.
Risden, E.L. *Heroes, Gods and the Role of Epiphany in English Epic Poetry*. Jefferson, NC: McFarland, 2008.
Robathan, Dorothy M. "Ovid in the Middle Ages." In *Ovid*, 191–209. Edited by J.W. Binns. London: Routledge, 1973.
Roberts, Gildas. "Worthy of Their Envy: The Literary Merits of Joseph of Exeter's Trojan Epic." *University of Cape Town Studies in English* 2 (1971): 13–23.
Robertson, D.W., Jr. *A Preface to Chaucer*. Princeton: Princeton University Press, 1962.
—. "Some Observations on Method in Literary Studies." In *Essays in Medieval Culture*, 73–84. Princeton: Princeton University Press, 1980.
Robinson, Jon. *Court Politics, Culture and Literature in Scotland and England, 1500–1540*. Aldershot: Ashgate, 2008.
Rohrberger, Mary. "*The Kingis Quair*: An Evaluation." *Texas Studies in Literature and Language* 2 (1960): 292–302.
Root, R.K. "Chaucer's Dares." *Modern Philology* 15 (1917): 1–22.
Rordorf, Willy. "An Aspect of the Judeo-Christian Ethic: The Two Ways." In *The "Didache" in Modern Research*, 148–64. Edited by Jonathan A. Draper. Arbeiten zur Geschichte des Antiken Judentums und des Urchristentums 37. Leiden: Brill, 1996.
Rosati, Gianpiero. "Statius, Domitian and Acknowledging Paternity: Rituals of Succession in the *Thebaid*." In *The Poetry of Statius*, 175–93. Edited by Johannes J.L. Smolenaars, Harm-Jan van Dam, and Ruurd R. Nauta. MGRLL 306. Leiden: Brill, 2008.
Rose, Martial, and Julia Hedgecoe. *Stories in Stone: The Medieval Roof Carvings of Norwich Cathedral*. New York: Thames and Hudson, 1997.
Ross, D.J.A. *Alexander Historiatus: A Guide to Medieval Illustrated Alexander Literature*. London: Warburg, 1963.
Rouse, Mary A., and Richard H. Rouse. "Prudence, Mother of Virtues: The Chaplet des virtus and Christine de Pizan." *Viator* 39 (2008): 185–228.
Rovane, Carol A. "The Epistemology of First-Person Reference." *The Journal of Philosophy* 84 (1987): 147–67.
Roy, Bruno. "A la Recherche des Lecteurs Médiévaux du De amore d'André le Chapelain." *Revue de l'Université d'Ottawa/University of Ottawa Quarterly* (1985): 45–73.
Rozenski, Steven, Jr. "Henry Suso's Horologium Sapientiae in Fifteenth-Century France: Images of Reading and Writing in Brussels Royal Library MS IV 111." *Word & Image* 26 (2010): 364–80.
Russell, J. Stephen. *Chaucer and the Trivium: The Mindsong of the Canterbury Tales*. Gainesville: University Press of Florida, 1998.
—. *The English Dream Vision: Anatomy of a Form*. Columbus: Ohio University Press, 1988.
Sabourin, Leopold. *The Psalms: Their Origin and Meaning*. New York: Alba House, 1974.
Sadlek, Gregory M. *Idleness Working: The Discourse of Love's Labor from Ovid through Chaucer and Gower*. Washington, DC: Catholic University of America Press, 2004.
Saenger, Paul. *Space between Words: The Origins of Silent Reading*. Stanford: Stanford University Press, 1997.
Salmon, P.B. "The 'Three Voices' of Poetry in Mediaeval Literary Theory." *Medium Aevum* 30 (1961): 1–18.
Salter, Elizabeth. "The 'Troilus Frontispiece'." In *Troilus and Criseyde: A Facsimile of Corpus Christi College Cambridge MS 61*, introduced by M.B. Parkes and Elizabeth Salter, 15–23. Cambridge: D.S. Brewer, 1978.
Scaglione, Aldo. "The Classics in Medieval Education." In *The Classics in the Middle

Ages, 343–62. Edited by Aldo S. Bernardo and Saul Levin. Medieval & Renaissance Texts & Studies 69. Binghamton, NY: Center for Medieval and Early Renaissance Studies, 1990.

Scanlon, Larry, and James Simpson, eds. *John Lydgate: Poetry, Culture, and Lancastrian England*. Notre Dame: University of Notre Dame Press, 2006.

Scarisbrick, J.J. *Henry VIII*. New ed. New Haven: Yale University Press, 1997.

Scattergood, John. [V.J.]. Introduction to *The Works of Sir John Clanvowe*, 9–31. Edited by V.J. Scattergood. Lanham, MD: Rowman and Littlefield, 1975.

—. *John Skelton: The Career of an Early Tudor Poet*. Dublin: Four Courts Press, 2014.

—. "Skelton's *Garlande of Laurell* and the Chaucerian Tradition." In *Chaucer Traditions: Studies in Honour of Derek Brewer*, 122–38. Edited by Ruth Morse and Barry Wineatt. Cambridge: Cambridge University Press, 1990.

Scheps, Walter. "Chaucerian Synthesis: The Art of the *Kingis Quair*." *Studies in Scottish Literature* 8 (1971): 143–65.

—. "*The Golden Targe*: Dunbar's Comic *Psychomachia*." *Papers on Language and Literature* 11 (1975): 339–56.

—, and J. Anna Looney. *Middle Scots Poets: A Reference Guide to James I of Scotland, Robert Henryson, William Dunbar, and Gavin Douglas*. Boston: G.K. Hall, 1986.

Schirmer, Walter. *John Lydgate: A Study in the Culture of the XVth Century*. Translated by Ann E. Keep. London: Methuen, 1961.

Schreiber, Earl G. "Venus and the Mythographic Tradition." *JEGP* 74 (1975): 519–35.

Sedgwick, Walter Bradbury. "The *Bellum Troianum* of Joseph of Exeter." *Speculum* 5 (1930): 49–76.

Seltman, Charles. *The Twelve Olympians*. New York: Crowell, 1960.

Seznec, Jean. *The Survival of the Pagan Gods*. New York: Harper, 1953.

Shannon, E.F. *Chaucer and the Roman Poets*. Cambridge, MA: Harvard University Press, 1929.

Shannon, Laurie. "Minerva's Men: Horizontal Nationhood and the Literary Production of Googe, Turbervile, and Gascoigne." In *The Oxford Handbook of Tudor Literature, 1485–1603*, 437–54. Edited by Mike Pincombe and Cathy Shrank. Oxford: Oxford University Press, 2009.

Sheffler, David. "Education and Schooling." In *Handbook of Medieval Culture: Fundamental Aspects and Conditions of the European Middle Ages*, 384–405. 3 vols. Edited by Albrecht Classen. Berlin: De Gruyter, 2015.

Shelton, Jo-Ann. *As the Romans Did: A Sourcebook in Roman Social History*. Oxford: Oxford University Press, 1988.

Shuffleton, Frank. "An Imperial Flower: Dunbar's *The Golden Targe* and the Court Life of James IV of Scotland." *Studies in Philology* 72 (1975): 193–207.

Shutters, Lynn. "Confronting Venus: Classical Pagans and Their Christian Readers in John Gower's *Confessio Amantis*." *The Chaucer Review* 48 (2013): 38–45.

Silverstein, Theodore. "The Fabulous Cosmogony of Bernard Silvestris." *Modern Philology* 46 (1948–9): 92–116.

Simpson, James. "The Economy of Involucrum: Idleness in *Reason and Sensuality*." In *Through a Classical Eye: Transcultural and Transhistorical Visions in Medieval English, Italian, and Latin Literature in Honour of Winthrop Wetherbee*, 390–414. Edited by Andrew Galloway and R.F. Yeager. Toronto: University of Toronto Press, 2009.

—. "The Other Book of Troy: Guido delle Colonne's *Historia destructionis Troiae* in Fourteenth- and Fifteenth-Century England." *Speculum* 73 (1998): 397–423.

—. *Sciences and the Self in Medieval Poetry: Alan of Lille's* Anticlaudianus *and John Gower's*

Confessio Amantis. CSML 25. Cambridge: Cambridge University Press, 1995.
Smalley, Beryl. *English Friars and Antiquity in the Early Fourteenth Century*. New York: Barnes & Noble, 1960.
—. *The Study of the Bible in the Middle Ages*. Notre Dame: University of Notre Dame Press, 1964.
Smith, Jeremy J. *Older Scots: A Linguistic Reader*. STS, 5th ser. 9. Edinburgh: STS, 2012.
Smith, Sr. Mary Frances. *Personification of Wisdom in Middle English Literature*. Washington, DC: Catholic University of America Press, 1935.
Smits, Edmé R. "A Medieval Supplement to the Beginning of Curtius Rufus's *Historia Alexandri*: An Edition with Introduction." *Viator* (1987): 89–124.
Solomon, Jon. "The Vacillations of the Trojan Myth: Popularization and Classicization, Variation and Codification." *International Journal of the Classical Tradition* 14 (2007): 482–534.
Solterer, Helen. *The Master and Minerva: Disputing Women in French Medieval Culture*. Berkeley: University of California Press, 1993.
Southern, R.W. *Medieval Humanism and Other Studies*. New York: Harper, 1970.
—. *Robert Grosseteste: The Growth of an English Mind in Medieval Europe*. Oxford: Clarendon Press, 1986.
—. *Scholastic Humanism and the Unification of Europe: Volume 1: Foundations*. Oxford: Blackwell, 1995.
Sowell, Madison U. Introduction to *Dante and Ovid: Essays in Intertextuality*, 1–8. Edited by Madison U. Sowell. MRTS 82. Binghamton, NY: Center for Medieval and Early Renaissance Studies, 1991.
Spearing, A.C. "Dreams in *The Kingis Quair* and the Duke's Book." In *Charles d'Orléans in England: 1415–1440*, 123–44. Edited by Mary-Jo Arn. Cambridge: D.S. Brewer, 2000.
—. *Medieval Autographies: The "I" of the Text*. Notre Dame: University of Notre Dame Press, 2012.
—. *Medieval Dream Poetry*. Cambridge: Cambridge University Press, 1976.
—. *The Medieval Poet as Voyeur: Looking and Listening in Medieval Love-Narratives*. Cambridge: Cambridge University Press, 1993.
—. "The Medieval Poet as Voyeur." In *The Old Daunce: Love, Friendship, Sex and Marriage in the Medieval World*, 57–86. Edited by Robert R. Edwards and Stephen Spector. Albany: State University of New York Press, 1991.
—. "Prison, Writing, Absence: Representing the Subject in the English Poems of Charles d'Orléans." *Modern Language Quarterly* 53 (1992): 83–99.
—. *Textual Subjectivity: The Encoding of Subjectivity in Medieval Narratives and Lyrics*. Oxford: Oxford University Press, 2005.
Spitzer, Leo. "Note on the Poetic and the Empirical 'I' in Medieval Authors." *Traditio* 4 (1946): 414–22.
Stahl, William Harris, and Richard Johnson, with E.L. Burge. *Martianus Capella and the Seven Liberal Arts*, vol. 1. Records of Civilization: Sources and Studies 84. New York: Columbia University Press, 1971.
Stapleton, M.L. *Harmful Eloquence: Ovid's Amores from Antiquity to Shakespeare*. Ann Arbor: University of Michigan Press, 1996.
Stark, Rodney. *The Rise of Christianity: A Sociologist Reconsiders History*. Princeton: Princeton University Press, 1996.
Stearns, Marshall W. "A Note on Henryson and Lydgate." *Modern Language Notes* 60 (1945): 101–3.

Steltman, Charles. *The Twelve Olympians*. New York: Crowell, 1960.
Stevens, Martin. "The Performing Self in Twelfth-Century Culture." *Viator* 9 (1978): 193–218.
Stock, Brian. *The Implications of Literacy: Written Language and Models of Interpretation in the Eleventh and Twelfth Centuries*. Princeton: Princeton University Press, 1983.
—. *Myth and Science in the Twelfth Century: A Study of Bernard Silvester*. Princeton: Princeton University Press, 1972.
Stritmatter, Roger. "Triangular Numbers in Henry Peacham's *Minerva Britanna*: A Study in Jacobean Literary Form." *Brief Chronicles* 4 (2012–13): 89–116.
Strohm, Paul. *Politique: Languages of Statecraft between Chaucer and Shakespeare*. Notre Dame: University of Notre Dame Press, 2005.
Strong, David. "Supra-Natural Creation in Dunbar's 'The Golden Targe'." *Philological Quarterly* 82 (2003): 149–66.
Struck, Peter T. "Allegory and Ascent in Neoplatonism." In *The Cambridge Companion to Allegory*, 57–70. Edited by Rita Copeland and Peter T. Struck. Cambridge: Cambridge University Press, 2010.
Suggs, M. Jack. "The Christian Two Ways Tradition: Its Antiquity, Form, and Function." In *Studies in New Testament and Early Christian Literature: Essays in Honor of Allan P. Wikgren*, 60–74. Edited by David Edward Aune. Leiden: Brill, 1972.
Sullivan, J.P. *Martial: The Unexpected Classic – A Literary and Historical Study*. Cambridge: Cambridge University Press, 1991.
Summers, Joanna. *Late-Medieval Prison Writing and the Politics of Autobiography*. Oxford: Clarendon Press, 2004.
Summit, Jennifer. *Memory's Library: Medieval Books in Early Modern England*. Chicago: University of Chicago Press, 2008.
Synan, Edward A. "A Goliard Witness: The *De nuptiis Philologiae et Mercurii* of Martianus Capella in the *Methamorphosis Golye Episcopi*." *Florilegium* 2 (1980): 121–45.
Szendrei, Janka. "On the Prose Historia of St. Augustine." In *The Divine Office in the Latin Middle Ages: Methodology and Source Studies, Regional Developments, Hagiography*, 430–43. Edited by Margot E. Fassler and Rebecca A. Baltzer. Oxford: Oxford University Press, 2000.
Tarrant, Richard J. "Ovid." In *Texts and Transmission: A Survey of the Latin Classics*, 257–84. Edited by L.D. Reynolds. Oxford: Clarendon Press, 1983.
—. "Ovid and Ancient Literary History." In *The Cambridge Companion to Ovid*, 13–33. Edited by Philip Hardie. Cambridge: Cambridge University Press, 2002.
Tatlock, John S.P. "The Epilog of Chaucer's *Troilus*." *Modern Philology* 18 (1921): 625–59.
Taylor, Jerome. Introduction to *The Didascalicon of Hugh of St. Victor: A Medieval Guide to the Arts*, 3–39. Translated by Jerome Taylor. New York: Columbia University Press, 1961.
Temperini, Lino. *Assisi, Romana e Medievale: Profilo-Storico-Archeologica*. Rome: Franciscanum, 1985.
Teviotdale, Elizabeth. "Music and Pictures in the Middle Ages." In *Companion to Medieval and Renaissance Music*, 179–88. Edited by Tess Knighton and David Fellows. Berkeley: University of California Press, 1992.
Thiébaux, Marcelle. *The Stag of Love: The Chase in Medieval Literature*. Ithaca, NY: Cornell University Press, 1974.
Tilley, E. Allen. "The Meaning of Dunbar's *The Golden Targe*." *Studies in Scottish Literature* 10 (1973): 220–31.
Tolkien, J.R.R. "On Fairy Stories." In *The Tolkien Reader*, 3–84. New York: Ballantine, 1966.

Too, Yun Lee, ed. *Education in Greek and Roman Antiquity*. Leiden: Brill, 2001.
Tonry, Kathleen. "John Skelton and the New Fifteenth Century." *Literature Compass* 5/4 (2008): 721–39.
Townsend, David. Introduction to *The Alexandreis: A Twelfth-Century Epic, Walter of Châtillon*, 11–22. Translated by David Townsend. Peterborough, Ont.: Broadview, 2007.
Traube, Ludwig. *Vorlesungen und Abhandlungen*, vol. 2. Edited by Paul Lehman. Munich: Beck, 1911.
Traver, Hope. "The Four Daughters of God: A Mirror of Changing Doctrine." *PMLA* 40 (1925): 44–92.
—. *The Four Daughters of God: A Study of the Versions of the Allegory with Special Reference to Those in Latin, French and English*. Bryn Mawr College Monographs 6. Bryn Mawr, 1907.
Travis, Peter. "Affective Criticism, the Pilgrimage of Reading, and Medieval English Literature." In *Medieval Texts and Contemporary Readers*, 201–15. Edited by Laurie A. Finke and Martin Shichtman. Ithaca, NY: Cornell University Press, 1987.
Triggs, Oscar Lovell. Introduction to *The Assembly of Gods*, vii–lxxvi. Edited by Oscar Lovell Triggs. English Studies 1. Chicago: University of Chicago Press, 1895.
Trout, John. *The Voyage of Prudence: The World View of Alan of Lille*. Washington, DC: University Press of America, 1979.
Tucker, Melvin J. "The Ladies in Seklton's 'Garland of Laurel'." *Renaissance Quarterly* 22 (1969): 333–45.
Turner, Denys. "Allegory in Christian Late Antiquity." In *The Cambridge Companion to Allegory*, 71–82. Edited by Rita Copeland and Peter T. Struck. Cambridge: Cambridge University Press, 2010.
Tuve, Rosamond. *Allegorical Imagery: Some Medieval Books and Their Posterity*. Princeton: Princeton University Press, 1966.
Twycross, Meg. *The Medieval Anadyomene: A Study in Chaucer's Mythography*. Medium Aevum Monographs ns 1. Oxford: Blackwell, 1972.
Universal Short-Title Catalogue. http://www.ustc.ac.uk/.
van Buuren, Catherine. "The Chepman and Myllar Texts of Dunbar." In *William Dunbar, 'The Nobill Poyet': Essays in Honour of Priscilla Bawcutt*, 24–39. Edited by Sally Mapstone. East Linton, UK: Tuckwell Press, 2001.
Van Deusen, Nancy, ed. *The Place of the Psalms in the Intellectual Culture of the Middle Ages*. Albany: SUNY Press, 1999.
van Dorsten, J.A. "The Leyden 'Lydgate Manuscript'." *Scriptorum* 14 (1960): 315–25.
van Heijnsbergen, Theo. "Dunbar, Scott and the Making of Poetry." In *William Dunbar, 'The Nobill Poyet': Essays in Honour of Priscilla Bawcutt*, 108–33. Edited by Sally Mapstone. East Linton, UK: Tuckwell Press, 2001.
Varner, Eric R. *Mutilation and Transformation: Damnatio memoriae and Roman Imperial Portraiture*. Monumenta Graeca et Romana 10. Leiden: Brill, 2004.
Vignaux, Paul. *Philosophy in the Middle Ages: An Introduction*. Translated by E.C. Hall. New York: Meridian, 1959.
Vitz, Evelyn Birge, Nancy Freeman Regalado, and Marilyn Lawrence, eds. *Performing Medieval Narrative*. Cambridge: D.S. Brewer, 2005.
von Hendy, Andrew. "The Free Thrall: A Study of *The Kingis Quair*." *Studies in Scottish Literature* 2 (1964): 141–51.
von Simson, Otto. *The Gothic Cathedral: Origins of Gothic Architecture and the Medieval Concept of Order*. 3rd ed. Bollingen Series 48. Princeton: Princeton University Press, 1988.

Wack, Mary Frances. *Lovesickness in the Middle Ages: The* Viaticum *and Its Commentaries.* Philadelphia: University of Pennsylvania Press, 1990.

Wagner, David L. "The Seven Liberal Arts and Classical Scholarship." In *The Seven Liberal Arts in the Middle Ages*, 1–31. Edited by David L. Wagner. Bloomington: Indiana University Press, 1983.

Wakelin, Daniel. "Stephen Hawes and Courtly Education." In *The Oxford Handbook of Tudor Literature, 1485–1603*, 53–68. Edited by Mike Pincombe and Cathy Shrank. Oxford: Oxford University Press, 2009.

Wallace, Rex E. *An Introduction to Wall Inscriptions from Pompeii and Herculaneum.* Wauconda, IL: Bolchazy-Carducci, 2005.

Warden, John, ed. *Orpheus: The Metamorphoses of a Myth.* Toronto: University of Toronto Press, 1982.

Waswo, Richard. "Our Ancestors, the Trojans: Inventing Cultural Identity in the Middle Ages." *Exemplaria* 7 (1995): 269–90.

Watson, Patricia. "*Praecepta* Amoris: Ovid's Didactic Elegy." In *Brill's Companion to Ovid*, 141–65. Edited by Barbara Weiden Boyd. Leiden: Brill, 2002.

Webster, Graham. *The British Celts and Their Gods under Rome.* London: Batsford, 1986.

Wedel, Theodore Otto. *Astrology in the Middle Ages.* Mineola, NY: Dover, 2005.

Wehrle, Jan. "Dreams and Dream Theory." In *Handbook of Medieval Culture: Fundamental Aspects and Conditions of the European Middle Ages*, 329–46. 3 vols. Edited by Albrecht Classen. Berlin: De Gruyter, 2015.

Wei, Ian P. *Intellectual Culture in Medieval Paris: Theologians and the University c.1100–1330.* Cambridge: Cambridge University Press, 2012.

Wells, Whitney. "Stephen Hawes and *The Court of Sapience*." *The Review of English Studies* 6 (1930): 284–94.

Welsford, Enid. *The Court Masque: A Study in the Relationship between Poetry and the Revels.* Cambridge: Cambridge University Press, 1927.

Wenzel, Siegfried. "The Pilgrimage of Life as a Late Medieval Genre." *Mediaeval Studies* 35 (1973): 370–88.

—, trans. *Preaching in the Age of Chaucer: Selected Sermons in Translation.* Washington, DC: Catholic University of America Press, 2008.

Wetherbee, Winthrop. "Genius and Interpretation in the 'Confessio Amantis'." In *Magister Regis: Studies in Honor of Robert Earl Kaske*, 241–60. Edited by Arthur Groos et al. New York: Fordham University Press, 1986.

—. "Learned Mythography: Plato and Martianus Capella." In *The Oxford Handbook of Medieval Latin Literature*, 335–55. Edited by Ralph J. Hexter and David Townsend. Oxford: Oxford University Press, 2012.

—. *Platonism and Poetry in the Twelfth Century: The Literary Influence of the School of Chartres.* Princeton: Princeton University Press, 1972.

—. "The Study of Classical Authors from Late Antiquity to the Twelfth Century." In *The Cambridge History of Literary Criticism: Volume 2*, 99–144. Edited by Alastair Minnis and Ian Johnson. Cambridge: Cambridge University Press, 2005.

Wheeler, Stephen. "Before the 'aetas Ovidiana': Mapping the Early Reception of Ovidian Elegy." *Hermathena* 177/178 (2004, 2005): 9–26.

Whitman, Jon. "Present Perspectives: Antiquity to the Late Middle Ages." In *Interpretation and Allegory: Antiquity to the Modern Period*, 33–70. Edited by Jon Whitman. Leiden: Brill, 2003.

—. "A Retrospective Forward: Interpretation, Allegory, and Historical Change." In *Interpretation and Allegory: Antiquity to the Modern Period*, 3–29. Edited by Jon Whitman. Leiden: Brill, 2003.

Wilkinson, L.P. *Ovid Recalled*. Cambridge: Cambridge University Press, 1955.
Willard, Charity Cannon. *Christine de Pizan: Her Life and Works*. New York: Persea, 1984.
Williams, George. "The 'Troilus and Criseyde' Frontispiece Again." *Modern Language Review* 57 (1962): 173–8.
Williams, Janet Hadley. "Dunbar and His Immediate Heirs." In *William Dunbar, 'The Nobill Poyet': Essays in Honour of Priscilla Bawcutt*, 85–107. Edited by Sally Mapstone. East Linton, UK: Tuckwell Press, 2001.
Wilson, Janet. "Poet and Patron in Early Fifteenth-Century England: John Lydgate's *Temple of Glas*." *Parergon* 11 (1975): 25–32.
Wisnovsky, Robert, Faith Wallis, Jamie C. Fumo, and Carlos Fraenkel, eds. *Vehicles of Transmission, Translation, and Transformation in Medieval Textual Culture*. Turnhout: Brepols, 2011.
Wittkower, Rudolf. "Transformations of Minerva in Renaissance Imagery." *Journal of the Warburg Institute* 2 (1939): 194–205.
Woods, Marjorie Curry. "Experiencing the Classics in Medieval Education." In *The Oxford History of Classical Reception in English Literature: Volume 1 (800–1558)*, 35–51. Edited by Rita Copeland. Oxford: Oxford University Press, 2016.
Young, Karl. *The Origin and Development of the Story of Troilus and Criseyde*. The Chaucer Society, Second Series 41. London: Kegan Paul, 1908.
Zander, Friedrich. *Stephen Hawes' "Passetyme of Pleasure" verglichen mit Edmund Spenser's "Faerie Queene" unter Berücksichtigung der allegorishcen Dichtung in England*. Rostock: Carl Hinstorffs, 1905.
Zeeman, Nicolette. "Mythography and Mythographical Collections." In *The Oxford History of Classical Reception in English Literature: Volume 1 (800–1558)*, 121–50. Edited by Rita Copeland. Oxford: Oxford University Press, 2016.
Ziolkowski, Jan M. "Epic." In *Medieval Latin: An Introduction and Bibliographic Guide*, 547–55. Edited by F.A.C. Mantello and A.G. Rigg. Washington, DC: Catholic University of America Press, 1996.
Zuwiyya, Z. David, ed. *A Companion to Alexander Literature in the Middle Ages*. BCCT 29. Leiden: Brill, 2011.

Index

Abelard, Peter   91, 97–8
  Historia calamitatum   40 n.91, 91, 97, 99
Achilles   120 n.1, 128–9, 131, 132, 137–8, 143, 149, 150, 180–1, 183, 212, 213, 222, 224 n.45
Achitophel   76–7
Acts of the Apostles   76, 166–7
Adelard of Bath
  De eodem et diverso   95
Aeolus/Eolus   116, 186, 188–9, 191, 194, 197, 200, 212 n.16
Aeschines   115, 132
Aeschylus
  Oresteia: Eumenides   41, 121
Alan of Lille   53
  Anticlaudianus   64 n.59, 66, 98–101, 111, 112–13, 119, 131 n.32, 139 n.50, 192, 218, 249
  De planctu Naturae   59, 60–1, 64 nn. 58 and 59, 66, 69 n.72, 94, 201, 218
Alcuin of York   47–8, 85–6, 94, 216 n.27
  De dialectica   86
  De orthographia   86
  Dialogus de rhetorica et virtutibus   86
  Grammatica   86
  Missa de Sancta Sapientia   47–8, 49, 55, 249
Alexander of Macedon   131–4, 143 n.69, 181
Alexander de Villedieu
  Doctrinale   220 n.42
allegory/allegorical   5, 7, 8, 33 n.69, 37–8, 42 n.101, 43, 55, 58, 59, 70, 71, 73, 74, 79 n.92, 91–2, 95–7, 98, 99, 100, 102 n.74, 103, 104–5, 106, 108 n.86, 111, 113, 114, 124 n.9, 125, 142–3, 151, 152, 153, 154 n.89, 155, 158, 161, 198–9, 200, 223–4, 228 n.54, 240, 243, 245, 248, 249, 251, 252
  allegoresis   38, 42
Amans   181–2, 223
  see also *amans* under Ovid, *Amores*
Amor   6, 46–7, 49–50, 51, 74 n.78, 80, 202, 218, 224 n.45, 230, 235

  see also Book 2 metrum 8 under Boethius, *CP* and Sapientia-Amor/*sapienta-amor* under Sapientia/Sapience/Sapyence
Andreas Capellanus
  De arte honeste amandi   217
antiqui   4
Aphrodite   5, 203
  see also Venus
Apollo   3, 20, 34, 36, 122, 138, 180–1, 183–4, 188–9, 191, 218–19
Apollodorus
  The Library   203, 213 n.17
Apuleius
  De deo Socratis   172
Aquinas, see Thomas Aquinas
Arachne   136, 148, 206–8
Aratus
  Phaenomena   167, 205 n.5
Aristotle   23 n.43, 25 n.51, 63 n.57, 77, 87 n.31, 115, 133
Armstrong, Rebecca   214
L'Art d'Amours   216 n.28
The Assembly of Gods   8, 163, 185, 185–95, 197, 200, 202, 227, 250
Athena   19, 22, 35, 41–2, 81 nn.1 and 2, 109, 120–1, 120 n.1, 124 n.9, 142, 146–8, 159, 182, 183, 186, 187, 187 n.45, 196–202, 203
  birth   19, 19 n.25
  Erichthonius   203 n.1
  founding of Athens   109, 184
  opposes Aphrodite   203, 210
  patroness   35, 41, 42, 81 n.2, 120, 124 n.9, 128, 129, 168, 203, 225, 250
  see also Minerva, Pallas, and Tritonia
Atropos/Attropos   60, 191–2, 194, 195
  as Dethe   192, 194–5
Augustine   14 n.9, 25, 38, 47, 50, 62, 76, 84, 85, 86, 168, 170, 178, 179, 182, 185, 188, 250
  Confessions   62 n.55, 76
  De civitate Dei   63 n.57, 171–4, 175–6, 177, 178 n.29, 184

De doctrina Christiana 38 n.86, 47, 57, 84, 86 n.29, 107, 108
De ordine 84, 86 n.29
De Trinitate 30 n.65,
"Letter 1*A" 171 n.21
Augustus, Roman Emperor 18, 20, 21, 144, 162 n.1, 205, 212, 224 n.45, 255
Ayres, Philip
Cupids addresse to the Ladies 254

Bacchus 39 n.89, 92, 174, 177, 190, 201, 218, 219, 224
Bawcutt, Priscilla 196
Bede 17, 85
Benedict of Nursia 85
Benjamin Minor 42 n.101
Benoît de Sainte-Maure
Roman de Troie 133, 138, 139
Benson, C. David 141 n.59, 142, 149, 150, 179
Bernard of Clairvaux 50, 97–8
"In festo Annunciationis Beatae Mariae Verginis: Sermo I" 104–5
Tractatus de diligendo Deo 50, 52, 62, 67, 71
Bernard Silvestris 5
Commentary on Martianus Capella 95, 110–11,
Commentum super sex libros Eneidos Virgilii 5–6, 7, 8, 40 n.93, 68, 110, 236
"interiores animi potentias" 7, 42, 43, 59, 238, 245, 252
Cosmographia 30, 52–5, 64 n.59, 94, 98, 100, 111, 138 n.50, 249, 253 n.7, 255
Bersuire, Pierre 28 n.57, 38
De formis figurisque 65, 67, 68, 110, 111, 184–5, 229 n.58, 242 nn.88 and 90
Metamorphosis Ovidiana Moraliter 38–9, 40 n.93, 68 n.71
Boccaccio, Giovanni 6, 53, 130 n.26, 248
Amorosa Visione 29 n.61
De mulieribus claris 146 n.76, 153, 186
Il Filocolo 130 n.24
Il Filostrato 179, 226 nn.50 and 51
Genealogie deorum gentilium 40 n.93, 204 n.3, 229 n.58
Teseida 6, 68 n.71, 109, 124, 177 n.28, 219 n.39, 224 n.46
Arcita 177
Bodel, Jean
La Chanson des Saxons 131
Boethius 6, 57, 193 n.50
De consolatione Philosophiae 6, 7, 40 n.93, 60 nn.48 and 50, 64 n.59, 65–7, 93–4, 160, 181, 233, 236–7, 240, 241, 242, 243 n.92, 245, 248, 251
Book 2 metrum 8 6, 46–7, 55, 80, 201, 202, 230
in Maximianus' Elegy 3 219–20
Boffey, Julia 114 n.93, 116, 228 n.55, 234 n.72, 239 n.80, 241
Bonaventure
Commentaria in quatuor libros sententiarum Magastri Petri Lombardi 11 n.1
De reduction artium ad theologiam 88

Cadmus 122, 124, 125, 223–4
Calliope 75, 78, 79, 80, 141, 209, 221
Cambridge, Corpus Christi College Ms. 61 12–14
Cambridge, Corpus Christi College Ms. 406 138 n.50
Cambridge, Trinity College Ms. R.3.19 187 n.44
Cambridge, Trinity College Ms. R.3.21 102
Cambridge, Trinity College Ms. R.14.9 95 n.54
Cambridge, University Library Ms. F.f.6.33 42 n.101
Cambridge, University Library Ms. Gg.4.27 230 n.61, 231 n.64
Cambridge, University Library Ms. K.k.6.26 42 n.101
Cambridge, University Library Ms. Mm.1.18 95 n.54
Cames, Gérard 90
caritas 47, 50, 172, 249
Carmina Burana 218, 251
"De Phyllide et Flora" 222
"Ecce, chorus virginem" 221–2
"Ianus annum circinat" 218–19
Carruthers, Mary 8 n.16, 11, 12 nn.4 and 6, 17 n.16, 23 n.43
Caseau, Béatrice 169
Cassiodorus 4, 84–5, 86, 87, 113
Institutions divninarum et humanarum 84, 90, 113 n.91
Variarum libri XII 4 n.7
The Castle of Persevererance 105 n.79
catalog of deities 178–85, 190, 195, 200, 251
Caxton, William 101 n.69, 102, 118 n.102, 152 n.83, 230
The Recuyell of the Historyes of Troye 140
Chance, Jane 33, 38, 39 n.89, 40, 143, 193 n.50
Charles d'Orléans 226, 231 n.66, 239
Fortunes Stabilnes 8, 204, 239–46
Chartres, Bibliothèque Municipale Ms. 497 95 n.55

Chaucer, Geoffrey 1, 11–14, 23, 26, 53, 70, 116–17, 118, 138, 139 n.54, 153, 181, 185, 197, 198, 229, 233, 239 n.82, 240 n.85, 241, 250, 251
  Anelida and Arcite 64 n.58, 196, 220 n.41
  Boece 150 n.79
  The Book of the Duchess 11, 58, 70 nn.73 and 76, 76 n.86, 103, 186 n.40, 217, 232
  The Canterbury Tales
    The General Prologue 106
    The Knight's Tale 124, 224 n.46, 232, 248
    The Miller's Tale 70 n.74, 226 n.50
    The Physician's Tale 219
    The Wife of Bath's Prologue 36–7, 39, 223 n.44
  "Chaucers Wordes unto Adam" 23 and n.44
  The Complaint of Mars 39
  "Fortune" 237
  The House of Fame 11, 58, 79, 106, 107 n.84, 114, 118 n.102, 118, 200 n.64, 227, 248
  The Legend of Good Women 217, 232
  The Parliament of Fowls 39, 58, 61, 63 n.56, 64 n.58, 66, 106, 107, 227, 232
  The Romaunt of the Rose 224
  Troilus and Criseyde 11, 24 n.48, 37, 39, 70 n.75, 77 n.88, 118 n.103, 129–30, 131, 141, 142, 150 n.79, 177, 178–9, 181, 182 n.34, 185, 224–6, 227, 230, 232, 242 n.89, 242
The Chepman and Myllar Prints 199
Christine de Pizan 142, 151, 186
  Epistre d'Othea 7, 121, 142–9, 150, 153, 155, 160, 187, 250
Cicero 32, 64 n.59, 82–3, 111
  De natura deorum 32–3, 177
  De officiis 83
  De oratore 83
  Tusculanae disputations 83
Claassen, Jo-Marie 247
Clanvowe, Sir John 26, 29 n.58
  Boke of Cupid 232
  The Two Ways 26–7, 28–9, 32, 72 n.77
Classical Reception Studies 4–5, 17
classicism, medieval 4, 5, 16–17, 198, 247, 248–9, 252, 255
  see also Classical Reception Studies and mythography
Clio 113, 136, 141
Cologny, Foundation Martin Bodmer, Cod. Bodmer 86 130 n.27

Cologny, Foundation Martin Bodmer, Cod. Bodmer 87 130 n.27
Columkille 85
Constantine, Roman Emperor 162–3, 169–70, 171, 176
Constantine the African
  Viaticum 217
Copeland, Rita 4, 24 n.48, 42 n.101, 57
Corinthians, First Letter to 25 n.51, 27, 32, 172
The Court of Sapience 7, 66, 82, 101–13, 118, 153, 186, 242, 249
Criseyde/Cresseid 37, 76 n.85, 77 n.89, 224–5, 226
Cupid 3, 37, 58, 72, 77, 96–7, 184–5, 189–90, 197, 201, 208, 209–10, 211, 212, 219, 220, 221, 222, 226, 228, 233–4, 254
  see also God of Love
cupiditas 47, 168, 220, 233, 251
Curtius, Ernst Robert 4 n.5, 14, 16–17, 66–7, 86

Dante Alighieri 78, 118, 130
  Commedia 104, 118 n.103, 208 n.10, 230, 237
  De vulgari eloquentia 139 n.52
  "The Letter to Can Grande" 23 n.43
Dares Phrygius
  De exicidio Troiae historia 35, 130 n.27, 134–5, 137, 140, 141, 180
De deorum imaginibus libellus 229 n.58
De septem septenis 88
The Debate of the Body and Soul 186 n.41
demon/*daemon* 7, 136 n.44, 163, 168, 169, 171–8, 179–80, 183–4, 185, 190, 201
Deuteronomy, Book of 47, 168
DeVries, David 200
Diana 5, 36, 37, 38, 58, 72–3, 74, 75, 77, 79, 80, 173, 188–9, 209, 214, 249
Dictys Cretensis
  Ephemeridos belli Troiani 35, 134–5, 141, 180
The Didache 27 n.54
Diomedes/Diomede 41, 120, 122, 124, 128, 203, 209, 211, 225, 253
Domitian, Roman Emperor 121, 126–8
  Equus Domitiani 126
  see also Martial and Suetonius
Douglas, Gavin 7, 75
  The Palice of Honoure 7, 44, 75–80, 104, 113, 114, 151, 198, 199, 249
dream/dream–vision 2–3, 5, 7, 12, 18, 29 n.61, 37, 57, 58–60, 71, 72–3, 75–6, 77, 79–80, 95–7, 101, 104, 107 n.84, 114,

116–18, 127, 135, 136, 139, 140–1, 148–9, 151, 152–3, 161, 181, 183, 185–6, 193, 195, 196–7, 198, 200, 201, 223, 226, 227–9, 231, 233–8, 240–1, 243–4, 247, 248, 249, 250, 251, 252, 253
    see also *somnium*
Dunbar, William   75, 195–6
    The Golden Targe   8, 163, 195, 196–202, 218, 251
    "I that in heill was"   23 n.44, 199 nn.61 and 62
Dunchad
    Glossae in Martianum   94

Ebin, Lois   24 n.44, 57 n.40, 59
Ecclesiastes, Book of   44, 207 n.9, 235
Ecclesiasticus, Book of   7, 29, 30–1, 44, 45, 49, 51, 65, 67, 69, 110
Edinburgh, National Library of Scotland, Adv. Ms. 35.6.7   231 n.65
Ehrhart, Margaret J.   3–4, 57, 136 n.44, 140, 141 n.59
epiphany/epiphanic   51, 122, 127, 129, 233, 238
Les Eschéz d'Amours   55, 56, 57, 59, 60 n.48, 61 n.52, 64 n.58, 74 n.78
Eutropius
    Breviarium ab urbe condita   168 n.7
Evrart de Conty
    Livre des Eschez Amoureux Moralisés   56, 59 n.45
Excidium Troiae   35
Exodus, Book of   163–4, 165, 166

Feiss, Hugh   47
First Vatican Mythographer   110
Flora   75, 221, 222
Fortuna/Fortune   3, 4 n.5, 46, 60, 67–8, 70, 76, 77, 99, 103, 124, 136 n.76, 153, 156–7, 189–90, 200 n.64, 221, 231, 232 n.70, 233, 236–8, 239, 240, 241, 242, 243–4, 245, 251
Four Daughters of God   101, 102 n.74, 104–5, 153
Fulgentius
    Expositio Virgilianae continentiae   40 n.93, 79 n.91
    Mitologiae   40 n.93, 64–5, 67, 68–9, 79, 109, 110, 111, 140, 183 n.36, 184, 185, 242, 248

Galen
    Exhortatio ad artes addiscendas   83
Genesis, Book of   42 n.101, 45
Genius   3, 4 n.5, 63 n.56, 73, 181–3, 186 n.40, 217 n.33, 222–4, 253

Geoffrey of Monmouth
    Historia regum Britannie   35–6, 138
Geoffrey of Vinsauf
    Poetria nova   23–4, 24 n.48, 25 n.51, 38 n.50
Glossae aevi Carolini in Libros I–II Martiani Capellae   94
God of Love   217 n.33, 222, 223, 226, 240
    see also Cupid
Godfrey of St. Victor
    Fons Philosophiae   87–8
Gordian III, Roman Emperor   168–9, 178
Gower, John   14 n.9, 116–17, 118, 153, 181, 197, 198, 202, 250
    Confessio Amantis   63 n.56, 73, 181–3, 185, 186, 192, 195, 201, 234, 240
grammatica   12 n.6, 17, 40 n.101, 82, 85, 86, 88, 90, 92, 93, 100, 130
Gregory the Great   90
Gregory of Tours
    Historia Francorum   93
Green, Richard Hamilton   3, 6
Griffiths, Jane   56 n.29, 57, 59 n.45, 61 n.52, 62 n.54, 117
Grosseteste, see Robert Grosseteste
Guido delle Colonne
    Historia destructionis Troiae   139, 140, 141, 149, 150, 180–1, 183, 184, 185, 195, 202, 226 nn.50 and 51, 250
Guillaume de Lorris, see *Le Roman de la Rose*

Harvey, E. Ruth   101, 105–6
Hasler, Antony   76, 77 n.87, 79 n.92, 160 n.94
Hawes, Stephen   75, 102, 140, 151–2, 187 n.44, 199
    The Example of Vertu   7, 102, 121, 152–4, 161, 250
    The Pastime of Pleasure   7, 102 nn.71 and 73, 121, 154–61, 186 n.38, 250
Haydock, Nickolas   37, 79, 118 n.102
Hector   128–9, 137, 142, 143, 144, 146, 148–50, 156, 157
Hekster, Oliver   127
Henry V, King of England   139, 140 n.55, 141, 151
Henry VII, King of England   151, 152, 154 n.89, 155, 160, 161
Henry VIII, King of England   152, 161
Henry of Kirkestede
    Catalogus de libris autenticis et apocrifis   64 n.59
Henryson, Robert   37, 76 n.85, 77, 140
    The Testament of Cresseid   37, 77 n.89, 196, 226 n.51

Herrad of Hohenbourg
  Hortus deliciarum 88–90
Hesiod 116
  Theogony 19 n.25
Heywood, Jasper
  Thyestes 252–3, 254
Heywood, Thomas
  "Vpon the Avthor and his Minerva" 253
Hilary of Poitiers
  De Trinitate 30 n.65
Hildegard of Bingen 48, 50, 53
  Explanatio Symboli Sancti Athanasii 50
  Scivias 49 n.13
  Symphonia
    "Karitas" 49
    "O ignis Spiritus Paracliti" 49, 254
    "O quam mirabilis" 53
    "O virtus Sapientie" 48–9, 66
Historia Augusta 168 n.7
Hoccleve, Thomas
  Letter of Cupid 58, 232
  Mother of God 232
Homer 5, 116, 123, 139, 180
  The Iliad 41, 60 n.48, 81 n.1, 120, 122, 124, 128–9, 130, 150, 203, 224 n.45
  The Odyssey 7, 41, 81, 120–1, 122
Homeric Epigrams 81 n.1
Homeric Hymns 19 n.25, 41, 81 n.1, 120, 203
Horace 64 n.59, 216
  Ars poetica 204
Hugh of Fouilloy
  Aviarium 108 n.86, 245 n.96
Hugh of St. Victor
  Didascalicon 63 n.57, 68 n.70, 86–7, 98, 248
humanism, medieval 53 n.25, 97–8, 141 n.61

idol/idolatry 7–8, 34, 38 n.86, 162, 163–8, 169, 173, 175–8, 179, 180–1, 183–5, 186, 188, 191–3, 195, 196, 201–2, 203, 230 n.60, 250–1, 255
Ilias Latina 128–9, 130, 135–6, 137, 139 n.52
Irvine, Martin 11, 12 n.6, 17 n.16
Isidore of Seville 17, 35
  Etymologiae 35 n.75, 37 n.83, 84–5, 179–80, 181, 182, 184, 202, 245 n.96, 250

Jack, R.D.S. 200
Jacques de Longuyon
  "Les Vœux du paon" 143 n.69
Jaeger, C. Stephen 8 n.16, 86, 87, 98, 230
James I, King of Scotland 226, 231–2, 239 n.82, 243 n.92
  The Kingis Quair 8, 204, 231–9, 240, 241, 242, 245, 251

James, Letter of 27–8
Jean de Meun, see *Le Roman de la Rose*
Jerome 57, 86, 173
John, Gospel of 30–1
John of Hauville
  Architrenius 100, 131 n.32, 138 n.50
John Rylands University Library English Ms. 1 140 n.55
John of Salisbury
  Metalogicon 86, 87–8, 95, 98
John Scotus Eriugena
  Annotationes in Marcianum 94
"Jolly Jankin" 26 n.50
Joseph of Exeter 131, 134
  Frigii Daretis Yliados libri sex 134–8, 139, 150
Juan Rodriguez del Padrón
  Siervo libre de amor 68 n.71
Judgment of Paris 4, 55–6, 59, 63–9, 71, 72, 74, 80, 136, 139, 140, 141 n.59, 148, 203, 206, 209, 212, 218, 221, 242, 249
Julian, Roman Emperor 171
Juno 2, 16, 20–1, 34, 55, 58, 59, 63, 67, 68–9, 72, 80, 92, 110–11, 121, 135, 136, 137, 139, 148, 156, 188 n.46, 212, 221, 226 n.51
Jupiter/Jove 5, 19, 20–1, 36, 52, 63, 65, 92, 93, 108, 110–11, 121, 122, 123, 125, 126, 127, 134 n.39, 135, 138, 173, 175, 177, 178, 179, 192 n.49, 209, 212 n.16, 215, 218, 253, 254
  see also Zeus

Kings, First Book of 153, 165, 197

Lactantius
  Divinarum Institutiones 29 n.60, 33–5, 176, 178, 183 n.36, 184, 205 n.5
[Lactantius]
  De ave phoenice 42 n.101
Lafferty, Maura 132, 134 nn.38 and 40
Langland, William
  Piers Plowman 105 n.79
Leiden, Leiden University Vossius Germ. Gall. Q.9 1, 247
Leviticus, Book of 47, 168
Lewis, C.S. 75, 102 n.74, 124 n.9, 160 n.94
liberal arts/*artes liberales* 7, 12 n.6, 23, 25, 38 n.86, 81–90, 91–101, 103, 104, 106, 108, 111, 112–13, 114, 115, 117, 118, 119, 120, 153, 156, 159, 161, 192 n.48, 214, 249–50, 255
  quadrivium 84, 92, 93, 95, 112
  trivium 84, 86, 87, 91–2, 93, 95, 112
  see also *grammatica*
London, British Library Ms. Additional 29729 58, 102

INDEX 303

London, British Library Ms. Harley 682 240 n.83, 245
London, British Library Ms. Harley 2251 102
London, British Library Ms. Harley 4431 144–7
London, British Library Ms. Royal 18 D.II 140 n.55
Lotman, Maria-Kristiina 128
Love, Nicholas
  The Mirrour of the Blessed Lyf of Jesu Christ 105 n.79
lovesickness 217, 219, 226, 227, 231, 234
Lucan 130
  De bello civili 123, 129, 131, 132, 134 n.39
Luke, Gospel of 45, 47, 172, 176
Lyall, R.J. 200
Lydgate, John 1, 55, 116–17, 118, 151, 153, 155, 186 n.38, 197, 198, 202, 250
  Complaynt of a Loveres Life 232
  Reson and Sensuallyte 7, 44, 55–74, 75, 79, 80, 102, 136, 193, 200, 201, 219, 249
  The Temple of Glas 8, 204, 226–31, 240, 242, 251
  Troy Book 7, 139–42, 149–50, 151, 183–5, 187 nn.44 and 45, 192, 195, 226 n.51, 242
Lyndsay, David
  Papyngo 196, 199 n.63

Macrobius
  In somnium Scipionis 36, 37–8, 112 n.90, 114 n.97
  Saturnalia 64 n.59,
Major, John
  Historia maioris Britanniae 231 n.65
Map, Walter
  De nugis curialium 218, 219
Mark, Gospel of 47, 172, 175
Mars 6, 16, 20, 36–7, 38, 39, 41, 73, 77, 81, 91, 127 n.18, 133, 134 n.38, 135, 136, 141, 144, 146, 149, 156–7, 173, 178, 179, 181, 190, 197, 201, 211
Martial 126, 130
  Epigrams 127–8
Martianus Capella
  De nuptiis Philologiae et Mercurii 7, 36, 40 n.93, 65, 81–2, 86, 87, 90, 91–101, 106, 109, 110, 111–12, 113, 118–19, 156, 204, 242, 249
  see also *magistra artium liberalium* under Minerva
Martin of Tours 134 n.40, 175
Matthew, Gospel of 26, 47, 72 n.77, 107, 172, 175

Maximianus
  Elegies 219–21
McCall, John P. 179
Meditationes vitae Christi 104
Medusa, see under Minerva
Mercury 5, 36, 39 n.89, 55, 58, 60, 63, 67, 68, 69, 72, 87, 91–2, 96, 98, 112, 116, 123, 134 n.38, 136, 139, 175, 208–9, 218
  see also the Judgment of Paris
Methamorphosis Golye episcopi 95–8, 118–19, 249
Minerva
  Bellona 133–4
  birth 19, 22, 41, 52, 108, 110–11, 112 n.90, 253–4
  contemplative wisdom 7, 68, 69, 75, 78, 81, 148, 242, 249
  etymology 21–2
  magistra artium liberalium 81–2, 91–3, 96, 98–101, 103, 104, 106, 111–13, 114–15, 116, 118–19, 120, 156, 192 n.48, 214, 235, 249, 250, 252–3, 254
  mater principis 146, 150
  Medusa 63–4, 65, 109 n.88, 123, 124–5, 126, 127, 129 n.23, 133, 209
  Neptune 109, 120, 123, 184, 190, 207, 209
  olive 16, 93, 108, 109, 120, 133, 135, 206, 213 n.18
  owl 19, 64 n.58, 108, 109, 240, 241, 242–3, 245–6, 251
  Palladium 20, 35, 120, 127 n.18, 135, 136, 139, 175–6
  patroness
    arts and artisans 18–19, 20, 22–3, 81
    cities 20–1, 22, 34, 35, 41, 109, 120–1, 132, 133, 135, 148, 157, 168, 171, 180, 184–5, 207, 224
    physicians 18, 19
    poets 20, 23
    teachers and students 18, 20
  Philosophia 7, 65–6, 190, 234–5, 236–7, 245 n.96
  Raison 65–6, 74 n.78, 190
  Roman 14, 15–17, 18–22, 32, 41
    Capitoline Triad 20–1, 110–11, 121
    Quinquatrus 20, 23, 121, 204 n.4
  Sapientia 7, 44, 52–5, 63–4, 65, 67, 69, 76–7, 80, 81, 96, 108–9, 110–13, 190
  seven (heptad) 111–13
  Sulis-Minerva 19, 168–9, 178
Venus
  allied 7, 8, 175, 184–5, 204, 209–15, 219–26, 226–46, 251–2, 254–5

304 INDEX

opposed   203–4, 206–9, 218–19 and see the Judgment of Paris
warfare   6, 7, 20, 22–3, 41, 63, 81, 91, 112, 123, 124, 125–7, 128–9, 133, 135, 136, 137–8, 146–8, 149, 150, 156–8, 159–60, 161, 168, 187, 190, 192, 197, 200–1, 203, 206, 208, 213, 220
weaving   41, 183, 206–7, 213, 222, and see Arachne
see also Athena, Pallas, and Tritonia
mirror   78, 79
moderni   4
Mora-Lebrun, Francine   138
Morpheus   152, 186, 194
Moses   29, 163, 164, 173
Muses   78, 79, 93, 96, 141, 209, 252
mythography   5, 7, 14, 17, 32–43, 64–5, 68, 95 n.54, 110–11, 140–1, 142–3, 222, 224, 229–30, 240, 242

Natura/Nature   3, 30, 53, 54–5, 58, 59–62, 63, 64, 66–7, 69, 71–2, 73, 74, 75–6, 98, 99, 100, 101 n.68, 105, 107 n.84, 112, 153, 191, 197, 200 n.64, 201–2, 222, 228, 237–8, 240, 249, 254
Neckam, Alexander
   Commentum super Martianum   95
   Novus Avianus   57 n.39
Neptune   109, 120, 123, 173–4, 184, 188–9, 190, 191, 207, 209
Newlands, Carole E.   126
Newman, Barbara   30, 44, 49 n.13, 53 n.23, 61 n.51
Nicea, Council of   170
   Nicene Christianity   163, 170, 171, 178
Nicolas de Orbellis   82, 84, 101
Nievergelt, Marco   155
nine worthies   143, 160
novus homo   98, 100, 113, 119
Noys   30, 53–5, 66, 98, 99, 100, 110–11, 112
The N-Town Play   26 n.52, 105 n.79

O Antiphons   45
   see also "O Sapientia" under Sapientia/Sapience/Sapyence
Odysseus/Ulysses   41, 81 n.2, 120, 121, 128, 214
Ogilvie, R.M.   20
Ostia   19, 21, 22–3
Othea   141, 142, 143, 144–5, 146, 148, 149, 187–8, 189–91, 192, 193, 195, 200, 150
Ovid   7, 8, 14 n.9, 38, 40 nn.93 and 94, 51, 64 n.59, 78, 79 n.92, 129–30, 139, 180, 203–6, 208 n.10, 215–18, 219, 220, 221, 222, 224, 228 n.54, 231, 232, 239, 246, 251, 254, 255
   Amores   39, 143, 209–12, 214, 217, 225 n.48
      amans   210–12, 217, 225 n.48
   Ars amatoria   136 n.44, 212–14, 217, 224, 225, 226, 227
      praeceptor amoris   211 n.15, 212–14, 217, 222, 224, 225 n.48, 226
   Epistulae ex Ponto   205 n.5, 206
      cantor deorum   206, 251
   Fasti   19 n.25, 20, 23, 81, 206
   Heroides   35, 206, 209, 217
   Metamorphoses   41, 61 n.52, 64 n.58, 128, 131, 206, 210, 215, 218
      Arachne   206–8
      Cadmus and Thebes   122, 224
      Ceyx and Alcione   11, 186 n.40, 217
      Mercury, Aglauros, and Herse   208–9, 226
      Minerva and Muses   209
      Orpheus and Eurydice   217
      Perseus   111 n.88, 123
      Proserpina   245 n.96
      Pyramus and Thisbe   217
      Trojan War   125, 209
      Venus and Mars   39 n.87
   Remedia amoris   217, 224 n.45
   Tristia   130 n.24, 204–5, 206
The Owl and the Nightingale   64 n.58
Oxford, Bodleian Library Ms. Arch. Selden. B.24   232
Oxford, Bodleian Library Ms. Digby 222   95 n.54
Oxford, Bodleian Library Ms. Fairfax 16   57 n.41, 58

Pallas   58, 63, 65, 74 n.78, 91, 93, 96, 108, 110–11, 112, 114–16, 117, 118, 119, 122, 123, 125, 127, 128–9, 132, 133, 135, 137, 139, 146–8, 149, 155, 156, 159–60, 161, 180, 183, 184, 187, 197, 200–1, 206 n.8, 207, 209, 211–12, 213, 218–19, 221, 223, 224, 225, 226 n.51, 229–30, 242, 251, 252, 253–4
see also Athena, Minerva, and Tritonia
Parlement of the Thre Ages   143 n.69, 186 n.41
Paulinus of Nola   178
   Carmina   174
pax deorum   162, 164, 171, 178
Peacham, Henry
   Minerva Britanna   253–4
Pervigilium Veneris   248
Petrarch, Francesco   130
   Africa   219
   Rerum vulgarium fragmenta

Sonnet 132 11
Sonnets 2 and 3   226 n.50
Philologia/Philology   87, 91, 92, 96, 97, 98, 101, 112, 218
Philosophia/Philosophy   6, 7, 44, 46–7, 60 n.50, 65–6, 88–90, 95, 108, 187, 190, 193 n.50, 233, 235, 236–7, 241–2, 243, 245 n.96, 248
pilgrimage   26, 62 n.54, 101, 106, 151, 155, 161, 193
Plato   25, 27, 36, 55, 76 n.86, 90, 115
  Republic   42 n.101, 60 n.48, 208 n.10
  Symposium   5
Pluto   188, 189–90, 192
Pompeii   19, 21, 22
Prince, Gerald   2, 70 n.76
Prosper of Aquitaine
  Epigrams   29 n.60
Proverbs, Book of   7, 30–1, 44, 45 n.5, 67, 69, 86, 104, 107, 113 n.91
Prudentia   61, 66, 98–100
prudentia/prudence   25, 32, 45, 47, 48, 50, 52, 67, 76, 80, 93, 109, 121, 141–2, 144, 149–50, 153, 161, 180, 189–90, 202, 235, 249, 250, 254
  see also *sapientia*/sapience
Prudentius   111, 169, 178, 188, 250
  Contra Symmachum   169, 176, 192
  Peristephanon
    10 Sancti Romani Martyris dicta   177–8, 179, 181, 190
    14 Passio Agnetis   176–7, 178, 195
  Psychomachia   186, 192
Psalms, Book of   104, 165–6, 173, 181, 185
psychomachia   99, 186, 192, 194, 198, 201, 240, 250

Quintilian   116,
  Institutio oratoria   83, 121 n.3, 128, 205 n.5
Quintus Curtius Rufus
  Historia Alexandri   132

Rabanus Maurus
  De clericorum institutione   12 n.6
  De universo libri viginti duo   245 n.96
Raison   65–6, 73, 74 n.78, 190, 223
  see also Ratio and Reson/Resoun/Reason
Ratio   98–9, 100
  see also Raison and Reson/Resoun/Reason
read/reading/readers   1–3, 5–6, 8, 11–14, 23 n.43, 28–9, 37 n.83, 38–9, 40, 44, 45, 50, 52, 55, 56, 57, 58–9, 60–1, 63–9, 70–2, 73–4, 75, 76, 77, 78, 79, 84, 85, 87–8, 93, 95 n.56, 98, 100, 106–7, 109, 110, 112, 114, 117, 118, 124 n.9, 126, 127–8, 130, 131–2, 134–5, 138, 139–40, 141–2, 144, 146, 149–50, 153–4, 155 n.90, 156, 167, 178 n.29, 179, 187, 188 n.46, 199, 200–1, 202, 203–4, 205, 207 n.9, 208 n.10, 211 n.115, 214, 215–16, 223, 224 nn.45 and 46, 227, 229, 230–1, 232–3, 236–7, 239 n.82, 241, 245, 247, 248–9, 253, 254–5
  kernel-and-shell metaphor   42, 71, 72, 73, 74
  see also allegoresis
reception and transformation   4–5, 14, 16–17, 32, 33, 38, 43, 44, 56, 58, 69, 82, 119 n. 105, 186 n.38, 199, 115–18, 220 n.42, 230–1, 232, 245, 248–9, 254–5
Remigius of Auxerre
  Commentum in Martianum Capellam   92 n.45, 93, 94, 109 n.87, 110, 111, 112 n.90
Reson/Resoun/Reason   62, 66, 71, 103, 192, 193–5, 197, 201, 228, 240, 243, 251
  see also Ratio and Raison
Richard de Bury
  Philobiblon   42, 64 n.59
Rigg, A.G.   134
Risden, Edward   122 n.6
Robert Grosseteste
  De artibus liberalibus   88
  Le chateau d'amour   105 n.80
Le Roman de la Rose   56, 59, 60 n.48, 73, 78, 198, 217, 222–4, 227,
Romans, Letter to   167
Rome   4, 19, 20–1, 22, 35, 85, 117, 120, 131, 162 n.1, 168, 169, 171, 173, 176, 177, 192 n.49, 204 n.4, 205
"The Ruin"   17

Sapientia/Sapience/Sapyence   7, 30, 44–5, 47, 48, 49, 50, 51–3, 54, 55, 61, 62, 67, 69, 71, 76–7, 80, 81, 86, 101, 103, 104, 105–6, 107, 108, 109, 110–11, 113, 115, 142, 153–4, 157, 183, 190, 197, 202, 249, 253, 254
  creatrix   48, 53, 54, 81
Sapientia-Amor/*sapientia-amor*   47, 49–50, 51–2, 230, 234, 238, 245, 249, 251
"O Sapientia"   45, 49, 52, 55, 67, 80, 202
sapiential/sapience   22 n.41, 25–6, 27–8, 31 n.66, 32, 44, 45 n.5, 47–8, 50, 51, 52, 63, 65, 80, 81, 83, 90, 103 n.77, 104 n.77, 109, 110, 166, 180, 204, 207 n.9, 230, 235, 251, 254
  sapientia et fortitudo/wisdom and fortitude   91, 143, 149, 160, 161
  see also *prudentia*/prudence
Scheps, Walter   200

Scrope, Stephen
  The Epistle of Othea   142 n.65, 154 n.87
Second Vatican Mythographer   40 n.91,
  65 n.63, 68 n.71, 111 n.88, 184
Sedulius
  Carmen Paschale   29 n.60
Seneca (the Elder)
  Controversiae   204 n.4, 215 n.23
Seneca (the Younger)   252–3
Seznec, Jean   5, 33, 35 n.76
Shannon, Laurie   252
Sidney, Sir Philip
  "Defense of Poesie"   23 n.44
Simpson, James   56 n.29, 57, 60 n.52,
  70 n.76, 100 n.67, 181 n.33
Sinon   76–7
Skelton, John   75, 113–14, 151, 199, 252
  The Garland of Laurel   82, 113, 114–19, 160,
    250
Solomon, King of Israel   52, 77, 80, 103, 111,
  153, 165, 197, 249
Solterer, Helen   4, 91 n.42
somnium   103, 104, 197, 201–2, 114 n.97, 227,
  231
  see also dream/dream–vision
Sophia, see Sapientia/Sapience/Sapyence
Spearing, A.C.   2–3, 75 n.83, 227, 232 n.70,
  239 nn.81 and 82, 243 n.92
Statius   42, 123, 126, 130
  Silvae   126
  Thebaid   42, 123–6, 127, 129, 131, 138, 149,
    224 n.46
Suetonius
  De vita Caesarum   121, 127–8
Sulpicius Severus   175, 178
  De vita beati Martini   175, 177, 184
Suso, Henry
  Horologium   50–2, 55, 62, 69, 71, 103, 107,
    108 n.85, 111, 240 n.85, 249

Tabellae Sulis   168–9, 178
Tarrant, Richard   205
Temple of Minerva, Assisi   15–17, 18, 83 n.10,
  167 n.6
Thebes   42, 122, 123–5, 131, 132–3, 144, 148,
  157, 206, 223, 224
Theodulf of Orleans   17
  Carmina   216 n.27
  De libros quos legere solebam   216 n.27
  *De septem liberalibus in quadam pictura
    depictis*   94
Theophilus
  On Diverse Arts   48 n.9
Theseus   124–5, 126, 157, 224 n.46

Thierry of Chartres
  Heptateucon   94–5
Third Vatican Mythographer
  De diis gentium et illorum allegoriis
    40 n.91, 65, 67, 68, 95, 110, 112 n.90, 185,
    200, 242 nn.88 and 90
Thomas Aquinas   17
  Summa Theologiae   25–6, 28, 29, 47
three temptations   28, 29, 153
threefold life   68, 226 n.51
Tiberinus   18
Tilley, E. Allen   200, 201
Tolkien, J.R.R   24, 102 n.73
translatio   56–7
Tritonia   112, 123, 124–6, 128–9, 137, 180
  see also Athena, Minerva, and Pallas
Troilus   77 n.89, 137, 156, 177, 179, 224–5, 226,
  228, 242
Troilus frontispiece   12–14
Troy   20, 35–6, 120, 131, 132, 134, 135, 138, 139,
  141 n.59, 143, 144, 148, 149, 157, 175–6, 179,
  180, 183
  Troia Nova   35–6, 138, 139, 253
Tuve, Rosamond   144
Tydeus   41–2, 123–4, 125–6, 127, 138, 149

Venus   1, 2–3, 5–6, 7, 28 n.57, 29 n.61, 34,
  35, 36–7, 38, 55, 58, 59, 63, 64 n.58, 67–8,
  69, 72, 73, 75, 77–8, 79, 80, 96–7, 99, 135,
  136, 137, 139, 148, 156, 173, 175, 184–5, 197,
  200, 201
  Bacchus   174, 218, 224
  birth   68, 241–2
  concordia   230
  Cupid   72, 77, 96–7, 208, 211, 220
  Genius   181–2
  hunting   136 n.44
  Mars   39, 73, 77–8, 173, 181
  Minerva
    allied   7, 8, 175, 184–5, 204, 209–15,
      219–26, 226–46, 251–2, 254–5
    opposed   203–4, 206–9, 218–19 and see
      the Judgment of Paris
  Temple   155, 158, 226 n.51
  see also Aphrodite and Cupid
Vincent of Beauvais   78 n.90, 79, 88
Virgil   40 nn. 93 and 94, 43, 64 n.59, 79,
  126 n.12, 130, 139, 180, 209–10, 216
  Aeneid   5, 11, 18, 19, 35, 40 n.93, 64 n.58,
    78, 79 nn. 91 and 92, 120, 131, 134 n.38,
    156, 157 n.91, 188 n.46, 235 n.75
Vitruvius
  De architectura   21, 83
"Vpon Temse"   1–3, 5, 67, 247–8

Walsingham, Thomas
  De archana deorum   40 n.93, 65, 68, 110, 206 n.8, 242 nn.88 and 90
Walter of Châtillon
  Alexandreis   121, 131–4, 135, 138, 150, 150
William of St. Thierry   97–8
wisdom   21–32, passim
  defined   22
  etymology   22 n.39
  fear of the Lord   29, 42 n.101, 86 n.29, 107, 166
  of the flesh   26–8, 204, 250
  of the spirit   26–8, 113, 204, 250
  see also *prudentia*/prudence and *sapientia*/sapience
Wisdom, Book of   7, 24, 30, 34, 44, 45, 52, 166, 167, 173
Wisdom (Middle English play)   31–2
writing   4, 5, 11–14, 20, 23–4, 32, 33, 36 n.83, 42, 47, 51, 70–1, 80, 83, 87–8, 90, 91, 93, 95, 98, 100–1, 106, 115, 121, 124 n.9, 134, 138, 141, 142–3, 148, 155, 178, 185, 189 n.47, 195, 200–1, 204–6, 215, 219, 222, 225 n.48, 227, 228, 230, 232, 239, 241
Wyer, Robert
  Lepistre de Othea   142 n.65, 144 n.73
Wynkyn de Worde   102 n.73, 114, 152, 187 n.44, 230

Zeus   19, 41, 42 n.101, 60 n.48, 168 n.6, 203
  see also Jupiter/Jove